1 & 2 CHRONICLES

THE NIV
APPLICATION
COMMENTARY

From biblical text . . . to contemporary life

THE NIV APPLICATION COMMENTARY SERIES

EDITORIAL BOARD

General Editor
Terry Muck

Consulting Editors
Old Testament

Tremper Longman III　　　　　*Robert Hubbard*
John H. Walton　　　　　　　*Andrew Dearman*

Zondervan Editorial Advisors

Stanley N. Gundry
Vice President and Editor-in-Chief

Jack Kuhatschek　　　　　　*Verlyn Verbrugge*
Senior Acquisitions Editor　　　Senior Editor

1 & 2 CHRONICLES

THE NIV
APPLICATION
COMMENTARY

From biblical text . . . to contemporary life

ANDREW E. HILL

ZONDERVAN™

GRAND RAPIDS, MICHIGAN 49530 USA

ZONDERVAN™

The NIV Application Commentary: 1 and 2 Chronicles
Copyright © 2003 by Andrew E. Hill

Requests for information should be addressed to:

Zondervan. *Grand Rapids, Michigan 49530*

Library of Congress Cataloging-in-Publication Data

Hill, Andrew E.
    1 and 2 Chronicles / Andrew E. Hill.
        p. cm. — (The NIV application commentary)
    Includes bibliographical references and indexes.
    ISBN: 0–310–20610–3
    1. Bible. O.T. Chronicles — Criticism, interpretation, etc. I. Title. II. Series.
BS1345.52 .H55 2003
222'.6077 — dc21   2002013637
                                        CIP

This edition printed on acid-free paper.

Printed in the United States of America

---

03 04 05 06 07 08 09 /❖ DC/ 10 9 8 7 6 5 4 3 2 1

The NIV Application Commentary Series

When complete, the NIV Application Commentary
will include the following volumes:

Old Testament Volumes

Genesis, John H. Walton
Exodus, Peter Enns
Leviticus/Numbers, Roy Gane
Deuteronomy, Daniel I. Block
Joshua, Robert Hubbard
Judges/Ruth, K. Lawson Younger
1-2 Samuel, Bill T. Arnold
1-2 Kings, Gus Konkel
1-2 Chronicles, Andrew E. Hill
Ezra/Nehemiah, Douglas J. Green
Esther, Karen H. Jobes
Job, Dennis R. Magary
Psalms Volume 1, Gerald H. Wilson
Psalms Volume 2, Gerald H. Wilson
Proverbs, Paul Koptak
Ecclesiastes/Song of Songs, Iain Provan
Isaiah, John N. Oswalt
Jeremiah/Lamentations, J. Andrew Dearman
Ezekiel, Iain M. Duguid
Daniel, Tremper Longman III
Hosea/Amos/Micah, Gary V. Smith
Jonah/Nahum/Habakkuk/Zephaniah,
    James Bruckner
Joel/Obadiah/Malachi, David W. Baker
Haggai/Zechariah, Mark J. Boda

New Testament Volumes

Matthew, Michael J. Wilkins
Mark, David E. Garland
Luke, Darrell L. Bock
John, Gary M. Burge
Acts, Ajith Fernando
Romans, Douglas J. Moo
1 Corinthians, Craig Blomberg
2 Corinthians, Scott Hafemann
Galatians, Scot McKnight
Ephesians, Klyne Snodgrass
Philippians, Frank Thielman
Colossians/Philemon, David E. Garland
1-2 Thessalonians, Michael W. Holmes
1-2 Timothy/Titus, Walter L. Liefeld
Hebrews, George H. Guthrie
James, David P. Nystrom
1 Peter, Scot McKnight
2 Peter/Jude, Douglas J. Moo
Letters of John, Gary M. Burge
Revelation, Craig S. Keener

To see which titles are available,
visit our web site at www.zondervan.com

Contents

NIV Application Commentary
Series Introduction

THE NIV APPLICATION COMMENTARY SERIES is unique. Most commentaries help us make the journey from our world back to the world of the Bible. They enable us to cross the barriers of time, culture, language, and geography that separate us from the biblical world. Yet they only offer a one-way ticket to the past and assume that we can somehow make the return journey on our own. Once they have explained the *original meaning* of a book or passage, these commentaries give us little or no help in exploring its *contemporary significance*. The information they offer is valuable, but the job is only half done.

Recently, a few commentaries have included some contemporary application as *one* of their goals. Yet that application is often sketchy or moralistic, and some volumes sound more like printed sermons than commentaries.

The primary goal of the NIV Application Commentary Series is to help you with the difficult but vital task of bringing an ancient message into a modern context. The series not only focuses on application as a finished product but also helps you think through the *process* of moving from the original meaning of a passage to its contemporary significance. These are commentaries, not popular expositions. They are works of reference, not devotional literature.

The format of the series is designed to achieve the goals of the series. Each passage is treated in three sections: *Original Meaning, Bridging Contexts,* and *Contemporary Significance.*

THIS SECTION HELPS you understand the meaning of the biblical text in its original context. All of the elements of traditional exegesis—in concise form—are discussed here. These include the historical, literary, and cultural context of the passage. The authors discuss matters related to grammar and syntax and the meaning of biblical words.[1] They also seek to explore the main ideas of the passage and how the biblical author develops those ideas.

---

1. Please note that in general, when the authors discuss words in the original biblical languages, the series uses a general rather than a scholarly method of transliteration.

After reading this section, you will understand the problems, questions, and concerns of the *original audience* and how the biblical author addressed those issues. This understanding is foundational to any legitimate application of the text today.

Bridging Contexts

THIS SECTION BUILDS a bridge between the world of the Bible and the world of today, between the original context and the contemporary context, by focusing on both the timely and timeless aspects of the text.

God's Word is *timely*. The authors of Scripture spoke to specific situations, problems, and questions. The author of Joshua encouraged the faith of his original readers by narrating the destruction of Jericho, a seemingly impregnable city, at the hands of an angry warrior God (Josh. 6). Paul warned the Galatians about the consequences of circumcision and the dangers of trying to be justified by law (Gal. 5:2–5). The author of Hebrews tried to convince his readers that Christ is superior to Moses, the Aaronic priests, and the Old Testament sacrifices. John urged his readers to "test the spirits" of those who taught a form of incipient Gnosticism (1 John 4:1–6). In each of these cases, the timely nature of Scripture enables us to hear God's Word in situations that were *concrete* rather than abstract.

Yet the timely nature of Scripture also creates problems. Our situations, difficulties, and questions are not always directly related to those faced by the people in the Bible. Therefore, God's word to them does not always seem relevant to us. For example, when was the last time someone urged you to be circumcised, claiming that it was a necessary part of justification? How many people today care whether Christ is superior to the Aaronic priests? And how can a "test" designed to expose incipient Gnosticism be of any value in a modern culture?

Fortunately, Scripture is not only timely but *timeless*. Just as God spoke to the original audience, so he still speaks to us through the pages of Scripture. Because we share a common humanity with the people of the Bible, we discover a *universal dimension* in the problems they faced and the solutions God gave them. The timeless nature of Scripture enables it to speak with power in every time and in every culture.

Those who fail to recognize that Scripture is both timely and timeless run into a host of problems. For example, those who are intimidated by timely books such as Hebrews, Galatians, or Deuteronomy might avoid reading them because they seem meaningless today. At the other extreme, those who are convinced of the timeless nature of Scripture, but who fail to discern its timely element, may "wax eloquent" about the Melchizedekian priesthood to a sleeping congregation, or worse still, try to apply the holy wars of the Old Testament in a physical way to God's enemies today.

The purpose of this section, therefore, is to help you discern what is timeless in the timely pages of the Bible—and what is not. For example, how do the holy wars of the Old Testament relate to the spiritual warfare of the New? If Paul's primary concern is not circumcision (as he tells us in Gal. 5:6), what *is* he concerned about? If discussions about the Aaronic priesthood or Melchizedek seem irrelevant today, what is of abiding value in these passages? If people try to "test the spirits" today with a test designed for a specific first-century heresy, what other biblical test might be more appropriate?

Yet this section does not merely uncover that which is timeless in a passage but also helps you to see *how* it is uncovered. The authors of the commentaries seek to take what is implicit in the text and make it explicit, to take a process that normally is intuitive and explain it in a logical, orderly fashion. How do we know that circumcision is not Paul's primary concern? What clues in the text or its context help us realize that Paul's real concern is at a deeper level?

Of course, those passages in which the historical distance between us and the original readers is greatest require a longer treatment. Conversely, those passages in which the historical distance is smaller or seemingly nonexistent require less attention.

One final clarification. Because this section prepares the way for discussing the contemporary significance of the passage, there is not always a sharp distinction or a clear break between this section and the one that follows. Yet when both sections are read together, you should have a strong sense of moving from the world of the Bible to the world of today.

THIS SECTION ALLOWS the biblical message to speak with as much power today as it did when it was first written. How can you apply what you learned about Jerusalem, Ephesus, or Corinth to our present-day needs in Chicago, Los Angeles, or London? How can you take a message originally spoken in Greek, Hebrew, and Aramaic and communicate it clearly in our own language? How can you take the eternal truths originally spoken in a different time and culture and apply them to the similar-yet-different needs of our culture?

In order to achieve these goals, this section gives you help in several key areas.

(1) It helps you identify contemporary situations, problems, or questions that are truly comparable to those faced by the original audience. Because

contemporary situations are seldom identical to those faced by the original audience, you must seek situations that are analogous if your applications are to be relevant.

(2) This section explores a variety of contexts in which the passage might be applied today. You will look at personal applications, but you will also be encouraged to think beyond private concerns to the society and culture at large.

(3) This section will alert you to any problems or difficulties you might encounter in seeking to apply the passage. And if there are several legitimate ways to apply a passage (areas in which Christians disagree), the author will bring these to your attention and help you think through the issues involved.

In seeking to achieve these goals, the contributors to this series attempt to avoid two extremes. They avoid making such specific applications that the commentary might quickly become dated. They also avoid discussing the significance of the passage in such a general way that it fails to engage contemporary life and culture.

Above all, contributors to this series have made a diligent effort not to sound moralistic or preachy. The NIV Application Commentary Series does not seek to provide ready-made sermon materials but rather tools, ideas, and insights that will help you communicate God's Word with power. If we help you to achieve that goal, then we have fulfilled the purpose for this series.

The Editors

General Editor's Preface

WHY SHOULD WE HAVE HOPE that the future will bring good? The world is at war. Environmental resources are disappearing at an alarming rate. Signs of cultural decline—crime rates, increasing fragmentation of society, immorality—are increasing. Individual well-being plummets as depression and suicide rates rise. Where is the hope in all that?

Andrew Hill, in this excellent commentary, tells us that Chronicles explains why we should have hope. Chronicles, he tells us, is a theology of hope written long before Jürgen Moltmann even thought of the phrase. Hope, Chronicles tells us, rests not in world peace or in environmental restoration or in cultural rejuvenation, although all of those things are welcome. Chronicles tells us hope rests in the Lord.

But how can we communicate that hope to hopeless generations? The pernicious character of hopelessness is that it closes us off to even the most legitimate harbingers of hope. We hear but do not understand; we read but do not comprehend. Feeling becomes disconnected from the facts. How, then, does the Chronicler do it?

(1) He does it by retelling in some detail the story of God's chosen people up to this point. The Chronicler begins with Adam and traces the line of descent through the twelve tribes and the conquest of Canaan. The story is by no means told dispassionately. (Can any story be told dispassionately?) By his selection of certain incidents and his omission of others, it is obvious that the author wants this story to come across well. The characters are true heroes; the events are inspiring acts of God. King David's strengths are stressed while his failures are forgotten. God's acts of judgment are redemptive, not punitive.

By the way the story is told, it becomes obvious that the hearers are meant to focus on the big picture, the community of people who have gone before, not on themselves. Even when talking to individuals (e.g., God to Solomon in 2 Chron. 7), God talks about "my people" and what they should do. Of course, this also meant that the focus of the story was on God and not self. The story is about God and his chosen people.

The lesson as far as hope is concerned is that hopelessness feeds on self-absorption. Hope, by contrast, feeds on other-absorption, to some extent the human community, but especially on God.

(2) The second technique the Chronicler uses is to restrict his call to action to the realm of the implicit. One comes away from a reading of Chronicles

with a commitment to act, but nowhere does the Chronicler explicitly call for action. Why does he do that?

A story well told transports us from our outsider status to full involvement. We become a part of the story by reading about it and becoming inspired by it. In 1 Chronicles 12:17, men from the tribe of Benjamin come to join David's army. David expects them to not just fight as soldiers but to join the story: "If you have come to me in peace, to help me, I am ready to have you unite with me."

They were not expected to just join in the story; they were expected to join for the specific reason of making the story line better for future generations. It is clear that David himself did what he did so that his son, heir, and successor, Solomon, would have an even greater kingdom to rule over (1 Chron. 28–29). Clearly, the Chronicler's theory is that hope comes from pointing away from the self toward God, toward others, and toward the future.

(3) One final strategy: The Chronicler sets the venue for discovering and recapturing hope. The venue is not the home or the marketplace. It is neither the nation or the world. All of these venues are susceptible to the dangers of self-absorption.

No, the Chronicler's venue is worship, liturgical and otherwise. Worship is the antithesis of self-absorption. Worship is God-absorption. It defeats hopelessness. It makes us hope.

Terry C. Muck

Author's Preface

THE RECOVERY OF "story" in our postmodern culture bodes well for the rediscovery of Chronicles by the Christian church. The books of Chronicles retell the story of Davidic kingship in ancient Israel. The story is told as a theology of hope for a despairing Jewish community in postexilic Judah. The writer rehearses Israel's past as proof-positive that God's promises are utterly reliable—not a "pocketful of divine mumbles," as his audience suspects. The stories of kings like David, Solomon, Hezekiah, and Josiah are surety of sorts that the long-awaited "righteous Branch" will indeed "sprout from David's line" (Jer. 33:15; cf. Ezek. 34:23–24).

Hope is always in vogue; indeed, hope "springs eternal" for fallen people in a fallen world—never more so than now. The moral bankruptcy of a consumer culture, the oppression and persecution of millions in the name of religion, the failure of humanist philosophy in education and politics, the devaluation of human life in the form of state-sponsored infanticide, and the emerging threat of global terrorism make our world a rather grim place to live. It is in this context that the Christian church awaits the second advent of that "righteous Branch"—that Son of David. In so doing, we embrace Paul's exhortation to "have hope" through the encouragement of the Scriptures written in the past to teach us (in this case, 1–2 Chronicles; cf. Rom. 15:4).

A discerning reader will notice that I have attempted (perhaps crudely) to imitate aspects of the literary approach of Chronicles, especially the narrative style that utilizes lists, appeals to a wide range of bibliographic sources, and emphasizes the theme of worship. Beyond this, I have made a conscious effort to bring three lenses to bear on the text of Chronicles: those of historical awareness, literary appreciation, and theological perspective.

(1) To read the books of Chronicles as *history* means that we understand this portion of the Bible as the chronological record of key events and significant characters affecting a nation (in this case, Israel) and institutions (in this case, the Davidic dynasty and Solomon's temple). Often this includes an explanation of both the cause(s) and the effect(s) of these events, and for the books of Chronicles God is always "first cause." In keeping with the nature of Hebrew narrative, however, 1–2 Chronicles depicts "a God who has chosen to do nothing apart from human participation."[1]

---

1. Ken Mathews, "Preaching Historical Narrative," in *Reclaiming the Prophetic Mantle*, ed. G. L. Klein (Nashville: Broadman, 1992), 41.

(2) To read the Bible as *literature* means that we understand the books of Chronicles as the *story* of human experience and a commentary on the great issues of life. These great issues may be summarized in questions such as these: What really exists? What is good and bad behavior? What really matters and what matters most?[2] The literary approach to biblical narrative is one that explores the story as an experience with enduring relevance and considers the biblical story "as an invitation to share an experience."[3]

(3) To read the Bible as *theology* means that we understand the books of Chronicles as the revelation of God (in his immanence and transcendence) and as his redemptive plan to reclaim creation and restore humanity to the "garden." In the case of Chronicles, the historical narrative "bears witness to God as the architect of a universal kingdom which was foreshadowed by Israel's monarchy."[4] Specifically, the recitation of the story of the Davidic dynasty in ancient Israel anticipates the reign of that ultimate "son of David" (Matt. 1:1).

The books of Chronicles are a sermon without explicit application. The writer expected his audience to tease out the implications and applications of his retelling of Hebrew history on the basis of their prior knowledge of this history (from the synoptic parallels in 1–2 Samuel and 1–2 Kings) and their own theological understanding (informed by priestly instruction and temple worship). Although less opaque than the Chronicler (I trust), I have copied his sermonic style in the sense that I offer the reader categories of personal and corporate application of the message of Chronicles with the design that he or she might tease out that specific application of the biblical text appropriate for his or her local context.

I have outlined the literary units of Chronicles in broad chronological strokes, seeking to maintain the historical flow of the narrative as much as possible. This means some literary units will be (several times in certain cases) longer than other pericopes of Chronicles. Naturally, the reader is expected to isolate a particular text in those expanded literary units for preaching or teaching (whether a chapter or a clearly delineated subunit of a chapter). The highly repetitive nature of the narrative in Chronicles permits this kind of selectivity in identifying texts for preaching and teaching without compromising the essential message of the two books. The broad-based categories for contemporary application have been crafted to be compatible with almost any literary unit within that given section of the outline of 1–2 Chronicles.

---

2. Leland Ryken, *How to Read the Bible As Literature* (Grand Rapids: Zondervan, 1984), 58.
3. Ibid., 34.
4. Mathews, "Preaching Historical Narrative," 41.

Unlike Shakespeare's King John, who lamented that "life is as tedious as a twice-told tale," the author of Chronicles encourages us to enter his retelling of Israelite history like Bunyan's pilgrim named "Hopeful." This fellow traveler became Hopeful by observing the behavior and listening to the speech of Christian and Faithful during their suffering at the fair. Like Hopeful, our encounter with the faithful of God portrayed in Chronicles should prompt us to "love a holy life and long to do something for the honor and glory of the name of the Lord Jesus"[5]—that Son of David whom the Chronicler longed to see. So then, let the "pilgrimage" through Chronicles begin!

Finally, by way of acknowledgments, I wish to thank Zondervan for the opportunity to contribute the NIV Application Commentary Series, especially general editor Terry Muck and senior acquisitions editor Jack Kuhatschek. My appreciation extends to the rest of the Zondervan editorial and production staff as well for their good work in seeing the manuscript through into print. I commend Zondervan for their initiative with the NIV Application Commentaries—biblical interpretation is incomplete without application, and this is the distinctive feature of this commentary series. As an Old Testament scholar, I am hopeful that this series will result in an awakening of sorts to the fact that there is still an important place for the preaching and teaching of the First Testament in the Christian church.

As always, I am grateful for my wife Teri—thanks to her partnership I have come to understand even more clearly that "yours, O LORD, is the greatness and the power and the glory and the majesty and the splendor, for everything in heaven and earth is yours" (1 Chron. 29:11).

Beyond this, both Teri and I are grateful to our son, Jesse Andrew, for his challenge to keep the first great commandment *first*—and thus learn to love and worship our God as King David did, who desired only to "dwell in the house of the LORD ... to gaze upon the beauty of the LORD" (Ps. 27:4).

Andrew E. Hill
Wheaton, Illinois
Yom Kippur, 2001

---

5. John Bunyan, *The Pilgrim's Progress in Modern English* (North Brunswick, N.J.: Bridge-Logos, 1998), 186.

Figures

Abbreviations

AB	Anchor Bible
ABD	*Anchor Bible Dictionary*
ANEP	*The Ancient Near East in Pictures Relating to the Old Testment*
ANET	*Ancient Near Eastern Texts Relating to the Old Testment*
BA	*Biblical Archaeologist*
BST	The Bible Speaks Today
BTB	*Biblical Theology Bulletin*
CBC	Cambridge Bible Commentary
CBQ	*Catholic Biblical Quarterly*
CEV	Contemporary English Version
DSBOT	Daily Study Bible of the Old Testament
EBC	*Expositor's Bible Commentary*
FCI	Foundations of Contemporary Interpretation
FOTL	Forms of the Old Testament Literature
GKC	Gesenius-Kautzsch-Cowley *Hebrew Grammar*
HAT	Handbuch zum Alten Testament
ICC	International Critical Commentary
IDB	*Interpreter's Dictionary of the Bible*
Interp	*Interpretation*
ISBE	*International Standard Bible Encyclopedia*
JBL	*Journal of Biblical Literature*
JETS	*Journal of the Evangelical Theological Society*
JPSV	Jewish Publication Society Version of the Tanakh (Hebrew Scriptures)
JSOT	*Journal for the Study of the Old Testament*
JSOTSup	Journal for the Study of the Old Testament Supplement Series
KJV	King James Version
MT	Masoretic Text
NAC	New American Commentary
NBD	*New Bible Dictionary*
NCBC	New Century Bible Commentary
NEB	New English Bible
NIV	New International Version
NIVAC	NIV Application Commentary

Abbreviations

NJB	New Jerusalem Bible
NJPSV	New Jerusalem Publication Society Version
NKJV	New King James Version
NLT	New Living Translation
NRSV	New Revised Standard Version
OBT	Overtures to Biblical Theology
OTL	Old Testament Library
OTWSA	*Die Ou Testamentiese Werkgemeenskap in Suid-Afrika*
RSV	Revised Standard Version
SBLDS	Society of Biblical Literature Dissertation Series
SBLMS	Society of Biblical Literature Monograph Series
TBC	Torch Bible Commentaries
ThTo	*Theology Today*
TOTC	Tyndale Old Testament Commentaries
TrinJ	*Trinity Journal*
TynBul	*Tyndale Bulletin*
VT	*Vetus Testamentum*
VTSup	Vetus Testamentum Supplement Series
WBC	Word Biblical Commentary
WTJ	*Westminster Theological Journal*
ZAW	*Zeitschrift für die alttestamentliche Wissenschaft*

Introduction

THE BIBLE INFORMS US that one night in ancient Persia a sleepless King Xerxes (KJV Ahasuerus) ordered the reading of "the book of the chronicles," presumably as an antidote for his insomnia (Est. 6:1). It is important to note that the document read to Xerxes was not the same book of the chronicles serving as the focus of our study. Yet, the Persian chronicles were no doubt similar to the Hebrew chronicles in structure and contents since both belonged to the royal annal tradition of ancient Near Eastern literature. Precisely because of this correspondence, I fear the books of Chronicles are often relegated to the same category of medicinal remedy ascribed to those Persian chronicles—that of "literary tranquilizer."

But we have not heard the end of the story. Before drawing hasty conclusions or relying on first impressions as we begin our study of Chronicles, we must return to ancient Persia and see if King Xerxes indeed journeyed to "the land of Nod." Happily, I am pleased to report that Xerxes' sedative failed. Rather than drift off into sleep at the reading of the Persian chronicles, his interest was piqued, and he was drawn into an intriguing recital—a story of profound personal relevance. I trust the same will be true of our review of the Hebrew Chronicles.[1]

The church's neglect of Chronicles is understandable, though not excusable, for a number of reasons. I will briefly mention but two of the several factors that have conspired to rob the church of its once-hyphenated legacy. Naturally, I refer to what was known for centuries as the Judeo-Christian religion. According to the apostle Paul, the Gentile church may be compared to a wild olive shoot grafted into the nourishing sap of the tap-root of believing Israel (Rom. 11:17–24). During the past two centuries the impact of Westernization and the influence of dispensational theology have combined to sever the "wild branch" of the (North American) church from the "cultivated olive tree" of Jewish religion.[2]

---

1. The "book of the chronicles" to which Xerxes made reference was probably some type of logbook recording the daily events of the royal court. It was from this source that the king's "honor role" was compiled, permitting the crown to reward the memorable deeds of loyal subjects. According to Joyce Baldwin (*Esther* [TOTC; Downers Grove, Ill.: InterVarsity Press, 1984], 89), the king may have given up all hope of sleeping that night and instead decided to make up arrears in reviewing the records of his reign.

2. See the discussion of "The Roots and the Branches" in Marvin R. Wilson, *Our Father Abraham: Jewish Roots of the Christian Faith* (Grand Rapids: Eerdmans, 1989), 3–16.

What does this mean for the study of the books of Chronicles? Proponents of dispensational theology would have us believe that the Old Testament is Israel's history, not the church's. By dispensationalism, I mean the theological stance that assumes the old covenant belonged exclusively to the nation of Israel. According to this approach, the implementation of the new covenant in Christ has rendered the old covenant obsolete and its stipulations are no longer binding on the Christian church.[3] Chronicles, however, invites the reader to view God's progressive revelation within the movements of Israel's history through the lens of continuity—not contrast. The word of God to King David through the prophet Nathan indicated his royal dynasty would be established "forever" (2 Sam. 7:16). The writer of the Chronicles considered this promise still operative in the national life of Israel some six centuries later (1 Chron. 17:14). Curiously, one of the key New Testament titles for the church's Messiah is the Old Testament epithet for Israel's messiah, "Son of David" (cf. Matt. 9:27; Acts 13:32–34; Rom. 1:3; Rev. 5:5; 22:16). This is only one simple illustration of the overlap between the old and new covenants assumed by the New Testament writers.

If the Christian reader somehow manages to overcome the siren song of those espousing the partition of the old and new covenants, there remains the shoals of "occidentalism." Industrialization and urbanization have had a profound effect on Western thought and culture. The citizenry of many Western nations, including the United States, enjoy unparalleled personal freedom and unprecedented economic prosperity. Individualism and materialism carry a price tag, however, and the cost has been staggering. The culture of narcissism that characterizes Western society has been described as an abyss of affluent individualism resulting in alienation and loneliness, boredom in pursuit of sensation, obsession with personal convenience, and insatiable consumerism.[4] In fact, the postmodern condition of North America has been diagnosed as that of a society "cast adrift" in a time of "cultural winter."[5]

---

3. Exemplified in the statement, "the Old Testament is not our testament" (Gordon D. Fee and Douglas Stuart, *How to Read the Bible for All Its Worth*, 2d ed. (Grand Rapids: Zondervan, 1993], 151). On traditional and progressive dispensationalism, see further Herbert W. Bateman, ed., *Three Central Issues in Contemporary Dispensationalism: A Comparison of Traditional and Progressive Views* (Grand Rapids: Kregel, 1999); Craig A. Blaising and Darrell L. Bock, *Progressive Dispensationalism* (Grand Rapids: Baker, 2000).

4. The assessment of Robert H. Bork, *Slouching Towards Gomorrah: Modern Liberalism and American Decline* (New York: HarperCollins, 1996), 1–13. Bork's critique of radical individualism and radical egalitarianism in American culture is penetrating, though hardly startling. Pundits in the social science sector have been sounding similar warnings for decades, quite apart from the apocalyptic forecasts of secular "seers" like George Orwell and Alvin Toffler or Christian "prophets" like A. W. Tozer and Jacques Ellul.

5. See J. Richard Middleton and Brian J. Walsh, *Truth Is Stranger Than It Used to Be: Biblical Faith in a Postmodern Age* (Downers Grove, Ill.: InterVarsity Press, 1995), 26–27. Sadly,

Like it or not, we find ourselves living in a society that craves a future without a past. Increasingly, North American culture is characterized by a "centripetal individualism" that scorns any communal record framed in the "preterit tense" because of it preoccupation with self-gratification in the "present tense." Yet 1–2 Chronicles encourage us both to restore our sense of historicity and to reclaim the essence of our social identity. They reinforce the former by emphasizing the epithet "the God of our fathers" (some twenty-five times, e.g., 1 Chron. 12:17), a reminder that God remains the God of our ancestors in the faith. Chronicles bolsters the latter by linking individual identity with group solidarity through the genealogical records and cross-generational accounts of temple worship and related service responsibilities (e.g., 2 Chron. 31:16–18).

There is a sense in which even the form of the literature in Chronicles is a problem for many modern readers. The books of Chronicles are one type of story, a sequential narrative tracing the history of kingship in Israel. According to Leland Ryken, a story may be driven by a documentary impulse (i.e., telling *what* happened) or a literary impulse (telling in detail *how* it happened). In either case, the writer seeks to draw the reader into a shared experience with the characters of the story.[6]

By contrast, contemporary society has abandoned the shared experience of the connected narrative for a functional database consisting of "factoids." The factoid is a piece of decontextualized information capable of being stockpiled in a massive arsenal of personal or corporate knowledge, given our multiple technologies for storing, retrieving, and publishing data. And yet, the strategies of contemporary epistemology promote triviality and incoherence, removing knowledge from the sphere of education and learning and placing it in the arena of entertainment or power politics.[7] The information explosion made possible by ever more sophisticated electronic technologies has so fragmented and tribalized knowledge that our contemporaries now cry for some "metanarrative" that will bring universal meaning and coherence to the human experience.[8]

Ironically, the metanarrative our postmodern culture needs is nothing more than a universal "story" in which to root truth and reality. Alas, postmodernism has found no story large enough to include all the islands of human knowledge and experience. In step with the contemporary mania for

---

rampant *Technicism* and *Economism* within the Pacific-rim nations suggests Asian culture will soon mirror that of the West (cf. ibid., 22).

6. Ryken, *How to Read the Bible As Literature*, 33.

7. See Neil Postman's chapter entitled "A Peek-a-Boo World" in *Amusing Ourselves to Death* (New York: Viking Penguin, 1985), 64–80.

8. Middleton and Walsh, *Truth Is Stranger*, 69–71.

data, 1–2 Chronicles give us "facts" about Israelite history: names, dates, places, events, and so on. But this two-volume book is also a connected narrative, a story if you will. Chronicles is a story about a God who chooses one nation to bless all nations. Chronicles is also about a people banished from God's "promised land" because of sin and rebellion but restored to that privileged position by his gracious response to their repentance and renewed faith. According to C. S. Lewis, a good story "leaves things where it did not find them."[9] Chronicles is a "good story" because it "finds" the Hebrews in exile in Babylonia but "leaves" the Hebrews regathered in Jerusalem and Judah (according to the word of the Lord spoken by Jeremiah the prophet and orchestrated by the God of heaven, 2 Chron. 36:22–23).

In one sense Chronicles repeats the story of Genesis and the story of the entire Bible and offers a "metanarrative" for all of human history: the story of "paradise lost" and the journey toward "paradise regained." My task as a "literary escort" through the "story" of Chronicles is to help the reader navigate the historical and cultural distance between the then (postexilic Israel) and the now (twenty-first-century world).

Successful navigation of any kind is dependent on accurate directional instruments. The "true north" compass point for this study is the assumption that the relevance of Chronicles for the modern reader must be based on some theological principle or principles demonstrating the continuity between the Old and New Testaments. Several examples of those theological axioms bridging the covenants are noted below, including:

- similarity in doctrinal emphases, especially human sinfulness (e.g., Ps. 14:1–3; Prov. 14:12; cf. Rom. 3:23; 6:23)
- correspondence in essential message, that of "good tidings" or "good news" of God's freedom, release, and favor, and forgiveness (e.g., Isa. 40:9; 41:27; 52:7; 61:1; cf. Matt. 4:23; 9:35)
- consistent application of typology as a basic hermeneutic for understanding the relationship of the two covenants. Typology is literary foreshadowing and a method of biblical interpretation that establishes formal correspondence between Old Testament events, persons, objects, or ideas and similar New Testament events, persons, objects, or ideas by way of prototype. The Old Testament correspondent is identified as the "type"; the term "antitype" is used for the New Testament correspondent expressing the Old Testament truth more completely (e.g., the priesthood of Melchizedek [Gen. 14:17–24; Ps. 110:4] is the prototype of the superior priesthood of Jesus Christ

---

9. C. S. Lewis, *A Preface to Paradise Lost* (New York: Oxford Univ. Press, 1942), 133.

[Heb. 7:1–22]; the sacrificial worship of Israel [Lev. 1–7] is a shadow of the reality of Christ's "once for all sacrifice" [Heb. 10:1–18]).

- overlap in ultimate purpose, namely, making sinful humanity wise unto salvation through faith in God (e.g., Gen. 15:6; Hab. 2:4; cf. Rom. 1:17; 5:1; Eph. 2:8; 2 Tim. 3:15)
- identical understanding of the appropriate human response to God's revelation, one of loving God and obedience to his Word (e.g., Deut. 5:10; 6:5; 1 Sam. 15:22; Ps. 119:9; cf. Matt. 28:20; John 14:23; 1 Cor. 7:19; 1 John 5:2–3)

Finally, this study takes seriously the principles of biblical theology articulated in several of the New Testament letters concerning the value of the Old Testament for the church. Paul, the apostle to the Gentiles, indicated to Timothy that "all Scripture is God-breathed and is useful for teaching, rebuking, correcting and training in righteousness" (2 Tim. 3:16). By "all Scripture," Paul understood what we now call the Old Testament (cf. "the holy Scriptures" in 3:15), since that collection of Jewish literature was the church's only complete canon at the time he penned his letters. More specifically, Paul recognized that those things written in the past (i.e., the Old Testament) were meant to teach and warn us so that we might have hope and stand firm in the Christian faith (cf. Rom. 15:4; 1 Cor. 10:11).

Granted, there are two Testaments in our Bible. But we have *one* Bible, and the God of the Old Testament is the very same God of the New Testament (cf. Ps. 33:11; James 1:17).[10]

The English poet and Nobel laureate Rudyard Kipling once quipped:

> I keep six honest serving men
> (They taught me all I knew);
> Their names are What and Why and When
> And How and Where and Who.[11]

I have enlisted the help of Kipling's worthy companions here as guides for our orientation to the books of Chronicles. Our journey ushers us into Israel's past, but a detached analysis of ancient history is not our final destination. Rather, our ultimate goal is active participation in the record of Israel's

---

10. My position for understanding the relationship between the Old Testament and the New Testament is one of "biblical theology" as articulated by John Bright: "the true conclusion of Israel's history, and the fulfillment of her faith, lies in Christ and his gospel" (*The Authority of the Old Testament* [repr. Grand Rapids: Baker, 1975], 126). This means the church must recognize the entire Old Testament as valid or normative Scripture by virtue of its inspiration and of its relevance and authority to the church through its theology.

11. Rudyard Kipling, "The Elephant's Child" (from "Chapter Headings" of the "Just-So Stories" [*Rudyard Kipling's Verse*; New York: Doubleday, Doran & Co., 1931]), 678.

pilgrimage of faith in God, recognizing their story is really our own. Much like Xerxes, who rewarded Mordecai's loyalty upon hearing the chronicles of his own reign (Est. 6:1–3), we seek that kind of personalized investment in the records of the Hebrew monarchies that instills the desire to respond accordingly to the God who rules over all kingdoms and nations—all history (2 Chron. 20:6).

Lest we become victims of the same self-absorption that plagued the Chronicler's generation, it is imperative we remember that the universal theological truths derived from our study have both *individual* and *corporate* application. Even further, our appropriation of timeless biblical principles for the life and practice of contemporary Christianity must consider seriously the next generation of faithful—since by definition "today" is the threshold of "tomorrow."

What Are the Chronicles?

Literary Character

AS LITERARY HISTORY, the books of Chronicles supplement the records of Samuel and Kings. The books of 1–2 Samuel and 1–2 Kings are considered part of the "Primary History of the Old Testament" (i.e., Genesis through Kings), a connected narrative tracing the rise and fall of the nation of Israel. Chronicles, however, belongs to the "Secondary History of the Old Testament" (i.e., Chronicles, Ezra, Nehemiah, Esther). These books retell the same story from the vantage point of the postexilic period. In addition, they update the story by reporting the plight of those Hebrews who returned to Judah after the Exile and those who remained in Babylonia.

The Chronicler rehearses the history of Israel from the patriarchs (by way of genealogy) through the fall of the southern kingdom of Judah to Babylonia. As theological history, the Chronicles provide commentary on the faithfulness of God in fulfilling his covenant promises (esp. the Abrahamic covenant [Gen. 12:1–3] and the Davidic covenant [2 Sam. 7:4–17]). In addition, the Chronicles emphasize the centrality of the temple and legitimize the authoritative roles of the priestly and Levitical orders within the community. Finally, the books give considerable attention to the contributions of the Hebrew united and Judahite monarchies to the religious life of Israel.

As a literary work, the Chronicles may be broadly classified as history. According to Burke Long, "history" is an extensive and continuous written composition, based on source materials and devoted to a particular subject or time period.[12] Above all, history is concerned with chronology and cause-

---

12. According to the definition of Burke O. Long, *1 Kings: With an Introduction to Historical Literature* (FOTL 9; Grand Rapids: Eerdmans, 1984), 250.

effect relationships. More specifically, the books are truly "chronicles" in terms of literary style. The "chronicle" as a literary form is a prose composition consisting of a series of reports or selected events in third-person style, arranged and dated in chronological order.[13] The Chronicles are not "annals" in the strict sense of the literary form, since they are not a concise year-by-year reporting of events pertaining to a particular institution (e.g., monarchy or temple).

The Chronicles represent a rich collection of literary types, including:

- genealogy (1 Chron. 3:1–9)
- list or catalog (1 Chron. 9:3–23; 2 Chron. 4:19–22)
- report (2 Chron. 9:1–12)
- letter (2 Chron. 30:6–9)
- prayer (1 Chron. 17:16–27)
- speech and sermon (1 Chron. 22:5–16; 2 Chron. 32:9–15)
- prophetic revelation (1 Chron. 17:4–14)
- song (1 Chron. 16:7–36)

This combination of literary forms and the well-developed plot structure of the two books confirm Chronicles as a work of considerable artistic merit.[14]

The vocabulary of Chronicles shows a tendency to use stock phrases and standardized expressions when addressing the need for a balance between the heart and form of worship (e.g., "rejoicing" and "serving God" with a pure heart, 1 Chron. 28:9; 29:9, 19; "generous giving" and "faithfulness," e.g., 1 Chron. 29:9, 14, 17; and "thankfulness" and "joyful celebration" in worship, e.g., 1 Chron. 16:4, 7; 23:30). Finally, in keeping with the conventions of ancient historiography, the language in sections of Chronicles is highly formulaic. Several of the more prominent formulas are listed below:

- adoption formula ("I will be his father, and he will be my son," e.g., 1 Chron. 17:13; 28:6)
- authorization formula (statement identifying the proper authority behind a given procedure, usually with "person X said/wrote/commanded . . . ," e.g., 1 Chron. 9:22)
- covenant formula (usually includes the word "covenant," e.g., 2 Chron. 15:12–13; 23:16)
- date formula (reference to a specific year of a king's reign for the purpose of locating an event chronologically, e.g., 2 Chron. 23:1; 34:3)

---

13. See ibid., 246 (although Long prefers to identify the Old Testament books of Chronicles as "history").

14. On the discussion of "plot" in Chronicles see Richard L. Pratt, "First and Second Chronicles," in *A Complete Literary Guide to the Bible*, ed. L. Ryken and T. Longman III (Grand Rapids: Zondervan, 1993), 199–202.

- intimidation formula (usually includes the word "fear," e.g., 1 Chron. 14:17; 2 Chron. 14:14)
- reassurance formula ("do not be afraid or discouraged," e.g., 1 Chron. 22:13; 28:20)
- regnal résumé (an introductory and/or concluding summary of the reign of a king of Israel or Judah, including such elements as: accession age formula, length and place of reign formula, identification of queen mother formula, theological review formula, citation formula, death and burial formula, succession formula)[15]

Historical Focus

THE GENEALOGIES OF 1 Chronicles trace the heritage of covenant faith from Adam to David, with particular attention given to the Hebrew patriarchs and the twelve sons of Jacob. The actual history addressed in Chronicles spans the Hebrew monarchy from the close of Saul's reign to the Babylonian captivity of Judah (ca. 1020–586 B.C.). The accounts of David's and Solomon's kingships are focused on events and figures associated with the ark of the covenant as well as the preparations for and the construction and dedication of Yahweh's temple.

The Chronicler's history of the divided kingdoms virtually ignores the northern entity, the rival kingdom of Israel. The narrative summarizing the exploits of the kings of the southern monarchy extols their role as religious reformers and worship leaders in the temple festivals. The books of Chronicles conclude with this same emphasis on Yahweh's temple, expressed in the edict of Cyrus, king of Persia. His decree permitted the return of the Hebrew exiles to Palestine and the eventual rebuilding of their sanctuary (ca. 538 B.C., cf. 2 Chron. 36:22–23).

Reliability

EVEN A CASUAL reading of the Chronicles reveals that the writer exercised considerable freedom in selecting, arranging, and modifying the extensive source material from which he composed his history. This condition has led many biblical scholars to disparage the integrity and historical reliability of the Chronicler's record. In fact, the accuracy of the book of Chronicles has been called into question more than any other book of the Old Testament except Genesis. Specific accusations leveled against the validity of the Chronicler's history include:

---

15. For a complete catalog of formulaic language in the Old Testament historical books, see the "Glossary" in Long, *1 Kings*, 264–65; S. J. De Vries, *1 and 2 Chronicles* (FOTL 11; Grand Rapids: Eerdmans, 1989), 437–39.

- the bias shown in omitting material from Kings related to the northern kingdom
- the neglect of the sins of David and the apostasy of Solomon
- the overemphasis on the favorable character traits of the Hebrew kings
- the tendency to modify material from Samuel and Kings in moralizing and theologizing terms (e.g., 2 Sam. 24:1 compared with 1 Chron. 21:1)
- the addition (or fabrication?) of historical material not found in Samuel–Kings (e.g., 2 Chron. 33:18–20)
- the inclination to enlarge (or exaggerate?) the numbers reported in the parallel accounts of Samuel–Kings (e.g., 2 Sam. 10:18 compared with 1 Chron. 19:18)

Scholars who are committed to the trustworthiness of the books of Chronicles as a historical document have responded to these charges with a variety of arguments. For example, the Chronicler's omission of materials from Samuel–Kings should not be understood as intentional deception. Rather, the writer assumes the reader's working knowledge of the earlier Hebrew histories. This allows the compiler carefully and deliberately to select only those excerpts that have direct bearing on the religious life of the Israelite community or promote the theology of hope the Chronicles are intended to convey.

Likewise, the skeptical stance toward the historical accuracy of the Chronicler's "additions" to the history of the Hebrew kings is unwarranted. The insertion of new materials was simply the result of his wide appeal to sources outside the Samuel–Kings narrative. Many of these sources are identified by name and may actually represent older traditions than those underlying the Samuel–Kings narratives. More important, archaeological data and extrabiblical historical materials have corroborated the Chronicler's record in those instances where the different sources converge or overlap.[16]

Several explanations have been offered for the Chronicler's "embellishment" of the numbers and statistics taken from the parallel Samuel–Kings narrative (see fig. 1). Clearly, some of the numerical discrepancies can be attributed to scribal error (e.g., 2 Kings 24:8; 2 Chron. 36:9, see NIV note). Others reflect a literary approach that prefers rounding off of totals rather

---

16. Cf. J. M. Myers, *I Chronicles* (AB 12; Garden City, N.Y.: Doubleday, 1965), 240; S. Japhet, "The Historical Reliability of Chronicles," *JSOT* 33 (1985): 83–107. See further M. P. Graham, K. Hoglund, and S. McKenzie, eds., *The Chronicler As Historian.* (JSOTSup 238; Sheffield: Sheffield Academic Press, 1997); K. Peltonen, *History Debated: The Historical Reliability of the Chronicler in Pre-critical and Critical Research* (Göttingen: Vandenhoeck & Ruprecht, 1996).

than exact readings. It is even suggested that the Chronicler may have introduced the ancient equivalent of allowing for inflation in his numerology (since he was writing some five hundred years after the time of David). Finally, it is possible that portions of the books of Chronicles may have been based on older (and perhaps more reliable?) Hebrew texts and manuscripts than the Samuel–Kings accounts.

The Chronicler's modification of the historical narratives of Samuel–Kings proves more difficult to assess. Here the concept of Yahweh's continuing and progressive revelation in Hebrew history and the consequent development of Hebrew theology aids our understanding of the Chronicler's use of the ancient sources. For instance, 2 Samuel 24:1 states that the Lord incited David to take a census, whereas the parallel account in 1 Chronicles 21:1 attributes the instigation to Satan. This seems an unmistakable example of later development of Hebrew theology regarding the "agency of Satan" in Yahweh's sovereign design to test motive and punish sin among humanity (cf. the role of Satan in Job 1–2; Daniel's expansion of Hebrew understanding of resurrection from the dead in Dan. 12:2 based on Isa. 26:19).

Another category of conflicting reports in Samuel–Kings and Chronicles parallels finds its solution by analogy to the New Testament quotation of Old Testament passages. The New Testament writers both quoted and interpreted Old Testament texts for specific theological purposes. It appears that the Old Testament writers under the inspiration of the Holy Spirit also made appeal to earlier documents at their disposal in a similar fashion. This kind of interpretive quotation has sometimes been labeled "inspired exposition."[17] Apparently, God is free to interpret his own record!

A Sermon?

THE BOOKS OF Chronicles are widely acknowledged as "sermonic" literature by biblical commentators. In fact, Williamson describes the Chronicler's work as a "levitical sermon" that both warns and encourages his audience.[18] By "sermon" we mean preaching, whether an oral or written public address.

---

17. As understood by S. L. Johnson, *The Old Testament in the New* (Grand Rapids: Zondervan, 1980). For a discussion of variant readings in the Samuel–Kings and Chronicles parallels, see J. Barton Payne, "Validity of Numbers in Chronicles," *Near East Archaeological Society Bulletin* 11 (1978): 5–58 (esp. 39–51) and the pertinent sections of his commentary, "1, 2 Chronicles," in *EBC* (Grand Rapids: Zondervan, 1988), 4:302. For a more strained approach harmonizing these variant readings, see G. L. Archer, *Encyclopedia of Bible Difficulties* (Grand Rapids: Zondervan, 1982).

18. H. G. M. Williamson, *1 and 2 Chronicles* (NCBC; Grand Rapids: Eerdmans, 1982), 33.

	Higher	Lower	Content Specifics	Parallel Passage	Evaluation of Chronicles
(a)		1 Chron. 11:11	300 slain by Jashobeam, not 800	2 Sam. 23:8	Scribal error
(b)	18:4		Hadadezer's 1000 chariots and 7000 horsemen, not 1000 chariots and 700 horsemen	8:4	Correct
(c)	19:18a		7000 Syrian charioteers slain, not 700	10:18a	Correct
(d)		19:18b	and 40,000 foot soldiers, not horsemen	10:18b	Correct
(e)	21:5a		Israel's 1,100,000 troops, not 800,000	24:9a	Different objects
(f)		21:5b	Judah's 470,000 troops, not 500,000	24:9b	More precise
(g)		21:12	Three years of famine, not seven	24:13	Correct
(h)	21:25		Ornan paid 600 gold shekels, not 50 silver	24:24	Different objects
(i, j)	2 Chron 2:2, 18		3,600 to supervise temple construction, not 3,300	1 Kings 5:16	Different method of reckoning
(k)	2:10		20,000 baths of oil to Hiram's woodmen, not 20 kors (= 200 baths)	5:11	Different objects
(l)	3:15		Temple pillars 35 cubits, not 18	7:15	Scribal error
(m)	4:5		Sea holding 3000 baths, not 2000	7:26	Scribal error
(n)		8:10	250 chief officers for building temple not 550	9:23	Different method of reckoning
(o)	8:18		450 gold talents from Ophir, not 420	9:28	Correct or scribal error
(p)		9:16 (Chron. is same)	300 gold bekas per shield, not 3 minas	10:17	Different method of reckoning
(q)		9:25	4000 stalls for horses, not 40,000	4:26	Correct
(r)	22:2		Ahaziah king at age 42 years not 22	2 Kings 8:26	Scribal error
(s)		36:9	Jehoiachin king at age 8, not 18	2 Kings 24:8	Scribal error

Compared with its parallels, Chronicles is the same once, higher 10 times, and lower 7 times. Total disagreements: 19 (j repeats i) out of 213 parallel numbers.

Fig. 1. Numbers in Chronicles That Disagree with Old Testament Parallels

Rex Mason has identified the essential characteristics of a preached sermon as follows. A sermon:

- must appeal to some recognized source of authority
- proclaims some theological teaching about the nature, character, promises, works, or power of God
- calls for some kind of response on the part of the audience (e.g., penitence or obedience to some specific instruction)
- often employs rhetorical devices designed to arouse the interest of the audience and draw them into the message (e.g., wordplay, hypothetical question, illustration, literary device like simile or metaphor, anecdote, humor).[19]

Admittedly some scholars are more cautious in their analysis of Chronicles as a "sermon." They prefer to restrict the literary form known as Levitical or priestly sermon to isolated speech units in the books and in certain cases reject the description "sermon" for something more generic like "address" or "oracle."[20] Quite apart from these technicalities related to the definition and extent of the sermonic literary form of Chronicles, the term *sermon* seems most appropriate for characterizing the books because:

- the Chronicler makes repeated references to authoritative literary sources, especially other histories of Israel and prophetic writings (see "The Chronicler's Sources," below)
- according to Selman, the Chronicler's message hinges on two words from God that emphasize divine promise and fulfillment: the Davidic covenant (1 Chron. 17:3–14) and God's response to Solomon's prayer at the dedication of the temple (2 Chron. 7:11–22; see also "Chronicles As a Biography of God," below)
- the books are filled with literary devices and rhetorical features (see "Literary Character," above, and "The Composition of the Chronicles," below)[21]

The issue of audience response proves more difficult to assess. Michael Wilcock claims that the Chronicles are a sermon encouraging right rela-

---

19. Rex Mason, "Some Echoes of the Preaching in the Second Temple? Tradition Elements in Zechariah 1–8," *ZAW* 96 (1984): 223–25.

20. E.g., Roddy Braun (*1 Chronicles* [WBC 14; Waco, Tex.: Word, 1986], xxv) prefers "prophetic oracle," while William M. Schniedewind (*The Word of God in Transition: From Prophet to Exegete in the Second Temple Period* [JSOTSup 97; Sheffield: Sheffield Academic Press, 1995, 80ff.) distinguishes between the Chronicler's "prophetic speeches" and "Levitical prayers."

21. See further my article "Patchwork Poetry or Reasoned Verse? Connective Structure in 1 Chronicles XVI," *VT* 33 (1983): 97–101.

tionship between God and his people.[22] Yet in one way, the Chronicles are a sermon without an application, since the Chronicler makes no direct reference to his own time period. The response of the audience, however, is implicitly assumed everywhere in the Chronicler's sermon. The audience's intuited understanding of the preacher's application is a key ingredient of the art of biblical narrative. It also a subtle but most powerful technique for penetrating the heart and mind of hearer (or reader) with the truth claims of the preacher's message.

Two characteristics of biblical narrative are especially pertinent to the Chronicler's subliminal approach to eliciting the desired response from his audience. (1) The first is connected with the idea of plot development in storytelling. The plot of a story is a coherent sequence of related events moving toward closure. The essence of a story plot is conflict moving toward resolution.[23] By his careful selection and arrangement of the narrative events associated with the Israelite monarchies the Chronicler has encouraged his audience to consider the history as a type of commentary on the rise and fall of Davidic kingship in Israel. For the Chronicler, the resolution of this conflict (i.e., the seeming failure of the divine promise concerning the Davidic covenant) is found in the continuity of Hebrew worship of the God of Abraham and in the restoration of the Hebrews to the land of Israel under Cyrus king of Persia.[24]

(2) The other characteristic is linked to the role the Chronicler plays as the "narrator" of the events in his retelling of Israel's history. The narrator of a story speaks in the third person, leaving personal judgment and moral commentary to the subtle influences of literary structure and the dialogue of the main characters in the story. As narrator, the Chronicler persuades the audience to understand the history of Israel from his viewpoint, a viewpoint different from those of the participants in the story. Point of view is crucial for the interpretation of the narrative because it is the ideological lens through which the audience comprehends the events of the story line. The Chronicler's viewpoint reflects the perspective of God and the ideology of the Hebrew Bible, making Chronicles a theological commentary on Israelite history. In fact, Raymond Dillard has described Chronicles as a "tract," a religious pamphlet designed to renew Israel's hope in God and restore right worship of him.[25]

---

22. Michael Wilcock, *The Message of Chronicles* (BST; Downers Grove, Ill.: InterVarsity Press, 1987), 14.

23. On plot, plot types, and conflict motifs in biblical narrative, see Ryken, *How to Read the Bible As Literature*, 33–86.

24. For insightful comments on narrative structure in Chronicles, see Kenneth A. Mathews, "Preaching Historical Narrative," 27–31.

25. Raymond B. Dillard, *2 Chronicles* (WBC 15; Waco, Tex.: Word, 1987), xviii.

Introduction

The intrusion of the prophetic voice in the Chronicler's history is another way in which the books may be classified as sermonic literature. More than a dozen prophetic speeches are scattered throughout Chronicles, addressed to both the Hebrew kings and people alike (see fig. 2). The Chronicler's purpose for inserting the prophetic speeches matches that of Jehoshaphat's speech to Judah, an exhortation to his audience to believe in God and the word of his prophets so they might be "successful" as his covenant people (2 Chron. 20:20).

Name	Reference	Title	Audience
Amasai	1 Chron. 12:18	chief	King David
Nathan	1 Chron. 17:1–15	prophet	King David
Shemaiah	2 Chron. 12:5–8	prophet	King Rehoboam, officials
Azariah	2 Chron. 15:1–7	none	King Asa
Hanani	2 Chron. 16:7–9	seer	King Asa
Zedekiah	2 Chron. 18:9–10	prophet	King Jehoshaphat, Ahab
Micaiah	2 Chron. 18:12–22	prophet	Kings Jehoshaphat, Ahab
Jehu	2 Chron. 19:1–3	seer	King Jehoshaphat
Jahaziel	2 Chron. 20:14–17	Levite	King Jehoshaphat, all Judah
Eliezer	2 Chron. 20:37	none	King Jehoshaphat
Elijah	2 Chron. 21:12	prophet	King Jehoram
Zechariah	2 Chron. 24:20–22	priest	the people
Anonymous	2 Chron. 25:7–8	man of God	King Amaziah
Anonymous	2 Chron. 25:15–16	prophet	King Amaziah
Obed	2 Chron. 28:9–11	prophet	Israelite army
Huldah	2 Chron. 34:22–28	prophetess	King Josiah
Neco	2 Chron. 35:20–21	pharaoh of Egypt	King Josiah

Fig. 2. Prophetic Speeches in Chronicles[26]

---

26. Adapted from Schniedewind, *The Word of God in Transition*, 123. Note that Schniedewind distinguishes between the prophetic speeches of "prophets" and "inspired messengers" on the basis of "inspiration formulas."

In fact, Schniedewind has suggested that these prophetic speeches in Chronicles represent a new kind of "prophecy" in later biblical literature—"the inspired interpretation" of earlier prophetic texts.[27] The basic functions of these prophetic speakers in Chronicles included interpretation of historical events (e.g., Shemaiah's speech in 2 Chron. 12:5–8), warning (e.g., Jahaziel's speech in 20:14), and exhortation (e.g., Zechariah's speech in 24:20–21). The Chronicler was also careful to emphasize the key themes of the earlier Hebrew prophetic tradition, namely:

- the divine retribution associated with the blessings and curses conditioning Yahweh's covenant relationship with Israel (e.g., 1 Chron. 28:9; 2 Chron. 7:13–14)
- the call to return to Yahweh in genuine repentance (e.g., 2 Chron. 12:6–12; 15:4)

Concerning the former, Williamson has noted that the Chronicler only cites prophetic literary sources when referring to a "good" king of Judah.[28] He further suggests that this may be the Chronicler's way of shifting the thrust of the prophetic message from divine judgment to divine blessing. As to the latter, it seems the Chronicler recites the illustrations of past repentance on the part of the Israelites as concrete examples to assure postexilic Judah of God's continued response of merciful forgiveness to those who return to him.

A Morality Play?

MICHAEL WILCOCK HAS suggested Chronicles might be understood as a drama of sorts, a "morality play" in the guise of historical narrative.[29] By "morality play," we mean a dramatization of a conflict between good and evil or right and wrong from which an ethical lesson may be drawn. Granted, one might identify a cast of characters in the narrative of Chronicles, complete with heroes like David and Solomon and villains like Ahaz and Manasseh. What better setting for the staging of a drama than Jerusalem, King David's Zion and the city of God? Or could one imagine a more elaborate prop than the temple of Yahweh or more distinctive costuming than the priestly wardrobe of its ministers? But Chronicles may be considered drama for other reasons, especially for its sermonic style, the frequent intrusion of the prophetic voice, and the theme of divine retribution.

---

27. Schniedewind, *The Word of God in Transition*, 128–29.
28. Williamson, *1 and 2 Chronicles*, 19.
29. Wilcock, *The Message of Chronicles*, 15–16.

The sermonic style of the Chronicler's narrative contributes to its classification as a type of "morality play." Mason has identified several characteristics of preaching embedded in the literature of Chronicles (see above the Chronicles as "A Sermon?").[30]

According to Henry Sloane Coffin, preaching is the presentation of "truth through personality to constrain conscience at once."[31] Chronicles is both sermon and morality play, in that the Levitical preacher articulates God's truth as witnessed in Israel's history for the sake of mobilizing the conscience of his audience. The conscience is that human faculty or innate principle of right and wrong that prompts self-awareness of moral goodness (or its lack) in one's intentions and conduct. The portraits of good and evil in the Chronicler's character studies of the Israelite kings call attention to the human "heart" (the word occurs more than thirty-five times in the two books). The Chronicler understood that a person's will is inclined toward good or evil as it is informed by the character of the conscience, whether deadened by sin or enlivened by faith in God. This explains the emphasis in his "preaching" on God's work of probing the human heart to test motive and encourage loyalty among the faithful (e.g., 1 Chron. 28:9; 29:17–18).

The recital of Judah's history (the southern kingdom) underscores another key message for postexilic Jerusalem. This message is the principle of divine retribution associated with the blessings and curses conditioning Yahweh's covenant with Israel. Beyond its sermonic style and prophetic interjection, Chronicles is a morality play because it showcases "a God of inflexible justice."[32] The Chronicler's story of the Judahite monarchy substantiates his work as a "morality play" for two reasons. (1) It validates the thesis of divine retribution as an undergirding principle shaping Israelite history: The wicked have "perished" and the righteous have "prospered" over the centuries (cf. Ps. 1:3, 6). (2) The example of Davidic kingship stands as a warning to postexilic Judah that the retribution principle is not dormant but still operative in the life of the covenant community.

Lest the community suffer "spiritual paralysis" over the threat of divine retribution, the Chronicler also offers select case studies illustrating the divine alternative to covenant curses. One such case study is the account of King Manasseh's reign (2 Chron. 33:1–9). Even as God's justice cannot fail, neither can God's grace, as attested in the repentance of Manasseh (cf. 2 Chron.

---

30. Rex Mason, *Preaching the Tradition: Homily and Hermeneutics after the Exile* (Cambridge: Cambridge Univ. Press, 1990), 257.

31. Henry Sloane Coffin, *Evangelistic Preaching* (New York: Board of National Missions, n.d.), 6.

32. Wilcock, *The Message of Chronicles*, 15.

33:10–13). The Chronicler recognizes that his audience must have an understanding of the retribution principle or they are doomed to repeat past failures. Hence, respect for divinely appointed authority figures and obedience to the covenant stipulations are essential for the success of the postexilic community. A replay of the Babylonian exile is unthinkable!

Why Were the Chronicles Compiled?

THE DISPOSITION OF the Chronicler's audience is much like that of the psalmist who lamented, "How long, O LORD? Will you forget me forever?" (Ps. 13:1). A cloud of despair and a shroud of doubt hung over postexilic Judah because of the apparent failure of Zerubbabel and others to inaugurate the new covenant promised by Jeremiah (Jer. 31:31–34). This new covenant also pledged that a David-like king would rise to power in Israel (Jer. 33:15; Ezek. 37:24) and that God's people would be infused with a new heart and a new spirit (Ezek. 36:26–27). Later the prophets Haggai and Zechariah predicted that God would shake the nations and overthrow kingdoms and Jerusalem would once again enjoy renown as a wealthy commercial hub and an international worship center (Hag. 2:7, 22; Zech. 14:16).

This hope for Israelite restoration projected by the prophets has been deferred for two hundred years by the time of the Chronicler. The Hebrews are convinced that God has reneged on his covenant promises. Victimized by a martyr complex and paralyzed by self-pity, the contemporaries of the Chronicler would have found comfort in the words of the seventeenth-century English satirist Alexander Pope:

> Hope springs eternal in the human breast:
> Man never Is, but always To be blest.[33]

Indeed, the exiles under Assyria and Babylonia are over for the minority of Hebrews who have returned, but Judah remains a struggling and insignificant political and cultural "backwater" under Persian domination. National and political life are overshadowed by the pagan "superpowers" of Persia and Greece. The religion of the Jews is challenged by the rival temple cult of the Samaritans on Mount Gerizim, the great cult of Ahura Mazda among the Persians, and the Greek mystery religions. It is against this backdrop that the Chronicler offers a "theology of hope" to postexilic Judah, couched in the annals of earlier Israelite history. He seeks to assure the Jewish community of faith that the present distress will soon pass and give way to God's restoration of Israel, according to the theocratic ideal expressed in Chronicles.

---

33. Alexander Pope, "Essay on Man," in *Collected Poems* (London: Dent & Sons, 1924), 184.

Chronicles As a Biography of God

THE PURPOSE OF Chronicles is only secondarily to rekindle hope through the retelling of the history of Israel, especially the story of Hebrew kingship. Its primary purpose is to tell the story of the God of history, more specifically, the biography of the God of Israel's history. The Chronicler's biography of God includes "chapters" addressing the themes of his:

- sovereign rule as Creator (cf. 2 Chron. 20:6)
- providential intervention as Sustainer (cf. 2 Chron. 20:12)
- election of Israel (1 Chron. 16:13, 17)
- faithfulness to his covenant promises (1 Chron. 17:18–24)
- responsiveness to prayer (2 Chron. 6:40; 7:12)
- justice (2 Chron. 19:7)
- goodness (2 Chron. 30:18–20)
- mercy (2 Chron. 30:9)

The "biography" as a literary form in the ancient world was a stylized account of the public and professional life of a significant individual in a given society. The "life story" of certain key political or religious figures was important as a model or example of the distinctive norms and values shared by that group or society. The primary purpose of the biography was to reshape or change the life of the reader through a literary encounter with a significant character portrayed as an ideal representative of the community. The Chronicler's biography or "life of God" has a similar purpose. The "public life" of God, so to speak, is "chronicled" as one of absolute faithfulness to his promises made to Israel as his chosen people, especially David and his heirs (2 Chron. 6:14–15). The Chronicler reminds his audience that the God of Israel seeks a similar response as his eyes range throughout the earth looking for "those whose hearts are fully committed to him" (16:9).

Chronicles As a Theology of Hope

THE HOPE OFFERED by the Chronicler, however, is not simply "religious escapism" accomplished through a fixation on certain theological abstractions about God. Rather, the essence of hope is concretized for the Chronicler in the response of authentic worship of this God of history. The Chronicler is enough of a psychologist to recognize that hope is largely the by-product of a proper relationship of the self with the Transcendent,[34] thus enabling the

---

34. See the discussion of Kierkegaard's existential psychology in S. L. Jones and R. E. Butman, *Modern Psychotherapies: A Comprehensive Christian Appraisal* (Downers Grove, Ill.: Inter-Varsity Press, 1991), 279–81, esp. the level of the *religious stage* in his theory of human

individual to engage in the necessary tussle with the fundamental polarities of life, *infinitude and finitude* and *eternity and temporality*.[35]

The Chronicler is also enough of a theologian to realize that an authentic worship response to the God of Israel's history is crucial to gaining any integrated perspective on time and circumstance (cf. Ps. 73:15–17, 23–26). Time is the domain of God; past, present, and future belong to ʾel ʿolam ("the Eternal God," cf. Gen. 21:33; Isa. 40:28; 57:15). Likewise, circumstance is also God's province in that he knows all things (Job 28:23–24) and sustains and directs all creation (Job 12:10; 33:4; Ps. 139:16). Essentially, the Chronicler offers hope to postexilic Judah in the form of instruction for worship renewal. Specific aspects of worship emphasized in this "spiritual renewal workshop" include:

- the recognition that worship is an attitude, a condition of heart and mind, more than ritual (cf. 1 Chron. 28:9; 2 Chron. 6:10–11, 31, 33)
- the significance of worship as "word," seen in the emphasis on oath-taking, prayer, songs of praise and thanksgiving, confession, and liturgical responses (cf. 1 Chron. 15:29; 16:4, 9, 23, 36, 40; 17:16–27; 2 Chron. 15:15)
- the importance of formal corporate worship because of the benefits associated with belonging to a worship community (2 Chron. 7:8–10)
- the necessity of keeping a liturgical calendar as a reminder that time and life belong to God (2 Chron. 30:15–27)
- the contribution of music as the "universal language" of worship (2 Chron. 5:13; 29:28, 30; 30:21)
- the reinforcement of theological truth through sign and symbol (e.g., the ark of the covenant and the presence of God, 2 Chron. 5:7–14)
- the value of modeling in worship through priestly leadership and mediation (1 Chron. 15:11–15; 16:4–6; 28:21)
- the principle of lay participation in corporate worship (1 Chron. 16:36; 29:17–18; 2 Chron. 7:4–5; 31:10; 35:7)

Like the psalmist before him, the Chronicler understands that ultimately hope must be placed in God (Ps. 42:5, 11; 43:3) because hope issues from God alone (Ps. 62:5). Indeed, God our Savior is "the hope of all the ends of the earth" (Ps. 65:5).

The Chronicler's remedy for overcoming spiritual malaise remains a potent medicine for God's people today. The essential ingredients of the Chronicler's antidote are as contemporary as that of modern psychotherapy as it engages

---

development (i.e., "a trusting personal relationship with the transcendent God of the Christian faith," 280).

35. Ibid., 280.

the dysfunction spawned in our culture of narcissism—a variety of interrelated cognitive and behavioral strategies targeting self-absorption.[36] The Chronicler's prescription for moving his audience off "self-center" reads like this:

- shift the focus from self to God through the experience of worship renewal (2 Chron. 6:18–21; cf. Ps. 73:13–28)
- contextualize the role of the individual in the larger community of faith (i.e., the notion of many members in one body, whether Israel in the Old Testament or the church in the New Testament, cf. 2 Chron. 7:14)
- develop a cross-generational blueprint for spiritual growth and development (i.e., focused strategies promoting the welfare of the "next generation"; e.g., David's extensive preparations assuring the success of his son Solomon, 1 Chron. 28–29)
- gain long-range perspective by locating the individual (i.e., the immediate personal concerns of the postexilic Hebrews at the time of the Chronicler) on the continuum of the community's history (i.e., "God's-story" of redemption for all creation through the nation of Israel; note the numerous occurrences of the phrase "the God of our fathers" in Chronicles, e.g., 1 Chron. 12:17; 29:18)

Chronicles As a Call to Worship

LITURGICALLY, THE CALL to worship is an invitation, a summoning of the assembly of the faithful into God's presence. The call to worship is a call to celebration, praising God for who he is as the only true God and thanking him for what he has done to restore the pre-Fall creation order and to redeem fallen humanity. Certain portions of the books of Chronicles emphasize temple worship, especially the pilgrimage festivals, and they are presented as a model for worship in postexilic Judah. Some of these texts still have currency for use as a call to worship for our contemporary church settings (e.g., 1 Chron. 29:10–13; 2 Chron. 7:14).

But there is another sense in which the entirety of 1 and 2 Chronicles is a call to worship because in retelling the story of Israel's history we have a "biography of God" (or even an "autobiography," since God inspired the writing of the Chronicles by his Holy Spirit, see above). In telling the story of the God of history, and more specifically the God of Israel's history, this

---

36. It seems the Chronicler's methods have parallels in several of the modern psychotherapies, including: *existential therapy* (especially suited for individuals confronting personal crises), *transactional analysis* (with its emphasis on experience in a group therapy format), and even *family therapy* (stressing the importance of clearly defined structures and roles, including clarity concerning hierarchical relationships; see Jones and Butman, *Modern Psychotherapies*, 278–300, 324–45, 349–72).

biography reveals who God is and what he has done for Israel and ultimately for all the nations. Once we have entered into God's presence through the literary portal of "salvation history" as narrated in Chronicles, what can our response be but one of praise and thanksgiving!

> Give thanks to the LORD, call on his name;
>> make known among the nations what he has done.
> Sing to him, sing praise to him;
>> tell of all his wonderful acts.
> Glory in his holy name;
>> let the hearts of those who seek the LORD rejoice.
>> (1 Chron. 16:8–10)[37]

When Were the Chronicles Compiled?

THE CHRONICLES, ALONG with Ezra-Nehemiah, are probably the latest books of the Old Testament in respect to the date of composition. The time of writing for the Chronicles is usually assigned to the postexilic period of Hebrew history. Dates range anywhere from the reforms of the prophets Haggai and Zechariah (ca. 515 B.C.) to well into the Greek period (sometime between 300 and 160 B.C.).

The last dated event in Chronicles is the record of the decree issued by the Persian King Cyrus permitting the Jews to return to Palestine from exile in Babylonia (ca. 538 B.C.; cf. 2 Chron. 36:22–23). If Zerubbabel's genealogy is ordered in chronological sequence, however (cf. 1 Chron. 3:17–21), then seven generations are counted from the exile of King Jehoiachin (ca. 597 B.C.) to the Chronicler's own era. This internal evidence moves the date of (at least the genealogical portion of) Chronicles nearer 450 B.C. (assuming a twenty-year generation). The widely acknowledged associations between Chronicles and Ezra–Nehemiah (whether or not one identifies Ezra as the Chronicler) also suggest a similar date.[38] Given the uncertainties in

---

37. The topic of worship is developed more fully below in the chapter addressing the role of the Levites as facilitators of worship education (1 Chron. 6) and the chapter portraying King David as a worship leader (21:1–29:9).

38. Many commentators recognize a two-stage compilation of the books. Braun suggests the rebuilding of the second temple (ca. 515 B.C.) as the occasion for the initial stratum of Chronicles (i.e., 1 Chron. 10–2 Chron. 36:21), reaching final form about 350 B.C. (i.e., the addition of the genealogies [1 Chron. 1–9] and the epilogue [2 Chron. 36:22–23]). Given the emphasis on the Levitical priesthood and temple worship, it seems more likely that the reforms of Ezra (including the rehabilitation of the priesthood) and the dedication of the city wall rebuilt by Nehemiah (Neh. 12) were the occasions prompting the writing of the core history of Chronicles (ca. 450 B.C.).

559 B.C.	Accession of Cyrus in Persia
539	Babylon falls to Cyrus (Dan. 5:30–31)[39]
538	Edict of Cyrus (Ezra 1:1–4)
537?	Jews return under Sheshbazzar and Zerubbabel (Ezra 1:11; 2:2)
536	Second Temple foundation set (Ezra 3:8)
530	Accession of Cambyses
522	Accession of Darius I
520–518	Haggai and Zechariah preach to Judah (Hag. 1:1; Zech. 1:1, 7; 7:1)
515	Second temple completed (Ezra 6:15)
490	Battle of Marathon; Malachi preaches?
485	Accession of Xerxes
478	Esther becomes Xerxes' queen (Est. 2:16)
465	Accession of Artaxerxes I
458	Ezra arrives in Jerusalem (Ezra 7:8–9)
445	Nehemiah arrives in Jerusalem (Neh. 2:11)
432	Nehemiah's return to Susa (Neh. 13:6)

Fig. 3. Postexilic Israelite Chronology

approximating the length of a biblical generation, it seems reasonable to assign the compilation of Chronicles in its final form to a date between 450 and 400 B.C.

How Were the Chronicles Compiled?

As History

THE CHRONICLER MAY be favorably compared to the New Testament Gospel writer Luke as both a historian and a theologian. As a historian Luke gathered materials (including eyewitness accounts), investigated other historical sources, interviewed eyewitnesses, and set down in writing an "orderly account" of the life of Jesus Christ (Luke 1:1–4; cf. Acts 1:1–2). Luke's Gospel is a blend of prose and poetry and combines third-person reporting with first-person speech (esp. conversations, prayers, and songs). Finally, Luke

---

39. It appears as if "Darius the Mede" in Dan. 5:30–31 is a local name for Cyrus.

was heavily dependent on the early church's use of the Old Testament as the source book for identifying Jesus as the Messiah.[40]

Likewise, the Chronicler wrote a chronologically ordered account of Israel's history (from Adam to his own day) based on a careful analysis of existing historical sources. Further, the Chronicler's history of Israel is a blend of prose and poetry and combines third-person narrative with first-person speech (esp. in conversations, prayers, psalms, and letters). Lastly, the Chronicler was also dependent on those earlier Scriptures contained in the Hebrew Bible (notably the books of Samuel, Kings, Psalms, Isaiah, and Jeremiah).

As Theology

AS A THEOLOGIAN, Luke emphasized the theme of God's salvation for both Jew and Gentile rooted in the new covenant established by the death, burial, and resurrection of Jesus Christ. Luke's history is a theology of hope centered in the good news of the kingdom of God, inaugurated by the teaching and work of Jesus as Messiah. Luke was also an apologist of sorts, since he sought to legitimize Jesus of Nazareth as the long-awaited Messiah and the church of Jesus Christ as the rightful heir of the covenant promises given to the Israelites.[41]

In much the same way, the Chronicler's recitation of Israel's history is grounded in the theology of the covenants associated with Abraham, Moses, and David. The Chronicler's history is also a theology of hope, assuring the restoration of Israel as God's chosen people on the record of his past faithfulness to the Hebrews in word and deed. Finally, the Chronicler served as an apologist. He sought to establish the continuity between postexilic Judah and preexilic Israel as the covenant community of Yahweh. Moreover, he demonstrated the legitimacy of the Levitical priesthood as the rightful heirs of the divine authority previously invested in the kings and prophets of Israel.

The Chronicler's Sources

LIKE ANY OTHER historical work, ancient or modern, Chronicles makes use of earlier and contemporary documents. Like his New Testament counterpart Luke, the Chronicler is a model research historian, carefully citing the resources informing his edition of Israelite history. The sources identified by the Chronicler are sorted below according to literary category:

---

40. See I. Howard Marshall, *Luke: Historian and Theologian* (Grand Rapids: Zondervan, 1970), esp. 53–76. For a more detailed assessment of the Chronicler's historiographical method, see Graham, Hoglund, and McKenzie, *The Chronicler As Historian*.

41. Marshall, *Luke: Historian and Theologian*, 77–102.

Introduction

1.Genealogical records
- descendants of Simeon (1 Chron. 4:33)
- descendants of Gad (1 Chron. 5:17)
- descendants of Benjamin (1 Chron. 7:9)
- descendants of Asher (1 Chron. 7:40)
- all Israel (1 Chron. 9:1)
- gatekeepers (1 Chron. 9:22)
- Rehoboam (2 Chron. 12:15)

2.Letters and official documents
- David's temple plans (1 Chron. 28:11–12)
- Sennacherib's letter (2 Chron. 32:9–20)
- Hezekiah's Passover letter (2 Chron. 30:6–12)
- proclamation of Cyrus (2 Chron. 36:22–23)

3.Other histories
- the book of the kings of Israel (1 Chron. 9:1; 2 Chron. 20:34)
- the book of the annals of King David (1 Chron. 27:24)
- the book of the kings of Judah and Israel (2 Chron. 16:11; 25:26; 28:26; 32:32)
- the annotations on the book of the kings (2 Chron. 24:27)
- the book of the kings of Israel and Judah (2 Chron. 27:7; 35:27; 36:8)
- the annals of the kings of Israel (2 Chron. 33:18)
- the directions written by David king of Israel and by his son Solomon (2 Chron. 35:4)

4.Prophetic writing
- the records of Samuel the seer (1 Chron. 29:29)
- the records of Nathan the prophet (1 Chron. 29:29; 2 Chron. 9:29)
- the records of Gad the seer (1 Chron. 29:29)
- the prophecy of Ahijah the Shilonite (2 Chron. 9:29)
- the visions of Iddo the seer (2 Chron. 9:29)
- the records of Shemaiah the prophet (2 Chron. 12:15)
- the records of Iddo the seer (2 Chron. 12:15)
- the annotations of the prophet Iddo (2 Chron. 13:22)
- the annals of Jehu son of Hanani (recorded in the book of the kings of Israel) (2 Chron. 20:34)
- (the events of Uzziah's reign) recorded by the prophet Isaiah son of Amoz (2 Chron. 26:22)
- the vision of the prophet Isaiah son of Amoz (in the book of the kings of Judah and Israel) (2 Chron. 32:32)
- the records of the seers (2 Chron. 33:19)

There is considerable debate in the literature as to the number, nature, and content of these sources since many of the titles suggest considerable overlap. More important is the relationship of the Chronicler's resources to the anterior texts of the books Samuel and Kings. It is now argued that many of the Chronicler's bibliographic citations do not represent independent sources but are variant names for the two primary sources of 1–2 Kings' corpus ("the book of the annals of the kings of Judah" [e.g., 1 Kings 14:29] and "the book of the annals of the kings of Israel" [e.g., 1 Kings 15:31).[42]

The Chronicler's modification of Kings' royal annal formula to include the name "Israel" should not be construed as deception or misrepresentation (e.g., 1 Kings 15:23 refers to "the book of the annals of the kings of Judah"; the parallel citation in 2 Chron. 16:11 cites "the book of the kings of Judah and Israel").[43] Rather, the expansion of the formula is in keeping with the Chronicler's purpose to unify the Hebrew tribes after the demise of the divided monarchies. Similarly, the Chronicler highlights the important role of the prophets as a positive force in the Judahite monarchy by interpolating references to them as advocates of repentance when the narrative in Kings preserves no prophetic intervention.[44]

There is no doubt that the Chronicler makes use of historical sources no longer extant (e.g., the references to genealogical records). It is more significant to recognize, however, that the Chronicler relies principally on biblical books already established in the Hebrew canon for his retelling of Israel's history (especially Samuel, Kings, and Psalms). This fact is important for two reasons: First, it affirms the high regard of the Chronicler for the received Scriptures of the Hebrew Bible; second, it provides insight into the exegetical tradition of the later biblical writers as it relates to the selection, arrangement, and reshaping of excerpts from those earlier canonical documents.[45]

The Place of Chronicles in the Canon

THE HEBREW TITLE of the book is literally "the words of the days" or "the events" of the monarchies. The Hebrew title is characteristically taken from the first verse, but here the title phrase is actually found in 1 Chronicles 27:24.

---

42. See the discussion of the Chronicler's sources in H. G. M. Williamson, *1 and 2 Chronicles*, 17–21 (cf. the elaboration on Williamson's thesis in D. M. Howard Jr., *An Introduction to the Old Testament Historical Books* [Chicago: Moody Press, 1993], 238–42).
43. See the discussion of the name "Israel" in the parallel source citations of Kings and Chronicles in Howard, *An Introduction to the Old Testament Historical Books*, 240–41.
44. Michael Fishbane, *Biblical Interpretation in Ancient Israel* (Oxford: Clarendon, 1985), 387.
45. See ibid., 385–403.

Like Samuel and Kings, 1 and 2 Chronicles were originally one book. Chronicles follows Ezra–Nehemiah in the Hebrew Bible, suggesting it either was accepted into the Old Testament canon at a later date or was viewed as an appendix to the Writings collection since it supplemented the histories found in Samuel and Kings. The text was divided into two books when the Hebrew Bible was translated into Greek.

The English version adopts the order of the LXX in placing Chronicles among the historical books after Kings and before Ezra–Nemehiah. The books are called "The Things Omitted" in the Greek Old Testament, a reference to the things passed over by the histories of Samuel and Kings (see Appendix A on the synoptic relationship of Samuel/Kings and Chronicles).[46] The English title "Chronicles" is a shortened form of Jerome's suggestion that the books be called "a chronicle of the whole divine history."[47] The reference to the death of the priest Zechariah by Jesus suggests that these books were considered canon at his time and were located at or near the end of that collection (Matt. 23:35; cf. 2 Chron. 24:20–22).

The Chronicler is a theologian, religious teacher, and historian. His interpretive and apologetic history of Israel is designed to awaken covenant faith and evoke hope in the beleaguered postexilic Jewish community. The larger structure of Chronicles highlights this hopefulness in that the first book opens with the building of the temple (with Gentile help) and the second book closes with the edict of a Gentile king commanding the building of the Second Temple (cf. 2 Chron. 36:22–23). An expanded version of this tagline, the so-called Cyrus colophon in 2 Chronicles, appears in Ezra 1:1–3. The repetition of the decree of Cyrus serves to bridge the records of Ezra and Nehemiah with the history of the Chronicler. The connection of the Ezra–Nehemiah reforms with Israel's "temple history" reinforces the Chronicler's theocratic ideal and the expectations of a "new exodus."

The Composition of Chronicles

IT IS GENERALLY assumed that the historical materials of Chronicles were spliced together in two distinct stages. The original work consisting of 1 Chronicles 10 through 2 Chronicles 34 was probably compiled in conjunction with the prophetic ministries of Haggai and Zechariah about 500 B.C.

---

46. Commentators have lamented this disparaging for Chronicles in the LXX, contending that it has contributed to the neglect of the unique contents and message of the books (e.g., Braun, *1 Chronicles*, xix).

47. See the article by Gary N. Knoppers and Paul B. Harvey Jr., "Omitted and Remaining Matters: On the Names Given in the Book of Chronicles in Antiquate," *JBL* 121 (2002): 227–43.

It is even possible this rewriting of Israel's "royal history" was commissioned as part of the celebration surrounding the completion of the Second Temple. The second stage of compilation saw the addition of 1 Chronicles 1–9 and 2 Chronicles 35–36, perhaps in association with the reforms of Ezra and Nehemiah (ca. 450–400 B.C.).

The genealogies of 1 Chronicles 1–9 preface the review of the monarchies of David and Solomon. The section makes important contributions to the overall plan and purpose of the book in several ways, including:

- calling attention to the unity of "all Israel," a necessary theme after the fall of the divided monarchies
- confirming God's election of Israel and demonstrating the divine fulfillment of the covenant promise made to Abraham and Sarah concerning "a great nation" (cf. Gen. 12:1–3)
- legitimizing the royal and priestly leadership of the nation (given the particular focus on the tribes of Judah and Levi).

The section outlining the reigns of kings Saul and David presents a study of contrasts (1 Chron. 10–29). Saul's disobedience, failure, and neglect of the ark of the covenant serve as a foil for David's faithfulness, triumphs, and careful attention to the ark of God and Israel's worship. The reign of King Solomon is summarized in the next major unit of the history (2 Chron. 1–9). The theme of promise and fulfillment related to the Davidic covenant ties the story of Solomon to the preceding narrative, with David cast as a "second Moses" and Solomon a "second Joshua." The concluding block of material reviews the history of Judah in view of God's promise to "forgive and heal" when the Israelites "humble themselves and pray and seek" God (2 Chron. 7:14), emphasizing the reigns of Hezekiah and Josiah. Both are idealized as Davidic and Solomonic type figures because of their attention to the cleansing of the temple and the restoration of proper worship in Jerusalem (2 Chron. 10–36).

Where Were the Chronicles Compiled?

THE PROVENANCE OR geographical setting for the writing of the Chronicles is unspecified. Since the Chronicler has written a theology of hope for postexilic Judah, it seems likely the compiler was a member of the restoration community. Further, the books seek to legitimize the priestly corps attending to the duties associated with temple liturgy and to reestablish Jerusalem as the authentic site of Hebrew worship. This makes it probable that the author of Chronicles was also a resident of postexilic Jerusalem.

Who Compiled the Chronicles?

Authorship

THE CHRONICLES ARE an anonymous composition. The stylistic and linguistic similarities with Ezra–Nehemiah have led many biblical scholars to conclude a single "Chronicler" was responsible for all four books. Following the Jewish tradition assigning the Chronicles to Ezra the scribe (Babylonian Talmud, *Baba Batra* 15a), W. F. Albright championed the view that Ezra and the Chronicler were the same person.[48] At one time there was an overwhelming consensus that Ezra and Chronicles were the product of a single author, but the identification of the Chronicler with Ezra the scribe has not been universally accepted.

More recent biblical research has questioned the literary ties between Chronicles and Ezra–Nehemiah.[49] The comprehensive analysis of the Chronicler's language has led most Old Testament scholars today to acknowledge the unity of the two books of Chronicles but reject the idea of common authorship of Ezra–Nehemiah. Now the tendency is to separate Chronicles from Ezra–Nehemiah and recognize the two works as distinct compositions.[50] Thematic differences such as the lack of Davidic messianism, "second exodus" overtones, and the "pan-Israelite" emphasis in the latter are also cited as reasons for this detachment. At present it seems best to accept the books of Chronicles as a unified composition written by an unknown "Chronicler." The writer's pointed interests in the temple and its priestly and Levitical personnel suggest he himself is a priest or Levite employed in the service of the temple. The exact relationship of the Chronicler's writings to the books of Ezra–Nehemiah remains an open question.

The Chronicler As Pastor

THE CHRONICLER IS both a historian and a theologian. As a historian the Chronicler selects and arranges historical information following the conventions of historiography, whether ancient or modern. His account of Israel's history utilizes sources, contains unifying themes, emphasizes the role of key individuals (e.g., kings and prophets) as "history makers," and takes note

---

48. William F. Albright, "The Date and Personality of the Chronicler," *JBL* 40 (1921): 104–14.

49. See the watershed study of Sara Japhet, "The Supposed Common Authorship of Chronicles and Ezra-Nehemiah Investigated Anew," *VT* 18 (1968): 330–71; cf. her *I and II Chronicles* (OTL; Louisville: Westminster John Knox, 1993), 23–28.

50. E.g., J. A. Thompson, *1, 2 Chronicles* (NAC 9; Nashville: Broadman & Holman, 1993), 29.

of causality in the events of human history. As a theologian the Chronicler assumes God's sovereignty and his providential activity in created order, emphasizing themes related to the divine-human relationship like covenant and temple worship.

But perhaps more important, the Chronicler is also a pastor and an exegete. As a pastor the Chronicler's purpose is both instruction and exhortation. His narrative is a sermon, an exposition on the pattern of failure and judgment, grace and restoration in Israel's history. According to Wilcock, "its object is the fostering of a right relationship between God and his people."[51] Two methods are especially important to the Chronicler as an interpreter of Israel's history: (1) a form of biblical typology (i.e., formal correspondence between persons, institutions, and/or events of earlier biblical history with the same of later biblical history by way of foreshadowing), and (2) and what is now known as innerbiblical exegesis (i.e., the Bible's citation of itself as a historical and theological source).[52] In each case, the Chronicler's exegetical method assumes the supremacy of the earlier Hebrew Scriptures and models the principle of permitting Scripture to interpret Scripture.[53]

Audience

THE RESIDENTS OF postexilic Jerusalem and the surrounding province of Judah are the Chronicler's audience. Although they are several generations removed from those Jews who repatriated the land after the Babylonian exile, the memory of that catastrophe lingers. The emphasis on "all Israel" (the phrase occurs forty times in the Chronicles) suggests the writer has the entire nation in mind, including the political leadership, the religious leadership, and the general populace. The theme of "all Israel" in the Chronicler's history also suggests an attempt to heal wounds of schism among the Hebrew tribes as a result of the division caused by the competing monarchies of Israel and Judah. The twin themes of the Davidic covenant and temple worship serve

---

51. Wilcock, *The Message of Chronicles*, 14; cf. Darrell L. Bock on Luke as historian, theologian, and pastor (*Luke* [NIVAC; Grand Rapids: Zondervan, 1996], 21).

52. On the Chronicler as interpreter, see Martin J. Selman, *1 Chronicles* (TOTC 10a; Downers Grove, Ill.: InterVarsity Press, 1994), 27–45, esp. 40–43.

53. Specifically, the exegetical approach identified with the Chronicler is that of *haggadic* exegesis (i.e., exposition that is primarily theological and moral; cf. Fishbane, *Biblical Interpretation in Ancient Israel*, 380–403). The theological transformation of the accounts of Samuel and Kings by the Chronicler represents a reshaping of an earlier biblical tradition for the purpose of addressing a new historical situation. This reinterpretation of earlier Scriptures by a later biblical writer is an Old Testament example of what S. Lewis Johnson has identified in the New Testament as the work of the Holy Spirit in "inspired exposition" (*The Old Testament in the New*, 39–51).

to remind the Israelites that their unity is assured by divine promise and demonstrated in their common worship of Yahweh, the God of the covenant. Thanks to Kipling's "six trusted servants," we are now ready to begin our pilgrimage into the history, literature, and theology of Chronicles. I use the word "pilgrimage" because a pilgrimage is a journey made to a sacred place as an act of devotion. The Chronicler invites us into a "sacred place" of sorts, the stage of human history. The stage of human history is sacred in one sense because it is the arena of God's redemptive activity.

To read and study history is to read and study theology, because the God of the Bible is the Sovereign Lord of history. Furthermore, to read and study Scripture is an "act of devotion." The psalmist asserts that "great are the works of the LORD, studied by all who delight in them" (Ps. 111:2 NRSV). In fact, the righteous person delights in the law of the Lord and meditates on that law day and night (1:2). So then, our journey into Chronicles is indeed a "pilgrimage."

So like Xerxes of old at the recital of the Persian chronicles, may the biblical writer's retelling of Israel's history pique our interest and draw us into God's intriguing story of redemption—a story of eternal significance with profound personal relevance.

Outline of Chronicles

I. **Genealogical Prologue (1 Chron. 1–9)**
   A. Patriarchs (1 Chron. 1:1–2:2)
   B. Israel's Sons (2:3–3:24)
   C. Families of Judah (4:1–23)
   D. Simeon (4:24–43)
   E. Reuben, Gad, Manasseh (ch. 5)
   F. Levi (ch. 6)
   G. Issachar, Benjamin, Naphtali, Ephraim, Asher (ch. 7)
   H. Saul (ch. 8)
   I. Returning Exiles (9:1–34)
   J. Saul's Genealogy (9:35–44)

II. **United Monarchy (1 Chron. 10–2 Chron. 9)**
   A. King Saul and King David Contrasted (chs. 10–12)
      1. Saul's Death (ch. 10)
      2. David's Ascension to the Throne (chs. 11–12)
   B. David Returns the Ark of the Covenant (chs. 13–17)
      1. The Journey of the Ark from Kiriath Jearim to Kidon (ch. 13)
      2. David's Dynasty (14:1–7)
      3. David Defeats the Philistines (14:8–17)
      4. The Ark Enters Jerusalem (chs. 15–16)
      5. The Davidic Covenant (ch. 17)
   C. David's Conquests (chs. 18–20)
      1. David Expands His Territorial Holdings (18:1–13)
      2. David's Cabinet (18:14–17)
      3. David Defeats the Ammonites (19:1–20:3)
      4. Renewed War with the Philistines (20:4–8)
   D. David's Preparations for the Temple (21:1–29:9)
      1. David's Census (21:1–22:1)
      2. Securing Materials (22:2–19)
      3. Duties for the Levites (ch. 23)
      4. Priestly Divisions (ch. 24)
      5. Temple Singers (ch. 25)
      6. Temple Gatekeepers (ch. 26)
      7. Military and Political Officials (ch. 27)

        8. Architectural Plans (ch. 28)
        9. Gifts for Temple Construction (29:1–9)
    E. David's Farewell and Death (29:10–30)
    F. Solomon's Reign (2 Chron. 1–9)
        1. Solomon's Kingship (ch. 1)
        2. Construction of the Temple (2:1–5:1)
        3. Dedication of the Temple (5:2–7:22)
        4. Solomon's Activities (chs. 8–9)

III. **Early History of Judah (chs. 10–32)**
    A. Four Kings and the Prophetic Voice (10:1–21:3)
        1. Rehoboam (chs. 10–12)
        2. Abijah (13:1–14:1a)
        3. Asa (14:1b–16:14)
        4. Jehoshaphat (17:1–21:3)
    B. Judah and the Dynasty of Ahab (21:4–23:21)
        1. Jehoram (21:4–20)
        2. Ahaziah (22:1–9)
        3. Athaliah and Joash (22:10–23:21)
    C. Three Kings and the Decline of Judah (chs. 24–26)
        1. Joash (ch. 24)
        2. Amaziah (ch. 25)
        3. Uzziah (ch. 26)
    D. Three Kings and the Assyrian Threat (chs. 27–32)
        1. Jotham (ch. 27)
        2. Ahaz (ch. 28)
        3. Hezekiah (chs. 29–32)

IV. **Later History of Judah (33:1–36:21)**
    A. Three Kings and Repentance (33:1–36:1)
        1. Manasseh (33:1–20)
        2. Amon (33:21–25)
        3. Josiah (34:1–36:1)
    B. Four Kings and the Exile of Judah (36:2–21)
        1. Jehoahaz (36:2–4)
        2. Jehoiakim (36:5–8)
        3. Jehoiachin (36:9–10)
        4. Zedekiah (36:11–14)
        5. Fall of Jerusalem (36:15–21)

V. **Epilogue: The Decree of Cyrus (36:22–23)**

Select Bibliography

Achtemeier, E. *Preaching from the Old Testament*. Louisville: Westminster John Knox, 1989.

Ackroyd, P. R. "History and Theology in the Writings of the Chronicler." *Concordia Theological Monthly* 38 (1967): 501–15.

_____. *I and II Chronicles, Ezra, Nehemiah*. TBC. London: SCM, 1973.

_____. "The Chronicler As Exegete." *JSOT* 2 (1977): 2–32.

_____. "The History of Israel in the Exilic and Post-Exilic Periods. Pages 320–50 in *Tradition and Interpretation*. G. W. Anderson, ed. Oxford: Clarendon, 1979.

_____. "The Chronicler in His Age." JSOTSup 101. Sheffield: Sheffield Academic Press, 1991.

Albright, W. F. "The Date and Personality of the Chronicler." *JBL* 40 (1921): 104–24.

Allen, L. C. *1, 2 Chronicles*. Communicator's Commentary 10. Waco, Tex.: Word, 1987.

_____. "Kerygmatic Units in 1 and 2 Chronicles." *JSOT* 41 (1988): 21–36.

_____. *1, 2 Chronicles*. Mastering the Old Testament 10. Dallas: Word, 1993.

_____. "The First and Second Books of Chronicles." Pages 297–659 in Vol. 3 of *The New Interpreter's Bible*. Leander E. Keck, gen. ed. Nashville: Abingdon, 1999.

Alter, R. *The David Story*. New York: Norton, 1999.

Alter, R., and F. Kermode, eds. *A Complete Literary Guide to the Bible*. Cambridge, Mass.: Harvard Univ. Press, 1987.

Berquist, J. L. *Judaism in Persia's Shadow*. Minneapolis: Augsburg Fortress, 1995.

Braun, R. "Solomon, the Chosen Temple Builder: The Significance of 1 Chronicles 22, 28, and 29 for the Theology of Chronicles." *JBL* 95 (1976): 581–90.

_____. "A Reconsideration of the Chronicler's Attitude Toward the North." *JBL* 96 (1977): 59–62.

_____. "Chronicles, Ezra and Nehemiah: Theology and Literary History." Pages 52–64 in *Studies in the Historical Books of the Old Testament*. J. A. Emerton, ed. VTSup 30. Leiden: Brill, 1979.

_____. *1 Chronicles*. WBC 14. Waco, Tex.: Word, 1986.

Brueggemann, W. *David's Truth*. Philadelphia: Fortress, 1985.

Campbell, A. F. *The Ark Narrative*. Missoula, Mont.: Scholars Press, 1975.

Coggins, R. J. *The First and Second Books of Chronicles*. CBC. Cambridge: Cambridge Univ. Press, 1976.

Curtis, E. L. *The Books of Chronicles*. ICC. Edinburgh: T. & T. Clark, 1910.

Davies, W. D., and L. Finkelstein, eds. *Cambridge History of Judaism: Introduction, Persian Period*. Cambridge: Cambridge Univ. Press, 1984.

De Vries, S. J. *1 and 2 Chronicles*. FOTL 11. Grand Rapids: Eerdmans, 1989.

Dillard, R. B. "The Reign of Asa (2 Chr 14–16)." *JETS* 23 (1980): 207–18.

_____. "The Chronicler's Solomon." *WTJ* 43 (1981): 207–18.

_____. "Reward and Punishment in Chronicles: The Theology of Immediate Retribution." *WTJ* 46 (1984): 164–72.

_____. "The Chronicler's Jehoshaphat." *TrinJ* 7 (1986): 17–22.

_____. *2 Chronicles*. WBC 15. Waco, Tex.: Word, 1987.

Dumbrell, W. J. "The Purpose of the Books of Chronicles." *JSOT* 27 (1984): 257–66.

Endres, J. C., et al., eds. *Chronicles and Its Synoptic Parallels in Samuel, Kings, and Related Biblical Texts*. Collegeville, Minn.: Liturgical Press, 1998.

Fishbane, M. *Biblical Interpretation in Ancient Israel*. Oxford: Clarendon, 1985.

Freedman, D. N. "The Chronicler's Purpose." *CBQ* 23 (1961): 436–42.

Goldingay, J. "'That You May Know That Yahweh is God': A Study of the Relationship Between Theology and Historical Truth in the Old Testament." *TynBul* 23 (1972): 58–93.

_____. "The Chronicler as Theologian." *BTB* 5 (1975): 99–121.

Graham, M. P., K. Hoglund, and S. McKenzie, eds. *The Chronicler As Historian*. JSOTSup 238. Sheffield: Sheffield Academic Press, 1997.

Hooker, P. K. *First and Second Chronicles*. Westminster Bible Companion. Louisville: Westminster John Knox, 2001.

Howard, D. M. Jr. *An Introduction to the Old Testament Historical Books*. Chicago: Moody Press, 1993.

Japhet, S. "The Historical Reliability of Chronicles." *JSOT* 33 (1985): 83–107.

_____. *I and II Chronicles*. OTL. Louisville: Westminster John Knox, 1993.

Johnson, M. D. *The Purpose of the Biblical Genealogies*. 2d ed. Cambridge: Cambridge Univ. Press, 1988.

Johnstone, W. *1 and 2 Chronicles (Volume 1): 1 Chronicles 1–2 Chronicles 9: Israel's Place Among the Nations*. JSOTSup 253. Sheffield: Sheffield Academic Press, 1998.

_____. *1 and 2 Chronicles. (Volume 2): 2 Chronicles 10–36: Guilt and Atonement*. JSOTSup 254. Sheffield: Sheffield Academic Press, 1998.

Knoppers, G. *1 Chronicles*. AB 12. New York: Doubleday, 2002.

Long, V. P. *The Art of Biblical History*. FCI 5. Grand Rapids: Zondervan, 1994.

Mason, R. "Some Echoes of the Preaching in the Second Temple? Tradition Elements in Zechariah 1–8." *ZAW* 96 (1984): 221–35.

———. *Preaching the Tradition: Homily and Hermeneutics after the Exile.* Cambridge: Cambridge Univ. Press, 1990.

Mathews, K. A. "Preaching Historical Narrative." Pages 19–50 in *Reclaiming the Prophetic Mantle: Preaching the Old Testament Faithfully.* G. L. Klein, ed. Nashville: Broadman, 1992.

McConville, J. G. *I and II Chronicles.* DSBOT. Philadelphia: Westminster, 1984.

Merrill, E. H. *1, 2 Chronicles.* Bible Study Commentary. Grand Rapids: Zondervan, 1988.

Myers, J. M. *I Chronicles.* AB 12. 2d. ed. New York: Doubleday, 1986.

———. *II Chronicles.* AB 13. 2d ed. New York: Doubleday, 1986.

Newsome, J. D. "Toward a New Understanding of the Chronicler and His Purposes." *JBL* 94 (1975): 204–17.

———. *A Synoptic Harmony of Samuel, Kings, and Chronicles.* Grand Rapids: Baker, 1986.

North, R. "Theology of the Chronicler." *JBL* 82 (1963): 369–81.

Payne, J. B. "1, 2 Chronicles." *EBC*, 4: 303–562. Grand Rapids: Zondervan, 1988.

Peltonen, K. *History Debated: The Historical Reliability of the Chronicler in Pre-critical and Critical Research.* Göttingen: Vandenhoeck & Ruprecht, 1996.

Petersen, D. L. *Late Israelite Prophecy: Studies in Deutero-Prophetic Literature and in Chronicles.* SBLMS 23. Missoula, Mont.: Scholars Press, 1977.

Pratt, R. L. "First and Second Chronicles." Pages 193–205 in *A Complete Literary Guide to the Bible.* L. Ryken and T. Longman III, eds. Grand Rapids: Zondervan, 1993.

Rudoph, W. *Chronikbücher.* HAT. Tübingen: J. C. B. Mohr, 1995.

Sailhamer, J. *First and Second Chronicles.* Everyman's Bible Commentary. Chicago: Moody Press, 1983.

Selman, M. J. *1 Chronicles.* TOTC 10a. Downers Grove, Ill.: InterVarsity Press, 1994.

———. *2 Chronicles.* TOTC 10b. Downers Grove, Ill.: InterVarsity Press, 1994.

Thompson, J. A. *1, 2 Chronicles.* NAC 9. Nashville: Broadman & Holman, 1994.

Throntveit, M. A. *When Kings Speak: Royal Speech and Royal Prayer in Chronicles.* SBLDS 93. Atlanta: Scholars Press, 1987.

Tuell, S. S. *First and Second Chronicles.* Interpretation. Louisville: Westminster John Knox, 2001.

Vaughn, A. G. *Theology, History and Archaeology in the Chronicler's Account of Hezekiah.* Atlanta: Scholars Press, 1999.

Bibliography

Wilcock, M. *The Message of Chronicles*. BST. Downers Grove, Ill.: InterVarsity Press, 1987.

Williamson, H. G. M. *Israel in the Book of Chronicles*. Cambridge: Cambridge Univ. Press, 1977.

_____. "Eschatology in Chronicles." *TynBul* 28 (1977): 115–54.

_____. *1 and 2 Chronicles*. NCBC. Grand Rapids: Eerdmans, 1982.

Wilson, R. R. *Genealogy and History in the Biblical World*. New Haven, Conn.: Yale Univ. Press, 1977.

_____. "Between 'Azel' and 'Azel': Interpreting Biblical Genealogies." *BA* 42 (1979): 11–22.

Wright, J. W. "Guarding the Gates: 1 Chronicles 26:1–19 and the Roles of Gatekeepers." *JSOT* 48 (1990): 69–81.

_____. "The Legacy of David in Chronicles: The Narrative Function of 1 Chronicles 23–27." *JBL* (1991): 229–42.

1 Chronicles 1:1–2:2

❧

ADAM, SETH, ENOSH, ²Kenan, Mahalalel, Jared, ³Enoch, Methuselah, Lamech, Noah.

⁴ The sons of Noah:
Shem, Ham and Japheth.

⁵ The sons of Japheth:
Gomer, Magog, Madai, Javan, Tubal, Meshech and Tiras.

⁶ The sons of Gomer:
Ashkenaz, Riphath and Togarmah.

⁷ The sons of Javan:
Elishah, Tarshish, the Kittim and the Rodanim.

⁸ The sons of Ham:
Cush, Mizraim, Put and Canaan.

⁹ The sons of Cush:
Seba, Havilah, Sabta, Raamah and Sabteca.
The sons of Raamah:
Sheba and Dedan.

¹⁰ Cush was the father of
Nimrod, who grew to be a mighty warrior on earth.

¹¹ Mizraim was the father of
the Ludites, Anamites, Lehabites, Naphtuhites,
¹²Pathrusites, Casluhites (from whom the Philistines came) and Caphtorites.

¹³ Canaan was the father of
Sidon his firstborn, and of the Hittites, ¹⁴Jebusites, Amorites, Girgashites, ¹⁵Hivites, Arkites, Sinites, ¹⁶Arvadites, Zemarites and Hamathites.

¹⁷ The sons of Shem:
Elam, Asshur, Arphaxad, Lud and Aram.
The sons of Aram:
Uz, Hul, Gether and Meshech.

¹⁸ Arphaxad was the father of Shelah,
and Shelah the father of Eber.

¹⁹ Two sons were born to Eber:
One was named Peleg, because in his time the earth was divided; his brother was named Joktan.

²⁰Joktan was the father of
> Almodad, Sheleph, Hazarmaveth, Jerah, ²¹Hadoram,
> Uzal, Diklah, ²²Obal, Abimael, Sheba, ²³Ophir, Havilah
> and Jobab. All these were sons of Joktan.

²⁴Shem, Arphaxad, Shelah,
²⁵Eber, Peleg, Reu,
²⁶Serug, Nahor, Terah
²⁷and Abram (that is, Abraham).

²⁸The sons of Abraham:
> Isaac and Ishmael.

²⁹These were their descendants:
> Nebaioth the firstborn of Ishmael, Kedar, Adbeel, Mib-
> sam, ³⁰Mishma, Dumah, Massa, Hadad, Tema, ³¹Jetur,
> Naphish and Kedemah. These were the sons of Ishmael.

³²The sons born to Keturah, Abraham's concubine:
> Zimran, Jokshan, Medan, Midian, Ishbak and Shuah.

The sons of Jokshan:
> Sheba and Dedan.

³³The sons of Midian:
> Ephah, Epher, Hanoch, Abida and Eldaah.

All these were descendants of Keturah.

³⁴Abraham was the father of Isaac.

The sons of Isaac:
> Esau and Israel.

³⁵The sons of Esau:
> Eliphaz, Reuel, Jeush, Jalam and Korah.

³⁶The sons of Eliphaz:
> Teman, Omar, Zepho, Gatam and Kenaz;
> by Timna: Amalek.

³⁷The sons of Reuel:
> Nahath, Zerah, Shammah and Mizzah.

³⁸The sons of Seir:
> Lotan, Shobal, Zibeon, Anah, Dishon, Ezer and Dishan.

³⁹The sons of Lotan:
> Hori and Homam. Timna was Lotan's sister.

⁴⁰The sons of Shobal:
> Alvan, Manahath, Ebal, Shepho and Onam.

The sons of Zibeon:
> Aiah and Anah.

⁴¹The son of Anah:
> Dishon.

The sons of Dishon:
Hemdan, Eshban, Ithran and Keran.
⁴²The sons of Ezer:
Bilhan, Zaavan and Akan.
The sons of Dishan:
Uz and Aran.
⁴³These were the kings who reigned in Edom before any
Israelite king reigned:
Bela son of Beor, whose city was named Dinhabah.
⁴⁴When Bela died, Jobab son of Zerah from Bozrah succeeded him as king.
⁴⁵When Jobab died, Husham from the land of the Temanites
succeeded him as king.
⁴⁶When Husham died, Hadad son of Bedad, who defeated
Midian in the country of Moab, succeeded him as king.
His city was named Avith.
⁴⁷When Hadad died, Samlah from Masrekah succeeded him
as king.
⁴⁸When Samlah died, Shaul from Rehoboth on the river succeeded him as king.
⁴⁹When Shaul died, Baal-Hanan son of Acbor succeeded him
as king.
⁵⁰When Baal-Hanan died, Hadad succeeded him as king. His
city was named Pau, and his wife's name was Mehetabel
daughter of Matred, the daughter of Me-Zahab.
⁵¹Hadad also died.

The chiefs of Edom were:
Timna, Alvah, Jetheth, ⁵²Oholibamah, Elah, Pinon,
⁵³Kenaz, Teman, Mibzar, ⁵⁴Magdiel and Iram. These
were the chiefs of Edom.

²·¹These were the sons of Israel:
Reuben, Simeon, Levi, Judah, Issachar, Zebulun, ²Dan,
Joseph, Benjamin, Naphtali, Gad and Asher.

Original Meaning

BIBLICAL SCHOLARS HAVE long noted that the genealogies of the prologue to Chronicles (1 Chron. 1–9) are a mini-commentary of sorts on the book of Genesis. This understanding is largely based on the phrase "these are the generations of," which provides a structural framework for the narratives of Genesis (e.g., Gen. 5:1; 10:1 RSV). In most cases, the Chronicler borrows from earlier genealogical sources and pares the listings to a register of names only (e.g., Gen. 5:1–32; cf. 1 Chron. 1:1–4). God is everywhere assumed but nowhere mentioned in genealogies. The Chronicler also takes it for granted that his audience knows well the stories and personalities associated with the names logged in the genealogies. This fact is important to understanding the rest of the Chronicles as well. The highly selective retelling of Israel's history presupposes the Chronicler's audience knows their Hebrew Bible.

Selman has noted that the pivot points of the introductory genealogy are names of great significance in the early history of God's people, including Adam (1:1), Noah (1:4), Abraham (1:27, 28, 32, 34), and Israel (or Jacob, 1:34; 2:1). Further, he has observed that each section of the genealogy is arranged in such a way that the person providing the link from Adam to Israel is mentioned last in each generation.[1] This means that the sequence of names does not always correspond with birth order as presented in the Genesis narratives.

More important are the theological threads unifying this opening genealogy. (1) The nations are introduced in such a way that all peoples are placed inside rather than outside the purposes of God's electing love. (2) The nation of Israel lies at the center of the genealogical scheme. Thus, the Israel of the Chronicler's day is united with the earlier Israel and with the nations.

The genealogical prologue found in 1 Chronicles 1–9 contains the most extensive and complex genealogies of the Bible. According to Robert Wilson, "a genealogy is a written or oral expression of the descent of a person or persons from an ancestor or ancestors."[2] Particular terminology is sometimes used to characterize the composition of biblical genealogies, such as:

- breadth, a listing of a single generation of descendants from a common ancestor (e.g., 2:1)
- depth, a listing of successive generations, commonly four to six (e.g., 3:10–16)
- linear, displaying depth alone (e.g., 2:10)
- segmented, displaying both breadth and depth (e.g., 3:17–24)
- descending, or proceeding from parent to child (e.g., 9:39–44)
- ascending, or moving from child to parent (e.g., 9:14–16)[3]

---

1. Selman, *1 Chronicles*, 89–90.

2. Robert Wilson, *Genealogy and History in the Biblical World* (New Haven, Conn.: Yale Univ. Press, 1977), 9.

3. Ibid., 18–26; cf. Braun, *1 Chronicles*, 1–5; Howard, *An Introduction to the Old Testament Historical Books*, 249–51.

The basic purpose of the genealogy is to identify kinship relationships between individuals, families, and people groups. Marshall Johnson has isolated nine distinct functions that genealogies serve in the Old Testament:

- demonstrate existing relationships between Israel and neighboring tribes by establishing common ancestors (e.g., the relationship of Lot's descendants to Israel, Gen. 19:36–38)
- connecting isolated traditions of Israelite origins into a coherent literary unit by means of an inclusive genealogical system (e.g., the *toledot* formulas in Genesis [5:1; 10:1; etc.])
- bridge chronological gaps in the biblical narratives (e.g., Ruth 4:18–22)
- serve as chronological controls for the dating of key Old Testament events (e.g., the date of the book of Esther in relationship to the Babylonian exile, Est. 2:5–6—although the selective nature of biblical genealogies may compromise the accuracy of the genealogy as a chronological device)
- perform a specific political and/or military function, as in the taking of a census (e.g., Num. 1:3–46)
- legitimize an individual or family in an office or enhance the stature of an individual by linkage to an important clan or individual of the past (e.g., Zeph. 1:1)
- establish and preserve the ethnic purity of the Hebrew community, as in the case of the records found in Ezra and Nehemiah (e.g., Ezra 7)
- assert the importance of the continuity of God's people through a period of national calamity (prominent in Chronicles, e.g., the line of David in 1 Chron. 3:17–24)
- express order, structure, and movement in history according to a divinely prearranged plan (e.g., identifying Haman, the son of Hammedatha, as an Agagite, Est. 3:1, 10).[4]

It is evident the genealogies of 1 Chronicles 1–9 serve multiple purposes, especially in legitimizing the authority of Levitical priesthood as the rightful successors to the royal authority of Davidic kingship and in asserting the continuity of the Hebrew people through the national distress of the Babylonian exile. There is even a sense in which the juxtaposition of certain genealogies (e.g., that of Esau and Israel or Saul and David) works to express movement in history according to God's redemptive plan.

A child was named immediately upon birth during Old Testament times, and the name was usually chosen by the mother (e.g., Gen. 35:18;

---

4. Marshall D. Johnson, *The Purpose of the Biblical Genealogies*, 2d ed. (Cambridge: Cambridge Univ. Press, 1988), 77–82.

1 Sam. 1:20).[5] The ancients understood the name to signify the essence of a thing or a person. The naming process involved knowledge of the thing or person named and power over that entity once the name was ascribed (e.g., Pharaoh's naming Joseph as Zaphenath-Paneah, Gen. 41:45).

Since the name denoted essential being, a child's name was chosen with great care. A person's name revealed the character and personality as well as the reputation, authority, vocation, and even the destiny of the bearer. At times unusual circumstances surrounding the birth inspired a child's name (e.g., Isaac, Gen. 21:6−7; Samuel, 1 Sam. 1:20). On occasion the shifting fortunes in a person's life situation or the transformation of a person's character prompted a name change (e.g., Jacob becomes Israel, Gen. 32:28; Naomi becomes Mara, Ruth 1:20).

Many Old Testament names are theophoric; that is, they contain some element of a divine name or title indicating one's religious loyalty (e.g., Josiah [= "Yahweh will give"], 1 Chron. 3:14; Elkanah [= "God has created"], 1 Chron. 6:23; Merib-Baal ["the Lord/Baal contends"], 1 Chron. 8:34). All this is a part of the worldview of the Chronicler's audience. The genealogy is not simply a catalog of the names of dead ancestors. Rather, it represents a rich history of family, clan, and nation told and retold through the life and story represented by the personal names of individuals who form an integral part of the larger story of the Israelite community.

The Chronicler's panoramic sweep of ancient history from Adam to Noah to Abraham and Israel transports the audience into the accounts of the book of Genesis. There the emphasis was on God's dealings with humanity both in terms of creation and redemption. The same is true for the Chronicler, especially as he traces the names of key players in the unfolding drama of God's redemptive plan for humanity. The stories behind the names in the genealogies may hint at themes and ideas important to the Chronicler. For example, Enoch "walked" with God (1 Chron. 1:3; cf. Gen. 5:24), a repeated phrase in the Chronicler's evaluation of the kings of Judah (e.g., 2 Chron. 17:3; 21:12; etc.). Perhaps Nimrod the "mighty warrior" (1 Chron. 1:10; cf. Gen. 10:8−9) inspires the descriptions of the mighty warriors of David's day (e.g., 1 Chron. 12:8, 21, 28, etc.).

The reference to Noah, his sons, and their descendants further develops the links between the Chronicler's genealogical prologue and the Genesis narratives (1 Chron. 1:4−27). The proliferation of people (groups) registered under the names of Japheth, Ham, and Shem calls to mind the creation mandate to populate the earth (Gen. 1:28) and later echoed to those survivors of

---

5. The custom of naming (the male child) at the time of circumcision (eight days after birth) is a later Jewish practice (cf. Luke 1:59; 2:21).

the great Flood (Gen. 9:7). The genealogy of Noah also functions to introduce Abraham through the line of Shem (1 Chron. 1:17, 27).

Equally important are the great theological themes the story of Noah
establishes, themes that course through the rest of the Bible—especially the
covenant relationship with God (Gen. 9:11) and the twin truths of God's
judgment of human sin and rebellion and his sustaining grace in preserving
the righteous (Gen. 6:7–8).

In terms of recorded material, Abraham (1 Chron. 1:28–33) receives less
attention in the opening genealogy than does Esau and Seir (1:34–54).
Nonetheless, the family of Abraham is located strategically in the middle of
the listing of names from Adam (1:1) to Israel (2:1) and appropriately paired
with the family of Esau as a foil, illustrating contrasting responses to covenant
relationship with Yahweh. If we keep in mind the stories represented by the
names, in one sense the genealogy of Abraham is flanked by destruction:
Noah and the Flood at the front end and Esau and the eventual obliteration
of the Edomites on the other.

Not coincidentally, the listing of the twelve sons of Israel follows the
genealogy of Esau, a reminder that the Hebrews persist as the people of
God. Although the Chronicler gives Abraham prominence as the father of
the Israelites, the genealogy has included all the descendants of Abraham as
confirmation of God's fulfillment of the promise to make Abraham the father
of many nations (cf. Gen. 17:3–6). Interestingly, the genealogy of Abraham
mentions Keturah, the concubine of Abraham (1 Chron. 1:32; v. 28 assumes
knowledge of Hagar and Sarah as wives of Abraham). The citation is unusual
in that Old Testament genealogies primarily document family history from
male descendant to male descendant without reference to mothers. Theologically, however, this name and the other names of women in the Chronicler's genealogies may be a subtle reference to their role in the "offspring of
the woman" theology for restoring humanity to Eden (Gen. 3:15–16). This
theme is continued in both Kings and Chronicles, as the mothers of the
Judahite kings (only) are recorded in accession formulas.

The genealogies of Esau and Edom combine four separate catalogs, each
with Esau as the common element (1 Chron. 1:35–54). The list of Esau's
descendants (vv. 35–37; cf. Gen. 36:10–14) is followed by that of Seir,
ancient neighbors of the Edomites and ancestors of the Horites (vv. 38–42;
cf. Gen. 14:6; 36:20–28; Deut. 2:12, 22). The record of Edomite rulers
(1 Chron. 1:43–54; cf. Gen. 36:31–43) attests the prominence of that nation
in Old Testament history (cf. Num. 20:14–21; Jer. 49:7–22). Indeed, the
legacy of the Edomites was entwined with Israel from the birth of Esau (Gen.
25:23–26) to the ruin of Edom during the early postexilic period for aiding
and abetting the Babylonians in the sack of Jerusalem (cf. Ps. 137:7).

The extensive register of names demonstrates that Esau has multiplied, but "that was as nothing compared to the miracle that God had worked for his brother's family."[6] The repetition of the fact that each Edomite king "died" is significant as well. The Edomite kings died, and in one sense so did the nation of Edom, as it was destroyed or absorbed by the Nabatean Arabs (sometime between 550 and 400 B.C.). The kings of Judah died as well, but the people of Israel survived the collapse of Davidic kingship, returned to Jerusalem, and rebuilt the city. The Chronicler's juxtaposition of Esau's and Israel's genealogies may be an allusion to the prophet Malachi's assessment of the twins with respect to covenant relationship with God: "I have loved [chosen] Jacob, but Esau I have hated [rejected]" (Mal. 1:2–3).

The final passage of the section simply lists the twelve sons of Jacob, later named Israel (Gen. 32:28; see chart below). The Chronicler only uses the name "Israel" for the patriarch in the retelling of his history of God's people. Since a change of name in the Old Testament often indicates a change in one's character or station in life, it may be that the Chronicler suggests the same for the remnant of the Israelites after the Exile.

Like Jacob, they too have experienced a transformation in that the Babylonian exile has cured God's people of the sin of idolatry. The catalog of the twelve sons of Israel sets the stage for the remainder of the genealogies comprising the prologue of Chronicles. Both Zebulun and Dan are slighted by the Chronicler, and Naphtali's descendants are mentioned in a single verse (7:13). This selectivity in the presentation of the genealogical records further underscores the Chronicler's pointed interests in the lineage of Judah and the institution of kingship and the lineage of Levi and the office of the priesthood.

THE GENEALOGIES OF 1 Chronicles 1–9 suggest an important point of transition between the Chronicler's context and our own related to the psychosocial conflict known as an "identity crisis."[7] According to Erikson, "identity" may refer to the sense of sameness or continuity between one's past and present selves, the integration of one's private and public selves, or the relationship between one's present self and one's future self.[8] In a nondiagnostic sense, an identity crisis may be described

---

6. Selman, *1 Chronicles*, 93.

7. Understanding the term *identity crisis* in the less technical sense of "an aggravated life crisis rather than a psychological disorder"; see W. E. Atwater, *Adolescence*, 2d ed. (Englewood Cliffs, N.J.: Prentice-Hall, 1988), 138.

8. See Erik H. Erikson, *Identity: Youth and Crisis* (New York: W. W. Norton, 1968), esp. "The Life Cycle: Epigenesis of Identity," 91–141.

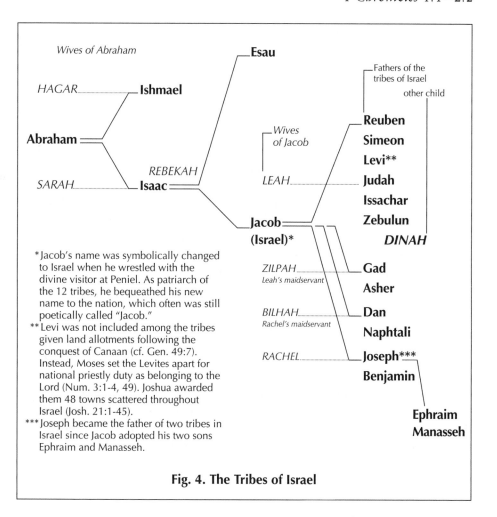

Wives of Abraham

Esau

Fathers of the tribes of Israel

other child

HAGAR............**Ishmael**

Reuben

Wives of Jacob

Simeon

Abraham ═

Levi**

REBEKAH

LEAH............

Judah

SARAH............**Isaac** ═

Issachar

Zebulun

Jacob ═

(Israel)*

DINAH

*Jacob's name was symbolically changed to Israel when he wrestled with the divine visitor at Peniel. As patriarch of the 12 tribes, he bequeathed his new name to the nation, which often was still poetically called "Jacob."

ZILPAH............

Leah's maidservant

Gad

Asher

**Levi was not included among the tribes given land allotments following the conquest of Canaan (cf. Gen. 49:7). Instead, Moses set the Levites apart for national priestly duty as belonging to the Lord (Num. 3:1-4, 49). Joshua awarded them 48 towns scattered throughout Israel (Josh. 21:1-45).

BILHAH............

Rachel's maidservant

Dan

Naphtali

RACHEL............

Joseph***

***Joseph became the father of two tribes in Israel since Jacob adopted his two sons Ephraim and Manasseh.

Benjamin

Ephraim

Manasseh

Fig. 4. The Tribes of Israel

as a personal sense of confusion about one's defining characteristics and social role. On the individual level this confusion may involve a loss of continuity with one's basic personality traits or some form of disconnection with one of the distinctive selves of personhood (e.g., the private self with the public self). The nation addressed by the Chronicler demonstrates a "collective identity," especially with respect to the notion of continuity or sameness between past, present, and future "self." At the corporate level, then, an identity crisis may signify the dislocation of an entity from the constituting principles outlined in its original charter.

The Chronicler's audience is plagued by such a crisis. Israel's "identity" both in terms of a crucial defining characteristic and consequent social role had been associated with Davidic kingship for several centuries. The Babylonian exile and its aftermath has disrupted Israelite continuity with this basic "personality trait" and resulted in a state of national confusion concerning the identity of the Jews as the people of God.

All Israelites were keenly aware of the several important elements contained in their constituting charter or covenant, especially the divine promise about perpetual Davidic kingship and the central role of Israel among the nations (2 Sam. 7:5–16). Neither are true for the Jews at the time of the Chronicler's writing. The symptoms of this identity crisis in postexilic Israel are evidenced in numerous ways, including the abandonment of corporate religious ideals for personal comforts (cf. Neh. 13:15–18; Hag. 1:3–11) and the spirit of malaise that characterizes the Israelite approach to other basic principles of their covenantal charter, such as tithing, social justice, and interracial marriage (cf. Ezra 9:1–2; Neh. 5:1–11; Mal. 3:5–9).

According to McConville, the basic function of the biblical genealogy is to demonstrate that the divine promises and purposes are still operative in God's overall plan.[9] The Chronicler counters the identity crisis in postexilic Israel, in part, by appealing to the genealogical history of the Jews. The recitation of the ancient genealogies serves to build historical and theological connections between postexilic Israel and her earliest ancestors, reestablishing the continuity of the later community with the true "people of God." The links to Adam and Noah affirm the realization of the divine purposes related to the creation mandate for filling the earth and ruling over it (Gen. 1:26–28). Likewise, the ligature to Abraham and Israel (i.e., Jacob) assures the postexilic Jewish community that they are the heirs of the covenant promises of God made to the patriarchs and matriarchs of Israel (Gen. 12:1–3; 17:3–14; 26:3–4; etc.).

Theologically for the Chronicler, the issue is the continuity of Yahweh's kingship over creation and all the nations, not merely Davidic kingship in Israel. For this reason, he frames the retelling of the history of Israel between the genealogy excerpted from the Table of Nations (1 Chron. 1; cf. Gen. 10) and the decree of King Cyrus of Persia (2 Chron. 36:22–23). The "nations" serve as the bookends for the story of kingship in Israel, indicating that they

---

9. J. Gordon McConville, *I and II Chronicles* (DSBOT; Philadelphia: Westminster, 1984), 7; we must not overlook the cultural significance of the genealogy, however, in the "honor" and "shame" society of the biblical world. For example, the honor to which one is born into is "ascribed" honor. Honor that has been achieved or earned is understood as "acquired" honor. The genealogies of Chronicles include both the idea of "ascribed" honor (e.g., Er as Judah's "firstborn" son, 2:3) and "acquired" honor (e.g., Nimrod who became known as a "mighty warrior" for his exploits, 1:10). It is important to note that "shame" may be acquired as well, as in the case of Achar (or Achan, 2:7; cf. John Pilch, *Introducing the Cultural Context of the Old Testament* [New York: Paulist, 1991], 52–53).

too stand inside the unfolding plan of God's redemption of fallen creation. In addition, Israel's role as the "elect of God" remains secure in the reality of God's sovereignty over all the peoples of the earth. God has chosen one nation so he might bless all nations. The opening genealogy of Chronicles is a simple reminder of that fact. Israel's identity crisis during the postexilic period is primarily a matter of poor theology, not bad psychology.

Ultimately, the Chronicler's recitation of genealogies is a lesson in God's faithfulness to the word of his covenant promise. Israel's worth and dignity, her "identity" so to speak, lies outside the changing circumstances of history and in the character and plan of God Almighty. This truth sets the stage for one of the key themes of the books of Chronicles, the proper worship of Yahweh as the Lord of creation, the Sovereign of the nations, and the God of Israel.

IDENTITY CONFUSION. The identity crisis in postexilic Judah was only secondarily a matter of historical circumstance. Granted, Davidic kingship no longer defined Israel, and the Persian Empire still controlled the fate of the Jewish people. Yet the real crisis in postexilic Judah was one of theological understanding. The Chronicler's generation had misinterpreted the message of the earlier prophets concerning the nature and the timing of the restoration of Israel. This misunderstanding of God's revelation for the future of Israel led to a distorted perception of the current situation confronting God's people. Like the first generation of expatriates who returned from Babylonia, they had expected much but had experienced little (Hag. 1:9). Naturally, blame was displaced away from unkept individual or corporate covenant responsibilities and onto God and his failure to make good on the word of his promises (cf. Hag. 1:4; Zech. 7:5–7; Mal. 3:14).

Specifically, the several generations of Jews from the time of Haggai and Zerubbabel to the Chronicler had been expecting the reinstatement of Davidic kingship and the restoration of national Israel (cf. Hag. 2:20–22). Clearly this is what Jeremiah and Ezekiel predicted after the return from Babylonian captivity (cf. Jer. 33:15–22; Ezek. 34:20–25). Later, the prophets Zechariah and Malachi essentially told their constituencies to "hang in there," for God would soon inaugurate the new Davidic kingdom and restore the fortunes of Israel (i.e., "the day is coming"; cf. Zech. 12:10; 13:1; Mal. 3:1; 4:1). But by the time of Ezra and Nehemiah, there is no longer any mention of a Davidic king or a restored Hebrew nation. The postexilic community has resigned itself to hierocratic or priestly rule as well as economic and political subordination in the vast Persian Empire.

Whether verbalized or not, the Chronicler's audience suspects that God's word has failed.[10] All this suggests that the identity crisis in postexilic Judah is surely one of compounded disenfranchisement—both in a psychological rootlessness, fostering insecurity and alienation (since the "present self" of the Hebrew nation is divorced from its "past self" as an autonomous monarch), and in a theological discontinuity, resulting in apathy and despair (since the "present self" of the Hebrew nation has lost any hope of actualizing the prophetic word that promised the restoration of the "future self" of Israel).

The Chronicler's response to this identity crisis proves valuable as a model for the contemporary reader of the Bible. The context of his message parallels that of modern society, given the religious pluralism, ethnic diversity, and philosophical relativism that characterized the sprawling Persian Empire. Likewise, human nature is a constant since we are prone to the same syndrome of "victimization" evident in the behavior of our earliest ancestors (e.g., Adam was a "victim" of the woman's hasty impulse and Eve was a "victim" of the serpent's smooth talk; cf. Gen. 3:12–13).[11]

Furthermore, the prophets from Moses to Jesus recognized that the Word of God was susceptible to human manipulation and warned against exchanging divine truth for human traditions (cf. Deut. 13:3; 16:19; Mark 7:8–9). Finally, an important part of the Christian message promulgated by the church during the interim between the advents of Christ is that of "waiting" for the return of God's Son from heaven (1 Thess. 1:9–10; cf. 2 Peter 3:4). Thus, we see that in certain respects the ancient and the modern worlds are not all that different. What then might we learn from the Chronicler as we encounter and respond to the "identity crises" besetting the people of God today?

Before developing a biblical template for countering human crises based on the example of the Chronicler's strategy, it may be helpful to recall our

---

10. It is interesting that the Chronicler opts not to appeal to the dreams and visions of Daniel for an explanation in the delay of the promised Davidic kingdom and restoration of Israel. A careful reading of Daniel indicates a series of four world empires must come and go before God implements his "kingdom program" (cf. Dan. 2, 7, 8). At the time of the Chronicler the Jews are in Stage Two (the Persian period) of that four-stage historical development (with the Babylonian period preceding and the empires of Greece and Rome to follow). To his credit the Chronicler pinpoints the root cause of postexilic Judah's identity crisis, the demise of Davidic kingship. His two-pronged approach includes both genealogical recitation and historical review. It is possible that the Chronicler already anticipates the spiritual and ethical nature of God's coming kingdom (in Jesus Christ as the Son of David) and chooses deliberately to avoid any reference to the more nationalistic portrayal in the book of Daniel.

11. On the topic of "victim status" in postmodern North America, see Robert H. Bork, *Slouching Towards Gomorrah*, 80–82.

definition of this psychological conflict. Previously, we explained an identity crisis as a personal or collective sense of confusion about one's defining characteristics and social role. Such confusion may be individual in nature, as seen in the agony of Jeremiah's conflict with ideals of the prophetic office and the reality of the human response to the divinely prompted message (cf. Jer. 20:7–18). Thus, for the individual this identity confusion may result in the loss of continuity with the basic traits of one's self or personhood (e.g., the "persecution" paranoia eroding Jeremiah's self-esteem [Jer. 20:7–10] and his "death-wish" conflicting with his will for self-preservation [20:14–18]).

Or such confusion may be experienced in a corporate manner, as in the case of Israel's penchant for the idolatry and immorality of the Baal cult in flagrant violation of the stipulations of the Mosaic covenant (e.g., Hos. 4:16–18; Amos 2:4–5). At the collective level this identity confusion may signify the dislocation of an entity or a nation from the constituting principles outlined in its original charter (e.g., the radical monotheism prescribed for worship in the Sinai covenant in opposition to the polytheism characteristic of the ancient world). In either case, the Chronicler offers the contemporary reader helpful guidelines for resolving those conflicts.

(1) *Approach the crisis directly.* One of the defining characteristics of ancient Israel was Davidic kingship. The idolatry of God's people eventually led to the Babylonian exile and the loss of the foundational institutions of Israelite life—the monarchy and the temple. Upon their return from the Babylonian captivity, the Persians permitted the restoration of the temple only. The horrific trauma and the nightmarish aftermath of the Exile (memorialized in the book of Lamentations) evoked the identity crisis in postexilic Judah.

The Chronicler employs a two-pronged approach to the theme of the Davidic dynasty, including both genealogical recitation (emphasizing the tribes of Judah and Levi) and historical review (focusing primarily on the Judahite monarchy). His direct approach affirms the importance of the issue for the restoration community. In so doing he acknowledges that the crisis is real and establishes a bond of empathy with his audience. This in turn lends a sense of credibility and genuineness to his message and makes the transition to an alternative form of community governance (i.e., priestly authority instead of royal authority) a more bearable experience for the people.

(2) *Isolate the cause rather than treat the symptoms of the crisis.* Earlier we characterized Chronicles as a "theology of hope" for the beleaguered Jews residing in postexilic Jerusalem. The writer, however, does not attempt to manipulate emotions by inducing guilt or raising false expectations. Nor does he seek to motivate or inspire the people by means of self-help "pop psychology." Rather, he encourages his audience with sound doctrine in the form of a

biography of God, emphasizing his sovereign rule as Creator, his providential intervention as Sustainer, and his unconditional election of Israel (see Introduction, "Chronicles As a Biography of God"). Ultimately, human crises are theological in nature in that they are generally related to the idea of theodicy (or the problem of evil in relationship to the goodness of God). The psalmist recognized that intimate knowledge and proper worship of God are essential for gaining some perspective on the "crookedness" of life in a fallen world (Ps. 73:16–17, 26, 28).

The Chronicler is well aware of this biblical truism, so he too steers his audience to the person and character of God for an explanation of and a solution to their crisis. The New Testament is consistent with the Old Testament pattern as the apostle Paul coached Titus to "encourage others" by teaching sound doctrine (Titus 1:9).

(3) *Locate the crisis within a larger historical and theological framework, a metanarrative.* Walsh and Middleton regard a metanarrative as a grounding or legitimating "story" (i.e., a narrative or tradition) that shapes the worldview and guides the practice of a given community.[12] A metanarrative possesses a "mythic" quality that accounts for a given way of life and that is taken as the normative expression for that way of life. The concept of metanarrative is under attack in our postmodern society. We see a pervasive incredulity toward metanarratives because given the current emphasis on pluralism and diversity in North American culture, no metanarrative is comprehensive enough to include the experiences and realities of all people.[13]

The Chronicler uses the literary form of the genealogy to locate postexilic Judah in a larger historical framework—a metanarrative. By definition, an identity crisis is rooted in the self, whether the personality of an individual or a particular social group. The metanarrative functions to divert attention away from "self" to those common ideas and experiences shared by all people for all time. By resorting to the genealogy, the Chronicler is able to move his audience off "center," so to speak—off self-pity and narcissistic introspection. Perspective and insight on the present are gained when an acute problem is situated in a larger context. The loss of Davidic kingship in postexilic Judah pales in comparison to the loss of Edenic fellowship with God when David, Judah, and Israel are placed in a metanarrative that includes Adam and Noah. The "story" of postexilic Judah is hardly unique when viewed against the "story" of humanity.[14]

---

12. Middleton and Walsh, *Truth Is Stranger Than It Used to Be*, 69–70.

13. Ibid., 70–71.

14. There is a sense in which the Old and New Testaments continually call the reader to consider the biblical metanarrative, whether in divine epithets like "the God of Abraham, Isaac and Jacob" (Ex. 3:16) or in simple admonitions like "remember" (e.g., Deut. 5:15;

(4) Link the metanarrative to the work and words of God. It is not enough to locate any given human predicament in a larger historical context. The metanarrative must have a substantial theological orientation as well. Only then will it possess an intrinsic authority that supersedes the rival claims of some remarkable personal experience or the long-standing tradition of any social group. Only then will the "legitimating story" exhibit a moral universality that is inherently just and practically feasible. Only this kind of metanarrative is comprehensive enough to embrace, order, and explain the unity and diversity of all creation.

For the Chronicler, the theological locus of the biblical metanarrative is the God of Israel. Especially important to the formation of the theological baseline for his metanarrative are the words of God emphasizing divine promise and fulfillment. The Davidic covenant (1 Chron. 17:3–14) and God's response to Solomon's prayer of dedication after completing the temple are strategic examples (2 Chron. 7:11–22). Granted, important theological ideas are only implicitly represented in the personal stories of the names cited in the genealogical records. They become explicit, however, in the Chronicler's highly selective recital of Israelite history. This is especially the case in his depiction of God in the numerous prayers scattered throughout the accounts of the kings of Judah (e.g., 1 Chron. 29:10–13; 2 Chron. 20:6–12).

The Chronicler's theology of hope is credible for the Jewish restoration community because the God of Israel has proven faithful to his Word across the generations from Adam to all those listed in his genealogy—the prominent and the obscure. Perhaps more important, the great deeds of God including the work of creation, the Exodus from Egypt, and most recently the prompting of Cyrus king of Persia to rebuild the temple of Yahweh in Jerusalem are now documented and inscripturated (2 Chron. 36:22–23). Thus the Chronicler's metanarrative has the currency of canonical status in the Jewish community.

By appealing to those books and records already a part of the Hebrew Bible as resources for his preaching and teaching, the Chronicler offers his audience the flawless, true, and eternal Word of God himself (Ps. 18:30; 33:4; Isa. 40:8). Such is the pattern for apostolic preaching in the New Testament (cf. Acts 2; 7; 13; 15), and so it remains for preaching and teaching in the church today. The unfolding drama of God's redemption of humanity as recorded in Scripture continues to provide the legitimate metanarrative for the Christian faith (2 Tim. 3:15–16).

---

2 Tim. 2:8). The Bible is careful to locate the individual believer in a community of faith that spans generations, hence the description of God as one who is faithful and merits praise through all generations (Ps. 100:5; Eph. 3:21).

1 Chronicles 2:3–3:24

꧁

THE SONS OF Judah:

Er, Onan and Shelah. These three were born to him by a Canaanite woman, the daughter of Shua. Er, Judah's firstborn, was wicked in the LORD's sight; so the LORD put him to death. ⁴Tamar, Judah's daughter-in-law, bore him Perez and Zerah. Judah had five sons in all.

⁵The sons of Perez:

Hezron and Hamul.

⁶The sons of Zerah:

Zimri, Ethan, Heman, Calcol and Darda—five in all.

⁷The son of Carmi:

Achar, who brought trouble on Israel by violating the ban on taking devoted things.

⁸The son of Ethan:

Azariah.

⁹The sons born to Hezron were:

Jerahmeel, Ram and Caleb.

¹⁰Ram was the father of

Amminadab, and Amminadab the father of Nahshon, the leader of the people of Judah. ¹¹Nahshon was the father of Salmon, Salmon the father of Boaz, ¹²Boaz the father of Obed and Obed the father of Jesse.

¹³Jesse was the father of

Eliab his firstborn; the second son was Abinadab, the third Shimea, ¹⁴the fourth Nethanel, the fifth Raddai, ¹⁵the sixth Ozem and the seventh David. ¹⁶Their sisters were Zeruiah and Abigail. Zeruiah's three sons were Abishai, Joab and Asahel. ¹⁷Abigail was the mother of Amasa, whose father was Jether the Ishmaelite.

¹⁸Caleb son of Hezron had children by his wife Azubah (and by Jerioth). These were her sons: Jesher, Shobab and Ardon. ¹⁹When Azubah died, Caleb married Ephrath, who bore him Hur. ²⁰Hur was the father of Uri, and Uri the father of Bezalel.

²¹Later, Hezron lay with the daughter of Makir the father of Gilead (he had married her when he was sixty years

old), and she bore him Segub. ²²Segub was the father of
Jair, who controlled twenty-three towns in Gilead.
²³(But Geshur and Aram captured Havvoth Jair, as well
as Kenath with its surrounding settlements—sixty
towns.) All these were descendants of Makir the father
of Gilead.

²⁴ After Hezron died in Caleb Ephrathah, Abijah the wife of
Hezron bore him Ashhur the father of Tekoa.

²⁵ The sons of Jerahmeel the firstborn of Hezron:
Ram his firstborn, Bunah, Oren, Ozem and Ahijah.
²⁶Jerahmeel had another wife, whose name was Atarah;
she was the mother of Onam.

²⁷ The sons of Ram the firstborn of Jerahmeel:
Maaz, Jamin and Eker.

²⁸ The sons of Onam:
Shammai and Jada.
 The sons of Shammai:
Nadab and Abishur.

²⁹ Abishur's wife was named Abihail, who bore him Ahban
and Molid.

³⁰ The sons of Nadab:
Seled and Appaim. Seled died without children.

³¹ The son of Appaim:
Ishi, who was the father of Sheshan.
Sheshan was the father of Ahlai.

³² The sons of Jada, Shammai's brother:
Jether and Jonathan. Jether died without children.

³³ The sons of Jonathan:
Peleth and Zaza.
 These were the descendants of Jerahmeel.

³⁴ Sheshan had no sons—only daughters.
He had an Egyptian servant named Jarha. ³⁵Sheshan
gave his daughter in marriage to his servant Jarha, and
she bore him Attai.

³⁶ Attai was the father of Nathan,
Nathan the father of Zabad,
³⁷ Zabad the father of Ephlal,
Ephlal the father of Obed,
³⁸ Obed the father of Jehu,
Jehu the father of Azariah,

³⁹ Azariah the father of Helez,
Helez the father of Eleasah,
⁴⁰ Eleasah the father of Sismai,
Sismai the father of Shallum,
⁴¹ Shallum the father of Jekamiah,
and Jekamiah the father of Elishama.

⁴² The sons of Caleb the brother of Jerahmeel:
Mesha his firstborn, who was the father of Ziph, and his
son Mareshah, who was the father of Hebron.

⁴³ The sons of Hebron:
Korah, Tappuah, Rekem and Shema. ⁴⁴Shema was the
father of Raham, and Raham the father of Jorkeam.
Rekem was the father of Shammai. ⁴⁵The son of Shammai was Maon, and Maon was the father of Beth Zur.

⁴⁶ Caleb's concubine Ephah was the mother of Haran, Moza
and Gazez. Haran was the father of Gazez.

⁴⁷ The sons of Jahdai:
Regem, Jotham, Geshan, Pelet, Ephah and Shaaph.

⁴⁸ Caleb's concubine Maacah was the mother of Sheber and
Tirhanah. ⁴⁹She also gave birth to Shaaph the father of
Madmannah and to Sheva the father of Macbenah and
Gibea. Caleb's daughter was Acsah. ⁵⁰These were the
descendants of Caleb.

The sons of Hur the firstborn of Ephrathah:
Shobal the father of Kiriath Jearim, ⁵¹Salma the father of
Bethlehem, and Hareph the father of Beth Gader.

⁵² The descendants of Shobal the father of Kiriath Jearim were:
Haroeh, half the Manahathites, ⁵³and the clans of
Kiriath Jearim: the Ithrites, Puthites, Shumathites and
Mishraites. From these descended the Zorathites and
Eshtaolites.

⁵⁴ The descendants of Salma:
Bethlehem, the Netophathites, Atroth Beth Joab, half
the Manahathites, the Zorites, ⁵⁵and the clans of scribes
who lived at Jabez: the Tirathites, Shimeathites and
Sucathites. These are the Kenites who came from Ham-
math, the father of the house of Recab.

^{3:1} These were the sons of David born to him in Hebron:
The firstborn was Amnon the son of Ahinoam of
Jezreel;
the second, Daniel the son of Abigail of Carmel;

² the third, Absalom the son of Maacah daughter of Talmai king of Geshur;

the fourth, Adonijah the son of Haggith;

³ the fifth, Shephatiah the son of Abital;

and the sixth, Ithream, by his wife Eglah.

⁴ These six were born to David in Hebron, where he reigned seven years and six months.

David reigned in Jerusalem thirty-three years, ⁵and these were the children born to him there:

Shammua, Shobab, Nathan and Solomon. These four were by Bathsheba daughter of Ammiel. ⁶There were also Ibhar, Elishua, Eliphelet, ⁷Nogah, Nepheg, Japhia, ⁸Elishama, Eliada and Eliphelet—nine in all. ⁹All these were the sons of David, besides his sons by his concubines. And Tamar was their sister.

¹⁰ Solomon's son was Rehoboam,

Abijah his son,

Asa his son,

Jehoshaphat his son,

¹¹ Jehoram his son,

Ahaziah his son,

Joash his son,

¹² Amaziah his son,

Azariah his son,

Jotham his son,

¹³ Ahaz his son,

Hezekiah his son,

Manasseh his son,

¹⁴ Amon his son,

Josiah his son.

¹⁵ The sons of Josiah:

Johanan the firstborn,

Jehoiakim the second son,

Zedekiah the third,

Shallum the fourth.

¹⁶ The successors of Jehoiakim:

Jehoiachin his son,

and Zedekiah.

¹⁷ The descendants of Jehoiachin the captive:

Shealtiel his son, ¹⁸Malkiram, Pedaiah, Shenazzar, Jekamiah, Hoshama and Nedabiah.

¹⁹ The sons of Pedaiah:

Zerubbabel and Shimei.

The sons of Zerubbabel:

Meshullam and Hananiah.

Shelomith was their sister.

²⁰ There were also five others:

Hashubah, Ohel, Berekiah, Hasadiah and Jushab-

Hesed.

²¹ The descendants of Hananiah:

Pelatiah and Jeshaiah, and the sons of Rephaiah, of

Arnan, of Obadiah and of Shecaniah.

²² The descendants of Shecaniah:

Shemaiah and his sons:

Hattush, Igal, Bariah, Neariah and Shaphat—six in all.

²³ The sons of Neariah:

Elioenai, Hizkiah and Azrikam—three in all.

²⁴ The sons of Elioenai:

Hodaviah, Eliashib, Pelaiah, Akkub, Johanan, Delaiah

and Anani—seven in all.

Original Meaning

THE TRIBE OF JUDAH heads the Chronicler's genealogical prologue, selectively tracing the lineage of the twelve sons of Jacob (also called Israel). Although the list of Israelite tribes has some affinities with the genealogical record of Genesis 46:8–25, this ordering of the tribes is unique to the Old Testament and the rest of Chronicles. According to Williamson, the seemingly disorderly presentation of the materials indicates the writer's primary interest lay outside tracing the family tree of the tribe of Judah.[1]

What does seem clear is the emphasis on three of the twelve Israelite tribes: Judah, Levi, and Benjamin. Presumably this is the case because these three tribes were the dominant Hebrew tribes during the restoration period when the Chronicler composed his history of Israelite kingship. Broadly outlined, the genealogical prologue showcases Judah, followed by a review of half the northern Israelite tribes. Next Levi is emphasized, again followed by an overview of the other half of the northern Israelite tribes. The genealogical prologue then concludes with the family tree of Saul the Benjamite.

---

1. Williamson, *1 and 2 Chronicles*, 48.

More attention is given to Judah than any of the other Israelite tribes. This is the case for several reasons, but two stand out. (1) In general, the emphasis on the tribe of Judah demonstrates that the purposes of God's election to provide righteous leadership through Judah were still at work despite Judah's unfaithfulness that led to the catastrophe of the Babylonian exile. (2) Specifically, as noted by Selman, the genealogy of Judah highlights the family of David and implicitly evokes thoughts of the Davidic covenant.[2] For it was through this covenant of kingship that God would be glorified as the ruler of Israel and the nations and Israel would enjoy "rest" in the land granted to the descendants of Abraham (2 Sam. 7:8–11; cf. Gen. 12:1–3).

The royal family of David (3:1–24) is sandwiched between records of the other sons of Judah (2:1–55 and 4:1–23) in a highly stylized literary structure. The chiastic or inverted "A/B" pattern of this section has been widely recognized by biblical commentators and can be diagrammed as follows:

Introduction (2:3–9)
    Shelah (2:3–4)
    Perez (2:5–8)
    Jerahmeel, Ram, and Caleb (2:9)
        A Descendants of Ram (2:10–17, including David)
            B Descendants of Caleb (2:18–24)
                C Descendants of Jerahmeel (2:25–33)
                C' Descendants of Jerahmeel (2:34–41)
            B' Descendants of Caleb (2:42–55)
        A' Descendants of Ram (3:1–24, including David and
           his descendants)
Conclusion (4:1–23)
    Perez (4:1–20)
    Shelah (4:21–23)

The lineage of Ram, son of Hezron, is deliberately divided into two separate lists and placed as "bookends" for the family tree of Judah. The overall effect is to highlight the clan of Hezron and the family of Ram, the ancestors of King David (cf. 2:15; 3:1). The artistic structure of the genealogy forcefully conveys the Chronicler's theological conviction that the royal family of David was destined to play a key role in the restoration of postexilic Judah. This prominence accorded to David in the Judahite genealogy suggests that the Chronicler has expectations for the reestablishment of Davidic kingship in postexilic Judah. In light of earlier prophetic statements about

2. Selman, 1 Chronicles, 94.

David's dynasty, I am inclined to agree with Allen's hunch that the Chronicler's hope for the restoration community includes "messianic expectations."[3]

Portions of the family tree of Judah have parallels elsewhere in the Old Testament, notably 2:3 (Gen. 38:7); 2:10–12 (Ruth 4:19–22); 3:1–4a (2 Sam. 3:2–5); 3:4b (2 Sam. 5:5); 3:5–8 (2 Sam. 5:14–16). The genealogies of Judah are segmented in that they contain lists of names representing both breadth (i.e., a list of single generations of descendants from a common ancestor, e.g., 2:6, 25) and depth (a listing of successive generations, e.g., 2:10–12). All of the genealogies of Judah are descending; that is, they list names moving from parent to child (e.g., 2:3). By way of special features, the genealogies include birth report (noting the name of the mother, e.g., 2:17), name list (e.g., 2:5), ranking formula (e.g., 2:3, 13), register (i.e., official records calling attention to persons associated with formal institutions like kingship, e.g., 3:1–4, 5–8), and tally (e.g., 3:4).[4]

Judah to Hezron (2:3–8)

JUDAH WAS THE fourth son born to Leah, Israel's (or Jacob's, 2:1) first wife (Gen. 35:23). The Chronicler's register of five sons born to Judah agrees with the lists found in Genesis 46:12 and Numbers 26:19–22. Both of those genealogies end with Hezron and Hamul, the sons of Perez. The Chronicler's genealogy also places an emphasis on Perez and his son Ram, since they are ancestors of King David (cf. 1 Chron. 2:15).

Clearly the writer of Chronicles presupposes his audience's familiarity with story of Judah's marriage to the Canaanite woman named Shua, the tragic death of her first two sons (Er and Onan), and his eventual seduction by his own daughter-in-law Tamar (cf. Gen. 38). The Chronicler also seems to be aware of Jacob's blessing of Judah as the tribe of the "scepter" since the royal family of David is the focal point of his genealogical record of Judah (cf. Gen. 49:10).

This brief portion of Judah's family tree (2:3–4) contains a number of subtle theological ideas that become themes or motifs for the Chronicler's genealogical prologue. For instance, the birth reports calling attention to the mothers of Judah's sons (daughter of Shua, v. 3, and Tamar, v. 4) are a recurring feature of the genealogical prologue. The Chronicler effectively uses the birth report to promote his agenda of "inclusivism" in the face of the growing separatistic nationalism of the later postexilic period. This literary vehicle enables the Chronicler to give prominence not only to women in the

---

3. Leslie C. Allen, *1, 2 Chronicles* (Communicator's Commentary 10; Waco, Tex.: Word, 1987), 43.

4. De Vries, *1 and 2 Chronicles*, 35–44.

genealogical prologue but also to non-Hebrew women like the Canaanite Shua, the Geshurite Maacah (3:2), or the Egyptian Bithiah (4:18).

As Selman has noted, these birth reports also allow the Chronicler to record God's providential activity in mixed marriages (2:3; cf. 2:12, 17; 4:18). The Chronicler likewise anticipates the Matthean genealogy of Jesus Christ, which includes men and women and Jews and Gentiles, marking him as the true "Son of Man" (Matt. 1:2–16).[5] Other theological themes embedded in this list of Judah's sons include the demotion of the firstborn son (2:3; cf. 5:1), God's just punishment of wickedness among the Hebrew people as his elect (2:3; cf. 5:26), and God's faithfulness in sustaining the line of Judah (2:4; cf. 4:10).

The concluding section of this genealogical unit lists the descendants of Judah's twin sons, Perez and Zerah (2:5–9). Implicit in the envelope construction that frames the section with the name of Hezron (2:5, 9) is the story of God's election of the second-born twin Zerah (cf. Gen. 38:27–30). Four of Zerah's sons, including Ethan, Heman, Calcol, and Darda, are identified as famous wise men (1 Chron. 2:6; cf. 1 Kings 4:31). It appears that both Ethan and Heman were associated with the temple musical guilds as well (Ps. 88; 89).

We know from Joshua (Josh. 7:1, 18) that Carmi was the son of Zimri (1 Chron. 2:6). The name Achar (2:7) is a wordplay on the word for "trouble" (Heb. ᶜoker) and associates Achan with King Ahab as a "troubler of Israel" (Josh. 7:24–26; cf. 1 Kings 18:17). The term "violate" (Heb. maᶜal, 1 Chron. 2:7) is often translated "unfaithful" in Chronicles (e.g., 5:25; 10:13; 2 Chron. 12:2; 29:6), and this unfaithfulness led to the Babylonian exile (2 Chron. 36:14). It is David, the son of Jesse, who will rise as the model of faithfulness to God and provide the ultimate solution to Israel's maᶜal.

Descendants of Ram (2:9–17)

THE FAMILY TREE of Ram is listed first even though he was not the firstborn son of Hezron (2:10; cf. v. 9). The Chronicler showcases Ram because his interest in Judah centers on the clan of Hezron and the family of David through Ram (2:13–17). The roster of names from Ram to Jesse (2:10–12) repeats the genealogy of Ruth (Ruth 4:19–22). The Chronicler has listed David as the seventh son of Jesse (1 Chron. 2:15), while he is numbered the eighth son in 1 Samuel 16:10–13; 17:12. Payne speculates that a son (unnamed in the Bible) was born to Jesse between Ozem and David but died prematurely, making David the seventh living son at the time the genealogical record was composed.[6]

---

5. Selman, *1 Chronicles*, 96.
6. Payne, "1, 2 Chronicles," 4:334.

Only the Chronicler identifies Zeruiah and Abigail as sisters of David (2:16). The precedent for intermarriage within David's family is recorded in Abigail's union with an Ishmaelite (2:17). Interestingly, Jether the father of Amasa is regarded as an Israelite in 2 Samuel 17:25 (probably a textual corruption; cf. textual note in the NIV with reference to the LXX). We also learn from this passage that Zeruiah and Abigail were step-daughters of Jesse, born to David's mother by a previous marriage to Nahash (2 Sam. 17:25). The three sons of Zeruiah (Abishai, Joab, and Asahel) and the son of Abigail (Amasa) were famous warriors during the reign of King David (2 Sam. 2:18–19; 19:13).

Descendants of Caleb (2:18–24)

ANALYSIS OF CALEB'S genealogy is complicated by two factors: The genealogy is divided into several sections (2:18–24, 42–55; 4:1–8), and there is some question as to whether or not Caleb son of Hezron (2:18) and Caleb son of Jephunneh are distinct individuals (cf. Num. 13:6). The Chronicler rightly does not equate Caleb with Caleb the spy of the Exodus narrative (cf. 4:15). This section of Caleb's genealogy (spelled Kelubai or Chelubai in 2:9, cf. NIV text note) is unusual because the birth reports referencing his wives and concubines provide the literary structure of the passage (2:18, 19, 21, 24). Unlike most of the other rosters of descendants of Judah, the family tree of Caleb also includes reports recording the settlement of territory in Gilead (2:22).

The key descendant of the first unit of Caleb's family tree is Bezalel (2:18–20). Along with Oholiab, Bezalel was a divinely appointed and anointed architect and craftsman assigned to the design and building of the Mosaic tabernacle and its furniture (Ex. 31:2; 35:30). No doubt, the lineage of Bezalel is juxtaposed with that of David's to emphasize the legitimate connection between the worship in the earlier institution of the tabernacle and worship in the later institution of the temple. It seems best to understand Jerioth as the daughter of Caleb and Azubah (so NEB, NJB), not his concubine wife (so NIV, NRSV).[7]

The second section of Caleb's family registry shifts the focus back to Hezron (2:21) and preserves genealogical connections between descendants of Judah and Gileadites, who settled in northern regions of the Transjordan (2:21–23). The historical significance of the relationship is now lost, although Selman has suggested the report may allude to David's marriage to Maacah, the daughter of Talmai king of Geshur (1 Chron. 3:2 = 2 Sam. 3:3), or to the resettlement of Judahites in the region after the Babylonian exile.[8]

---

7. Cf. Williamson, *1 and 2 Chronicles*, 52–53.
8. Selman, *1 Chronicles*, 98.

It is also possible the geographical data included in the genealogy is of special interest to the postexilic community of the Chronicler's day. The repeated phrase "Makir father of Gilead" (2:21, 23) forms an envelope for this portion of the genealogy. The phrase "father of [place name]" is a frequent formula in Chronicles for identifying the founder of a city or a prominent leader of that city (e.g., 4:14). Havvoth Jair (2:23) was a region of northern Gilead that included between thirty (Judg. 10:4) and sixty cities (Josh. 13:30; 1 Kings 4:13). The association of Aram with Geshur is probably a reference to Aram Maacah (cf. 1 Chron. 19:6), not the Aramean kingdom centered in Damascus.[9]

The concluding birth report (2:24) appears to be a continuation of the genealogy of Caleb recorded in 2:18–19. The MT seems garbled at this point because Ephrath has previously been identified as a wife of Caleb (2:19). Most commentators tend to emend the text on the basis of the LXX and Latin Vulgate and understand Ashhur to be the son of Caleb and Ephrath (with the phrase "Abijah the wife of Hezron" considered a misplaced parenthetic statement identifying the unnamed daughter of Makir, 2:21).[10]

Descendants of Jerahmeel (2:25–41)

THE GENEALOGY OF Jerahmeel shares the emphasis on women with the preceding family tree of Caleb (cf. 2:26, 29, 31, 34, 35). The Chronicler's strong interest in the role of non-Hebrews in the genealogical prologue surfaces as well in the reference to the Egyptian Jarha (2:34). The names of Jerahmeel's descendants have no Old Testament parallels, making analysis virtually impossible. It appears the clan of Jerahmeel may have lived on Judah's southern frontier, given the reference to the "Negev of Jerahmeel" (1 Sam. 27:10; 30:29). The genealogy is a combination of two lists (2:25–33, 34–41), evidenced by the summary formula found in verse 33 ("these were the descendants of Jerahmeel"). The second section features an extensive name list (2:36–41), although nothing is known of Elishama (v. 41).

Most likely this name list was composed to certify Elishama as a descendant of Hezron and Jerahmeel for some (now unknown) reason. Ahijah (2:25) may have been Jerahmeel's first wife, not his fifth son since Atarah is named as "another wife" (2:26).[11] Since Sheshan had only daughters (2:34), Ahlai must have been one of his daughters (2:31).

9. On the time frame for the Aramean expansion, see Williamson, *1 and 2 Chronicles*, 53.
10. E.g., Braun, *1 Chronicles*, 37 n. 24.
11. So Selman, *1 Chronicles*, 98.

Descendants of Caleb (2:42–55)

THIS EXTENSION OF CALEBITE genealogy begun in 2:18–24 and continued in 4:1–7 has little in common with the other lists of Caleb's descendants. The rosters range across the territory of Judah geographically, and there is hardly any overlap between the persons mentioned in this record and those names found in the others. The genealogy consists of two distinct sections, each one probably representing a separate literary source.

The first section is framed by opening and closing formulas, much like the unit listing the descendants of Jerahmeel (i.e., "the sons of . . . ," 2:42, and "these were the descendants of . . . ," 2:50a; cf. 2:25, 33). Caleb's descendants are ordered in a three-part arrangement according to their different mothers, including an unnamed wife (2:42–45), a concubine named Ephah (2:46–47), and a concubine named Maacah (2:48–50a). The purpose of the section seems to be the identification of Hebron and environs with Caleb, although Joshua connects Hebron with Caleb son of Jephunneh—not Caleb son of Hezron (cf. Josh. 14:13; 15:13). The apparent splicing of the two Caleb traditions is also seen in the naming of Acsah as Caleb's (son of Hezron) daughter (cf. Josh. 15:16; Judg. 1:13). As in the case with the descendants of Jerahmeel, the expression "the father of [place name]" may be a title of leadership rather than founder of the settlement (cf. 1 Chron. 2:31).

The second section (2:50b–55) continues the family tree of Hur, born to Caleb and Ephrathah (2:19; cf. 4:4b). Each of the three sons of Hur is identified as the founding father or important chieftain of a well-known Judahite city (2:50–51). The geographical focal point of the unit stretches from Kiriath Jearim, a border city between Judah and Benjamin (2:50; cf. Josh. 15:60; 18:14–15) to Bethlehem (1 Chron. 2:51).

The reference to Bethlehem is a natural prelude to the family tree of David beginning in the next section of the Judahite genealogy (ch. 3). The records of the clans of Kiriath Jearim (2:53–55) appear to be genealogical fragments attached to the line of Shobal, given his association with the city (2:52). According to Thompson, the aim of the Chronicler is to connect previously unrelated and diverse tribal elements into the mainstream of the tribe of Judah.[12] Whether this is prompted by theological or political motivations is unclear. Thompson may well be right that this section of the Calebite genealogy reflects a time when fringe groups on the southern border of Judah were amalgamated into the tribal life of Judah. If so, this becomes yet another example of the Chronicler's concern for policies promoting "inclusion" rather than "exclusion" in postexilic Judah.

---

12. Thompson, *1, 2 Chronicles*, 66.

Commentators regularly emend the name Haroeh (2:52) to Reaiah on the basis of the parallel in 4:2.[13] Identification of the city or region of Manahath (2:52) is problematic, although Benjamites were carried captive there (cf. 8:6). It may have been associated with Edomite territory since Manahath was a descendant of the Shobal, one of the descendants of Seir (1:40).

David had two Ithrites among his mighty men, Ira and Gareb, perhaps associated with the city of Jattir (2:53; cf. 2 Sam. 23:38; 1 Chron. 11:40). References to the Zorathites and Eshtaolites (1 Chron. 2:53), both cities originally allotted to the tribe of Dan (Josh. 15:33; 19:41), suggest the gradual expansion of the tribe of Judah into that region. Netophah is a well-attested town near Bethlehem, from which two of David's mighty men hailed (2 Sam. 23:28–29; 1 Chron. 11:30) and which was settled by Levitical singers during the restoration period (Ezra 2:22; Neh. 12:28). It is difficult to determine if the "clans of the scribes" (1 Chron. 2:55) refers to a scribal guild (comparable with the guilds mentioned in 4:14, 21, 23) or a gentilic expression identifying another clan (cf. "the Sophrite clans," NJB). The relationship of the Kenites (2:55) and the Recabites is uncertain (cf. 2 Kings 10:15; Jer. 35).

Royal Family of David (3:1–24)

THE FAMILY OF David is the feature attraction of Judah's genealogy. The Chronicler's emphasis on David stems from his knowledge of prophetic statements about the unbreakable covenant God made with David and the reestablishment of Davidic kingship in Israel (cf. Jer. 33:19–22). He then offers this hope to his audience through the repetition of the word of the Lord to Nathan announcing the Davidic covenant (1 Chron. 17:4–14, esp. vv. 10–14; cf. 2 Sam. 7:4–16). The record of the royal line continues the genealogy tracing David's ancestry from Ram to Jesse (1 Chron. 2:10–17). The chapter divides naturally into three distinct sections: David's children (3:1–9), the kings of Judah (3:10–16), and the postexilic descendants of David (3:17–24).

David's sons are registered in two lists according to the capital city in which they were born: Hebron (3:1–4) or Jerusalem (3:5–9). The genealogy highlights birth reports citing the name of the mother (e.g., 3:1), concluding tallies (e.g., 3:4), and name lists (e.g., 3:5). Chronicles reports the parallel record of David's sons born in Hebron with only minor variation (e.g., Daniel is mentioned as the son of Abigail, not Kileab, cf. 2 Sam. 3:2–5). The roster of sons born to David in Jerusalem differs more noticeably from the Samuel parallel (2 Sam. 5:14–16) and the Chronicler's internal parallel

---

13. E.g., Braun, *1 Chronicles*, 38 n. 52a; Williamson, *1 and 2 Chronicles*, 55.

(1 Chron. 14:3–7). For example, this list enumerates the four sons of Bathshua (probably an alternative spelling of Bathsheba, 3:5) and includes the names of Nogah and Eliphelet (not found in the parallel lists in 2 Sam. 5). Shimea (1 Chron. 3:5) and Shammua (2 Sam. 5:14; 1 Chron. 14:4) are variations on the name of the firstborn son of Bathsheba.

The birth reports citing the name of the individual mothers of David's sons recall the annals of the kings of Judah, where similar information is preserved (e.g., 1 Kings 15:2). Theologically, the practice reflects the association of the "offspring of the woman" promise (Gen. 3:15) with the line of David (cf. 2 Sam. 7:16). Tamar (1 Chron. 3:9) is mentioned because she is the only daughter of David; her story is known from 2 Samuel 13.

The Chronicler reports the complete list of Davidic kings reigning in the southern kingdom of Judah during the period of the divided Hebrew monarchies (3:10–16). Naturally, Athaliah (the evil queen who reigned between the regimes of Ahaziah and Joash) is omitted as a non-Davidide. Azariah (3:12) is also known as Uzziah (2 Chron. 26:1). The parallel accounts in 2 Kings omit Johanan, the firstborn son of Josiah (1 Chron. 3:15). Shallum (3:15) is the throne name of Jehoahaz (2 Kings 23:31; Jer. 22:11).

Jehoiachin (1 Chron. 3:16), the next to last king of Judah, was taken captive by King Nebuchadnezzar and exiled as a prisoner of war in Babylonia (2 Kings 24:15). His release from prison upon the ascension of Evil-Merodach (2 Kings 25:27–30) serves as the postscript for the book of Jeremiah (Jer. 52:31–34) and rekindled hope for the restoration of the Davidic monarchy after the Babylonian exile.[14] It is for this reason that the Chronicler introduces the last section of the Davidic genealogy with King Jehoiachin "the captive" (1 Chron. 3:17). Payne admits that the Chronicler's birth order of Josiah's sons is difficult to harmonize with the age formulas in 2 Kings 23:31, 36; 24:18; he assumes a scribal error in the transmission of the numbers.[15]

The final section of the royal genealogy contains the register of the post-exilic descendants of David (3:17–24).[16] The eight generations counted after the Exile may be suggestive, perhaps identifying contemporaries of the Chronicler.[17] The key figures of the list include Shenazzar, probably the same "prince of Judah" named Sheshbazzar, who led the initial wave of Jewish emigrants back to Jerusalem with the help of King Cyrus of Persia (cf. Ezra 1:8–11), and Zerubbabel, who headed up a second Hebrew migration from Persia sometime later (Ezra 2:2). Zerubbabel, son of Shealtiel (through Peda-

---

14. For the text of the Jehoiachin ration tablet, see D. Winton Thomas, ed., *Documents from Old Testament Times* (New York: Harper & Row, 1961), 84–86; also *ANET*, 308.

15. Selman, *1 Chronicles*, 100.

16. On the numerous textual problems, see Sara Japhet, *I and II Chronicles*, 99–102.

17. See Braun's genealogical chart, *1 Chronicles*, 52.

iah, 1 Chron. 3:17–19), served as governor of postexilic Judah for a time (cf. Zech. 4:6–10). It was Haggai's blessing of Zerubbabel as God's "signet ring" that overturned Jeremiah's curse on the line of King Jehoiachin and restored royal authority to the descendants of David (Hag. 2:23; cf. Jer. 22:28–30).

According to Selman, these postexilic descendants of David are the corporate incarnation of a living hope for the eventual restoration of Davidic kingship in Israel.[18] This hope is exemplified even in the names of Zerubbabel's children, such as Meshullam ("Restored," 1 Chron. 3:19), Hananiah ("Yahweh is merciful," 3:19), Shelomith ("Peace," 3:19), Hashubah ("Yahweh has considered," 3:20), Ohel ("Tent" [of Yahweh], 3:20), Berekiah ("Yahweh has blessed," 3:20), Hasidiah ("Yahweh is love," 3:20), and Jushab-Hesed ("Covenant love returns," 3:20).[19]

THE DEATHBED BLESSING of Jacob over his son Judah anticipated Israelite kingship, as the "scepter" was promised to the tribe of Judah (Gen. 49:10). Centuries later this pledge was realized in the covenant of kingship God granted to David and his descendants (2 Sam. 7:4–17; 1 Chron. 17:4–15). Chronicles revives hopes for Davidic kingship by setting the tribe of Judah and the family of David as the centerpiece of the genealogical prologue. This reminder of the Davidic dynasty rekindled expectations for a resumption of the monarchy by rehearsing David's family tree.

The Chronicler assumes that God will sprout a shoot from the "stump of Jesse" to govern the postexilic community in righteousness (in keeping with Isa. 11:1, 4). The family of David and the restoration of kingship is not, however, the primary emphasis of the Chronicler. Rather, his emphasis is on God's faithfulness in preserving the tribe of Judah and the family of David. Historically speaking, there was good reason for the line of David to have been snuffed out by the Babylonian conquest and Exile. Nevertheless, God kept the family tree of David alive.

The roots of Israel's genealogical tree run deep, beyond the Hebrew patriarchs and matriarchs back to the faithful of God remembered in that universal history of earliest humanity. More than that, the Chronicler reminds his audience that the branches of Israel's family tree are numerous and full, generation after generation sustaining the legacy of those twelve tribes descended from Jacob. Wilcock has rightly noted that there is great value in tracing the

18. Selman, *1 Chronicles*, 101.
19. Cf. Braun, *1 Chronicles*, 54.

genealogical roots of a people uprooted by exile and later transplanted by waves of emigrants returning to their homeland.[20] In a real sense, postexilic Judah is rootless, with kingship but a memory and the institution of the temple and the office of the priest but a shadow of former times. The genealogical prologue serves the important purpose of grafting the postexilic Hebrew community into the family tree of her ancestors.

Establishing both the hereditary and the spiritual continuity between the past and present generations of Hebrews is important for several reasons. Two are crucial to the Chronicler's message. (1) The Chronicler summons the postexilic community to move beyond tribalism and territoriality and to find unity in the stronger bond of faith in God as his people.[21]

(2) The Chronicler calls each postexilic generation of Israelites to stand in readiness and to serve the restoration effort as needed. This is especially true for the family of David, should the opportunity for the reestablishment of Israelite kingship materialize. The New Testament genealogy identifying Jesus Christ as the "Son of David" is all that more remarkable when viewed in light of Chronicles. Not only did God preserve the line of David until "the time had fully come" (Gal. 4:4), but also he sustained that spirit of readiness and obedience in the descendants of David—namely, Mary and Joseph (cf. Matt. 1:24; Luke 1:38).[22]

Finally, the Chronicler uses the literary form of genealogy with great skill and considerable confidence. He is intentional in where he wants to take his audience through the vehicle of the records of Israel's family tree. The genealogical prologue works for the Chronicler because his audience is familiar with the story of Hebrew history, in many cases even the names of the "cast of thousands" participating in that story.

As Wilcock has observed, the Chronicler simply interprets and applies "facts" that his first audience knows already.[23] He writes to a people steeped in its own history and well-schooled in its own Scriptures. His audience understands the overarching story of covenant history and Israel's role in God's redemptive plan for the nations. They grasp, if you will, the *metanarative* of Old Testament revelation. The premium placed on teaching the words and deeds of God to the next generation by the Israelites assures the Chronicler that the "preaching" of names is enough; his audience knows "the rest of story" (cf. Deut. 4:9–10; 6:2, 7; Ps. 78:5–6).

---

20. Wilcock, *The Message of Chronicles,* 29–30.
21. Ibid., 30–31.
22. On the theme of readiness see Allen, *1, 2 Chronicles,* 43–44.
23. Wilcock, *The Message of Chronicles,* 25.

RETELLING THE STORY. The Chronicler's genealogical prologue fails as a literary device today because the story of the Old Testament has no currency in our post-Christian or postbiblical society. Beyond this, the genealogical prologue proves extraneous because any story told with names only is incomprehensible in a postmodern culture that bases reality on the emotive narration of personal experiences. The fragmentation and trivialization of knowledge, the individualization of learning, and the tribalization of human experience in postmodern culture denies universal relevance to any story—let alone a story told through the seemingly endless register of names in a genealogy.

Sadly, the shadow of postmodernity grows steadily longer and darker over the Christian subculture. As one prominent biblical scholar has noted, "the Bible has become a springboard for personal piety and meditation, not a book to be read."[24] According to the (unscientific) results of biblical literacy tests given to Christian young people over the past several years, there is an emerging trend of an alarming lack of basic Bible knowledge. Though many youth (and adults) in the church use the Bible on a regular basis, few seem to know its stories.

Small wonder, then, that the genealogical prologue of Chronicles is better known as an antidote for insomnia in the church rather than a soaring and profound theology of hope for a beleaguered community of faith adrift in a sea of religious and cultural pluralism. How much less the appreciation for Matthew's genealogy (Matt. 1:1–17) as the story of Jesus as the "Son of Man," or truly representative human being, when Christian youth cannot even identify Matthew as one of Jesus' apostles from a list of New Testament names! The church's historical roots are withering in terms of basic knowledge of the biblical story of redemption and the essentials of church history. Nothing short of a "catechetical revolution" in Christian education in the home, the church, and the academy will thaw the "cultural winter" brought about by the increasingly imperialistic worldview of postmodernism.[25]

Neil Postman's radical response to what may be called the "discrete" or fragmented learning of postmodernism is to teach every subject as history because every subject has a history.[26] Knowledge of one's ideological roots is as important as knowledge of one's genealogical roots, perhaps more so.

---

24. Gary M. Burge, "The Greatest Story Never Read," *Christianity Today* 43/9 (Aug. 9, 1999): 45.

25. Cf. Middleton and Walsh, *Truth Is Stranger Than It Used to Be*, 22–27.

26. Neil Postman, *Technopoly* (New York: Vintage Books, 1992), 189–90.

For the sake of personal identity and self-awareness, not only is it essential to know where one's family comes from but also where one's ideas originate. We must know where our world comes from, the source of what Postman calls our moral and aesthetic sensibilities. The teaching of subjects as historical continuities contextualizes knowledge. Or as Postman argues, "the history of subjects teaches connections; it teaches that the world is not created new each day, that everyone stands on someone else's shoulders."[27]

Educational theory and practice as outlined in the Old Testament understood this principle well. The aim or purpose of Hebrew education is encapsulated within the revelation given to Abraham concerning the destruction of Sodom and Gomorrah (Gen. 18:19, in context immediately following the divine promise of an heir, 18:10–15). Here God bids Abraham to direct his children (and subsequent descendants) in "the way of the LORD."

Generally speaking, "the way of the LORD" refers to knowledge of and obedience to the will of God as revealed through act and word in Old Testament history. The way or will of God for humanity reflects his personal character and attributes. As human beings love their neighbors as themselves (Lev. 19:18), practice righteousness and justice (Gen. 18:19), and pursue holiness (Lev. 11:44), they walk in the way of the Lord in that they mirror God's character.

More specifically, "the way of the LORD" denotes the particular content of the series of covenant agreements or treaties Yahweh made with his people Israel. These covenants formed the basis of Israel's relationship to Yahweh and were characterized by a stylized literary pattern that included legislation or stipulations necessary for maintaining that relationship (e.g., Ex. 20–23). Often the covenant or treaty concluded with the promise of blessings or curses conditioned by Israel's obedience (or lack thereof!) to the specific covenant stipulations (e.g., Deut. 28).

Thus, Hebrew education was essentially instruction in covenant obedience or "keeping the way of the LORD" (cf. Gen. 18:19). Moses summarized the basic components of this covenant obedience in his farewell address to the Israelites as "to love the LORD your God, to walk in his ways, and to keep his commands, decrees and laws" (Deut. 30:16). Later, the psalmist condensed this covenant content of Old Testament education in the phrase "the law of the LORD" (Ps. 119:1).

Since the Israelites recognized Yahweh as the God of history, providentially active in the course of human events, history too became part of the

---

27. Ibid., 190. Note the disdain for such ideas in contemporary society as illustrated in the lyrics of the music of popular culture (e.g., "standing on the shoulders of giants leaves me cold"; R.E.M., *Document* [International Record Syndicate, Inc., 1987], from Track 10, "King of Birds").

content or curriculum of Hebrew education. The recitation and festal remembrance of divine acts in human history were instructive as to the nature of God and his purposes in creation. Naturally, the parade example of this historical trajectory in Hebrew education is the Passover, which celebrated the Exodus from Egypt (cf. Ex. 12–13; esp. 12:24–27; 13:11–16).

In time, the Hebrew poetic and wisdom traditions and the prophetic tradition were included in the covenant content of Old Testament education. The wisdom tradition served as a practical commentary on the law or covenant legislation while the prophetic tradition functioned as a theological commentary on Old Testament law. Like the legal tradition associated with the covenants, both wisdom and prophecy were rooted in the behavioral outcomes of loving God and doing righteousness and justice (cf. Prov. 1:3; 2:9; Hos. 6:6; Mic. 6:8).

Walter Brueggemann has offered a perceptive analysis of education in the Old Testament, connected to the major divisions of the Hebrew Bible: the Law or Torah, the Prophets, and the Writings (especially wisdom literature). His paradigm merits consideration as the church rethinks Christian education in a postmodern society. He views Israelite education in the Old Testament as a "nurturing in passion"—for loving God and maintaining covenant relationship with him.[28] This means instruction in Old Testament times was "religious education" in that it was a quest for the transcendent, "moral education" in that it stressed behavioral outcomes, and "historical education" in that it stressed the historical continuity of divine revelation.[29]

Brueggemann identifies the primary way of knowing in Old Testament education as that of the *ethos of the community* or the fundamental religious truths embraced by the Hebrew people.[30] These basic spiritual tenets are preserved in the law or Torah and the historical books of the Old Testament. The learner or initiate enters the community of faith by assimilating the accepted and trusted truths of the Israelites by means of a basic set of modalities, including religious tradition by rote (Deut. 6:7–9), dialogue (esp. in the form of catechism or question and answer, (Ex. 12:24–28), storytelling (Deut. 4:9–10; cf. Ps. 105), and sign and symbol (esp. in the office of the priesthood and the institution of the tabernacle, Ex. 25–40).

---

28. Walter Brueggemann, "Passion and Perspective: Two Dimensions of Education in the Bible," *ThTo* 42 (1985): 173.

29. Cf. Thomas H. Groome, *Christian Religious Education* (San Francisco: Harper & Row, 1980), 22–23; J. Elias, ed., *Psychology and Religious Education* (Bethlehem, Pa.: Catechetical Communications, 1975), 65–82.

30. Walter Brueggemann, *The Creative Word* (Philadelphia: Fortress, 1982), 30–31; for another perspective on education in biblical times emphasizing the Hebrew wisdom tradition, see James L. Crenshaw, *Education in Ancient Israel* (New York: Doubleday, 1998).

A second way of knowing, described as the *pathos of God*, disrupts the consensus of the truth accepted and established by the community. For Brueggemann, the Israelite prophets interrupt the continuity of the foundational truth of the Torah—intrusively challenging the consensus of truth in the community. This disruption of consensus is necessary because God may reveal new truth to the community (e.g., Isa. 42:9), or the human power structures within society may subvert or suppress the established truth of the community (e.g., 1 Kings 21:22). The prophets teach this new truth (or reinterpretation of the established truth) through dream, vision, oracle, poetic language, and personal object lesson (or living parable). This disruption prompted by the prophetic literature often "lay outside the rationality of their culture," and educationally it required the learner to experience a certain "marginality" in respect to social status and economic power.[31]

Brueggemann's third category of knowing is that of the *logos of God*, or discernment rooted in the wisdom literature of the Old Testament. The disclosure of established truth in the Torah and the disruption of this truth by the Prophets is mediated by the wisdom of God. This is essential for the educational process because it means "not everything is up for grabs."[32] Also, the discernment fostered by the Hebrew wisdom books encourages a synthesis that recognizes the interconnectedness of all of life. This means wisdom affirms human dependence on God, yet preserves and fosters the dignity of human initiative, investigation, and reflection—all the while nurturing the mystery of God's inscrutability.

Finally, Brueggemann identifies *obedience* as a mode of knowledge. Moses set life before the people of Israel in the form of obedience to divine directives (Deut. 30:15–16). Obedience to God reassures faith and leads to communion with God. For Brueggemann, the discernment of wisdom finds its fulfillment in obedience because it ends in doxology.[33] Obedience to God means his Word is the final Word. After probing the mysteries of life and death and faith in God, the learner ultimately must offer praise and worship to the sovereign Ruler of creation.

The Chronicler's genealogical prologue works for his audience because they have been initiated into the shared secret of the community of faith— covenant relationship with Yahweh, the covenant maker. They have also experienced the disruption of the Babylonian exile, as threatened by the prophets. For these reasons, they are in a position to embrace the "wisdom" of the Chronicler's theology of hope rooted in God's faithfulness over the

---

31. Brueggemann, *The Creative Word*, 47, 50.
32. Ibid., 87.
33. Ibid., 88–89.

course of their history as illustrated in the genealogical record. Appropriately, the Chronicler calls his contemporaries to respond to his "historical sermon" with praise and worship of the God of their Hebrew ancestors.

According to Brueggemann, the story of Israel's redemption by Yahweh in the Exodus from Egypt is the "bottom line" of Hebrew education rooted in the truth of the Torah.[34] As the foundation of Hebrew epistemology and the theological center of the Old Testament, the Torah is the religious primer for Hebrew children. Thus, they have no need to invent world-forming secrets, "but they are invited to share in a secret already trusted and relied upon."[35] That "secret" is the story of God's power, justice, and grace in the Exodus from Egypt preserved in the Torah.

The parallels to the redemptive story of Jesus Christ as the "Passover lamb" for the church in the New Testament are patently obvious (cf. John 1:29; 1 Cor. 5:7). What better way to play to a postmodern audience craving some sort of highly personal yet deeply mysterious experience than inviting old and young alike to share in a tried and trustworthy secret taught through the medium of the biblical story of redemption?

34. Ibid., 26–27.
35. Ibid., 18.

1 Chronicles 4:1–23

THE DESCENDANTS OF Judah:

Perez, Hezron, Carmi, Hur and Shobal.
²Reaiah son of Shobal was the father of Jahath, and Jahath
the father of Ahumai and Lahad. These were the clans
of the Zorathites.
³These were the sons of Etam:
Jezreel, Ishma and Idbash. Their sister was named
Hazzelelponi. ⁴Penuel was the father of Gedor, and
Ezer the father of Hushah.

These were the descendants of Hur, the firstborn of
Ephrathah and father of Bethlehem.
⁵Ashhur the father of Tekoa had two wives, Helah and
Naarah.
⁶Naarah bore him Ahuzzam, Hepher, Temeni and
Haahashtari. These were the descendants of Naarah.
⁷The sons of Helah:
Zereth, Zohar, Ethnan, ⁸and Koz, who was the father of
Anub and Hazzobebah and of the clans of Aharhel son
of Harum.

⁹Jabez was more honorable than his brothers. His mother
had named him Jabez, saying, "I gave birth to him in pain."
¹⁰Jabez cried out to the God of Israel, "Oh, that you would
bless me and enlarge my territory! Let your hand be with me,
and keep me from harm so that I will be free from pain." And
God granted his request.

¹¹Kelub, Shuhah's brother, was the father of Mehir, who was
the father of Eshton. ¹²Eshton was the father of Beth
Rapha, Paseah and Tehinnah the father of Ir Nahash.
These were the men of Recah.

¹³The sons of Kenaz:
Othniel and Seraiah.
The sons of Othniel:
Hathath and Meonothai. ¹⁴Meonothai was the father of
Ophrah.

Seraiah was the father of Joab,

the father of Ge Harashim. It was called this because its people were craftsmen.
15 The sons of Caleb son of Jephunneh:

Iru, Elah and Naam.

The son of Elah:

Kenaz.
16 The sons of Jehallelel:

Ziph, Ziphah, Tiria and Asarel.
17 The sons of Ezrah:

Jether, Mered, Epher and Jalon. One of Mered's wives gave birth to Miriam, Shammai and Ishbah the father of Eshtemoa. 18(His Judean wife gave birth to Jered the father of Gedor, Heber the father of Soco, and Jekuthiel the father of Zanoah.) These were the children of Pharaoh's daughter Bithiah, whom Mered had married.
19 The sons of Hodiah's wife, the sister of Naham:

the father of Keilah the Garmite, and Eshtemoa the Maacathite.
20 The sons of Shimon:

Amnon, Rinnah, Ben-Hanan and Tilon.

The descendants of Ishi:

Zoheth and Ben-Zoheth.
21 The sons of Shelah son of Judah:

Er the father of Lecah, Laadah the father of Mareshah and the clans of the linen workers at Beth Ashbea, 22Jokim, the men of Cozeba, and Joash and Saraph, who ruled in Moab and Jashubi Lehem. (These records are from ancient times.) 23They were the potters who lived at Netaim and Gederah; they stayed there and worked for the king.

THE SECTION LISTING the other clans of Judah splices several short and independent genealogical units as an addendum to the register of Judah's sons (cf. 2:3–3:24). The supplemental information about these additional descendants of Judah may have been included so as not to slight other members of the tribe, given the emphasis on the royal line issuing from David (3:1–24). None of the genealogies has any Old Testament parallel. The obscurity of these records is attested by the number of textual problems associated with the personal and place names in the genealogies.

As to literary structure, six distinct genealogical units can be discerned: the clans of Hur and Ashhur, descendants of Perez (4:1–8), Jabez (4:9–10), Kelub (4:11–12), the clans of Othniel and Caleb (4:13–16), the clan of Erzah and others (4:17–20), and the clan of Shelah (4:21–23). The formula "father of [personal/place name]" is also a regular feature of the passage, betraying an interest in the localities associated with the lesser clans of Judah (cf. 4:3, 4, 5, 11, 12, 14, 17, 18, 19, 21). Finally, the genealogies include an unusual series of notations emphasizing women (4:3, 5, 17, 18, 19), prayer (4:9–10), and occupations (4:14, 21, 23).

Clans of Hur and Shobal (4:1–8)

THE INITIAL PORTION of the genealogical appendix to the tribe of Judah contains supplementary materials tracing the clans of Hur and Shobal to Perez. The lists appear to be a collection of fragments brought together for the sake of completing the genealogies of Hur and Shobal begun in 2:50, 52 (note the repeated formula "the sons/descendants of Hur" in 2:50a and 4:4b). Thompson correctly notes that this expansion of the Hur and Shobal genealogies was intended to explain the origins of the Zorathites.[1] The village of Zorah is important to the Chronicler because it was resettled by Judeans after the Babylonian captivity (Neh. 11:29). This emphasis is in keeping with the Chronicler's theme of establishing the continuity of the restoration community with past Israelite history. Zorah was one of several border cities fortified by Rehoboam when the Hebrew united monarchy split into the northern and southern kingdoms (2 Chron. 11:10).

The genealogy of Etam (4:3–4) appears to be an unrelated intrusion in the registers of Hur and Shobal (note the NIV follows the LXX and Vulgate and reads "sons of Etam" rather than the Heb. "father of Etam"). Braun has suggested that these verses preserve the names of the descendants of Hur's third son Hareph (cf. 2:51).[2] Like the city of Zorah, Etam (4:3) and Tekoa (4:5) were also among the cities of Judah "militarized" by Rehoboam when the Hebrew monarchy divided into rival kingdoms (2 Chron. 11:5–10). Perhaps these names are important to the Chronicler because of resettlement patterns noted in connection with Zorah.

The name Hazzelelponi (4:3) is a curiosity but should be retained as original to the text. Women (wives as well as sisters) are featured in the Chron-

1. Thompson, *1, 2 Chronicles*, 72.
2. Braun, *1 Chronicles*, 44.

icler's genealogies, and the formula introducing the name of this "sister" has a parallel in 7:15 ("his sister's name was Maacah").

The expression "father of" common to the genealogies in this section (e.g., "Penuel was the father of Gedor," 4:4) may be understood in the sense of ancestor and/or as "settler" or even "founding father" of a town or village. Thus it is possible that Penuel (4:4) and Jered (4:18) were cofounders of the city of Gedor (or Jedur?). The name Hushah is attached to the village of Hushan (some five miles west of Bethlehem), and two of the members of David's elite guard are identified as "Hushathites" (2 Sam. 21:18; 23:27; cf. 1 Chron. 11:29; 20:4; 27:11). Again, the Chronicler's selection of genealogical materials here seems to be motivated by his concern to establish continuity between the restoration community and earlier Israelite history.

The genealogy of the clans of Ashhur (4:4b–8) poses problems when compared to the genealogy of Caleb son of Hezron in 2:18–24. The former identifies Hur as the son of Caleb and Ashhur as the son of Hur (4:4–5), while the latter suggests Ashhur is the son of Hezron and Hur is the son of Caleb (2:19, 24). Most commentators accept the alteration "and Caleb married Ephrathah" for "Hezron died in Caleb Ephrathah" in 2:24 (in agreement with 2:19 and supported by the LXX and the Vulgate). This means Ashhur was the younger brother of Hur.

The descendants of Ashhur are listed according to his two wives, who are cited by name (Helah and Naarah, 4:5). The inclusion of the names of women in Old Testament genealogies is significant; unfortunately, it is impossible to ascertain the reason why their names are important to this genealogical record. The clan name Haahashtari is unusual in that the name carries the definite article ("the Ahashtarites") and is widely recognized as a Persian loanword (cf. *haʾaḥašteranim*, Est. 8:10, 14).

Jabez (4:10–11)

THIS NOTE ON Jabez intrudes abruptly in the genealogy of Judah. The brief account is an independent literary unit and is theological in character. Nothing is known of his brothers, and there is no apparent connection between Jabez and the place Jabez mentioned in 2:55.[3] There is a play on words with the name Jabez (*yaʿbeṣ*) as a result of the "pain" (*beʿoṣeb*) his mother endured during his birth. Jabez is remembered as an "honorable" man, more so than his brothers. Thompson is probably correct in connecting Jabez's "honor" with his earnest prayers.

Given the ancient belief that one's name represented an individual's character and in some cases personal destiny, Jabez prayed that God would over-

---

3. Williamson, *1 and 2 Chronicles*, 59.

turn any curse associated with his name into blessing (cf. Gen. 38:15).[4] Two of his four petitions focus on physical circumstances (expanded territorial holdings and freedom from pain) and two deal with his relationship to God (blessing and protection). The efficacy of prayer to the God of Israel is an important theme in Chronicles (cf. 1 Chron. 5:20–22; 2 Chron. 20:6–12). The Chronicler seeks to remind his audience that God's responsiveness to prayer in the past is an invitation to offer prayers addressing present needs and concerns.

---

4. Thompson, *1, 2 Chronicles*, 73. On the petition of Jabez as a model for prayer, see Bruce Wilkinson, *The Prayer of Jabez* (Sisters, Ore.: Multnomah, 2000). Wilkinson is to be commended for introducing millions of readers to Chronicles, and his invitation to pray to the God of the Bible is certainly in keeping with the Chronicler's message. The premise of this best-selling book is that ordinary Christians need to reach for an extraordinary life by seeking God's blessing. The prayer of Jabez is treated as a four-part formula for divine blessing: seeking to be blessed by God, seeking greater personal "territory," depending on God's power for significant ministry, and fleeing temptation. This prayer formula is offered as a model of prayer for divine blessing and is supported by the guarantee that God always answers this daring prayer. The work, however, begs a critique that places the Jabez prayer formula (or "mantra") in the larger context of Scripture.

Although unmentioned, the language of the prayer is difficult. (1) It is unclear whether this opening statement of the prayer should be read as a conditional clause ("if you truly bless me," so NJB) or a wish ("Oh that you would bless me," so NIV). (2) The final clause can be changed from "so that I will be free from pain" (so NIV) to read "that I may not cause pain" (only NKJV).

The undertones of the "health and wealth gospel" sounded in what some critics call a "self-help" book play well to the consumer culture of North America. But one wonders how the ordinary Christian in Asia or Africa might understand this interpretation of the prayer of Jabez. The suggestion that God's blessing can be reduced to a formula is simplistic and borders on the irreverent (since God is not to be approached as a "cosmic slot machine," cf. Job 41:11). The emphasis on abundant personal blessing in the Jabez prayer formula certainly runs counter to the prayer Jesus taught his disciples requesting only "daily bread" (Matt 6:11). (In fact, after reading Wilkinson, one might wonder why Jesus taught his disciples another prayer instead of just giving them the Jabez prayer!) The Jabez prayer formula also seems to gloss over Paul's exhortation to look out for the interests of others (Phil. 2:4). Finally, the Jabez prayer formula fails to mention virtues like perseverance in the face of suffering or faithful service in humble and thankless situations—standard fare in the Christian life for many servants of Christ's gospel (although this criticism has been addressed in part in the author's sequel, *Secrets of the Vine: Breaking Through to Abundance* [Sisters, Ore.: Multnomah, 2001]).

More specifically on the content and structure of the Jabez prayer, see Larry Pechawer, *The Lost Prayer of Jabez* (Joplin, Mo.: Mireh, 2001), who concludes that the only request of the prayer is "more pasture land" (61). In part, his analysis is based on the alternate pointing of the Heb. word *mera'ah* ("from evil") so as to read *mir'eh* ("pasture land"), thus rendering the prayer: "Now Jabez cried out to the God of Israel, saying, 'If you would only bless me, then enlarge my territory that your hand may be with me, and provide me with pasture land so that I will not be in distress'" (59).

Kelub (4:11–12)

THE NAME KELUB is sometimes rendered Chelub (so NRSV). None of the persons included in this genealogy are mentioned elsewhere in the Old Testament, and Chelub's parents are unidentified. Several of the ancient versions read Caleb instead of Chelub (e.g., LXX, Vulgate, Syriac). Many modern commentators are inclined to emend Chelub to Caleb based on this evidence.[5] It seems more prudent, however, to agree with Williamson and retain the name Chelub as an otherwise unknown Old Testament figure.[6]

The name Ir Nahash (4:12) means "city of the craftsman" and may account for the verses that follow mentioning craft guilds (4:14 ["craftsmen"]; 4:21 ["linen workers"]; 4:23 ["potters"]). The importance of this independent genealogical unit seems to be the connection of Chelub to the "men of Recah," an as yet unidentified place.[7]

Clans of Othniel and Caleb (4:13–16)

THE KENIZZITES, or descendants of Kenaz, were apparently independent southern clans absorbed into the tribe of Judah. Kenaz was the younger brother of Caleb and the father of Othniel (cf. Josh. 15:17; Judg. 1:13; 3:9, 11). Caleb, son of Jephunneh, is also identified as a Kenizzite (Num. 32:12; Josh 14:6, 14). Caleb was one of the twelve spies sent into Canaan to reconnoiter the land before the Israelite conquest (Num. 13:6, 30; 14:6). Along with Joshua, Caleb returned with a favorable report and was commended by God for his faith and duly rewarded with an inheritance in the land of Canaan (Num. 14:24; Deut. 1:36).

Othniel, Caleb's nephew (or younger brother, as in the NIV), was known for his conquest of Debir at the behest of Caleb (for which he received Caleb's daughter Acsah in marriage, Josh. 15:16–17). Othniel was also known for his leadership as a judge in delivering the Israelites from the king of Aram (Judg. 3:9–11). The Chronicler includes the genealogies of Othniel and Caleb because both were responsible for expanding the boundaries of Israel during the days of the judges. Their example was meant to encourage postexilic Judah by reminding the people that God was still capable of enlarging the borders of diminished Judah through the efforts of faithful individuals.

The name Meonothai is restored (4:13) on the basis of the LXX and Vulgate in the genealogy because of an error of haplography. The name Ge Harashim (4:14) means "the valley of the craftsmen" and was located with a

---

5. Braun, *1 Chronicles*, 56.

6. Williamson, *1, 2 Chronicles*, 60.

7. The LXXb reads "Rechab," possibly connecting 4:12 with 2:55 (so Braun, *1 Chronicles*, 57).

cluster of villages including Lod and Ono, some thirty miles northwest of Jerusalem (cf. Neh. 11:35). Some commentators connect this reference to "craftsmen" with the Kenites, perhaps indicating this people group had been displaced to the north.[8] The phrase "the son of Elah: Kenaz" (NIV) may be rendered "these *are* the sons of Kenaz" with only a slight transposition of words.[9] If this reading is correct, then the section begins and ends with an envelope construction calling attention to "the sons of Kenaz." In either case, the name Kenaz frames the genealogy (4:13–15).

This section of genealogies is comprised of independent fragments and appears to be disconnected with the larger context of the additional clans of Judah. Some commentators suggest the passage is a possible continuation of the Calebite genealogy (4:13–15).[10] Only the name Ziph is known among the sons of Jehallelel, a city southeast of Hebron later associated with David when he was a fugitive hiding from King Saul (1 Sam. 23:14–16; 26:2; Ps. 54; cf. Josh. 15:55). Perhaps the Chronicler includes these former Hebrew cities south of Judah's postexilic border in anticipation of the restoration of this territory to the holdings of Judah.

Clan of Ezrah (4:17–20)

APART FROM THE (disputed) locations of Gedor, Soco, and Zanoah, nothing is known of people or places mentioned in 4:17–18. All three names are listed as villages belonging to the tribal allotment of Judah, suggesting a kinship relationship between the village and its founder (cf. Josh. 15:34, 48, 58). Keilah and Eshtemoa (1 Chron. 4:19) are also known from the record of Judah's tribal allotment (Josh. 15:44, 50). Keilah's history was linked to the rivalry between Saul and David (1 Sam. 23:1–6), and the town was apparently resettled and rebuilt by returnees from the Babylonian captivity (cf. Neh. 3:17–18). Eshtemoa was one of the cities in the hill country of Judah and was apparently loyal to David, as the elders of the town received booty from David's plundering of the Amalekites (1 Sam. 30:28).

This section of the extended Judahite genealogy is interesting because of the prominent place it gives to women, especially Miriam (a Calebite relative of Ezrah, 4:17) and Bithiah (daughter of Pharaoh, 4:18). There is some question as to whether or not "Pharaoh" is a royal title in this context. At the very least it suggests the inclusion of Egyptian elements within the tribe of Judah. The example of interracial marriage may have been an apologetic of sorts for the legitimacy of offspring from non-Hebrew mothers during the Chronicler's era.

---

8. E.g., Thompson, *1, 2 Chronicles*, 74.
9. Braun, *1 Chronicles*, 56 n. 15c.
10. Williamson, *1, 2 Chronicles*, 60.

Nothing is known of Shimon and his descendants or Ishi and his descendants (4:20). The names must have held some significance for the Chronicler's audience; perhaps they were ancestors of some of those Hebrews returning from Babylonian captivity.

Clan of Shelah (4:21–23)

THE REFERENCE TO SHELAH, the oldest surviving son of Judah, echoes 2:3 and forms an inclusion or envelope construction marking 2:3–4:23 as a larger literary unit. According to Williamson, this passage sheds welcome light on the existence of guilds of craftsmen in ancient Israel (e.g., linen workers (4:21] and potters [4:23]).[11]

The parenthetical statement attesting the antiquity of the genealogy (4:22) and the reference to the king (4:23) indicate these records date from the preexilic period of Israelite history. The names Lecah, Laadah, Beth Ashbea, Jokim, Cozeba, Saraph, and Netaim are unique to this passage in the Bible. The rendering of the clause "who ruled in Moab" is problematic. The Hebrew word $b^c l$ can mean to "rule over" or "to marry" (here in combination with preposition *le*, so the Targum reads "who married Moabites"; cf. NRSV, "who married into Moab"). Still others suggest a scribal error confusing $p^c l$ with $b^c l$ and translate accordingly, "who *worked* in Moab."[12] It is possible the word "there" in 4:23 indicates the potters moved to Lehem (perhaps Bethlehem?) in rotating shifts for a period of royal service.

Bridging Contexts

WE HAVE ALREADY observed that the Chronicler's genealogical prologue has been written for the Hebrew restoration community. Broadly understood, the genealogies served to legitimize the restoration community as the heirs of God's promises made to the patriarchs and kings of Israel and to bolster the morale of those resettling Judah. Beyond these general purposes, each section of the genealogical prologue contributes to a specific theme developed in the retelling of Israelite history. For instance, this particular section both fills the gaps and completes the genealogy of Judah begun in chapter 2. The emphasis on Judah in the genealogical prologue mirrors the centrality of Davidic kingship in the Chronicler's account of Israelite history.

---

11. Ibid., 60–61; cf. Michael Wilcock, *The Message of Chronicles*, 33–34, on "Irnahash" as a town devoted to a particular industry (i.e., a "city of bronze").

12. Selman, *1 Chronicles*, 102.

Equally important is the sensitivity the Chronicler subtly expresses to his target audience. Judah was preeminent among the tribes of Israel because this line would be the fountainhead for the institution of kingship and eventually the Messiah himself (Gen. 49:8–12). The ancestors and descendants of King David, however, represent only one family among the many clans in the tribe of Judah. Numerous non-Davidic families and clans of Judah are numbered among those Jewish expatriates who have made the journey back to Palestine from Babylonia. The Chronicler encourages certain of these "lesser clans" of the tribe of Judah by noting their resettlement patterns in his genealogical review. No doubt this strategy of personalizing the record by referencing particular clans and families who have resettled Judah after the Babylonian exile is aimed at achieving full participation in the restoration initiative.

In keeping with his previously established literary pattern, the Chronicler adds the dimension of personal story to the ledger of names in his genealogy by giving us occasional "snapshots" of life experiences for certain characters in the record. One vignette tells the story of a man named Jabez ("pain"), who is liberated from the neurosis of an ill-fated name by the power of prayer (4:9–10).[13] A second preserves the record of an interracial marriage between Mered and Bithiah, the daughter of Pharaoh (4:17–18) According to Allen, this was the Chronicler's way of raising a prophetic voice against the encroaching attitudes of "apartheid and xenophobia" in "isolationist" postexilic Judah.[14] A third and recurrent narrative expansion in the section simply celebrates the virtue of labor by emphasizing crafts and guilds (4:14, 21, 23; perhaps an echo of the creation mandate to "subdue" the earth in the broadest sense of the word, Gen. 1:28). Wilcock aptly concludes that the entire passage (4:1–23) showcases the Chronicler's concern to combine "practical facts" and "spiritual truths."[15]

The one-line report of Mered's marriage to Bithiah, daughter of Pharaoh, attests a significant Egyptian influence in this segment of the genealogy of Judah. This mixing of Hebrew and Egyptian populations is not surprising since historically the Judean Negev served as a buffer zone between the kingdom of Egypt and the Levant. That Bithiah is identified as a "daughter of Pharaoh" is so extraordinary that it is often dismissed by commentators as "extremely unlikely," given Egyptian custom and biblical tradition.[16] Others suggest that the use of the title "Pharaoh" is simply a later Hebrew euphemism for an "Egyptian lady."[17]

---

13. Allen, *1, 2 Chronicles*, 47–48.
14. Ibid., 44–45.
15. Wilcock, *The Message of Chronicles*, 33–34.
16. Japhet, *I and II Chronicles*, 115.
17. "Bithiah," in *ISBE*, 1:520.

A word of caution is in order here. There is no need to discount the authenticity of the Chronicler's record. Like the nation of Judah, Egypt in the fifth century B.C. was not the empire it was prior to the rise of Nebuchadnezzar and the Babylonians. As the political fortunes of kingdoms change, transformation of social customs and cultural traditions occurs as well. The marriage of Mered and Bithiah must be understood in this context, not the context of earlier Middle Kingdom Egypt.

Quite apart from the exact meaning of the phrase "daughter of Pharaoh," it is clear that the name Bithiah (lit., "daughter [or worshiper] of Yahweh") seems to designate a person who has converted to the worship of the Hebrew God Yahweh. This fact may betray a decidedly "progressive" theological stance on the part of the Chronicler since there is no trace of the criticism of marriage to foreign wives characteristic of the response of Ezra and Nehemiah to interracial marriage (Ezra 10).

Wilcock interprets this genealogical footnote listing the children born of a non-Jewish mother as evidence of the Chronicler's openness to relationships between Israel and other nations, thereby adding "an evangelistic breadth of vision" to his practicality and piety.[18] Perhaps this is in reaction to the hardline attitudes toward interracial marriage adopted as a result of the earlier reforms of Ezra and Nehemiah. Although these harsh social and religious reforms were necessary at the time, the Chronicler's reference to interracial marriage may be a warning of sorts lest the unhealthy attitude of particularism crystallize in the restoration community.

It is possible to infer that the Chronicler takes the Abrahamic covenant and the words of the preexilic prophets to heart. Israel has been placed at the crossroads of the ancient world to bless the nations (Gen. 12:1–3) by sharing the light of God's revelation with them (e.g., Isa. 49:6; 51:4). Later Jewish history suggests xenophobia eventually triumphed over the Chronicler's subliminal appeal for evangelistic openness as a fervently nationalistic Judaism continued to develop through the intertestamental period. This would not be overturned until the ministry of Jesus Christ, who sought out men and women, sinners and saints, Jew and Samaritan and Gentile alike—the very people comprising his genealogical ancestry (cf. Matt. 1:2–17).

Contemporary Significance

A WIDENESS OF HEART. The Chronicler's subtle exhortation to his postexilic audience for an "evangelistic openness" to relationships with non-Jews calls to mind the parable Jesus told about

---

18. Wilcock, *The Message of Chronicles,* 34.

the good Samaritan (Luke 10:25–37). The story is well known and often told. The question raised in applying the parable to the contemporary setting still haunts the Christian and the Christian church: "Who is my neighbor?"

The question posed by the thoughtful reading of the parable of the good Samaritan has been fittingly answered in recent years by any number of capable Christian thinkers and writers. For instance, John Stott has rightly emphasized imitating the compassion of Christ for people in need through responsible Christian social concern—doing good to the widest spectrum of human beings in urgent need.[19] Terry Muck challenges the Christian to extend the principle of "loving one's neighbor" to include the rapidly growing membership of the non-Christian religions in pluralistic North America.[20] Finally, John Piper has reminded us that the parable of the good Samaritan is not about "self-esteem" as our narcissistic culture might suggest; rather, it is about "God-esteem" that enables the Christian to be devoted to pursuing the happiness of others.[21]

There may be, however, another way in which we might apply the question of befriending a neighbor raised by the parable of the good Samaritan. Leslie Allen has observed "the Chronicler had a wideness of heart which we do well to ponder and seek to emulate."[22] In fact, Allen challenges us to translate the Chronicler's openness of mind and softness of heart into "multi-denominational awareness."[23] Given recent developments in evangelical Christianity, I might even extend Allen's thesis to a "multi-tradition awareness"—that is, a wideness of heart and a spirit of charity among the major traditions of Christianity: Protestant, Roman Catholic, and Orthodox.

A new spirit of ecumenical dialogue and cooperation is emerging in Christianity as the church of Jesus Christ forges ahead into the new millennium.[24] The dialogue between Protestant, Roman Catholic, and Orthodox Christians has been prompted by the "culture wars" of recent decades. The spiritual and moral decay of North American society—what has been called our culture of

---

19. John Stott, "Who Is My Neighbor?" in *The Challenge of Christ's Compassion* (London: Inter-Varsity Press, 1975), 16–17.

20. Terry C. Muck, *Those Other Religions in Your Neighborhood* (Grand Rapids: Zondervan, 1992), esp. 32–34.

21. John Piper, *Desiring God* (Sisters, Ore.: Multnomah, 1996), 277–86.

22. Allen, *1, 2 Chronicles*, 71.

23. Ibid.

24. For example, see Charles Colson and Richard Neuhaus, eds., *Evangelicals and Catholics Together: Toward A Common Mission* (Dallas: Word, 1995); James S. Cutsinger, ed., *Reclaiming the Great Tradition: Evangelicals, Catholics and Orthodox in Dialogue* (Downers Grove, Ill.: Inter-Varsity Press, 1997).

disbelief—is making allies of the three great Christian traditions.[25] Christians have begun to recognize that the "fight" against the tide of godless secularism and pluralistic relativism precludes "fighting" against each other. Beyond this, the Christian church is in the midst of rediscovering and reclaiming important elements of its rich heritage, including music, prayer, spiritual formation, and worship, not to mention exciting new ventures of cooperation in matters of social concern, virtue and morality, and evangelism.[26]

Such dialogue is not without problems, especially as it relates to matters of sound biblical doctrine and the practice of Christian worship. Much work remains in establishing the common Christian ground held by the three great Christian traditions. Yet, given his concern for the socioeconomic and spiritual well-being of "all the tribes of Israel," I believe the Chronicler would affirm these recent initiatives for dialogue and cooperation. Indeed, Paul exhorts Christians to "do good to all people, especially to those who belong to the family of believers" (Gal. 6:10). There is also little doubt that the great cloud of witnesses that continues to assemble in the heavenly realm includes saints from the Protestant, Roman Catholic, and Orthodox Christian traditions.

25. See Stephen L. Carter, *The Culture of Disbelief: How American Law and Politics Trivialize Religious Devotion* (New York: Anchor Books, 1994).

26. For examples, see Kenneth Collins, ed., *Exploring Christian Spirituality: An Ecumenical Reader* (Grand Rapids: Baker, 2000); William A. Dyrness, *Learning About Theology from the Third World* (Grand Rapids: Zondervan, 1990); and Robert E. Webber, *Ancient Future Faith* (Grand Rapids: Baker, 1999).

1 Chronicles 4:24–43

THE DESCENDANTS OF Simeon:

Nemuel, Jamin, Jarib, Zerah and Shaul; ²⁵Shallum was Shaul's son, Mibsam his son and Mishma his son.

²⁶The descendants of Mishma:

Hammuel his son, Zaccur his son and Shimei his son.

²⁷Shimei had sixteen sons and six daughters, but his brothers did not have many children; so their entire clan did not become as numerous as the people of Judah. ²⁸They lived in Beersheba, Moladah, Hazar Shual, ²⁹Bilhah, Ezem, Tolad, ³⁰Bethuel, Hormah, Ziklag, ³¹Beth Marcaboth, Hazar Susim, Beth Biri and Shaaraim. These were their towns until the reign of David. ³²Their surrounding villages were Etam, Ain, Rimmon, Token and Ashan—five towns—³³and all the villages around these towns as far as Baalath. These were their settlements. And they kept a genealogical record.

³⁴Meshobab, Jamlech, Joshah son of Amaziah, ³⁵Joel, Jehu son of Joshibiah, the son of Seraiah, the son of Asiel, ³⁶also Elioenai, Jaakobah, Jeshohaiah, Asaiah, Adiel, Jesimiel, Benaiah, ³⁷and Ziza son of Shiphi, the son of Allon, the son of Jedaiah, the son of Shimri, the son of Shemaiah.

³⁸The men listed above by name were leaders of their clans. Their families increased greatly, ³⁹and they went to the outskirts of Gedor to the east of the valley in search of pasture for their flocks. ⁴⁰They found rich, good pasture, and the land was spacious, peaceful and quiet. Some Hamites had lived there formerly.

⁴¹The men whose names were listed came in the days of Hezekiah king of Judah. They attacked the Hamites in their dwellings and also the Meunites who were there and completely destroyed them, as is evident to this day. Then they settled in their place, because there was pasture for their flocks. ⁴²And five hundred of these Simeonites, led by Pelatiah, Neariah, Rephaiah and Uzziel, the sons of Ishi, invaded the hill country of Seir. ⁴³They killed the remaining Amalekites who had escaped, and they have lived there to this day.

Original Meaning

THE SOURCES FOR the Chronicler's genealogy of Simeon include the records pertaining to Israel's (i.e., Jacob) second son by Leah found in Genesis 46:10; Exodus 6:15; Numbers 26:12–14; and Joshua 19:2–8. The lists of descendants in Genesis 46:10 and Exodus 6:15 name six sons of Simeon, while Numbers 26:12–14 and 1 Chronicles 4:24 omit the name Ohad and cite only five sons. The Chronicler is unique among all the biblical sources in naming the third son Jarib instead of Jachin.

The Chronicler's placement of Simeon's genealogy between that of Judah (2:2–4:23) and Levi (6:1–81) may be explained on historical grounds since Simeon's allocation of land in Canaan was carved out from the large tract of land granted to Judah (Josh. 19:2–9). Furthermore, some of the Levitical cities were originally towns and villages belonging to the territory of Simeon (1 Chron. 6:65). The destiny of Simeon and Judah was also entwined socially and politically. By the time of David, the towns and villages within the territory of Simeon were recognized as Judean holdings (1 Chron. 4:31). According to Braun, it is the Chronicler's interest in "all Israel" and his attachment to the ideal of the twelve-tribes motif that motivates his inclusion of Simeon in the tribal lists of Israel long after it has disappeared as a geographical and political entity.[1]

The genealogy demonstrates both breadth (the listing of a single generation of descendants from a common ancestor, e.g., 4:24) and depth (the listing of successive generations, e.g., 4:25–27). The passage reflects a three-part structure typical of the genealogical records of the lesser Hebrew tribes: the genealogy proper (4:24–27), settlements (4:28–33), and leaders and conquests (4:34–43). Numerous subfeatures of the genealogy have been identified: the name list (a catalog of proper names, whether person or places, e.g., 4:28–31), the muster roll (a list of fighting men, e.g., 4:34–37) and tally (a cardinal number attached to the genealogical record, e.g., 4:42), and a battle report (a summary of a military encounter, e.g., 4:41–43).[2]

The Chronicler's attention to detail in the reporting of precise numbers and specific geography further heightens the tension between the ideal of a bygone era and the actual situation of the postexilic period. Rather than discourage his audience, the Chronicler seeks to bolster hope by helping his contemporaries grasp "the real meaning of grace."[3] The record of Israel's past serves as a barometer of sorts, indicating the full measure of covenant blessings God is capable of bestowing on the current generation of Jews.

---

1. Braun, *1 Chronicles*, 68.
2. See further De Vries, *1 and 2 Chronicles*, 50–51.
3. Wilcock, *The Message of Chronicles*, 35.

The genealogy of Simeon highlights the family of Shaul through several generations. In so doing, the record offers a partial explanation for the subordinate position of the tribe of Simeon in relation to the tribe of Judah. Shimei, the grandson of Shaul, fathered sixteen sons and six daughters, but his brothers "did not have many children" (4:27a). Thus, the clan of Shaul was not as populous as the people of Judah (4:27b). Interestingly, Shaul's mother was an unnamed Canaanite woman (Gen. 46:10; Ex. 6:15). One wonders if this fact is incidental to the Chronicler's purposes or if it conveys a theological message. Given the highly selective nature of the genealogies in Chronicles, the latter seems more likely.

The question remains, however, as to the writer's intent. Perhaps the Chronicler is making a pejorative statement about intermarriage among God's people, resulting in the lack of offspring among the Simeonites. Or maybe the postexilic historian emphasizes the lineage of Shaul as an example of Yahweh's universal love for the nations, similar to the story of Ruth. No doubt the faithful among the Chronicler's audience discern both messages in this notation.

The middle unit of Simeon's record (4:28–33) contains a catalog of settlements and a reference to a genealogical record placed emphatically at the end of the section (4:33). According to Thompson, the Chronicler "wanted to stress that Simeon once had its own official registration and was part of the total Israel."[4]

This memory of Simeon's former independence from Judah is important for two reasons. (1) The example of geographical expansion is a reminder of the reality that territorial boundaries were always shifting, given the rise and fall of political fortunes in the ancient world. In the past the nation of Israel prospered materially and expanded geographically in accordance with her collective obedience to the stipulations of Yahweh's covenant. The Chronicler understands that the earth is the Lord's (Ps. 24:1) and that as owner of the land, God can restore to Israel what he once gave them (e.g., Deut. 1:8; 3:18; 8:10). Likewise, Israel has received the land as a divine gift by faith in Yahweh's covenant promises, and so by means of covenant renewal Israel can again be restored in the land of her ancestors (cf. Neh. 9:36–37; 10:28–39).[5]

(2) The account serves as an exhortation to those postexilic Jews still inhabiting the very same towns and villages settled by the descendants of Simeon (cf. Neh. 11:26–29). Theologically, the Chronicler's selective portrayal of Simeon shows that historical circumstances have not thwarted God's

---

4. Thompson, *1,2 Chronicles*, 76. Note his literal translation, "and *their* genealogical registration was *theirs*" (1 Chron. 4:33).

5. Cf. Walter Brueggemann, *The Land* (Philadelphia: Fortress, 1977), esp. 67–70 ("The Land As Threat") and 151–58 ("Separatism As a Way to Save the Land").

initiative in the ideal of the twelve tribes of Israel. The presentation of Simeon as one of the twelve, given the historical reality of the tribe of Simeon as a nonentity by the time of the Chronicler, mirrors the situation for all the Israelite tribes in one sense after the Exile. The boundaries of the ancient Israelite territories have been radically altered, if not erased altogether. Tribal and clan distinctions have been blurred by numerous deportations and generations of intermarriage. But "all Israel" as the people of God continue to possess a portion of the land of God's promise—the covenant inheritance bequeathed to Abraham's descendants (Gen. 12:1–3).

The third section of the genealogy (4:34–43) stresses the expansion and settlement of land to the west (vv. 39–41) and southeast (vv. 42–43) of the original Simeonite territory by the descendants of Shimei. The place name "Gedor" (v. 39) is problematic since the LXX reads Gerar, and that site is more appropriately situated to the offspring of Ham.[6] The term "Hamites" (vv. 40–41) refers generally to the Philistine or Canaanite people groups in this context. The Meunites are variously associated with the Amalekites and Sidonians (Judg. 10:12) and the Philistines (2 Chron. 26:7) in the Old Testament. Depending on the resource consulted, the Meunites are identified with "Maon," a town in the hill country of Judah (Josh. 15:55), or a site about eleven miles south of Gaza (modern day Ma'in).[7] It is unclear whether the hill country of Seir refers to an area of the southern Negev or to Edomite holdings south and east of the Dead Sea. The Amalekites (possibly descendants of Esau, cf. Gen. 36:12, 16) were a pastoral-nomadic people group of the Negev and Sinai, defeated first by Saul (1 Sam. 15:7–8) and later by David (30:1–18; 2 Sam. 8:12; cf. 1 Chron. 18:11). Historically, all were people groups hostile to Israel.

The passage offers insight on the process of genealogical enrollment in ancient Israel—apparently a two-stage process of entering names (v. 38, perhaps connected to a tribal oral tradition [NIV, "listed ... by name"]) and then cataloging the names according to some scheme of arrangement (4:41, perhaps on the basis of a census taking [NIV, "names were listed"]).[8] The theme of pastureland for the flocks and herds of the Simeonites is repeated three times in the brief account (vv. 39, 40, 41). Curiously, the closest lexical parallels to

---

6. According to Selman, *1 Chronicles*, 104, the name Gedor may be the Geder of Josh. 12:13. R. J. Coggins (*The First and Second Books of the Chronicles* [CBC; Cambridge: Cambridge Univ. Press, 1977], 32), however, cautions against the tendency to identify every unknown place with a well-known site with a similar name.

7. The Aramaic Targum and the Latin Vulgate translate "their dwellings" for "Meunites" on the basis of the Arabic "ma'an," meaning "tent" or "dwelling" (so NJB).

8. Japhet, *I and II Chronicles*, 124–25.

the Chronicler's language are those psalms identifying the Israelites as the sheep of God's pasture (e.g., Ps. 37:3; 74:1; 79:13; 95:7; 100:3). The military tone of the unit echoes the prophetic blessing of Jacob over Simeon as one given to anger and violence (cf. Gen. 49:5–7). Finally, the phrase "completely destroyed" (1 Chron. 4:41) is reminiscent of the conquest of Canaan (cf. Deut. 7:2; Josh. 2:10; 6:21).

Theologically, the focus of this third section of Simeon's genealogy is faithfulness—the faithfulness of God's Word concerning the destiny of Simeon as uttered by Jacob (Gen. 49:5–7), the faithfulness of the Simeonites in possessing the land allotted to them by Joshua (note the correspondence of the place names between Josh. 19:2–9 and 1 Chron. 4:28–33), the faithfulness of God in helping the Simeonites overcome their enemies (cf. Deut. 1:30; 3:22), and the faithfulness of Shimei's family in trusting God for the expansion of the Simeonite tribal holdings (1 Chron. 4:38–43). These are all important examples of a faithful God blessing his faithful people—a necessary history lesson for the Chronicler's audience.

GLORIFYING THE PAST (**or future**). The Chronicler uses the genealogy of Simeon to address a phenomenon common to the human experience, namely, the tendency to glorify the past. Each generation is troubled by the disparity perceived between their understanding of the ideal life and their observation of reality. Often the idealized life is associated with the past, the notion of "the good old days." Sometimes the actual or the contemporary situation is discounted against the future, in the sense that those things yet to come are presumed to be better than present conditions. In either case, the assumption is that the virtue of current circumstances pales when compared to the golden past or the silver-lined future.

Such dissatisfaction with life in the "present tense" is basic to fallen human nature. In fact, the garden temptation of Eve may be reduced to feelings of doubt implanted by the serpent, prompting a disaffection for her present situation (Gen. 3:1–7). The human penchant for reliving the past and yearning for the future is surely symptomatic of our pride in our own ability to alter circumstances and our impatience with the plan of God. The human capacity for selective remembrance and forgetfulness also permits the glorification of the past to the point where memory and imagination are blurred. Such reconstructions create a nostalgic experience or "homesickness" for the past.[9]

---

9. For a modern sociology of nostalgia, including a discussion of the differences between a "nostalgic experience" (i.e., a personally experienced past) and an "antiquarian feeling" (i.e.,

The Bible dispels the myth that the past is better than the present, as the Hebrew sage cautions against even asking such questions (Eccl. 7:10). Jesus himself indicated each day has enough trouble of its own, so worrying about the future is futile (Matt. 6:34). The Bible also discourages living in the future because tomorrow is uncertain and the future is unknown to finite mortals (cf. Matt. 24:42; James 4:13–16). Essentially, that means we must live in "this day"—as recognized by the Jews (e.g., Deut 30:15; Josh. 24:15; Ps. 118:24; Eccl. 5:18–20) and affirmed by the teaching of the New Testament (e.g., Matt. 6:11; Luke 19:9; Acts 22:16; Heb. 3:13).

Jacques Ellul goes so far to say that the present is all we have since people forget the past and are unable to penetrate the future.[10] Although he overstates the case, his emphasis on "living in the present" is an important insight. C. S. Lewis aptly noted the same some years earlier when Screwtape informed Wormwood that the business of "the Father [of Lies]" was to get people away from the eternal and from the Present (since freedom and actuality are offered to humans only in the Present).[11] This was best accomplished, according to Screwtape, by encouraging people to live in the Future since it is unknown and irreal (and thus least like eternity). Escapism into the Past had limited value for Screwtape because people have some real knowledge of the Past and it resembles eternity in its determinate nature. This is why the act of remembering the works and words of God in the past is so important to biblical theology. It is one of the keys to understanding the concept of the "eternal" in the contemporary setting.

---

a powerful, even knowledgeable identification with some previous period of history), see Fred Davis, *Yearning for Yesterday* (New York: Free Press, 1979), esp. 8–26. According to Davis's distinctions, the Chronicler evokes antiquarian feelings in his audience in his retelling of the storied days of the Hebrew monarchy. Davis's categorization of the "ascending orders of nostalgia" is also helpful in assessing the Chronicler's approach to historiography. First Order nostalgia is a positively toned evocation of the lived past in the context of some negative feeling toward the present (or impending circumstances). Second Order nostalgia moves from sentimentality about the past to some reflective and empirically oriented evaluation of the nostalgic experience (i.e., some estimate of the truth and accuracy of the nostalgic claim). Third Order nostalgia not only questions issues of historical accuracy related to the nostalgic claim but also critically analyzes (or objectifies) the nostalgic feeling itself. Applying Davis's rubrics for nostalgia to antiquarian feelings suggests the Chronicler is primarily seeking to evoke First Order feelings for the past in his audience. The question remains whether or not he is skilled enough as a psychologist to subtly move his audience to Second and Third Order reflection on the nostalgic claims of the Hebrew monarchy as theological preparation for the messianic kingdom. Personally, I suspect that he is both an astute theologian and psychologist, given his understanding of the Exile as an event for which there is "no remedy" (2 Chron. 36:16).

10. Jacques Ellul, *Reason for Being: A Meditation on Ecclesiastes*, trans. Joyce M. Hanks (Grand Rapids: Eerdmans, 1990), 69.

11. C. S. Lewis, *The Screwtape Letters* (New York: Macmillan, 1961), 77–78.

Despite the danger of escapism into memories, the Bible invites reflection on the past because the act of remembering is inherently educational. Israel's primary mode of knowing is narrative or story, and only remembering the story of her past will keep Israel true to her divine calling.[12] Centuries earlier Moses challenged his audience to "ask . . . about the former days" (Deut. 4:32). The invitation was rhetorical in that Moses proceeded to recite specific events of Israelite history to prove a point. Essentially, that point is the truth that the Lord is God and that he has chosen Israel (cf. Deut. 4:36–37). The power of God and the uniqueness of Israel as his people are rooted in divine acts of deliverance and the word of covenant revelation. These deeds and words of God are manifest throughout the course of Hebrew history as recorded in the Old Testament. In fact, the book of Deuteronomy provides a course of theological instruction based on the remembrance of the past.[13]

The Chronicler offers his people a similar invitation. In general, his recitation of Hebrew history is a theology of hope couched in the call to remember the words and deeds of God connected with the Davidic covenant. Specifically here, the genealogy of Simeon is intended to stir the memory of postexilic Israel because they too have assumed they are living in the days of "small things" (cf. Zech. 4:10).

But the summons to remember in the world of the Old Testament is more than nostalgia, the sentimental yearning for some past and irrecoverable period of history. Remembering in the Old Testament is an active cognitive commitment with behavioral outcomes, "an intellectual activity that is relational and personal."[14] For the Chronicler this act of remembering is relational in that it is a communal exercise as a result of Yahweh's covenant with Israel (cf. 1 Chron. 16:12, 15–16). That remembering is a highly personal activity for the Chronicler is evident in the recording of numerous prayers, each one presuming an individual faith commitment to God (e.g., 2 Chron. 6:42).

For the Chronicler the memory of Simeon is both retrospect (meditation on the past) and prospect (anticipation for the future). The God who prospered the initiatives of the Simeonites is the very same God who stirred Cyrus to rebuild the Jerusalem temple. Thus, careful reflection on the history of Israel serves two purposes. (1) It instills confidence in the future. Postexilic Israel has every reason to believe that the pattern of God's activity in history will continue. (2) It functions as a catalyst in the restoration community. The religious vitality and social mobilization of Israel is always conditioned by her ability to remember the words and deeds of God (cf. Deut. 8:18; Neh. 4:14).

---

12. Brueggemann, *The Creative Word*, 37–38.
13. Ibid., 19–32.
14. H. Eising, "זָכַר," *TDOT*, 4:65.

Whether as an antidote for times of individual and national distress (Ps. 77:11–12), as spiritual therapy prompting repentance and confession of sin (Ps. 25:6–7), or as an act of worship encouraging service to others in the name of God (Deut. 15:12–15), this activity of remembrance is essential to proper relationship with God.

Finally, the genealogical record of Simeon is also a legacy, something transmitted or received from ancestors. The Jews of the Chronicler's Jerusalem are the heirs of a rich inheritance. The legacy of Simeon is a strong faith in the God of their father Jacob, a God of unswerving faithfulness to the Simeonites and to all Israel. Only faith in the God of Simeon can enable restoration Judah to overcome the gulf between the Davidic ideal and the reality of Persian domination.

THE INCONGRUITY BETWEEN **the ideal and the actual.** The tension between the biblical ideal and the reality of present circumstances remains a struggle for God's faithful. Like the psalmist, the Christian at times still asks the question, "How long, O LORD?" (Ps. 13:1).

The New Testament addresses the incongruity between the ideal and the actual on several levels. The book of Hebrews affirms doctrinally that Jesus Christ is truly Son of Man and that God has put everything subject under him, though we do not now see everything subject to Christ (Heb. 2:8). John the apostle takes a more pastoral and reflective approach when he acknowledges we are children of God, but what we will be has not yet been made known (1 John 3:2). Lastly, Paul dramatizes the visceral strain of reconciling the ideal and actual when he laments what a wretched creature he is as he is torn by the war between sin and righteousness raging within (Rom. 8:22–24). Each aspect of the dichotomy between the ideal and the actual is important because it reminds us that the issue is a complex one. It also indicates that any resolution aimed at reconciling the polarity must be multifaceted, taking into consideration our intellect, our psyche, and our emotions.

We have learned that the Chronicler is attempting to reconcile the historical distance and theological disparity between the Davidic ideal and the reality of Persian occupation of Judah for a discouraged audience in postexilic Jerusalem. The New Testament mentions other kinds of tensions between the biblical ideal and actual human experience that have the potential to produce similar feelings of anxiety and despair in individual believers and in the Christian community at large. Note, for example, the ongoing conflict between the kingdom of light and the kingdom of darkness (cf. Col. 1:13), sound doctrine compromised by false teaching (e.g., 2 Tim. 1:13; Titus 2:1;

cf. 2 Tim. 4:3; 2 Peter 2:1), and an ethic of social justice eroded by oppression and prejudice (e.g., 2 Thess. 3:13; cf. James 2:5−6). Some mediation of the biblical ideal and present reality is essential because the unresolved tension poses a threat to personal faith and spiritual growth. The greater the discontinuity between the ideal and the actual, the more room for seeds of doubt to germinate, undermining one's hope in God and robbing one of the joy of the Lord.

The Chronicler understands the importance of dealing with the historical and theological distance between the Davidic ideal and the life situation of his audience. He basically seeks to resolve the dilemma by appealing to past faithfulness as documented in the Scriptures, recording earlier Hebrew history: (1) the faithfulness of God to his Word and to his people Israel, and (2) the faithfulness of God's people in believing his covenant promises and in obeying his covenant stipulations. Two other partial solutions for spanning the gap between the ideal and the actual are implicit in the Chronicler's message: The idea of waiting on God seems everywhere tacit in the two books, given his emphasis on prayer.

Like the psalmist the Chronicler subtly encourages his contemporaries to take heart and wait for the Lord (cf. Ps. 27:14). His numerous references to personal and corporate worship experiences during the days of Israelite kingship also echo the psalmist's understanding that entering the sanctuary of God in worship brings some perspective to polarity between the ideal and the actual (cf. Ps. 73:16−17).

The New Testament seeks to harmonize the ideal with the actual in a similar manner. For example, "faithful" is an epithet for God and Jesus Christ in Paul's letters (e.g., 1 Cor. 1:9; 2 Cor. 1:18). Much like Chronicles, the book of Hebrews appeals to the example of people faithful to God—that great cloud of witnesses who have preceded us (Heb. 12:1; cf. Phil. 3:17). Unlike Chronicles, the New Testament *explicitly* calls on the Christian to wait on God for a final resolution to the polarity between the biblical ideal and the present reality (e.g., Rom. 8:23, 25; 1 Cor. 1:7). Although less forceful, the idea that worship mediates the tensions between the ideal and the actual seems to be embodied in New Testament injunctions related to prayer (e.g., Matt. 6:9−10; James 5:13−16; 1 John 5:14−15).

In addition, the New Testament presents a more definitive statement of eschatology expressly intended to engender hope in the Christian (1 Thess. 4:13; Titus 2:13; Heb. 6:9). Perhaps most important, God has given his Holy Spirit to the Christian "as a deposit, guaranteeing what is to come" (2 Cor. 5:5). This specific and personal work of the Holy Spirit mediates the biblical ideal and present reality by affirming the believer as an heir of the promises of God in Christ (cf. Gal. 4:6; Eph. 3:16).

But what does all this mean, practically speaking? (1) Human frailty and finitude prevent any complete reconciliation of the biblical ideal and the present reality on this side of the second advent of Christ. This does not, however, lead us to despair. Rather, those who have put their faith in God's Son have the assurance that ultimately they "will never be put to shame" (cf. Rom. 9:33; cf. 5:5). (2) Because we possess the treasure of God's mercy in jars of clay, it is plain to all that it is God's power and not human ingenuity that enables the Christian to cope with the tension of life's polarities (cf. 2 Cor. 4:7). As we overcome the incongruence between the biblical ideal and the present reality by the help of the Holy Spirit, God is the One who is glorified!

1 Chronicles 5

THE SONS OF Reuben the firstborn of Israel (he was the firstborn, but when he defiled his father's marriage bed, his rights as firstborn were given to the sons of Joseph son of Israel; so he could not be listed in the genealogical record in accordance with his birthright, ²and though Judah was the strongest of his brothers and a ruler came from him, the rights of the firstborn belonged to Joseph)—³the sons of Reuben the firstborn of Israel:

Hanoch, Pallu, Hezron and Carmi.

⁴The descendants of Joel:

Shemaiah his son, Gog his son,
Shimei his son, ⁵Micah his son,
Reaiah his son, Baal his son,
⁶and Beerah his son, whom Tiglath-Pileser king of Assyria took into exile. Beerah was a leader of the Reubenites.

⁷Their relatives by clans, listed according to their genealogical records:

Jeiel the chief, Zechariah, ⁸and Bela son of Azaz, the son of Shema, the son of Joel. They settled in the area from Aroer to Nebo and Baal Meon. ⁹To the east they occupied the land up to the edge of the desert that extends to the Euphrates River, because their livestock had increased in Gilead.

¹⁰During Saul's reign they waged war against the Hagrites, who were defeated at their hands; they occupied the dwellings of the Hagrites throughout the entire region east of Gilead.

¹¹The Gadites lived next to them in Bashan, as far as Salecah:

¹²Joel was the chief, Shapham the second, then Janai and Shaphat, in Bashan.

¹³Their relatives, by families, were:

Michael, Meshullam, Sheba, Jorai, Jacan, Zia and Eber—seven in all.

¹⁴These were the sons of Abihail son of Huri, the son of Jaroah, the son of Gilead, the son of Michael, the son of Jeshishai, the son of Jahdo, the son of Buz.

¹⁵ Ahi son of Abdiel, the son of Guni, was head of their
family.

¹⁶ The Gadites lived in Gilead, in Bashan and its outlying vil-
lages, and on all the pasturelands of Sharon as far as
they extended.

¹⁷All these were entered in the genealogical records during
the reigns of Jotham king of Judah and Jeroboam king of
Israel.

¹⁸The Reubenites, the Gadites and the half-tribe of Man-
asseh had 44,760 men ready for military service—able-bodied
men who could handle shield and sword, who could use a
bow, and who were trained for battle. ¹⁹They waged war
against the Hagrites, Jetur, Naphish and Nodab. ²⁰They were
helped in fighting them, and God handed the Hagrites and all
their allies over to them, because they cried out to him during
the battle. He answered their prayers, because they trusted in
him. ²¹They seized the livestock of the Hagrites—fifty thousand camels, two hundred fifty thousand sheep and two thousand donkeys. They also took one hundred thousand people
captive, ²²and many others fell slain, because the battle was
God's. And they occupied the land until the exile.

²³The people of the half-tribe of Manasseh were numerous;
they settled in the land from Bashan to Baal Hermon, that is,
to Senir (Mount Hermon).

²⁴These were the heads of their families: Epher, Ishi, Eliel,
Azriel, Jeremiah, Hodaviah and Jahdiel. They were brave warriors, famous men, and heads of their families. ²⁵But they were
unfaithful to the God of their fathers and prostituted themselves to the gods of the peoples of the land, whom God had
destroyed before them. ²⁶So the God of Israel stirred up the
spirit of Pul king of Assyria (that is, Tiglath-Pileser king of
Assyria), who took the Reubenites, the Gadites and the half-
tribe of Manasseh into exile. He took them to Halah, Habor,
Hara and the river of Gozan, where they are to this day.

THE CHRONICLER HAS taken great care to establish the primacy of the tribe of Judah as the "true center" of Israel (2:3–4:23).[1] For him the Davidic covenant makes the tribe of Judah the true center of the Israelites both historically and theologically. The focus of the genealogical prologue now moves east to the tribes of the Transjordan: Reuben, Gad, and the half-tribe of Manasseh. The literary structure of each tribal record here is similar to that of the genealogy of Simeon, featuring a three-part pattern: the genealogical register, related geographical materials, and select historical notes. As stated previously, the Chronicler's concern for the story of all the Israelite tribes is necessary to present a complete historical overview of Israel to his postexilic audience. The "twelve tribes" genealogical prologue is also important given the Chronicler's theological emphasis on the restoration community as the representation of "all Israel."

The Chronicler has spliced three originally independent tribal lists into a unified record of Israelite occupation of the Transjordan. In addition to the contiguous location of the three tribes east of the Jordan River, the clause "lived next to them" (5:11) logically joins Gad with Reuben in a sociological context. The repeated reference to all three of the Transjordan tribes (5:18, 26) also emphasizes the common heritage and shared experience of Reuben, Gad, and East Manasseh. More tragically, the destinies of the three tribes are entwined historically and theologically since all were exiled by the Assyrians (5:6, 22, 26).

Reuben (5:1–10)

THE CHAPTER MAY be divided into five distinct sections: the genealogy of Reuben (5:1–10), the genealogy of Gad (5:11–17), a historical note on the war against the Hagrites (5:18–22), the genealogy of the half-tribe of Manasseh (5:23–24), and the summary statement of sin and exile (5:25–26). The purpose of the passage is twofold. (1) The account explains the prominence of the tribe of Judah even though Reuben was the firstborn son of Jacob (renamed Israel). (2) The record contributes to the Chronicler's goal of including all the tribes of Israel in the ideal "all Israel" identity he seeks to establish for the postexilic community.

Reuben was the firstborn son of Jacob by Leah (Gen. 29:32). The name Reuben means "he [the LORD] has seen my misery," so pronounced by Leah with the hope of gaining Jacob's love and respect. The Chronicler recites

---

1. See Myers, *I Chronicles*, 35, on the importance of Judah as the tribe of King David and the home of Israel's national political and religious institutions.

Reuben's crime of engaging in sexual intercourse with his father's concubine (Bilhah) in order to explain the prominence of Judah and the Joseph tribes in later Israelite history (35:22; cf. 49:3–4). From Judah came the "ruler" (*nagid*, 1 Chron. 5:2), no doubt a reference to King David. And to Joseph's sons, Ephraim and Manasseh, was transferred the firstborn rights of Reuben (Gen. 48:5–20). Implied in this forfeiture of the birthright is the "double share" due the firstborn son on the basis of Mosaic law (Deut. 21:15–17). Selman notes that the double share divided between Ephraim and Manasseh underscores the fact that the northern tribes had not lost their ancient privileges (cf. 2 Chron. 28:5–15; 30:1–12).[2]

The four sons of Reuben listed in the genealogy (5:3) agree with the parallel references (Gen. 46:9; Ex. 6:14; Num. 26:5). The later pronouncement of Moses over the tribe of Reuben was a "mixed" blessing that called for the historical continuity of the tribe but not its numerical proliferation (Deut. 33:6).

The genealogy of Joel (5:4–6) is probably a fragment from a longer Reubenite genealogy and has no parallel elsewhere in the Old Testament. Ackroyd suggests the list may represent a line of Reubenite chieftains.[3] The name Baal (5:5) has led to speculation concerning the possible influence of Canaanite religion on the descendants of Reuben. The reference to the Assyrian exile of Beerah (5:6) is the first of three phases of Reubenite history arranged in reverse chronological order. The historical setting is probably the campaign of Tiglath-Pileser into Galilee and the Transjordan in 733–732 B.C. during the reign of Pekah (cf. 2 Kings 15:29). The Chronicler spells the Assyrian king's name Tilgath-Pilneser (1 Chron. 5:6; cf. NIV note; also 2 Chron. 28:20).[4] Pul (see 1 Chron. 5:26) was his Babylonian throne name (cf. 2 Kings 15:19).

The second phase of Reubenite history cited is that of northern expansion during an unspecified earlier time, perhaps during the reign of David or Solomon (cf. 1 Sam. 30:28). Aroer (1 Chron. 5:8) on the Arnon River was built by Gad (Num. 32:34) and served as a border city between the tribes of Gad and Reuben (Josh. 13:16, 25). The sites of Nebo and Baal Meon to the northwest were ascribed to Reuben's territorial inheritance (Num. 32:38; Josh. 13:16). According to the Mesha Stone, Mesha king of Moab wrested control of Aroer, Nebo, and Baal Meon from Israel around 830 B.C.[5] Later

---

2. Selman, *1 Chronicles*, 105.

3. Peter R. Ackroyd, *I and II Chronicles, Ezra, Nehemiah* (TBC; London: SCM, 1973), 36.

4. The metathesis or shifting of consonants is attested elsewhere in Chronicles (e.g., *almuggim* [1 Kings 10:11] to *algummim* [2 Chron. 9:10]), perhaps for euphonic reasons (see Williamson, *1 and 2 Chronicles*, 64).

5. On the Mesha Stone see Andrew Dearman, ed., *Studies in the Mesha Inscription and Moab* (Archaeology and Biblical Studies 2; Atlanta: Scholars Press, 1989).

Hebrew prophets confirm the control of the region by Moab (cf. Isa. 15:2; Ezek. 25:9).

The reference to lands east of Gilead approaching the Euphrates River (5:9) suggests a pastoral-nomadic existence for some of the clans of Reuben. Traditionally Gilead is the region of the Transjordan between the Arnon and Yarmuk Rivers and originally settled by the tribe of Gad (Josh. 13:25). This may help explain the gradual absorption of Reuben by Gad. No king, judge, or prophet emerged from Reuben, and the group gradually faded from Israelite tribal history.

Another expansionist phase of Reubenite history is associated with the reign of King Saul in the eleventh century B.C. (5:10). The reference to Saul may foreshadow the genealogy of Benjamin developed in chapter 8. The Hagrites are often identified as Arab tribes and associated with Hagar and her son Ishmael (cf. Gen. 25:12–18). They settled east of Gilead and apparently had ties to the Moabites; like the Moabites they were classified as enemies of Israel (cf. Ps. 83:6).

Interestingly, the Chronicler omits any further references to earlier Reubenite history, especially episodes like the rebellion of Dathan and Abiram against Moses (Num. 26:9).

Gad (5:11–22)

THE UNIT OF Gad contains two distinct parts. The first pertains to the tribe of Gad (5:11–17), while the second refers collectively to the two and one-half tribes located in the Transjordan (5:18–22). The genealogy of Gad is unusual in that it begins with a geographical note (5:11) and omits materials from the other Gadite genealogies (e.g., Gen. 46:16; Num. 26:15–18; 1 Chron. 12:9–13). This emphasis on the territorial holdings of Gad forms an envelope for the genealogical record. Bashan (5:11–16) is the region east of the Sea of Galilee stretching from the Yarmuk River northward to Mount Hermon.

During Old Testament times Bashan was an extremely fertile plateau and was renowned for its grain harvests and served as pasturage for cattle (cf. Deut. 32:14) and as a source of timber (cf. Isa. 2:13). The desire for control of this highly productive real estate led to repeated warfare between Israel and Aram.

Salecah (5:11) was a city on the southeastern perimeter of Bashan that was captured by the Israelites from King Og (Deut. 3:10) and included in the tribal allotments of Gad and Reuben (Josh. 12:5–6). (On Gilead, see comments on 1 Chron. 5:9.) The "villages [lit., daughters, 5:16]" of Bashan may have been walled cities and numbered as many as sixty (cf. 1 Kings 4:13). The reference to Sharon (1 Chron. 5:16) is probably a town or region also mentioned in the text of the Moabite Stone.[6] The Chronicler's emphasis on the geographical boundaries of Gad may call attention to the fulfillment of Moses' earlier blessing on the tribe (Deut. 33:20–21).

The chieftains or leaders of Gad listed are unknown to the rest of the Old Testament, but the reference to Joel as the "chief" (lit., "head") may be another echo of Moses' blessing, where the "heads of the people" are mentioned (cf. Deut. 33:21). Some commentators count only three chieftains of Gad, since certain of the ancient versions render "Shaphat" as the noun "judge" rather than a proper name (i.e., "Janai the judge"; cf. Braun, "Janai judged").[7] The genealogy records seven clans, all sons of Abihail (1 Chron. 5:13–14). Like the seven clans of East Manasseh (5:24), these names are unknown elsewhere in the Bible. The genealogy listed in 5:14 were the ancestors of Abihail, not his descendants. Likewise, Ahi (5:15) was the forefather of Abihail.

There is some question concerning the reference to "Jotham king of Judah" in the chronological footnote (5:17) since the Transjordan tribes were part of the northern kingdom. The reference may suggest separate genealogical registers compiled by each of the divided monarchies or even a synchronistic chronicle composed in two columns.[8] It seems more likely that events in Israel were simply synchronized historically by reference to the occupant of the Judahite throne. In any case, the census mentioned dates to around 750 B.C.

The battle report of the coalition of Transjordan tribes against the Hagrites (5:18–22) has its parallel in the report of the exile of those two and one-half tribes into Assyria attached to the East Manasseh genealogy (5:25–26). The passage probably represents a summary of expansion during the period of the united monarchy by the coalition of Transjordan Israelite tribes against the Hagrites, not an account of a single battle or event. The Hagrites, along with the Moabites, Edomites, and Ishmaelites, were among the traditional enemies of Israel located in the Transjordan (cf. Ps. 83:6).

Some conjecture the Hagrites are descendants of Abraham's concubine Hagar.[9] This remains difficult to substantiate, given available data. Three

---

6. Ibid., 179–80.

7. Braun, *1 Chronicles*, 69, 71.

8. On this hypothetical source, see further T. N. D. Mettinger, *Solomonic State Officials* (Lund: Gleerup, 1971), 39.

9. According to Eugene H. Merrill, *1, 2 Chronicles* (Bible Study Commentary; Grand Rapids: Zondervan, 1988), 32, the Transjordan tribes ended up as refugees in the Habor (Khabur) River valley, a tributary of the Euphrates River. The towns of Halah, Habor, and Hara cited by the Chronicler remain unidentified. Gozan may be the modern day Tell Halaf on the Habor River.

Arab tribes (Jetur, Naphish, and Nodab) are allied with the Hagrites (cf. Gen. 25:15; 1 Chron. 1:31). The combined muster tally of 44,760 soldiers for the tribes of Reuben, Gad, and East Manasseh is less than half the muster tally of the second post-Exodus census for those tribes (136,930; see Num. 26:7, 18, 34; cf. the 120,000 for the Transjordan tribes in David's census, 1 Chron. 12:37).

More than the size of the muster tallies, the Chronicler's focus is on the theology of warfare. The war with the Hagrites and their allies was God's battle (5:22). The men of Reuben, Gad, and East Manasseh trusted in God and prayed to him, and he answered their prayers by helping them in battle (5:20–21). The themes of trust in God, prayer in battle, and God's help in gaining victory are repeated throughout Chronicles (e.g., 12:19; 15:26; 2 Chron. 20:15; 25:8; 32:10). The booty inventory (1 Chron. 5:21–22) lends tangible support to the theological principle that God delivers those who trust in him. This report is the foil or counterpoint for the report of the Assyrian exile concluding this section of the genealogical prologue (5:25–26).

East Manasseh (5:23–26)

LIKE THE GENEALOGY of Gad, this section contains two distinct units. The first pertains to the tribe of East Manasseh (5:23–24), while the second refers collectively to the two and one-half tribes located in the Transjordan (5:25–26). The material was probably excerpted from an earlier military census and deliberately separated from the text devoted to West Manasseh (cf. 7:14–19). Naturally this prompts biblical commentators to assume this portion of the Chronicler's genealogical prologue was arranged geographically. The account of Manasseh is similar to the previous documentation of Gad in its emphasis on the extensive boundaries and numerical size of the tribe. Unlike the pericope treating the tribe of Gad, however, the passage preserving information about Manasseh includes no genealogical list. The attention given to the size and prowess of the tribe of Manasseh recalls the patriarchal blessing that Joseph would be a "fruitful vine" (Gen. 49:22; cf. 48:15–16).

The East Manasseh record is a clan list. The seven clan leaders mentioned are unknown to the rest of the Old Testament. Two of the names perhaps have parallels: Epher (5:24) may be the Hepher and Azriel (5:24) may be the Asriel cited in the Pentateuchal version of Manasseh's genealogy (Num. 26:31–32). The adjectives "brave" and "famous" suggest these men were both heads of clans and military commanders. The Chronicler juxtaposes human strength and greatness with the commentary that these leaders were "unfaithful" to God (1 Chron. 5:25). Like the psalmist, he knows that God delights not in human strength but in those who trust in his unfailing love (cf. Ps. 20:7; 147:10).

There is some question as to whether the concluding passage (5:25–26) refers to the tribe of Manasseh only or represents a summary statement assessing the spiritual character of all the Transjordan tribes. Curtis is probably correct in recognizing that the verses function both as a conclusion to the brief material on East Manasseh and the larger record of the Transjordan.[10]

The Chronicler's account agrees with the books of Kings on the northern kingdom's sin of idolatry (2 Kings 17:7). The writer also correctly understood the "vomit theology" laid out by Moses in the book of Leviticus (Lev. 18:24–30). Once the Israelites became guilty of the sins for which God punished the Canaanites, the Israelite occupation of the land of covenant promise was in jeopardy. Despite repeated warnings by God's prophets, the tribes of the northern kingdom persisted in their idolatry (2 Kings 17:13–15). The result was the Assyrian exile (17:23).[11]

The Chronicler's consistent understanding of God's sovereignty is worth noting. It is God who stirred the spirit of the king of Assyria to judge the sin of Israel (1 Chron. 5:26). Likewise, it is God who stirred the spirit of the king of Persia to permit the Jews to return to their covenant homeland (cf. 2 Chron. 36:22–23).

WE HAVE ALREADY established the fact that one of the purposes of the Chronicler's genealogical prologue is to bolster morale in postexilic Judah. His retelling of Israel's past is, in part, also a theology of hope for Israel's future. In addition to exhortation, the genealogical prologue is also intended as instruction to the restoration community. Following the example set by Moses in his "historical sermon" to the second generation of Israelites delivered from Egypt (Deut. 4:9), the writer of Chronicles assumes there is something universal about the personal stories of his ancestors. The genealogies of the Transjordan tribes record just such experiences.

According to Wilcock, this section of the genealogy preserves two experiences of opposite kinds.[12] These contrasting experiences are principal themes in Chronicles, and they essentially characterize the history of Israel in the Old Testament (cf. 1 Chron. 14:10; 18:13; 2 Chron. 13:12). The first of these antithetical experiences is victory in battle and the expansion of tribal boundaries because God helps his people (specifically victory over the Hagrites and their allies). The second experience, as tragic as the first was

---

10. E.g., Edward L. Curtis, *The Books of Chronicles* (ICC; Edinburgh: T. & T. Clark, 1910), 120.
11. Braun, *1 Chronicles*, 78.
12. Wilcock, *The Message of Chronicles*, 36.

triumphant, is defeat at the hands of enemies and exile from the land of covenant promise (namely, the conquest of Israel by the king of Assyria, 1 Chron. 5:26)—something anticipated by Moses and cited as a threat in his historical sermon to the generation of Israelites about to enter the land of Canaan (cf. Deut. 4:25–31).

Like Moses, the Chronicler is concerned that the Israelites not suffer the latter experience by repeating the history of an earlier generation corrupted by idolatry and destroyed for unbelief (Deut. 1:35; 2:14–15; cf. Heb. 3:15–19). If that lesson from history were not enough, the writer drives the point home by recounting the sin of Reuben that led to his loss of the blessing normally reserved for the firstborn son (1 Chron. 5:1–2). The Chronicler must warn his audience of spiritual complacency spawned by an attitude of arrogance rooted in Israel's election as God's "firstborn" (Ex. 4:22; cf. Deut. 9:5). Selman offers the sober reminder that status before God is not a right inherited but a matter of privilege earned by obedience to the word of God.[13]

As his final exclamation point, the Chronicler adds a second warning, again echoing the instruction of Moses concerning the pitfalls of human achievement. Material prosperity may undermine faith in God as it induces a type of "spiritual amnesia" that causes people to forget that God has authored their success (cf. Deut. 8:10–11). It was important for the Transjordan tribes to remember that the expansion of their tribal boundaries, numerical increase, and material wealth were due to God's help, not self-help (1 Chron. 5:20).

The Chronicler, however, does not teach by negative example only. He also outlines the necessary ingredients for "victory" as divinely understood. His formula for divine help leading to spiritual success includes prayer to God and trust in God (5:21). Both are recurrent themes in the Chronicles, especially prayer to God in military contexts, since the battle belongs to him anyway (e.g., 2 Chron. 14:11–15; 32:20–21; cf. 20:15; 25:8). Interestingly, both are connected (at least implicitly) to the spiritual defeat (and exile) of the northern tribes (1 Chron. 5:25).

Prayer *to* God is central to Hebrew theology because the Old Testament record indicates that God hears (cf. 2 Chron. 30:20, 27; 34:27) and answers the prayers of those who invoke his name (cf. 1 Chron. 14:10, 14; 21:26, 28). To trust *in* God is to place confidence in or to depend on him as one's sole resource for help in circumstances of distress and need (cf. 2 Chron. 13:18; 14:11; 16:7–8; 32:10). Also, to trust *in* God is to acknowledge that he is the source of all blessing and that God extends that goodness to people accord-

---

13. See Selman, *1 Chronicles*, 105, on the recurring theme of the demotion of the firstborn in Chronicles (cf. Deut. 4:40).

ing to his mercy, not human merit. The prophet Habakkuk aptly understood trusting God as rejoicing in the Lord quite apart from the circumstances of prosperity or poverty (Hab. 3:17–18; cf. Paul's reflection on "contentment" in the Lord "whether living in plenty or in want," Phil. 4:12).

The failure and defeat of the Transjordan tribes of Reuben, Gad, and East Manasseh was not so much neglect of the act of prayer and the posture of trust as it was the substitution of other gods for the God of Abraham as the object of that prayer and trust (5:25). According to Moses, the outcome of such behavior is predictable. God is a jealous God, tolerating no rival (Deut. 4:24), and his only possible response to idolatry among the Israelites is destruction and banishment from the land (4:25–26).

 FINISHING THE RACE. The Chronicler has previously cast the tribe of Judah as the geographical and theological center of the Israelite tribes (2:3–4:23). In part, the genealogical prologue assesses the surrounding tribal units on the basis of their adherence to the ideal of kingship embodied in David (i.e., unswerving loyalty to God alone and a lover of his law). In a way, the Chronicler plays the role of a press-box commentator watching a long-distance race, since his attention is fixed on the "starts" and "finishes" of the tribes across the history of Israelite and Judean monarchies. In the previous section, the success of the tribe of Simeon is implicitly attached to their association with Judah (cf. 4:31). Although absorbed by Judah as the larger political unit geographically, they retained an identifiable tribal genealogical presence because they clung to the Davidic ideal. Allen regards the clans of Simeon as "survivors" who finished the race, noting that they persisted to the day of the Chronicler (4:43).[14]

Conversely, Allen has labeled the Transjordan tribes "losers" since they rejected the Davidic ideal and were exiled into Assyria, where they remained to the day of the Chronicler (5:26). In other words, they started the race and even "ran well" for a time (note their success recorded in 5:10, 18–22). Alas, they did not "stay with" God and finish the race but "strayed after" other gods and forfeited the prize of tribal unity in the land of covenant promise.

In one sense, the "start" for the Transjordan tribes of Reuben, Gad, and East Manasseh was ominous from the outset. The Transjordan regions of Gilead and Bashan were taken from Sihon king of the Amorites and Og king of Bashan prior to the invasion of Palestine under Joshua (Num. 21:21–31). Later, the leaders of the tribes of Reuben, Gad, and East Manasseh requested

---

14. Allen, *1, 2 Chronicles*, 52–53.

permission from Moses to settle in the areas of Gilead and Bashan because they were well suited for raising livestock (Num. 32:4; cf. Josh. 12:6). At first Moses took offense to the petition, comparing these three tribal units to the faithless first generation of Israelites delivered from Egypt (cf. Num. 32:14–15). Finally he consented to a conditional inheritance of the territory east of the Jordan River for these tribes, contingent on their full participation with their brother tribes in the conquest of the land of Canaan (Num. 32:20–22, 30; cf. Josh. 1:12–15).

A critical reading of the Joshua narrative suggests a certain selfish immediacy in the request for an inheritance in the Transjordan, since these tribes sought to establish themselves in the regions of Gilead and Bashan before they had actually earned their inheritance (Num. 32:16–19). The building of an altar in the Transjordan by the eastern tribes after Joshua had discharged them from their military obligations to the rest of the tribes nearly precipitated a civil war (Josh. 22:10–12). The episode raised suspicions concerning religious apostasy and tribal unity—a foreshadowing of what the future would bring. According to the Chronicler, Reuben, Gad, and East Manasseh eventually did turn away from the altar of the Lord and prostituted themselves to other gods (1 Chron. 5:25). The Lord did call them to account for their rebellion; their sin did find them out (Josh. 22:23; cf. Num. 32:23–24).

The apostle Paul further develops this analogy between the life of faith in Christ and a footrace by appeal to the running events associated with the athletic games of the Greek world in New Testament times (e.g., 1 Cor. 9:26). In fact, this is Paul's own epitaph as he writes what might be considered his last will and testament to Timothy: "I have finished the race, I have kept the faith" (2 Tim. 4:7). Paul deeply desires to achieve this goal and is able to see it through to the end by the grace of God and the power of the Holy Spirit (cf. Acts 20:24).

Paul, no doubt, took his example from Jesus, who had this same sense of mission in his earthly ministry, finishing what the Father had commissioned him to do (cf. John 4:34; 5:36; 17:4). In fact, Jesus told a story about the need to estimate the cost of finishing a building project lest one be subject to ridicule for starting but failing to complete such an undertaking (Luke 14:28–30). Both Paul and Peter were able to exhort fellow believers to "press on" in erecting that tower of faith in God because they recognized that the necessary resources for finishing the task were already "bankrolled" in the redemptive work of Jesus Christ (Phil. 3:12–14; 2 Peter 1:3). Hence, completion of the "project" is certain (cf. Phil. 2:12–13; 2 Peter 1:10–11)!

The goal of maintaining a covenant relationship with Yahweh for the Israelite tribes was threatened by rivals, the gods of the peoples of the land (5:25). Sadly, the Israelites succumbed to the siren songs of deities like

Asherah, Baal, Chemosh, and Molech (cf. 2 Chron. 23:17; 24:18). Finishing the race of faith in Christ today is no less challenging than it was for God's people in the Old Testament world. We must resist the lure of alternative forms of idolatry, such as the gods of money, efficiency, power, competition, famous people, and so on.[15] Unlike the "theistic" tendency of culture during Old Testament times that assumed the existence of a divine realm and its convergence with humanity, the contemporary Christian contends with a society given to agnosticism and atheism. This has prompted one social critic to describe American public life as a "culture of disbelief," where God is a little more than a "hobby."[16]

Perhaps even more disturbing are the pluralistic trends of postmodern thought that interpret religion as the ideological by-product of social engineering. Furthermore, the very concepts of "starting" and "finishing" anything are treated with skepticism and contempt today because the "objectivity" of historical events is devalued in favor of the "subjectivity" of personal experience.[17] Small wonder the church struggles to "coach" Christians in the subtleties of running the race of faith in Christ, given the impact of these adverse running conditions on the "track of life." Simply stated, the keys to staying on course and finishing the race for Israel were prayer and trust in God (1 Chron. 5:20). What about the New Testament strategy for completing the race of faith in Jesus Christ? How does the new covenant complement the Chronicler's advice for surviving, even emerging victorious from the battles of spiritual warfare?

One way in which the New Testament enhances the message of Chronicles is that of example through character study. The New Testament letters illustrate a variety of "starts" and "finishes" within that early community of Christian faith, giving it an almost photo album-like quality. For instance, we have the account of the life of the apostle Paul, introduced to us as the chief of sinners (cf. 1 Tim. 1:16) but transformed into the apostle of the Gentiles (Acts 9:15). The name Demas is associated with the more tragic story of one who apparently started well (cf. Col. 4:14) but who quit the race and deserted Paul because "he loved this world" (2 Tim. 4:10).

The New Testament also tracks the encouraging record of John Mark, one who started well but then faltered along the way (Acts 12:25; 13:13; cf. 15:38–39). Yet in the end he proved himself a faithful servant of Christ and

---

15. On the idolatries of contemporary culture, see Marva J. Dawn, *Reaching Out Without Dumbing Down* (Grand Rapids: Eerdmans, 1995), 41–56.

16. See Carter, *The Culture of Disbelief*, 23–43.

17. See Bork, *Slouching Towards Gomorrah*, 66–82, on how the rise of radical egalitarianism fosters a "victim status" mentality that removes any need for corporate accountability or personal responsibility.

a useful coworker in Paul's ministry (2 Tim. 4:11). There are even those singular role models who started well and finished in like manner. Naturally people like Simeon and Anna come to mind, each remembered for a lifetime of devotion and faithful service to God (cf. Luke 2:25, 36). Lest these biographies be dismissed as quaint reminiscences of a bygone day, it is important to remember that the cultural context of the New Testament world was much like that of our own: a world driven by greed and materialism, a world given to sensuality and moral decay, a world awash in ideological relativism and religious pluralism. So the greater question is: What points of commonality do these New Testament biographies share with the Chronicler's story of the Transjordan tribes of Israel?

When the two key ingredients of the Chronicler's formula for success in running the race of faith are unpacked in the light of the New Testament, it is apparent the new covenant serves to make explicit what was implicit in the old covenant. (1) There is indeed a "race" to be run, whether in battle against the Hagrites (1 Chron. 5:10) or against "the powers of this dark world and against the spiritual forces of evil" (Eph. 6:12).

(2) The race has a "finish line," and there is a prize to be won, whether "rest" in the land of covenant promise (1 Chron. 23:25; cf. Heb. 3:11) or the gift of God, which is eternal life (Rom. 6:23).

(3) The act of prayer itself is a constant reminder that the battle belongs to the Lord (2 Chron. 20:15) and that it will be won in the power of God's Spirit, not human strength (Zech. 4:6; cf. Phil. 4:13). Prayer also reminds us that the race cannot be run on "cruise control." The faith pilgrimage includes barriers, hurdles, trials, and setbacks. Such are used by God to encourage faith and strengthen hope since we know that although we will have trouble in the fallen world, Jesus Christ has overcome all such troubles (Rom. 5:3–5; cf. John 16:33).

(4) Finally, finishing the race brings glory to God and proclaims "the gospel of God's grace" to all those spectators on the sidelines still uncertain about Christianity (cf. Acts 20:24).

The notion of finishing the race informs the Chronicler's understanding of what it means to trust in God as well. The words "trust in God" may not be construed as a magical formula ensuring instant and constant success in personal endeavors. The race of life is not "fixed" in the sense that it is a mechanical process, like windup toys on a slotted miniature speedway oval. The expression "trust in God" connotes the ongoing responsibility for the believer in the Lord to maintain that faith relationship with the Almighty. The Transjordan tribes lost sight of this truth and became unfaithful in their relationship to God so that his only alternative was to send them into exile (1 Chron. 5:25–26).

Paul himself ran the race of faith in Christ with great vigor, focus, and self-discipline lest he become a "loser," one disqualified for the prize (1 Cor. 9:27). This would suggest that exercise or "training in godliness" is a staple in a biblical spiritual fitness program (cf. 1 Tim. 4:8). Specific exercises in the biblical regimen for godliness includes transforming the mind (Rom. 8:6), taming one's speech (cf. James 3:8), controlling the passions of the body (Rom. 12:1–2), harnessing one's emotions (James 1:19–20), and maintaining proper motives (Phil. 2:3). This also indicates attention must be given to the instruction of the next generation since we learn from both covenants that the race of faith in God stretches beyond any one lifetime and any single generation (e.g., Deut. 4:9–10; Eph. 6:1–4).

Finally, there is a communal aspect to trusting in God. The faith venture for Israel was cooperative on a clan and tribal level, even as the Transjordan tribes pooled their resources and expanded their borders through military conquest (1 Chron. 5:18). Likewise, the New Testament teaches that the church of Jesus Christ is one body, comprised of many individual members (1 Cor. 12:12). The diversity of gifts possessed in some measure by all Christians is the work of one Spirit and is given graciously for the purpose of nurturing and unifying the one body of Christ—his church (cf. Eph. 4:3–5, 12–13). There is no greater expression of righteousness in the Bible than trust in God because those who do so will never be put to shame (Rom. 5:5; 9:33).

1 Chronicles 6

T HE SONS OF Levi:

Gershon, Kohath and Merari.
2 The sons of Kohath:
Amram, Izhar, Hebron and Uzziel.
3 The children of Amram:
Aaron, Moses and Miriam.
The sons of Aaron:
Nadab, Abihu, Eleazar and Ithamar.
4 Eleazar was the father of Phinehas,
Phinehas the father of Abishua,
5 Abishua the father of Bukki,
Bukki the father of Uzzi,
6 Uzzi the father of Zerahiah,
Zerahiah the father of Meraioth,
7 Meraioth the father of Amariah,
Amariah the father of Ahitub,
8 Ahitub the father of Zadok,
Zadok the father of Ahimaaz,
9 Ahimaaz the father of Azariah,
Azariah the father of Johanan,
10 Johanan the father of Azariah (it was he who served as
priest in the temple Solomon built in Jerusalem),
11 Azariah the father of Amariah,
Amariah the father of Ahitub,
12 Ahitub the father of Zadok,
Zadok the father of Shallum,
13 Shallum the father of Hilkiah,
Hilkiah the father of Azariah,
14 Azariah the father of Seraiah,
and Seraiah the father of Jehozadak.
15 Jehozadak was deported when the LORD sent Judah and
Jerusalem into exile by the hand of Nebuchadnezzar.

16 The sons of Levi:
Gershon, Kohath and Merari.
17 These are the names of the sons of Gershon:
Libni and Shimei.

¹⁸ The sons of Kohath:

Amram, Izhar, Hebron and Uzziel.

¹⁹ The sons of Merari:

Mahli and Mushi.

These are the clans of the Levites listed according to their fathers:

²⁰ Of Gershon:

Libni his son, Jehath his son,

Zimmah his son, ²¹Joah his son,

Iddo his son, Zerah his son

and Jeatherai his son.

²² The descendants of Kohath:

Amminadab his son, Korah his son,

Assir his son, ²³Elkanah his son,

Ebiasaph his son, Assir his son,

²⁴ Tahath his son, Uriel his son,

Uzziah his son and Shaul his son.

²⁵ The descendants of Elkanah:

Amasai, Ahimoth,

²⁶ Elkanah his son, Zophai his son,

Nahath his son, ²⁷Eliab his son,

Jeroham his son, Elkanah his son

and Samuel his son.

²⁸ The sons of Samuel:

Joel the firstborn

and Abijah the second son.

²⁹ The descendants of Merari:

Mahli, Libni his son,

Shimei his son, Uzzah his son,

³⁰ Shimea his son, Haggiah his son

and Asaiah his son.

³¹ These are the men David put in charge of the music in the house of the LORD after the ark came to rest there. ³² They ministered with music before the tabernacle, the Tent of Meeting, until Solomon built the temple of the LORD in Jerusalem. They performed their duties according to the regulations laid down for them.

³³ Here are the men who served, together with their sons:

From the Kohathites:

Heman, the musician,

the son of Joel, the son of Samuel,

³⁴ the son of Elkanah, the son of Jeroham,
the son of Eliel, the son of Toah,
³⁵ the son of Zuph, the son of Elkanah,
the son of Mahath, the son of Amasai,
³⁶ the son of Elkanah, the son of Joel,
the son of Azariah, the son of Zephaniah,
³⁷ the son of Tahath, the son of Assir,
the son of Ebiasaph, the son of Korah,
³⁸ the son of Izhar, the son of Kohath,
the son of Levi, the son of Israel;

³⁹ and Heman's associate Asaph, who served at his right hand:
Asaph son of Berekiah, the son of Shimea,
⁴⁰ the son of Michael, the son of Baaseiah,
the son of Malkijah, ⁴¹the son of Ethni,
the son of Zerah, the son of Adaiah,
⁴² the son of Ethan, the son of Zimmah,
the son of Shimei, ⁴³the son of Jahath,
the son of Gershon, the son of Levi;

⁴⁴ and from their associates, the Merarites, at his left hand:
Ethan son of Kishi, the son of Abdi,
the son of Malluch, ⁴⁵the son of Hashabiah,
the son of Amaziah, the son of Hilkiah,
⁴⁶ the son of Amzi, the son of Bani,
the son of Shemer, ⁴⁷the son of Mahli,
the son of Mushi, the son of Merari,
the son of Levi.

⁴⁸Their fellow Levites were assigned to all the other duties of the tabernacle, the house of God. ⁴⁹But Aaron and his descendants were the ones who presented offerings on the altar of burnt offering and on the altar of incense in connection with all that was done in the Most Holy Place, making atonement for Israel, in accordance with all that Moses the servant of God had commanded.

⁵⁰ These were the descendants of Aaron:
Eleazar his son, Phinehas his son,
Abishua his son, ⁵¹Bukki his son,
Uzzi his son, Zerahiah his son,
⁵² Meraioth his son, Amariah his son,
Ahitub his son, ⁵³Zadok his son
and Ahimaaz his son.

⁵⁴These were the locations of their settlements allotted as their territory (they were assigned to the descendants of Aaron who were from the Kohathite clan, because the first lot was for them):

⁵⁵They were given Hebron in Judah with its surrounding pasturelands. ⁵⁶But the fields and villages around the city were given to Caleb son of Jephunneh.

⁵⁷So the descendants of Aaron were given Hebron (a city of refuge), and Libnah, Jattir, Eshtemoa, ⁵⁸Hilen, Debir, ⁵⁹Ashan, Juttah and Beth Shemesh, together with their pasturelands. ⁶⁰And from the tribe of Benjamin they were given Gibeon, Geba, Alemeth and Anathoth, together with their pasturelands.

These towns, which were distributed among the Kohathite clans, were thirteen in all.

⁶¹The rest of Kohath's descendants were allotted ten towns from the clans of half the tribe of Manasseh.

⁶²The descendants of Gershon, clan by clan, were allotted thirteen towns from the tribes of Issachar, Asher and Naphtali, and from the part of the tribe of Manasseh that is in Bashan.

⁶³The descendants of Merari, clan by clan, were allotted twelve towns from the tribes of Reuben, Gad and Zebulun.

⁶⁴So the Israelites gave the Levites these towns and their pasturelands. ⁶⁵From the tribes of Judah, Simeon and Benjamin they allotted the previously named towns.

⁶⁶Some of the Kohathite clans were given as their territory towns from the tribe of Ephraim.

⁶⁷In the hill country of Ephraim they were given Shechem (a city of refuge), and Gezer, ⁶⁸Jokmeam, Beth Horon, ⁶⁹Aijalon and Gath Rimmon, together with their pasturelands.

⁷⁰And from half the tribe of Manasseh the Israelites gave Aner and Bileam, together with their pasturelands, to the rest of the Kohathite clans.

⁷¹The Gershonites received the following:
From the clan of the half-tribe of Manasseh
they received Golan in Bashan and also Ashtaroth,
together with their pasturelands;
⁷²from the tribe of Issachar
they received Kedesh, Daberath, ⁷³Ramoth and Anem,
together with their pasturelands;

⁷⁴from the tribe of Asher

they received Mashal, Abdon, ⁷⁵Hukok and Rehob,
together with their pasturelands;

⁷⁶and from the tribe of Naphtali

they received Kedesh in Galilee, Hammon and
Kiriathaim, together with their pasturelands.

⁷⁷The Merarites (the rest of the Levites) received the
following:

From the tribe of Zebulun

they received Jokneam, Kartah, Rimmono and Tabor,
together with their pasturelands;

⁷⁸from the tribe of Reuben across the Jordan east of Jericho

they received Bezer in the desert, Jahzah, ⁷⁹Kedemoth
and Mephaath, together with their pasturelands;

⁸⁰and from the tribe of Gad

they received Ramoth in Gilead, Mahanaim, ⁸¹Heshbon
and Jazer, together with their pasturelands.

ALONG WITH JUDAH and Benjamin, Levi was one of the three prominent tribes in the Chronicler's retelling of Israelite history. The importance of Levi is attested both by its central position in the tribal genealogies and its length, second only to the register of Judah (2:3– 4:23). It has been suggested that the overall design of the Chronicler's genealogical preface was patterned after the layout of the camp of the Hebrew tribes following the Exodus.[1] This not only helps explain the centrality of the family tree of Levi in the genealogical records of Chronicles but also underscores the theological significance of that tribe for all Israel. According to the instructions of Moses, Levi encamped in the very midst of the Hebrew tribes, and centered among the priests and clans of Levites was the tabernacle and the sacred ark (Num. 1:47–2:34).

The genealogy may be divided into two sections: Levitical genealogies (6:1–53) and the settlement of the priests and Levites (6:54–81). Each section treats the priests and Levites separately: the genealogy of the high priests (6:1–15), the genealogies of the three Levitical orders (6:16–30), the Levitical singers (6:31–47), priestly duties (6:48–53), the settlement of the priests (6:54–60), and the settlement of the Levites (6:61–81).

---

1. Allen, *1, 2 Chronicles*, 60.

The genealogical trees of Levi are segmented in that they contain lists of names representing both breadth (i.e., a list of a single generation of descendants from a common ancestor, e.g., 6:1–3) and depth (a listing of successive generations, e.g., 6:4–15). Some of the genealogies are descending, listing names from parent to child (e.g., 6:1–15); others are ascending, listing names from child to parent (e.g., 6:33–47). Williamson has helpfully diagrammed a sevenfold pattern that accents the high priests:[2]

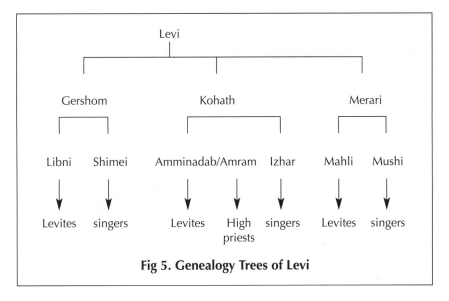

Fig 5. Genealogy Trees of Levi

We have already learned that genealogical lists serve a number of theological purposes in the biblical narrative, especially legitimizing an individual or a family in an office or enhancing the stature of an individual, clan, or tribe by linkage to an important figure of the past.[3] Such is the case with the descendants of Levi as they mediate the worship of God for all Israel through the priesthood. As Wilcock has noted, "Levi thus provides religious leadership which acts as a binding force through the length of Israel's history and the breadth of its territory."[4]

More specifically, central to the religious leadership provided by the tribe of Levi was "making atonement for Israel" (6:49). Selman has observed that out of all the families of the tribal lists, only the lines of David and Aaron trace their lineage from the patriarchs to the Exile. In both cases these genealogies are preceded by examples of Israelite unfaithfulness resulting in national

---

2. Williamson, *1 and 2 Chronicles,* 69.
3. Johnson, *The Purpose of the Biblical Genealogies,* 77–82.
4. Wilcock, *The Message of Chronicles,* 38.

catastrophe. Selman concludes that the tribes of Judah and Levi "seem to be the means through which even covenant-breaking sins could be atoned for (6:49; cf. 2 Chron. 36:22–23)."[5]

The Priestly Line of Levi (5:1–15)

THE SONS OF LEVI (Gershon, Kohath, and Merari) are always ordered according to age (cf. Gen. 46:11; Ex. 6:16; Num. 3:17). The focus of the initial genealogy of Levi, however, is Kohath (1 Chron. 6:2) since he was the ancestor of the Aaronite high priests (6:3). The listing of the Aaronite high priests preserves twenty-one generations from Eleazar to Jehozadak, but it is not a complete genealogical record (e.g., Eli [1 Sam. 14:3] and Jehoiada [2 Kings 11:9] are missing). The first six generations of the register (Levi to Phineas) have been extracted from the family record of Moses and Aaron (Ex. 6:16–25).

The genealogy highlights two priests with anecdotes: Azariah, who served as priest in Solomon's temple (6:10), and Jehozadak, who was deported to Babylonia at the time of Jerusalem's exile (6:15). Both events were watersheds in Israelite history. The erection of a permanent sanctuary for the worship of Yahweh in Jerusalem redefined the Levitical priesthood, while the Babylonian exile indelibly marked Israelite history and theology.

Critics have challenged the authenticity of the Chronicler's Levitical genealogy, citing among other problems the "artificial" linkage of Zadok (6:8) to the Aaronite priesthood. Outside of the names of his father Ahitub (2 Sam. 8:17), his son Ahimaaz (2 Sam. 15:36), and his grandson Azariah (1 Kings 4:2), we know nothing of Zadok apart from the Chronicler's record. Given this lack of external verification, Selman has charged that it is arbitrary to disparage the genealogical records of Chronicles as confused or inaccurate.[6] In fact, the Chronicler's genealogy agrees precisely with Ezra's listing of the Levitical family tree from the generations of Aaron to Meraioth (6:3–6) and Azariah to Seraiah (6:11–14; cf. Ezra 7:5; Neh. 11:11). Many of the other names cited by the Chronicler are attested elsewhere in the biblical record (e.g., Azariah, cf. 1 Kings 4:2; Amariah, cf. Ezra 7:3; Shallum, cf. Ezra 7:2).

When the integrity of Chronicles is challenged, we must insist, like Myers, that "the Chronicler's story is accurate wherever it can be checked, though the method of presentation is homiletical."[7] Stated more simply, Chronicles is reliable biblical history preached as a sermon.

No doubt the Chronicler's list of priestly names elicits a variety of responses from his audience as they replay the biblical stories connected

---

5. Selman, *1 Chronicles*, 108.
6. Ibid., 109.
7. Myers, *I Chronicles*, lxiii.

with each character. For example, the tragic account of the deaths of Nadab and Abihu (6:3) for violating the order of sacrifice in their drunkenness is a sober reminder of God's holiness and the dire consequences of covenant disobedience (cf. Lev. 10:1–11). Phinehas (6:4) distinguished himself as a champion of faithfulness to Yahweh in his righteous response to Israel's idolatry at Baal Peor (Num. 25:7–9). His zeal for the Lord's honor resulted in a covenant of peace and everlasting priesthood for his descendants (Num. 25:10–13). The high priest Hilkiah (1 Chron. 6:13) found the Book of the Law that precipitated the social and religious reforms of King Josiah (2 Chron. 34:14).

The horrific onslaught of Nebuchadnezzar against the kingdom of Judah included the priesthood, for the chief priest Seraiah (6:14) was among those Hebrew officials executed by the king of Babylon after the fall of Jerusalem (2 Kings 25:18–21). Yet it was his son Jehozadak who was father to the high priest Jeshua, leader of the Hebrew repatriation of Judah after the Babylonian captivity (Ezra 3:2; 5:2).

The story of triumph or tragedy attached to each name of the Levitical genealogy serves to exhort and admonish the Chronicler's audience. More than that, they plant seeds of hope for the imminent installation of the kingdom of that royal priest after the order of Melchizedek, who will destroy the enemies of the Israelites (Ps. 110:4).

The Sons of Levi (6:16–30)

THIS SECTION OF the genealogy introduces the three sons of Levi, each one as a founding ancestor of a major division of the Levitical corps: Gershon, Kohath, and Merari.[8] The Chronicler's source for the listing is the record of the Levitical clans found in Numbers 3:17–20 (cf. Ex. 6:16–19). The genealogies of Levi's descendants demonstrate breadth (or horizontal relationship of offspring from a common ancestor) for two successive generations for each of Levi's three sons (1 Chron. 6:16–19). Furthermore, they demonstrate depth (or the listing of successive generations) in recording seven generations of Gershonites (6:20) and Merarites (6:29). The clan genealogies appear to descend (i.e., arranged from father to son) to the time of Saul and David (given the reference to Samuel's sons in 6:28 [cf. 1 Sam. 8:2–3] and the reference to Asaiah in 1 Chron. 6:30 [cf. 15:6]).

The genealogy of the Kohathite clan presents numerous problems. Amminadab is listed as a fifth son of Kohath (6:22), but his name is not found in any of the other family trees of Levi. In addition, the lengthy and intricate

---

8. Generally the Chronicler prefers Gershom for the more familiar Gershon. The NIV reads "Gershon" for "Gershom" in 6:16, 17, 20, 43, 62, and 71 (see textual note on 6:16).

roster of descendants of Kohath includes five Elkanahs (6:23, 25, 26 [2x], 27).[9] Most biblical scholars assume Amminadab is another name for one of Kohath's other four sons (perhaps Ishar?).[10] Scholars also tend to assume that the relationships for the descendants of Korah are horizontal rather than vertical (6:22–23), thus compressing the descending genealogy of Kohath into seven generations like those of Gershon and Merari.[11] The hypothetical reconstruction is speculative and proves unconvincing. It seems better to recognize the integrity of each genealogical record, harmonize the data where possible given parallel sources, but acknowledge our understanding of all the horizontal and vertical relationships in the extensive lists of names in Chronicles may be only partial in some cases.

The family tree of Samuel (6:26–28) has been added to the clan of Kohath's genealogy in basic agreement with 1 Samuel 1:1 and 8:2.[12] The name of Samuel's firstborn son, Joel, has been rightly added to the NIV text of Chronicles on the basis of the parallel passages (see NIV textual note on 1 Chron. 6:28). The tragic record of the unfaithfulness of Samuel's sons to the commands of the Mosaic covenant and their heritage as priests is found in 1 Samuel 8:2–3. As a result of their corrupt leadership, the Israelites requested a king to rule the tribes (1 Sam. 8:4–5). Another descendant of Samuel, his grandson Heman, was a temple music director (1 Chron. 6:33). Perhaps the Chronicler is seeking to call to mind the era of Samuel, an era that parallels his own in that prior to Samuel, "the word of the LORD was rare; there were not many visions" (1 Sam. 3:1).

The Temple Musicians (6:31–47)

KING DAVID'S PREPARATIONS for a permanent sanctuary for the worship of Yahweh necessitated a reorganization of the nonpriestly Levites, whose services were no longer required as porters, assemblers, and custodians of the portable sanctuary. The Chronicler summarizes the reassignment of Levitical duties under the dual headings of music for the house of God (6:31–32) and duties related to the tabernacle (6:48). The families of Heman, Asaph, and Ethan, each representing one of the three sons of Levi, were appointed as music directors for temple worship. Apparently the Levitical musicians split the duties of the music ministry between the "house of the LORD" in Jerusalem where "the ark came to rest" (6:31; cf. 15:1–3) and the tabernacle in Gibeon (cf. 16:39–42) until the completion of Solomon's temple (6:32).

---

9. For example, the NIV drops one of names for Elkanah as a redundancy (see text note).
10. E.g., Selman, *1 Chronicles*, 110–11.
11. Cf. Williamson, *1 and 2 Chronicles*, 72, on the orthographic (or spelling) variants between the sources.
12. Japhet, *I & II Chronicles*, 440.

Heman (6:33) oversaw the ministry of music in the house of the Lord (6:31; cf. 15:16–17). He was among those charged to sound the bronze cymbals when the ark of the Lord entered Jerusalem (15:19). Elsewhere we learn his responsibilities included the accompaniment of sacred songs with both trumpets and cymbals (16:42). The superscription of Psalm 88 credits the composition to Heman. Finally, Heman and the other musicians were given the expanded role of "prophesying" to musical accompaniment (1 Chron. 25:1). The context there (25:2–3) suggests that the combined activity of singing and playing an instrument is construed in some technical sense as "prophesying" (esp. since the musicians are composing temple psalmody).[13]

The genealogy of Heman is traced through twenty-two generations of the clan of Kohath of the tribe of Levi (6:33–38). This impressive family tree is both a statement of the authority vested in the musical guild of Heman and the continuity of his leadership extending back to the origins of the Mosaic covenant. The list of Heman's ancestors is essentially the same register of Kohathite descendants found earlier in 6:22–28 (except it is arranged in ascending order instead of descending order). Neither genealogy is comprehensive since Assir son of Korah and Elkanah son of Assir (6:22–23) are omitted in the latter register. Although certain names may be interchangeable (e.g., Uzziah [6:24] and Azariah [6:36]; cf. 2 Kings 15:1 with 2 Chron. 26:1), the variations between the genealogies suggest the word "son" (Heb. *ben*) should be broadened in certain cases to imply "descendant" or "relative" (cf. Zephaniah son of Tahath [1 Chron. 6:36–37] with Uriel son of Tahath [6:24]).

Asaph was appointed the first associate of Heman ("served at his right hand," 6:39); his genealogy is traced through fifteen generations of the clan of Gershon of the tribe of Levi (6:39–43). Along with Heman, Asaph sounded the bronze cymbals celebrating the arrival of the ark of the covenant in Jerusalem (15:19). In addition to the one dozen psalms accredited to the Asaph guild, the Chronicler also ascribes the psalm commemorating the entrance of the ark of the Lord into the city of David to Aspah (16:7; cf. Pss. 50; 73–83). Attempts to connect Shimei son of Jahath (1 Chron. 6:42) with Shimei son of Gershon (6:17) require textual emendations based on hypothetical reconstructions and prove unconvincing.[14]

Ethan headed a third musical guild as a result of the reorganization of the Levites by King David (6:44–47; cf. 15:16–17). Like Heman and Asaph, he too sounded the bronze cymbals when David paraded the ark of the covenant

---

13. Selman, *1 Chronicles*, 112.
14. E.g., Williamson, *1 and 2 Chronicles*, 73–74.

into Jerusalem (16:19). The superscription of Psalm 89 credits that composition to Ethan. Ethan is replaced by Jeduthun as one of three primary temple musicians in 1 Chronicles 16:42 and 25:1. Either Jeduthun and Ethan are one in the same individual, or Jeduthun has succeeded Ethan as a director of one of the Levitical musical guilds for some unknown reason.

Ethan's genealogy is traced through Mushi, son of Merari, son of Levi (6:47). Ethan's family tree is the briefest among the directors of the three temple musical guilds, counting only twelve generations. Unlike the genealogy of Heman, however, there is little correspondence between the line of Ethan and the previous listing of descendants of Merari since it highlights the clan of Mushi's brother Mahli (cf. 6:19, 29–30).

Priestly Duties (6:48–49)

THE BLESSING OF the tribes of Israel highlights a twofold function for the descendants of Levi: "watching over" God's Word through the teaching of the Mosaic law to the Israelites and guarding Yahweh's covenant with Israel by attending to the sacrificial rituals of Hebrew worship (Deut. 33:8–11). Here the Chronicler distinguishes between the "fellow Levites" (1 Chron. 6:48) and the priesthood descended from Aaron with respect to liturgical duties. The context indicates the Chronicler differentiates between the Levitical musicians (6:31–47) and the priests assigned to perform the sacrificial liturgy of the sanctuary (6:48–49). While the Levites were called to assist the priests in numerous ways (cf. 1 Chron. 23:28–31; 2 Chron. 30:16; 35:11), the sacrificial altar was the exclusive domain of the Aaronic priesthood (cf. Num. 18:1–7).

The Chronicler summarizes the work of the Levites broadly as "all the other duties of the ... house of God" (6:48; cf. Num. 3:6–9). Elsewhere the Chronicler specifies that the temple service performed by the Levites included overseeing the courtyards and side (storage) rooms, the purification of all sacred things, handling all the tasks related to grain offerings and the Table of Presence, along with their duties as temple singers and musicians (cf. 1 Chron. 23:28–31). The priests were responsible for the altar of burnt offering, the altar of incense, and the work of the Most Holy Place in general, under the threat of divine wrath against all Israel should they shirk their responsibilities (6:49; cf. Num. 18:5).

The goal of the priestly sacrificial ministry was "making atonement for Israel" (6:49). The word "atonement" (Heb. *kpr*) essentially means "to cover." God ordained that sin be "covered" by means of animal sacrifice, whether offered for individuals (e.g., Lev. 4:29, 31) or the entire nation of Israel on the Day of Atonement (cf. Lev. 16). The sacrificial offerings were symbolic of atonement since "it is impossible for the blood of bulls and goats to take away sin" (Heb. 10:4). King David knew well that sin was covered by confession and repentance before a merciful God, offering sacrifices of a broken spirit and a contrite heart to God (Ps. 51:1–4, 16–17). Such confession and repentance was a "sacrifice of prayer"—hence the reference to the altar of incense in the context of the priests making atonement for Israel (Ex. 30:10; cf. Rev. 8:3). Prayer and forgiveness are vitally linked in the Chronicler's theology of atonement (cf. 2 Chron. 7:14; 33:18–19). The section closes with special emphasis on the fact that the priesthood served in compliance with the demands of the Mosaic law (1 Chron. 6:49).

The High Priests (6:50–53)

THE LIST OF high priests is an abbreviated version of the descendants of Aaron found previously (6:3–8). The register of names completes the thought of verse 49, given the reference to Aaron and the duties associated with the high priests. Zadok was a contemporary of David (2 Sam. 15:27; 19:11), while Ahimaaz was the high priest during a portion of Solomon's reign (1 Chron. 6:8–9). Breaking the list of high priests off at this juncture is logical because David reorganized the priesthood (6:31–32) and Solomon built the temple where divinely ordained priestly tasks were performed (6:49).

The reference to Zadok son of Ahitub (6:8; cf. 2 Sam. 8:17) is problematic since the records of his ancestry are in conflict with other genealogical records of the Israelite priesthood (cf. "Ahimelech son of Ahitub" in 1 Sam. 22:9, 20). Ackroyd regards the insertion of Zadok into the lineage of Aaron a "pious fiction" on the part of the Chronicler in an attempt to legitimize the presence of a renegade Jebusite priest in the Levitical line.[15] It is entirely possible, however, that both are correct, assuming the Bible refers to two different individuals with the name Ahitub.[16]

The Levitical Cities (6:54–81)

THE CHRONICLER'S LIST of Levitical cities is parallel to Joshua's allotment of towns to the Levites (Josh. 21:5–39). Scholars continue to debate whether Chronicles is dependent on Joshua or vice versa, or if both lists originate from a common source.[17] The list in Chronicles tends to abridge the version found in Joshua (e.g., omitting certain of the explanatory notes ["Arba

---

15. Ackroyd, *I and II Chronicles, Ezra, Nehemiah*, 40.

16. On the basis of 1 Sam. 14:3 and 1 Chron. 24:3 it is possible to reconstruct Ahimelech's lineage to Ithamar through Ahitub I, son of Phinehas, son of Eli, son of Ithamar, son of Aaron. This would make Zadok son of Ahitub II, a later descendant of Eleazar, son of Aaron.

17. Braun, *1 Chronicles*, 98–99.

was the forefather of Anak," Josh. 21:11] and the summary tallies of cities allotted to the Levitical clans; cf. Josh. 21:24, 25, 31, etc.). The omission of the references to Dan (1 Chron. 6:61, 69; cf. Josh. 21:5, 23) may represent the modernizing of the register by the Chronicler in an attempt to reflect the tribal realities of his own day rather than bias on his part.

Minor variations may be detected in the two lists, attributable to copyist error and the Chronicler's inclination to both abbreviate and update earlier records. In some cases, the Joshua parallel is helpful in restoring incomplete or confusing portions of the Chronicler's record (e.g., the NIV inserts "first" before "lot" in 6:54 on the basis of "first lot" in Josh. 21:10; it restores "Juttah" [6:59] and "Gibeon" [6:60] to the list of Kohathite settlements on the basis of Josh. 21:16–17 to bring the tally of towns from eleven to thirteen, as cited in the summary statement).

The Chronicler also reorders the Levitical settlement list from Joshua, placing the allotment of towns for the descendants of Aaron first (6:54–60; cf. Josh. 21:9–19). The emphatic position of the Aaronides no doubt calls attention to the centrality of the priestly line in postexilic Judah, given the collapse of Davidic kingship. Although the three clans of Levi are listed by birth order (Gershom/Gershon, Kohath, Merari in 6:1, 16), the roster of Levitical cities is (apparently) ordered by the fall of the lot (Kohath, Gershom/Gershon, Merari; cf. Josh. 14:2; 21:4–7).

The list of Levitical cities serves as an important reminder that the tribe of Levi received no inheritance of land when the Israelites settled Canaan. Rather, they received forty-eight cities scattered across the territorial claims of the other Hebrew tribes (Josh. 21:41–42). The Levitical cities stood as a permanent testimony to the reality that the Lord was the share and inheritance of Aaron and his descendants (Num. 18:20). In addition to the allotment of cities from the Israelite tribes among whom they lived, the inheritance of the priests and Levites included the tithes of the Israelites as their means of support in return for performing the service of worship on behalf of the nation (Num. 18:21–24).

The Chronicler has retained only two of the explanatory notes from the parallel list of Levitical cities in Joshua. Both are references to "a city of refuge" (6:57, 67), and both occur in a shortened form (cf. "a city of refuge for one accused of murder," Josh. 21:13, 21, 27, 32, 38). The city of refuge was a safe haven from the avenger of blood for a person who committed accidental manslaughter (Josh. 20:2–6). Six of the forty-eight Levitical settlements were designated as cities of refuge, three on the east side of the Jordan River (Golan, Ramoth in Gilead, and Bezer) and three on the west side of the Jordan River (Kedesh, Shechem, and Hebron, cf. Josh. 20:7–9). In one sense, the city of refuge was a place where "righteousness and peace kiss each other" in a practical way (cf. Ps. 85:10). Is the Chronicler perhaps calling the priests and Levites living in the towns and villages of the postexilic province of Judah to a similar kind of ministry of reconciliation?

SELF-PRESERVATION IS ONE of the basic instincts or impulses of a healthy self-concept. Given this fundamental human trait, Crenshaw has observed that "the urge to secure human existence through the use of reason is universal."[18] The need for people to cope with the complex realities of daily existence for the purpose of sheer survival gave rise to the idea of a sapiential or wisdom tradition. This desire to gain mastery over life through the powers of observation and analysis naturally extends to social units, whether family, clan, tribe, or nation. In fact, the wisdom tradition is one pervasive characteristic of ancient and modern societies.

The idea of wisdom as a database of accumulated knowledge necessary for the success of individuals and societies as they cope with ever-changing circumstances of ordinary life is predicated on two assumptions. (1) It assumes that the innate capacities of human beings for observation, analysis, and reflection enable people to discover what is "right and just and fair—every good path" (Prov. 2:9). It is worth noting here the emphasis on acquiring knowledge and wisdom through the discipline of learning in the prologue to Proverbs (1:1–7).

(2) The idea of wisdom also presupposes that the fundamental principles of this accrued insight into successful living can be taught to the next generation (cf. Prov. 4:1–9). It is the concept of "the fear of the LORD," however, that distinguished Hebrew wisdom from its ancient counterparts. For Israel, wisdom could not be separated from the knowledge of God because he was the source and dispenser of insight and understanding (cf. 1:7; 2:5–6).

The Levitical priesthood was appointed to fulfill this very function as a professional class of ministers devoted to the task of perpetuating the law of Moses and facilitating the worship of the Hebrew nation as the people of God (cf. Ex. 29:44). Originally, the priests (and Levites) were but one of several classes of leaders invested with divine authority for the governing of God's people. The king eventually became Yahweh's anointed agent to rule the people justly, judge in righteousness, defend the poor and needy, and deliver Israel from her enemies (cf. Ps. 72). In addition, the priest, the sage, and the prophet are ascribed prominent roles in Israelite society (cf. Jer. 18:18; Ezek. 7:26). Each one was responsible for a domain of the national life and policy

---

18. James L. Crenshaw, *Old Testament Wisdom: An Introduction* (Atlanta: John Knox, 1981), 12.

of Israel: The priest oversaw the sphere of religion, the sage was influential in the political arena as adviser to the king, and the prophet functioned as the social conscience of the kingdom.

Even as kingship was linked to the tribe of Judah (Gen. 49:9–10), the priesthood was the destiny for the tribe of Levi. According to the farewell blessing of Moses, the Thummim and Urim belonged to the descendants of Levi (Deut. 33:8). That is, God chose to make his will known at times through mechanical means superintended by the high priest (cf. Lev. 8:8; Num. 27:21). Further, the Levites were charged to "watch over" the word of God and "guard" Yahweh's covenant (Deut. 33:9). Finally, the Levites were authorized to "teach" God's law to Israel and to "offer" sacrifices on Yahweh's altars (Deut. 33:10).

The duty of teaching God's law is implicit in the Chronicler's recitation of the Levitical genealogies (cf. 2 Chron. 15:3). The task of offering sacrifices to make atonement for all Israel is central to the Chronicler's understanding of the Levitical priesthood (1 Chron. 6:49). By faithfully discharging these twin duties of teaching the law and offering sacrifices to make atonement for Israel, the Levitical priesthood fulfilled their role as the keepers of Israel's tradition and the guardians of Yahweh's covenant.

The Chronicler well understands that by default, the priests and Levites now constitute the primary leadership office in the restoration community. The Exile brought an end to kingship in Israel. It appears that even the prophetic voice fell silent not long after the construction of the Second Temple (ca. 515 B.C.) at the prompting of Haggai and Zechariah. Naturally, the role of the sage has shifted from that of political adviser to that of scholar-teacher and scribe in the Jewish academic community. Until such a time when God will raise up another king like David, the fate of the nation of Israel lies in the hands of the descendants of Levi.

WORSHIP EDUCATION. The Chronicler makes several theological statements to his audience in the special emphasis on the family tree of Levi. (1) The genealogical record of the tribe of Levi reminds postexilic Judah that the institution of the temple and the rituals of sacrificial worship remain central to the life of the Jewish community. For this reason the writer is careful to admonish his audience by reporting the unfaithfulness and defilement of the temple that led to the Exile (5:25; 9:1; 2 Chron. 36:14).

(2) The priests and Levites of the restoration community are the legitimate heirs of the divine commission to serve as the ministers of temple worship. As descendants of Levi, they are entitled to serve the people of Israel

according to the organizational pattern established by King David in what Wilcock calls the "continuing fruit of the priesthood" (cf. 1 Chron. 23–26).[19]

(3) The priests and Levites rightfully play a key leadership role in post-exilic Judah, given the demise of the kingship. As members of one of the God-ordained "offices" surviving the Babylonian exile, it is imperative the Levitical corps step forward to fill the leadership vacuum. The recognition of this leadership by the people of the restoration community is demonstrated in the installation ceremony for the priests and Levites after completing the Second Temple (cf. Ezra 6:18).

The Chronicler recognizes, however, that the role of the priests and Levites as worship leaders goes beyond the sheer maintenance of the form and order of the sacrificial liturgy. The essence of their ministry is "making atonement for Israel," mediating a right relationship with God. That the crucial task of the priests and Levites is one of spiritual formation is attested by the emphasis on the "heart" in Chronicles. For it is God who searches the heart (28:9), and it is God who grants pardon to those who set their heart on seeking him (2 Chron. 19:3).

According to the farewell blessing of Moses, Israel's right relationship with God was to be accomplished primarily through the teaching ministry of the Levitical corps (Deut. 33:10). The curriculum for this educational initiative in "spiritual literacy" is the law of God. Only through the knowledge of and obedience to that law can a right relationship with him be established and maintained (cf. 2 Chron. 34:31).

In fact, the farewell sermon of Moses equated the "law" of God with the "precepts" of God (Deut. 33:10). This means that a right relationship with God ultimately involves the disposition of the heart and a lifestyle in agreement with the holiness of God, since precepts are defined as authoritative instructions shaping behavior. Naturally implicit in all this is turning to God in repentance and placing one's utter confidence in him (2 Chron. 7:14; 20:20). As a sidebar, in the order of the Levitical duties cited in the blessing of Moses for the tribe of Levi, teaching precedes the ministry of offering sacrifices—perhaps testimony to the fact that "functional" worship response of obedience must enlighten the "form" of the worship ritual.

The inauguration of the new covenant in Christ has not made the Chronicler's message obsolete. As the Dutch theologian Ridderbos has observed: "God speaks to us through the Scripture not to make us scholars, but to make us Christians.... What Scripture does intend is to place us as humans in a right

---

19. Wilcock, *The Message of Chronicles*, 46–47. On the ministry of the Levitical priesthood, see Roland deVaux, *Ancient Israel: Religious Institutions* (New York: McGraw–Hill, 1965), 345–405; Andrew E. Hill, *Enter His Courts with Praise!* (Grand Rapids: Baker, 1996), 138–54.

position to God."[20] Neither has the basic formula changed for establishing that right relationship with God. Turning to God in repentance and faith in the word and work of Jesus Christ are still the prerequisites for entering the fellowship of God's people (Acts 3:19; Rom. 3:22, 25). Clearly, spiritual formation is still an issue of the heart in the New Testament (cf. Rom. 10:10; Eph. 6:6). Finally, a lifestyle of obedience to the commands of God remains the litmus test of true spirituality (cf. 1 John 2:3; 5:3).

Beyond these parallels between the messages of Chronicles (and the Old Testament) and the New Testament, the two rely on the same "delivery system." In both cases, the audience receives the message by means of instruction from a divinely ordained authority figure. In upbraiding the priests of Jerusalem in postexilic Judah, Malachi lamented that they had abandoned their ministry of "true instruction" that "turned many from sin" (Mal. 2:6). Historically, the church of Jesus Christ has promulgated his gospel in a similar manner, that of instruction by clergy invested with the office gift of pastor-teacher and by laypeople endowed with the spiritual gift of teaching (cf. Rom. 12:7; 1 Cor. 12:28; Eph. 4:11). The goal, or "preferred outcome" educationally speaking, of this instruction is consistent with that of the priestly ministry: freeing people from bondage to sin through a knowledge of God's truth about the human condition and his redemptive plan to remedy our plight (cf. John 8:32; 2 Tim. 3:14–16).

This logical comparison between the Old Testament priest and the New Testament pastor-teacher as educator deserves more careful examination. The Old Testament priest served the nation of Israel in numerous ways pedagogically, especially as a worship role model for the people, a teacher and interpreter of God's law for the religious community, and a director of worship education.[21] Likewise, the New Testament recognizes the pastor-teacher as a worship role model in the church (cf. Titus 1:8). Since the Reformation, the dominant role of the pastor-teacher in Protestant circles has been that of teacher and interpreter of God's Word (cf. 1 Tim. 4:12; 2 Tim. 4:3). It seems, however, the analogy breaks down when we consider worship education. Despite the growth and impact of the recent worship renewal movement, worship education is a truant subject in the Christian education curriculum of many evangelical churches.

In his classic essay on worship, Tozer has tendered the thesis that worship is the missing gem in the crown of the evangelical church.[22] Tozer pro-

20. Hermann Ridderbos, *Studies in Scripture and Its Authority* (Grand Rapids: Eerdmans, 1978), 23–24.

21. Hill, *Enter His Courts with Praise!* 147–48.

22. A. W. Tozer, *Worship: The Missing Jewel* (Camp Hill, Pa.: Christian Publications, 1992).

poses to restore that missing jewel, in part, through the teaching of sound doctrine. Granted, the biblically based knowledge of God's character is vital to restoring the element of mystery essential to Christian worship. And I concur fully with Tozer that "admiration, fascination, and adoration" are the natural Spirit-prompted responses of the worshiping heart to God's work in creation and redemption.[23]

I would suggest, however, there is still something "missing" in Tozer's plan for restoring worship in the evangelical church. The missing component of which I speak is worship education itself—that is, formal instruction in the history, theology, and practice of Christian worship. This may be what Tozer advocates implicitly in his emphasis on the teaching of sound biblical doctrine. Nonetheless, the implicit must be taken to the next level. Explicit and systematic worship education must complement the teaching of sound Bible doctrine.

This is hardly a revolutionary idea. The catechisms of the Middle Ages included worship instructions, and Luther's *Smaller Catechism* included lessons devoted to worship education. More recently, Robert Webber has called for formal worship education as part of the Christian education in the church. In fact, worship education heads the lists of Webber's nine proposals for worship renewal among evangelical worshipers.[24] I can only echo his appeal to make a study of the biblical, historical, and theological sources of Christian worship at all age levels a matter of priority in our evangelical churches. I affirm the need for worship education because

> the heart of worship renewal is a recovery of the power of the Holy Spirit Who enables the congregation to offer praise and thanksgiving to God. The value of studying the history and theology of worship is that it provides us with insights into the work of the Holy Spirit in the past and allows us to be open to His work in the present. In this way the Holy Spirit may lead us into ways of Worship.[25]

Perhaps this is the forgotten legacy of the tribe of Levi for the church—a ministry of worship education that prompts worship renewal.

---

23. Ibid., 22–24.
24. Robert E. Webber, *Worship Old and New* (Grand Rapids: Zondervan, 1982), 193.
25. Ibid., 196.

1 Chronicles 7

THE SONS OF Issachar:

Tola, Puah, Jashub and Shimron—four in all.
²The sons of Tola:

Uzzi, Rephaiah, Jeriel, Jahmai, Ibsam and Samuel—
heads of their families. During the reign of David, the
descendants of Tola listed as fighting men in their
genealogy numbered 22,600.
³The son of Uzzi:

Izrahiah.

The sons of Izrahiah:

Michael, Obadiah, Joel and Isshiah. All five of them
were chiefs. ⁴According to their family genealogy, they
had 36,000 men ready for battle, for they had many
wives and children.
⁵The relatives who were fighting men belonging to all the
clans of Issachar, as listed in their genealogy, were
87,000 in all.
⁶Three sons of Benjamin:

Bela, Beker and Jediael.
⁷The sons of Bela:

Ezbon, Uzzi, Uzziel, Jerimoth and Iri, heads of
families—five in all. Their genealogical record listed
22,034 fighting men.
⁸The sons of Beker:

Zemirah, Joash, Eliezer, Elioenai, Omri, Jeremoth, Abijah, Anathoth and Alemeth. All these were the sons of
Beker. ⁹Their genealogical record listed the heads of
families and 20,200 fighting men.
¹⁰The son of Jediael:

Bilhan.

The sons of Bilhan:

Jeush, Benjamin, Ehud, Kenaanah, Zethan, Tarshish and
Ahishahar. ¹¹All these sons of Jediael were heads of families. There were 17,200 fighting men ready to go out
to war.
¹²The Shuppites and Huppites were the descendants of Ir,
and the Hushites the descendants of Aher.

¹³ The sons of Naphtali:

Jahziel, Guni, Jezer and Shillem—the descendants of Bilhah.

¹⁴ The descendants of Manasseh:

Asriel was his descendant through his Aramean concubine. She gave birth to Makir the father of Gilead. ¹⁵Makir took a wife from among the Huppites and Shuppites. His sister's name was Maacah.

Another descendant was named Zelophehad, who had only daughters.

¹⁶Makir's wife Maacah gave birth to a son and named him Peresh. His brother was named Sheresh, and his sons were Ulam and Rakem.

¹⁷ The son of Ulam:

Bedan.

These were the sons of Gilead son of Makir, the son of Manasseh. ¹⁸His sister Hammoleketh gave birth to Ishhod, Abiezer and Mahlah.

¹⁹ The sons of Shemida were:

Ahian, Shechem, Likhi and Aniam.

²⁰ The descendants of Ephraim:

Shuthelah, Bered his son,
Tahath his son, Eleadah his son,
Tahath his son, ²¹Zabad his son
and Shuthelah his son.

Ezer and Elead were killed by the native-born men of Gath, when they went down to seize their livestock. ²²Their father Ephraim mourned for them many days, and his relatives came to comfort him. ²³Then he lay with his wife again, and she became pregnant and gave birth to a son. He named him Beriah, because there had been misfortune in his family. ²⁴His daughter was Sheerah, who built Lower and Upper Beth Horon as well as Uzzen Sheerah.

²⁵ Rephah was his son, Resheph his son,
Telah his son, Tahan his son,
²⁶ Ladan his son, Ammihud his son,
Elishama his son, ²⁷Nun his son
and Joshua his son.

²⁸ Their lands and settlements included Bethel and its surrounding villages, Naaran to the east, Gezer and its villages to

the west, and Shechem and its villages all the way to Ayyah and its villages. ²⁹Along the borders of Manasseh were Beth Shan, Taanach, Megiddo and Dor, together with their villages. The descendants of Joseph son of Israel lived in these towns.

³⁰The sons of Asher:

Imnah, Ishvah, Ishvi and Beriah. Their sister was Serah.

³¹The sons of Beriah:

Heber and Malkiel, who was the father of Birzaith.

³²Heber was the father of Japhlet, Shomer and Hotham and of their sister Shua.

³³The sons of Japhlet:

Pasach, Bimhal and Ashvath.

These were Japhlet's sons.

³⁴The sons of Shomer:

Ahi, Rohgah, Hubbah and Aram.

³⁵The sons of his brother Helem:

Zophah, Imna, Shelesh and Amal.

³⁶The sons of Zophah:

Suah, Harnepher, Shual, Beri, Imrah, ³⁷Bezer, Hod, Shamma, Shilshah, Ithran and Beera.

³⁸The sons of Jether:

Jephunneh, Pispah and Ara.

³⁹The sons of Ulla:

Arah, Hanniel and Rizia.

⁴⁰All these were descendants of Asher—heads of families, choice men, brave warriors and outstanding leaders. The number of men ready for battle, as listed in their genealogy, was 26,000.

THIS SECTION OF the Chronicler's genealogical prologue contains the final installment of Hebrew tribal lists, broadly classified as northern and in certain cases Transjordan tribes. This treatment of six Israelite tribes is remarkably brief (forty verses) when compared to the preceding register of Levites (eighty-one verses). Yet the listing is in keeping with the Chronicler's overall purpose in the retelling of Israelite history. The inclusion of both the prominent and obscure northern Hebrew tribes is necessary for presenting a complete historical overview of Israel to the restoration community.

The genealogical record of the northern tribes is also important given the Chronicler's theological emphasis on "all Israel," perhaps on the basis of

Ezekiel's prophecy of the two sticks (representing Israel and Judah) being rejoined as one stick after the Exile (Ezek. 37:15–23). Moreover, the accounts of the northern tribes provide the Chronicler with an appropriate entree to his primary theme, kingship in Israel. The introduction of the tribe of Benjamin permits the logical expansion of the tribal genealogy in chapter 8 and naturally leads into the family of Saul, the first king of Israel.

Portions of the northern tribe genealogies have parallels in Genesis 46 and Numbers 26. The Chronicler's genealogies, however, include names omitted in the other biblical accounts and at times demonstrate the same fluidity characteristic of Old Testament genealogical records in general (e.g., the Chronicler lists three sons of Benjamin [7:6] while Gen. 46:21 counts ten and Num. 26:38–39 records five). These variations suggest the Chronicler has access to other (unknown) sources, probably tribal census reports and clan genealogies. The military overtone of his genealogies, including muster rolls with tallies (e.g., 1 Chron. 7:2, 5, 7), prompts many scholars to connect the records with King David's ill-fated military census (2 Sam. 24; cf. 1 Chron. 21) or even his conscripting of troops at Hebron (cf. 1 Chron. 12:23–37).[1]

There is an accounting problem in enumerating the Chronicler's ideal twelve tribes. Both Dan and Zebulun are listed as sons of Israel (or Jacob) in 2:1 but are omitted in listing of the northern tribes here. Instead, the so-called half-tribes or Joseph tribes of Manasseh (5:23–26; 7:14–19) and Ephraim (7:20–29) round out the ideal twelve tribes. Interestingly, geographical information is preserved only for the Joseph tribes. Presumably for the Chronicler the province of postexilic Judah is idealized both nationally as the representation of the twelve tribes of Israel and geographically as the land of the covenant promise stretching from "the river of Egypt to the great river, the Euphrates" (Gen. 15:18).

As in the case with the rejoining of the sticks of Israel and Judah into a single stick, the Chronicler finds support for his projection of idealized boundaries upon the restoration community in the visions of Ezekiel, who predicted as much for regathered Israel (Ezek. 47:15–20). The Chronicler rightly recognizes that the disparity between the prophetic ideal and contemporary reality in postexilic Judah is inconsequential for the God who swore to make good on his covenant promises (Ezek. 47:14).

Issachar (7:1–5)

ISSACHAR WAS THE ninth son of Jacob, the fifth son born to him by Leah (Gen. 30:17). His name means "hired workman," and Jacob's deathbed blessing of Issachar plays on that meaning in predicting that Issachar's descendants

---

1. Selman, *1 Chronicles*, 114.

will toil in forced labor gangs (Gen. 49:15). Issachar is often paired with Zebulun in lists of the Israelite tribes (e.g., Deut. 33:18–19). The tribe of Zebulun is absent from this tribal register, but the list does agree with the ordering of the earlier reference to the twelve sons of Israel (1 Chron. 2:1).[2] Williamson detects no particular significance in the sequence of tribal names in this passage, apart from the fact the list simply reflects the order of the Chronicler's source.[3]

The genealogy of Issachar is both descending (i.e., parent to child) and segmented (i.e., it demonstrates breadth in listing a single generation of descendants as well as depth in citing successive generations from a common ancestor). The muster tallies (7:2, 4, 5) suggest the record originally belonged to a military census from the time of David (see 7:3).

The names of Issachar's four sons match those lists found in Genesis 46:13 and Numbers 26:23–24. This genealogy consists of four sections, each introduced by the phrase "the son(s) of": the constituent families of the tribe (7:1), the sons of Tola (7:2), the sons of Uzzi (7:3–4), and other tribal members (7:5).[4] Most of the Chronicler's record of Issachar has no parallel elsewhere in the Old Testament, although Tola is named as a judge at the time of Abimelech (Judg. 10:1). This Tola is identified as the son of Puah and the grandson of Dodo, several generations removed from Issachar and his four sons. Some speculate that Michael the father of Omri (1 Chron. 27:18) could be the Michael the son of Izrahiah (7:3). There seems to be general agreement that the reference to David (7:2) indicates that the purpose of the tribal lists is to accent the role of King David in uniting the tribes of Israel.

That the tribal lists of Issachar are incomplete is attested simply by checking the math of the muster tallies, since the total cited (87,000 in 7:5) is greater than the sum of the tallies of 7:2, 4 (58,600). The sheer size of the muster tallies has led some scholars to understand the Hebrew word *ʾelep* as "captain" or "chief" rather than "1,000" (thus, e.g., understanding the census of Tola as "22 chiefs, 600 fighting men").[5] One must also understand the number "five" (7:3) to include Izrahiah and his four sons or one must read "five sons of Uzzi" by deleting the phrase "sons of" before the name Izrahiah (as a scribal error of dittography). These and other textual and interpretive problems aside, Issachar was the largest tribal unit recorded in ancient Israel apart from Judah (cf. 2 Sam. 24:9; 1 Chron. 21:5). This accounts for the inclusion of the explanatory reference to the many wives and children in the clan of Izrahiah (7:4).

---

2. Braun, *1 Chronicles*, 103.

3. Williamson, *1 and 2 Chronicles*, 76.

4. On the *lamed* of introduction (*welibne*), see GKC § 143e.

5. E.g., Payne, "1, 2 Chronicles," 4:357–58. Note also the reference to "200 chiefs" of Issachar in 12:32.

Benjamin (7:6–12)

BENJAMIN WAS THE youngest son of Jacob and the second son born to Rachel, who died giving birth to him (Gen. 35:19, 24). The name Benjamin was given to the boy by his father and means literally "son of the right hand." But Rachel, with her dying breath, named the child Ben-Oni ("son of my sorrow," 35:18).

The genealogy of Benjamin lacks the characteristic introductory phrase "the sons of," restored as an error of haplography in the ancient versions and certain English versions (e.g., NIV, NRSV). The listing also seems out of place since the genealogy of Benjamin resumes in chapter 8 after the register of the remaining northern tribes. Finally, there is little correspondence between the names of the Chronicler's record and those of Genesis 46:21 and Numbers 26:38–41 (only the name Bela is common to all three sources).[6] It does seem likely that the names Shuppim and Huppim in 1 Chronicles 7:12 are the Muppim and Huppim in Genesis 46:21 and the Shephupham and Hupham in Numbers 26:39. This combination of unusual features connected with the personal names has led some scholars to conjecture that the section has suffered textual corruption either through scribal error or editorial rearrangement.[7]

Rather than suppose scribal errors have corrupted the text, it may well be that the Chronicler's variation is deliberate for the sake of emphasizing the entry in the list of northern tribes. The tribe of Benjamin was a transitional group in terms of Israelite geography, buffering Judah in the south and the rest of the tribes to the north. The insertion of the Benjamite genealogy at this juncture serves to introduce the more extensive family tree of Benjamin that follows in chapter 8. The highlighting of Benjamin calls to mind the fact that this tribe was also the transitional tribe of Hebrew kingship. King Saul hailed from Benjamin, and the Chronicler uses his genealogy and royal history as a preface to the history of the Davidic dynasty.

No doubt the muster roll of Benjamin is a continuation of the military census serving as the Chronicler's source of information. Selman aptly notes that this census may have been based on David's Hebron assembly (12:23–37). Most Benjamites, however, were still loyal to the house of Saul after David's accession (cf. 12:29), thus explaining the diminished number of Benjamite clans listed here as compared with earlier texts.[8]

---

6. See the helpful chart in Braun, *1 Chronicles*, 108.
7. E.g., Braun (*1 Chronicles*, 106, 109) restores the tribe of Dan in the list by emending 7:12.
8. Selman, *1 Chronicles*, 114–15.

Naphtali (7:13)

BILHAH WAS ONE of Jacob's concubines and the mother of Naphtali (Gen. 46:24–25). The four clans of Naphtali match the records of Genesis 49:24 and Numbers 26:48–49 (with the exception of Shallum for Shillem in the Chronicler's listing). The brevity of the genealogy is noteworthy, prompting Williamson to speculate on the possibility of "extensive scribal loss" in the source(s) the Chronicler is relying on.[9] This may also account for the omission of the genealogies of Dan and Zebulun in the tribal records of Chronicles.

Manasseh (7:14–19)

MANASSEH AND EPHRAIM were the sons of Joseph by his Egyptian wife, Asenath (Gen. 41:50–51). Manasseh and Ephraim are the so-called half-tribes or Joseph tribes of Israel. First Chronicles preserves separate genealogies for the Transjordan clans of Manasseh (5:23–26) and the western clans of Manasseh (7:14–19). This section of the tribal genealogy is in disarray, seemingly at variance with itself internally and externally with other Old Testament sources. Unlike the other tribal records in this passage, the registers of descendants from Manasseh and Ephraim are not connected with the military census of David.

It is also important to recognize that the genealogy of Manasseh may have been separated from its original location for theological purposes (since it appears that 7:14–19 served as an introduction to 5:23–26).[10] While not accounting for all the problems in harmonizing the available biblical data, it is helpful to remember that the Chronicler has selected and arranged genealogical materials from a number of ancient sources for theological purposes related to the postexilic restoration of Judah.

The Chronicler evidently knows the census list of Numbers 26:29–33 and the tribal allotment register of Joshua 17:1–13. Even these sources, however, do not permit a complete reconstruction of Manasseh's genealogy. Certain of the names of Manasseh's descendants are common to the records of Numbers and Joshua (e.g., Makir, Gilead, Zelophehad). Many others are unknown to the other biblical genealogies (e.g., Maacah, Peresh, Sheresh, Ulam). Rather than assuming sloppy work by the ancient scribes in this section, it seems more prudent to recognize that the Chronicler's genealogy is based in part on a reliable source independent of known Old Testament sources. Recent biblical scholarship continues to verify the integrity of the

---

9. Williamson, *1 and 2 Chronicles*, 78.
10. Ibid., 79.

Chronicler's work as a historian. There is no reason why that same charity should not apply to his genealogies.[11]

The Chronicler has included genealogical records of the Joseph tribes primarily in order to round out the ideal number of the twelve tribes. The appeal to the historical tribal associations of the nation of Israel is an important argument in his agenda to cast the restoration of Judah as an "all Israel" event. By subtly calling attention to the territory of Manasseh through the separation of the genealogy into the Transjordan and Western Manasseh clans, the Chronicler extends the "ideal" of all Israel to the tribal boundaries established by priestly allotment in the land of covenant promise (cf. Josh. 17).[12]

One of the historical sidebars of this section is the reference to Asriel's Aramean mother (Manasseh's unnamed concubine, 7:14). Such mixed marriages were outlawed as part of the social and religious reforms initiated by Ezra and Nehemiah (Neh. 13:3, 23–30). In contrast to Rudolph's suggestion that the reference to Manasseh's Aramean concubine was designed to discredit the descendants of Manasseh,[13] this seems to be yet another example of the Chronicler's openness to the nations in affirming God's sovereignty in fulfilling the "blessings" clause of the Abrahamic covenant (Gen. 12:3).

Ephraim (7:20–29)

THE SEQUENTIAL TREATMENT of the two Joseph tribes is logical, fitting the biblical pattern of treating Ephraim and Manasseh as a related sociopolitical entity (cf. Deut. 34:2). Often Ephraim is placed first when paired with Manasseh because of Jacob's blessing of Ephraim prior to Manasseh (over the protest of Joseph), though Manasseh was the older of the brothers (Gen. 48:20). The Chronicler's order of Manasseh followed by Ephraim is explained on the basis of geographical location of the northern tribes, since

---

11. Some of the internal confusion of Manasseh's genealogy may be clarified by recognizing words like "sister" (7:15, 18 NIV) are better understood less technically as simply "relative" in this context (so Selman, *1 Chronicles*, 116). For a more comprehensive analysis see D. Edelman, "The Manassite Genealogy in 1 Chronicles 7:14–19," *CBQ* 53 (1991): 179–201. Seven of the thirteen clans of the tribe of Manasseh are attested in the Samaria ostraca, extrabiblical commodities receipts recorded on potsherds dating to the eighth century B.C. (see further Klaas A. D. Smelik, *Writings from Ancient Israel* [Louisville: Westminster John Knox, 1991], 55–62).

12. The emphasis on tribal descent cannot be understood in absolute terms, as mingling of the tribes through intermarriage occurred through the passing of time. For example, the Judahite clan of Hezron married into the Manassite clan of Makir (1 Chron. 7:14; cf. 2:21). Makir also took a wife from one of the clans of Benjamin (cf. 1 Chron. 7:7, 12, 15–16). See further Merrill, *1, 2 Chronicles*, 36.

13. See W. Rudolph, *Chronikbücher* (HAT; Tübingen: J. C. B. Mohr, 1955), 64.

the genealogy of Western Manasseh (7:14–19) connects more naturally with the list of Transjordan clans of Manasseh recorded earlier (5:23–26). The section combines three literary units: the genealogy of Ephraim through Joshua (7:20–21a, 25–27), interrupted by a historical footnote concerning Ezer and Elead (7:21b–24), and capped by a name list of settlements occupied by the tribe of Ephraim (7:28–29).

The Chronicler's genealogy of Ephraim corresponds to the tribal list of Numbers 26:35–36 only in the name and position of Shuthelah. The vertical genealogy is a feature unique to the Chronicler (i.e., "A, his son B, his son C, etc."; cf. the Kohathite genealogies, 6:22–28, 33–38). The genealogy concludes with Joshua son of Nun, descendant of Ephraim and successor of Moses (7:27; cf. Deut. 34:9). The reference to Joshua is in keeping with the Chronicler's emphasis on the Israelite conquest and occupation of the land of covenant promise. The historical anecdote sandwiched between the two halves of the genealogy seems to serve the same purpose. The reference to Gath (1 Chron. 7:21) is probably the Gittaim mentioned in 2 Samuel 4:3, and the account probably dates to the Israelite settlement in Canaan.[14] The Ephraim in this narrative must be a later descendant of the clan patriarch Ephraim (7:20).

The story of Ezer and Elead is unique to Chronicles. Commentators are quick to note that the historical interlude serves etiological purposes, explaining the name Beriah (or "misfortune," 7:23 [similar to the Jabez story, 4:9–10]) and the place name Uzzen Sheerah (7:24). The Chronicler, however, inserts the account as an example of temporary loss and setback overcome providentially by human initiative. What better way to remind his audience that the setback of the Exile was only temporary? The addendum to the historical footnote celebrating Sheerah as the builder of Beth Horon is remarkable for the prominence accorded a woman, but not out of character for the Chronicler. This story too, emphasizing the accomplishments of an individual, serves to encourage each member of the postexilic community to become involved in restoring Israel to its former glory.

The phrase "the descendants of Joseph" (7:29) indicates that the name list of settlements includes geographical information pertinent to both Manasseh and Ephraim. This recital of the towns and villages occupied by the Joseph tribes roughly corresponds to Joshua 16–17. It is possible the cities represented the southern and northern limits of the combined territories of Manasseh and Ephraim.

---

14. The phrase "native-born men of Gath" (7:21) simply identifies the assailants as members of the indigenous population. The use of the verb "went down" is well chosen because the Ephraimites descended from the hills to the lowlands to raid cattle (so Japhet, *I and II Chronicles*, 181).

Specifically, Bethel (7:28) was conquered by the Joseph tribes (Judg. 1:22) but was assigned to Benjamin as a border city (Josh. 18:22). The occupation of Gezer (1 Chron. 7:28) suggests the time of the united monarchy and marks the eventual success of the Israelites in wresting real estate from the Canaanites (cf. Josh. 16:10). The political control of Shechem (1 Chron. 7:28) shifted according to historical period. Shechem lay within the territory of Manasseh (Josh. 17:7), but it may have been one of those cities in Manasseh set aside as a haven for Ephraimites (cf. Josh. 16:9). The location of Ayyah (1 Chron. 7:28) is unknown.

The Ephraimite cities of Beth Shan, Taanach, Megiddo, and Dor were properly located in the territories of Issachar and Asher. According to Joshua 17:11–13, these cities remained bastions of Canaanite influence. Japhet contends the Chronicler includes the Joseph-tribes settlement report for the sake of harmonizing Israelite historical geography with the list of Levitical cities located in the territories of Manasseh and Ephraim (cf. 6:67, 71).[15] It seems equally important to the Chronicler that the earlier records of the incomplete conquest and occupation of Canaan under Joshua be brought to satisfactory closure.

Asher (7:30–40)

ASHER WAS THE son of Zilpah, the handmaid of Leah (Gen. 46:18). The genealogy apparently combines the first- and second-generation clan names from several earlier sources, including Genesis 46:17–18 (cf. Num. 26:44–46, which names only three sons of Asher), an unknown source that cites additional descendants of Asher, and the muster roll of Asher from the military census of King David (1 Chron. 7:40). Structurally, the genealogy of Asher mirrors the opening register of Issachar, tracing only one clan in the segmented genealogy (Beriah, 7:31).

As in 2:1–2. Asher concludes the tribal list. Asher is cited after Naphtali and Gad in that passage, but here Asher is preceded by the tribes of Manasseh and Ephraim. The tribe of Asher settled the region of western Galilee, so it is possible the military census that served as the primary source for the Chronicler catalogued the tribes on the basis of geographical location moving from east to west. The attrition in the muster roll to 26,000 (7:40) from 41,500 (Num. 1:40–41) and 53,400 (26:47) testifies to the misfortunes experienced by this tribe.

---

15. Japhet, *I and II Chronicles*, 185.

THE NATURE OF the message of the genealogical prologue in Chronicles is emotional as much as it is theological. The Chronicler wants to bolster morale and encourage participatory ownership of the postexilic restoration effort by appealing to the collective identity of Israel embodied in the names filling the genealogical rolls. The problem for him is twofold. (1) How does one motivate the individual to become proactive in the initiatives to restore Judah and Jerusalem, given the emphasis on corporate or national identity in ancient Israel? (2) Once the individual has been spurred into action, how does one ensure that the newly found imagination and energy will be applied to community as well as to self-interests?

This is the challenge facing the Chronicler: motivating the individual while maintaining the value of corporate responsibility in the covenant community. He chooses to do that in a couple of ways in the genealogical prologue, effectively using the powerful medium of personal story to engage and elicit a response from his audience. One cannot help but wonder if the Chronicler's blending of genealogy and report or story is not the literary precursor of the catalog of "faithful witnesses" recorded in the book of Hebrews 11.

One type of story inserted strategically throughout the genealogies by the Chronicler is known in terms of literary form as the *anecdote* or the *exploit report*. This historical sidelight records a significant event or experience in the life of a person listed in the genealogy.[16] A striking example of the *anecdote* is the story of Jabez, who changes the course of his own destiny as a result of his faithful prayers to God (4:9–10). The *exploit report* records a deed or event in the life of one person that has ramifications for the entire family or clan, whether for their welfare or hurt. For example, the adventures of the brave but idolatrous warriors of Manasseh resulted in exile in Assyria for the members of that Joseph tribe (5:24–26). By the same token, the Gadite warriors extended the tribal boundaries and increased the agricultural prosperity of the people because they trusted in God (5:20–22).

This section of the Chronicler's genealogical prologue offers examples of both the anecdote and the exploit report. In each case the stories feature women, and the parallel accounts focus attention on the entwined histories of the Joseph tribes of Manasseh and Ephraim. (1) The first story is little more than a one line allusion to an episode of the post-Exodus desert wanderings of Israel (7:15b; cf. Num. 27:1–11). The mere fact that Zelophehad's name appears in the Chronicler's genealogy of Manasseh centuries later

---

16. Cf. De Vries, *1 and 2 Chronicles*, 427, 430.

is testimony to the precedent-setting efforts of his enterprising daughters. Not only did they secure an inheritance of property in the land of covenant promise for the family, but also their bold and counterculture request was responsible for preserving the name of sonless Zelophehad for posterity (cf. Num. 27:4). (1) The story of Sheerah, the half-tribe's counterpart of Zelophehad's daughters, is no less striking as we learn she was the founder of three Ephraimite cities (7:24).

We have already noted an openness on the part of the Chronicler to relationships between Israel and other nations (cf. 4:18). Now we uncover an emphasis on precedent-setting initiatives by women in the genealogical prologue that suggests the Chronicler is seeking to encourage women to become active in the restoration of postexilic Jerusalem. Allen has aptly reflected that "we would do well to ponder and emulate" such wideness of heart and openness of mind.[17]

 INCLUSIVISM. No doubt there are those among the Chronicler's audience who question the value of reciting the names and stories rehearsing the departed glory and checkered history of the Israelite tribes. Other biblical texts from the postexilic period indicate the Chronicler faced a problem similar to that of our own postmodern era, an incredulity toward any metanarrative.[18] That is, society validates (even celebrates) the experience of the individual but voids the notion that any universal concept or common story exists in which that corporate experience might be framed and given meaning or coherence.

Fundamentally, the problem is the same for fallen people in fallen cultures in any century. How does a society establish a shared vision that affirms individual expression but retains group solidarity? What sociological mechanism encourages a meaningful and productive relationship between the "one" and the "many" in a group or social unit? Historically, societies have relied on some form of "law" to regulate individual behavior and appealed to some type of "authority figure" (e.g., political and/or religious) to stabilize and direct the individuals confederated into a group.[19]

---

17. Allen, *1, 2 Chronicles*, 71.
18. E.g., "What did we gain by carrying out his requirements?" Mal. 3:14; cf. Middleton and Walsh, *Truth Is Stranger Than It Used to Be*, 70–81; see also the Contemporary Significance section of 2:3–3:24.
19. On the "law of human nature," see C. S. Lewis, *Mere Christianity* (New York: Macmillan, 1952), esp. 17–30.

The genealogical prologue of the Chronicler suggests an Old Testament principle broad enough to encompass the individual (whether Hebrew or non-Hebrew, man or woman, royal or peasant) and sufficiently compelling in its ideology to unify diverse people groups. For the Chronicler the only viable metanarrative or universal story for Israel is the Abrahamic covenant (Gen. 12:1–3; cf. 1 Chron. 1:28). This term *covenant* is central to the discussion of metanarrative or universal story. The purpose of law is to regulate existing relationships in a society by orderly means (i.e., the application of its monopoly of force). By contrast, the purpose of covenant is "to create new relationships in accordance with stipulations given in advance" (e.g., marriage).[20]

Briefly stated, God's covenant with Abram (later renamed Abraham) and Sarai (later renamed Sarah) is a story of the relationship between the one and the many in both vertical (theological) and horizontal (sociological) dimensions. This treaty of grant established a new relationship between God and the "parents" of the nation of Israel, so much so that Abraham has the title "friend of God" elsewhere in Scripture (cf. 2 Chron. 20:7; Isa. 41:8; James 2:23). The Abrahamic covenant established a new relationship with all humanity as well, seen in the attendant blessing of the nations (Gen. 12:3). The Chronicler's repeated references to non-Hebrew individuals in the genealogical prologue emphasizes this fact.

One fundamental fallacy of postmodernity is the denial of a metanarrative or universal story expansive enough to include all the "islands" of human knowledge and experience.[21] Postmodernism's skepticism toward a metanarrative of any sort must ignore, however, a universal reality printed daily in every newspaper and broadcast each evening in news programs around the world—the evil bent of the human heart. The question is not whether a metanarrative capable of explaining and unifying human experience exists. Rather, the question is whether there is a universal story capable of overcoming the metanarrative of what the Bible describes as the fall of humanity, the story of "paradise lost" (cf. Gen. 3). The Chronicler would quickly answer, "Of course! Surely you know the story of Abraham and Sarah!"

The contemporary Christian reader of the Bible, however, may not be impressed with the Chronicler's answer. After all, Abraham and Sarah belonged to the old covenant, and the new covenant has been established in Jesus Christ for some twenty centuries now. Wilcock's reminder concerning the application of the message of Chronicles to the life of the church

---

20. George E. Mendenhall, *The Tenth Generation* (Baltimore: Johns Hopkins Univ. Press, 1973), 200.

21. On "metanarrative" in postmodernism see Middleton and Walsh, *Truth Is Stranger Than It Used to Be*, 69–71.

proves helpful in our discussion: "In changing circumstances, seek the unchanging principles."[22]

The changing circumstances in terms of Old Testament history include Israel's relationship to the surrounding nations, given the ever-shifting political landscape of the ancient Near East. The constant amid the rise and fall of Israel's political fortunes is God's promise to Abraham and Sarah to build a great nation through them and to bless all nations through that socioreligious entity (Gen. 12:1–3). Isaiah the prophet brings even greater definition to the Abrahamic covenant with his pronouncements that Israel is God's instrument for bringing "light to the nations" and "salvation to the ends of the earth" (cf. Isa. 42:1–4; 45:22; 51:4–5). Stated differently, God's election of Israel is for the sake of "inclusion," choosing one nation to bless all nations and to establish them among God's people (cf. Jer. 12:15–16).[23]

The new covenant echoes this message of "good news" for all people, seen in Simeon's confession of Jesus as "a light for revelation to the Gentiles" (Luke 2:24) and in the sermons of the John the Baptist proclaiming salvation for all humankind (Luke 3:6). Likewise, the kingdom parables of Jesus illustrate the "inclusiveness" of God's plan of redemption as the "seed" of the gospel is sown throughout the world (Matt. 13:38). Jesus Christ, then, is the mediator of a new covenant (Heb. 9:15), and it is through this covenant that God is reconciling the world to himself (2 Cor. 5:19), thus creating that new relationship and establishing that new metanarrative for all of human history: the story of "paradise regained."

The inclusive nature of the covenants, old and new, permits the application of an unchanging biblical principle to changing historical and cultural circumstances—the principle of inclusion itself! The theme of including the Gentiles in the covenant promises to Israel encases the message of the entire Bible, much like an envelope or even bookends. The opening chapters of Genesis introduces the table of nations (Gen. 10) and God's promise to bless all nations (12:1–3), and the concluding book of the Bible depicts the nations surrounding the throne of God in worship (Rev. 5:9–10; 7:9–10; etc.).

It is not enough, however, to merely recognize such inclusivism as one of the themes that unifies the two covenants of our one Bible. The greater questions of application at both the macro-level and the micro-level remain: What does the church do with its knowledge of this theme of inclusion in

---

22. Wilcock, *The Message of Chronicles*, 38.

23. Cf. Christopher J. H. Wright, *Knowing Jesus Through the Old Testament* (Downers Grove, Ill.: InterVarsity Press, 1992), 46–54; see further Aida B. Spencer and William D. Spencer, *The Global God* (Grand Rapids: Baker, 1998); Walter C. Kaiser, *Mission in the Old Testament: Israel As a Light to the Nations* (Grand Rapids: Baker, 2000).

biblical theology? How does the individual Christian develop and implement a practical theology of inclusion in daily life?

At the macro-level, it seems that the church established on the confession that Jesus is the Christ simply needs to reaffirm those "first principles" that have defined its history:

- a capacity for worship that transcends all human convention, facilitating a corporate experience that enables all believers to encounter the holiness and mystery of the Godhead and thereby empowering them for acts of service to a needy world[24]
- a fervent heart for evangelism, recalling on a regular basis the biblical teaching that the good news of God's plan of redemption is for all people (2 Peter 3:9) because God does not delight in the death of any wicked person (Ezek. 18:23, 32)
- a compassionate spirit that promotes reconciliation through Christ, who reconciles all things to himself (Col. 1:20) and brings harmony and healing to all those relationships in disrepair, whether racial, intergenerational, or familial (2 Cor. 5:18–20; cf. Luke 1:17)
- a vision for ministry that unleashes all the gifts of the Holy Spirit so that the entire body of Christ might be built up (Eph. 4:12)[25]
- a community of fellowship rooted in mutual love (John 13:34–35), constantly seeking the common ground of "one hope ... one Lord, one faith" (Eph. 4:4–5)

---

24. On the "worship response" of service, see Robert E. Webber, *Common Roots* (Grand Rapids: Zondervan, 1978), 101–2; Andrew E. Hill, *Enter His Courts with Praise!* 157.

25. There is a sad twist of irony in the application of the Chronicler's principle of ethnic and racial inclusivism to contemporary evangelical settings. Rather than promoting the principle of unity and inclusion in the body life of the church, disagreement over the place of certain of the *charismata* of the Holy Spirit in the life of the church continues to foster attitudes of exclusivism that lead to division and schism among Christians. Even more sardonic is the so-called "inclusive language debate" as it relates to the practice of Bible translation (but one item in the larger category of "gender issues" confronting popular culture in North America and hence the church). Once again, "well-meaning" Christians in both camps (i.e., the egalitarians and the complementarians) have managed to controvert the biblical principles of unity and inclusion into partisan flag-waving and sectarian sparring (see further, D. A. Carson, *The Inclusive Language Debate* [Grand Rapids: Baker, 1998]). Meanwhile, a generation of young people thoroughly immersed in postmodernism (the millennial generation, 1982–2000) continues its drift after the siren of popular culture as the evangelical church minds (or mines?) its pronouns (see further Leslie Newbigin, *The Gospel in a Pluralist Society* [Grand Rapids: Eerdmans, 1989], as well as the "redemptive hermeneutic'" of William J. Webb, *Slaves, Women, and Homosexuals: Exploring the Hermeneutic of Cultural Analysis* [Downers Grove, Ill.: InterVarsity Press, 2001]).

At the micro-level, each of us can learn a lesson from the Chronicler's "wideness of heart and openness of mind." Jesus taught that Christians are known by their love for each other (John 13:34–35) and their tendency to do acts of kindness for those who cannot repay in like manner (Luke 14:12–14). The Chronicler would approve of such Christian "charity." (I choose the term *charity* deliberately, known to us from the KJV, esp. 1 Cor. 13:13.) It signifies love in action for the benefit of others, not some amorphous and selfish feeling or gratifying personal experience that now passes for "love" in our culture.

The Chronicler would approve of the notion of "Christian charity" because he has already grasped the Old Testament principles on which the theology of Christian charity rests. (1) The Chronicler understands that with God there is no partiality or respect of persons since all human beings are created in his image (2 Chron. 19:7; cf. Deut. 1:17; 10:17). Since the charge to Israel was to be holy even as God is holy (Lev. 11:44), it is only natural that the Chronicler would apply this precept to human relationships. The New Testament echoes this sentiment about God who "does not show favoritism but accepts [people] from every nation who fear him and do what is right" (Acts 10:34–35). Likewise, Christians are not to show favoritism (or discrimination) when dealing with others in any venue (James 2:1; cf. Eph. 6:9; Col. 3:25).

(2) The Chronicler is apparently a subscriber to the "good neighbor policy" found in the Mosaic law: "Love your neighbor as yourself" (Lev. 19:18). Again, the New Testament affirms this Old Testament principle. In fact, Jesus extends the coverage of the "good neighbor policy" to include enemies, persecutors, and non-Jews as well (Matt. 5:43–44). There is even a "rider" attached to the policy in the form of a parable that extends coverage to people like Samaritans, indeed, anyone in need (Luke 10:25–37). The apostle Paul went so far as to instruct Christians to "consider others better than yourselves" (Phil. 2:3; cf. Rom. 12:3).

The prophet Micah declared that God requires the faithful to act justly and to love mercy (as the outcome of walking humbly with God, Mic. 6:8). For the prophet Isaiah specific acts of justice and mercy include encouraging the oppressed and pleading the cases of orphans and widows (Isa. 1:17). The New Testament offers similar instruction, emphasizing simple deeds like the provision of food and clothing for those in need (Matt. 10:42; James 2:14–17). Practically speaking, the Chronicler's wideness of heart and openness of mind demonstrates itself in deeds of social service and social action as exemplified in the book of Amos (see Fig 6 on the following page).

The key to proper development of Christian social concern is sound biblical doctrine, especially a doctrine of God that recognizes him as the Creator

Social Service	Social Action
Relieve Human need (5:12)	Remove the causes of human need (8:4–6)
Philanthropic activity (4:5; 6:4–7)	Political and economic activity (5:10–11, 15)
Ministering to individuals/ families (4:1; 5:6–7)	Transforming the structures of society (4:4–5; 7:7–9)
Works of mercy (4:1; 6:4–7)	Quest for justice (2:6–8; 5:7, 24; 6:12)

Fig. 6. Social Concern in Amos's Teaching[26]

and sustainer of creation, deliverer of his people, merciful God of all nations, and a God who hates evil and loves justice because he is concerned for the whole of humankind. It includes a doctrine of humanity that understands that all persons are God's creatures and that the reality of cause and effect in human social experience is due to sin. But as one values human beings created in the image of God, the desire to serve them increases.

Although the Chronicler would agree that sound doctrine informs our sense of Christian "charity," I suspect he would still challenge us, Levitical preacher that he is, to personalize our theology of inclusiveness by looking after "orphans and widows in their distress" (i.e., attending to the socially disadvantaged and oppressed among all people groups; cf. James 1:27). I can imagine his joy among the assembly of the righteous from every nation, tribe, people, and language before God's throne—knowing that the gender and ethnic diversity sprinkled through his genealogies of ancient Israel are but a portent of what God will do among the nations through the gospel of Jesus Christ (cf. Rev. 7:9)!

---

26. Andrew E. Hill and John H. Walton, *A Survey of the Old Testament*, 2d ed. (Grand Rapids: Zondervan, 2000), 485.

1 Chronicles 8:1–9:1a

❧

BENJAMIN WAS THE father of Bela his firstborn,
Ashbel the second son, Aharah the third,
²Nohah the fourth and Rapha the fifth.
³The sons of Bela were:
Addar, Gera, Abihud, ⁴Abishua, Naaman, Ahoah, ⁵Gera,
Shephuphan and Huram.
⁶These were the descendants of Ehud, who were heads of
families of those living in Geba and were deported to
Manahath:
⁷Naaman, Ahijah, and Gera, who deported them and
who was the father of Uzza and Ahihud.
⁸Sons were born to Shaharaim in Moab after he had
divorced his wives Hushim and Baara. ⁹By his wife
Hodesh he had Jobab, Zibia, Mesha, Malcam, ¹⁰Jeuz,
Sakia and Mirmah. These were his sons, heads of families. ¹¹By Hushim he had Abitub and Elpaal.
¹²The sons of Elpaal:
Eber, Misham, Shemed (who built Ono and Lod with its
surrounding villages), ¹³and Beriah and Shema, who
were heads of families of those living in Aijalon and who
drove out the inhabitants of Gath.
¹⁴Ahio, Shashak, Jeremoth, ¹⁵Zebadiah, Arad, Eder,
¹⁶Michael, Ishpah and Joha were the sons of Beriah.
¹⁷Zebadiah, Meshullam, Hizki, Heber, ¹⁸Ishmerai, Izliah and
Jobab were the sons of Elpaal.
¹⁹Jakim, Zicri, Zabdi, ²⁰Elienai, Zillethai, Eliel, ²¹Adaiah,
Beraiah and Shimrath were the sons of Shimei.
²²Ishpan, Eber, Eliel, ²³Abdon, Zicri, Hanan, ²⁴Hananiah,
Elam, Anthothijah, ²⁵Iphdeiah and Penuel were the sons
of Shashak.
²⁶Shamsherai, Shehariah, Athaliah, ²⁷Jaareshiah, Elijah and
Zicri were the sons of Jeroham.
²⁸All these were heads of families, chiefs as listed in their
genealogy, and they lived in Jerusalem.

²⁹Jeiel the father of Gibeon lived in Gibeon.
His wife's name was Maacah, ³⁰and his firstborn son was
Abdon, followed by Zur, Kish, Baal, Ner, Nadab,

³¹Gedor, Ahio, Zeker ³²and Mikloth, who was the father
of Shimeah. They too lived near their relatives in
Jerusalem.

³³Ner was the father of Kish, Kish the father of Saul, and
Saul the father of Jonathan, Malki-Shua, Abinadab and
Esh-Baal.

³⁴The son of Jonathan:
Merib-Baal, who was the father of Micah.

³⁵The sons of Micah:
Pithon, Melech, Tarea and Ahaz.

³⁶Ahaz was the father of Jehoaddah, Jehoaddah was the
father of Alemeth, Azmaveth and Zimri, and Zimri was
the father of Moza. ³⁷Moza was the father of Binea;
Raphah was his son, Eleasah his son and Azel his son.

³⁸Azel had six sons, and these were their names:
Azrikam, Bokeru, Ishmael, Sheariah, Obadiah and
Hanan. All these were the sons of Azel.

³⁹The sons of his brother Eshek:
Ulam his firstborn, Jeush the second son and Eliphelet
the third. ⁴⁰The sons of Ulam were brave warriors who
could handle the bow. They had many sons and grand-
sons—150 in all.

All these were the descendants of Benjamin.

⁹:¹All Israel was listed in the genealogies recorded in the
book of the kings of Israel.

THE GENEALOGY OF the tribe of Benjamin functions as a sequel to the brief listing of Benjamites
found in 7:6–12. It also serves as an introduction
to the genealogy of Saul in 9:35–44. Wilcock has
suggested the expansion of the Benjamite genealogy is due to the fact that
Benjamin was a "royal" tribe, given the anointing of Saul as Israel's first king.[1]
It is true that the focus of Chronicles is the idea of Israel's kingship, whether
located in the tribe of Benjamin or Judah. Selman has countered that the
allocation of additional space in the Chronicler's record for the tribe of Benjamin is more likely an issue of geography, especially the settlement of the
tribe in and around Jerusalem (8:6, 12, 13, 28, 32).[2] Japhet observes that the

1. Wilcock, *The Message of Chronicles*, 44.
2. Selman, *1 Chronicles*, 44–45.

geographical principle governing the genealogical prologue confirms Selman's argument. She depicts the sequence as a circle beginning with Judah (2:3–4:23) that widens to include the peripheral tribes and then returns to the center (Jerusalem, ch. 9) through the tribe of Benjamin (ch. 8).[3]

The tribal territory of Benjamin is important since it represents a portion of the covenant promise made to Abraham about a specific geographical region (Gen. 12:1–3). The very fact that this piece of real estate remains a part of the postexilic province of Judah is testimony to the Chronicler's audience that God has been faithful to his Word.

Beyond that, however, the tribes of Benjamin and Judah essentially formed the southern kingdom of Judah and later the postexilic province of Judah. Selman has recognized a parallel between Judah as the first tribe listed in the genealogical prologue and Benjamin as the last tribe mentioned in that both lists emphasize tribal geography.[4] Not only do these two tribes form the core of the restoration community geographically and numerically, but also they are partners in preserving Israel's social and political identity and maintaining the Hebrew religious tradition.

The Benjamite genealogy is loosely connected to the tribal lists of Genesis 46:21; Numbers 26:38–41; and 1 Chronicles 7:6–12. At least superficially, it appears 1 Chronicles 8 relies on the text in Numbers whereas 1 Chronicles 7:6–12 has affinities to the precursor text in Genesis. We have learned previously that the genealogy of Benjamin in 1 Chronicles 7:6–12 is based on a military census (see comments). The emphasis on the "heads of families" (8:6, 10, 13, 28) in the Benjamite roster here suggests a civil register of some sort, perhaps even related to clan territorial allotments. The divergent materials (e.g., deportation reports, 8:6; battle reports, 8:13) indicate the Chronicler is utilizing a source that is already a compilation of earlier records.

No two Benjamite lists are the same, and only Bela is common to all four rolls. No doubt some of the variation in the lists is due to corruption in textual transmission. In addition, differences may be further accounted for by recognizing that genealogies represent a blend of records from differing historical time periods, prompted by particular documentary impulses.[5]

---

3. Japhet, *I and II Chronicles*, 189.

4. Selman, *1 Chronicles*, 118.

5. It is not within the scope of this commentary series to treat textual problems in any detail. For a discussion of the pertinent issues, see the textual notes in Braun, *1 Chronicles*, and Japhet, *I and II Chronicles*. On the differences between the genealogies of Benjamin found in 7:6–12; 8:28–38; and 9:35–44, Wilcock has aptly commented: "Alert and intelligent people who were prepared to let such 'contradictions' stand as part of a historical record presumably had sound reasons for doing so" (*The Message of Chronicles*, 44).

The genealogy itself divides neatly into two segments: the settlement of Benjamite families (8:1−28) and the genealogy of Saul's family (8:29−40). A more precise structure of the passage is marked by noting the geographical setting for each of the Benjamite clans: the descendants of Benjamin and Ehud in Geba (8:1−7); the descendants of Shaharaim in Moab, Ono, and Lod (8:8−13); the descendants of Ahio and others in Aijalon and Jerusalem (8:14−28); and the ancestors of Saul in Gibeon (8:29−40). Finally, Japhet offers a more detailed outline of the chapter also based on the geographical emphasis of the passage:

Introduction (8:1−2)
Genealogy and episode of the sons of Bela (8:3−7)
Genealogy and episodes of Shaharaim (in Moab, 8:8−11; and west of the Jordan, 8:12−14)
Benjamites living in Jerusalem (8:15−28)
Benjamites living in Gibeon (8:29−32)
Family tree of Ulam (8:33−40).[6]

The genre of the biblical genealogy is classified generally as a "list." Specific literary elements identified in the Benjamite register include tribal rosters (e.g., 8:14−27), episodes from tribal history (e.g., 8: 6b−7a), birth reports (e.g., 8:8−10), settlement reports (e.g., 8:6b, 8a), name lists (characterized by the formula "sons of X," e.g., 8:30−31), ranking formulas (8:1−2), muster rolls (8:38, 39−40a), and family tree (of Ulam tracing lineage back to Saul's family, 8:33−40).[7]

The Families of Bela and Ehud (8:1−7)

THE FOCAL POINT of the genealogy is the clan of Ehud more than the family tree of the tribal patriarch Benjamin. The phrase "heads of families" (8:6, 10, 13, 28) refers to a clan leader (note the additional modifier in v. 28, "chiefs" [*ra³sim*]). Although this register has several names in common with the parallel sources (e.g., Bela, Ashbel, Gera), the introductory verses cannot be harmonized with Genesis 46:21; Numbers 26:38−41; or 1 Chronicles 7:6. Williamson comments that this is not surprising since "the differences will reflect alterations in which clans were prominent at a given period."[8] Although extensive commentary on textual problems lies outside the purpose of this series, the NIV footnote to the name Abihud in 1 Chronicles 8:3 deserves comment. It is indeed possible that "Gera, Abihud" should be read "Gera the

6. Japhet, *I and II Chronicles*, 189−90.
7. On the literary form of the Benjamite genealogy, see De Vries, *1 and 2 Chronicles*, 83−88.
8. Williamson, *1 and 2 Chronicles*, 83.

father of Ehud," thus connecting the Chronicler's genealogy with Ehud the left-handed judge (cf. Judg. 3:15). This would explain the emphasis on the sons of Ehud in the genealogy.[9]

The Ehud clan of Benjamites is associated with Geba (8:6), one of the cities allotted to Benjamin as part of the tribal inheritance of Canaan supervised by Joshua (Josh. 18:24). The city was fortified by King Asa as a border post between Judah and the northern kingdom of Israel (1 Kings 15:22). Later, the city is mentioned as one of the sites having a high place desecrated by King Josiah as part of his religious reforms (2 Kings 23:8). The reference here probably reflects a preexilic time period since the postexilic returnees settled in Micmash (the northern neighbor of Geba, cf. Neh. 11:31). The modern town of Jiba is located about six miles north of Jerusalem.

The deportation (or migration?) of Ehud's sons to Manahath (8:7) cannot be placed historically, given the limited data available. The biblical record suggests tribal migrations as a result of natural calamities (e.g., famine; cf. Ruth 1:1) and expulsions as a result of intertribal and intratribal strife (cf. Judg. 20). Manahath was a Judean village, probably modern-day Mahnah (four miles southwest of Jerusalem). Even less clear is the identity of those heads of families deported, the person or persons responsible for the deportation, and the relationship of Gera (1 Chron. 8:7) to Gera (8:3, 5). The text of 8:7 is difficult to unravel and may have suffered at the hand of copyists. The NIV translation is widely accepted, though other renderings are viable.[10]

The Family of Shaharaim (8:8–13)

THE SETTING FOR the episodes concerning the family of Shaharaim is Moab (8:8). Nothing else is known of Shaharaim apart from the Chronicler's genealogy. Moab was a satellite state under Israelite control during the reigns of David and Solomon (cf. 2 Sam. 8:2). Moab regained its autonomy at the time of King Joram during the divided kingdom period of Israel's history (2 Kings 3:5). Though not the same person, the name Mesha (1 Chron. 8:9) was also the name of the Moabite king who revolted against King Joram of Israel (2 Kings 3:4). The name Malcam (1 Chron. 8:9) is related to the god Molech of the Ammonites (cf. 1 Kings 11:7). The use of these names indicates both their popularity and the acculturation of the Israelites while in Moab. The story of Shaharaim undoubtedly reflects a time of peaceful relations and free movement between the nations of Israel and Moab (as in the story of Ruth) or a time when Moab was controlled by the Israelites.

---

9. Cf. Selman, *1 Chronicles,* 119.

10. Cf. the NRSV, " . . . and Gera, that is, Heglam" (NIV, " . . . and Gera, who deported them"). See further Braun, *1 Chronicles,* 121 n. 7b.

The Benjamite genealogy includes the curious report that sons were born to Shaharaim by a third wife, Hodesh, after he had divorced two other of his wives (8:8). The marital problems precipitating the divorces are not mentioned. This anecdote is in keeping with the Chronicler's style, however, of personalizing the genealogies with sidebars that highlight unusual events or call attention to "marginalized" people (like women and non-Hebrews). One wonders if the report of sons born to Shaharaim after divorcing Hushim and Baara had special application for the Chronicler's audience in light of the divorces enforced by Ezra and Nehemiah as part of their reforms (cf. Ezra 10:11–17). One of the divorced women, Hushim, is given prominence in the register because she was the mother of Elpaal, whose descendants are the focal point of the next section of the genealogy.

The reference to Shemed as the one "who built Ono and Lod" (8:12) should be understood as having rebuilt or perhaps fortified the cities of Ono and Lod. Both Ono and Lod had a long history, known from Egyptian records prior to the Hebrew conquest of Canaan.[11] The two cities were resettled in the postexilic period by descendants of families who had lived there previously (Ezra 2:33; Neh. 7:37), including Benjamites (Neh. 11:35).

There is some question as to how Ono and Lod became cities of Benjamin when they were originally part of the tribal allotment of Dan (i.e., "the area facing Joppa"; Josh. 19:46). As the tribe of Ephraim gained in influence, it took control of the cities of Ono and Lod. Since Benjamin shared a border with Ephraim, it seems likely that the two cities were absorbed by Benjamin and Judah at the division of the monarchy.

The city of Aijalon (8:13) was also originally a part of the tribal allotment given to Dan (Josh. 19:42). The city lay on the border with Ephraim, however, and it seems the tribe of Ephraim controlled Aijalon from early times (cf. Judg. 1:35). Aijalon was strategically located on the most important trade route in the Shephelah (thirteen miles northwest of Jerusalem). King Rehoboam fortified the city as a border post against Philistine aggression (2 Chron. 11:10), but the city was later captured by the Philistines during the reign of King Ahaz (28:18). The settlement of Benjamites in Aijalon may be traced to the time when the city was controlled by Judah during the reign of Rehoboam. The conquest of Gath (1 Chron. 8:13) by the Benjamites cannot be placed historically, given the terseness of the battle report.

The Descendants of Elpaal (8:14–28)

THE RELATIONSHIP BETWEEN the rosters of the families of Shaharaim (8:8–13) and Elpaal (8:14–28) to the genealogies of Bela and Ehud (8:1–7) is

---

11. Thompson, *1, 2 Chronicles*, 100.

unclear. Like Saul's genealogy that follows (8:29—40), the lists probably represent independent sources. Little is known about those individuals included in the genealogy since most of the names occur only here in the Bible. Perhaps geography is an organizing principle in the splicing together of the Benjamite materials since there is a general movement from the periphery of the territory of Benjamin to the city of Jerusalem. Williamson also notes that the genealogy demonstrates movement toward the family of Elpaal, whose descendants lived in Jerusalem (8:28).[12] In each case, emphasis on Jerusalem fits the pattern of the Chronicler's interest in the resettlement and rebuilding of the city of David.

The listing of the family of Shaharaim emphasizes the expansion of tribal boundaries by the Benjamites (8:13). This may have occurred at various times in Israelite history, especially during the reigns of David in the united monarchy and Rehoboam and Josiah during the divided monarchy of Judah. The lack of data prevents any precise dating of the rebuilding of Ono and Lod and the taking of Gath. The listing of the family of Elpaal emphasizes the mingling between the tribes of Benjamin and Judah. According to Myers, the tendency for the mixing of Benjamites and Judahites in the same location arose after the division of the Israelite monarchy.[13] Such a development is not surprising given the commission for both Benjamin and Judah to displace the Jebusites and take the city of Jerusalem, a border city between the two tribes (cf. Josh. 15:63; Judg. 1:21).

The dual themes of tribal expansion and tribal unity are important to the Chronicler's theology of hope for postexilic Judah. In fact, he illustrates that the city of Jerusalem belongs to all Israel by naming citizens from several tribes resettling there after the Exile (9:3).

The Family of Saul (8:29—40)

THE CONCLUDING GENEALOGY fits the pattern of the previous listings in that the key figure is mentioned near the middle of the family roster. In this case, the central character of the last section of Benjamin's genealogy is Saul—the most famous of all the Benjamites. The greater portion of Benjamin's family tree (8:29—38) is repeated in the parallel passage recording the genealogy of Saul found in 9:35—44 (see comments).

The pattern of identifying clans of Benjamin with particular geographical locations continues as well, with the family of Jeiel connected with Gibeon. The biblical Gibeon is associated with modern el-Jib, some six miles northwest of Jerusalem. The city was part of Benjamin's tribal allotment

12. Williamson, *1 and 2 Chronicles*, 84.
13. Myers, *I Chronicles*, 61.

(Josh. 18:25) and was assigned to the network of Levitical cities (Josh. 21:17). Prior to the conquest of Canaan, Gibeon was a Canaanite enclave eventually absorbed by the tribe of Benjamin as the result of an unwise treaty with the Gibeonites (cf. Josh. 9). This fact suggests Saul's ancestry included Canaanites.

In light of this, some scholars have understood the reference to Gibeon (8:29) as a subtle theological foil to the reference to Jerusalem (8:28), signifying Saul was unfit for kingship.[14] This seems an overreading of the geographical data, however, since 10:13 explicitly states Saul was unfit for the throne of Israel because of his unfaithfulness to Yahweh. More likely the Chronicler devotes time to the Benjamites of Gibeon because their descendants helped rebuild the walls of Jerusalem after returning from exile (Neh. 3:7) and resettled Gibeon (Neh. 7:25).

The name Jeiel (8:29) is usually restored on the basis of the LXX and the parallel in 1 Chronicles 9:35 (so NIV). The phrase "father of Gibeon" should be understood as a civic or military leader, not the founder of the city (cf. textual note in NIV). According to Thompson, the name Maacah (8:29) indicates Jeiel's intermarriage with an Aramean (a non-Hebrew group).[15] If true, this would help explain Saul's tendencies toward religious syncretism since his father Kish was the product of a "mixed" marriage.

Apart from the implications for this blending of the religious traditions of Baalism and Yahwism in Saul's family, the mention of Maacah is in keeping with the Chronicler's penchant for selecting genealogical materials that call attention to women and/or non-Hebrews. The theme of Israel as a "light" to the nations is integral to the Chronicler's theology of hope. Like the list of names associated with Bela (8:3–5), it is unclear whether the catalog of names cited after Abdon (9:30) are sons or relatives of Jeiel.

The naming of Kish (8:33) prompts the recitation of the genealogy of King Saul (8:33–38). The list is the most extensive record of Saul's family in the Bible and is repeated (with minor variations) in 9:39–44 as an introduction to the death of King Saul (ch. 10). It seems likely that the name Ner should be added (8:30) on the basis of the LXX (so the NIV), which means Ner was probably the name of both Saul's uncle (8:30) and grandfather (8:33). The LXX reads the name Bokeru (8:38) as "firstborn son" (i.e., "Azrikam, his firstborn"). The retention of the "Baal" names in the genealogy indicates both the antiquity of the source and the integrity of the scribal transmission (since the offensive name of Yahweh's rival was not purged from the roster). For instance, Esh-Baal (8:33) is also known as Ishvi (1 Sam. 14:49) and Ish-

---

14. E.g., Thompson, *1, 2 Chronicles*, 101.
15. Ibid.

Bosheth (2 Sam. 4:1), and Merib-Baal (1 Chron. 8:34) is called Mephibosheth (2 Sam. 4:4). The names from Micah on (8:34) are unknown to the rest of Old Testament history apart from the parallel register in 9:39–44.

The genealogy of Benjamin concludes with references to Azel and his sons and the sons of Eshek, the brother of Azel (8:38–40). The listing of the family of Eshek appears somewhat unrelated to the rest of the section and probably represents an independent military census, given the muster roll of bowmen (8:40).[16] Benjamin was one of tribes instrumental in the restoration of Judah and Jerusalem after the Babylonian exile (cf. 9:3). The Chronicler's genealogy of Benjamin is both a reminder to the postexilic Benjamites of their noble heritage and a call to emulate their example of faith and intertribal cooperation.

First Chronicles 9:1a concludes the genealogical prologue. It references "all Israel" and has its parallel in the introduction to the genealogical prologue listing the twelve sons of Israel (or Jacob, 2:1–2). The idea of "all Israel" is a key theme for the Chronicler because unity among the returnees from the Exile is essential for any sustained initiative aimed at restoring Judah and Jerusalem to its former glory. This explains the title of the source book for the genealogical record, "the book of the kings of Israel" (cf. 2 Chron. 20:34).[17] For the Chronicler, the ideal of kingship is a divinely appointed king shepherding the one people of God (embodied in King David and projected to the messianic king; cf. Jer. 33:25–26; Ezek. 34:23–24).

A RECURRING THEME in our analysis of Chronicles is the message of hope for postexilic Judah couched in the retelling of the story of Israelite kingship. Despite the delay of nearly two centuries, the Chronicler is hopeful that kingship will be restored in postexilic Judah. That hope is not utopian wishful thinking or sentimental daydreaming but confidence in the Word of God that promised a revived Davidic monarchy (cf. Jer. 33:15; Amos 9:11). The certainty of the Chronicler's conviction that God will make good that promise spoken through the prophets informs the structure of the genealogical prologue.

---

16. According to Japhet's historical reconstruction (*I and II Chronicles*, 198–99), Micah (8:35) may have been a contemporary of King Solomon. If the ten generations between Micah and Ulam are an uninterrupted accounting of Micah's descendants, then Ulam and his sons would have lived near the end of the seventh century B.C. (before the destruction of Jerusalem).

17. E.g., Braun, *1 Chronicles*, 129–30; Williamson, *1 and 2 Chronicles*, 87.

The compilation of tribal genealogies (chs. 4–7) is encased in an envelope featuring Judah (chs. 2–3) and Benjamin (ch. 8), the two "royal" tribes of Israel. It is the idea of kingship that inspires the Chronicler's retelling of Hebrew history. He knows beyond doubt that Israel's destiny is tied to a royal figure of some future time. I suspect the Chronicler is hopeful that kingship will again emerge in Israel during his lifetime. His questions penetrate the subsequent centuries of Jewish history even to the time of Christ's postresurrection ascension into the glory of heaven: "Lord, are you at this time going to restore the kingdom to Israel?" (Acts 1:6).

The shift from word to image as a vehicle of communication as a result of the technology revolution in our society has diminished our awareness of and appreciation for the sophistication of the Chronicler's literary effort. The retelling of a story already well known by the audience for the purpose of bolstering morale is a tall order for any writer, no matter the century. Beyond that, the Chronicler chooses to use the genre of list or genealogy to retell Israel's history. Yet through that medium he has subtly enhanced his message of hope by strategically selecting those tribal records that include anecdotes and brief reports scattered through the lists of names.

For example, the Chronicler teaches us something about prayer in the example of Jabez (4:9–10), wideness of heart in the attention given to the "marginalized" (e.g., the emphasis on women in the registers of Manasseh and Ephraim; 7:14–16, 24), and fresh starts by the grace of God in lists of those resettling Jerusalem after the Exile (9:1b–34). Here in the Benjamite genealogy he does it by reporting examples in which families from the tribe have experienced and overcome adversity.

Specifically, the genealogical record reports four episodes that may be construed as misfortune for the tribe of Benjamin, including the deportation of descendants of Ehud from Geba (8:6), the divorce of Hushim and Baara by Shaharaim (8:8), the tragedy of Saul's kingship (implicitly in the reference to Israel's first king in 8:33), and the brave warriors of Ulam's family who are no more (8:40; according to Japhet's historical reconstruction of Micah's lineage Ulam and his sons were most likely casualties of the Babylonian conquest of Judah and Jerusalem).[18]

Yet, in 9:3 we read that some from the tribe of Benjamin joined other Jews in resettling the Persian imperial province of Judah and rebuilding the city of Jerusalem. The memoirs of Ezra and Nehemiah confirm the role of Benjamin in the restoration community (cf. Ezra 1:5; Neh. 11:4, 7–9). Was this a chance stroke of good fortune for the tribe of Benjamin? Or was this simply testimony to the tenacious spirit and exceptional ability of certain fam-

---

18. Japhet, *I and II Chronicles*, 198–99.

ilies of the Benjamites? Or did the tribe of Benjamin overcome adversity by the gracious help of the sovereign God of Israel?

Obviously these questions are rhetorical in nature. But we must take note that this profound biblical truth may be grasped only through theological extrapolation. The Chronicler nowhere makes such claims; the message is tacit or even subliminal for his audience, given their knowledge of their own history and Scriptures. We might add this is an example of good pedagogical method, encouraging the listener or the reader to draw lessons and principles for personal edification inductively from known materials. In a sense, the writer invites his audience to do "biblical theology" by remembering other portions of the Hebrew Scriptures germane to his theme of hope for a restored Israel. No doubt the Chronicler had in mind texts like Psalm 42:5, 11; 43:5: "Why are you downcast, O my soul? . . . Put your hope in God."

Or in view of the grim memory of the Exile and the halting restoration effort in postexilic Judah, perhaps the Chronicler expects his audience to call to mind Lamentations 3:21–23:

> Yet this I call to mind
>   and therefore I have hope:
> Because of the LORD's great love we are not consumed,
>   for his compassions never fail.
> They are new every morning;
>   great is your faithfulness.

CUP OF SORROW/CUP OF JOY. Part of the story of the Bible is the conflict between faith in God (and the truth he has disclosed through general and special revelation) and false gods and false teaching espoused by humanistic philosophies and superstitious religions. In the Old Testament we learn that Jeremiah battled counterfeit prophets who preached a message of false hope based on visions of their own creation (Jer. 14:14; 23:16). Centuries later Jesus warned his followers that false prophets and even false Christs would rise up and deceive many (Matt. 24:4–14). Soon after, his apostles encountered stiff opposition to the truth of God in their own ministries, prompting them to admonish and instruct God's people on the subject of false teachers and false teaching in their letters (e.g., 2 Cor. 11:13; 1 Tim. 1:3; 6:3; 2 Peter 2:1).

Typically, we tend to associate false teaching with heretical belief and practice related to the basic tenets of our Christian creed. Historically such false doctrine has included denying the deity of Christ, denying the effects of the Fall in the nature of persons, investing other "holy books" with the divine authority of the Bible, and adding some form of "law" or "works" to the grace of God for salvation. The assault on foundational Bible truths by false teachers and the spread of their false doctrine became the catalyst for the early creedal responses to heresy (e.g., the Councils of Nicea, Chalcedon). Not surprisingly, these and other distortions of biblical teaching persist today as the spirit of antichrist remains active in the world (1 John 4:1–3).

In addition, new challenges to Christian orthodoxy have surfaced. Issues related to gender roles and sexual orientation now divide the church, fallout from the "culture wars" that continues to fragment society and alienate people groups. The pluralism unleashed by postmodernism recognizes all belief systems as equally valid (whether true or not is unimportant since relativism makes "truth" superfluous). By the same token, the multicultural agenda of postmodernism insists that every culture is of equal intrinsic value. Hence, "there is no exclusive truth. There is no superior culture."[19]

As a result Christianity and Western civilization are only as valid as Hinduism and Eastern civilization or animism and African civilization in the new cultural order. Even more disturbing is the perspectivist approach to literature advocated by postmodernism, divesting texts of any meaning and coherence apart from that determined by each reader. At best, the Bible can mean only what the individual reader predisposes the text to mean. At worst, the Bible is meaningless because it is impossible for language to articulate a reality that is unknowable.[20]

Beyond this, in recent decades the church has had to combat an equally insidious false teaching that promotes health, wealth, and happiness—all the while eschewing pain, suffering, and adversity as symptoms of a "stunted" spiritual development.[21] Rather than exhorting God's faithful to overcome adversity like the Chronicler, these false teachers preach "another gospel" that claims the "truly spiritual" person is exempt from adversity. This "have-it-all" philosophy combines the misapprehension of biblical teaching concerning "success" and "prosperity" with the social agenda of modern liberalism that seeks to eradicate all pain and suffering for the citizens of "democracy."[22]

This gospel of "gain with no pain" must ignore the biblical stories featuring the adversity and suffering of God's people. What place for Joseph wrongly accused and imprisoned (Gen. 39:11–20)? What place for the widow

19. David W. Henderson, *Culture Shift* (Grand Rapids: Baker, 1998), 192.

20. See esp. ch. 13, "Leaving Meaning Behind," in ibid., 184–99.

21. For a historical overview and theological assessment of the "prosperity gospel" movement, see Bruce Barron, *The Health and Wealth Gospel* (Downers Grove, Ill.: InterVarsity Press, 1987).

22. Cf. Bork, *Slouching Towards Gomorrah*, 82.

Naomi, who changed her name to "bitterness" (Ruth 1:20)? What place for fugitive David, who fled the wrath of King Saul in the caves of the Judean desert (1 Sam. 23:14)? What place for the apostle Paul who boasted of his weaknesses (2 Cor. 11:30; 12:7–10)? What place for the apostle John exiled to the island of Patmos (Rev. 1:9)? Each one is a graduate of what Gene Edwards has called "God's sacred school of submission and brokenness."[23]

The gospel of "gain with no pain" must also ignore the teaching of Jesus. On more than one occasion he made it clear to his disciples that they should anticipate adversity and persecution because "a student is not above his teacher, nor a servant above his master" (Matt. 10:24; cf. John 15:20). Shortly before his own arrest Jesus declared to his followers, "In this world you will have trouble. But take heart! I have overcome the world" (John 16:33). Christian "triumphalism" is forged in the crucible of the cross of Jesus Christ (Matt. 16:24; cf. 1 Cor. 1:17; Col. 2:15).

The psalmist asks the question: "How can I repay the LORD for all his goodness to me?" He then answers his own question by declaring: "I will lift up the cup of salvation and call on the name of the LORD" (Ps. 116:12–13). Henri Nouwen reminds us that the "cup of salvation" is both "the cup of joy" and "the cup of sorrow." His study of the life of Christ as recorded in the Gospels and his years of ministry to the "marginalized" of society taught him that "the cup of sorrow is also the cup of joy, that precisely what causes us sadness can become the fertile ground for gladness. . . . Only when we fully realize that the cup of life is not only a cup of sorrow but also a cup of joy will we be able to drink it."[24]

Paul understood the paradox of the cup of sorrow and the cup of joy, recognizing that as coheirs with Christ, the child of God must share in his sufferings in order to share in his glory (Rom. 8:17). Elsewhere, Paul praised "the God of all comfort," who comforts the faithful in all their troubles, not the God who removes all trouble from their lives (2 Cor. 1:3–6). Peter echoes Paul in calling the Christian to rejoice in sharing the sufferings of Christ so that we may be "overjoyed when his glory is revealed" (1 Peter 4:13). Fortunately, we are called to overcome adversity for only a "little while" (5:10), knowing we can commit ourselves to our faithful Creator, who both comforts us in our suffering and enables us to overcome our adversity (2 Cor. 1:3, 10–11; 1 Peter 4:19). This is the cup Jesus offered his disciples: "Can you drink the cup. . . ?" (Matt. 20:22).

---

23. Gene Edwards, *A Tale of Three Kings* (Wheaton, Ill.: Tyndale, 1992), 13.

24. Henri J. M. Nouwen, *Can You Drink the Cup?* (Notre Dame, Ind.: Ave Maria Press, 1996), 51.

1 Chronicles 9:1b–44

THE PEOPLE OF Judah were taken captive to Babylon because of their unfaithfulness. ²Now the first to resettle on their own property in their own towns were some Israelites, priests, Levites and temple servants.

³Those from Judah, from Benjamin, and from Ephraim and Manasseh who lived in Jerusalem were:

⁴Uthai son of Ammihud, the son of Omri, the son of Imri, the son of Bani, a descendant of Perez son of Judah.

⁵Of the Shilonites:

Asaiah the firstborn and his sons.

⁶Of the Zerahites:

Jeuel.

The people from Judah numbered 690.

⁷Of the Benjamites:

Sallu son of Meshullam, the son of Hodaviah, the son of Hassenuah;

⁸Ibneiah son of Jeroham; Elah son of Uzzi, the son of Micri; and Meshullam son of Shephatiah, the son of Reuel, the son of Ibnijah.

⁹The people from Benjamin, as listed in their genealogy, numbered 956. All these men were heads of their families.

¹⁰Of the priests:

Jedaiah; Jehoiarib; Jakin;

¹¹Azariah son of Hilkiah, the son of Meshullam, the son of Zadok, the son of Meraioth, the son of Ahitub, the official in charge of the house of God;

¹²Adaiah son of Jeroham, the son of Pashhur, the son of Malkijah; and Maasai son of Adiel, the son of Jahzerah, the son of Meshullam, the son of Meshillemith, the son of Immer.

¹³The priests, who were heads of families, numbered 1,760. They were able men, responsible for ministering in the house of God.

¹⁴Of the Levites:

Shemaiah son of Hasshub, the son of Azrikam, the son of Hashabiah, a Merarite; ¹⁵Bakbakkar, Heresh, Galal

and Mattaniah son of Mica, the son of Zicri, the son of
Asaph; [16]Obadiah son of Shemaiah, the son of Galal,
the son of Jeduthun; and Berekiah son of Asa, the son of
Elkanah, who lived in the villages of the Netophathites.
[17]The gatekeepers:

Shallum, Akkub, Talmon, Ahiman and their brothers,
Shallum their chief [18]being stationed at the King's Gate
on the east, up to the present time. These were the
gatekeepers belonging to the camp of the Levites.
[19]Shallum son of Kore, the son of Ebiasaph, the son of
Korah, and his fellow gatekeepers from his family (the
Korahites) were responsible for guarding the thresholds
of the Tent just as their fathers had been responsible for
guarding the entrance to the dwelling of the LORD. [20]In
earlier times Phinehas son of Eleazar was in charge of
the gatekeepers, and the LORD was with him.
[21]Zechariah son of Meshelemiah was the gatekeeper at
the entrance to the Tent of Meeting.

[22]Altogether, those chosen to be gatekeepers at the thresholds numbered 212. They were registered by genealogy in
their villages. The gatekeepers had been assigned to their
positions of trust by David and Samuel the seer. [23]They and
their descendants were in charge of guarding the gates of the
house of the LORD—the house called the Tent. [24]The gatekeepers were on the four sides: east, west, north and south.
[25]Their brothers in their villages had to come from time to
time and share their duties for seven-day periods. [26]But the
four principal gatekeepers, who were Levites, were entrusted
with the responsibility for the rooms and treasuries in the
house of God. [27]They would spend the night stationed
around the house of God, because they had to guard it; and
they had charge of the key for opening it each morning.

[28]Some of them were in charge of the articles used in the
temple service; they counted them when they were brought in
and when they were taken out. [29]Others were assigned to take
care of the furnishings and all the other articles of the sanctuary, as well as the flour and wine, and the oil, incense and
spices. [30]But some of the priests took care of mixing the
spices. [31]A Levite named Mattithiah, the firstborn son of Shallum the Korahite, was entrusted with the responsibility for
baking the offering bread. [32]Some of their Kohathite brothers

were in charge of preparing for every Sabbath the bread set out on the table.

³³Those who were musicians, heads of Levite families, stayed in the rooms of the temple and were exempt from other duties because they were responsible for the work day and night.

³⁴All these were heads of Levite families, chiefs as listed in their genealogy, and they lived in Jerusalem.

³⁵Jeiel the father of Gibeon lived in Gibeon.

His wife's name was Maacah, ³⁶and his firstborn son was Abdon, followed by Zur, Kish, Baal, Ner, Nadab, ³⁷Gedor, Ahio, Zechariah and Mikloth. ³⁸Mikloth was the father of Shimeam. They too lived near their relatives in Jerusalem.

³⁹Ner was the father of Kish, Kish the father of Saul, and Saul the father of Jonathan, Malki-Shua, Abinadab and Esh-Baal.

⁴⁰The son of Jonathan:

Merib-Baal, who was the father of Micah.

⁴¹The sons of Micah:

Pithon, Melech, Tahrea and Ahaz.

⁴²Ahaz was the father of Jadah, Jadah was the father of Alemeth, Azmaveth and Zimri, and Zimri was the father of Moza. ⁴³Moza was the father of Binea; Rephaiah was his son, Eleasah his son and Azel his son.

⁴⁴Azel had six sons, and these were their names:

Azrikam, Bokeru, Ishmael, Sheariah, Obadiah and Hanan. These were the sons of Azel.

THIS CONCLUDING GENEALOGY explains the genealogical introduction of the Chronicler's history. The list of families resettling Jerusalem after the Babylonian exile joins the present to the past. It is through this extensive prologue cataloging the names of Hebrew ancestors that the restoration community is directly linked to the twelve patriarchs of Israel. As noted elsewhere, the purpose of the genealogical introduction was twofold: (1) to legitimize the restoration community as the rightful heirs of the promises made to the patriarchs and kings of Israel, and (2) to bolster the morale of those Hebrews returning to Judah from Babylonia and inspire full participation in the restoration initiative.

Families Resettling Jerusalem (9:1b–34)

THE PARAGRAPH STRUCTURE at the beginning of the section is rendered variously, frequently broken at 9:1b (so NIV, NLT) or at 9:2 (so NRSV, NKJV). The repetition of "Israel" in 2:1 and 9:1a suggests an envelope construction encasing the genealogies of 2:1–9:1a as a complete literary unit. First Chronicles 9:1a makes reference to a "book" containing genealogical records, perhaps a royal census list identified by the Chronicler as the resource for his own genealogical catalog.[1] The genealogy as a whole calls attention to the priests, Levites, and temple personnel resettling Jerusalem. The citations to the tribe of Benjamin at the beginning of the list serve as a bridge between the genealogy of Benjamin (ch. 8) and the account of Saul's kingship (9:35–10:14, including the Chronicler's final genealogy, the Benjamite lineage of King Saul in 9:35–44).

Biblical commentators have noted the similarities between 9:1–17 and Nehemiah 11:3–19. It is unclear whether Nehemiah and Chronicles share a common source or if one of the accounts is the source of the other.[2] The genealogy itself is segmented in that it demonstrates both breadth (the listing of a single generation from a common ancestor, e.g., 9:5) and depth (the listing of successive generations, e.g., 9:4). In addition to the common genealogical subfeatures identified previously (e.g., the tally [a cardinal number attached to the genealogical record, 9:6]), this genealogy also includes the subgenera of job description and schedule (e.g., 9:22–28).[3]

The introduction (9:2–3) to the list of people resettling Judah after the Babylonian exile subtly confirms the linkage of the postexilic Jewish community with earlier national Israel. The parallel in Nehemiah 11:4 mentions only two tribes (Judah and Benjamin), whereas the Chronicler cites the representatives of four tribes in the resettlement of Jerusalem (Judah, Benjamin, Ephraim, and Manasseh). His reference to people returning to "their own property" (*ʾaḥuzzah*) translates a term used rarely in Chronicles (elsewhere only 1 Chron. 7:28; 2 Chron. 11:14; 31:1). This word may be used to describe "ancestral property" and is associated with the Israelite settlement of Canaan as prescribed by Moses (e.g., Lev. 14:34; 25:10) and implemented by Joshua (Josh. 22:4, 9, 19).

The Chronicler's report of the reoccupation of Jerusalem (9:3) is another important tie between the present and the past for the postexilic community. The resettling of Jerusalem is a sure sign of God's blessing and a hopeful

---

1. Note that Selman, *1 Chronicles*, 122, and Braun, *1 Chronicles*, 130, prefer the conjectural emendation "the book of the kings of Israel *and Judah*" in 9:1 as an error of haplography (contra NIV, "the book of the kings of Israel").

2. See the discussions in Myers, *I Chronicles*, 67–71; Selman, *1 Chronicles*, 123–24.

3. On terminology related to the elements and formulas of the genealogical genre see the glossary in De Vries, *1 and 2 Chronicles*, 426–39.

omen since the prophetic promises for the rebuilding of the nation of Israel are centered in the city of David (Isa. 44:26, 28; Jer. 33:16).

The Chronicler abbreviates the list of descendants of Judah (9:4–6) found in the parallel of Nehemiah 11:4–6. It is possible that the names of the family leaders Uthai and Asaiah are alternate forms of Athaiah (Neh. 11:4) and Maaseiah (Neh. 11:5) respectively. The Chronicler also adds the family of Jeuel, an otherwise unknown Judahite leader. But the genealogy does correspond to the three traditional branches of the tribe of Judah recognized elsewhere, including the clans of Perez, Shelah (the "Shilonites" for the Chronicler), and Zerah (cf. Num. 26:20). The difference in tabulations (468 in Neh. 11:6 and 690 in 1 Chron. 9:6) may be due to the breadth of the census takings ("men" specified in Neh. 11:6, "people" in 1 Chron. 9:6). The Chronicler's total may also reflect the growth in the families of Judah from the earlier census of Nehemiah.

The Chronicler's list of the descendants of Benjamin (9:7–9) contains even more variation from the parallel account in Nehemiah 11:7–9 than the Judahite genealogy. The two genealogies have only one name in common (Sallu), and Chronicles lists four family heads while Nehemiah cites only one. Numerous solutions have been proposed for reconciling the differences in the two records, but suffice to say that each writer makes selective use of a common and more complete genealogical record.[4] As with the genealogy of Judah, the totals for the census of the Benjamites increase slightly from 928 (Neh. 11:8) to 956 people counted (1 Chron. 9:9).

Characteristic of the Chronicler's style, the list of priestly descendants resettling Jerusalem (9:10–13) is also abbreviated when compared to the parallel account in Nehemiah 11:10–14. In addition, Chronicles cites six heads of families whereas Nehemiah mentions only five. The Chronicler's list also shows some variation in the spelling of certain names. The number of priests has increased significantly (1,760 in 1 Chron. 9:13) over the tally in Nehemiah (1,192 in Neh. 11:12–14). Both census takings, however, number less than half of the priests who initially returned from exile (4,289; cf. Ezra 2:36–39 = Neh. 7:39–42). This may indicate even priests were reluctant to live in the ruined shell of Jerusalem upon return from Babylonia (cf. Neh. 11:1–2). Selman and others are correct in suggesting that the phrase "official in charge of the house of God" is an equivalent for "high priest" (1 Chron. 9:11; cf. 2 Chron. 31:10, 13).[5]

As one might expect, the Chronicler (9:14–16) slightly expands the genealogy of the Levites when compared to the parallel in Nehemiah 11:15–

4. See Thompson, *1, 2 Chronicles*, 105–6.
5. Selman, *1 Chronicles*, 127.

18, mentioning seven family leaders among the eighteen names listed (versus six family leaders and sixteen names in Nehemiah). This may be the result of an updating of the records in Chronicles. Curiously, the Chronicler omits any tally (whereas 284 Levites are counted in Neh. 11:18).

The families of Shemaiah, Mattaniah, and Obadiah are emphasized because they represent the important descendants of the Levitical tribal organization, Merari, Asaph, and Jeduthun. Asaph and Jeduthun are significant because they were heads of musical guilds organized by King David for temple worship (cf. 1 Chron. 25:1–3). According to Nehemiah 12:28–29, the villages of the Netophathites were home to the Levitical singers. The town of Netophath was located only about three miles southeast of Bethlehem; historically it was connected with Caleb (1 Chron. 2:54) and David (2 Sam. 23:28–29).

The Chronicler's section on the gatekeepers is an extensive expansion of a single verse in Nehemiah (Neh. 11:19). The gatekeepers are numbered with the Levites (1 Chron. 9:26) and form a separate class in the catalog of priests, Levites, and other temple ministers and servants. In addition to their Levitical descent, this listing emphasizes their exemplary behavior in heeding the call to live in Jerusalem (9:22, 25) and in their self-sacrificing spirit as they willingly accept additional tasks (9:26–32). The essential function of a gatekeeper was "guarding the thresholds of the Tent . . . the entrance to the dwelling of the LORD" (9:19).

Four chief gatekeepers are identified, as there were four entrances to the temple precincts. A gate was located on each of the cardinal compass points, with the east gate being the most important. This gate was the King's Gate and faced the entrance to the temple sanctuary (9:18; cf. Ezek. 46:2). According to 1 Chronicles 26:13, the gate assignments of the chief gatekeepers were originally determined by the casting of lots. The gatekeepers worked their shifts in pairs for seven-day periods (9:25), and in all they manned twenty-two stations around the clock (26:17–18). The census of Nehemiah tallies 172 gatekeepers (Neh. 11:19), and by the time of the Chronicler that total has increased to 212 gatekeepers (1 Chron. 9:22).

Selman has conveniently outlined the section treating the gatekeepers according to the basic aspects of their temple ministry: authority (9:17–23), leadership (9:24–27), and tasks (9:28–32).[6] The authority of the gatekeepers rested in their genealogical association with the Levites through Korah (9:18–19) and their spiritual association with Phinehas, who supervised the gatekeepers during the days of Moses (9:20; cf. Num. 25:7–13). As if to emphasize the point by "name-dropping," the Chronicler adds the fact that

---

6. Ibid., 129.

the position of gatekeeper itself was formally constituted by the likes of Samuel and David (1 Chron. 9:22; cf. 23:4–5).

The gatekeepers provided leadership in the day-to-day operations of the temple by continually guarding the premises and its contents and opening the gates for temple services every morning (9:27). In addition, the gatekeepers supported the temple ministries by maintaining the furniture and the implements used in the worship rituals and by preparing the ingredients required for the priestly sacrifices and offerings (9:29–30).

It has been suggested the anomalous inclusion of the unnamed temple musicians is a concession to a group of disgruntled Levites who feel they have been slighted by their more prominent associates.[7] But it seems more likely they are included for the sake of completeness in the recitation of priestly ministries connected with the temple.[8] The word translated "musicians" (so NIV, NLT) literally signifies "singers" (so NKJV, NRSV). It is unclear if the singers are the Levites mentioned in 9:14–16 or gatekeepers (9:17–32) who double as temple musicians. The singers are exempt from work routinely associated with the Levitical job description since they minister "night and day" (much like the gatekeepers, 9:27; cf. Ps. 134:1; Isa. 30:29). Interestingly, the Chronicler's stylized genealogical record of all Israel, past and present, represents the religious ideal for God's people. The focal point of the genealogies is Jerusalem and the services of temple worship orchestrated by the priests and Levites.[9]

The conclusion to the list of people resettling Jerusalem (9:34) essentially repeats 8:28 (with the addition of the word "Levite"). The verse serves as a transition between the Levitical musicians (9:33) and the genealogy of Saul (9:35–44). Most commentators note the echo of "Jerusalem" marks an inclusion with 9:3 and forms an envelope construction for the section (an "artistic touch," according to Japhet[10]).

Braun remarks how striking it is that this postexilic genealogy cites no Judahite connected with the Davidic ideal since King David dominates the remaining history of 1 Chronicles.[11] Actually this should come as no surprise since as early as Malachi's day prophetic appeal to the family of David ceased, implying they were no longer a factor in the restoration community.[12] The Chronicler seems to assume the fate of postexilic Judah

---

7. Braun, *1 Chronicles*, 142.

8. So Japhet, *I and II Chronicles*, 217.

9. On the Chronicler's preoccupation with worship see Wilcock, *The Message of Chronicles*, 45–46.

10. Japhet, *I and II Chronicles*, 218.

11. Braun, *1 Chronicles*, 144.

12. See Andrew E. Hill, *Malachi* (AB 25D; New York: Doubleday, 1998), 71.

lies in the hands of the priests and Levites for an interim period until such time as God raises up a successor to the Davidic ideal (cf. Jer. 33:17; Ezek. 34:23–24; 37:25).

Genealogy of Saul (9:35–44)

THIS GENEALOGY REPEATS the register of Saul's family tree (with minor variations) found in 8:29–38 as one segment of the genealogy of Benjamin. Japhet has noted that the parallel passage of the genealogy of Saul in 9:35–44 preserves three names not found in 8:29–38: Jeiel (9:35; cf. 8:29), Ner (9:36; cf. 8:30), and Mikloth (9:37; cf. 8:32).[13] Beyond this, there are variants in six of the names recorded in the two genealogies: Zeker/Zechariah (8:31/9:37), Shimeah/Shimeam (8:32/9:38), Merib-Baal/Meribaal (8:34/9:40, lit.), Tarea/Tahrea (8:35/9:41), Jehoaddah/Jarah (8:36/9:42), and Raphah/Rephaiah (8:37/9:43). These minor variations may be explained as either textual corruption (e.g., Jaʿadah/Jaʿarah) or to an ongoing process of transformation of names because of language changes over time.[14] See further comments on 8:29–40, above.

THE CONCLUDING GENEALOGY fixes attention on an issue common to God's people in both the old and new covenants, namely, leadership during an interim or transition period. The prophets Jeremiah and Ezekiel predicted a royal figure would arise after the Exile and rule in righteousness after the example of King David (Jer. 33:15 ; Ezek. 34:23). The restoration process in postexilic Israel has been underway for more than a century by the time the Chronicler writes, but the Davidic ideal is still unrealized. The concluding genealogy indicates the Levitical priests assume they are the interim caretakers of the destiny of regathered Israel until such time as the Davidic prince establishes his rule.

In part, this hierocracy (rule by a priestly class) is based on the legitimacy of recognized "office gifts" ordained by God for the political and spiritual direction of Israel. Specifically mentioned are the offices of priest, sage, and prophet (cf. Jer. 18:18; Ezek. 7:26). The role of the priest is primarily one of instructor in the law of God, offering both exhortation and rebuke. This educational function of the priesthood is necessary in order to ready God's people to receive the future rule of the Davidic prince. The emphasis on the sacred duties for each of the priestly guilds recorded in the final genealogy

13. Japhet, *I and II Chronicles*, 218.
14. Cf. ibid., 219.

suggests they take Malachi's earlier message to heart and apply themselves to proper ministry and instruction (cf. Mal. 2:1−9).

A similar situation faces the church today as God's people await the second advent of Jesus Christ, promised to those who witnessed his ascension and the sure hope of the church in every generation (Acts 1:11; 1 Thess. 4:16−17). The crisis of leadership during the interim period is averted by the bestowal of a new set of "office gifts" designed to instruct and direct the church of God until such time the Son of David returns to establish his kingdom of righteousness. As in the case of the Old Testament, God has ordained by his Holy Spirit that some should serve the church in leadership roles: apostles, prophets, evangelists, and pastor-teachers (Eph. 4:11).

According to Paul, these "office gifts" also have a didactic function, expressly designed "to prepare God's people for works of service, so that the body of Christ may be built up" (Eph. 4:12). Since there is one Spirit (4:4), it is clear that the same Holy Spirit empowering leadership in the church also enabled those exercising "office gifts" in ancient Israel.[15] Unlike the Old Testament, however, the New Testament brings an added dimension to the work of the Holy Spirit among the people of God in the form of a variety of "spiritual gifts" distributed to every Christian "for the common good" (of the church as the body of Christ, 1 Cor. 12:7). The Chronicler's genealogy links the different orders of the priesthood to particular responsibilities and ministry tasks (1 Chron. 9:10−21). So too, each one should use whatever gift he or she has received to serve others, faithfully administering God's grace in its various forms (1 Peter 4:10).

FRESH STARTS. The concluding genealogy of the Chronicler's prologue has proven a rich lode for biblical commentators in mining theological nuggets for life application. One important lesson—and a recurring theme in Chronicles—is the fact that the Babylonian exile did not annul God's covenant of grant with Abraham and Sarah (Gen. 12:1−3). God is eternally faithful to his Word (cf. Ps. 111: 5). The roster of postexilic inhabitants of Jerusalem only serves to affirm the assertion of

---

15. The topic of the work of the Holy Spirit in the Old Testament is a difficult one and requires a separate study. Essentially, what is explicit in the New Testament concerning the work of the Holy Spirit is implicit in the Old Testament (apart from the "baptism of the Holy Spirit" [Acts 1:5]) and the universal and more permanent distribution of spiritual gifts among the people of God [1 Cor. 12:7−12]; cf. Leon J. Wood, *The Holy Spirit in the Old Testament* (Grand Rapids: Zondervan, 1976); Wilf Hildebrandt, *An Old Testament Theology of the Spirit of God* (Peabody, Mass.: Hendrickson, 1995).

Lamentations that the mercies of God are indeed new every morning and his faithfulness is surely great (Lam. 3:22–23). For this reason the Hebrew poet was certain that God's people "are not cast off by the Lord forever" (Lam. 3:31). The Chronicler offers the resettlement of Jerusalem as indisputable proof that the hope kindled among the exiles for the eventual restoration of Israel has not been misplaced.

A second vital truth emerges from the Chronicler's concluding genealogy, namely, that divine restoration makes human reconciliation possible. This is demonstrated in the common resettling of Israelites formerly identified and separated by the political descriptors "northern tribes" and "southern tribes."[16] Most likely the Chronicler recognizes the resettlement of Jerusalem as the fulfillment of Ezekiel's prophecy concerning the joining of the two sticks etched with the names "Israel" and "Judah" (Ezek. 37:15–28).

The biblical principle of reconciliation also illustrates a basic attribute of God, his oneness. Even as God is One as Creator and Father, so he works to bring this ideal of "oneness" to the human experience in marriage and family and in the life of the religious community (cf. Mal. 2:10, 15). The biblical teaching of human reconciliation through divine restoration is a welcome message in our age of ever-widening "gaps" between people, whether age, race, or gender, and of broken family and marital relationships.

A third lesson is the cogent reminder that the Chronicler's genealogies speak to the church as much as they spoke to postexilic Israel because in our times of smallness and defeatism, we need to recall those biblical declarations indicating that we too are the heirs of God's promises for restoration (Rom. 8:17; Gal. 4:7; 2 Peter 1:4).[17] This is essentially the modus operandi of the writer to the Hebrews in the New Testament. This letter seeks to encourage Christians in the throes of doubt and despair because of both persecution and false teaching by reminding them of their location in the "spiritual genealogy," that "great cloud of witnesses" who are our ancestors in faith in God's promises (Heb. 12:1).

Perhaps most significant, however, is the idea that the story of Israel is a story of "fresh starts" by God's grace.[18] In fact, the story of the Bible is the story of God making and remaking, "doing new things" (Isa. 43:19; cf. Jer. 31:22). Whether by raising up a courageous judge, a righteous king, or a fiery prophet, God lovingly "jump-starts" his relationship with the nation of Israel over and over again after their covenant failures (cf. Deut. 30:3; Jer. 33:25–26).

16. So Allen, *1, 2 Chronicles*, 75–76.
17. See McConville, *I and II Chronicles*, 13.
18. See Thompson, *1, 2 Chronicles*, 107.

The Psalms indicate the faithful individual also experiences the compassion of God in the assurance of a fresh start after a lapse into doubt or sin (cf. Ps. 30:5; 40:3; 51:12). Even the Hebrew system of marking time is imprinted with the principle of "fresh starts" by God's grace in the celebration of the New Moon festival—a new beginning in pilgrimage with God each month (Num. 10:10; 28:11–14). God never hesitates or wearies of "returning" to his people when they "return" to him—and he is always careful to leave in his wake the blessing of new beginning (Zech. 1:3; Mal. 3:7; cf. Hos. 6:1–2).

The New Testament, especially the Gospels and Acts, tells a similar story. There one reads of dramatic examples of "fresh starts," people whose lives are changed because of an encounter with Jesus of Nazareth. Whether blind or lame, fisherman or prostitute, Jew or Samaritan, those touched by the ministry of Jesus Christ experience a "fresh start" by God's grace. The radical transformation of these new beginnings is underscored by the verbs used in connection with the ministry of Jesus. The Gospel accounts employ numerous terms to describe the metamorphosis in people who "meet" Jesus, including "cleansed" (Luke 17:14), "cured" (Mark 1:42), "forgiven" (Matt. 9:2), "healed" (Luke 4:40), and "restored" (Mark 3:5). In commenting on this idea of a "fresh start" by God's grace, perhaps with his own remarkable experience in mind, the apostle Paul says that if anyone is in Christ, that person is a new creation; "the old has gone, the new has come" (2 Cor. 5:17).

The story of "fresh starts" initiated by the grace of God is not confined to biblical history. As one reads church history, whether patristic, Byzantine, medieval, Reformation, or modern, there is a delightful repetition in the annals of Christian faith. The biographies of scholastics like Jerome and Aquinas, mystics like John of the Cross and Teresa of Avila, monastics like St. Francis and Mother Teresa, reformers like Calvin and Luther, revivalists like Wesley and Whitefield, and evangelists like Moody and Graham all have at least one chapter in common—a life given a fresh start by the grace of God. In one sense, church history is the never-ending story of new beginnings for the "bride" of Jesus Christ as God continues to build, revive, and purify the church through ordinary people empowered for extraordinary service by the Holy Spirit.

These new beginnings, flashing like meteor showers across the timeline of church history, testify to the faithfulness of God through the ages. They also confirm the biblical affirmation that God shows his gracious love to a thousand generations (Ex. 20:6). But perhaps most significant, they foreshadow that grand finale showcasing God's marvelous capacity for "fresh starts"—the re-creation of heaven and earth!

He who was seated on the throne said, "I am making everything new!" Then he said, "Write this down, for these words are trustworthy and true." (Rev. 21:5; cf. Isa. 65:17)

The reality that God is a God of "fresh starts" means there is always hope for people in a tired and dismal world desperate for the chance to start over. The degree of futility connected with the "fresh starts" manufactured by secular culture (i.e., diet crazes, fashion fads, pop-culture trends, exotic therapies, etc.) may be measured by the frequency of their turnover—almost weekly! The enduring message of the church is one of hope that does not disappoint (Rom. 5:5), of lasting righteousness and salvation (Isa. 51:6, 8). The lifestyle of the Christian is one of "hopeful joy" while awaiting that "blessed hope"—the glorious appearing of our Lord and Savior Jesus Christ (Rom. 12:12; Titus 2:13).

1 Chronicles 10–12

‌❧

NOW THE PHILISTINES fought against Israel; the Israelites fled before them, and many fell slain on Mount Gilboa. ²The Philistines pressed hard after Saul and his sons, and they killed his sons Jonathan, Abinadab and Malki-Shua. ³The fighting grew fierce around Saul, and when the archers overtook him, they wounded him.

⁴Saul said to his armor-bearer, "Draw your sword and run me through, or these uncircumcised fellows will come and abuse me."

But his armor-bearer was terrified and would not do it; so Saul took his own sword and fell on it. ⁵When the armor-bearer saw that Saul was dead, he too fell on his sword and died. ⁶So Saul and his three sons died, and all his house died together.

⁷When all the Israelites in the valley saw that the army had fled and that Saul and his sons had died, they abandoned their towns and fled. And the Philistines came and occupied them.

⁸The next day, when the Philistines came to strip the dead, they found Saul and his sons fallen on Mount Gilboa. ⁹They stripped him and took his head and his armor, and sent messengers throughout the land of the Philistines to proclaim the news among their idols and their people. ¹⁰They put his armor in the temple of their gods and hung up his head in the temple of Dagon.

¹¹When all the inhabitants of Jabesh Gilead heard of everything the Philistines had done to Saul, ¹²all their valiant men went and took the bodies of Saul and his sons and brought them to Jabesh. Then they buried their bones under the great tree in Jabesh, and they fasted seven days.

¹³Saul died because he was unfaithful to the LORD; he did not keep the word of the LORD and even consulted a medium for guidance, ¹⁴and did not inquire of the LORD. So the LORD put him to death and turned the kingdom over to David son of Jesse.

¹¹:¹All Israel came together to David at Hebron and said, "We are your own flesh and blood. ²In the past, even while Saul was king, you were the one who led Israel on their mili-

tary campaigns. And the LORD your God said to you, 'You will shepherd my people Israel, and you will become their ruler.'"

³When all the elders of Israel had come to King David at Hebron, he made a compact with them at Hebron before the LORD, and they anointed David king over Israel, as the LORD had promised through Samuel.

⁴David and all the Israelites marched to Jerusalem (that is, Jebus). The Jebusites who lived there ⁵said to David, "You will not get in here." Nevertheless, David captured the fortress of Zion, the City of David.

⁶David had said, "Whoever leads the attack on the Jebusites will become commander-in-chief." Joab son of Zeruiah went up first, and so he received the command.

⁷David then took up residence in the fortress, and so it was called the City of David. ⁸He built up the city around it, from the supporting terraces to the surrounding wall, while Joab restored the rest of the city. ⁹And David became more and more powerful, because the LORD Almighty was with him.

¹⁰These were the chiefs of David's mighty men—they, together with all Israel, gave his kingship strong support to extend it over the whole land, as the LORD had promised— ¹¹this is the list of David's mighty men:

Jashobeam, a Hacmonite, was chief of the officers; he raised his spear against three hundred men, whom he killed in one encounter.

¹²Next to him was Eleazar son of Dodai the Ahohite, one of the three mighty men. ¹³He was with David at Pas Dammim when the Philistines gathered there for battle. At a place where there was a field full of barley, the troops fled from the Philistines. ¹⁴But they took their stand in the middle of the field. They defended it and struck the Philistines down, and the LORD brought about a great victory.

¹⁵Three of the thirty chiefs came down to David to the rock at the cave of Adullam, while a band of Philistines was encamped in the Valley of Rephaim. ¹⁶At that time David was in the stronghold, and the Philistine garrison was at Bethlehem. ¹⁷David longed for water and said, "Oh, that someone would get me a drink of water from the well near the gate of Bethlehem!" ¹⁸So the Three broke through the Philistine lines, drew water from the well near the gate of Bethlehem and carried it back to David. But he refused to drink it; instead, he

poured it out before the LORD. [19]"God forbid that I should do this!" he said. "Should I drink the blood of these men who went at the risk of their lives?" Because they risked their lives to bring it back, David would not drink it.

Such were the exploits of the three mighty men.

[20]Abishai the brother of Joab was chief of the Three. He raised his spear against three hundred men, whom he killed, and so he became as famous as the Three. [21]He was doubly honored above the Three and became their commander, even though he was not included among them.

[22]Benaiah son of Jehoiada was a valiant fighter from Kabzeel, who performed great exploits. He struck down two of Moab's best men. He also went down into a pit on a snowy day and killed a lion. [23]And he struck down an Egyptian who was seven and a half feet tall. Although the Egyptian had a spear like a weaver's rod in his hand, Benaiah went against him with a club. He snatched the spear from the Egyptian's hand and killed him with his own spear. [24]Such were the exploits of Benaiah son of Jehoiada; he too was as famous as the three mighty men. [25]He was held in greater honor than any of the Thirty, but he was not included among the Three. And David put him in charge of his bodyguard.

[26]The mighty men were:

    Asahel the brother of Joab,
    Elhanan son of Dodo from Bethlehem,
[27]Shammoth the Harorite,
    Helez the Pelonite,
[28]Ira son of Ikkesh from Tekoa,
    Abiezer from Anathoth,
[29]Sibbecai the Hushathite,
    Ilai the Ahohite,
[30]Maharai the Netophathite,
    Heled son of Baanah the Netophathite,
[31]Ithai son of Ribai from Gibeah in Benjamin,
    Benaiah the Pirathonite,
[32]Hurai from the ravines of Gaash,
    Abiel the Arbathite,
[33]Azmaveth the Baharumite,
    Eliahba the Shaalbonite,
[34]the sons of Hashem the Gizonite,
    Jonathan son of Shagee the Hararite,

³⁵ Ahiam son of Sacar the Hararite,
   Eliphal son of Ur,
³⁶ Hepher the Mekerathite,
   Ahijah the Pelonite,
³⁷ Hezro the Carmelite,
   Naarai son of Ezbai,
³⁸ Joel the brother of Nathan,
   Mibhar son of Hagri,
³⁹ Zelek the Ammonite,
   Naharai the Berothite, the armor-bearer of Joab son
   of Zeruiah,
⁴⁰ Ira the Ithrite,
   Gareb the Ithrite,
⁴¹ Uriah the Hittite,
   Zabad son of Ahlai,
⁴² Adina son of Shiza the Reubenite, who was chief of the
   Reubenites, and the thirty with him,
⁴³ Hanan son of Maacah,
   Joshaphat the Mithnite,
⁴⁴ Uzzia the Ashterathite,
   Shama and Jeiel the sons of Hotham the Aroerite,
⁴⁵ Jediael son of Shimri,
   his brother Joha the Tizite,
⁴⁶ Eliel the Mahavite,
   Jeribai and Joshaviah the sons of Elnaam,
   Ithmah the Moabite,
⁴⁷ Eliel, Obed and Jaasiel the Mezobaite.

^{12:1}These were the men who came to David at Ziklag, while
he was banished from the presence of Saul son of Kish (they
were among the warriors who helped him in battle; ²they were
armed with bows and were able to shoot arrows or to sling
stones right-handed or left-handed; they were kinsmen of Saul
from the tribe of Benjamin):

³Ahiezer their chief and Joash the sons of Shemaah the
Gibeathite; Jeziel and Pelet the sons of Azmaveth;
Beracah, Jehu the Anathothite, ⁴and Ishmaiah the
Gibeonite, a mighty man among the Thirty, who was a
leader of the Thirty; Jeremiah, Jahaziel, Johanan, Jozabad the Gederathite, ⁵Eluzai, Jerimoth, Bealiah, Shemariah and Shephatiah the Haruphite; ⁶Elkanah,

Isshiah, Azarel, Joezer and Jashobeam the Korahites;
⁷and Joelah and Zebadiah the sons of Jeroham from
Gedor.

⁸Some Gadites defected to David at his stronghold in
the desert. They were brave warriors, ready for battle and
able to handle the shield and spear. Their faces were the
faces of lions, and they were as swift as gazelles in the
mountains.

> ⁹ Ezer was the chief,
>   Obadiah the second in command, Eliab the third,
> ¹⁰ Mishmannah the fourth, Jeremiah the fifth,
> ¹¹ Attai the sixth, Eliel the seventh,
> ¹² Johanan the eighth, Elzabad the ninth,
> ¹³ Jeremiah the tenth and Macbannai the eleventh.

¹⁴These Gadites were army commanders; the least was a
match for a hundred, and the greatest for a thousand. ¹⁵It was
they who crossed the Jordan in the first month when it was
overflowing all its banks, and they put to flight everyone living in the valleys, to the east and to the west.

¹⁶Other Benjamites and some men from Judah also came
to David in his stronghold. ¹⁷David went out to meet them
and said to them, "If you have come to me in peace, to
help me, I am ready to have you unite with me. But if you
have come to betray me to my enemies when my hands are
free from violence, may the God of our fathers see it and
judge you."

¹⁸Then the Spirit came upon Amasai, chief of the Thirty,
and he said:

> "We are yours, O David!
>   We are with you, O son of Jesse!
> Success, success to you,
>   and success to those who help you,
>   for your God will help you."

So David received them and made them leaders of his raiding bands.

¹⁹Some of the men of Manasseh defected to David when he
went with the Philistines to fight against Saul. (He and his
men did not help the Philistines because, after consultation,
their rulers sent him away. They said, "It will cost us our heads

if he deserts to his master Saul.") ²⁰When David went to
Ziklag, these were the men of Manasseh who defected to him:
Adnah, Jozabad, Jediael, Michael, Jozabad, Elihu and
Zillethai, leaders of units of a thousand in Manasseh. ²¹They
helped David against raiding bands, for all of them were brave
warriors, and they were commanders in his army. ²²Day after
day men came to help David, until he had a great army, like
the army of God.

²³These are the numbers of the men armed for battle who
came to David at Hebron to turn Saul's kingdom over to him,
as the LORD had said:

²⁴ men of Judah, carrying shield and spear—6,800 armed
for battle;

²⁵ men of Simeon, warriors ready for battle—7,100;

²⁶ men of Levi—4,600, ²⁷including Jehoiada, leader of the
family of Aaron, with 3,700 men, ²⁸and Zadok, a brave
young warrior, with 22 officers from his family;

²⁹ men of Benjamin, Saul's kinsmen—3,000, most of whom
had remained loyal to Saul's house until then;

³⁰ men of Ephraim, brave warriors, famous in their own
clans—20,800;

³¹ men of half the tribe of Manasseh, designated by name to
come and make David king—18,000;

³² men of Issachar, who understood the times and knew what
Israel should do—200 chiefs, with all their relatives
under their command;

³³ men of Zebulun, experienced soldiers prepared for battle
with every type of weapon, to help David with undivided loyalty—50,000;

³⁴ men of Naphtali—1,000 officers, together with 37,000
men carrying shields and spears;

³⁵ men of Dan, ready for battle—28,600;

³⁶ men of Asher, experienced soldiers prepared for battle—
40,000;

³⁷ and from east of the Jordan, men of Reuben, Gad and the
half-tribe of Manasseh, armed with every type of
weapon—120,000.

³⁸All these were fighting men who volunteered to serve in
the ranks. They came to Hebron fully determined to make
David king over all Israel. All the rest of the Israelites were
also of one mind to make David king. ³⁹The men spent three

days there with David, eating and drinking, for their families had supplied provisions for them. [40]Also, their neighbors from as far away as Issachar, Zebulun and Naphtali came bringing food on donkeys, camels, mules and oxen. There were plentiful supplies of flour, fig cakes, raisin cakes, wine, oil, cattle and sheep, for there was joy in Israel.

THE STORY OF King Saul's death in 1 Chronicles 10 represents the selective appeal to an earlier source, namely, the defeat of Israel by the Philistines at Mount Gilboa as recorded in 1 Samuel 31:1–13. The parallel passage is faithfully reproduced with minor changes, except for key additions of 1 Chronicles 10:6 ("and all his house died together") and 10:14 ("So the LORD put him [i.e., Saul] to death and turned the kingdom over to David son of Jesse"). This chapter may be divided into three parts: the battle report of the war with the Philistines (10:1–7), the exploit report of the Jabeshites honoring Saul (10:8–12), and the Chronicler's theological appraisal of Saul's reign (10:13–14).[1]

The abruptness of the shift from the genealogical prologue to the narrative of Hebrew kingship is striking. The brevity of the Chronicler's account of King Saul's reign is arresting as well. (1) Note that David, not Saul, is the focus of the Chronicler's retelling of Israelite history. Saul's death is a tragic but necessary introduction to Davidic kingship. (2) The writer of Chronicles has assumed his audience is familiar with the reign of King Saul on the basis of the records preserved in Samuel. Interestingly, as Japhet has observed, "the factor of time-sequence" plays almost no role in this rendition of Israel's kingship.[2] (3) Finally, the theological appraisal explains the motive for this terse summary of Saul's reign: the transition of kingship from the house of Saul to the house of David because of Saul's disobedience to God's word (10:14).

Typically, the story of Saul's death at Gilboa is understood as a foil to the kingship of David or as a paradigmatic example of the unfaithfulness that led to the Babylonian exile. I am inclined to agree with Selman, who admits the narrative includes elements of both interpretive approaches but suggests the real purpose of the chapter is the emphasis on the Davidic covenant as the permanent theological foundation for the restoration of the postexilic Jewish community (and the rest of biblical history for that matter).[3]

---

1. See De Vries, *1 and 2 Chronicles*, 117.
2. Japhet, *I and II Chronicles*, 221.
3. Selman, *1 Chronicles*, 134; cf. Thompson, *1, 2 Chronicles*, 111.

Saul's Death (10:1–7)

THIS FIRST SECTION of chapter 10 recounts King Saul's death and its aftermath, the rout of Israel by the Philistines. Saul was anointed king over Israel in order to deliver God's people "from the hand of the Philistines" (1 Sam. 9:16). Ironically, Saul and his sons were killed by these very same Philistines. In the end, Israel actually lost more territory than it gained in these wars. The national hopes that fueled the fervent clamor for a king were dashed at Mount Gilboa (cf. 1 Sam. 8:20). The chant of victory slogans (e.g., "Saul has slain his thousands," 1 Sam. 18:7) gave way to the wail of the funeral dirges ("How the mighty have fallen!" 2 Sam. 1:19).

The dramatic narration of the inexorable "press" of the battle against King Saul and his sons (10:2) helps illumine the Chronicler's assessment of the conflict: "so the LORD put him [Saul] to death" (10:14). In like manner, the naming of Saul's slain sons (10:2; cf. 1 Sam. 31:6, where Saul's fallen sons are unnamed) foreshadows the Chronicler's commentary on the cessation of his royal dynasty (1 Chron. 10:6). The reference to Jonathan (10:2) no doubt stirs memories in the Chronicler's audience of Jonathan's covenant of friendship with David and King David's eulogy of King Saul and Jonathan (cf. 1 Sam. 20:16–17; 2 Sam. 1:17–27). Tragically, Jonathan was everything Saul was not, but the crown prince recognized that he would never succeed his father (cf. 1 Sam. 20:13–14).

The battle at Mount Gilboa was staged on the southeast side of the plain of Esdraelon. Selman has suggested that fear and desperation drove Saul to engage the enemy in a precarious position, a crossroads permitting the Philistines optimum use of their chariots (cf. 1 Sam. 28:4–5).[4] Japhet has observed that fear is a dominant emotion in the Samuel narrative, motivating Saul's actions and predetermining his defeat.[5] Samuel's word of doom to Saul from beyond the grave induced a paralyzing dread in the king, no doubt inciting his request to his armor-bearer to kill him before the Philistines could capture him (1 Chron. 10:4; cf. 1 Sam. 28:19–20).

Both Samuel and Chronicles agree as to the wounding of King Saul by Philistine archers (10:3; cf. 1 Sam. 31:3). The refusal of his armor-bearer to honor Saul's request to kill him with the sword prompts the first king of Israel to fall on his own sword. Whether the armor-bearer's reluctance is related to respect for the Lord's anointed (e.g., 1 Sam. 24:10; 26:11) or fear of retaliation by way of a blood-vengeance custom is uncertain. The Chronicler offers no theological commentary on the propriety of Saul's suicide, a rare occurrence

---

4. Selman, *1 Chronicles*, 134–35; cf. Y. Aharoni and M. Avi-Yonah, *The Macmillan Bible Atlas*, rev. ed. (New York: Macmillan, 1977), 64.

5. Japhet, *I and II Chronicles*, 223–24.

in the Bible.[6] Clearly, suicide was preferable to torture and public humiliation at the hands of a pagan enemy. The report of the desecration of Saul's body indicates his fear of abuse by the enemy is justified (1 Chron. 10:9–10). As Japhet has aptly commented, the suicide of the anonymous armor-bearer (10:5) underscores the bitter end of the battle against the Philistines.[7] The glory of Israel "lies slain on [the] heights" (2 Sam. 1:19).

Chronicles omits entirely the report of King Saul's death as told to David by the Amalekite (2 Sam. 1:1–16). Beyond this, the Chronicler inserts "and all his house died together" (1 Chron. 10:6) for "and all his men died together" in the Samuel parallel (1 Sam. 31:6). Most commentators acknowledge the "dynastic" implications of the change. As Williamson has explained, in the theological light of God's plans for Israel, "Saul's dynasty was judged, and was therefore to all intents and purposes at an end."[8] This does not mean that the Chronicler is unaware of the surviving descendants of King Saul, as some suggest.[9] Saul's fourth son, Esh-Baal, and his grandson, Merib-Baal, find their place in the Benjamite genealogy (1 Chron. 8:33–34; 9:39–40). But another has already been anointed king over Israel (1 Sam. 16:12–13), and for the Chronicler the direct and immediate theological outcome of the battle of Mount Gilboa is David's kingship over all Israel.[10]

The deaths of Saul and his sons at Mount Gilboa have the practical outcome of demoralizing the Israelite militia, who flee the battleground (1 Chron. 10:7; cf. 1 Sam. 31:6, where the clause "all his men died" should be probably be understood as a small cohort of mercenary soldiers, much like David's band of "mighty men," 2 Sam. 23:8–39). News of the rout also causes the nearby Israelite civilian population of the Jordan River valley (1 Chron. 10:7), and even the region beyond the Jordan (1 Sam. 31:7), to evacuate and abandon their villages and towns to the Philistine army.

Saul's Burial (10:8–12)

THE CHRONICLER'S NARRATIVE differs from the Samuel parallel in certain details of the reporting of Saul's death (cf. 1 Sam. 31:1–13). For example, Chronicles omits the beheading of Saul and the public exposure of Saul's corpse on the city wall of Beth Shan (cf. 31:9–10). The Chronicler adds the detail of Saul's head displayed as a trophy of war in the temple of Dagon.

---

6. Instances of suicide are rare in the biblical record. See further A. J. Droge, "Suicide," *ABD*, 6:225–31.

7. Japhet, *I and II Chronicles*, 224.

8. Williamson, *1 and 2 Chronicles*, 93.

9. Braun, *1 Chronicles*, 150.

10. Japhet, *I and II Chronicles*, 225.

Earlier the sword of Goliath had been preserved in the Israelite sanctuary as a souvenir of God's victory over the Philistines through the valor of David. Now King Saul's armor becomes a relic in the temple of Ashtoreth, symbolizing the Philistine triumph over the Israelites (31:10). More significantly in the minds of the Philistines, the booty is public testimony to the supremacy of Dagon and the Ashtoreths over Yahweh of the Hebrews.

The rescue of the exposed corpses of Saul and his sons by the valiant men of Jabesh Gilead (10:11—12) may have been prompted by King Saul's deliverance of Jabesh Gilead from the aggression of Nahash the Ammonite (1 Sam. 11:1—11). Burning is mentioned as a penalty for certain sexual sins in Mosaic law (e.g., Lev. 20:14; 21:9; cf. Gen. 38:24). The burning of human remains is mentioned elsewhere in the Old Testament only in Amos 6:10 (presumably to prevent the spread of plague during the siege of a city). The remains of Saul and his sons may have been burned (see 1 Sam. 31:12) as an act of purification since their corpses had been desecrated by pagan foes (see 1 Chron. 10:12, although the Chronicler omits the reference to the burning of the remains of Saul and his sons). This may have been necessary for an honorable burial of Israel's fallen king and princes.

The burial site under "the great tree in Jabesh" was an important local landmark and probably a sacred site. Fasting was a mourning custom in ancient Israel (10:12; cf. 2 Sam. 1:12; 3:35). The seven-day duration of the fast by the inhabitants of Jabesh Gilead attest their fierce loyalty and high regard for King Saul. Sometime later the remains of Saul and his sons are exhumed and removed to the family tomb of Kish at Zela in the territory of Benjamin (2 Sam. 21:12—14).

Demise of Saul's Dynasty (10:13—14)

THE CHRONICLER CONCLUDES the story of Saul's death with a unique theological commentary on Saul's reign. Saul fails miserably on three crucial counts: He was unfaithful, he did not keep the word of the Lord (including consultation with a medium or witch, cf. 1 Sam. 28:7—25), and he neglected to seek guidance from the Lord. Unfaithfulness and failure to seek the Lord are prominent themes in Chronicles and inevitably result in divine judgment (e.g., 2 Chron. 12:2, 14; 15:13; 26:16, 18; 28:19, 22).

Saul's tragic death serves as a grim reminder of God's sovereignty over Israel and all the nations—a theological truth not lost on the Chronicler's audience as they languish in the aftermath of the Babylonian exile. The Philistines were merely agents of God's just punishment of King Saul's disobedience (even as the Babylonians were instruments of divine judgment in the exile of Judah). Finally, the Chronicler's narrative of Saul's death has a twofold purpose: (1) The Israelite kingdom and kingship belong to God; (2) God had good reason for transferring the kingdom from the family of Saul to the family of David.

All Israel Supports David's Kingship (11:1–12:40)

THE THEME OF "all Israel's" recognition of David as king unifies chapters 11 and 12. The widespread support of David on the part of the tribes is emphasized at the beginning and the end of the passage, with 11:1–3 and 12:38–40 forming a type of envelope for the section. The unity of Israel achieved under David's rule is reinforced by references of loyalty by David's "mighty men" (11:10) and the tribal militia (12:23, 31). For the Chronicler, the unity of the Israelite tribes forged under King David is the operative template for a similar reunification of the Jews during the postexilic period as a result of God's promised restoration of the Davidic dynasty.

Commentators have observed a highly stylized arrangement of the Chronicler's material in this passage. The pericope effectively combines the "flashback" technique with the chiastic arrangement hinging on David's anointing as king over Israel in Hebron. According to Japhet, the historical and literary focal point of the two chapters is the accession of David.[11] The series of reports describing the tribal support for David interweaves accounts both prior to and contemporary with that key event. The chiastic structure may be outlined as follows:

A David enthroned in Hebron (11:1–3)
  B David conquers Jerusalem (11:4–9)
    C Support of David's mighty men (who came to Hebron) (11:10–47)
      D Support of David at Ziklag (12:1–7)
        E Men of Gad support of David at his desert stronghold (12:8–15)
        E' Men of Judah and Benjamin support David at his desert stronghold (12:16–18)
      D' Men of Manassesh support David at Ziklag (12:19–22)
    C' Divisions of tribal militia support David at Hebron (12:23–37)
A' Celebration of David's enthronement in Hebron (12:38–40)

David enthroned at Hebron (11:1–3). The account of David's accession to Saul's throne in Hebron faithfully represents the earlier parallel found in 2 Samuel 5:1–5. The Chronicler omits the record of David's age at accession

---

11. Ibid., 233.

(thirty), the length of his reign (forty years, 5:4), and the fact that he ruled in Hebron as the capital of a separate kingdom of Judah for a span of nearly eight years (5:5). The Chronicler assumes that knowledge on the part of his audience since his purpose is to idealize the Israelite unity achieved under David with the hope of instilling similar expectations in postexilic Judah. By way of Old Testament chronology, David's forty-year reign is dated tentatively from about 1010 to 970 B.C.

The report of "all Israel" gathering to lend support to David's kingship (11:1) is echoed throughout the narrative (11:4, 10; 12:38). According to Wilcock, the Israelites rightfully justify the installation of David as king over Israel for several good reasons. (1) They recognize their kinship with David as their own "flesh and blood" (11:1). (2) David has earned the loyalty of the Israelites by his prowess in battle as Saul's general (11:2). (3) The people enter a compact with David and accept him as their king by anointing him (11:3). (4) Finally, the people confess that all has been done in accordance with the word of the Lord spoken by Samuel (11:3).[12]

The passage references several key concepts connected with kingship after the Davidic ideal: the pastoral image of king as shepherd of the people (an echo of Ezekiel's promise that God would place a shepherd like David over his people once again, Ezek. 34:23–24), the "king" (*melek*) as "ruler" (*nagid*; the term has military connotations and calls to mind the language of the Davidic covenant, 2 Sam. 7:7–8), and the act of anointing (the public recognition of a divine commission for an office of leadership, cf. 1 Sam. 16:3, 12). Moreover, the historical and theological significance of Hebron as the site of David's accession to the Israelite throne cannot be overlooked. The ancient city of Hebron was home and burial ground for the patriarchs and matriarchs of Israel: Abraham and Sarah, Isaac and Rebekah, and Jacob and Leah (cf. Gen. 13:18; 23:19; 35:27; 49:30–32). No doubt implicit in the Chronicler's association of David with the patriarchal site of Hebron geographically is the splicing together of the Abrahamic and Davidic covenants theologically. The promise of a self-governed progeny thriving in the Promised Land finds its fulfillment in the Davidic dynasty.

David conquers Jerusalem (11:4–9). The account of David's conquest of the Jebusite city of Jerusalem has its parallel in 2 Samuel 5:6–10 (noting that 1 Chronicles omits the events reported in 2 Sam. 1–4). The Chronicler's version of the battle for Jerusalem differs from that of Samuel at several points. (1) "The king and his men" (2 Sam. 5:6) are identified as "David and all the Israelites" (1 Chron. 11:4). (2) The Jebusite retort to David's siege is abbreviated (2 Sam. 5:6; cf. 1 Chron. 11:5). (3) The emphasis in Samuel on

12. Wilcock, *The Message of Chronicles*, 54.

the tactic resulting in Israelite victory (infiltration by means of the city's water shaft, 2 Sam. 5:8) gives way to the elevation of Joab as chief and commander of David's army in 1 Chronicles 11:6. Both reports agree that David then rebuilds portions of Jerusalem and makes the city his royal residence.

According to the Chronicler, the conquest of Jerusalem is the first major act of David's kingship (11:4). This narrative is important to the purpose of portraying the development of a "united Israel" under King David's leadership. As Williamson notes, the Chronicler emphasizes that David's personal troops are not alone in their support of Saul's rival.[13] In fact, the section ends with this same theme: The professional soldiers, the Israelite militia, and all the people of Israel are of one mind in their support of David even before his coronation in Hebron (12:38).

That the writer's agenda is primarily a political one at this point is evident since no mention is made of the religious significance of Jerusalem as the eventual site of Yahweh's temple. Admittedly, there is a certain genius in David's annexation of the Jebusite city of Jerusalem. (1) He secures a neutral site for his capital city. This means David has no political obligations to any Israelite "special interest group," the likely result had he established his capital city in the territory of one of the twelve tribes. (2) David captures intact a functioning bureaucratic center. This means David need only place his own "civil servants" into a ready-made political infrastructure as he organizes his kingdom.

The reference to the city of Jerusalem as Jebus (11:4) appears to be the Chronicler's convention for identifying the city prior to Israel's occupation (perhaps to distance the name Jerusalem from the pagan Jebus). The prominence given to Joab in the Chronicler's version of the conquest of Jerusalem may be due to his fierce loyalty to King David, part of that "strong support" David enjoys from his cadre of military leaders (11:10; cf. 2 Sam. 11:14–17). The "supporting terraces" (*millo*ʾ) are generally recognized by archaeologists as step-terraces built by the Jebusites on the eastern slope of Mount Zion. In contrast to Saul's unfaithfulness (1 Chron. 10:13), David expands his base of power in Israel because "the LORD Almighty was with him" (11:9). The Chronicler rightly acknowledges David's faithfulness to God and his obedience to God's law as the standard by which his successors will be measured (2 Chron. 7:17).

David's mighty men (11:10–47). The roster of David's mighty men and the reports of their heroic exploits has its precursor in 2 Samuel 23:8–39. The original list of heroes demonstrates a three-part structure: the Three and their singular exploits (2 Sam. 23:8–12//1 Chron. 11:10–14) and the acts of the Three as a group (2 Sam. 23:13–17//1 Chron. 11:15–19), the exploits of

---

13. Williamson, *1 and 2 Chronicles*, 101.

two other warriors of special status (2 Sam. 23:18–23//1 Chron. 11:20–25), and the roster of all the mighty men (minus any reference to their deeds, 2 Sam. 23:24–39//1 Chron. 11:26–41a). The addendum to the Chronicler's roster of mighty men (1 Chron. 11:41b–47) represents another military source of unknown origin available to the writer. (On the geographical chiastic structure of chs. 11–12, see the comments on 12:1–7.)[14]

The lists of soldiers in both Samuel and the Chronicles parallel make reference to the "Three" and the "Thirty" (2 Sam. 23:8, 13, 17, 23; 1 Chron. 11:15, 20, 25). The "Three" are identified as the "chiefs" (*ro'š*) of the rest of the mighty men. The term probably signifies the role of general or commander within the cohort of the mighty men. The designation the "Thirty" is an idealized title for the complete unit of mighty men. No doubt these esteemed "tags" were intended to differentiate and elevate the best warriors from the rest of the professional military and the Israelite militia. The absence of Joab in the register of David's mighty men is conspicuous. We may surmise, however, on the basis of the report of the capture of Jerusalem, that Joab is the supreme commander (or "command-in-chief," NIV) of all of David's military forces (2 Sam. 8:16; 1 Chron. 11:6).

These elite troops are professional soldiers, not vulgar mercenaries. They live and die by the military code of their day—a code of honor that even prohibited the enjoyment of personal pleasures while on "active duty" (cf. 2 Sam. 11:11). David's "mighty men" (*haggibborim*) are the ancient equivalent of both the modern-day "special forces" military units and the "secret service," charged with the protection of our highest elected officials (note their roles as both irrepressible warriors in the face of overwhelming odds and as bodyguards to the king, 2 Sam. 23:23; 1 Chron. 11:25).

Beyond this, the unswerving loyalty of the cohort of mighty men to God and the king is rooted in the ideology of the Davidic covenant (cf. 2 Sam. 7:12; 1 Chron. 17:11). King David and his dynasty are the "lamp of Israel," and the mighty men serve with distinction and uncommon valor so that that "lamp" will not be extinguished (cf. 2 Sam. 21:17). The Chronicler's interest in these heroes is found in the "strong support" they give to David as king (1 Chron. 11:10). Their role is that of a catalyst or a type of a "patriotic glue" bonding "all Israel" in solidarity for David. The subsequent story of Solomon's succession to the throne is instructive in reconstructing the importance of the mighty men for the office of king, since their support is decisive in establishing Solomon as king of Israel (cf. 1 Kings 1:8, 36–38). The Chronicler recognizes that the survival of the postexilic community to which he writes

---

14. See further the helpful comparative chart of David's "mighty men" as listed in 2 Sam. 23 and 1 Chron. 11 in Braun, *1 Chronicles*, 161–62.

depends on this kind of unanimity of support for the leadership God might restore in Jerusalem.

The roster of David's mighty men begins with the names and exploits of those known as "the Three": Jashobeam, Eleazar, and Shammah (11:11–14). This trio of warriors are the most accomplished of all of David's military personnel, each known for deeds of singular valor against the Philistines—the nemesis of the united monarchy. Jashobeam is "chief of the officers" (11:11; or "chief of the Three," 2 Sam. 23:8). He earned his place at the head of David's elite military cohort by his single-handed defeat of three hundred Philistines in one encounter (1 Chron. 11:11). Eleazar distinguished himself with David in a battle against the Philistines at Pas Dammim (11:13). Most commentators agree that the report of Shammah (2 Sam. 23:9b–11a) has fallen out of the Chronicler's record as a result of scribal error.[15]

Perhaps the most striking feature of 11:11–14 is the theological assessment of the heroism of the Three, that "the LORD brought about a great victory" (11:14; cf. 2 Sam. 23:10, 12). The Chronicler's theology of hope for postexilic Judah rests not on the exploits of "mighty men" but on "the LORD strong and mighty, the LORD mighty in battle" (Ps. 24:8).

It is unclear whether the account of the three anonymous mighty men securing water for King David from the heavily guarded well at Bethlehem (11:15–19) should be connected with the names of David's heroes preceding or following the story. Japhet is probably correct in her assessment that this literary unit makes reference to the deeds of the previously mentioned Three, functioning as a group.[16] What is unmistakably clear is the Chronicler's emphasis on David's ability as a leader to inspire remarkable bravery and unshakable loyalty among his followers.

No doubt, the Chronicler's audience hears echoes of David's own exploits as a "mighty man" in the recounting of the deeds of his mighty men (e.g., 2 Sam. 18:6–7). The report is careful to note that the significance of such acts of heroism on the part of these warriors is not lost on David. The repetition of the king's refusal to drink the water obtained at great risk but instead pouring it out on the ground is testimony to the immense admiration and deep respect he has for these comrades (1 Chron. 11:19). Like the lifeblood of an animal sacrifice poured out onto the ground, David refuses the water because it is as precious as blood since his men have risked their very lives to secure it for him. As an aside, the reference to the Philistine garrison stationed at Bethlehem (11:16) indicates the extent of their penetration into the hill country of Israel during the days of Kings Saul and David (cf. 2 Sam. 8:1).

---

15. E.g., Selman, *1 Chronicles*, 142.
16. Japhet, *I and II Chronicles*, 243.

Next the Chronicler showcases two additional heroes of special status, ranking somewhere between the "Three" and the "Thirty" (11:20–25). The intrepid exploits of Abishai and Benaiah are well documented, especially their victories over the "best men" (^ʾ*ariʾel*, "champion" [lit., "lion of God"], 11:22) of Israel's enemies (cf. 1 Sam. 26:6; 1 Kings 2:35; 1 Chron. 2:16). Abishai is mentioned because of his place as leader of the Thirty (1 Chron. 11:20).[17]

Benaiah is accorded special honor because of his role as the chief of King David's bodyguards (11:25). We are unable to grasp the full significance of these elite military classifications of the Three and the Thirty in ancient Israel. There is clearly an important distinction between the two cohorts since the Chronicler readily notes the fame of Abishai and Benaiah among the Thirty, but he is most careful to preserve the fact that they are not numbered among the Three (11:21, 25).

The list of David's "mighty men" in 1 Chronicles 11:26–47 is longer than the parallel found in 2 Samuel 23:24–39. This probably explains the Chronicler's omission of the title "the Thirty" (1 Chron. 11:26; cf. 2 Sam. 23:24) and the concluding tally ("thirty-seven in all," cf. 2 Sam. 23:39). Selman notes a rough geographical order in the Chronicler's catalog of the mighty men: beginning with Judah (1 Chron. 11:26–30), then including the northern Israelite tribes (11:31–37), next identifying the non-Israelite warriors (11:38–41a), and finally an additional source citing those with connections to the Transjordan (11:41b–47).[18]

The differences in the two lists enumerating David's mighty men suggests not only the Chronicler's access to additional historical sources but also the natural fluidity in the composition of a group of military heroes during David's long reign. It is worth noting that the list of David's mighty men in Samuel concludes with "Uriah the Hittite" (2 Sam. 23:39; cf. 1 Chron. 11:41). One can only speculate as to the theological motivation the Chronicler might have in extending this register of David's "mighty men."

Early tribal support for David: Benjamin (12:1–7). This section of the larger literary unit (chs. 10–12) furthers the Chronicler's theme of the wide support King David enjoys from "all Israel." The purpose of chapter 12 seems to be that of telling the story of the building of David's "great army" (12:22). Additionally, the Chronicler seeks to demonstrate that David's backing combines the support of the military establishment and the general populace (12:38).

---

17. Reading the Greek and Latin textual variant "Thirty" for the MT "Three," following the NLT and NRSV.

18. Selman, *1 Chronicles*, 143.

Chapter 12 divides neatly into two parts: the defectors from Saul's army who join David while he is a fugitive as the rival king (12:1–22), and the assembly of the Israelite militia at Hebron for David's coronation (12:23–40). The Chronicler resorts to a familiar structure, the geographical chiasm.[19] In this case, he arranges the tallies of the tribal contingents lending support to David around three geographical locations:

A Hebron (11:10)
  B Ziklag (12:1)
    C Desert stronghold (12:8)
    C' Desert stronghold (12:16)
  B' Ziklag (12:20)
A' Hebron (12:23)

This material has no parallel in the Samuel narrative, suggesting the Chronicler preserves an untitled military document from the period of the united monarchy.

The account of the defection of certain warriors from the tribe of Benjamin to David's guerilla band dates to the time when David was seeking asylum among the Philistines (12: 1–7). According to 1 Samuel, David was granted haven in Ziklag by the Philistine prince Achish, and he lived there with his army of six hundred for sixteen months (1 Sam. 27:6–7). The fact that these defectors are kinsmen of King Saul is not lost on the Chronicler (1 Chron. 12:2). The ambidextrous skill of these Benjamite warriors as both slingers and bowmen is noteworthy. The addition of a contingent of twenty-three experienced soldiers to David's army does not seem too impressive to the modern reader. Yet we learn from the Amarna correspondence from an earlier historical period that a small cohort of experienced archers could turn the tide of a battle.[20]

Selman has noted that it is to David's credit that a former opponent, Ishmaiah (12:4), is admitted to the elite company of the Thirty warriors.[21] Some of the place names in the territory of Benjamin are readily identified (e.g., Gibeah, Anathoth, Gibeon), while the location of others remains uncertain (e.g., Gederah, Korah).

Early tribal support for David: Gad (12:8–15). Quite apart from the fact that Gad receives little attention in Chronicles, it is notable that members of this northerly tribe are found so far to the south. It seems likely that David's

19. Williamson, *1 and 2 Chronicles*, 105.
20. See William L. Moran, *The Amarna Letters* (Baltimore: Johns Hopkins Univ. Press, 1992), EA 71, 73, 82, 90, 93, 105, 127, 131, 139.
21. Selman, *1 Chronicles*, 145.

"stronghold in the desert" at this time is either Adullam (cf. 1 Sam. 22:1) or En Gedi (cf. 1 Sam. 24:1). The list of eleven Gadite defectors (1 Chron. 12:9–13) is framed by exploit reports emphasizing the caliber of the warriors joining David's ranks (12:8, 14–15). Unlike the archers and slingers from the tribe of Benjamin who are effective in battle from a distance (12:1–7), the Gadite soldiers excel in hand-to-hand combat because of their speed and strength. According to Williamson, the metaphorical comparison of the heroic qualities of warriors with animals (12:8) is commonplace in the ancient world to the degree that such designations often become titles for warriors.[22]

The concluding exploit report underscores the military prowess of the Gadite warriors in two ways. The first generalizes about the superior quality of these mercenaries in comparison to other soldiers (12:14). The second preserves the specific account of their remarkable crossing of the Jordan River, swollen by the springtime thawing of snows at the headwaters of Mount Hermon (12:15). Such a crossing of the Jordan River at flood stage was part of the miraculous entry of the Israelites into the land of Canaan subsequent to the Exodus (cf. Josh. 3:13–17). The latter portion of the concluding exploit report poses translation difficulties. Myers best captures the sense: "These were the ones who once crossed the Jordan in the first month when it had overflowed all its banks and made impassable all the lowlands to the east and to the west."[23]

Early tribal support for David: Benjamin and Judah (12:16–18). As in the preceding unit, the setting for this passage is David's "stronghold" (12:16). The site is unnamed, but some scholars suggest the fortress is located near En Gedi (cf. 1 Sam. 24:1).[24] The text recounts the story of a special group of soldiers from Benjamin and Judah who seek asylum with David. The motive for their shift in allegiance from Saul to David is unclear. David himself is suspicious of their intentions and challenges their loyalty under oath (12:17). His skepticism is well-founded in that during his flight from King Saul he was already betrayed by Doeg the Edomite (1 Sam. 22:22), the people of the village of Keilah (23:12), and the Ziphites (26:1).

There is some question as to the identity of Amasai (12:18) since he is associated with the Thirty warriors. Amasai may have been the Amasa appointed commander over the Israelite army by Absalom following his coup and ouster of King David from Jerusalem (2 Sam. 17:25). Amasa was eventually reinstated by David as a commander in his own army (only to be assassinated later by Joab, 2 Sam. 19:13; 20:9–10). The Chronicler's real

---

22. Williamson, *1 and 2 Chronicles*, 107.
23. Myers, *I Chronicles*, 92.
24. Thompson, *1, 2 Chronicles*, 124.

---

interest is not Amasai's place among the Thirty; rather, his emphasis is on his poetic speech. He well understands that the success of the restoration community depends on an oath of loyalty on the part of his audience to the current Davidic household. The checkered history of Israelite kingship is due in part to the divided loyalties of the twelve tribes, frequently resulting in schisms and eventually prompting the division of the monarchy into northern and southern states. The key to reestablishing the kingdom of Israel is unity among the tribes, and the catalyst for such unity is the house of David.

Implicit in David's oath (12:17, "may the God of our fathers see it and judge you") is the threat of a divine curse, an indication of the gravity of the situation David faces in terms of uncertain support during the period of his transition to the throne of Israel. The reference to the "Spirit" coming on Amasai (12:18; lit., "the Spirit clothed Amasai," cf. Judg. 6:34; 2 Chron. 24:20) signifies the anointing of God's Spirit and marks his speech as a type of prophetic utterance. The reference to the "Spirit" may also serve as the Chronicler's affirmation that God's Spirit remains among the people of postexilic Judah (cf. Hag. 2:5).

Amasai's speech makes oblique reference to the Davidic covenant in the clause "your God will help you" (cf. 17:7–14). Japhet has noted close parallels between David's speech challenging the loyalty of this group of defectors (12:17) and the speech of Amasai (12:18).[25] In response to David's question of allegiance, Amasai replies, "We are yours" (12:18a). The second half of Amasai's speech plays on the key words prompting David's skepticism, "peace" (*šalom*, trans. "success" 3x in 12:17–18) and "help" (*ʿzr*, 3x in 12:17–18). The Chronicler essentially tells his audience that "God helps those who help David and his descendants."

Early tribal support for David: Manasseh (12:19–22). The Chronicler assumes that his audience knows the story of the Philistine mistrust of David and the dismissal of his assistance as they muster for battle against the Israelites at Aphek (cf. 1 Sam. 29). The Philistine rejection of David's help as an ally against Saul's army may be understood as an act of divine providence on two scores. (1) David and his army are thus freed to pursue the Amalekites raiders who have plundered, burned, and taken captives from Ziklag during David's absence (cf. 1 Sam. 30). (2) The suspicion of David's motives on the part of the Philistines prompting their denial of his participation in the battle against King Saul means David is absolved from raising his hand against the Lord's anointed leader of Israel (cf. 1 Sam. 24:6, 10; 26:9).

The theme of "help" joins this passage with the preceding unit (12:16–18). Amasai's generalized prophecy of God's help in bringing about suc-

---

25. Japhet, *I and II Chronicles*, 265.

cess for David's kingship (12:18) is fulfilled specifically through the loyal "help" of others against the Amalekite bandits (12:21–22). Allen has noted this motif of "help" for David is further emphasized in the wordplay with the noun for "help" (*'ezer*) in the names of certain of the soldiers defecting to the rival king (e.g., Ahiezer, 12:3; Joezer, 12:6; Ezer, 12:9). The phrase "units of a thousand" (12:20, lit., "chiefs of thousands") is probably better understood as leaders of tribal clans (so JPSV). The statement reporting the great army amassed by David (12:22) serves as a summary for the entire section.

The equation of the size of David's army with the "army of God" proves difficult to assess (12:22). The phrase occurs elsewhere in the Old Testament only in Genesis 32:2. Selman suggests that its usage here hints at the idea of "unseen divine support" (as is the case in Genesis).[26] If this summary statement anticipates the census of the Israelite militia joining King David's army some eight years later at Hebron reported in the following section (12:23–40; cf. 2 Sam. 5:5), then David's army tallies 336,900 soldiers (plus an unspecified number of loyalists from the tribe of Issachar, 1 Chron. 12:32). This certainly constitutes a "great army," but even this total pales when compared to David's later (ill-advised) military census counting 800,000 troops in Israel and 500,000 troops in Judah (cf. 2 Sam. 24:9).

The tribes anoint David at Hebron (12:23–40). This tribal muster roll with tallies complements the preceding lists of individuals who side with David after the death of Saul. The record is another example of unique sources available to the Chronicler, since the passage has no parallel in the books of Samuel or Kings. The purpose of this report of the tribal gathering at Hebron is the transfer of Saul's kingdom to David (12:23; note the repetition of *sbb* ["turn over"] in 10:14 and 12:23). The Chronicler also notes that all this is done according to the word of the Lord (12:23). A poetic reflection on the coronation of David may be read in Psalm 89.

The muster roll names eleven tribes and two half-tribes, the most complete tribal register in the Old Testament. All this is further evidence in support of the Chronicler's basic premise that "all Israel" supports David's kingship (12:38). The muster roll begins with those tribes located in the southern regions (Judah, Simeon, Levi). It then proceeds to cite Benjamin (historically the transitional territory between the south and the north), and concludes with the northern tribes (with the Transjordan tribes of Rueben, Gad, and half of Manasseh capping the list). The tallies probably record the number of Israelite militia in contrast to the professional soldiers of the preceding reports, since the troops are identified as volunteers (12:38).

---

26. Selman, *1 Chronicles*, 147.

The small size of the tallies of the militia defecting to David from the southern tribes in contrast to the large tallies of militia from the northern tribes has puzzled interpreters. Perhaps the vast majority of volunteer troops in the south have already pledged their loyalty to David. The size of the tallies has also prompted alternative interpretations of the numbers. The word translated "thousand" (*’elep*) may indicate a military cadre or unit. Thus, it is possible to render the tally of Judah in this fashion: "the men of Judah, carrying shield and spear numbered six units with eight hundred armed men" (12:24).[27] Wenham has proposed reading the Hebrew *’lp* as *’allup*, meaning "chief" or "officer."[28] In this case Judah musters eight hundred troops under six officers. Finally, Payne argues against understanding the numbers as totals but rather as a list of officers: "six (commanders of) thousands, eight (commanders of) hundreds" (12:24).[29] According to this interpretation, a total of 398 Israelite officers (not 340,800 Israelite militia) attend David's coronation in Hebron.

The section concludes with representatives from the Hebrew tribes gathered at Hebron for the crowning of David as king over all Israel (12:38–40). The emphasis of the Chronicler on Israel as "the people of God" is seen in the various segments of Hebrew society joining in the coronation, including the professional military (12:1–22), the volunteer militia (12:23–37), and the rest of the Israelites (12:38). Chronologically, this closing paragraph completes the narrative begun in 11:1–3, the account of "all Israel" assembling at Hebron to anoint David as king. David's coronation sets the stage for the rest of the Chronicler's history, especially the relocation of the ark of the covenant in Jerusalem, Yahweh's covenant with David (chs. 13–17), and the rest of David's achievements as the great shepherd-king of Israel (chs. 18–29).

It is important to note that all who come to Hebron are "fully determined" to make David king. Literally the assembly of the Hebrews is of a "peaceable mind" or "undivided heart" (12:39). This wholehearted service to God and king is a repeated theme in Chronicles (cf. 28:9; 2 Chron. 19:9; 25:2). The three days of "eating and drinking" with King David are covenantal terms. It was customary in biblical times to conclude covenant ceremonies with celebrations that climaxed in a meal (e.g., Gen. 31:54; Ex. 24:11). The feast ratifies the compact or covenant brokered between David and the elders of Israel (1 Chron. 11:3). The duration of the ratification festival (three days) indicates the strength of Israel's support for David's kingship.

---

27. Myers, *I Chronicles*, 98.
28. John W. Wenham, "Large Numbers in the Old Testament," *TynBul* 18 (1967): 44–53.
29. Payne, "1, 2 Chronicles," 4:378.

The Chronicler is careful to report that the outcome of that tribal unity is "joy in Israel" (1 Chron. 12:40; cf. 29:22; 2 Chron. 7:8–10; 30:21–26). He is hopeful, no doubt, that this recipe for joy will be the experience of post-exilic Judah as well.

THE CHRONICLER WELL understands the truth of the old adage that "no one declares independence, only allegiance." The biblical world knows only two paths: the way of the righteous and the way of the wicked (Ps. 1). There is no neutrality when it comes to relationship with God. Both the Old and the New Testaments prescribe an unswerving loyalty to God. For example, the stipulations of the Sinai covenant make this unmistakably clear: "You shall have no other gods before me . . . for I, the LORD your God, am a jealous God" (Ex. 20:3–5); and "fear the LORD your God, serve him only . . . do not follow other gods" (Deut. 6:13–14).

Attempts to maintain divided loyalties are equally forbidden. We need only recall Elijah's rebuke of Israel in the contest with the prophets of Baal on Mount Carmel: "How long will you waver between two opinions? If the LORD is God, follow him; but if Baal is God, follow him" (1 Kings 18:21). The teachings of Jesus affirm simply but forcibly the exclusive nature of the relationship to God: "He who is not with me is against me," and "no one can serve two masters . . . you cannot serve both God and Money" (Matt. 6:24; 12:30).

The heroic story of David's passage from fugitive to king hinges on the principle of allegiance or loyalty. It was the disloyalty of King Saul that disqualified both him and his descendants from establishing a royal dynasty (10:13–14). In fact, the Chronicler registers three specific counts of disloyalty against King Saul: disobedience to God's word, consultation with a medium or witch, and a failure to inquire of God (10:13; cf. Saul's neglect of the ark of the covenant, 13:3). Impetuous Saul sought to balance his divided loyalties to both God and other (Canaanite) gods through the mediation of the prophet Samuel and mediums like the witch of Endor. In an ironic twist, God's final message to Saul—that of his impending death and the end of his dynasty—was conveyed through the spirit of the dead prophet by means of a terrified medium (cf. 1 Sam. 28). Disloyalty to God inevitably results in disaster, whether Saul on an individual level or Israel on a national level (cf. 1 Chron. 9:1).

By stark contrast, David's loyalty to God propels him into kingship. The next section of Chronicles preserves concrete examples of David's loyalty to God, including the return of the ark of the covenant (and hence Yahweh) to the national religious life of Israel (chs. 13–15), the reestablishment of

Yahweh and his saving deeds as the centerpiece of worship (ch. 16), and the prayer that David's dynasty will make known Yahweh as Israel's God to the nations (17:23–24).

David's loyalty to God also fosters a like-minded response to David himself among those who recognize him as the Lord's "anointed." This included the "disenfranchised" of Israel (e.g., 1 Sam. 22:2) and defectors from Saul's camp (e.g., 1 Chron. 12:2). Eventually David inspires the loyalty of all Israel (12:38). The ripple effect of his loyalty to God is not lost on the Chronicler. The subtext of his "sermon" on David's loyalty may be stated accordingly: Loyalty to God induces the mutual loyalty of the tribes to each other, which results in the blessing of God on Israel. For the Chronicler, nothing less than a similar formula is necessary to restore the postexilic community to the former greatness of Israel united under King David.

The Chronicler views loyalty to God as a catalyst for tribal unity. We must be careful, however, not to reduce this insight into a mechanistic cause-and-effect relationship dependent solely on the emotive and volitional human response of allegiance (to God and/or king). Allen reminds us that in chapters 11–12 we have the "triad of Israel, David, and God cooperating in beautiful harmony."[30] Clearly David is the focal point of the Israelite unity, but the Chronicler unmistakably credits David's success to the fact that "the LORD Almighty was with him" (11:9). Those defecting from Saul to join with the rival king do so because they also perceive that God's help rests with David (12:18). Not long afterward all Israel joins together to support David (12:38).

Ultimately, the issue is not one of allegiance conditioned by charismatic personality or military prowess. The psalmist provides ample warning against placing such trust in princes or warriors (Ps. 146:3; 147:10–11). No genuine or lasting help can be found with mortal leaders. Allegiance and loyalty must be rooted in an authority and in principles that transcend human ingenuity and strength. Greater than King Saul or King David is the idea of divinely ordained kingship in Israel (1 Sam. 10:1; 16:1, 13). Greater still is the God of Israel, who has established that sacred office for the purpose of shepherding his people (cf. Ps. 45). This formed the basis, in part, for David's loyalty to God and explains his reluctance to take any action against Saul despite the repeated attempts against his life by the tormented king (1 Sam. 18:11; 19:1).

David's loyalty is rewarded and enshrined in a divinely initiated treaty mediated by the prophet Nathan (2 Sam. 7; 1 Chron. 17). The divine promises incorporated into this covenant of grant provides for perpetual leadership for the Israelites through a Davidic dynasty, security and rest for Israel among the nations in the land bequeathed to Abraham and Sarah, and

---

30. Allen, *1, 2 Chronicles*, 91.

the blessing of God's presence with his people. We must remember that biblical theology tends to be practical theology because God is good (cf. Ps. 25:7–8; 34:8; 100:5). His goodness prompts him to seek the welfare of all through the instrument of Israel as his chosen people and through David as his chosen king (cf. Ps. 86; 89).

The immediately tangible benefits of loyalty to God for the tribes of Israel at David's accession to the throne included strength, resilience, mutual help in corporate solidarity (12:21–22), a single-mindedness of purpose (12:38), and national joy (12:40). Even as disloyalty to God results in the curse of punishment, so loyalty to God yields the blessing of unity (Ps. 133).

ON LOYALTY. The Chronicler preaches to a people in the throes of crisis, a crisis rooted in issues of allegiance to God and loyalty to each other as fellow Jews. A close reading of the prophets Haggai, Zechariah, and Malachi suggests that early postexilic Judah languishes in apathy and despair. The restoration community is disillusioned with God because they assume his Word had failed, since no David-like king has arisen to shepherd Israel as Jeremiah and Ezekiel promised (cf. Jer. 33:15; Ezek. 34:23–24). In addition, a selfish individualism hinders the development of community spirit as the Jews seek to rebuild after the Exile (Hag. 1:4–6; Mal. 1:12–14). Despite the zealous efforts of Ezra and Nehemiah some two generations earlier, their initiatives for religious and social reform seem to have little lasting impact on the Jerusalem and Judah of the Chronicler's day.

Two centuries prior to the Chronicler's "historical sermons," the prophet Jeremiah pleaded with the ancestors of these people. They too were mired in a crisis of loyalty, glibly dividing their allegiance to Yahweh on the one hand, and the Queen of Heaven on the other (cf. Jer. 7:18–19). Jeremiah forecasted disaster for Judah because of their idolatry, pride, and disregard for social justice (cf. 6:19; 7:9–11; 13:9–10). This was no idle threat on the part of God's watchman, as the message of the book of Lamentations testifies. The frightening reality of divine judgment took the form of a Babylonian invasion, resulting in the sack of Jerusalem and the exile of the Jews from the land of the covenant promise.

Seeking to avert an encore of that catastrophe, the Chronicler echoes Jeremiah's call to "stand at the crossroads and look; ask for the ancient paths" (Jer. 6:16). For Jeremiah the "ancient path" was the good way of obedience to God's law and faithfulness to Mosaic covenant (cf. Deut. 25:19; 33:12). For the Chronicler, the "ancient path" is one of similar fidelity and loyalty to God—as exemplified in the life of King David.

The writer of Chronicles appeals to David's example of fierce loyalty to God because the spirit of unity it inspired among the tribes of Israel. After all, support of the Israelite monarchy was essential to the success of the post-exilic community. The Chronicler's appeal to this earlier historical example is neither a wistful lapse into nostalgia nor a desperate manipulation of Hebrew history for the sake of concocting a magical formula for national success. If we may read accurately between the lines of the Chronicler's historical "sermon," he seems to be simply calling his audience to do the right thing—quite apart from the hope of any tangible reward for the individual or the larger community. For the Hebrews the right thing to do—from that first word of promise to Abraham and Sarah to the Mosaic covenant enacted at Sinai and beyond—is to respond to God with unswerving allegiance.

That loyalty to God is not a game chip by which we might barter for God's favor and blessing was clearly understood by the three Jewish servants of King Nebuchadnezzar. When commanded to disavow the true God and bow to an idol, upon threat of incineration, they refused. They shamelessly confessed to the king that whether God in his infinite wisdom and power chose to deliver them from their peril or not, their oath of loyalty was sworn to him alone (Dan. 3:16–18). As Bennett has compiled in *The Book of Virtues*:

> Our loyalties are important signs of the kinds of persons we have chosen to become. They mark a kind of constancy or steadfastness in our attachments to those other persons, groups, institutions, or ideals with which we have deliberately decided to associate ourselves.[31]

The Bible, however, is well aware of the relationship between one's loyalties extrinsically and one's character intrinsically long before the publication of Bennett's tome addressing the crisis of character in North American society. For example, Jesus likened the correspondence between the inward character and the outward behavior to the telltale quality of the fruit of trees (Matt. 12:33–37). Inevitably, the loyalties of our heart determine what we count as "treasure" in this life (6:21). To his credit, Bennett has aptly observed that the virtue of loyalty needs to be informed by "both the wisdom to know what the right thing to do is, and the will to do it."[32] The former was certainly no mystery for the Chronicler and his audience. From Moses to Micah, the instruction to the Israelites is consistent and may be easily summarized in two directives: to love God with one's entire being (Deut. 6:5; or "to walk humbly with ... God," Mic. 6:8) and to love one's neighbor as one's self (Lev. 19:18; or "to act justly and to love mercy," Mic. 6:8).

---

31. William J. Bennett, *The Book of Virtues* (New York: Simon & Schuster, 1993), 665.
32. Ibid.

That these truths are injunctions indicates the will is involved, not just the emotions. Nor is the desired response of obedience to God achieved by the sheer, fist-clenched determination of the suppliant. Rather, allegiance to God is "not too difficult" for the follower of Yahweh because it is accomplished by means of the cooperative work of God's Spirit (Zech. 4:6). The Chronicler's summons to show loyalty to God, subtly couched in the biography of King David, echoes Joshua's charge to "carefully obey" the law of Moses and anticipates Jesus' teaching about the greatest commandment in the law (Matt. 22:34–40).

The crisis of loyalty addressed by the Chronicler is not as far removed from the Christian church as we might think. Popular culture naturally infiltrates and influences the Christian subculture over the course of time. One example illustrates the point. The contemporary social doctrine of "political correctness" has created a "PC" mindset that now permeates popular culture. To be politically correct means to conform to a belief that language and practices that might offend another sociopolitical or religious group are to be eliminated. As Gaede has noted, the attitude of "tolerance" promoted by the "political correctness" movement erodes loyalty to the God of the Bible by denying the existence of moral and religious absolutes.[33]

This relativizing of God's truth as revealed in (Christian) Scripture mutes convictions and thus fosters a pseudo-neutrality that grants the "truth of Islam" or the "truth of Hinduism" as on equal footing with the "truth of Christianity." Hence, the Christian church is now embroiled in an intramural controversy involving the exclusive claims of the gospel of Jesus Christ and its implications for the doctrine of salvation in this age of religious pluralism.[34]

In addition to the problem of ambivalence, we also face the challenge of what may be called "competing loyalties." Veith has rightly observed that the postmodern emphases on pluralism and multicultural awareness have segmented or splintered society into hundreds of subcultures, creating a new tribalism.[35] Again, the Christian church has not escaped the effects of this new tribalism as the debates over issues like women's roles in the church, inclusive-language Bible translation, same-sex marriage, and the ordination of homosexual clergy attest. For these reasons alone, education in biblical

---

33. S. D. Gaede, *When Tolerance Is No Virtue* (Downers Grove, Ill.: InterVarsity Press, 1993), 20–30.

34. See the attempt to "objectify" the discussion by presenting the views of normative pluralism, inclusivism, salvation in Christ, and salvation in Christ alone as equally viable theological positions in Dennis L. Okholm and Timothy R. Phillips, eds., *More Than One Way?* (Grand Rapids: Zondervan, 1995).

35. Gene E. Veith, *Postmodern Times: A Christian Guide to Contemporary Thought and Culture* (Wheaton, Ill.: Crossway, 1994), 143–56.

morality remains an imperative for the millennial generation of the Christian church.

The Chronicler would have approved of Bennett's concern for "the time-honored task of the moral education of the young ... the training of the heart and mind toward good."[36] He would also agree with the emphasis placed on the need to couple sound instruction with modeling of moral example, although I suspect the Chronicler might take issue with limiting moral education to youth, since the Bible exhorts men and women, young and old, to the daily practice of godly virtues (Deut. 31:12; Titus 2:1–7).

What might that moral education look like in view of the Chronicler's message? The writing of a primer on moral education lies beyond the scope of this commentary, but I offer these basic categories that seem essential for consideration as a baseline for biblically informed moral education:

- a healthy understanding of what it means to "return" to God in repentance (cf. 2 Chron. 30:6). Only by taking personal responsibility of one's sin before God can the individual Christian and the Christian church prevent the insidious cancer of "victim status" that ravages the moral fiber of Western society.[37]
- a thorough knowledge of the Word of God, the Bible (2 Chron. 34:21). In the Old Testament, special attention should be given to the moral law of Moses in the Torah, the precepts of the book of Proverbs as a practical commentary on the Torah, the book of Psalms as an experiential commentary on the Torah, and select minor prophets (e.g., Hosea, Amos) as a hortatory commentary on the Torah. In the New Testament, the teachings of Jesus in the Gospels and the ethical imperatives of Paul in Romans (chs. 12–14) merit focused study.
- a program of discipleship that takes seriously Paul's charge to Timothy to "set an example for the believers in speech, in life, in love, in faith and in purity" (1 Tim. 4:12). The value of what Bennett calls "the moral power of quiet example" may be seen in both contemporary role models of the Christian faith and virtue and in historical personages, whether by character study of biblical figures or Christian auto/biography. We need the moral example of that "great cloud of witnesses" (Heb. 12:1).[38]
- a renewed emphasis on teaching the doctrine of the Holy Spirit, especially the biblical injunctions to "be filled with the Spirit" and to "pray in the Spirit on all occasions" (Eph. 5:18; 6:18).

---

36. Bennett, *The Book of Virtues*, 11.
37. Bork, *Slouching Towards Gomorrah*, 82.
38. Bennett, *The Book of Virtues*, 11.

The difference between King Saul and King David is that Saul failed to obey the Word of the Lord (1 Chron. 10:13), so that God's Spirit eventually departed from him (1 Sam. 16:14). In the end, it was the Spirit of God working through Amasai who engineered the coalition of tribal support for King David (1 Chron. 12:18). It is "'not by might, nor by power, but by my Spirit,' says the LORD Almighty" (Zech. 4:6).

1 Chronicles 13–17

D AVID CONFERRED WITH each of his officers, the commanders of thousands and commanders of hundreds. ²He then said to the whole assembly of Israel, "If it seems good to you and if it is the will of the LORD our God, let us send word far and wide to the rest of our brothers throughout the territories of Israel, and also to the priests and Levites who are with them in their towns and pasturelands, to come and join us. ³Let us bring the ark of our God back to us, for we did not inquire of it during the reign of Saul." ⁴The whole assembly agreed to do this, because it seemed right to all the people.

⁵So David assembled all the Israelites, from the Shihor River in Egypt to Lebo Hamath, to bring the ark of God from Kiriath Jearim. ⁶David and all the Israelites with him went to Baalah of Judah (Kiriath Jearim) to bring up from there the ark of God the LORD, who is enthroned between the cherubim— the ark that is called by the Name.

⁷They moved the ark of God from Abinadab's house on a new cart, with Uzzah and Ahio guiding it. ⁸David and all the Israelites were celebrating with all their might before God, with songs and with harps, lyres, tambourines, cymbals and trumpets.

⁹When they came to the threshing floor of Kidon, Uzzah reached out his hand to steady the ark, because the oxen stumbled. ¹⁰The LORD's anger burned against Uzzah, and he struck him down because he had put his hand on the ark. So he died there before God.

¹¹Then David was angry because the LORD's wrath had broken out against Uzzah, and to this day that place is called Perez Uzzah.

¹²David was afraid of God that day and asked, "How can I ever bring the ark of God to me?" ¹³He did not take the ark to be with him in the City of David. Instead, he took it aside to the house of Obed-Edom the Gittite. ¹⁴The ark of God remained with the family of Obed-Edom in his house for three months, and the LORD blessed his household and everything he had.

14:1Now Hiram king of Tyre sent messengers to David, along with cedar logs, stonemasons and carpenters to build a palace for him. 2And David knew that the LORD had established him as king over Israel and that his kingdom had been highly exalted for the sake of his people Israel.

3In Jerusalem David took more wives and became the father of more sons and daughters. 4These are the names of the children born to him there: Shammua, Shobab, Nathan, Solomon, 5Ibhar, Elishua, Elpelet, 6Nogah, Nepheg, Japhia, 7Elishama, Beeliada and Eliphelet.

8When the Philistines heard that David had been anointed king over all Israel, they went up in full force to search for him, but David heard about it and went out to meet them. 9Now the Philistines had come and raided the Valley of Rephaim; 10so David inquired of God: "Shall I go and attack the Philistines? Will you hand them over to me?"

The LORD answered him, "Go, I will hand them over to you."

11So David and his men went up to Baal Perazim, and there he defeated them. He said, "As waters break out, God has broken out against my enemies by my hand." So that place was called Baal Perazim. 12The Philistines had abandoned their gods there, and David gave orders to burn them in the fire.

13Once more the Philistines raided the valley; 14so David inquired of God again, and God answered him, "Do not go straight up, but circle around them and attack them in front of the balsam trees. 15As soon as you hear the sound of marching in the tops of the balsam trees, move out to battle, because that will mean God has gone out in front of you to strike the Philistine army." 16So David did as God commanded him, and they struck down the Philistine army, all the way from Gibeon to Gezer.

17So David's fame spread throughout every land, and the LORD made all the nations fear him.

15:1After David had constructed buildings for himself in the City of David, he prepared a place for the ark of God and pitched a tent for it. 2Then David said, "No one but the Levites may carry the ark of God, because the LORD chose them to carry the ark of the LORD and to minister before him forever."

³David assembled all Israel in Jerusalem to bring up the ark of the LORD to the place he had prepared for it. ⁴He called together the descendants of Aaron and the Levites:

⁵From the descendants of Kohath,
  Uriel the leader and 120 relatives;
⁶from the descendants of Merari,
  Asaiah the leader and 220 relatives;
⁷from the descendants of Gershon,
  Joel the leader and 130 relatives;
⁸from the descendants of Elizaphan,
  Shemaiah the leader and 200 relatives;
⁹from the descendants of Hebron,
  Eliel the leader and 80 relatives;
¹⁰from the descendants of Uzziel,
  Amminadab the leader and 112 relatives.

¹¹Then David summoned Zadok and Abiathar the priests, and Uriel, Asaiah, Joel, Shemaiah, Eliel and Amminadab the Levites. ¹²He said to them, "You are the heads of the Levitical families; you and your fellow Levites are to consecrate yourselves and bring up the ark of the LORD, the God of Israel, to the place I have prepared for it. ¹³It was because you, the Levites, did not bring it up the first time that the LORD our God broke out in anger against us. We did not inquire of him about how to do it in the prescribed way." ¹⁴So the priests and Levites consecrated themselves in order to bring up the ark of the LORD, the God of Israel. ¹⁵And the Levites carried the ark of God with the poles on their shoulders, as Moses had commanded in accordance with the word of the LORD.

¹⁶David told the leaders of the Levites to appoint their brothers as singers to sing joyful songs, accompanied by musical instruments: lyres, harps and cymbals.

¹⁷So the Levites appointed Heman son of Joel; from his brothers, Asaph son of Berekiah; and from their brothers the Merarites, Ethan son of Kushaiah; ¹⁸and with them their brothers next in rank: Zechariah, Jaaziel, Shemiramoth, Jehiel, Unni, Eliab, Benaiah, Maaseiah, Mattithiah, Eliphelehu, Mikneiah, Obed-Edom and Jeiel, the gatekeepers.

¹⁹The musicians Heman, Asaph and Ethan were to sound the bronze cymbals; ²⁰Zechariah, Aziel, Shemiramoth, Jehiel, Unni, Eliab, Maaseiah and Benaiah were to play the lyres

according to *alamoth,* ²¹and Mattithiah, Eliphelehu, Mikneiah, Obed-Edom, Jeiel and Azaziah were to play the harps, directing according to *sheminith.* ²²Kenaniah the head Levite was in charge of the singing; that was his responsibility because he was skillful at it.

²³Berekiah and Elkanah were to be doorkeepers for the ark. ²⁴Shebaniah, Joshaphat, Nethanel, Amasai, Zechariah, Benaiah and Eliezer the priests were to blow trumpets before the ark of God. Obed-Edom and Jehiah were also to be doorkeepers for the ark.

²⁵So David and the elders of Israel and the commanders of units of a thousand went to bring up the ark of the covenant of the LORD from the house of Obed-Edom, with rejoicing. ²⁶Because God had helped the Levites who were carrying the ark of the covenant of the LORD, seven bulls and seven rams were sacrificed. ²⁷Now David was clothed in a robe of fine linen, as were all the Levites who were carrying the ark, and as were the singers, and Kenaniah, who was in charge of the singing of the choirs. David also wore a linen ephod. ²⁸So all Israel brought up the ark of the covenant of the LORD with shouts, with the sounding of rams' horns and trumpets, and of cymbals, and the playing of lyres and harps.

²⁹As the ark of the covenant of the LORD was entering the City of David, Michal daughter of Saul watched from a window. And when she saw King David dancing and celebrating, she despised him in her heart.

¹⁶:¹They brought the ark of God and set it inside the tent that David had pitched for it, and they presented burnt offerings and fellowship offerings before God. ²After David had finished sacrificing the burnt offerings and fellowship offerings, he blessed the people in the name of the LORD. ³Then he gave a loaf of bread, a cake of dates and a cake of raisins to each Israelite man and woman.

⁴He appointed some of the Levites to minister before the ark of the LORD, to make petition, to give thanks, and to praise the LORD, the God of Israel: ⁵Asaph was the chief, Zechariah second, then Jeiel, Shemiramoth, Jehiel, Mattithiah, Eliab, Benaiah, Obed-Edom and Jeiel. They were to play the lyres and harps, Asaph was to sound the cymbals, ⁶and Benaiah and Jahaziel the priests were to blow the trumpets regularly before the ark of the covenant of God.

⁷That day David first committed to Asaph and his associates this psalm of thanks to the LORD:

⁸Give thanks to the LORD, call on his name;
    make known among the nations what he has done.
⁹Sing to him, sing praise to him;
    tell of all his wonderful acts.
¹⁰Glory in his holy name;
    let the hearts of those who seek the LORD rejoice.
¹¹Look to the LORD and his strength;
    seek his face always.
¹²Remember the wonders he has done,
    his miracles, and the judgments he pronounced,
¹³O descendants of Israel his servant,
    O sons of Jacob, his chosen ones.

¹⁴He is the LORD our God;
    his judgments are in all the earth.
¹⁵He remembers his covenant forever,
    the word he commanded, for a thousand generations,
¹⁶the covenant he made with Abraham,
    the oath he swore to Isaac.
¹⁷He confirmed it to Jacob as a decree,
    to Israel as an everlasting covenant:
¹⁸"To you I will give the land of Canaan
    as the portion you will inherit."

¹⁹When they were but few in number,
    few indeed, and strangers in it,
²⁰they wandered from nation to nation,
    from one kingdom to another.
²¹He allowed no man to oppress them;
    for their sake he rebuked kings:
²²"Do not touch my anointed ones;
    do my prophets no harm."

²³Sing to the LORD, all the earth;
    proclaim his salvation day after day.
²⁴Declare his glory among the nations,
    his marvelous deeds among all peoples.
²⁵For great is the LORD and most worthy of praise;
    he is to be feared above all gods.
²⁶For all the gods of the nations are idols,
    but the LORD made the heavens.

²⁷Splendor and majesty are before him;
    strength and joy in his dwelling place.

²⁸Ascribe to the LORD, O families of nations,
    ascribe to the LORD glory and strength,
²⁹   ascribe to the LORD the glory due his name.
  Bring an offering and come before him;
    worship the LORD in the splendor of his holiness.
³⁰Tremble before him, all the earth!
    The world is firmly established; it cannot be moved.
³¹Let the heavens rejoice, let the earth be glad;
    let them say among the nations, "The LORD reigns!"
³²Let the sea resound, and all that is in it;
    let the fields be jubilant, and everything in them!
³³Then the trees of the forest will sing,
    they will sing for joy before the LORD,
    for he comes to judge the earth.

³⁴Give thanks to the LORD, for he is good;
    his love endures forever.
³⁵Cry out, "Save us, O God our Savior;
    gather us and deliver us from the nations,
  that we may give thanks to your holy name,
    that we may glory in your praise."
³⁶Praise be to the LORD, the God of Israel,
    from everlasting to everlasting.

Then all the people said "Amen" and "Praise the LORD."

³⁷David left Asaph and his associates before the ark of the covenant of the LORD to minister there regularly, according to each day's requirements. ³⁸He also left Obed-Edom and his sixty-eight associates to minister with them. Obed-Edom son of Jeduthun, and also Hosah, were gatekeepers.

³⁹David left Zadok the priest and his fellow priests before the tabernacle of the LORD at the high place in Gibeon ⁴⁰to present burnt offerings to the LORD on the altar of burnt offering regularly, morning and evening, in accordance with everything written in the Law of the LORD, which he had given Israel. ⁴¹With them were Heman and Jeduthun and the rest of those chosen and designated by name to give thanks to the LORD, "for his love endures forever." ⁴²Heman and Jeduthun were responsible for the sounding of the trumpets

and cymbals and for the playing of the other instruments for sacred song. The sons of Jeduthun were stationed at the gate.

⁴³Then all the people left, each for his own home, and David returned home to bless his family.

¹⁷:¹After David was settled in his palace, he said to Nathan the prophet, "Here I am, living in a palace of cedar, while the ark of the covenant of the LORD is under a tent."

²Nathan replied to David, "Whatever you have in mind, do it, for God is with you."

³That night the word of God came to Nathan, saying:

⁴"Go and tell my servant David, 'This is what the LORD says: You are not the one to build me a house to dwell in. ⁵I have not dwelt in a house from the day I brought Israel up out of Egypt to this day. I have moved from one tent site to another, from one dwelling place to another. ⁶Wherever I have moved with all the Israelites, did I ever say to any of their leaders whom I commanded to shepherd my people, "Why have you not built me a house of cedar?" '

⁷"Now then, tell my servant David, 'This is what the LORD Almighty says: I took you from the pasture and from following the flock, to be ruler over my people Israel. ⁸I have been with you wherever you have gone, and I have cut off all your enemies from before you. Now I will make your name like the names of the greatest men of the earth. ⁹And I will provide a place for my people Israel and will plant them so that they can have a home of their own and no longer be disturbed. Wicked people will not oppress them anymore, as they did at the beginning ¹⁰and have done ever since the time I appointed leaders over my people Israel. I will also subdue all your enemies.

"'I declare to you that the LORD will build a house for you: ¹¹When your days are over and you go to be with your fathers, I will raise up your offspring to succeed you, one of your own sons, and I will establish his kingdom. ¹²He is the one who will build a house for me, and I will establish his throne forever. ¹³I will be his father, and he will be my son. I will never take my love away from him, as I took it away from your predecessor. ¹⁴I will set him over my house and my kingdom forever; his throne will be established forever.'"

¹⁵Nathan reported to David all the words of this entire revelation.

¹⁶Then King David went in and sat before the LORD, and he said:

"Who am I, O LORD God, and what is my family, that you have brought me this far? ¹⁷And as if this were not enough in your sight, O God, you have spoken about the future of the house of your servant. You have looked on me as though I were the most exalted of men, O LORD God.

¹⁸"What more can David say to you for honoring your servant? For you know your servant, ¹⁹O LORD. For the sake of your servant and according to your will, you have done this great thing and made known all these great promises.

²⁰"There is no one like you, O LORD, and there is no God but you, as we have heard with our own ears. ²¹And who is like your people Israel—the one nation on earth whose God went out to redeem a people for himself, and to make a name for yourself, and to perform great and awesome wonders by driving out nations from before your people, whom you redeemed from Egypt? ²²You made your people Israel your very own forever, and you, O LORD, have become their God.

²³"And now, LORD, let the promise you have made concerning your servant and his house be established forever. Do as you promised, ²⁴so that it will be established and that your name will be great forever. Then men will say, 'The LORD Almighty, the God over Israel, is Israel's God!' And the house of your servant David will be established before you.

²⁵"You, my God, have revealed to your servant that you will build a house for him. So your servant has found courage to pray to you. ²⁶O LORD, you are God! You have promised these good things to your servant. ²⁷Now you have been pleased to bless the house of your servant, that it may continue forever in your sight; for you, O LORD, have blessed it, and it will be blessed forever."

THE ACCOUNT OF King David's installation of the ark of the covenant in Jerusalem for the purpose of establishing a central religious shrine in Israel forms a single literary unit. Chapter 17 is often omitted in the discussion of the Chronicler's ark narrative and is treated in isolation as a distinct section. Yet, God's covenant with David stands appropriately as the conclusion to the ark narrative. In the first section (chs. 13–16), David aspires to build a suitable "house" for the ark of the covenant so that the name of Yahweh might be enthroned. Conversely, in the second section (ch. 17), God promises to build David's "house" into a royal dynasty. In each case, the objective is the same—establishing the greatness of the name of Yahweh (17:24).

More than explaining how the ark of the covenant came to be established at a permanent site in Jerusalem, the ark narrative tells the story of the transformation of the former Jebusite stronghold into the political and religious center of the Israelite monarchy.[1] The installation of the ark in a temporary shrine in Jerusalem was the second phase of this transformation. The first phase was the capture of the city itself by cunning and courage on the part of David's army (cf. 11:4–9). These two phases, along with the earlier report of David's being crowned as king by all Israel, are three essential elements to the preparations for the building of Yahweh's temple—a focal point of the Chronicler's interest in his retelling of Israel's history.

Broadly speaking, the Chronicler relies on the earlier parallel account of David's transfer of the ark of the covenant to center stage in the religious life of Israel found in 2 Samuel 5–6. His reordering and selective highlighting of those materials, however, once again demonstrate the Chronicler's literary purposes are primarily thematic and theological—not chronological.[2]

By way of genre identification, chapters 13–17 form a "report" or narrative consisting of a complex series of "reports" (with the exception of the composite psalm in ch. 16). The "report" is a brief, self-contained narrative subgenre describing a single event or situation.[3] Chapters 13–16 largely avoid dialogue, while the dialogue characterizing the report of chapter 17 features prophetic oracle and prayer. The story line hinges on the dramatic twist of David's failure in his first attempt to transfer the ark of Yahweh into Jerusalem and the irony of God's promising to build David's "house" before David has the opportunity to fulfill his desire to build God's "house." The passage may be divided into six smaller units:

---

1. Japhet, *I and II Chronicles*, 272.
2. Williamson, *1 and 2 Chronicles*, 113.
3. De Vries, *1 and 2 Chronicles*, 135, 426, 434.

1. First stage of the ark's transfer: from Kiriath Jearim to Kidon (13:1–14)
2. King David's fame spreads (14:1–17)
3. Jerusalem made ready for the entrance of the ark (15:1–24)
4. Second stage of the ark's transfer: the processional into Jerusalem (15:25–16:3)
5. Yahweh enthroned on Israel's praise (16:4–43)
6. Yahweh's covenant with David (17:1–27)

The centerpiece of this portion of the Chronicler's history is a piece of tabernacle furniture, the ark of the covenant. The ark was a rectangular chest made of acacia wood and overlaid with gold (cf. Ex. 25:10–22). The box measured 2.5 cubits long by 1.5 cubits high and 1.5 cubits wide (roughly 3.75 ft. x 2.5 ft. x 2.5 ft.; see fig. 7 [on the following page] for a drawing of the ark of the covenant). The ark rested on four short legs equipped with rings for transporting on a set of wooden poles, also overlaid with gold. The ark and its carrying poles were the only pieces of furniture in the Most Holy Place (26:31–35). The ark contained the stone tablets of the Decalogue, hence the name for this sacred chest—"the ark of the covenant" (Deut. 10:5). Also housed in the ark was a jar of manna from the desert wandering of the Israelites after the Exodus (Ex. 16:33), Aaron's rod (Num. 17:10), and later a complete book of the Law was placed beside the ark (Deut. 31:26; cf. Heb. 9:4).

Atop the ark was a lid of pure gold called the "atonement cover" (NIV) or "mercy seat" (NRSV; Ex. 37:6–9). Fixed at the ends of this lid were two cherubim facing each other, with wings outstretched. Above the cover of the box and between the cherubim is where God met with Israel (25:22). Thus, the ark became the symbol of God's presence in the midst of Israel. Since the ark also contained the law of Moses, it also symbolized the Mosaic covenant enacted at Sinai. David's concern for properly housing and attending to the ark of God represented his obedience to the law of Moses. According to Selman, this provided a natural lead-in to the announcement of the Davidic covenant for the Chronicler (ch. 17).[4] A third aspect of the ark's symbolism—the rule of God over Israel and all creation—will be developed in more detail later in this chapter.

First Stage of the Ark's Return (13:1–14)

THE OPENING SECTION of the Chronicler's ark narrative records the decision to retrieve the ark of God from Kiriath Jearim (13:1–4). These verses introduce the story of the ark's eventual entry into Jerusalem and have no parallel

---

4. Selman, *1 Chronicles*, 149.

The Ark of the Covenant was the centerpiece of the Israelite religion, a box covered with gold, 44 inches long by 26.4 inches wide and high, with carrying poles for the wilderness journey to the promised land. Centered within the Tabernacle (portable temple) it was later placed within Solomon's permanent temple.

Once a year the High Priest entered the Most Holy Place to appear before the Lord (Lev. 16:34). This part of the Day of Atonement ceremony included sprinkling of the blood from animals upon the cover of the Ark of the Covenant (Lev. 16:14). Israelite people prayed over animals to be sacrificed, placing upon them their own weaknesses and guilt (Lev. 16:21). Blood then, became a substance which embodied both physical and spiritual life, could be carried and actually positioned upon the very throne of Yahweh (God), the sacred space between the cherubim the lid of the ark.

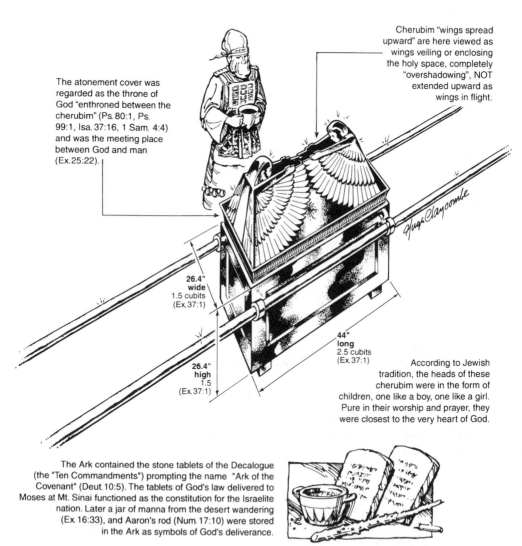

The atonement cover was regarded as the throne of God "enthroned between the cherubim" (Ps. 80:1, Ps. 99:1, Isa. 37:16, 1 Sam. 4:4) and was the meeting place between God and man (Ex. 25:22).

Cherubim "wings spread upward" are here viewed as wings veiling or enclosing the holy space, completely "overshadowing", NOT extended upward as wings in flight.

26.4" wide
1.5 cubits
(Ex. 37:1)

44" long
2.5 cubits
(Ex. 37:1)

26.4" high
1.5
(Ex. 37:1)

According to Jewish tradition, the heads of these cherubim were in the form of children, one like a boy, one like a girl. Pure in their worship and prayer, they were closest to the very heart of God.

The Ark contained the stone tablets of the Decalogue (the "Ten Commandments") prompting the name "Ark of the Covenant" (Deut. 10:5). The tablets of God's law delivered to Moses at Mt. Sinai functioned as the constitution for the Israelite nation. Later a jar of manna from the desert wandering (Ex. 16:33), and Aaron's rod (Num. 17:10) were stored in the Ark as symbols of God's deliverance.

Fig. 7. The Ark of the Covenant

in the Samuel account. The latter portion of this literary unit describes the journey of the ark from the house of Abinadab of Kiriath Jearim (or Baalah) to the threshing floor of Kidon (13:5–14). This account of the transfer of the ark is taken from 2 Samuel 6:2–11 with some variation. Three smaller units may be observed in this section: the journey of all Israel to Kiriath Jearim (13:5–6), the transportation of the ark in a processional (13:7–11), and the temporary deposit of the ark at the house of Obed-Edom (13:12–14).

We must recall that the ark of the covenant had been captured in battle by the Philistines when the Israelites foolishly assumed the symbol of God's presence at the vanguard of the army would guarantee a military victory (1 Sam. 4:11). Not long after their capture of the ark, the Philistines returned the sacred chest to the Israelites to stay the plagues the Lord inflicted on them (1 Sam. 5). The ark of God was returned to Beth Shemesh, but only briefly. God struck dead seventy of the villagers for their irreverence in peeking into the contents of the covenant box (6:19). Terrified, the leaders of Beth Shemesh sent the ark to Kiriath Jearim, where it was housed by Abinadab and guarded by his son Eleazar (7:1). It is at this point that the Chronicler picks up the story.

The book of 2 Samuel treats the transfer of the ark of God as a military event initially (2 Sam. 6:1). The Chronicler adds the details that David consults not only with his military leaders but also the religious leadership of Israel (priests and Levites) and the general populace (1 Chron. 13:2). The thirty thousand chosen to escort the ark (2 Sam. 6:1) are apparently representative of "all Israel" for the Chronicler (1 Chron. 13:5). The unity of "all Israel" under King David is a key theme in Chronicles; here it connects the preceding section (chs. 10–12) with the ark narrative (chs. 13–17).

David's call to "bring the ark of our God back to us" connotes a spiritual journey as much as it denotes a geographical one (13:3a). The site of Kiriath Jearim was located in the tribe of Judah (13:6), so the issue is not the physical presence of the ark of God. Japhet correctly discerns that David in fact admonishes the people in a spiritual sense: "Let us make the ark 'ours.'"[5] She substantiates her interpretation by the appeal to once again "inquire" of the ark, as it was neglected during Saul's reign (13:3b). The issue for Israel is the role of the ark "in God's worship, as an object of 'seeking.'"[6] The word "inquire" (*drš*) displays a wide range of meaning, including "seeking" God in the sense of "worship" (e.g., 2 Chron. 17:3). The full conclusion of the installation of the ark, as Japhet reminds us, "is not seen in its placement 'inside the tent' (1 Chron. 16:1//2 Sam. 6:17), but in the establishment of a permanent liturgy of worship before it" (described in 1 Chron. 16).[7]

---

5. Japhet, *I and II Chronicles*, 276.
6. Ibid.
7. Ibid.

Implicit in David's summons to restore the ark to its proper place in Israelite worship is the cause-and-effect link between Saul's demise and Israel's defeat by the Philistines and the neglect of the ark of God (13:3c). In fact, the writer probably intends his audience to recall the earlier theological assessment of King Saul as one who did not "inquire" (*drš*) of Yahweh (10:14). That sober reminder alone may have been enough to motivate the assembly of Israel to decide that "to return the ark" is the right thing to do (13:4).

Affirming the prominent theme of Israelite unity under King David, the Chronicler indicates in threefold repetition that "all the Israelites" participate with King David in the processional to return the ark of God (13:5, 6, 8). This phrase interprets the "thirty thousand men" chosen out of Israel to accompany the ark in the Samuel parallel as a throng representative of "all Israel" (cf. 2 Sam. 6:1).

The Chronicler's elaboration on the extent to which this multitude represents the breadth of the territory of Israel is noteworthy (13:5). Typically, the Old Testament boundaries or geographical poles for the land of Israel are Dan in the north and Beersheba in the south (cf. 21:2). The Chronicler's extreme definition of the borders of Israel extending from the Shihor River in Egypt (or the Nile) to Lebo Hamath (the city at the entrance to the territory of Hamath in Syria some forty-five miles north of Damascus) occurs elsewhere in the Old Testament only in Joshua 13:2−5. There the Shihor River and Lebo Hamath are the "bookends" for the territories still unconquered by the Hebrews prior to Joshua's death. The Chronicler may be making two statements in his appeal to the precursor text in Joshua: (1) The rarely used geographical description maximizes the sweeping extent of David's support; (2) it may offer commentary on Joshua 13:2−5 in the sense that under King David the conquest of Canaan is finally completed.

The point of departure for the processional transferring the ark of God to the central shrine in Jerusalem is Kiriath Jearim (1 Chron. 13:5). The city was a border town between Judah and Benjamin located approximately eight miles west of Jerusalem. The site was also known as Kiriath Baal and Baalah (Josh. 15:9; 18:14, 15; cf. 2 Sam. 6:2).

The portrayal of Yahweh as "the LORD, who is enthroned between the cherubim" (13:6) is an infrequent but powerful image of the God of the Hebrews (cf. 1 Sam. 4:4; 2 Kings 19:15). The idea of the mysterious and majestic presence of God enthroned between the cherubim of the ark of the covenant is based on the understanding that this is where God meets his people (Ex. 25:22). The idea behind God's "meeting" with Israel is comparable to that of a king holding audience with subjects—hence, the ark represented the throne of God on earth. The psalmist associates the enthronement of God between the cherubim of the ark with his sovereign rule of the nations (Ps. 99:1). Clearly, he wants to impress on his audience the fact that Yahweh is not a local deity after the fashion of the gods and goddesses of the pantheons of Israel's neighbors. Rather, the Lord Almighty is a universal deity, and his rule encompasses all of creation.

The NIV's expression, "the ark that is called by the Name," is interpretive (13:6d). The literal clause, "where [the] Name is called" is cryptic. Some commentators suggest the expression is a later addition to the text.[8] If Chronicles preserves a better version of original Hebrew text than Samuel, then the expression should be retained as original and probably signifies that the ark and the shrine housing it are the "local" manifestations of the divine presence—the "house" or residence of God, so to speak (cf. Deut. 12:11; 1 Kings 8:29).

There are numerous divergences between 2 Samuel 6:2–11 and 1 Chronicles 13:6–14. For instance, the MT of 2 Samuel 6:5 reads "celebrating before the LORD with all kinds of instruments made of pine" (see NIV text note). As a second example, the site of Uzzah's tragic death is the "threshing floor of Kidon" (1 Chron. 13:9), whereas the place name in Samuel is Nacon (2 Sam. 6:6); other witnesses identify the site as Nodan (4QSam[a]) or Nodab (LXX[b]). Williamson has noted these variants are of textual interest in the reconstruction of the original MT, but that reading theological significance into them is unwarranted.[9]

The deadly mishap involving Uzzah (13:9) dramatically and immediately changes the mood surrounding the transfer of the ark of the covenant. The festive enthusiasm and joyous celebration of the procession suddenly turn into confusion, despair, and mourning. Interestingly, the Chronicler avoids all comment on the response of the Israelites participating in the event. What is clear is that Uzzah is struck down and killed by the Lord (13:10). King David's response of both anger and fear to the tragedy is also readily reported (13:11–12). David's visceral reaction seems to be based on the assumption that Uzzah is an innocent victim and that God has capriciously shown his disapproval for the enterprise of transferring the ark.

The death of Uzzah resulting in the bungled transfer of the ark of the covenant is one of two failures of King David reported by the Chronicler (the other is the census-taking, 1 Chron. 21). In part, the explanation for David's failure is found in the repeated phrase "before God" (13:8, 10). David and Israel overlook the role of the ark as the "vehicle of God's presence in the midst of his people."[10] The awesome power and dreadful holiness of God have somehow been forgotten. Perhaps the euphoria of the celebration has dulled

---

8. Braun, *1 Chronicles*, 173.

9. Williamson, *1 and 2 Chronicles*, 115.

10. Japhet, *I and II Chronicles*, 279.

the "theological senses" of both king and people. The physical separation of the ark from the sacred shrine still located in Gibeon (cf. 1 Chron. 16:39; 21:29–30) may have contributed to an unhealthy familiarity with this piece of sacred furniture normally viewed but once a year by the high priest.

Whatever the reason, the fatal experience of Nadab and Abihu's profane behavior "before the LORD" has faded from memory (cf. Lev. 10:1–3). God is a consuming fire, and he will show himself holy before all people, even in the stumbling of oxen pulling a cart at the threshing floor of Kidon (cf. Ex. 24:17; Deut. 4:24; Heb. 12:29). The Chronicler's repetition of the word "break out" (*prṣ*) in this section of the narrative seems to draw attention to this terrifying dimension of God's character—perhaps as a necessary reminder to his audience (cf. 13:11; 14:11; 15:13).

A more complete explanation of David's failure ensues in the subsequent narrative, phase two of the transfer of the ark to Jerusalem. Here we learn that King David fails to "inquire" of the Lord as to the proper procedure for transporting the ark (15:13). According to Mosaic law, only the Levites were to carry the holy things of the tabernacle, and even they were not to touch the holy vessels against the threat of death (Num. 4:15). Accordingly, David orders the consecration of the priests to transport the ark by means of the carrying poles prescribed by pentateuchal law (1 Chron. 15:2–24; cf. Ex. 25:14). Ironically, David's neglect to inquire of the Lord mimics that of King Saul's (1 Chron. 10:14). Unlike Saul's habitual neglect of God, however, David's lapse is temporary and is remedied by his later entreaty for divine instruction in the transfer of the ark.

Selman has suggested King David and the other leaders are influenced by the Philistines and their use of a "new cart" to restore the ark to the Israelites, thus unwittingly perpetuating a pagan superstition (13:7; cf. 1 Sam. 6:7).[11] This may have indeed been the case. But it is not the central issue in understanding the outbreak of God's wrath and the slaying of Uzzah. According to Japhet, the touching of sacred objects was a sacrilege (see Num. 4:15). Consequently, "a sin of this kind is objective and absolute, the aspects of volition, intent, and moral consideration playing no role."[12] God's response to such desecration of the holy is consistent with the Chronicler's report (e.g., Num. 15:35; Josh. 7:25; 1 Sam. 6:19). Japhet further characterizes Uzzah's sin as one of disbelief and mistrust in the power of God, since it is for God and not human beings to protect the ark (the essential lesson of Shiloh, 1 Sam. 4–6).[13]

11. Selman, *1 Chronicles*, 153.
12. Japhet, *I and II Chronicles*, 280.
13. Ibid.

David's refusal to press on with his quest to transfer the ark to Jerusalem marks two important character traits of this beloved shepherd-king (13:13–14). (1) His disposition to deposit the ark at the nearest convenient location indicates his submission to God's will (cf. Ps. 40:8). (2) Whether out of abject fear or outright reverence, David refuses to manipulate God for personal advantage through control of the sacred symbol of divine presence (cf. Ps. 40:6; 51:6).

There is some question as to the identity of Obed-Edom. Some commentators have suggested he is a Philistine since he is associated with Gath (13:13; "Gittite" is related to Gath) and that David deliberately warehouses the ark with a "foreigner" as a sort of "guinea pig" to ensure that God's wrath has indeed subsided.[14] Others equate him with the Obed-Edom named by the Chronicler among the Levitical gatekeepers (15:18, 21).[15] There is no doubt, however, about the purpose of the Chronicler's report of God's blessing on the house of Obed-Edom for those three months the ark resides in his keeping. David and all Israel (as well as the Chronicler's audience) need to know that the transgression against God was not the transfer of the ark itself but the faulty way in which it was carried out. God demands proper "means" to achieve good and right "ends."

King David's Fame Spreads (14:1–17)

THE THREE REPORTS comprising chapter 14 are taken from 2 Samuel 5:11–25: (1) the assistance provided by King Hiram of Tyre for the building of David's palace (1 Chron. 14:1–2), (2) the children born to King David during the Jerusalem era of his reign (14:3–7), and (3) two successful military campaigns waged by King David against the Philistines (14:8–17).

The Chronicler's rearrangement of the Samuel narrative shifts these events of David's kingship out of strict chronological order. His editing of the Samuel parallel may have been motivated by theological reasons; that is, in contrast to King Saul's unfaithfulness, David's faithfulness, demonstrated in his seeking of the ark of God, is blessed by God (cf. 10:13). It is also possible that the "cutting and pasting" in Chronicles is a literary device the writer uses to account for the three-month time lapse between the first and second phases of the installation of the ark of the covenant in Jerusalem (cf. 13:14).[16]

King Hiram (Heb. *Huram,* most often in Chronicles) of Tyre was an ally of both David and Solomon (14:1–2). His name may be a shortened form of Ahiram. The dates for his rule of the Phoenician city-state of Tyre are

---

14. E.g., Japhet, ibid., 281; Selman, *1 Chronicles,* 154.
15. Thompson, *1, 2 Chronicles,* 129.
16. Braun, *1 Chronicles,* 178.

uncertain, although it is clear his reign overlaps that of David and Solomon since he was the "contractor" for the Jerusalem temple (2 Chron. 2:12–14). Most likely that Hiram ruled from about 980–950 B.C., but scholarly estimates vary widely.[17] Hiram's gift of construction materials and craftsmen for the building of David's palace may have been part of a trade agreement, much like that arranged later with Solomon (building supplies in exchange for food staples, 2 Chron. 2:15–16). Hiram's desire to "build a house" for David foreshadows the same motif in chapter 17, where David seeks to build a house for Yahweh but instead learns of Yahweh's desire to "build a house" for him.

The Jerusalem birth report and name list assume the audience's knowledge of the Hebron birth report and name list (2 Sam. 3:2–5). The list of David's children born in Jerusalem essentially repeats 2 Samuel 5:13–16, with the exception of two additional names: Elpelet and Nogah.[18] The omission of these names in Samuel may have been due to the untimely deaths of the children.[19] The genealogy in Chronicles also includes the names of the mothers of David's children as well as those of his daughters (1 Chron. 3:4b–9). Unlike King Saul's dynasty, which died out (10:6), David's house is a "fruitful vine" (cf. Ps. 128:3).

The news of David's being anointed as king of Israel prompts a Philistine invasion of Judah, presumably an attempt to dethrone him before their former vassal has sufficient time to solidify his power among God's people (14:8–12). The attack takes place at the Valley of Rephaim, a border region between the tribes of Benjamin and Judah, immediately southwest of Jerusalem (Josh. 15:8). Unlike King Saul, who "inquired" (*drš*) of the medium of Endor (1 Sam. 28:7), David "inquired" (*š?l*) of the Lord and was assured victory over the Philistines (1 Chron. 14:10). Previously God had "broken out" (*prṣ*) in anger against Uzzah (and Israel) for failing to respect his holiness (13:11); now God "breaks out" (*prṣ*) against the Philistines (14:11).

Earlier, the Israelites lost the ark of the covenant to the Philistines in the battle of Shiloh (1 Sam. 4:11). Here at Rephaim the Philistines abandon their gods on the battlefield, symbolic of their impotence before Yahweh, the true God (14:12). Rather than plunder the idols and parade them as trophies of war, David burns the relics of false worship in accordance with the law of Moses (Deut. 7:5; 12:3).

The Philistines launch a second offensive at the same location, although the interval of time between the two attacks is unspecified (14:13–16). As before, the narrative reports that David appropriately "inquires" of God as to

---

17. Cf. Selman, *1 Chronicles*, 156.
18. See the helpful comparative chart in Myers, *I Chronicles*, 107.
19. Payne, "1, 2 Chronicles," 4:338.

his response to the Philistine aggression (14:14). Once again, David is assured of God's help in battle, but this time the tactics are changed. Instead of meeting the enemy in a head-on clash, David is instructed to entrap the enemy by circling around the Philistine army. The divine signal for engaging the enemy is most unusual, as David and his army are cautioned to wait for the "sound of marching" in the treetops before attacking (14:15). The rustling of the leaves in the trees is most likely the Spirit of God, since David is told God will go before him in battle. The noise, perhaps akin to soldiers' feet rushing into battle, is designed to confuse the Philistine army (cf. 2 Kings 7:6). David and the Israelites rout the Philistines and drive them in a northwesterly direction away from Jerusalem through Gibeon (or Gibeah?; cf. "Geba" in 2 Sam. 5:25) to Gezer (1 Chron. 14:16).

The spread of David's fame and the fear of Yahweh among the nations are interrelated (14:17). As God blesses David's faithfulness, so David's success brings glory and honor to God. The Chronicler's report of David's growing reputation foreshadows the covenant blessing of God's promise to make David's name among the greatest of the world (17:8). Fittingly, the defeat of the Philistines at Rephaim reverses the outcome at Mount Gilboa and avenges the deaths of Saul and Jonathan, closing the story on that tragic first chapter in the history of Israelite kingship. Presumably the Chronicler intends this account of the reversal of fortune for Israel under King David as a message of hope and encouragement for his audience—"fodder" for possibility thinking on the part of his generation.

Jerusalem Made Ready for the Entrance of the Ark (15:1–24)

THIS SECTION FURTHERS the account of the transfer of the ark of the covenant by detailing the preparations made by David in response to the failure of his first initiative. The passage may be divided into three smaller units: the provisional preparations for transferring the ark (15:1–3), the summons and purification of the Levites (15:4–15), and the duty roster of the Levitical musicians (15:16–24). By way of literary genre the material is essentially considered report, with interesting subfeatures like the edict (i.e., a proclamation carrying the force of law, 15:2), the name list with tallies (15:5–10), and the duty roster (15:16–24). The material has no parallel in 1–2 Samuel. Yet, there is no need to assume the account is the Chronicler's invention. We have already seen that he has access to several sources not included in the books of Samuel and Kings.

Before we comment on this passage, J. A. Thompson makes an interesting observation. He has noted that the Chronicler's narrative devoted to the transfer of the ark of God gives careful attention to an object that *"had already ceased to exist* [italics his]" by the writer's own time.[20] That is, the Chronicler's audience has no opportunity to worship before the ark as did David because the sacred chest was lost or destroyed during the Exile. At least there is no record that this piece of furniture was part of the inventory of temple vessels and articles returned to Jerusalem under Persian auspices (cf. Ezra 1:7–11). Nor is there any evidence that a replica of the ark was constructed for use in Zerubbabel's temple by the postexilic community. Thompson correctly deduces that the issue is not the ark as a sacred object, but what that piece of furniture represents: the mobile presence of God among his people and his uncompromising holiness.[21]

The report of the "tent" David pitches for temporarily housing the ark (15:1) emphasizes the thoroughness of his preparations for transferring the ark (cf. 15:12). More important to the venture of relocating the ark of God in Jerusalem is the role of the Levites as porters (15:2). This time the ark is to be carried by the Levites, not driven on a cart (also noted in the Samuel parallel by "those . . . carrying the ark"; 2 Sam. 6:13). David has learned from his earlier mistake in transporting the ark, although the text is silent as to the source of the instruction. The tone and circumstance of David's lecture to the priests concerning their role in the transfer of the ark suggests God himself may have revealed this to David through the king's study of the Mosaic law (Deut. 10:8; 18:5; cf. 1 Chron. 15:13).

The Chronicler is careful to include the priests ("descendants of Aaron") and the "Levites" (15:4) in the assembly of "all Israel" (15:3). As noted previously, the military, religious, and civilian sectors of the population are consulted and incorporated into the processional for the transfer of the ark of God. The sons of Levi (Kohath, Merari, and Gershon) give their names to the three primary clans of the Levitical corps (Num. 3:17–20).

The Chronicler also lists three additional families in 15:8–10 (Elizaphan, Hebron, and Uzziel), all descendants of Kohath (cf. 6:18; 2 Chron. 29:13). Thompson has suggested these families have risen to a place of prominence either because of size or prestige.[22] Some commentators contend this section of the name list simply reflects those clans of the Levites who have assumed leadership roles during the Chronicler's own day. More clear is the role of the Kohathites in relationship to the ark of the covenant, since they were the clan charged by Moses to attend and transport the ark (Num. 3:31; 4:4–6, 15). In his appointment of the proper Levitical clan to transport the ark, King David again demonstrates his faithfulness to God's commands.

---

20. Thompson, *1, 2 Chronicles*, 130.
21. Ibid., 134–35.
22. Ibid., 135.

David's preparations for the transfer of the ark extend beyond the readying of a site for housing it to the personnel responsible for transporting and attending the sacred chest (15:11–15). David assigns the task of "consecrating" the priesthood to eight Levitical clan leaders (15:11), six of whom are included in the previous name list (Uriel, Asaiah, Joel, Shemaiah, Eliel, and Amminadab). The names of the two priests, Zadok and Abiathar, need not be considered secondary additions to the text (based on the influence of 2 Sam. 15:24–29).[23] Following the original pattern of priestly ordination, the priests would first purify themselves. In turn, they would then be fit to purify the rest of the Levitical priesthood (cf. Ex. 29; Lev. 8).

The word "consecrate" (15:12, 14) means to set things or persons apart from impurity and profane use and dedicate them to the service of God in holiness. Chronicles records the similar consecration of the Levitical priesthood during the reigns of Solomon (2 Chron. 5:11), Hezekiah (29:5), and Josiah (35:6). In each case, Selman has noted, God subsequently blesses the nation.[24] The act of consecration included ritual washing and abstinence from sexual relations (Ex. 19:14–15). Elsewhere we learn that priests and Levites are to avoid contact with corpses (Lev. 21:1–4) and are subject to more stringent requirements concerning marriage (21:13–15).

Interestingly, the Mosaic legislation threatens that God will "break out" (*paras*) against the Israelites if the ritual purity of the Mount Sinai precinct is violated (Ex. 19:24). This is the same term used in Chronicles to describe the Lord's anger against Uzzah (1 Chron. 13:11). The Chronicler makes it clear that faulty procedure that fails to recognize the holiness of God is responsible for the aborted attempt to transfer the ark (15:13). This time David and the religious leaders of Israel follow the prescriptions of the Mosaic code, calling for the priests to shoulder the ark on poles when transporting it (15:15; cf. Ex. 25:12–15; Num. 7:9). The necessity to obey the word of the Lord is a recurrent theme in Chronicles, since God's blessing is directly tied to Israel's observance of Mosaic law (cf. Deut. 28).

The concluding section of the report summarizing David's extensive preparations for the transfer of the ark to Jerusalem (15:16–24) showcases the priests and Levites as musicians, another theme in Chronicles. The purpose in David's appointments is simple: The Levitical corps is to provide appropriate music for the processional (15:16). The occasion of installing the ark in Jerusalem is to be celebratory and festive—the ark and God are to be "serenaded" into the city with joyous music. The king instructs the leaders of the Levites to divide their group into singers and musicians (15:16). The

---

23. Cf. Williamson, *1 and 2 Chronicles*, 124.
24. Selman, *1 Chronicles*, 163.

musicians are sorted into divisions on the basis of the instrument played (lyre, harp, or cymbal). The citation of Kenaniah as a musical director of sorts references his "skill" (or perhaps "musical knowledge"), suggesting the appointments of the Levites as singers and musicians may have been based on some type of audition (15:22).

Braun's chart comparing the two different but related lists of Levitical singers and musicians is most helpful.[25] List "A" (15:17—18) includes three leaders, eleven assistants, and two gatekeepers (reading 15:18 on the information supplied in 15:24 about Obed-Edom and Jehiah as gatekeepers, cf. 26:4). List "B" (15:19—24) records the same personnel with the addition of two more leaders (Azaziah and Kenaniah), two more gatekeepers (Berekiah and Elkanah), and seven priests assigned to blow trumpets (15:24). List "B" also rosters the Levites according to their musical instrument and perhaps the tunes to which the music was played (although the exact meaning of the words *"alamoth"* [15:20] and *"sheminith"* [15:21] is unclear; cf. the use of the terms in the headings of Ps. 6; 12; and 46).

The number and role of the gatekeepers is somewhat ambiguous (15:18, 23, 24). It was customary in the ancient world for doorkeepers to attend the various entrances of the palace complex, both to serve as guards and to welcome and announce those passing through the doors as part of the royal protocol. This may have been another way for David to show proper reverence to God as king as the ark enters the city of Jerusalem and is installed in the tent-sanctuary. On a more practical note, since the Levitical porters are carrying the ark on poles hoisted on their shoulders, the gatekeepers can see to it that another tragedy was averted by carefully directing the Levites as they crossed the thresholds of gates and doorways. The sacrifices offered along the way of the processional account for the inclusion of the priests in the Chronicler's Levitical duty roster (15:26; 16:1—2).

Second Stage of the Ark's Transfer: The Processional into Jerusalem (15:25—16:3)

THE CHRONICLER'S NARRATIVE now returns to the Samuel parallel (2 Sam. 6:12—16), with some variation. Notable in Chronicles is the emphasis on the priests and Levites in the logistics of the transfer of the ark. Chronicles also underscores the corporate effort of "all Israel" in the processional (1 Chron. 15:28; 16:3), whereas the perspective in Samuel is that of a heroic act on the part of King David (2 Sam. 6:12). The divine "help" afforded David (1 Chron. 15:26; cf. 12:18) is now extended to the Levitical corps as confirmation that this time the plans for the transfer of the ark are truly sanctioned by God.

David's priestly role in the processional is tacitly approved by the detailed reference to the king's garb: a linen robe and linen ephod (15:27; a vest or apron-like over-garment, like that of the Levites, cf. Ex. 39:27–29). Reflection on the event may have provided the impetus for David's psalm referencing the priesthood of Melchizedek (Ps. 110:4). Perhaps it is this experience that prompts the appointment of his sons as "priests" of some sort (cf. 2 Sam. 8:18).

By contrast, David earns the disapproval of his wife Michal (15:29), Saul's daughter. She "despises" (*bzh*) him for his joyous abandon in celebrating the transfer of the ark of God—to her own detriment, for as a result of rebuking the king, she is barren (2 Sam. 6:23). According to Selman, Michal is out of sympathy with David's and all Israel's concern for the ark.[26] In one sense she represents the last vestige of King Saul's "unfaithfulness," and her story provides yet further justification for God's rejection of Saul's dynasty.

This portion of the account concludes with the successful installation of the ark of God in a tent, a temporary structure erected by David for housing the ark until a permanent shrine can be built. The Jerusalem tent is not to be confused with the Mosaic tabernacle, apparently located at Gibeon during David's reign (cf. 16:39; 21:29).[27]

The "burnt offerings" (16:2) are sacrifices for sin and demonstrate dedication to God (cf. Lev. 1). The "fellowship offerings" signify the completion of a vow (David's vow to honor the Lord by attending to the ark, 1 Chron. 13:3; cf. Ps. 132) and thankfulness on the part of all Israel for the blessings of God in sustaining the nation and establishing David as king (cf. Lev. 3). The communal blessing and ritual meal are part of a covenant-renewal ceremony in the biblical world (cf. Ex. 24:11). By installing the ark in Jerusalem, David is reestablishing God's rule over Israel and Israel's loyalty to Yahweh's covenant with his chosen people. The relationship between God and Israel, the relationship of Israelite to Israelite, and the relationship of Israel to the nations are once again restored under the umbrella of the Mosaic covenant.

Yahweh Enthroned on Israel's Praise (16:4–43)

THE PSALM OF THANKSGIVING commemorating the installation of the ark in Jerusalem, in one sense, is the theological center of the Chronicler's retelling of Israel's history. The installation of the ark marks Israel's return to God

---

26. Selman, *1 Chronicles*, 166.

27. After the Israelite conquest of Canaan, the Mosaic tabernacle was located in Shiloh (Josh. 18:1). By the time of Samuel the tabernacle had been moved to Nob (1 Sam. 21:1). Saul's slaughter of the priests at Nob for their aiding and abetting the fugitive David probably occasioned the relocation of the tent-shrine in Gibeon (1 Sam. 22:1–19).

under David's leadership and a renewal of the nation's covenant loyalty to the God of their ancestors. The ark itself symbolizes the covenant agreement established by Yahweh with Israel at Mount Sinai. The Sinai treaty was mediated by the prophet Moses, and the written record of that binding pact was archived for Hebrew posterity in the sacred ark. The Chronicler's song of praise celebrates God as both covenant maker and covenant keeper, the lynchpin in his theology of hope for postexilic Judah.

King David's appointment of certain members of the Levites to attend the ark indicates a division of labor among the Levitical corps. One group of Levites and the priests are stationed at the shrine in Gibeon housing the Mosaic tabernacle (16:39; 21:29). The other group of Levites are stationed in Jerusalem to minister before the ark of the Lord (16:4). The word "minister" (šrt) means "devout service" or "faithful attendance to ritual." The duty rosters of 16:4—7 and 16:37—43 describe the postinstallation worship arrangements established for appropriately reverencing the presence of the ark in Jerusalem. The list of names in 16:5—6 is taken from the ledger of names found in 15:17—21. Presumably, those individuals omitted from that earlier catalog are assigned to duties in Gibeon.

The priestly and Levitical ministry centered in Gibeon remains one of maintaining the sacrificial worship of Israel. The Levitical ministry before the ark in Jerusalem is primarily musical in nature. Williamson has suggested the terms in 16:4 describing this ministry of music are related to the three types of songs in the anthology of the Psalms: "to make petition" (i.e., to invoke the Lord through psalms of lament), "to give thanks" (i.e., to sing the psalms of thanksgiving), and "to praise the LORD" (i.e., to laud God with the psalmic hymns).[28] The NIV obscures the introduction to the composite psalm (16:7) by implying that David writes this psalm of thanksgiving and gives it to Asaph and the Levites for performance. The Hebrew more precisely states that David first assigns the activity of "giving thanks" to the Lord to Asaph and his relatives (cf. NASB, NRSV).[29]

The psalm of thanksgiving (16:8—36) is a composite of selections from three psalms:

    1 Chronicles 16:8—22 = Psalm 105:1—15
    1 Chronicles 16:23—33 = Psalm 96:1—13
    1 Chronicles 16:34—37 = Psalm 106:1, 47—48

The psalmic composition, however, is not a random rearrangement of earlier poetic materials. The Chronicler has been influenced in his selection of

---

28. Williamson, *1 and 2 Chronicles*, 127.
29. Thompson, *1, 2 Chronicles*, 140.

poems from the Psalter by the vocabulary found in the immediate context of the narrative. Specifically, the account mentions several activities in connection with the installation of the ark, namely: "to make petition" (*zkr*), "to give thanks" (*ydh*), and "to praise" (*hll*). These three words are distributed throughout the composite psalm. Even more striking is the inverted parallelism or chiastic structure of the imperative forms of *ydh* and *šir* at the seams of the composite psalm:

"Give thanks to the LORD"	[Heb. *ydh*]	(1 Chron. 16:8 = Ps. 105:1)
"Sing to him"	[Heb. *šir*]	(1 Chron. 16:9 = Ps. 105:2
"Sing to the LORD"	[Heb. *šir*]	(1 Chron. 16:23 = 96:1b + 2b)
"Give thanks to the LORD"	[Heb. *ydh*]	(1 Chron. 16:34 = Ps. 106:1)

This broad connective structure that mirrors the activities of "giving thanks" and "singing" to the Lord testify to the deliberate and skillful poetic arrangement on the part of the compiler.[30]

The theological themes of the three divisions of the composite psalm rehearse the key emphases of 1–2 Chronicles as a "biography" of God (see the introduction). (1) The first unit (16:7–22) highlights God as a covenant maker and keeper and Israel's unique place among the nations as his elect (16:15–17). Without question, the emphasis in this extract from Psalm 105 on the "land of Canaan" as the inheritance of Israel is important to the Chronicler and his audience in the light of the recent Babylonian exile (1 Chron. 16:18). (2) The second unit (16:23–33) from Psalm 96 extols God as Creator and Sovereign over all the nations and over all their gods (1 Chron. 16:26, 30). (3) The third unit (16:34–36) from Psalm 106 praises the goodness and mercy of the God of salvation. Last, and not to be overlooked, the entire composite psalm repeats the covenant name Yahweh (NIV "LORD") some sixteen times.

The members of the division of the Levitical corps assigned to Jerusalem reflect the name-lists of previous material (15:17–21; 16:4–6). Like the priestly ministry performed in the tabernacle of Moses, the ministry of worship before the ark is also a daily activity for the Jerusalem priests and Levites (16:37). Obed-Edom and his sixty-eight associates probably minister at the newly established sanctuary in some sort of rotation for a set number of days, although this is unspecified in the Chronicler's account.

Obed-Edom apparently serves in the dual role of musician and gatekeeper (16:38; cf. 15:18, 21, 24). The relationship of this Obed-Edom to the

30. See further J. A. Loader, "Redaction and Function of the Chronistic 'Psalm of David,'" *OTWSA* 19 (1976): 69–75; Andrew E. Hill, "Patchwork Poetry or Reasoned Verse? Connective Structure in 1 Chronicles XVI," *VT* 33 (1983): 97–101.

Obed-Edom who housed the ark for three months after David's first attempt to transfer the ark failed is unclear (cf. 13:13).

Critical scholarship tends to dismiss the tradition of a tabernacle at Gibeon as an invention of the Chronicler designed to justify King Solomon's worship at Gibeon (16:39–42; 1 Kings 3:4; 2 Chron. 1:3). Such an argument is unnecessary, however, since we have already seen that the Chronicler has made use of other reliable historical sources in his retelling of Israelite history. The reference to the Gibeon sanctuary is important to the purpose of Chronicles because it demonstrates that King David has not neglected the Mosaic tabernacle. Likewise, the perpetuation of the morning and evening sacrifices commanded by the Torah is a further witness to David's adherence to the law of Moses (cf. Ex. 29:39). Perhaps more crucial from the Chronicler's perspective is establishing the historical and theological continuity between David's tent-shrine in Jerusalem and the Mosaic tent-shrine in Gibeon. It seems likely that implicit in Zadok's assignment to Gibeon as chief priest (1 Chron. 16:39) is the appointment of Abiathar as chief priest in Jerusalem (cf. 15:11).

Clearly the ministry of music on the part of the Levites is central to worship at both tent-sanctuaries. Both Heman and Jeduthun are known elsewhere as directors of Levitical musical guilds (cf. 25:1, 6; see also the headings of Ps. 39; 62; 77; 88). The musical refrain describing the thanksgiving of the Levites ("his love endures forever," 1 Chron. 16:41) emphasizes the covenant loyalty, faithfulness, and steadfast love of God for Israel. Selman has aptly commented that this refrain celebrating the enduring love of God (16:34, 41) lies at the heart of Old Testament praise and worship.[31]

The report of King David's departure to go home and bless his family (16:43) marks the Chronicler's return to the Samuel parallel (2 Sam. 6:19b–20a). The verse serves as a conclusion to the narrative preserving the story of the transfer of the ark of the covenant to Jerusalem. It also introduces the following chapter, since David's action foreshadows the covenant blessing God pronounces on the royal family.

The Davidic Covenant (17:1–27)

THE PROPHETIC ORACLE recounting God's promise to build David's into a royal dynasty has its precursor in 2 Samuel 7. The Chronicler's version, though directly dependent on the earlier account, contains numerous divergences that may be attributed to an alternative manuscript tradition or the tendency for Chronicles to contemporize.[32] Significant is the omission of the threat of punishment against the royal line for wrongdoing (cf. 2 Sam. 7:14).

---

31. Selman, *1 Chronicles*, 174.
32. See the discussion in Braun, *1 Chronicles*, 198–99.

It is unclear whether the Chronicler has assumed the fulfillment of the divine warning in the Babylonian exile or considered the menace moot since the monarchy is only a memory at the time of his writing.

This narrative genre is classified broadly as "report," specifically a prophetic commission report (17:3–15) and a prayer (17:16–27). The report contains a number of specialized formulas often found in prophetic literature, including the messenger formula ("this is what the LORD says," 17:4, 7), the word formula ("the word of God came," 17:3), the adoption formula ("I will be his father, and he will be my son," 17:13), the self-abasement formula ("who am I?" 17:16), and the covenant formula ("you made your people Israel your very own," 17:22).[33]

Chronicles is the story of two "houses": the house or dynasty of King David and the house or temple of God. According to Selman, the building blocks for the Chronicler's narrative are the two words from God—one blessing David's house (17:3–15) and the other blessing the house King Solomon built for Yahweh in Jerusalem (2 Chron. 7:11–22).[34] The passage may be divided into three logical units: David's plan (1 Chron 17:1–2), Nathan's oracle (17:3–15), and David's prayer (17:16–27).

The contextual relationship to the preceding and following materials is ideological rather than literary or chronological. (1) The formal installment of the ark of God in Jerusalem is preliminary to David's plan and all his preparations for building a permanent sanctuary for Yahweh (chs. 13–16). On this point, Williamson has noted that the remainder of 1 Chronicles is devoted to the single theme of the Jerusalem temple by noting the builder (ch. 17), setting the political conditions (chs. 18–20), drafting the plans and securing the materials (chs. 22; 28–29), and appointing the personnel (chs. 23–27).[35] (2) God's covenant with the house of David is understood as the natural outcome of Israel's covenant renewal with God as a part of the ark installment ceremony. (3) The divine promise to build a Davidic dynasty in Israel is played out in the Chronicler's subsequent record of the rise and fall of kingship in Israel (2 Chron. 1–36).

The Chronicler condenses the Samuel parallel (17:1–2 = 2 Sam. 7:1–3), omitting the reference to the "rest" enjoyed by King David (2 Sam. 7:1). That "rest" is only partial at best in terms of Israelite foreign policy. The Chronicler's emphasis on David's disqualification as builder of the temple because he is as a warrior (1 Chron. 22:8; 28:3) makes retention of the rest motif awkward contextually as well (cf. David's wars in chs. 18–20).

---

33. De Vries, *1 and 2 Chronicles*, 156–57.
34. Selman, *1 Chronicles*, 174.
35. Williamson, *1 and 2 Chronicles*, 132.

David's desire to build a temple for Yahweh is typical of royal behavior in the biblical world (17:1). In ancient Egypt and Mesopotamia kings erected monuments and built great temples as an act of homage to the deity responsible for establishing them on the throne.[36] It is only natural that David seeks to honor his God in like manner. Beyond this, David is shamed that Yahweh as the true king of Israel is confined to a tent-sanctuary while he himself enjoys the luxury of a palace of cedar (cf. 14:1 and the role of King Hiram in building David's palace).

Nathan enters the scene rather abruptly in the narrative (17:1–2). Along with his contemporary Gad (cf. 21:9), he is identified as a "prophet" or spokesperson for God. Nathan's role as God's messenger frames the oracle. First Nathan receives a message from God (17:3), then he responsibly discharges his commission by faithfully reporting the revelation verbatim to King David (17:15). The introductory and concluding verses referencing Nathan are more than bookends for the dynastic oracle promising perpetual kingship to the line of David. The "word of God" formula (17:3) and the technical term "revelation" (lit., "vision", 17:15; Heb. *ḥazon*) authenticate the divine origin of the message.

The idea behind the word "prophet" (*nabiʾ*) in the Old Testament world is that of a servant who stands in the council of the gods and then reports exactly what he heard as a divine messenger or herald. Nathan is a strategic religious-political adviser in the early Hebrew monarchy as evidenced by his role in securing Solomon's succession to David's throne (cf. 1 Kings 1). Elsewhere we learn that Nathan the prophet is also a court historian, since the Chronicler references his "records" (cf. 1 Chron. 29:29; 2 Chron. 9:29). The combined good intentions of King David and the blessing of the prophet Nathan, however, are rebuffed by God. Curiously, there is no reference here to any "inquiry" of the Lord, despite David's insistence that with the installation of the ark Israel will again inquire of God (cf. 1 Chron. 13:3).

The oracle hinges on word "build" (*bnh*). David will not build a temple for God (17:4), but God will build a royal dynasty from the family of David (17:10). Previously God's presence has not been localized permanently at one specific geographical site. Rather, God moved with his people Israel as they traveled from Egypt after the Exodus and slowly wrested the land of Canaan from the indigenous population (17:5–7). Eventually the Mosaic tent-shrine came to be located more or less permanently in Shiloh and later Gibeon (but with the understanding that Yahweh would one day choose a dwelling place for his name, cf. Deut. 14:24; 16:2). The phrase "from one dwelling place to

---

36. According to Henri Frankfort, the king in the ancient world could render no greater service than to build a house for his god (*Kingship and the Gods* [Chicago: Univ. of Chicago Press, 1978, reprint], 267; see esp. 267–74).

another" (1 Chron. 17:5) is difficult in Hebrew. The expression (lit., "from tent to tent and tabernacle") probably refers to the gradual replacement of the Mosaic tabernacle with another tent-sanctuary as the materials of the Exodus tent-shrine deteriorated over the intervening centuries from Moses to Samuel.

The idea of a permanent and centralized structure for the worship of Yahweh is not the issue in God's veto of David's plan to build a temple. The problem is not the erection of a temple for Yahweh, but David. David's legacy as a warrior means he will serve only as Solomon's contractor for the building of the temple (cf. 22:8; 28:3). It appears that the construction of a permanent sanctuary or temple for the worship of God is connected to Israel's secure position in the land of covenant promise (17:9–10). Unlike the era of the judges ("leaders," 17:10), the Israelites are no longer oppressed by the neighboring people groups. God enables David to achieve this relative peace and safety by cutting off and subduing Israel's enemies (17:8), as reported in the account of his successful military campaigns (chs. 18–20).

The promise of an offspring to succeed David on the throne of Israel echoes God's similar promise to Abraham and Sarah (cf. Gen. 12:1–3). King David has the assurance of God that despite his own death, his dynasty will be firmly established (1 Chron. 11:11). According to Selman, this marks the third reason why God amends David's proposal to build a temple in Jerusalem.[37] Yahweh's priority to build a house for David takes precedence over the construction of a permanent sanctuary. Lasting and appropriate Israelite worship of God must be founded on righteous leadership. The temple as "God's house" can have significance for God's people only after God has built "David's house."

The language of covenant adoption (17:13a) means the royal line of David will enjoy a privileged status as adopted sons of Yahweh (cf. Ps. 2:7; 89:27). The irrevocable steadfast "love" (*ḥesed*) of Yahweh means David's family will avoid the tragic experience of King Saul—divine disapproval and rejection (17:13b). The final verse of the dynastic oracle contains a significant divergence from the Samuel parallel, with the shift to "my [i.e., God's] house and my kingdom" (17:14) from "your [i.e., David's] house and your kingdom" (2 Sam. 7:16). Yahweh is the true king of Israel, and as Williamson has rightly noted, legitimate and successful kings will be those confirmed and established by God himself.[38]

Biblical commentators have noted a high degree of correspondence between David's prayer in 1 Chronicles 17:16–27 and its precursor in 2 Samuel 7:18–29. This is the first of several prayers offered to God by Israelite kings inserted in the Chronicler's retelling of Israelite history. In

---

37. Selman, *1 Chronicles*, 179.
38. Williamson, *1 and 2 Chronicles*, 136.

fact, this is a subtle agenda item of the Chronicler—to draw the people of postexilic Judah back into conversation with God through prayer. The emphasis on prayer fits naturally into his concern for worship renewal because prayer ultimately issues in the glory of God (17:24).[39]

Balentine has identified David's prayer as "formal prayer" or more liturgical-type prayer in contrast to "the single-response" type prayer or more conversational prayer of the Old Testament.[40] It has various elements. The *description* is an account of the situation or circumstance giving rise to the formal prayer. In this case, the oracle of Nathan announcing God's covenant with the house of David constitutes the description of the prayer (17:3–15).

The *introduction* to the prayer precedes its text and calls attention to the content of the prayer. The introduction to David's prayer is brief and implies that he has entered the newly constructed tent-shrine in Jerusalem to offer his supplication (17:16a).

The *invocation* or address to God (17:16b–19) sets the tone of the prayer. David's response to God's gracious overture to establish his dynasty forever is one of self-deprecation in comparison to Yahweh's benevolence. According to Japhet, David's self-abasement sets a tone of reconciliation for the prayer, a "resignation to the will of God" in the decision concerning the building of the temple.[41]

The *declaration* serves either to praise God or justify the suppliant's petition. Here in David's prayer the declaration (17:20–22) praises the uniqueness of God and his power as revealed in Hebrew history. The thumbnail sketch of Israelite history highlights the Exodus, when God "redeemed" a people for himself, and makes an allusion to the Conquest and settlement period of the judges in the phrase "driving out nations" (17:21).

David's *petition* is brief (17:23–24). He simply asks God to follow through and bring to completion what he has already promised: to raise up a descendant who will complete the task of building the temple and to establish firmly an everlasting Davidic dynasty.

The final structural element of the formal prayer is the *recognition* of God's response to the prayer (17:25–27). Unlike the Samuel parallel (cf. 2 Sam.

---

39. Japhet (*I and II Chronicles*, 337–38) has carefully documented the divergences in the two texts of the prayer of David; primary among them are the numerous changes in Chronicles in the divine names and titles. Among the twenty-five divine titles in the Samuel account and the twenty-three divine titles in the Chronicles account, only eight correspond exactly in the two versions. One explanation seems to be the growing sensitivity in later Judaism for the reverencing of certain divine names—to the point of not even writing them down.

40. Samuel E. Balentine, *Prayer in the Hebrew Bible* (OBT; Minneapolis: Fortress, 1993), 19–21.

41. Japhet, *I and II Chronicles*, 336.

7:29), David acknowledges that he has already received a partial answer to his prayer (1 Chron. 17:27). God has blessed David's house in that his divine promise will not fail (17:19, 23). Beyond this, God has blessed David in elevating him to king over Israel and enabling him to transfer the ark of the covenant to Jerusalem. The conclusion of David's prayer is a doxology of sorts, as the word "bless" (*brk*) occurs three times in the final verse (17:27). David understands all this is the gracious work of God, not the genius of human scheming or the chance of fate.

Doubtless, the Chronicler expects his audience to learn (or be reminded of) basic theological truths embedded in David's prayer. The first is a repeated message in Chronicles, given the emphasis on prayer in the books: God both hears and answers the prayers of the righteous by doing great things that ultimately bring glory to his name (17:19, 24, 26). The second is implicit in God's promise to build a lasting Davidic dynasty. The covenant granted to the house of David establishes the rule of God on earth in theological principle through the nation of Israel, apart from any literal descendant of David ruling over the autonomous nation of Israel. For the Chronicler "the divine kingdom was still effective despite the depravations of the exile and the foreign imperial rule of his own day."[42] The present reality of the kingdom of God embodied in the nation of Israel is the cornerstone of the Chronicler's theology of hope.

The repeated use of the word "forever" (*ʿolam*) points to the distant future and indicates the Chronicler's message is intended for another audience as well (17:23, 24, 27). Previously, the prophets Jeremiah and Ezekiel attached messianic expectations to the promises of the Davidic covenant (cf. Jer. 23:5; 30:9; 33:21; Ezek. 34:23; 37:24). The New Testament recognizes Jesus Christ as the ultimate fulfillment of those promises. He is the heir of David, and he inherited the throne of King David (Luke 1:32). Jesus is both the Son of David (Matt. 1:1) and the Son of God charged to build and oversee the very "house" of God (Heb. 3:6). God continues to build his "house," the church, through the Son of David—a spiritual house that will prevail against the opposition of hell itself (Matt. 16:18; Eph. 2:21; 1 Peter 2:5)!

Bridging Contexts

THE TABERNACLE or tent-shrine described in detail in Exodus 25–40 was designed to symbolize the active presence of God among his people. In fact, Exodus 25:8 specifies the basic purpose of this portable worship center as one of giving God an "address" in the Israelite community: "Then have them make a sanctuary for me, and I will dwell among them."

---

42. Selman, *1 Chronicles*, 176.

This sanctuary was also called the Tent of Meeting, because it was there that God convened his assemblies with Israel. The Levitical priesthood was ordained to represent the people before God and to mediate the divine presence in the covenant community. In one sense, God's presence associated with the tabernacle and symbolized in the cloud of glory that resided there (Ex. 40:34–38) was part of the developing "Immanuel theology" of the Old Testament. This progressive revelation of an incarnational divine presence aimed at restoring the intimate fellowship enjoyed by God and humanity in the pre-Fall garden experience. The "Immanuel theology" of the Old Testament was ultimately fulfilled in Jesus Christ (John 1:14; cf. Isa. 7:14).

King Solomon's prayer of dedication for the Jerusalem temple echoes this theme: "I have indeed built a magnificent temple for you, a place for you to dwell forever" (1 Kings 8:13). Interestingly, the parallel passage in Chronicles describes the function of the temple as a repository or resting place for the ark of the covenant—the very "footstool of our God" (1 Chron. 28:2). Thus, the ark was both "throne" and "footstool" of Yahweh (cf. 2 Kings 19:15). The Chronicler appropriately identifies the ark of the covenant as God's footstool because his divine presence was specifically associated with this piece of tabernacle furniture as the place where God met with his people: "There, above the cover [of the ark of the Testimony] between the two cherubim that are over the ark of the Testimony, I will meet with you" (Ex. 25:22).

Practically speaking during biblical times, the royal footstool supported a king's feet as he sat on his throne. According to Fabry, the installation of a royal throne and its footstool in a city or territory was also the equivalent of establishing residence and confirmed the ruler's permanent sovereignty in that domain.[43] The portrayal of a king seated on his throne with feet resting on the footstool represented, through symbol, the reality of royal authority in that city or region and the peace and prosperity enjoyed by the loyal subjects of the kingdom. In addition, the footstool was a sign of humility and servitude on the part of the conquered peoples within that king's realm.

By logical extension from the particular to the universal, the footstool motif associated with the ark of the covenant prescribed the realm of God moving outward in an ever-expanding circle. The jurisdiction of God included the Jerusalem temple housing the ark (Ps. 132:7), but extended to Mount Zion or the city of David where the temple was eventually built (Lam. 2:1), and ultimately reached out to the whole earth (Isa. 66:1).

Belief strives for embodiment in conventional and tangible modes of expression. For this reason, symbolism has been a part of biblical religion from

---

43. H.-J. Fabry, "הֲדֹם [stool]," *TDOT*, 3:328.

its beginnings because it is the vehicle of revelation and the language of faith. As vehicles of revelation, symbols summarize and interpret human experience and interaction with God. As part of the language of faith, symbols interpret the holy, the eternal, and the grace and righteousness of God.

Schaper understands symbolism as an object, act, or word that stands for, suggests, or represents something else.[44] Thus, a sign is something practical and visible that essentially conveys information leading to personal action. For instance, the fish is a religious sign in that as a badge or emblem it conveys information about one's identity as a Christian. Kooy has attempted to more precisely distinguish between sign and symbol in the Old Testament: "The religious symbol points beyond itself to reality, participating in its power, and makes intelligible its meaning. As such it goes beyond a sign or an image."[45] For example, the dove is a religious symbol since it incarnates the reality of the Holy Spirit (cf. Matt. 3:16). In other words, the sign may represent reality, whereas the symbol embodies it.

As ancient Israel's most beloved poet, King David is well acquainted with the value of symbolic language. He understands the power inherent in word pictures for communicating theological truths, whether the sterling character of God (Ps. 18:1–2, 25, 30–31) or the faltering faith of the righteous (51:7–8). For David, the procession of the ark of the covenant into Jerusalem for eventual installation in a central sanctuary is both sign and symbol. As a *sign*, the ark of covenant serves both as a reminder of Israel's Exodus experience and as a testimony of God's holy presence among his people. The return of that sign of divine immanence to the religious life of Israel will stir the people to action—of once again recognizing Yahweh's kingship by affirming their allegiance to him and demonstrating their loyalty to him by complying with the stipulations of his covenant.

As a *symbol*, the ark of the covenant embodies the theological truth of God's residency in the midst of Israel. More important, the footstool motif associated with the ark validates the reality of Yahweh's sovereign rule over creation and thus becomes an emblem of Israel's submission and loyalty to God as king. Based on the instructions of the prophet-priest Samuel, David knows that kingship in Israel can only succeed as the people acknowledge God's presence in their midst by the response of obedience to his commandments (1 Sam. 12:14–15). For King David, the processional celebrating the entry of the ark of the covenant into Jerusalem is a grand object lesson that dramatically portrays the vital relationship between the recognition of God's presence and God's rule.

---

44. Robert Schaper, *In His Presence* (Nashville: Thomas Nelson, 1984), 160.
45. Vernon H. Kooy, "Symbol," *IDB*, 4:472.

THE VALUE OF SYMBOLS. In an important book addressing communication theory and practice, Pierre Babin has analyzed the impact of technology on religious communication in this age of electronic media. He has identified two types of language: the conceptual and the symbolic. Conceptual language may be defined as that form of communication "that provides an abstract, limited, and fixed representation of reality."[46] Symbolic language is "full of resonances and rhythms, stories and images, and suggestions and connections."[47]

The rise of the media civilization is changing "our historical times into psychological times, and . . . those obliged to receive communication into those interested in receiving it."[48] This paradigm shift from conceptual to symbolic language has awakened an "interiority" in contemporary (postmodern) society that places an emphasis on feelings, imagination, and experience. Babin concludes his study of religious communication by prophetically calling the Christian church to rediscover the value of symbolic language for the sake of religious education in this postmodern electronic age.

Babin suggests two special ways the church might develop religious education in this audiovisual age: the way of beauty and the symbolic way.[49] The way of beauty is the development of a religious sensitivity to God's perfection that results in the spiritual experience of recognizing his goodness and beauty in the whole of creation—"the fullness of the cross that joins earth to heaven."[50]

Rather than offer explanation, the symbolic way employs the language of images and stories to free the spirit and move the heart. Symbolic language is more important for "the effect it produces on us . . . arousing a longing for hidden treasure."[51] Finally, Babin stresses the need for incorporating both conceptual and symbolic language in religious education. What he has called *stereo catechesis* must appeal to the heart and human feelings as well as inform the intellect and human reason. Only in this way can an orthodox knowledge and practice of the Bible be infused with a truly converted heart.

---

46. Pierre Babin, *The New Era in Religious Communication* (Minneapolis: Augsburg Fortress, 1991), 151.

47. Ibid., 149; on art as "indirect communication" see Robert E. Webber, "The Arts As Vehicles of Communication," in *The Complete Library of Christian Worship*, ed. R. E. Webber (Nashville: StarSong, 1994), 4:522–23.

48. Babin, *The New Era in Religious Communication*, 35.

49. Ibid., esp. chs. 6 and 7 (pp. 110–67).

50. Ibid., 113.

51. Ibid., 152.

According to Robert Webber, the paradigm shift in communications from conceptual language to symbolic language described by Babin also has profound implications for worship in the Christian church. As he carefully notes:

> The role of symbolism in a postmodern world is not to re-create the ceremonial symbolism of the medieval era, but to understand and apply the symbolism of atmosphere such as the sense of awe and reverence, to recover the beauty of space and the symbolic actions of worship, and to restore the sounds of music and the sights of the arts.[52]

Elevating the known to the unknown through symbolic language and action transports the worshiper into the mystery of the transcendent. In the terminology of art history, this mediation of God's presence and truth through symbol is one way artistic expression communicates divine "intervention" in the natural order.

Historically, ancient and modern societies have employed symbolic representation in artistic expression for several purposes, including:

- intervention—art as a means of representing supernatural powers, unseen spiritual forces, and the mystery of religious thought and experience, thus serving as a bridge to other dimensions of reality
- affiliation—art as a means of defining family and community relationships and to legitimize the right to rule of the leadership class(es) in a society
- documentation—art as a means of memorializing momentous events and recording significant traditions (e.g., creation stories, adventures of heroes, and exploits of the deities)
- aesthetic contemplation—art as a means of enhancing the physical environment and stimulating emotion, intuition, and imagination through a sense of beauty.[53]

The community of faith in ancient Israel and the early Christian church used signs and symbols in much the same way. By *sign* we mean a practical and visible representation of reality, whether a spiritual quality or characteristic, a biblical doctrine or truth, or even a key biblical figure. A sign conveys information that leads to personal action. For example, the sign of Christian baptism points to the theological idea of the "virtual" death, burial, and resurrection of the believer in Jesus Christ (cf. Rom. 6:3–4).

A *symbol* may be understood as a visual representation of an idea or a reality beyond or more than itself. The religious symbol points to a spiritual

52. Robert E. Webber, *Ancient Future Faith* (Grand Rapids: Baker, 1999), 107.
53. Lynn Mackenzie, *Non-Western Art: A Brief Guide*, 2d ed. (Englewood Cliffs, N.J.: Prentice-Hall, 2001), 1–2.

reality outside of itself, participates in its power, and makes intelligible its meaning. Genuine religious symbols are divinely created in the sense that they find their origin in Scripture. For example, the dove is a symbol of the reality of the empowering Holy Spirit (Matt. 3:16), and the sacrificial lamb is a symbol of the reality of the redemptive nature of Jesus Christ's life and ministry (John 1:29; Rev. 5:6). The biblical appropriation of artistic representation in sign and symbol for the purposes of intervention, affiliation, documentation, and aesthetic contemplation are summarized below.

Intervention. The images associated with God's intervention in the created order recorded in the Bible serve various purposes, such as revealing his nature, character, and work; acknowledging the existence of an unseen spiritual reality; indicating the pervasive effects of the Fall in creation; representing the mystery of life, death, and the future; validating God's redemptive plan for all creation; and demonstrating his supremacy over all dimensions of reality.

Specific examples of the symbolic representation of divine intervention in Scripture include the sign of the rainbow (as a reminder of divine judgment and a promise of divine mercy, Gen. 9:13–16), the ark of the covenant (pointing to the presence of God in Israel, Ex. 25:10–22), the Sabbath day (as a marker of God's holiness, 31:12–18), angels (as agents of divine protection, revelation, etc., 32:34; Matt. 1:20), the temple (as a house of prayer, 1 Kings 8:35–36; Matt. 21:13), Elijah the prophet (as the forerunner of Messiah, Mal. 4:5; Matt. 16:14), the dove (signifying the Spirit of God, Matt. 3:16), and the cross itself (as an emblem of self-denial and divine redemption, Matt. 10:38; 1 Cor. 1:17–18).

Affiliation. Affiliation is generally understood as a personal decision to associate as a member in a group or be received in close connection to a club or join an organization. The gospel of Jesus Christ calls people into affiliation with him as the Son of God and the church he continues to build throughout the world (cf. Matt. 16:18). This affiliation with the Christian church is demonstrated in a number of ways:

- becoming a disciple (lit., a follower of an [itinerant] teacher who obeys that person's teachings and in some cases gives up family and material possessions to travel with the teacher and practice his ways; cf. Mark 1:16–18)
- public witness or testimony confessing one's allegiance to Christ as a disciple (cf. Peter's confession, Matt. 16:16)
- the act of baptism (Matt. 28:19; Acts 2:41; Rom. 6:3–4) and other acts such as giving, prayer, and fasting (cf. Matt. 6:1–18)
- eating at the table of the Lord, breaking the bread and drinking the cup (1 Cor. 10:16–17).

Historically, the Christian church has used a variety of symbolic activities and visual representations to signify the membership or affiliation of believers. For example, wearing a white robe during Christian baptism signifies the cleansing of the believer of sin and guilt (cf. Rev. 3:4–5), giving the new believer a Christian name or even a white stone serves as a token of membership in the local church and the body of Christ universal (cf. Rev. 2:17), and gathering for the "breaking of bread" or eating the sacramental meal on a regular basis is a proclamation of the gospel of Jesus Christ (1 Cor. 11:23–26).

During times of persecution the church resorted to secret marks of identification and affiliation (e.g., the sign of the fish used as a motto or badge of identification, attesting initiation and membership in the church of Jesus Christ). The signs and symbols associated with the rituals of affiliation or membership in the church indicate fellowship in a community of like-minded people. The visual representations of affiliation reinforce a sense of belonging that includes mutual care and support, a new identity as a new creation in Christ, a new loyalty, initiation into a new family with responsibilities and obligations, and a new direction and purpose in life.

Documentation and instruction. Documentation through symbolic representation is a means of memorializing God's activity in human history. It is difficult to separate documentation and instruction in the biblical use of signs and symbols. By instruction we mean the use of visual images to teach biblical truth to those unable to read. This was especially true in the early church, when Christian symbols were a universal "sign language" facilitating literacy and communication across language and dialect barriers.

The use of sign and symbol was also important as a pedagogical device complementing oral and written teaching about God and spiritual truth through visual images. These images have the ability to elucidate and to compress truth into a simple and meaningful whole, in a form readily grasped and retained. The developments in educational theory emphasizing learning styles confirm the value of symbols for making an insight permanent because of the mnemonic qualities inherent in visual images.

For example, the Passover ceremony included the images of a lamb, unleavened bread, and doorposts dabbed with blood as memorials of God's activity in Hebrew history (Ex. 12). In addition, written instruction accompanied the symbols of the Exodus to carefully explain the meaning of the event theologically (13:1–13). Finally, a question-and-answer catechism designed to school the next generation in the deeds and words of God concluded the Passover ceremony (13:14–16). Not surprisingly, a similar pattern of *image + word + catechism* may be identified in the ceremony of the bread and the cup of the Lord's table (1 Cor. 11:17–34).

Aesthetic contemplation. The word "aesthetic" means "having a sense or appreciation of the beautiful" or "characterized by a love of beauty." The use of visual images is one means to enhance the environment of worship and stimulate emotion, intuition, and imagination through a sense of beauty. Artistic expression is linked to worship in the Old Testament in connection with the Mosaic tabernacle and later the temple of Solomon (Ex. 31:1–11; 1 Kings 6:14–36). In the New Testament, artistic expression is linked to worship especially in the depiction of heavenly worship in the book of Revelation (Rev. 21:9–27).

The arts generally, and artistic expression in sign and symbol specifically, bridge the natural and the spiritual world. The arts permit humanity as creatures of God to explore and express the mystery of God's transcendence and immanence as Creator and Redeemer (cf. Ps. 96:11–12; 97:5–6; Isa. 55:12).

Dangers associated with symbols. Church history testifies to the fact that the Christian utilization of symbolic representation through artistic expression poses certain risks. At times the distinction between the worship of God and the reverence shown images and objects often has been blurred in Christian practice.

- Chief among these risks are idolatry or the worship of a physical object as a god (cf. Ex. 20:3–5).
- A second risk is iconolatry, or the worship of images or icons (i.e., a flat, one-dimensional pictorial representation of Christ, another biblical figure, or later Christian saints in the formal Byzantine style).
- Another risk is misdirected veneration, the practice of honoring or showing reverential respect to an icon or an image with a ritual act of devotion. For example, in the Roman Catholic tradition reverence is paid to relics of the saints, in Orthodox traditions icons are venerated, and in some liturgical Protestant circles the worship processional includes the "Veneration of the Book" (i.e., the Bible). Unfortunately during church history, the lines between "veneration" and "worship" have been too easily blurred at times.
- Finally, at the level of popular culture, the overuse of Christian symbols as trendy adornment and decoration or for "bumper sticker" evangelism trivializes biblical truth and robs the symbol of its coded meaning.

Toward revaluing sign and symbol. The Christian church broadly speaking, and the evangelical church in particular, must begin to reconsider alternative forms of religious communication for worship, instruction, and evangelism that include sign and symbol or "symbolic language" as "modernism" gives way to "postmodernism." The descriptive thoughts below are offered by way

of summary as prompts for stimulating further thought and discussion, leading to more prescriptive responses to this thesis:

1. Sign and symbol are reemerging as important forms of communication in the Christian church as a result of the shift in our culture from
   conceptual to symbolic forms of communication.
2. Sign and symbol have a long history in the Christian church as a
   means for signifying affiliation, expressing divine intervention, complementing documentation and instruction, and aiding aesthetic contemplation.
3. Sign and symbol constitute indirect forms of communication. This
   nonverbal language is designed to complement, not replace, direct
   forms of communication (the spoken or printed word) in the church.
4. Artistic expression has not escaped the effects of the Fall. Note the
   risks associated with the use of sign and symbol outlined above. The
   Christian church and the Christian must continually consider and
   critically evaluate the role of sign and symbol as used in worship,
   instruction, and evangelism.
5. Sign and symbol may be effectively employed in the Christian church
   not only in worship but also in instruction (preaching and teaching)
   and evangelism.
6. Sign and symbol (including the symbolic use of colors) are readily
   connected to the cycles of Advent, Epiphany, Lent, Easter, Ascension,
   and Pentecost in the Christian year.

Belief strives for embodiment in conventional and tangible modes of
expression. For the sake of imparting the legacy of Christian worship, instruction, and evangelism to the generations now being raised in this age of technology and visual media culture, the church must rediscover the value of
symbolic communication.

1 Chronicles 18–20

I N THE COURSE of time, David defeated the Philistines and subdued them, and he took Gath and its surrounding villages from the control of the Philistines.

²David also defeated the Moabites, and they became subject to him and brought tribute.

³Moreover, David fought Hadadezer king of Zobah, as far as Hamath, when he went to establish his control along the Euphrates River. ⁴David captured a thousand of his chariots, seven thousand charioteers and twenty thousand foot soldiers. He hamstrung all but a hundred of the chariot horses.

⁵When the Arameans of Damascus came to help Hadadezer king of Zobah, David struck down twenty-two thousand of them. ⁶He put garrisons in the Aramean kingdom of Damascus, and the Arameans became subject to him and brought tribute. The LORD gave David victory everywhere he went.

⁷David took the gold shields carried by the officers of Hadadezer and brought them to Jerusalem. ⁸From Tebah and Cun, towns that belonged to Hadadezer, David took a great quantity of bronze, which Solomon used to make the bronze Sea, the pillars and various bronze articles.

⁹When Tou king of Hamath heard that David had defeated the entire army of Hadadezer king of Zobah, ¹⁰he sent his son Hadoram to King David to greet him and congratulate him on his victory in battle over Hadadezer, who had been at war with Tou. Hadoram brought all kinds of articles of gold and silver and bronze.

¹¹King David dedicated these articles to the LORD, as he had done with the silver and gold he had taken from all these nations: Edom and Moab, the Ammonites and the Philistines, and Amalek.

¹²Abishai son of Zeruiah struck down eighteen thousand Edomites in the Valley of Salt. ¹³He put garrisons in Edom, and all the Edomites became subject to David. The LORD gave David victory everywhere he went.

¹⁴David reigned over all Israel, doing what was just and right for all his people. ¹⁵Joab son of Zeruiah was over the army; Jehoshaphat son of Ahilud was recorder; ¹⁶Zadok son of

Ahitub and Ahimelech son of Abiathar were priests; Shavsha was secretary; ¹⁷Benaiah son of Jehoiada was over the Kerethites and Pelethites; and David's sons were chief officials at the king's side.

^{19:1}In the course of time, Nahash king of the Ammonites died, and his son succeeded him as king. ²David thought, "I will show kindness to Hanun son of Nahash, because his father showed kindness to me." So David sent a delegation to express his sympathy to Hanun concerning his father.

When David's men came to Hanun in the land of the Ammonites to express sympathy to him, ³the Ammonite nobles said to Hanun, "Do you think David is honoring your father by sending men to you to express sympathy? Haven't his men come to you to explore and spy out the country and overthrow it?" ⁴So Hanun seized David's men, shaved them, cut off their garments in the middle at the buttocks, and sent them away.

⁵When someone came and told David about the men, he sent messengers to meet them, for they were greatly humiliated. The king said, "Stay at Jericho till your beards have grown, and then come back."

⁶When the Ammonites realized that they had become a stench in David's nostrils, Hanun and the Ammonites sent a thousand talents of silver to hire chariots and charioteers from Aram Naharaim, Aram Maacah and Zobah. ⁷They hired thirty-two thousand chariots and charioteers, as well as the king of Maacah with his troops, who came and camped near Medeba, while the Ammonites were mustered from their towns and moved out for battle.

⁸On hearing this, David sent Joab out with the entire army of fighting men. ⁹The Ammonites came out and drew up in battle formation at the entrance to their city, while the kings who had come were by themselves in the open country.

¹⁰Joab saw that there were battle lines in front of him and behind him; so he selected some of the best troops in Israel and deployed them against the Arameans. ¹¹He put the rest of the men under the command of Abishai his brother, and they were deployed against the Ammonites. ¹²Joab said, "If the Arameans are too strong for me, then you are to rescue me; but if the Ammonites are too strong for you, then I will rescue you. ¹³Be strong and let us fight bravely for our people and the cities of our God. The LORD will do what is good in his sight."

¹⁴Then Joab and the troops with him advanced to fight the Arameans, and they fled before him. ¹⁵When the Ammonites saw that the Arameans were fleeing, they too fled before his brother Abishai and went inside the city. So Joab went back to Jerusalem.

¹⁶After the Arameans saw that they had been routed by Israel, they sent messengers and had Arameans brought from beyond the River, with Shophach the commander of Hadadezer's army leading them.

¹⁷When David was told of this, he gathered all Israel and crossed the Jordan; he advanced against them and formed his battle lines opposite them. David formed his lines to meet the Arameans in battle, and they fought against him. ¹⁸But they fled before Israel, and David killed seven thousand of their charioteers and forty thousand of their foot soldiers. He also killed Shophach the commander of their army.

¹⁹When the vassals of Hadadezer saw that they had been defeated by Israel, they made peace with David and became subject to him.

So the Arameans were not willing to help the Ammonites anymore.

²⁰:¹In the spring, at the time when kings go off to war, Joab led out the armed forces. He laid waste the land of the Ammonites and went to Rabbah and besieged it, but David remained in Jerusalem. Joab attacked Rabbah and left it in ruins. ²David took the crown from the head of their king—its weight was found to be a talent of gold, and it was set with precious stones—and it was placed on David's head. He took a great quantity of plunder from the city ³and brought out the people who were there, consigning them to labor with saws and with iron picks and axes. David did this to all the Ammonite towns. Then David and his entire army returned to Jerusalem.

⁴In the course of time, war broke out with the Philistines, at Gezer. At that time Sibbecai the Hushathite killed Sippai, one of the descendants of the Rephaites, and the Philistines were subjugated.

⁵In another battle with the Philistines, Elhanan son of Jair killed Lahmi the brother of Goliath the Gittite, who had a spear with a shaft like a weaver's rod.

⁶In still another battle, which took place at Gath, there was a huge man with six fingers on each hand and six toes on each foot—twenty-four in all. He also was descended from Rapha. ⁷When he taunted Israel, Jonathan son of Shimea, David's brother, killed him.

⁸These were descendants of Rapha in Gath, and they fell at the hands of David and his men.

KING DAVID ESTABLISHED an Israelite empire by expanding territorial boundaries through a series of military campaigns against neighboring nations. The Chronicler's retelling of David's wars is a highly selective summary of 2 Samuel 8—21, as noted in the outline below:

1 Chronicles 18 = 2 Samuel 8 (David's campaigns)
1 Chronicles 19 = 2 Samuel 10 (Ammonite war)
1 Chronicles 20:1a = 2 Samuel 11:1 (end of Ammonite war)
1 Chronicles 20:1b = 2 Samuel 12:26 (siege of Rabbah)
1 Chronicles 20:2–3 = 2 Samuel 12:30–31 (booty report from Rabbah)
1 Chronicles 20:4–8 = 2 Samuel 21:18–22 (exploits of David's warriors)

The Chronicler chooses to retain the narrative order of the original accounts but adds little new material. His exclusion of the story of David and Bathsheba is not an attempt to idealize the beloved king as much as it is in keeping with his pattern of emphasizing the public and political events associated with the kings of the Davidic dynasty. The summary statement of David's spoils of war in 1 Chronicles 18:11 agrees with 2 Samuel 8:11–12, although the Chronicler has omitted the report detailing the victory over the Amalekites.

The reports of David's wars serve as important background for the later episodes of Solomon's installation as David's successor and the building of the Jerusalem temple. The recounting of David's campaigns are included primarily for the purpose of explaining why David is prohibited from building Yahweh's temple: David is a warrior who has "shed much blood" (22:8; 28:3). According to Deuteronomy, God would choose a dwelling place for his name once the Israelites had "rest" from their enemies (Deut. 12:10; 25:19). That rest has not yet occurred.

The Chronicler picks up on this Deuteronomic theme, since it is the rest and safety won by David's wars that prompt King David to commission Solomon to build Yahweh's temple (22:9, 18; cf. 23:25). The repetition of the victory formula suggests divine approval of David's expansionist policy, almost as a type of "second" Joshua engaging in the conquest of the Promised Land (cf. 18:6, 13). Although a secondary emphasis, the booty David and his armies plunder from their enemies and subsequently dedicate to the Lord provides the funds for the eventual construction of the temple (18:8, 11; cf. 22:3, 14; 29:3).

The literary genre of this section may be identified as historical story and includes a variety of subgenres like the battle report (e.g., 18:1–6, 12–13; 19:16–19), booty lists (e.g., 18:7–11; 20:2–3), exploit report (e.g., 20:4, 5), and anecdote (e.g., 20:6–7).[1] Structurally, the literary unit of chapters 18–20 is loosely organized by the repetition of the conjunctive formula "in the course of time" (18:1; 19:1; 20:4). Allen has detected a more subtle structural marker in the repetition of the word "subdue" (*knc*) at the beginning and the end of the passage, creating a type of envelope construction for the account of David's wars (1 Chron. 18:1; 20:4 [NIV "subjugated"]; cf. 17:10).[2] This theme is reinforced by the repeated phrase "became subject to" (*ʿbd*) in each of the battle reports (18:2, 6, 13; 19:19).

Theologically, the retelling of David's wars and the subduing of the nations demonstrates a partial fulfillment of the covenant Yahweh granted David, an important theme in the Chronicler's theology of hope for postexilic Judah. The narrative also verifies David's role as a faithful servant in the fulfillment of the commission entrusted to him to provide a haven for the people of Israel (cf. 17:8–10).

David's Campaigns (18:1–13)

THE CHRONICLER INSERTS "Gath and its surrounding villages" for "Metheg Ammah" (see 2 Sam. 8:1, a site of unknown location), presumably to update the parallel source for his audience. The six hundred Gittites among David's mercenaries attests David's subjugation of Gath (2 Sam. 15:18; cf. 1 Kings 2:39–40, which suggests Gath is still under some degree of Israelite control when King Solomon ascends the throne). Strategically, subduing the Philistines secures the western flank of David's empire. The later delineation of the borders of Solomon's empire seems to indicate that the Philistine territory lies outside Israelite domain and remains an autonomous political entity (cf. 1 Kings 4:21). The Chronicler reports Israel's victory over Moab minus the account of David's cruel treatment of the Moabites (1 Chron. 18:2; cf. 2 Sam. 8:2). In both cases David apparently leaves local leadership in place but imposes annual tribute (at least on Moab) as a satellite state of Israel.

1. See further De Vries, *1 and 2 Chronicles*, 159–67.
2. Allen, *1, 2 Chronicles* (1987), 132–33.

The Chronicler preserves a more lengthy account of campaign against a coalition of Aramean states to the northeast (18:3–10). King Hadadezer has consolidated a kingdom that includes the regions of Beth Rehob, Zobah, and Hamath (located north and east of Dan and west of Damascus). The conflict between Israel and the Arameans is precipitated by Hadadezer's raising of a monument (or boundary stone?) to register his claim on territory along the Euphrates River (18:3; cf. "he went to establish his control" [NIV]). David opposes Hadadezer's declaration of sovereignty, perhaps because he has designs on controlling the trade route known as the King's Highway (running from Sela in Edom to the city of Hamath through Damascus; this would explain David's expansionist policy in the Transjordan against the Edomites, Moabites, and the Ammonites).

David deals Hadadezer a severe blow in a single battle but does not subdue the kingdom of Zobah. Chronicles reports that David captures 1,000 chariots (18:4; missing in the text of 2 Sam. 8:4 but restored in the NIV), 7,000 charioteers, and 20,000 foot soldiers.[3] The Arameans of Damascus, apparently in league with the kingdom of Zobah, marshal troops to aid Hadadezer in his engagement with the Israelites (1 Chron 18:5). David and his army strike down 22,000 troops sent from Damascus and as a result establish garrisons in that city. Like the Moabites (18:2), the Arameans of Damascus become a tribute-paying vassal state to Israel (18:6).

Among the spoils David takes from Hadadezer and the cities of Zobah are large quantities of bronze.[4] The Chronicler adds the fact that the booty is later used by Solomon in casting the bronze vessels for the temple (18:7–8). This not only provides further detail as to what became of the plunder, but also it is another way in which the Chronicler connects David to the preparations made for building Yahweh's temple.

The news of Israel's success against the kingdom of Zobah and the Arameans of Damascus prompts Tou, king of Hamath, to befriend King David with gifts of gold, silver, and bronze (18:9–10). This is likely more than a congratulatory gesture, although King Tou of Hamath (modern Hamah, 120 miles north of Damascus on the Orontes River) had been at war with King Hadadezer of Zobah. D. J. Wiseman has suggested that the mission of Tou's son Hadoram (Joram in 2 Sam. 8:10) is a diplomatic move and the gifts of precious metals are intended to forge some kind of political alliance between King Tou and King David.[5]

---

3. For a discussion of the textual problems related to the numbers in the battle report of 18:3–4, see Japhet, *I and II Chronicles*, 346–47.

4. Cf. ibid., 348, on the Chronicler's tendency "to 'modernize' the historical testimony" (in this case, the place names).

5. D. J. Wiseman, "'Is It Peace?'—Covenant and Diplomacy," *VT* 32 (1982): 311–26.

The survey of David's campaigns concludes with a brief report of the Edomite war (18:12–13). Edom becomes a satellite state of Israel like Aramean Damascus and Moab. Military garrisons are placed throughout Edom to ensure Israelite control of the territory. Although the text says nothing about Edomite tribute to Hebrew kings, it appears Edom is among the nations paying tribute to Israel during the reign of Solomon (cf. 1 Kings 4:21). The exploit report cites the heroics of Abishai (1 Chron. 18:12), but 2 Samuel 8:13 credits David and 1 Kings 11:15–16 vaunts Abishai's brother Joab. Selman is probably correct to note that each of these warriors would have had differing responsibilities during the Edomite war in the overall chain of command (with Joab the field general [cf. 1 Chron. 19:8] and Abishai chief of the Three [11:20–21; cf. 2 Sam. 20:6–7]).[6] Hence, all three play key roles in the victory over the Edomites.

More important to the Chronicler's message is the theological commentary found at the midpoint and end of the chapter (18:6, 13). The God who "gave David victory" is the God of the Chronicler and postexilic Judah. That same blessing of divine approval awaits those who dedicate themselves in expectant faith to the spiritual and physical restoration of Jerusalem, even as King David dedicates the silver and gold plundered in war to the work of the Lord (18:11).

David's Royal Cabinet (8:14–17)

THE NIV INCLUDES 18:14 in this section as an introduction to the catalog of King David's officers, recognizing the organizational structure as a demonstration of his "just and right" rule. Some scholars mark the paragraph break at 18:15, arguing that the summary statement characterizing David's reign better serves as the conclusion to the report of David's victories on the battlefield.[7] The theological assessment of David's reign may serve double duty, functioning as a summary statement to the report of David's wars and as an introduction to the roster of the king's primary advisers (so Japhet).[8] The remark does stress the fact that David rules over "all Israel," an important theme in the Chronicler's retelling of Israelite history. The statement also stresses that David's reign is one of justice and righteousness. According to Japhet, this confirms that David has satisfied the Israelites' expectations of the ideal king.[9] Doing what is "just and right" becomes the standard by which later kings are measured (cf. Jer. 22:15) and the model for future Davidic kingship (cf. Jer. 23:5).

---

6. Selman, *1 Chronicles*, 189.
7. E.g., ibid., 190.
8. So Japhet, *I and II Chronicles*, 351.
9. Ibid.

The list of royal cabinet members is borrowed directly from 2 Samuel 8:15–18 (cf. also 20:23–26). This naming of the royal bureaucracy is not directly related to the accounts of David's wars, but there are logical connections between territorial expansion and the need for administrative oversight of the Israelite empire. The source for the Israelite administrative model remains a topic of scholarly debate, with both Egyptian and Canaanite governments suggested as likely paradigms.[10] Selman correctly reminds us, however, that native Hebrew developments in the political structure of the Israelite empire should not be overlooked.[11]

Three distinct "departments" comprise David's royal cabinet: a war office, a priestly office, and an administrative office. Joab becomes David's general (cf. 2 Sam. 3:22–27) and is briefly displaced by Amasa after Joab disobeys the king's command and executes the rebel Absalom (2 Sam. 19:13). Joab later assassinates Amasa and usurps the role of general (2 Sam. 20:8–13). King David never forgives Joab for these two crimes and instructs Solomon, upon his accession to the throne, to execute Joab (cf. 1 Kings 2:34). Solomon then elevates Benaiah son of Jehoiada (1 Chron. 18:17) to the cabinet post of general (1 Kings 2:35).

Abiathar and Zadok (18:16) appear to function as joint high priests after the massacre of the priestly clan at Nob by King Saul (1 Sam. 22:20). The emergence of Zadok as a priestly figure in Israel is a matter of considerable scholarly discussion. It is possible David appoints Abiathar as a priestly representative for tribal Israel, while Zadok represents the remnant of an indigenous priesthood centered in Jerusalem that is absorbed by the Israelites when David conquers the city.[12] Since both Zadok and Abiathar are linked to one Ahitub, it is also possible that both escaped the massacre at Nob. In any event, Abiathar is later exiled as a result of his loyalty to Adonijah in the question of David's successor and Zadok becomes chief priest in Solomon's administration (1 Kings 2:26–27). It should be noted that the books of Kings and Chronicles remember Abiathar and Zadok as priests and key members of the royal cabinet of David and Solomon (1 Kings 4:4; 1 Chron. 18:16).

The cabinet post of "secretary" or "recorder" (NASB) may have been a position similar to that of the royal herald in the Egyptian court. The herald was a personal secretary to the pharaoh in charge of royal protocol and served as the public spokesman for the monarchy.[13] The cabinet office of "secretary"

---

10. E.g., Myers, *I Chronicles*, 138; George E. Mendenhall, "The Monarchy," *Interp* 29 (1975): 155–70.

11. Selman, *1 Chronicles*, 190.

12. Cf. Mendenhall, "The Monarchy," 165–66.

13. Cf. Myers, *I Chronicles*, 138.

functioned as the royal scribe and was responsible for all official correspondence (during the divided monarchy the duties of the secretary included financial oversight of temple funds and military conscription, cf. 2 Kings 12:10; 18:18; 25:19). The Kerethites and the Pelethites (1 Chron. 18:17)—that is, Cretan and Philistine mercenaries—serve as the royal bodyguard (cf. 2 Sam. 15:18; 20:7).

Controversy surrounds the role of David's sons in the royal cabinet at two levels. (1) There is some question as to whether the text refers to the "eldest sons" as officials of King David (so NEB) or to the sons of David as "chief officials" of the king (so NIV, NRSV). The latter reading is preferred by the majority of commentators and by this writer as well.[14]

(2) The Chronicler deviates from 2 Samuel 8:18 in identifying the sons of David as "chief officials" (*hari' sonim*, 1 Chron. 18:18) instead of "priests" (*kohanim*; cf. NIV "royal advisers"). Japhet argues that the sons of David are unacceptable to the Chronicler as "priests" because they are not of Levitical lineage.[15] Thompson contends the text of 2 Samuel 8:18 is corrupt in that the term for priest (*kohen*) was mistaken with the term for "administrator" (*soken*).[16] Selman seeks to mediate the extremes by suggesting David's sons are non-Levitical priests, who function as the king's personal priests or as "royal chaplains."[17]

There is little reason to doubt the text of 2 Samuel 8:18. It is also clear that King David violates several of the prescriptions for Hebrew kingship outlined by Moses (e.g., the prohibition against taking many wives, cf. Deut. 17:14–20). Why is it surprising that David would appoint his sons as "priests" of some sort when he himself usurped the role of priest on occasion (cf. 1 Chron. 15:27; 16:2–3)? Selman may be correct in his assumption that, as priests, David's sons have duties that differ from the Levitical priesthood.[18]

War Against the Ammonites (19:1–20:3)

THE PARALLEL ACCOUNT of the Ammonite war is found in 2 Samuel 10:1–19. The biblical record yields no account of an event or events resulting in a pact of friendship between David and the Ammonite king Nahash (1 Chron. 19:1–2). Selman has suggested the relationship may be "best explained by their common hostility toward Saul" (cf. 1 Sam. 11:1–2; 14:47).[19] The use of

---

14. E.g., Braun, *1 Chronicles*, 203, 205; Japhet, *I and II Chronicles*, 352.
15. Japhet, *I and II Chronicles*, 352.
16. Thompson, *1, 2 Chronicles*, 153.
17. Selman, *1 Chronicles*, 191.
18. Ibid.
19. Ibid., 193.

the word "kindness" (Heb. *ḥesed*) has covenant connotations and may imply some sort of informal treaty between David and Nahash. Hanun's treatment of David's entourage is interpreted as an annulling of the treaty and an act of belligerence threatening war.

David intends his commissioning of a delegation representing his administration at the "state funeral" in Ammon as a gesture of goodwill (19:2). The men are seized, however, and are accused of spying (19:3). The Samuel account reports that half of the beard of David's ambassadors is shaved off (2 Sam. 10:4). The Chronicler abbreviates the incident by summarizing, "Hanun ... shaved them" (1 Chron. 19:4). The beard was the symbol of manhood in the ancient world, so to shave off half the beard was both an insult to the Israelite emissaries and an affront to the virility of King David. The further humiliation of the Israelite dignitaries in the cutting of their robes is an act of open contempt for King David, publicly shaming him since ambassadors acted on behalf of the king. It is even possible the slashing of the garments to expose the men's buttocks is some sort of subtle mockery of David's own dancing (and public exposure) when the ark of the covenant was paraded into Jerusalem (2 Sam. 6:16, 20).

One wonders about the political savvy of the Ammonite king Hanun, given royal protocol in the ancient world. Does he really assume his disgraceful treatment of David's ambassadors will have no repercussions? The story recalls the ascension of and the counsel from royal advisers that Rehoboam later chooses to follow, which lead the nation of Israel into civil war (cf. 1 Kings 12). By the same token, if the death of King Nahash occurs during David's Transjordan campaigns against the Moabites (18:2) and the Edomites (18:12–13), then Hanun's suspicions about David's motives may have had some justification.[20]

The Ammonite preparations for war consist largely of hiring Aramean mercenaries (19:6–7). The soldiers are recruited from Aram Naharaim (a region north of the Euphrates River bounded by the Habur River), Aram Maacah (a small kingdom north and east of Lake Huleh), and Zobah (see comments on 18:3-6). The thousand talents of silver (19:6) translates into more than thirty-seven tons of the precious metal. This incredible sum speaks to the desperation of the Ammonites (although this may be another case where the number "1000" must be examined carefully). The idiom "to become a stench in [someone's] nostrils" (19:6) means to "make oneself repulsive"[21] or "to incur the wrath" of someone (so NJPSV).[22]

---

20. Cf. H. W. Hertzberg, *I and II Samuel* (OTL; Philadelphia: Westminster, 1964), 303–4.
21. Myers, *I Chronicles*, 133.
22. Braun's "when they knew they had offended David" is weak (*1 Chronicles*, 206).

David's response is swift and thorough: the mobilization of the entire Israelite army against the Ammonites under the command of Joab (19:8). The Arameans and the Ammonites are deployed in such a way that Joab is compelled to wage the war on two fronts: the Arameans in the open field (near Medeba in Moab south of Rabbah, cf. 19:7) and the Ammonites stationed just outside the city gates (presumably the capital of Rabbah, cf. 20:1).

Shrewdly, Joab positions his elite forces against the Aramean mercenaries, with the remaining forces pitted against the Ammonites (19:10–11). He also devises a "plan B," calling for the consolidation of the Israelite troops in case the battle should go against his army (19:12). Presumably this strategy will limit the fighting to a single front and thereby reduce casualties (and perhaps permit an organized retreat, should that be necessary).

Finally, Joab encourages his troops by reminding them they are fighting for all the Israelite people and "the cities of our God" (19:13a). This phrase, coupled with the command to "be strong and ... fight bravely," alludes to Yahweh's covenant with Israel and to the conquest of Canaan by Joshua (cf. Josh. 1:6–7). Joab concludes his precombat exhortation with a prayer, committing the outcome of the battle to the sovereignty and goodness of God (19:13b). Expressions of such trust in the providence of Yahweh are an important feature of the Chronicler's theology of hope for postexilic Judah (cf. 2 Chron. 19:11; 20:15; 32:7–8).

The answer to Joab's prayer comes almost immediately. The Aramean mercenaries flee their formation as the Israelites muster for battle, putting up little or no resistance. Witnessing the cowardice of the Arameans proves a devastating blow to the morale of the Ammonites, who likewise flee and retreat into the walled city. Joab chooses not to lay siege to the city of Rabbah but returns to Jerusalem (19:15b). It may have already been late in the year, and the winter rains would stymie any protracted siege of the city.

Joab's defeat of the coalition of Ammonite and Aramean armies is not decisive. Interestingly, Japhet notes that what was originally a mercenary enterprise for the Arameans has now become "the subject of Aramaean self-interest."[23] The Aramean troops sent from beyond the Euphrates River (19:16) are summoned to wage war with Israel in an attempt to check David's growing military strength. The reinforcements are sent by King Hadadezer of Zobah, both to restore national pride and to protect territorial boundaries from Israelite encroachment (this event represents a previous encounter between David and Hadadezer prior to Hadadezer's eventual capitulation, cf. 18:3–6).

The battle is fought at Helam, perhaps the site of Alma some thirty-five miles east of the Sea of Galilee (cf. 2 Sam. 10:16–17). The result of the bat-

---

23. Japhet, *I and II Chronicles*, 360.

tle is similar to the previous engagement led by Joab (1 Chron. 19:14—15). David is victorious as the Arameans again are routed and flee the battlefield (19:17—18). Shophach (or Shobach, 2 Sam. 10:16), Hadadezer's general, is killed in battle (1 Chron. 19:18).

More problematic are the discrepancies in the number of casualties (700 charioteers in 2 Sam. 10:18 versus 7000 charioteers in 1 Chron. 19:18).[24] The narrative indicates the "vassals of Hadadezer" make peace with David (19:19), suggesting Hadadezer's kingdom is not party to the treaty. This explains David's later declaration of sovereignty along the Euphrates River (cf. 18:3—6). The Aramean vassal states of Hadadezer become subject to David, but no mention is made of tribute (19:19). The unwillingness of the Arameans to partner with the Ammonites in any future campaigns suggests that the terms of Israel's treaty include a clause prohibiting such agreements.

The Ammonite campaign resumes in the spring of the following year, tactically a more opportune time to lay siege to a walled city (20:1). The Chronicler condenses his version of the conclusion of the Ammonite war from the accounts found in the Samuel parallels (2 Sam. 11:1; 12:26—31). Chronicles omits the lengthy (and lurid) story of David's tryst with Bathsheba (2 Sam. 11:2—12:25), although a hint of that royal scandal is retained in the cryptic reference to the king's decision to remain behind after sending Joab and the Israelite army off to war ("but David remained in Jerusalem," 1 Chron. 20:1b).

The transition from Joab's sacking of Rabbah (20:1c) to King David claiming the crown of the Ammonite king (20:2) is awkward. The Chronicler's abbreviated report of the defeat of the Ammonites assumes knowledge of the Samuel parallel (2 Sam. 12:26—29). There we learn that Joab and the Israelite troops besiege Rabbah and capture a portion of the city (the royal citadel, 2 Sam. 12:26). Joab then defers to military protocol and requests that David himself descend on Rabbah with additional forces and complete the conquest of the city (lest Joab be given credit as its conqueror, 2 Sam. 12:27—29). At this point the Chronicler rejoins the Samuel narrative with King David's seizing the crown of the Ammonite king, taking plunder from the city, and consigning the surviving Ammonite population to serve in forced labor gangs (1 Chron. 20:2—3).

Critics have questioned the accuracy of the biblical figures for the weight of the Ammonite crown (a talent of gold would weigh more than seventy-five pounds! 20:2). The piece in question is probably an ornamental tiara symbolizing Ammonite kingship and may have been displayed at certain royal occasions. Most likely this royal headdress is lifted to David's head

---

24. On the correctness of the Chronicler's figure in the battle report of 1 Chron. 19:18 see Payne, "1, 2 Chronicles" (4:402).

briefly by his personal attendants as a public declaration of Israel's sovereignty over Ammon. According to McCarter, establishing forced labor crews of captives "for the economic exploitation of the conquered territory" was a standard practice in the ancient world for victorious kings (20:3, "to labor with saws and with iron picks and axes").[25]

The report of the Israelite victory over the Ammonites ends abruptly, with David and his army returning to Jerusalem (20:3c). Clearly David takes his full revenge against King Hanun and the Ammonites for the humiliating treatment of his ambassadors. Nothing is said of the fate of the Ammonite king or the political status of Ammon after the war. Japhet has noted, however, that among Solomon's queens is Naamah (an Ammonite and Rehoboam's mother, 1 Kings 14:21, 31)—"a matter which no doubt should be interpreted politically."[26]

War Against the Philistines (20:4–8)

THE CHRONICLER RETURNS to the Philistine "problem" to conclude his summary of David's wars. The Philistines were the nemesis of the Israelites. The ongoing conflict stemmed primarily from the fact that the Israelites needed a seaport, as the kingdoms of Saul and David were landlocked. The narrative relates border skirmishes settled by duels between champion warriors more than full-scale war. According to Selman, "the duel was a recognized form of combat in Canaan and in the Philistines' original homeland in the Aegean."[27]

The Chronicler borrows the material from 2 Samuel 21:15–22 (which contains four exploit reports) with minimal editorial adaptation. Our passage consists of three exploit reports, each of which records a contest between an Israelite warrior and a Philistine warrior descended from the Rephaites (cf. NRSV, "descendants of the giants"). The Rephaim were people of enormous size and strength (e.g., Goliath was more than nine feet tall, 1 Sam. 17:4; Og king of Bashan required a bed [or sarcophagus?] thirteen feet in length, Deut. 3:11). The relationship of the Philistine Rephaites to the giants of the Transjordan, also called Rephaim or Anakim, is unclear (cf. Deut. 2:10–11).

The first exploit report relates the killing of Sippai by Sibbecai (20:4). Sibbecai is one of David's "mighty men" (11:29). The village of Gob is listed as the site of the contest according to 2 Samuel 21:18, while the Chronicler locates the battle at Gezer—perhaps another example of modernizing the report for his audience by citing a more well-known city in the same vicin-

---

25. P. Kyle McCarter, *II Samuel* (AB 9; New York: Doubleday, 1984), 313; on the administration of the Davidic state, see Myers, *I Chronicles*, 140; Selman, *1 Chronicles*, 197.

26. Japhet, *I and II Chronicles*, 365

27. Selman, *1 Chronicles*, 199.

---

ity. The Chronicler adds the comment "and the Philistines were subjugated" (1 Chron. 20:4).

The second exploit report records the victory of Elhanan (one of David's mighty men, 11:26) over Lahmi, the brother of Goliath (20:5). Problems arise when examining the parallel account (2 Sam. 21:19), because there Elhanan slays Goliath. The extensive scribal activity evident in the text of Samuel (including corruptions in that verse) have led some scholars to conclude that Chronicles preserves the correct rendering of the episode. Others have suggested that Goliath is a title, not a name, thus solving the apparent contradiction between Samuel and Chronicles. Selman speculates that the contest between Elhanan and Lahmi may have been a "round two" so to speak, after David killed Goliath.[28] The Samuel rendition locates the combat in Gob, but the Chronicler has omitted the site of the contest.

The third exploit report preserves the victory of David's nephew Jonathan over an unnamed Rephaite from Gath, who taunts Israel (20:6–7). The taunting of an enemy was an invitation or challenge to a duel. Apparently more memorable than the warrior's name, the biblical historian takes note of the man's extra digits on both hands and feet (cf. 2 Sam. 21:20).

One can only muse over the factors influencing the Chronicler's selective appeal to the summary accounts of the wars of King David. No doubt, the stories of the success of David and his army in the face of seemingly insurmountable odds are a source of inspiration for postexilic Judah. They are also a stirring reminder of the power of God to deliver his faithful servants from dark circumstances. The Chronicler's audience needs to hear that!

THE PECULIAR LITERARY genius of the Chronicler lies in his ability to retell Israelite history as a sermon. Understanding the report of David's wars against the Philistines, Moabites, Arameans, and Ammonites in chapters 18–20 merely as the glorification of the Israelites as champions of good triumphing over the sinister forces of evil misses the point. Rather, as McConville has pointed out, a key Old Testament truth in the Chronicler's proclamation to postexilic Judah through the recitation of David's wars is that to oppose Israel is to oppose God.[29]

We should not read this passage as justifying war, "holy war" or otherwise. Israel was, of course, constituted a theocracy at Mount Sinai and hence was an instrument of both divine justice and the light of divine revelation in the

28. Ibid.
29. McConville, *I and II Chronicles*, 65.

ancient world as a nation-state (cf. Ex. 19:6; Isa. 49:6). The Christian church as the people of God, however, is not a political entity and has no role in bearing arms—though the church is called to a ministry as salt and light in a dark world (Matt. 5:13–14; Eph. 5:8).

McConville is correct in his assessment that the aim of warfare for the armies of Israel is "not destruction itself, but the establishment, or re-establishment, of a right order in the world, i.e., an order in which the nations serve the true people of God (19:19), and therefore, implicitly, recognize God himself."[30] The Hebrew poets and prophets associate this right order in the world with the "day of the LORD" and understand it to include the worship of Yahweh in Jerusalem by the nations (cf. Ps. 45:17; 86:9; Isa. 56:7; Mal. 1:14). The Chronicler is not espousing a type of liberation theology, calling for postexilic Judah to revolt and throw off the yoke of their Persian oppressors. Rather, he seeks to incite a spiritual revolution. He envisions establishing (or reestablishing) right order in Israel (and ultimately the world) through prayer and the revitalization of temple worship. In a way, the Chronicler anticipates the startling teaching of Jesus about the kingdom of God being an ethical and spiritual one—not a material and political kingdom (cf. Matt. 5:1–12; 21:31–32; Luke 17:20–21).

The Chronicler also knows that the battle belongs to the Lord (2 Chron. 20:15). Victory in war is not contingent on the physical strength or strategic ploys of Israel's warrior-kings (cf. Prov. 21:31). Yahweh is the invincible warrior of Israel, not David. David himself knows Yahweh as a fortress, stronghold, deliverer, and shield (Ps. 144:1–2). Indeed, he is "the One who gives victory to kings" (Ps. 144:10). This too was established in the Exodus, when the Lord became a warrior for Israel against the Egyptians (Ex. 15:3). So Moses confidently instructed his people that "the LORD will fight for you; you need only to be still" (14:14).

It is in light of this background that the Israelite historians declare that "the LORD gave David victory wherever he went" (2 Sam. 8:6, 14; 1 Chron. 18:6, 13). It is on the basis of this knowledge that David's general Joab exhorts his troops to "fight bravely" as he prays for God to "do what is good in his sight" (1 Chron. 19:13). The result of numerous personal experiences is that God reaches "down ... from on high" and rescues David, so that the king himself sings of Yahweh as his deliverer (Ps. 144:7; cf. 3:7–8; 31:1, 15). The staunch testimony of David the warrior-shepherd echoes through the Chronicler's accounts of David the warrior-king: "The LORD who delivered me from the paw of the lion and the paw of the bear will deliver me from the hand of this Philistine [Goliath]" (1 Sam. 17:37).

---

30. Ibid.

CHRISTUS VICTOR. The warfare motif is not restricted to the Old Testament. The church at Ephesus learned about spiritual warfare from the apostle Paul, an ongoing cosmic battle between God and the unseen powers of evil (Eph. 6:11–12; cf. 2 Cor. 10:3–4). From one perspective, the theology of the entire New Testament can be understood in terms of "a titanic conflict between God and Satan."[31] More specifically, according to Ladd, the theology of the kingdom of God proclaimed in the Gospels and embodied in the church of Jesus Christ "is essentially one of conflict and conquest over the kingdom of Satan."[32] The eschatological kingdom of God ushered in at the *parousia* or second coming of Jesus Christ will result in a new heaven and earth and rid evil from God's creation once and for all (cf. Rev. 21:1–4). In fact, according to Paul, Jesus Christ will yield his kingdom to the Father only after he has defeated all dominions and powers, subdued all his enemies, and destroyed the last enemy—death (1 Cor. 15:21–26).

As was the case in the Old Testament with David's wars, so too the battle belongs to God in the New Testament era. King David sang with joyful confidence that "with God we will gain the victory" (Ps. 60:12).[33] In like manner, the apostle Paul rejoiced with the Corinthian church that God "gives us the victory through our Lord Jesus Christ" over sin and death (1 Cor. 15:57).

This biblical motif of warfare and the extensive military vocabulary applied to theological contexts in the Old and New Testaments have given rise to Aulén's "classic" idea of the atonement as a cosmic drama of divine conflict and victory. This so-called "Christus Victor" view of the atonement understands the redemptive work of Jesus Christ as a battle against and a triumph over the evil powers of the world.[34] The reason for the incarnation

---

31. George E. Ladd, "Kingdom of God," *ISBE*, 3:26.

32. George E. Ladd, *A Theology of the New Testament* (Grand Rapids: Eerdmans, 1974), 51; cf. Greg Boyd, *God at War: The Bible and Spiritual Conflict* (Downers Grove, Ill.: InterVarsity Press, 1997), 238, who identifies the unifying theme of Jesus' ministry as the conflict between the kingdom of God against the kingdom of Satan. The idea of God as a "warrior" is one of the "hard teachings" of the Bible. Despite all the difficulties associated with the concept ethically and theologically, Peter C. Craigie reminds us that "God as Warrior does provide hope for sinful humankind because 'God the warrior' did become "God the crucified" (*The Problem of War in the Old Testament* [Grand Rapids: Eerdmans, 1978], 43, 101–2). On the theme of God as the "divine warrior" in the Old and New Testaments, see Tremper Longman III and Daniel G. Reid, *God Is a Warrior* (Grand Rapids: Zondervan, 1995).

33. Note the superscription connects Ps. 60 with David's wars against Aram Naharaim and Aram Zobah.

34. Gustaf Aulén, *Christus Victor*, trans. A. G. Hebert (New York: Macmillan, 1969), 4–5.

---

was so that Christ might "destroy the devil's work" (1 John 3:8). It was by means of the cross that Jesus Christ "disarmed the powers and authorities . . . triumphing over them" (Col. 2:15).

The Chronicler's section treating David's wars serves to remind us that we, like David, need a comprehensive "warfare worldview." For many of us who trace our Christian heritage to the Reformation, this may entail a rethinking of the primary significance of Christ's death and resurrection. Since the time of Anselm (c. 1033–1109), Western Christianity has focused attention almost exclusively on the anthropological aspect of Christ's sacrificial ministry.[35] That is, Christ's death on the cross is understood in the juridical sense as a propitiation (i.e., the turning away of God's wrath by means of an offering) or "atonement for the sins of the people" (cf. Heb. 2:17). The cross of Christ satisfies the demands of God's holiness and justice as a payment delivering the Christian from slavery to sin and death (cf. Rom. 8:34; Heb. 7:25). The anthropological dimension of the cross emphasizes personal salvation, the individual Christian's redemption secured by the ransom of Christ's life (cf. Matt. 20:28; Mark 10:45).

Aulén, and more recently Boyd, have cogently argued that the cross should be viewed fundamentally from a theocentric perspective. By that Boyd means recognizing that "the cross is first and foremost a cosmic event— it defeats Satan."[36] The anthropological dimension of Christ's work (i.e., his substitutionary death for sinful humanity) is thus a consequence of this cosmic victory over the devil (cf. Heb. 2:14). Even more than reconciling fallen humanity to himself, through the cross of Christ, God reconciles to himself "all things, whether things on earth or things in heaven" (Col. 1:20). For Boyd, "the cross was a cosmic event that defeated the enemies of God, enthroned the Son of God, and thereby in principle liberated the whole cosmos from its bondage to an illegitimate evil ruler."[37]

But what about the application of this "warfare worldview" to contemporary Christianity? What does "Christus Victor" mean for Christians in the twenty-first century? An exhaustive answer to these questions is beyond the scope of our study. There are, however, important lessons to be learned from Aulén's proposal concerning the atonement.

For example, the Christus Victor understanding of Christ's cross offers an antidote for the self-absorption promoted by our culture of narcissism. The Christian subculture is not immune to the insidious influences of popular culture, sometimes falling prey to the same self-interest that now defines the

---

35. See Aulén on Anselm of Canterbury, ibid., 84–92.
36. Boyd, *God at War*, 241.
37. Ibid., 248.

American experience. The theocentric dimension of Christ's atonement brings perspective to "personal salvation" by placing "my redemption" in the larger context of God's universal and cosmic work of reconciling "all things" to himself. Such an approach discourages attitudes of egocentrism and ethnocentrism because the warfare worldview glorifies God as the Redeemer and locates the individual Christian among the people of God—a member of the body of Christ.

The Christus Victor theology reassures us as Christians that Christ will indeed build his church, "and the gates of Hades will not overcome it" (Matt. 16:18). C. S. Lewis predicted that in the final conflict between religions, "Hinduism and Christianity would offer the only viable options because Hinduism absorbs all religious systems, and Christianity excludes all others, maintaining the supremacy of the claims of Christ."[38] Lewis may be excused for failing to foresee the role of militant Islam in the "final conflict between religions," projecting into the future from his vantage point of the 1940s. He did correctly recognize, however, that the religious battle lines are ultimately drawn along the issues of inclusivity and tolerance versus exclusivity and intolerance. The pluralism and relativism of postmodernity has brought us to the very threshold of that final conflict between religions. As Christianity continues to be marginalized in our postmodern and post-Christian world, the reminder that Christ has defeated "the powers and authorities" is a wellspring of encouragement and hope for the church.

The New Testament indicates that the Christian life is spiritual warfare (Eph. 6:12). At the cross Christ defeated the enemies of God *de jure*, but the church awaits that day of consummation when all the enemies of God are destroyed *de facto*. During the interim, the Christian lives in the tension between "the now and the yet-to-come," for the "god of this age" (2 Cor. 4:4) still "prowls around like a roaring lion looking for someone to devour" (1 Peter 5:8).

Nevertheless, we are not defenseless as we await the blessed hope and glorious appearing of Jesus Christ (Titus 2:13). Christ has made gracious provision for us as we engage the "powers" in spiritual warfare, equipping us with everything needed for life and godliness (2 Peter 1:3). Those provisions for spiritual battle include the "full armor of God" (Eph. 6:13–17) and the enabling work of the indwelling Holy Spirit (6:18). Such armament and the aid of God's helping Spirit guarantees our victory against the evil one (6:16).

But such effective armament is of little value if it is not worn in battle (Eph. 6:11). The Christus Victor theology confronts the free agency of persons made in God's image and forces the issue of human responsibility. The

---

38. Cited in Walter Martin, *The New Age Cult* (Minneapolis: Bethany, 1989), 13.

Christian can be victorious in spiritual warfare with Satan only to the degree he or she declares allegiance to God and chooses to "put on the full armor of God" (6:11), to "stand firm" (6:14), to "take up" the shield of faith, the helmet of salvation, and the sword of the Spirit (6:16), and to "pray in the Spirit" (6:18). In fact, Aulén was persuaded "that no form of Christian teaching has any future before it except such as can keep steadily in view the reality of evil in the world, and go to meet the evil with a battle-song of triumph."[39] Clearly, the idea of Christus Victor and the warfare worldview brings new relevance to the lyrics of Isaac Watts's hymn "Am I a Soldier of the Cross?" (esp. verse 3):

> Are there no foes for me to face?
> Must I not stem the flood?
> Is this vile world a friend to grace,
> to help me on to God?

Finally, the idea of Christus Victor should revitalize our prayer life and our worship. Christ is now seated at God's "right hand" (Rom. 8:34; Col. 3:1; Heb. 1:3; 10:12; 12:2). As a result of his death and resurrection, Jesus has driven out the prince of this world. His enthronement at God's right hand is a position of power and authority over all God's enemies. The implications of this truth are profound, especially as we pray for God to "deliver us from the evil one" (Matt. 6:13). The cross means God is both willing and able to do just that, to deliver us from our true enemy. We are truly "more than conquerors" in all things because Christ has defeated all the "powers" (Rom. 8:37–39).

And what about our worship? One need only catch a glimpse of the heavenly worship portrayed in John's Apocalypse:

> Worthy is the Lamb, who was slain,
> to receive power and wealth and wisdom and strength
> and honor and glory and praise! (Rev. 5:12)

> To him who sits on the throne and to the Lamb
> be praise and honor and glory and power,
>   for ever and ever! (Rev. 5:13)

> Salvation belongs to our God,
> who sits on the throne,
> and to the Lamb. (Rev. 7:10)

---

39. Aulén, *Christus Victor*, 159.

1 Chronicles 21:1–29:9

ᐧᐧᐧ

S ATAN ROSE UP against Israel and incited David to take a
census of Israel. ²So David said to Joab and the commanders of the troops, "Go and count the Israelites
from Beersheba to Dan. Then report back to me so that I may
know how many there are."

³But Joab replied, "May the LORD multiply his troops a
hundred times over. My lord the king, are they not all my
lord's subjects? Why does my lord want to do this? Why
should he bring guilt on Israel?"

⁴The king's word, however, overruled Joab; so Joab left and
went throughout Israel and then came back to Jerusalem.
⁵Joab reported the number of the fighting men to David: In all
Israel there were one million one hundred thousand men who
could handle a sword, including four hundred and seventy
thousand in Judah.

⁶But Joab did not include Levi and Benjamin in the numbering, because the king's command was repulsive to him.
⁷This command was also evil in the sight of God; so he punished Israel.

⁸Then David said to God, "I have sinned greatly by doing
this. Now, I beg you, take away the guilt of your servant. I
have done a very foolish thing."

⁹The LORD said to Gad, David's seer, ¹⁰"Go and tell David,
'This is what the LORD says: I am giving you three options.
Choose one of them for me to carry out against you.'"

¹¹So Gad went to David and said to him, "This is what the
LORD says: 'Take your choice: ¹²three years of famine, three
months of being swept away before your enemies, with their
swords overtaking you, or three days of the sword of the
LORD—days of plague in the land, with the angel of the LORD
ravaging every part of Israel.' Now then, decide how I should
answer the one who sent me."

¹³David said to Gad, "I am in deep distress. Let me fall into
the hands of the LORD, for his mercy is very great; but do not
let me fall into the hands of men."

¹⁴So the LORD sent a plague on Israel, and seventy thousand men of Israel fell dead. ¹⁵And God sent an angel to

destroy Jerusalem. But as the angel was doing so, the LORD saw it and was grieved because of the calamity and said to the angel who was destroying the people, "Enough! Withdraw your hand." The angel of the LORD was then standing at the threshing floor of Araunah the Jebusite.

¹⁶David looked up and saw the angel of the LORD standing between heaven and earth, with a drawn sword in his hand extended over Jerusalem. Then David and the elders, clothed in sackcloth, fell facedown.

¹⁷David said to God, "Was it not I who ordered the fighting men to be counted? I am the one who has sinned and done wrong. These are but sheep. What have they done? O LORD my God, let your hand fall upon me and my family, but do not let this plague remain on your people."

¹⁸Then the angel of the LORD ordered Gad to tell David to go up and build an altar to the LORD on the threshing floor of Araunah the Jebusite. ¹⁹So David went up in obedience to the word that Gad had spoken in the name of the LORD.

²⁰While Araunah was threshing wheat, he turned and saw the angel; his four sons who were with him hid themselves. ²¹Then David approached, and when Araunah looked and saw him, he left the threshing floor and bowed down before David with his face to the ground.

²²David said to him, "Let me have the site of your threshing floor so I can build an altar to the LORD, that the plague on the people may be stopped. Sell it to me at the full price."

²³Araunah said to David, "Take it! Let my lord the king do whatever pleases him. Look, I will give the oxen for the burnt offerings, the threshing sledges for the wood, and the wheat for the grain offering. I will give all this."

²⁴But King David replied to Araunah, "No, I insist on paying the full price. I will not take for the LORD what is yours, or sacrifice a burnt offering that costs me nothing."

²⁵So David paid Araunah six hundred shekels of gold for the site. ²⁶David built an altar to the LORD there and sacrificed burnt offerings and fellowship offerings. He called on the LORD, and the LORD answered him with fire from heaven on the altar of burnt offering.

²⁷Then the LORD spoke to the angel, and he put his sword back into its sheath. ²⁸At that time, when David saw that the LORD had answered him on the threshing floor of Araunah the

Jebusite, he offered sacrifices there. ²⁹The tabernacle of the LORD, which Moses had made in the desert, and the altar of burnt offering were at that time on the high place at Gibeon. ³⁰But David could not go before it to inquire of God, because he was afraid of the sword of the angel of the LORD.

²²:¹Then David said, "The house of the LORD God is to be here, and also the altar of burnt offering for Israel."

²So David gave orders to assemble the aliens living in Israel, and from among them he appointed stonecutters to prepare dressed stone for building the house of God. ³He provided a large amount of iron to make nails for the doors of the gateways and for the fittings, and more bronze than could be weighed. ⁴He also provided more cedar logs than could be counted, for the Sidonians and Tyrians had brought large numbers of them to David.

⁵David said, "My son Solomon is young and inexperienced, and the house to be built for the LORD should be of great magnificence and fame and splendor in the sight of all the nations. Therefore I will make preparations for it." So David made extensive preparations before his death.

⁶Then he called for his son Solomon and charged him to build a house for the LORD, the God of Israel. ⁷David said to Solomon: "My son, I had it in my heart to build a house for the Name of the LORD my God. ⁸But this word of the LORD came to me: 'You have shed much blood and have fought many wars. You are not to build a house for my Name, because you have shed much blood on the earth in my sight. ⁹But you will have a son who will be a man of peace and rest, and I will give him rest from all his enemies on every side. His name will be Solomon, and I will grant Israel peace and quiet during his reign. ¹⁰He is the one who will build a house for my Name. He will be my son, and I will be his father. And I will establish the throne of his kingdom over Israel forever.'

¹¹"Now, my son, the LORD be with you, and may you have success and build the house of the LORD your God, as he said you would. ¹²May the LORD give you discretion and understanding when he puts you in command over Israel, so that you may keep the law of the LORD your God. ¹³Then you will have success if you are careful to observe the decrees and laws that the LORD gave Moses for Israel. Be strong and courageous. Do not be afraid or discouraged.

¹⁴"I have taken great pains to provide for the temple of the LORD a hundred thousand talents of gold, a million talents of silver, quantities of bronze and iron too great to be weighed, and wood and stone. And you may add to them. ¹⁵You have many workmen: stonecutters, masons and carpenters, as well as men skilled in every kind of work ¹⁶in gold and silver, bronze and iron—craftsmen beyond number. Now begin the work, and the LORD be with you."

¹⁷Then David ordered all the leaders of Israel to help his son Solomon. ¹⁸He said to them, "Is not the LORD your God with you? And has he not granted you rest on every side? For he has handed the inhabitants of the land over to me, and the land is subject to the LORD and to his people. ¹⁹Now devote your heart and soul to seeking the LORD your God. Begin to build the sanctuary of the LORD God, so that you may bring the ark of the covenant of the LORD and the sacred articles belonging to God into the temple that will be built for the Name of the LORD."

^{23:1}When David was old and full of years, he made his son Solomon king over Israel.

²He also gathered together all the leaders of Israel, as well as the priests and Levites. ³The Levites thirty years old or more were counted, and the total number of men was thirty-eight thousand. ⁴David said, "Of these, twenty-four thousand are to supervise the work of the temple of the LORD and six thousand are to be officials and judges. ⁵Four thousand are to be gatekeepers and four thousand are to praise the LORD with the musical instruments I have provided for that purpose."

⁶David divided the Levites into groups corresponding to the sons of Levi: Gershon, Kohath and Merari.

⁷Belonging to the Gershonites:
    Ladan and Shimei.
    ⁸The sons of Ladan:
    Jehiel the first, Zetham and Joel—three in all.
    ⁹The sons of Shimei:
    Shelomoth, Haziel and Haran—three in all.
    These were the heads of the families of Ladan.
    ¹⁰And the sons of Shimei:
    Jahath, Ziza, Jeush and Beriah.
    These were the sons of Shimei—four in all.

¹¹ Jahath was the first and Ziza the second, but Jeush and Beriah did not have many sons; so they were counted as one family with one assignment.

¹² The sons of Kohath:

Amram, Izhar, Hebron and Uzziel—four in all.

¹³ The sons of Amram:

Aaron and Moses.

Aaron was set apart, he and his descendants forever, to consecrate the most holy things, to offer sacrifices before the LORD, to minister before him and to pronounce blessings in his name forever. ¹⁴ The sons of Moses the man of God were counted as part of the tribe of Levi.

¹⁵ The sons of Moses:

Gershom and Eliezer.

¹⁶ The descendants of Gershom:

Shubael was the first.

¹⁷ The descendants of Eliezer:

Rehabiah was the first.

Eliezer had no other sons, but the sons of Rehabiah were very numerous.

¹⁸ The sons of Izhar:

Shelomith was the first.

¹⁹ The sons of Hebron:

Jeriah the first, Amariah the second, Jahaziel the third and Jekameam the fourth.

²⁰ The sons of Uzziel:

Micah the first and Isshiah the second.

²¹ The sons of Merari:

Mahli and Mushi.

The sons of Mahli:

Eleazar and Kish.

²² Eleazar died without having sons: he had only daughters. Their cousins, the sons of Kish, married them.

²³ The sons of Mushi:

Mahli, Eder and Jerimoth—three in all.

²⁴ These were the descendants of Levi by their families— the heads of families as they were registered under their names and counted individually, that is, the workers twenty years old

or more who served in the temple of the LORD. ²⁵For David had said, "Since the LORD, the God of Israel, has granted rest to his people and has come to dwell in Jerusalem forever, ²⁶the Levites no longer need to carry the tabernacle or any of the articles used in its service." ²⁷According to the last instructions of David, the Levites were counted from those twenty years old or more.

²⁸The duty of the Levites was to help Aaron's descendants in the service of the temple of the LORD: to be in charge of the courtyards, the side rooms, the purification of all sacred things and the performance of other duties at the house of God. ²⁹They were in charge of the bread set out on the table, the flour for the grain offerings, the unleavened wafers, the baking and the mixing, and all measurements of quantity and size. ³⁰They were also to stand every morning to thank and praise the LORD. They were to do the same in the evening ³¹and whenever burnt offerings were presented to the LORD on Sabbaths and at New Moon festivals and at appointed feasts. They were to serve before the LORD regularly in the proper number and in the way prescribed for them.

³²And so the Levites carried out their responsibilities for the Tent of Meeting, for the Holy Place and, under their brothers the descendants of Aaron, for the service of the temple of the LORD.

^{24:1}These were the divisions of the sons of Aaron:

The sons of Aaron were Nadab, Abihu, Eleazar and Ithamar. ²But Nadab and Abihu died before their father did, and they had no sons; so Eleazar and Ithamar served as the priests. ³With the help of Zadok a descendant of Eleazar and Ahimelech a descendant of Ithamar, David separated them into divisions for their appointed order of ministering. ⁴A larger number of leaders were found among Eleazar's descendants than among Ithamar's, and they were divided accordingly: sixteen heads of families from Eleazar's descendants and eight heads of families from Ithamar's descendants. ⁵They divided them impartially by drawing lots, for there were officials of the sanctuary and officials of God among the descendants of both Eleazar and Ithamar.

⁶The scribe Shemaiah son of Nethanel, a Levite, recorded their names in the presence of the king and of the officials: Zadok the priest, Ahimelech son of Abiathar and the heads of

families of the priests and of the Levites—one family being taken from Eleazar and then one from Ithamar.

> [7] The first lot fell to Jehoiarib,
>> the second to Jedaiah,
> [8] the third to Harim,
>> the fourth to Seorim,
> [9] the fifth to Malkijah,
>> the sixth to Mijamin,
> [10] the seventh to Hakkoz,
>> the eighth to Abijah,
> [11] the ninth to Jeshua,
>> the tenth to Shecaniah,
> [12] the eleventh to Eliashib,
>> the twelfth to Jakim,
> [13] the thirteenth to Huppah,
>> the fourteenth to Jeshebeab,
> [14] the fifteenth to Bilgah,
>> the sixteenth to Immer,
> [15] the seventeenth to Hezir,
>> the eighteenth to Happizzez,
> [16] the nineteenth to Pethahiah,
>> the twentieth to Jehezkel,
> [17] the twenty-first to Jakin,
>> the twenty-second to Gamul,
> [18] the twenty-third to Delaiah
>> and the twenty-fourth to Maaziah.

[19] This was their appointed order of ministering when they entered the temple of the LORD, according to the regulations prescribed for them by their forefather Aaron, as the LORD, the God of Israel, had commanded him.

[20] As for the rest of the descendants of Levi:
> from the sons of Amram: Shubael;
>> from the sons of Shubael: Jehdeiah.
> [21] As for Rehabiah, from his sons:
>> Isshiah was the first.
> [22] From the Izharites: Shelomoth;
>> from the sons of Shelomoth: Jahath.
> [23] The sons of Hebron: Jeriah the first, Amariah the second,
>> Jahaziel the third and Jekameam the fourth.

²⁴ The son of Uzziel: Micah;

from the sons of Micah: Shamir.

²⁵ The brother of Micah: Isshiah;

from the sons of Isshiah: Zechariah.

²⁶ The sons of Merari: Mahli and Mushi.

The son of Jaaziah: Beno.

²⁷ The sons of Merari:

from Jaaziah: Beno, Shoham, Zaccur and Ibri.

²⁸ From Mahli: Eleazar, who had no sons.

²⁹ From Kish: the son of Kish:

Jerahmeel.

³⁰ And the sons of Mushi: Mahli, Eder and Jerimoth.

These were the Levites, according to their families. ³¹They also cast lots, just as their brothers the descendants of Aaron did, in the presence of King David and of Zadok, Ahimelech, and the heads of families of the priests and of the Levites. The families of the oldest brother were treated the same as those of the youngest.

²⁵:¹David, together with the commanders of the army, set apart some of the sons of Asaph, Heman and Jeduthun for the ministry of prophesying, accompanied by harps, lyres and cymbals. Here is the list of the men who performed this service:

²From the sons of Asaph:

Zaccur, Joseph, Nethaniah and Asarelah. The sons of Asaph were under the supervision of Asaph, who prophesied under the king's supervision.

³As for Jeduthun, from his sons:

Gedaliah, Zeri, Jeshaiah, Shimei, Hashabiah and Mattithiah, six in all, under the supervision of their father Jeduthun, who prophesied, using the harp in thanking and praising the LORD.

⁴As for Heman, from his sons:

Bukkiah, Mattaniah, Uzziel, Shubael and Jerimoth; Hananiah, Hanani, Eliathah, Giddalti and Romamti-Ezer; Joshbekashah, Mallothi, Hothir and Mahazioth. ⁵All these were sons of Heman the king's seer. They were given him through the promises of God to exalt him. God gave Heman fourteen sons and three daughters.

⁶All these men were under the supervision of their fathers for the music of the temple of the LORD, with cymbals, lyres

and harps, for the ministry at the house of God. Asaph,
Jeduthun and Heman were under the supervision of the king.
⁷Along with their relatives—all of them trained and skilled in
music for the LORD—they numbered 288. ⁸Young and old
alike, teacher as well as student, cast lots for their duties.

⁹The first lot, which was for Asaph, fell
  to Joseph,
      his sons and relatives,   12
  the second to Gedaliah,
      he and his relatives and sons,   12
¹⁰the third to Zaccur,
      his sons and relatives,   12
¹¹the fourth to Izri,
      his sons and relatives,   12
¹²the fifth to Nethaniah,
      his sons and relatives,   12
¹³the sixth to Bukkiah,
      his sons and relatives,   12
¹⁴the seventh to Jesarelah,
      his sons and relatives,   12
¹⁵the eighth to Jeshaiah,
      his sons and relatives,   12
¹⁶the ninth to Mattaniah,
      his sons and relatives,   12
¹⁷the tenth to Shimei,
      his sons and relatives,   12
¹⁸the eleventh to Azarel,
      his sons and relatives,   12
¹⁹the twelfth to Hashabiah,
      his sons and relatives,   12
²⁰the thirteenth to Shubael,
      his sons and relatives,   12
²¹the fourteenth to Mattithiah,
      his sons and relatives,   12
²²the fifteenth to Jerimoth,
      his sons and relatives,   12
²³the sixteenth to Hananiah,
      his sons and relatives,   12
²⁴the seventeenth to Joshbekashah,
      his sons and relatives,   12

²⁵ the eighteenth to Hanani,
    his sons and relatives,   12
²⁶ the nineteenth to Mallothi,
    his sons and relatives,   12
²⁷ the twentieth to Eliathah,
    his sons and relatives,   12
²⁸ the twenty-first to Hothir,
    his sons and relatives,   12
²⁹ the twenty-second to Giddalti,
    his sons and relatives,   12
³⁰ the twenty-third to Mahazioth,
    his sons and relatives,   12
³¹ the twenty-fourth to Romamti-Ezer,
    his sons and relatives,   12

^{26:1} The divisions of the gatekeepers:

From the Korahites: Meshelemiah son of Kore, one of the sons of Asaph.
² Meshelemiah had sons:
Zechariah the firstborn,
Jediael the second,
Zebadiah the third,
Jathniel the fourth,
³ Elam the fifth,
Jehohanan the sixth
and Eliehoenai the seventh.
⁴ Obed-Edom also had sons:
Shemaiah the firstborn,
Jehozabad the second,
Joah the third,
Sacar the fourth,
Nethanel the fifth,
⁵ Ammiel the sixth,
Issachar the seventh
and Peullethai the eighth.
(For God had blessed Obed-Edom.)

⁶ His son Shemaiah also had sons, who were leaders in their father's family because they were very capable men. ⁷ The sons of Shemaiah: Othni, Rephael, Obed and Elzabad; his relatives Elihu and Semakiah were also able men. ⁸ All these were descendants of Obed-Edom; they

and their sons and their relatives were capable men with the strength to do the work—descendants of Obed-Edom, 62 in all.

⁹Meshelemiah had sons and relatives, who were able men— 18 in all.

¹⁰Hosah the Merarite had sons: Shimri the first (although he was not the firstborn, his father had appointed him the first), ¹¹Hilkiah the second, Tabaliah the third and Zechariah the fourth. The sons and relatives of Hosah were 13 in all.

¹²These divisions of the gatekeepers, through their chief men, had duties for ministering in the temple of the LORD, just as their relatives had. ¹³Lots were cast for each gate, according to their families, young and old alike.

¹⁴The lot for the East Gate fell to Shelemiah. Then lots were cast for his son Zechariah, a wise counselor, and the lot for the North Gate fell to him. ¹⁵The lot for the South Gate fell to Obed-Edom, and the lot for the storehouse fell to his sons. ¹⁶The lots for the West Gate and the Shalleketh Gate on the upper road fell to Shuppim and Hosah.

Guard was alongside of guard: ¹⁷There were six Levites a day on the east, four a day on the north, four a day on the south and two at a time at the storehouse. ¹⁸As for the court to the west, there were four at the road and two at the court itself.

¹⁹These were the divisions of the gatekeepers who were descendants of Korah and Merari.

²⁰Their fellow Levites were in charge of the treasuries of the house of God and the treasuries for the dedicated things.

²¹The descendants of Ladan, who were Gershonites through Ladan and who were heads of families belonging to Ladan the Gershonite, were Jehieli, ²²the sons of Jehieli, Zetham and his brother Joel. They were in charge of the treasuries of the temple of the LORD.

²³From the Amramites, the Izharites, the Hebronites and the Uzzielites:

²⁴Shubael, a descendant of Gershom son of Moses, was the officer in charge of the treasuries. ²⁵His relatives through Eliezer: Rehabiah his son, Jeshaiah his son, Joram his son, Zicri his son and Shelomith his son.

²⁶Shelomith and his relatives were in charge of all the treasuries for the things dedicated by King David, by the heads of families who were the commanders of thousands and commanders of hundreds, and by the other army commanders. ²⁷Some of the plunder taken in battle they dedicated for the repair of the temple of the LORD. ²⁸And everything dedicated by Samuel the seer and by Saul son of Kish, Abner son of Ner and Joab son of Zeruiah, and all the other dedicated things were in the care of Shelomith and his relatives.

²⁹From the Izharites: Kenaniah and his sons were assigned duties away from the temple, as officials and judges over Israel.

³⁰From the Hebronites: Hashabiah and his relatives—seventeen hundred able men—were responsible in Israel west of the Jordan for all the work of the LORD and for the king's service. ³¹As for the Hebronites, Jeriah was their chief according to the genealogical records of their families. In the fortieth year of David's reign a search was made in the records, and capable men among the Hebronites were found at Jazer in Gilead. ³²Jeriah had twenty-seven hundred relatives, who were able men and heads of families, and King David put them in charge of the Reubenites, the Gadites and the half-tribe of Manasseh for every matter pertaining to God and for the affairs of the king.

²⁷:¹This is the list of the Israelites—heads of families, commanders of thousands and commanders of hundreds, and their officers, who served the king in all that concerned the army divisions that were on duty month by month throughout the year. Each division consisted of 24,000 men.

²In charge of the first division, for the first month, was Jashobeam son of Zabdiel. There were 24,000 men in his division. ³He was a descendant of Perez and chief of all the army officers for the first month. ⁴In charge of the division for the second month was Dodai the Ahohite; Mikloth was the leader of his division. There were 24,000 men in his division. ⁵The third army commander, for the third month, was Benaiah son of Jehoiada the priest. He was chief and there were 24,000 men in his division. ⁶This was the Benaiah who

was a mighty man among the Thirty and was over the Thirty. His son Ammizabad was in charge of his division.

⁷The fourth, for the fourth month, was Asahel the brother of Joab; his son Zebadiah was his successor. There were 24,000 men in his division.

⁸The fifth, for the fifth month, was the commander Shamhuth the Izrahite. There were 24,000 men in his division.

⁹The sixth, for the sixth month, was Ira the son of Ikkesh the Tekoite. There were 24,000 men in his division.

¹⁰The seventh, for the seventh month, was Helez the Pelonite, an Ephraimite. There were 24,000 men in his division.

¹¹The eighth, for the eighth month, was Sibbecai the Hushathite, a Zerahite. There were 24,000 men in his division.

¹²The ninth, for the ninth month, was Abiezer the Anathothite, a Benjamite. There were 24,000 men in his division.

¹³The tenth, for the tenth month, was Maharai the Netophathite, a Zerahite. There were 24,000 men in his division.

¹⁴The eleventh, for the eleventh month, was Benaiah the Pirathonite, an Ephraimite. There were 24,000 men in his division.

¹⁵The twelfth, for the twelfth month, was Heldai the Netophathite, from the family of Othniel. There were 24,000 men in his division.

¹⁶The officers over the tribes of Israel:

over the Reubenites: Eliezer son of Zicri;
over the Simeonites: Shephatiah son of Maacah;
¹⁷over Levi: Hashabiah son of Kemuel;
over Aaron: Zadok;
¹⁸over Judah: Elihu, a brother of David;
over Issachar: Omri son of Michael;
¹⁹over Zebulun: Ishmaiah son of Obadiah;
over Naphtali: Jerimoth son of Azriel;
²⁰over the Ephraimites: Hoshea son of Azaziah;
over half the tribe of Manasseh: Joel son of Pedaiah;
²¹over the half-tribe of Manasseh in Gilead: Iddo son of Zechariah;
over Benjamin: Jaasiel son of Abner;

²² over Dan: Azarel son of Jeroham.

These were the officers over the tribes of Israel.

²³David did not take the number of the men twenty years old or less, because the LORD had promised to make Israel as numerous as the stars in the sky. ²⁴Joab son of Zeruiah began to count the men but did not finish. Wrath came on Israel on account of this numbering, and the number was not entered in the book of the annals of King David.

²⁵Azmaveth son of Adiel was in charge of the royal storehouses.

Jonathan son of Uzziah was in charge of the storehouses in the outlying districts, in the towns, the villages and the watchtowers.

²⁶Ezri son of Kelub was in charge of the field workers who farmed the land.

²⁷Shimei the Ramathite was in charge of the vineyards.

Zabdi the Shiphmite was in charge of the produce of the vineyards for the wine vats.

²⁸Baal-Hanan the Gederite was in charge of the olive and sycamore-fig trees in the western foothills.

Joash was in charge of the supplies of olive oil.

²⁹Shitrai the Sharonite was in charge of the herds grazing in Sharon.

Shaphat son of Adlai was in charge of the herds in the valleys.

³⁰Obil the Ishmaelite was in charge of the camels.

Jehdeiah the Meronothite was in charge of the donkeys.

³¹Jaziz the Hagrite was in charge of the flocks.

All these were the officials in charge of King David's property.

³²Jonathan, David's uncle, was a counselor, a man of insight and a scribe. Jehiel son of Hacmoni took care of the king's sons.

³³Ahithophel was the king's counselor.

Hushai the Arkite was the king's friend. ³⁴Ahithophel was succeeded by Jehoiada son of Benaiah and by Abiathar.

Joab was the commander of the royal army.

^{28:1}David summoned all the officials of Israel to assemble at Jerusalem: the officers over the tribes, the commanders of the divisions in the service of the king, the commanders of

thousands and commanders of hundreds, and the officials in charge of all the property and livestock belonging to the king and his sons, together with the palace officials, the mighty men and all the brave warriors.

²King David rose to his feet and said: "Listen to me, my brothers and my people. I had it in my heart to build a house as a place of rest for the ark of the covenant of the LORD, for the footstool of our God, and I made plans to build it. ³But God said to me, 'You are not to build a house for my Name, because you are a warrior and have shed blood.'

⁴"Yet the LORD, the God of Israel, chose me from my whole family to be king over Israel forever. He chose Judah as leader, and from the house of Judah he chose my family, and from my father's sons he was pleased to make me king over all Israel. ⁵Of all my sons—and the LORD has given me many—he has chosen my son Solomon to sit on the throne of the kingdom of the LORD over Israel. ⁶He said to me: 'Solomon your son is the one who will build my house and my courts, for I have chosen him to be my son, and I will be his father. ⁷I will establish his kingdom forever if he is unswerving in carrying out my commands and laws, as is being done at this time.'

⁸"So now I charge you in the sight of all Israel and of the assembly of the LORD, and in the hearing of our God: Be careful to follow all the commands of the LORD your God, that you may possess this good land and pass it on as an inheritance to your descendants forever.

⁹"And you, my son Solomon, acknowledge the God of your father, and serve him with wholehearted devotion and with a willing mind, for the LORD searches every heart and understands every motive behind the thoughts. If you seek him, he will be found by you; but if you forsake him, he will reject you forever. ¹⁰Consider now, for the LORD has chosen you to build a temple as a sanctuary. Be strong and do the work."

¹¹Then David gave his son Solomon the plans for the portico of the temple, its buildings, its storerooms, its upper parts, its inner rooms and the place of atonement. ¹²He gave him the plans of all that the Spirit had put in his mind for the courts of the temple of the LORD and all the surrounding rooms, for the treasuries of the temple of God and for the treasuries for the dedicated things. ¹³He gave him instructions for the divisions of the priests and Levites, and for all the

work of serving in the temple of the LORD, as well as for all the articles to be used in its service. ¹⁴He designated the weight of gold for all the gold articles to be used in various kinds of service, and the weight of silver for all the silver articles to be used in various kinds of service: ¹⁵the weight of gold for the gold lampstands and their lamps, with the weight for each lampstand and its lamps; and the weight of silver for each silver lampstand and its lamps, according to the use of each lampstand; ¹⁶the weight of gold for each table for consecrated bread; the weight of silver for the silver tables; ¹⁷the weight of pure gold for the forks, sprinkling bowls and pitchers; the weight of gold for each gold dish; the weight of silver for each silver dish; ¹⁸and the weight of the refined gold for the altar of incense. He also gave him the plan for the chariot, that is, the cherubim of gold that spread their wings and shelter the ark of the covenant of the LORD.

¹⁹"All this," David said, "I have in writing from the hand of the LORD upon me, and he gave me understanding in all the details of the plan."

²⁰David also said to Solomon his son, "Be strong and courageous, and do the work. Do not be afraid or discouraged, for the LORD God, my God, is with you. He will not fail you or forsake you until all the work for the service of the temple of the LORD is finished. ²¹The divisions of the priests and Levites are ready for all the work on the temple of God, and every willing man skilled in any craft will help you in all the work. The officials and all the people will obey your every command."

²⁹:¹Then King David said to the whole assembly: "My son Solomon, the one whom God has chosen, is young and inexperienced. The task is great, because this palatial structure is not for man but for the LORD God. ²With all my resources I have provided for the temple of my God—gold for the gold work, silver for the silver, bronze for the bronze, iron for the iron and wood for the wood, as well as onyx for the settings, turquoise, stones of various colors, and all kinds of fine stone and marble—all of these in large quantities. ³Besides, in my devotion to the temple of my God I now give my personal treasures of gold and silver for the temple of my God, over and above everything I have provided for this holy temple: ⁴three thousand talents of gold (gold of Ophir) and seven

thousand talents of refined silver, for the overlaying of the walls of the buildings, ⁵for the gold work and the silver work, and for all the work to be done by the craftsmen. Now, who is willing to consecrate himself today to the LORD?"

⁶Then the leaders of families, the officers of the tribes of Israel, the commanders of thousands and commanders of hundreds, and the officials in charge of the king's work gave willingly. ⁷They gave toward the work on the temple of God five thousand talents and ten thousand darics of gold, ten thousand talents of silver, eighteen thousand talents of bronze and a hundred thousand talents of iron. ⁸Any who had precious stones gave them to the treasury of the temple of the LORD in the custody of Jehiel the Gershonite. ⁹The people rejoiced at the willing response of their leaders, for they had given freely and wholeheartedly to the LORD. David the king also rejoiced greatly.

THE STORY OF DAVID'S preparations for the building of the Jerusalem temple is the first of three large blocks of connected narrative material in Chronicles. The protracted section recounts his extensive work in both "prefabricating" the structure of the temple and organizing the personnel responsible for the service of the sanctuary. The literary genre of this portion of the Chronicler's composition is usually classified as a combination of "report" and "account."[1] A *report* is a brief, self-contained prose narrative relating a single event or situation in the past. An *account* is a narrative form made up of a series of reports organized around a major event or significant theme. The list of reports documenting David's effort to make ready for the construction of Yahweh's temple include purchasing the land, securing the building materials, organizing and training the personnel, drafting the plans, and soliciting gifts from the people (see the outline below).

David ruled over Israel for forty years—roughly from 1010 to 970 B.C. (cf. 2 Sam. 5:4–5). In typical fashion, however, the Chronicler's arrangement of material reflects theological interests more than chronological or historiographical ones. Numerous themes and motifs emerge from his narrative, but three distinct emphases are especially pertinent to the circumstances of his own audience—the Jewish restoration community despairing of Judah's being "restored" (reduced to the equivalent of a "third world" nation after the Babylonian exile), as forecasted by the prophets Jeremiah and Ezekiel.

---

1. De Vries, *1 and 2 Chronicles*, 426, 434.

(1) The transition from the portable tent-shrine of Moses to the permanent sanctuary of Solomon is understood as a sign of God's faithfulness in keeping covenant with Israel. The Lord promised "rest" to Israel once they occupied and settled the land of Canaan (Deut. 12:10). God's promise of peace and safety was coupled with the divine designation for a single place for Israelite worship (12:11). The convergence of that rest and a demarcated worship site come to fruition under the leadership of King Solomon—whose very name means "peace." The unwavering faithfulness of God working through his servant David makes all this possible. The Chronicler knows that postexilic Jerusalem needs a "post-it note" reminding them of God's faithfulness—a sure word from the God who "remembers his covenant forever" (Ps. 111:5).

(2) The narrative emphasizes the complementary nature of the reigns of King David and King Solomon. Solomon is young and inexperienced, but energetic and talented. David is mature and experienced, but wizened and near death. Solomon will not be able to meet the demands of building Yahweh's temple without David's preparatory help. The model of collaboration exhibited by this father-son team is an important lesson for the Chronicler's audience—because for them, the restoration of Judah can only be accomplished as a cooperative venture.

(3) Despite the loss of kingship, the institution of the temple remains for the returned exiles, in the form of the rebuilt or second temple of Jerusalem. God is enthroned through worship, especially the praises of Israel (Ps. 22:3). The Israelites have learned this theological truth from David, who sought to implement the concept in the organization, training, and ministry of the Levitical musicians (1 Chron. 25:7). Praise is preoccupation with who God is and what he has done (cf. Ps. 135:1-7).

To "enthrone" God through praise (or worship) is to acknowledge God as King of all the earth and to recognize his sovereign rule over the destiny of the nations (cf. 47:6-8). To "enthrone" God through praise also is to admit that God has chosen "Jacob" and that he is the "God of Abraham" (cf. 47:4, 9). The Chronicler's account of King David's preparations for the building of Yahweh's temple is tantamount to a call to worship. As the postexilic community enthrones God in their praise and worship, they signify their hope in the reinstallation of Davidic kingship—and ultimately the righteous rule of God in the world (cf. Ezek. 37:24-28).

An outline of this continuous unit is as follows:

David's Census (21:1-22:1)
Preparations for the Temple (22:2-19)
Duties for Levites (ch. 23)

David's Census (21:1–22:1)

THE STORY OF DAVID'S census follows the structure of the synoptic parallel in 2 Samuel 24 but is somewhat longer and contains numerous variations peculiar to the literary and theological interests of the Chronicler. Chronicles disconnects the census narrative from its logical counterpart in Samuel, the anger of the Lord against Israel over King Saul's mistreatment of the Gibeonites (2 Sam. 21; note the Chronicler omits 2 Sam. 24:1a, "Again the anger of the LORD burned against Israel"). The report of David's sin in the census-taking is somewhat awkwardly placed in the Chronicler's narrative as well, following as it does the announcement of the Davidic covenant (1 Chron. 17) and the report of David's military victories (chs. 18–20).

The Chronicler, however, brings his own unique perspective to bear on the census. His primary concern is the relationship of the census-taking story to the centerpiece of his retelling of Israelite history—the Jerusalem temple. The eventual site for Yahweh's temple becomes the threshing floor David purchases in order to offer sacrifices to stay God's judgment against Israel for his sin in decreeing the census. The Chronicler emphasizes God's mercy and forgiveness in responding to David's prayer and sacrificial offering as he seeks atonement for the census-taking.

In retrospect, the purchase of the threshing floor becomes the foundational event for a series of actions by David to make ready for the building of Yahweh's temple. In the Chronicler's mind, what better place for God's permanent sanctuary than the site identified as the prime location for repentant prayer and divine absolution? As Thompson has aptly noted, God has empowered Israel to defeat their human enemies, and now he provides a place of atonement where they can (at least) hold at bay their spiritual enemy—Satan.[2]

The genre of David's census-taking is considered "historical story," after the pattern of David's campaign against the Ammonites (19:1–20:3). This story is a self-contained report that recounts how a particular event happened

---

2. Cf. Thompson, *1, 2 Chronicles*, 160.

by developing a simple plot with multiple episodes.[3] The structural relationship of Chronicles to the Samuel parallel is outlined below:

1 Chronicles	Event	2 Samuel
21:1–4a	David orders a census	24:1–4a
——	Census itinerary	24:4b–7
21:4b–7	Tally of the census	24:8–10
21:8–12	Method of judgment chosen	24:11–13
21:13–17	Divine judgment stayed	24:14–17
21:18–27	Temple site purchased	24:18–25
21:28–22:1	Conclusion	——

Braun has conveniently summarized the most significant variations between the accounts of the census-taking in Samuel and Chronicles.[4]

(1) The Chronicler refers to an "adversary" or "Satan" (so NIV for Heb. *śaṭan*, 21:1).
(2) Numerous alterations in the Chronicler's account actually increase David's culpability in calling for the census of the Israelites (e.g., 21:3, 8, 17).
(3) The story in Chronicles has a stronger emphasis on God's initiative (e.g., 21:9, 15, 26).
(4) Even as David's guilt is heightened by the Chronicler, so too his righteousness in seeking God's mercy to stay the judgment and in his securing of the site of the future temple.
(5) Chronicles places more dramatic emphasis on the intervention of the angel of Yahweh in the sequence of events related to divine judgment.
(6) There is a variance is the tally in Chronicles (1,570,000 militia, 21:5) when compared to the tally in Samuel (1,300,000 militia, 2 Sam. 24:9).
(7) The Chronicler reports God's acceptance of David's prayer and sin offering with fire from heaven, just like Elijah's sacrifice in the contest with the prophets of Baal (cf. 1 Kings 18:38). It is this divine approval that becomes the basis for claiming this threshing floor as the future temple site.
(8) Finally, the Chronicler's account is overlaid with subtle allusions to other Old Testament events concerned with altars and holy places.

The story of David's census-taking consists of three main episodes, to which the Chronicler has appended a conclusion: (1) David orders Joab to

---

3. De Vries, *1 and 2 Chronicles*, 431.
4. Braun, *1 Chronicles*, 216–18.

count the Israelites (21:1–7); (2) God is displeased with David's census and sends his judgment against Israel (21:8–17); (3) God stays his wrath against Israel by means of David's sacrificial offering at the threshing floor of Araunah and his securing of that site for the future temple of Yahweh (21:18–27). The conclusion (21:28–22:1) explains the Chronicler's omission of geographical, chronological, and other details from the earlier parallel in Samuel. The writer artfully develops the spiritual backdrop for the narrative by placing emphasis on the linkage of the location of David's atonement for the sin of the census with the future site of the temple of Yahweh.

Episode 1 (21:1–7). The first episode offers no rationale for David's census, although Joab's objections are duly noted. Essentially there were two reasons for a census-taking in the biblical world: to levy taxes (e.g., Ex. 30:12; Num. 3:40–51) or to register adult males for military service (e.g., Num. 26:1–4). Joab's report to King David indicates that the purpose of this census is the latter (1 Chron. 21:5). Most likely the tally of the census (1,570,000 fighting men) should be understood as 1,100 units or cohorts (of an unspecified number of soldiers) of militia or even 1,100 "chiefs" or "outstanding warriors" (for the Heb. *ʾalapim*, "thousand").[5]

The harmonization of the tallies given in 2 Samuel 24:9 with those of the Chronicler (1 Chron. 21:5) proves more difficult, but both the rounding off of totals and the omission of certain tribes in the latter tally help explain the variances.

More significant theologically is the Chronicler's understanding of the role of Satan in inciting David to take the census of Israel (21:1). The word "Satan" is simply the transliteration of the Hebrew word meaning "adversary" (*śaṭan*); in the Old Testament it is not so much a personal name as it is a role or function. The NIV, however, understands "Satan" as a personal name, the personification of the adversarial function. The fact that the Chronicler attributes the inciting of David's census to Satan and not to the Lord (as in 2 Sam. 24:1) reveals subtle developments in Old Testament theology from the time of David to that of the Chronicler. As a result of God's progressive revelation during those intervening centuries, the Hebrews came to understand the agency of Satan in relationship to God and the problem of evil. That is, as sovereign Lord, it is God's prerogative to use Satan as his agent of testing and/or judgment to accomplish his redemptive purposes in the created order.[6] This fact, however, does not absolve David of his personal guilt in the matter.

---

5. Payne, "1, 2 Chronicles," 4:407.

6. See the helpful discussion in Selman, *1 Chronicles*, 202–4. For a more complete presentation of the complex interplay of divine judgment and mercy in this chapter see McConville, *I and II Chronicles*, 72–74.

Episode 2 (21:8–17). This episode opens with David's confession that he has "sinned greatly" (21:8). Yet the exact nature of David's sin eludes us. Perhaps he is guilty of some breach of ritual in taking the census since those enrolled for military service were required to pay a ransom of a half-shekel (cf. Ex. 30:12). More likely, however, it seems that the offense is not so much a breach of ritual protocol as it is David's motive. Joab's strenuous objection to the king's request suggests that David orders the census as a tribute to his own strength and power rather than a testimony to God as the true warrior of Israel and the builder of Israel's army (21:3).

This episode also introduces Gad the prophet as David's "seer" (21:9; *ḥozeh*, the title denotes the official diviner of the royal court). God sends him to David in response to the king's initial prayer of repentance for his action (21:8), and he offers the king three possible punishments as divine judgment for the folly of numbering of Israel (21:10–12). David opts for the punishment of shortest duration and the one most directly controlled by God (21:13). There is a cruel irony in this, though, as God strikes Israel—the very object of David's foolish pride.[7]

The reaction of David and the elders of Israel to the sight of the destroying angel suggest they expected greater leniency in submitting to three days of the sword of Yahweh (21:16; note, however, the angel's sword remains drawn until 21:27!). Only then is David fully aware of the depth of his sin and the horrific consequences of his choice of punishment. All this brings David full circle to reiterate his admission that the census was his doing and that the people of Israel are "sheep," that is, innocent (21:17).

Episode 3 (21:18–27). This episode continues the involvement of Gad as a mediator in appeasing God's wrath against Israel on account of David's census (21:18). Later Gad helps David organize the Levitical musicians (2 Chron. 29:25); he also writes a history of David's reign (1 Chron. 29:29). The Chronicler interprets the divine command through Gad to build an altar at the site of Araunah's threshing floor as legitimizing a new altar for the sacrificial worship of the central shrine (cf. 21:28–29). The dire urgency of the situation is seen in the fact that the destroying angel is already at the threshing floor, presumably ready to kill Araunah and his sons (21:20).

The fire sent from heaven on the altar in answer to David's prayer of mercy is reminiscent of Elijah's contest with the prophets of Baal at Mount Carmel (1 Kings 18:38). The sign of this fire confirms God's approval of David's atoning prayer and sacrificial offerings, as evidenced by the staying of the plague (21:26–27).

7. Cf. Allen, *1, 2 Chronicles*, 140.

We must not forget that the sacrificial ritual prescribed by the Mosaic law was God's means of providing atonement for the sin of his people. Naturally, genuine repentance is a necessary requisite for the ritual act, as David well knows (cf. Ps. 51). McConville has smartly observed that this passage helps us make a distinction, in terms of maintaining an undisturbed relationship with God, between cost that is subjective and cost that is objective.[8] The subjective cost of enjoying fellowship with God is the penitence and intercession by the one who seeks to restore relationship with God (as in David's case here). The objective cost is the divinely ordained sacrificial ritual for atoning for individual and national sin among God's people. The temple itself was the symbol of that objective cost for the nation of Israel (cf. 2 Chron. 7:12).

The difference in the price paid for Araunah's threshing floor as recorded in the parallel accounts of the transaction is usually attributed to the cost differential between the threshing floor proper (fifty shekels of silver, 2 Sam. 24:24) and the tract of adjacent land required beyond the site for the altar in order to accommodate the entire temple complex (six hundred shekels of gold, 1 Chron. 21:25). The NIV follows the MT in breaking the paragraph at 21:26, although most biblical commentators understand the report of the destroying angel sheathing his sword (21:27) as the logical conclusion of the episode addressing the staying of divine judgment against Israel.

Conclusion (21:28–22:1). The Chronicler adds a conclusion to this story to demonstrate the God-ordained continuity between worship centered in the Mosaic tabernacle (located in Gibeon) and the future temple of Yahweh in Jerusalem. The answer to David's prayer for God's mercy by the sign of fire sent from heaven upon the altar is presented as divine confirmation of this shift in the location for Israel's worship center (21:26). The theological addendum also explains why the Israelite sanctuary is transferred from Gibeon to Jerusalem, since David is unable to go to Gibeon to inquire of the Lord because of the "destroying angel" (cf. 21:16).

The continuity in Israelite worship from the Mosaic tabernacle to the Solomonic temple is further solidified by the association of the temple site with Mount Moriah, the place of Abraham's near sacrifice of Isaac (2 Chron. 3:1; cf. Gen. 22:2). God's responsiveness to David's prayer and burnt offerings indicate that this site, in one sense, has already become a house of prayer and a temple for sacrifices (cf. 2 Chron. 7:12). The emphatic position of the phrase "to be here" [*zeh hu᾿*] in the syntax of the original language further underscores David's understanding that this is to be the site for the new altar and the new house of God (22:1). As Wilcock has noted, the threshing floor

---

8. McConville, *1 and II Chronicles*, 75.

of Araunah becomes the meeting place of divine wrath and divine mercy—foreshadowing the cross of Christ.[9]

Toward bridging contexts. King David's preparations for the Jerusalem temple highlight two great theological continuities between the Old and New Testaments: the theme of leadership and the theme of worship. Two cues from this section about the debacle of David's census that point toward the contemporary significance of the larger literary unit (21:1–29:9) are the ideas of that biblical leadership must take responsibility for decision-making—whether good or bad—and that worship is a form of spiritual warfare.

Preparations for the Temple (22:2–19)

THE REPORT OF David's preparations for building the temple have no parallel in the books of Samuel or Kings. In fact, while there are allusions in the earlier texts, there are no parallels for this entire literary unit (chs. 22–29). Yet, Selman has noted that the thematic framework for these chapters is borrowed from 1 Kings 2:1–12, which begins with David's impending death (1 Chron. 22:5) and concludes with the formulaic summary of David's reign (29:26–20).[10]

In 22:2–19 the spotlight shifts from a focus on David alone (cf. ch. 21) to a wider angle that highlights the relationship between David and his son and successor, Solomon. Repeated words and phrases indicate that the chapter is all about providing materials and preparing Solomon and Israel's leaders to build the temple of Yahweh ("build" [*bnh*] occurs nine times, 22:2, 5, 6, 7, 8, 10, 11, 19; the verb to "provide" or "make preparation" [*kwn* in the Hiphil] occurs five times in 22:3, 5, 14). David's "extensive preparations" (22:5) for the temple included readying Solomon to accept the charge to build a house for God (22:6–13), making provision for the building materials and skilled laborers (22:14–16), and establishing support for the project among the leadership of Israel (22:17–19). No doubt the Chronicler regards this concern for preparation before embarking on the work of God an important lesson for his own audience.

David conscripts workers and gathers materials (22:2–5). The emphasis in this paragraph is on the comprehensive nature of David's preparations for the building of the temple. The proximity of his own death and Solomon's youth and inexperience combine to motivate David's remarkable effort to organize the labor and secure the raw materials for the monumental project. In one sense, David is the prefabricator of Solomon's temple. The Chroni-

---

9. Wilcock, *The Message of Chronicles*, 95–96.
10. Selman, *1 Chronicles*, 214.

cler stresses the great quantities of materials involved as justification for the superlatives used to describe the edifice on the drawing board—"magnificence" and "splendor" (note the repetition of Heb. *larob*, "great, more, many" in 22:3, 4, 5).

Four types of craftsmen are drafted into service as laborers for the temple project: stonecutters, masons, carpenters, and metal workers (22:2, 15; cf. 2 Chron. 2:17–18). The "aliens" (1 Chron. 22:2) are non-Israelite inhabitants of territories occupied and controlled by Israel. David's conscription of "aliens" fits the pattern in the ancient Near East of using prisoners of war and subjugated people as forced laborers for major building projects. Typically, the resident aliens were free citizens with limited legal rights. They enjoyed the rights of assistance, protection, and religious participation in the Israelite community under Mosaic law (Deut. 14:29; 16:11, 14; 24:14). The alien was under divine protection, and the Israelites were to love aliens as themselves, since they had been aliens once in Egypt (Deut. 10:18–19). It is assumed these legal principles inform the Israelite treatment of the aliens levied in the labor details. We know from the register of David's cabinet members that Adoniram is supervisor of the forced labor units, a position he held under kings Solomon and Rehoboam as well (2 Sam. 20:24; cf. 1 Kings 12:18).

The temple craftsmen work with four types of raw materials: stone, iron, bronze, and wood (22:2–4). The gifts of gold, silver, and semiprecious and precious stones for the decoration of the temple are reported at the end of this larger section (29:1–9). The stone was probably limestone quarried near Jerusalem. Previously it was reported that some of the bronze taken as booty in David's wars was given to the sanctuary treasuries (18:8, 11). David's defeat of the Philistines may have provided the iron for the building project (cf. 12:19–22).

Some of the raw materials were probably secured through trade agreements of some sort, much like Solomon's bartering with the king of Phoenician Tyre for additional lumber with payments of grain (1 Kings 5:10–12). The cedar timbers imported from the Sidonians and Tyrians are one of the temple's outstanding features (cf. 1 Chron. 17:1, 6). These logs are one of the defining characteristics of the second temple as well (cf. Ezra 3:7). Selman has reminded us, however, that the magnificence and splendor of Yahweh's temple is not about the celebration of the edifice as an architectural wonder.[11] Rather, the temple is a theological statement to the nations (1 Chron. 22:5) about God's faithfulness to his covenant with David and the embodiment of his kingdom in the Israelite monarchy.

---

11. Ibid.

David's charge to Solomon (22:6–16). The suggestion that chapters 22–29 are an expansion of the report of David's "last days" in office has considerable merit (cf. 1 Kings 2:1–12).[12] If this is indeed the case, the events narrated in 1 Chronicles 22 and 28–29 may have taken place during a brief coregency shared by David and Solomon after the coup of Adonijah (1 Kings 1). It is likely, then, that David's counsel recorded here in 1 Chronicles 22:6–16 is a private charge to his son Solomon to build Yahweh's temple, in anticipation of the later public commissioning of the crown prince (cf. 28:9–10). The section contrasts David as a "man of wars" with Solomon as a "man of peace and rest" (22:9) and is laden with allusions to Joshua's succession of Moses as Israel's leader (cf. Deut. 31; Josh. 1).

While the introduction to David's charge to Solomon (22:7–10) contains no explicit references to 2 Samuel 7 or 1 Chronicles 17, the passage is generally understood to be a commentary of sorts on the Davidic covenant. The prophet Nathan's announcing the Davidic dynasty has been amplified in three ways: David may not build Yahweh's temple, Solomon may build the temple because the land now has "rest," and Solomon is recognized as the heir of the promise for the continuation of Davidic kingship (cf. 17:11).

The prohibition restraining David as the builder of the temple (22:8) is not mentioned in the formulation of the Davidic covenant (cf. 2 Sam. 7; 1 Chron. 17). It is often suggested that David's disqualification as the builder is the result of some type of ritual uncleanness because he "shed much blood" (1 Chron. 22:8). Yet the reports of David's wars sound no indictment of his military campaigns but rather place them in the context of doing God's bidding in bringing "rest" to the land (cf. 1 Kings 5:3–4). Possibly David's disqualification is simply a foil to heighten the peace and rest secured by David but enjoyed by Solomon as the necessary preconditions for building the temple (cf. Deut. 12:11). Selman appropriately informs us that Yahweh's temple not only points to God's gift of peace and forgiveness to Israel (and the nations) but also stands as a symbol of his faithfulness in keeping promises about the land bequeathed to Abraham—only fully realized during King Solomon's reign.[13]

The repetition of theme and the transfer of royal authority from David to Solomon reflect the commissioning of Joshua by Moses as his successor (22:11–13; cf. Deut. 31; Josh. 1). For example, both Moses and David are disqualified from achieving their ultimate goals, while both Joshua and Solomon lead God's people into an era of "rest" and "blessing." Beyond this, the language of David's charge to Solomon clearly demonstrates the influence of the

---

12. E. Ball, "The Co-regency of David and Solomon (1 Kings 1)," *VT* 27 (1977): 268–79.
13. Selman, *1 Chronicles*, 215.

parallel event. Specifically, the invocation "the LORD be with you" (1 Chron. 22:11) occurs in both accounts of Moses' charge to Joshua (cf. Deut. 31:6, 8, 23; Josh. 1:5, 9). The statement "when [the LORD] puts you in command" has parallels in Deuteronomy 31:14, 23 and Joshua 1:9. Likewise, the exhortations to "be strong . . . do not be afraid" (1 Chron. 22:13) have their counterparts in Deuteronomy 31:7, 23; Joshua 1:6, 7, 9. All this has led some to identify David as a "second" Moses and Solomon as a "second" Joshua. Whether addressed to Joshua or Solomon or the Christian servant today, the exhortation has retained its currency!

The phrase "discretion and understanding" (*śekel ubinah,* 22:12) occurs elsewhere only in King Hiram's letter to King Solomon, affirming these qualities in David's successor (2 Chron. 2:12). This expression combines the ideas of intelligence and insight. As in the case of Joshua's commission, however, true wisdom is connected to obedience to God's law (Josh. 1:7–8). King Solomon himself prays for such wisdom as he begins the task of building Yahweh's temple (cf. 1 Kings 3:6–9). This emphasis on law-keeping provides the theological foundation for the Chronicler's retribution principle (i.e., divine blessing or curse based on the response to God's law) since Solomon's success is conditioned by observance of the law (cf. 1 Chron. 28:9).

David's actual charge to Solomon to build the temple is an invocation or prayer that offers encouragement, delineates the task at hand, and gives assurance of divine help. This threefold structure has been identified as the pattern in what is called the "induction into office" formula in Old Testament literature. Typically, the induction formula begins with a word of encouragement to the one about to enter the office. It then includes a description of the task to which the individual is called and concludes with the promise of divine accompaniment as enablement for the successful completion of the commission (cf. Moses' charge to Joshua, Josh. 1:6–9).[14] In this case, the installation of office formula authorizes or establishes Solomon as the builder of Yahweh's temple. The installation formula reminds Solomon (and the Chronicler's audience) that God's call invariably includes the means to accomplish it—even as Moses learned when God called him and equipped him to deliver Israel from Egypt (cf. Ex. 3–4).

Many scholars consider the astronomical amounts of gold and silver that David provides for the temple project a form of hyperbole common in the biblical world (22:14; cf. NIV text notes: 3,750 tons of gold and 37,500 tons of silver). To these scholars, the hyperbole means that David gathers materials in quantities "beyond measure" or that he spares no expense in making extravagant provisions for Yahweh's temple. Payne, one of the few commentators

---

14. Braun, *1 Chronicles,* 222.

willing to assert the factuality of the fabulous amounts of precious metals stockpiled by David, says that "the historical reliability of these two passages in 1 Chronicles is better explained by 'the special providence of God, in bestowing on His servant David a weight of riches commensurate with their intended employment for the house of His glory.'"[15]

Whether or not the Chronicler's figures are a literary device or reflect reality, most biblical commentators miss the main focus, which is not on the opulence of the temple but on David's understanding of the inestimable worth of God (cf. Ps. 68). More practically, the inventory of materials and roster of ready workers mean that any delay in commencing with the building project is unnecessary because everything is in place to begin construction (22:14–15). The repetition of two elements of the installation formula framing David's charge to Solomon reinforce his commission as temple builder ("now begin the work," 22:16b) and acknowledge that the project will succeed only with God's help ("the LORD be with you," 22:16c).

David's charge to Israel's leaders (22:17–19). Following the private charge to Solomon, David issues a royal edict (22:17) to all the leaders of Israel, who are expected to "help" Solomon—a tacit admission that undertaking a building project of this magnitude demands the full support of the nation. The word "help" (*ʿezer*) recalls the "help" David received earlier from the people of Israel (cf. 12:1, 18 [2x], 21, 22). The occasion for this summons to the leaders is unknown, although it may have been associated with the general assembly of the nation to witness David's public charge to Solomon (28:1, 8). Previously Moses indicated that a God-given "rest" from their enemies was a precondition for building a sanctuary for the Lord (Deut. 12:10–11). Through the rule of King David God has granted that "rest" (*nawaḥ*) so that the land of the covenant promise is now subject to the Lord and his people (1 Chron. 22:18).

The same contingency for success given to Solomon applies to the leaders of Israel (cf. 22:12). They too must "seek" the Lord, recognizing that this is the act of obedience to God's law, not a search for divine guidance.[16] David envisions two distinct purposes for the temple as the sanctuary of God: housing the sacred vessels and furniture essential to Israel's worship, especially the ark of the covenant, and exalting the name of the Lord before his people and the nations (22:19; cf. 2 Chron. 5:5 on the "sacred furnishings" of the Tent of Meeting that are transferred to the temple). The rhetorical question affirming God's presence with the leaders assures them that God's interests do not lie with Solomon alone (22:18; cf. 22:11). The phrase "God be with you" is

---

15. Payne, "1 Chronicles," 4:412.
16. Selman, *1 Chronicles*, 218.

a covenant formula and has implications for the "Immanuel" theology that will continue with the temple even as it began with the tabernacle (cf. Ex. 25:8).

Toward bridging contexts. King David's preparations for the building of the Jerusalem temple highlight two great theological continuities between the Old and New Testaments: the theme of leadership and the theme of worship. One theme from chapter 22, in which David takes steps to secure both the raw materials and labor for building the temple, that points toward the contemporary significance of the larger literary unit (21:1–29:9) is the understanding that Yahweh will be exalted among the nations (22:5). From the beginning, God's redemptive plan has been directed to the nations—starting with the promise to bless all nations through Abram and Sarai (Gen. 12:1–3), being fulfilled in the incarnation of Jesus Christ, who is the light of revelation for the nations and the glory of Israel (Luke 2:30–32), and evident eternally in the worship of people from every nation (Rev. 5:9–10).

Duties for the Levites (23:1–32)

CHAPTER 23 OPENS the Chronicler's report of David's organization of the temple personnel, the Levites, and the priests (chs. 23–26). Note the structure of this section: David gathers the officials, the priests, and the Levites for the purpose of administrative reorganization (23:2); then the rest of the account treats those three leadership classes in reverse order (Levites, ch. 23; priests, ch. 24; other officials, chs. 25–27). Following the introductory verse serving as a general heading or title of sorts to the extended narrative (23:1), the passage may be subdivided into three descriptive units: the census and table of organization for the Levites (23:2–6a), the genealogical table of the Levites (23:6b–24), and the duty roster of the Levites (23:25–32).

Introduction (23:1). To identify the introductory verse as a title may be somewhat misleading since the story line recounting David's gathering of all Israel for Solomon's anointing and coronation as successor to the throne of Israel is resumed in 28:1. The general heading provides an entrée into the rest of the Chronicler's account of David's reign (23:2–29:30) by explaining the series of organizational moves by David that permit the successful transition of power to his son. Selman connects the heading implicitly to the Davidic covenant because David's organization of the priests and Levites links his "house" or dynasty with the God's "house" or temple (1 Chron. 17).[17]

This means that neither the kingship nor the temple is an independent institution; both partner in establishing God's kingdom in Israel. The heading should not be regarded as a chronological statement, since Solomon has

17. Ibid.

already been commissioned as the next king (at least privately, cf. 22:11–13).[18] The heading also assumes the reader's knowledge of the court intrigue and bloodshed that has accompanied Solomon's accession to the throne (cf. 1 Kings 1–2). The expression "old and full of years" is an epithet connoting great honor and places David among the Old Testament heroes of the faith (e.g., Abraham, Gen. 25:8; Isaac, 35:29; Moses, Deut. 34:7; Job, Job 42:17).

The census of the Levites (23:2–6a). The report of the census of the Levites provides the background for the subsequent registers of the three sons of Levi. David organized the Levites according to four distinct categories of labor: the work of the temple, officials and judges, gatekeepers, and musicians (23:3–5). Three of the four Levitical guilds are treated later as David prepares for the building of the temple, again in reverse order (see chs. 25–26). In addition to the legal functions of those Levites appointed as judges, it is possible that those described as "officials" have record-keeping responsibilities. The Levites assigned to the work of the temple assist the priests with the sacrificial rituals and certain aspects of temple worship (perhaps their duties are prescribed in 23:28–31). The roster of the Levites by family represents another strata of organization, namely, a genealogical one (23:6b–24).

This census should not be seen as a contradiction to the ill-advised military census previously ordered by David and implemented by Joab (ch. 21). The purpose of this census of the Levites is to establish a rotation of Levitical service for temple worship. The tallies for the four Levitical guilds are given in descending numerical order and total 38,000 Levites.

The exceedingly large numbers recorded in the census have raised numerous questions of interpretation. For instance, the number of Levites at the time of Moses is reported as 8,580 (Num. 4:36, 40, 44). The number of Levites defecting to David at Hebron after Saul's death is listed as 4,600 (1 Chron. 12:27). According to Ezra, only 733 Levites return to Israel during the repatriation of the land after the Babylonian exile (Ezra 2). Furthermore, Chronicles lists only a total of 288 musicians and 93 gatekeepers (1 Chron. 25:7–31; 26:8–11). This has led many biblical commentators to regard this report of the swollen ranks of the Levites as some sort of "ideal" temple service corps for the Chronicler. Others view this as one of those places where the word "thousand" (Heb. *ʾelep*) should be understood as a "clan" or "group" (i.e., twenty-four clans of temple Levites).[19]

David's census targeting Levites thirty years of age and older (23:3) coincides with the age qualification of the Mosaic census of the Levites (Num.

---

18. See Thompson, *1, 2 Chronicles*, 169, on the possibility of a coregency between David and Solomon, based on Egyptian models.

19. Selman, *1 Chronicles*, 223.

4:3). We know from census-takings in other Old Testament texts that service in the Levitical corps began at age twenty (e.g., 2 Chron. 31:17; Ezra 3:8) or even age twenty-five (cf. Num. 8:24). The Chronicler actually reports two different ages as the baseline for Levitical service in David's census (age thirty, 23:3; age twenty, 23:24, 27). Perhaps the Chronicler splices together sources that represent different traditions of Levitical service based on need at the time, or certain tasks performed by the Levites require men with more maturity and experience.

The three sons of Levi (23:6b–24). The genealogical table of Levi highlights his three sons in keeping with the order found elsewhere: Gershon, Kohath, and Merari (cf. Ex. 6:17–18; Num. 3–4; 1 Chron. 6). Apart from Moses (1 Chron. 23:15–17), each family in the register is represented by three generations of descendants. The expression "heads of families" (23:24) in Chronicles denotes clan leaders or family elders (cf. 27:1). The census counts twenty-two families, nine each from Gershon and Kohath and four from Merari. The lack of harmonization with the twenty-four divisions of Levites enumerated later (chs. 24–25) and the twenty-two families of Levites outlined in the genealogical table suggest that this list dates to a different time period.[20] We have already seen that the practice of annotating genealogies is common in Chronicles, so these expansions need not be regarded as secondary additions to the record.

The Gershonites (23:7–11) head all the lists of Levi's sons, although Libni is identified as Gershon's first son elsewhere (Ex. 6:17; Num. 3:18; 1 Chron. 6:17). Perhaps Ladan is an alternate name for Libni or Ladan is a descendant of Libni, who becomes a prominent figure among the Levites in latter times (cf. 1 Chron. 26:21). The annotation to the names of Jeush and Beriah is a curious application of administrative pragmatism to the division of labor among the Levites, in this case counting two families as one (23:11). It appears that the Shimei mentioned in 23:9 is the brother of Ladan, while the reference to Shimei in 23:10 seems to continue the genealogy of the second son of Gershon (23:7).

Aaron and Moses are sons of Amram of the Kohathites (23:12–20). The line of Aaron is excluded from the Levitical census as the high priestly family (23:13). Aaron was "set apart" (*bdl*) or singled out for holy service to God and his people. The family of Moses, however, was numbered among the Levites (23:14). Unlike Aaron's family, the family of Moses receives no special status despite his standing as a "man of God." This title signifies one chosen and sent by God as a prophet or a human agent of divine revelation and an example of holiness.

---

20. See the helpful genealogical charts in Braun, *1 Chronicles*, 232–34.

The fourfold list of duties prescribed for Aaron and his descendants is the most comprehensive statement of priestly function in Chronicles and is perhaps a commentary on the anointing of Aaron and his sons (23:13; cf. Ex. 30:30). Both the priests and the Levites are called "to minister" before the Lord and "pronounce blessings" in his name (cf. Deut. 10:8). Allen's poignant insight calls attention to this priestly blessing as it "formed a bridge between temple worship and mundane life back home."[21] The distinctive service of the priests consists of consecrating holy things and of offering sacrifices (23:13). The priests are responsible to sanctify the vessels and furniture of the Lord's sanctuary and to maintain the holy status of these objects as they are utilized in worship (cf. Ex. 30:22–29). The expression "offer sacrifices" (lit., "burn incense" or "go up in smoke," Heb. *qtr*) refers in general to the various types of ritual sacrifices superintended by the priests (e.g., Lev. 1:9; 2:2; 3:5).

The genealogy of Merari is the shortest of the three sons of Levi, representing only four families (23:21–23). The reference to Eleazar (23:22) suggests that his family line, despite the lack of any male heir, is legitimately continued through his daughters on the basis of the inheritance regulations decreed by Moses (Num. 27:4–11; 36:6–9).

The summary statement concluding the register of the Levitical heads of families emphasizes the meticulous nature of the census, registered by name and counted individually (23:24).[22] The similarities between 23:4 and 23:24 in vocabulary and theme indicate that the genealogical tables of the Levitical families are intended to augment the first group of Levites mentioned in the census (23:4). Presumably the Chronicler's reference to the census age of twenty represents a harmonization with the standard practice of the numbering of all Israelites established by Moses (cf. Num. 1:3). It is possible that the census age of thirty cited earlier (1 Chron. 23:3) applies to Levites assigned to specific tasks or that those Levites between the ages of twenty and thirty serve some kind of apprenticeship until they reach the mandatory age for full participation in the Levitical service corps.

The duties of the Levites (23:25–32). The preceding verse (23:24) serves double duty in that it closes the genealogical tables by summarizing the methodology of the census-taking and directly introduces the unit describing the functions of the Levites. A change in historical circumstances necessitates the reorganization of the Levites. Originally the Levites were porters for the tent-shrine and its furnishings (23:25–27; cf. Num. 3–4). The shift from a portable to a permanent sanctuary for Israel's worship of Yahweh means that the duties for the Levites must be reassigned. David anticipates this need

---

21. Allen, *1, 2 Chronicles*, 160.
22. Japhet, *I and II Chronicles*, 417–18.

---

to restructure the duty roster of the Levites, perhaps on the basis of Moses' prediction that one day Israel will worship at a central sanctuary (note the emphasis on "rest" in the king's speech, 1 Chron. 23:25; cf. Deut. 12:10).

In general, the Levites assist the priests in the service of the temple (23:28a). They are charged to help the priests minister before the Lord in three distinct realms: guarding the temple precincts (23:28b), cleaning and maintaining the precincts (23:28c), and aiding the priests in the daily sacrificial rituals (23:29). This duty roster for the Levites is less detailed than the catalog of Levitical services found earlier in the Chronicler's narrative (cf. 9:28–32).

In addition to their role as a supporting cast to the priesthood, the Levites are also in charge of the music that accompanies the rituals of temple worship (23:30–31). The key idea of the passage is the contribution of the Levites to the continuity of Israelite worship through the faithful discharging of their responsibilities, first in the Tent of Meeting and then in the temple of David and Solomon (23:32). The subordination of the Levites to the priests characteristic at David's time seems to have changed by the postexilic period, when priest and Levite seem to function more as equals in the service of the second temple.[23]

Toward bridging contexts. King David's preparations for building the Jerusalem temple highlight two great theological continuities between the Old and New Testaments: the theme of leadership and the theme of worship. Two cues from 1 Chronicles 23 reporting David's organization of the Levites for ministry in the temple that point toward the contemporary significance of the larger literary unit (21:1–29:9) are the importance of a delegation of responsibilities as a leadership principle and the relationship between God's faithfulness to his people and the faithful service of those who minister to his people in his name.

The Divisions of the Priests (24:1–31)

CHAPTER 24 IS part of a larger unit (chs. 23–26) addressing the various groups of Levites and their duties in the temple. The chapter consists of a report of the allotment process for determining the division of labor for the service of temple worship (24:1–5), a register of the twenty-four priestly divisions (24:6–19), and a second register of the twenty-four Levitical courses responsible for assisting the priests in the temple liturgy (24:20–31). Rather than enumerating the specific duties to be performed by the priests and Levites,

---

23. So concludes Julia M. O'Brien in a detailed study of the issue: *Priest and Levite in Malachi* (SBLDS 121; Atlanta: Scholars Press, 1990).

the Chronicler places emphasis on the organization of the temple personnel into divisions and the ordering of those divisions in a systematic service rotation. The identification of the priests as simply one segment of the larger Levitical corps is in keeping with the postexilic understanding of the relationship between the priests and the Levites.

The descendants of Aaron (24:1–19). The emphasis here is not one of liturgical function but rather one of organization for service (24:1–5). This is another case where the Chronicler has assumed the audience's knowledge of the priestly duties associated with the sacrificial worship of the temple. The writer's concern is twofold: the formal sanctioning of that duty roster by King David (24:3) and the propriety of carefully ordering priestly service by means of lot-casting (24:5).

The list of Aaron's descendants repeats information found elsewhere (e.g., Ex. 6:23; 1 Chron. 6:3) but omits certain details like the cause of death for Nadab and Abihu. Rather than suppressing information (as Williamson contends), the Chronicler omits such facts because his audience is no doubt thoroughly acquainted with that tragic story.[24] The essential datum for the writer is the role that the remaining sons of Aaron play as the progenitors of the priestly clans still superintending temple liturgy during the Chronicler's day. Beyond the wrath of God evident in the judgment of Nadab and Abihu, the Chronicler desires his audience to rejoice in God's grace in preserving Eleazar and Ithamar so that the priesthood might be built through them.

David relies on Zadok, a descendant of Eleazar, and Ahimelech, a descendant of Ithamar (cf. 18:16), for assistance. Zadok is a prominent priestly figure serving under both David and Solomon (1 Kings 1:8, 2:35).[25] The reference to Ahimelech is a bit unusual since often Zadok is paired with Abiathar in contexts addressing priestly concerns (cf. 2 Sam. 15:35; 1 Kings 4:4). Selman suggests the mention of Abiathar's son Ahimelech (cf. 2 Sam. 8:17) may reflect the disaffection of David with Abiathar in the aftermath of Adonijah's revolt (cf. 1 Kings 1:7–8).[26]

The reference to "drawing lots" underscores the impartiality of the method in the assignment of priestly duties (24:5; cf. v. 31). Since the heads of families from Eleazar outnumber the heads of families from Ithamar by two to one (24:4), the alternating draw affects the appointments to service rotation

---

24. Williamson, 1 and 2 Chronicles, 163, also sees a contradiction between David's appointment of the priestly divisions (24:3) and the reference to lot-casting (24:5). Presumably, however, David appoints the priestly divisions while the lot-casting determines the allocation of duties to those divisions.

25. For a concise overview of the controversy surrounding Zadok's genealogical roots, see Eugene E. Carpenter, "Zadok 1," ISBE, 4:1169–70.

26. Selman, 1 Chronicles, 231.

for only the first sixteen lots. The remaining eight assignments automatically fall to families of Eleazar.

The exact meaning of the titles "officials of the sanctuary" and "officials of God" is unclear (24:5). The phrases may be understood in apposition, so as to clarify the nature of their position or the character of their service ("there were many qualified officials serving God," so NLT). The latter phrase ("officials of God") may even have a superlative meaning, signifying that the "officials of the sanctuary" are "outstanding leaders."[27]

Shemaiah the scribe is mentioned only here (24:6) in the biblical records. The scribal tradition's association with the priestly class has a long history in the Old Testament, however, perhaps dating to the writing and preserving of the records of tribal allotments under the direction of Joshua (cf. Josh. 18–21). By analogy to the institution of the Israelite monarchy with its royal "recorder" and royal "secretary" (2 Sam. 8:16–17), it seems logical that the institution of the Israelite priesthood also had its official record keepers.

It is not clear if the names listed in the priestly register represent individuals or families or both. Many of the names found in the roster occur only here, so it is possible that the contents of the priestly rota (a fixed order of persons or duties) represent the divisional structure of the priesthood at the time of the writer. The name Jehoiarib (24:7) is known from the genealogy of Mattathias as an ancestor of the Maccabees (1 Macc. 2:1). This has prompted some biblical scholars to date this priestly rota to the Maccabean era. Granting the assumption that the name refers to one and the same person, this point alone is insufficient to establish a second century B.C. date for the entire list.

Beyond this, the prologue to Sirach suggests that a threefold Hebrew canon of Scriptures containing the Law, Prophets, and Other Books was already recognized a generation before the Maccabean heroes.[28] The name Abijah (24:10) is known from the Gospel records since Zechariah, the father of John the Baptist, is a priest from this division (Luke 1:5). Zechariah's encounter with the angel Gabriel left him unable to speak (and hence unable to pronounce the priestly blessing of 1 Chron. 23:13) until his wife Elizabeth gave birth to the child (Luke 1:63–64). Zechariah's "post-partum" song or prophetic blessing (the *Benedictus*) remains an important element in the daily prayers of the Prayer Book tradition of the church.

As a counter to critics who observe that Nehemiah reports a priesthood of four classes or divisions gradually developing into twenty-one or twenty-two priestly courses, Selman has suggested that Chronicles represents the ideal priestly

---

27. Thompson, *1, 2 Chronicles*, 173.
28. See the discussion in Williamson, *1 and 2 Chronicles*, 164.

division rather than the actual figure (cf. Neh. 7:39–42; 10:1–8).[29] It is possible, however, that the priestly rota has expanded to twenty-four divisions by the time of the Chronicler (some two to four generations after Nehemiah). According to Myers, the assigning of groups of priests to specific periods or "watches" of service was a well-known practice in the ancient world.[30] The twenty-four divisions of the priestly duty roster accords with later Jewish practice of priestly service on a lunar calendar of forty-eight weeks, with each course or division serving a week at a time twice during the year.

The rest of the Levites (24:20–31). The roster of additional Levitical families updates the register found in 23:6–23 and assumes the reader's knowledge of that list. This section reporting the divisions of the priests is understood as a supplement to the report of David's organization of the Levites (ch. 23), both by the heading ("as for the rest of the descendants of Levi," 23:20) and by the overlap in content. The chief differences between this roster of Levites and the previous one is the omission of the family of Gershom (23:7–11) and the addition of another name in six of the Levitical families. The extension of certain Levitical families by one name suggests the addition of a generation to the roster of names. The inclusion of ten other names in this list of "the rest of the Levites" may be an update of sorts reflecting the situation of the writer's time.[31] The concluding report of the enrollment of the Levites by lot serves to link this unit (24:20–31) with the rota of priests (24:1–19).

Toward bridging contexts. King David's preparations for building the Jerusalem temple highlight two great theological continuities between the Old and New Testaments: the theme of leadership and the theme of worship. First Chronicles 24, reporting David's organization of the priests into divisions for rotational ministry in the temple, points toward the contemporary significance of the larger literary unit (21:1–29:9) by drawing attention to the need for competent leadership in corporate worship.

The Temple Musicians (25:1–31)

THIS SECTION IS devoted to the rostering and duties of the temple musicians, the first of several special classes of Levites. The passage suggests that singing in the temple liturgy was typically accompanied by the playing of musical instruments. As in the case with the priests, the Levitical musicians are ordered in families and arranged in twenty-four courses (cf. 24:20–31).

---

29. Selman, *1 Chronicles*, 229–30.

30. Myers, *I Chronicles*, 167–68.

31. There are textual difficulties in 24:26–27. The NIV (following the Vulgate) reads the Heb. *beno* as a proper name "Beno," the son of Jaaziah. Braun (*1 Chronicles*, 237) understands the word lit. as "his son" (i.e., Jaaziah as the son of Mushi).

The first unit (25:1–7) identifies the three Levitical families comprising the corps of temple musicians (Asaph, Heman, and Jeduthun) and summarizes their assigned duties. David charges the Levitical singers and musicians to perform "the ministry of prophesying" (with instrumental accompaniment, 25:1) and to provide the music ministry for the temple of the Lord (25:6). The second unit orders the assignment (and perhaps rotation) of duties as determined by lot-casting (25:8–31). The Mosaic law contains no explicit instructions concerning temple choirs, but their ministry is sanctioned by the word of David's prophets—Nathan and Gad (cf. 2 Chron. 29:25). Selman is probably correct in his assessment that the Chronicler has described an ideal Levitical structure and ministry from an earlier era.[32] Perhaps he intends to encourage a similar ministry of musical prophecy and praise among the Levitical singers of the second temple.

The three musical guilds (25:1–7). The Chronicler traces the origin of the temple music ministry in three Levitical families: Asaph, Heman, and Jeduthun (25:1). There is a sense in which these families represent musical guilds, as witnessed in their contribution to the Psalms (cf. Ps. 73–89). Perhaps each family or guild has its own distinctive musical style or repertoire, or some other distinctive feature (note, e.g., the musical notations introducing the psalms of the Asaph and Korah collections, Ps. 73–89).

There seems to be some fluidity in the membership of the core families responsible for the music ministry of the temple since Ethan replaces Jeduthun in another of the Chronicler's lists of Levitical musicians (cf. 15:19), and the sons of Korah are connected with nearly a dozen different psalms (Ps. 42; 44–49; 84–85; 87–88).[33] David's organization of a corps of Levitical temple musicians is important to the legitimacy of music in worship as temple liturgy developed. This is another way for the Chronicler to connect his present with Israel's past, especially since the postexilic community is still bereft of Davidic kingship. For the Chronicler, the community is still linked to Davidic kingship, at least indirectly, through the temple worship he organized.

The basic genre of the literary unit is considered "a register" (an official record listing persons or items with regard to the identifying characteristics of the domain of their vocation or function). The register is composed of a "roster" (a list of personal names within a related group, including assigned duties or offices, 25:1–6) and a "rota" (a fixed order of persons or duties; see 25:9–31).[34] Scholars debate the nature and the primacy of the sources comprising this pericope (e.g., are 25:1–7 the product of composite

---

32. Selman, *1 Chronicles*, 234.

33. It is possible that Ethan and Jeduthun are one in the same person; see "Jeduthun" in *NBD*, 545.

34. De Vries, *1 Chronicles*, 206, 435.

authorship? Are 25:8—31 secondary additions to the report?). A full discussion of such questions lies outside the scope of this commentary.[35]

King David appoints the temple musicians in consultation with "commanders of the army" (25:1a). Although strong associations between musicians and the military are known in the ancient world, it is unclear whether these consultants are military personnel or Levitical officers, since the meaning of the word "army" (Heb. *ṣaba'*) is flexible. Japhet is probably correct in understanding the expression "the officers of the host of the service" as the chief Levitical officers.[36] According to the Chronicler, the task or function of the temple musicians is "the ministry of prophesying" (1 Chron. 25:1b). This musical ministry of prophesying is accompanied by particular instrumentation, namely "harps, lyres and cymbals." These same instruments are mentioned later as an important part of the ministry of music in the temple, but in reverse order (25:6; cf. Ps. 150:3—5).

The terms "prophesy" (*nb'*, 25:1, 2, 3) and "seer" (*ḥozeh*, 25:5) are associated with the classical prophets. Selman summarizes by saying either this Levitical prophecy "supplied messages direct from God in the manner of the classical prophets" (cf. Jahaziel in 2 Chron. 20:14—17) or their musical praise is seen as "prophecy" in that "it proclaimed God's word with God's authority."[37] The latter view seems more in keeping with the context of the Levitical ministry of "prophecy" in the form of teaching or the exposition of Mosaic law (cf. Deut. 33:10). It also fits the Chronicler's modus operandi of reconnecting the postexilic community to the key offices of king and prophet through temple worship. In fact, he may be calling the Levitical musicians of his day to revitalize their temple ministry by reminding them of their heritage.

Music and singing are connected with Hebrew liturgy from its inception in the covenant code ratified at Mount Sinai. God's deliverance of Israel from slavery in Egypt was the redemptive event that prompted worship in song throughout Hebrew history. The Song of Moses and the Song of Miriam are the precursors of later praise hymns and songs of thanksgiving celebrating Yahweh's activity in history (Ex. 15:1—21). In fact, another song of Moses was sung as an oath of witness or testimony to covenant renewal with God (Deut. 31:19; 31:30—32:47).

Singing to instrumental accompaniment seems to be the norm in the Old Testament. Such music was a part of the temple dedication (Ps. 30), Sabbath worship (Ps. 92), temple worship (2 Chron. 29:28; Ps. 100:2), and other special festivals (Isa. 30:29). It is not surprising that David organizes the

---

35. See further Braun, *1 Chronicles*, 243—46; Japhet, *I and II Chronicles*, 437—39.
36. Japhet, *I and II Chronicles*, 439.
37. Selman, *1 Chronicles*, 235.

Levitical musical guilds responsible for the music of the temple liturgy since he himself accounts for nearly half of the songs in the Psalter (cf. 2 Sam. 23:1). No doubt, his example of exuberant and skillful musicianship serves the Levitical corps well as they direct the worship of Israel.

The three families of musicians trace their lineage to Levi. Asaph is a descendant of Gershom, a son of Levi (6:39). Jeduthun is identified as a Levite; his ancestry is not traced, although the name appears in the titles of three psalms (Ps. 39; 62; 77). Heman is a descendant of Kohath, another son of Levi (1 Chron. 6:33; cf. Ps. 88). The four sons of Asaph, the six sons of Jeduthun, and the fourteen sons of Heman account for the twenty-four divisions of temple musicians. Each is under the supervision of their father.

The priority of Asaph is assumed by virtue of his order in the register and his close association with King David (25:2). The name Jesarelah (25:14) is a variant of Asaph's son Asarelah listed earlier (25:2). The name Shimei is added to the list of Jeduthun's sons on the basis of manuscript evidence preserved in the Greek Old Testament. The title "seer" (25:5) given to Heman is a synonym for "prophet" in the Old Testament. Elsewhere the same title is applied to Asaph (2 Chron. 29:30) and Jeduthun (35:15).

The reference to Heman's fourteen sons and three daughters (25:5) is no doubt included as a demonstration of God's blessing of his family for his faithful service as a temple musician. In a curious use of wordplay, it appears that the last nine names of Heman's sons (with some modification) may be read as a poem (25:4). The first five names in the register may represent a compilation of five incipits (or first lines of poems). Thus, according to Williamson, "it may be suggested that members of five separate families or sections of the guilds were called, perhaps playfully, after the openings of the Psalms which they were regularly accustomed to sing."[38]

The twenty-four divisions of Levitical musicians (25:8–31). The opening verse bridges the two sections of the chapter in the collective reference to the preceding roster of Levitical musicians ("young and old, teacher and student") and in the introduction of the lot-casting for assigned duties. The casting of lots is also the method used to determine the order of ministry for the priestly divisions (24:31) of the Levites and the gate assignments for the gatekeepers (26:13). The Israelites considered the drawing of lots (24:5) as an impartial selection process as well as a divinely superintended one, since they understood that the decision of the lot is from the Lord (Prov. 16:33).[39] It is unclear whether the lot-casting determines the composition and ministry routine of the Levitical singers or their rotation of liturgical service.

38. Williamson, *1 and 2 Chronicles*, 167.
39. On the method of lot-casting see Japhet, *I and II Chronicles*, 447–48.

Unlike the divisions of the priests who minister in the temple for two weeks at time in a staggered service rotation, there seems to be no parallel for this rotation of service among the Levitical singers. It is interesting to note, however, that according to Nehemiah there were Levitical musicians and singers living outside of the city of Jerusalem who were summoned to the city for special worship-related events—perhaps implying those Levites off their rotation of musical ministry were called back into duty during festive occasions (Neh. 12:28–29).

The rota of twenty-four divisions of Levitical musicians is actually one long sentence (25:9–31). Unlike the register of the priests (ch. 24) and the Levitical gatekeepers (ch. 26), the Levitical singers are identified first by family affiliation according to three main branches (25:1–7) and then by the ordering of divisions (25:8–31). This register lacks any concluding remarks, in contrast to the register of the Levites (ch. 23) and the priests (ch. 24).

The tally of 288 Levitical musicians (25:7) assumes the overlap of the earlier list (25:1–7) with the stereotyped registration of twenty-four divisions of temple singers. In fact, each of the names in the family rota of Levitical musicians occurs in the rota of twenty-four divisions of temple servants (with some variance in spelling). The report of the installation of the ark of the covenant in Jerusalem confirms that each Levitical ensemble consists of twelve musicians, including nine who play harps or lyres, two who play trumpets, and one assigned to cymbals (cf. 15:19). The reference to "young and old alike, teacher as well as student" (25:8) suggests a conservatory-like environment with emphasis on technique and skill level through training and rehearsal in addition to scheduled appearances for music ministry in the temple liturgy.

Toward bridging contexts. King David's preparations for building the Jerusalem temple highlight two great theological continuities between the Old and New Testaments: the theme of leadership and the theme of worship. First Chronicles 25 on David's organization of the temple musicians points toward the contemporary significance of the larger literary unit (21:1–29:9) by affirming the importance of music in the worship of Yahweh.

The Temple Gatekeepers (26:1–32)

THIS CHAPTER CONTINUES the lengthy section on the organization of the Levites and civil service corps under David (23:2–27:34). This passage contains two basic units: the register of Levitical gatekeepers and their duties (26:1–19), and a second register of other Levites and a list of their corresponding duties (26:20–32). The essential genre of the chapter is "register" (see comments on 25:1–7 for definition).[40]

---

40. De Vries, *1 Chronicles*, 434.

What do the temple gatekeepers actually do? The shift from the portable shrine of the Mosaic tabernacle to the permanent sanctuary of Solomon's temple makes the duties of certain Levites obsolete. Specifically, sons of Levi were originally the porters for the tabernacle, with the Gershonites and Merarites responsible for assembling, dismantling, and transporting the tabernacle materials and the Kohathites responsible for the installation and transportation of the tabernacle furnishings (cf. Num. 4). According to Thompson, the Levitical gatekeepers are a paramilitary security force who play three significant roles in the Jerusalem temple: They have oversight of the governance of the temple precinct, they are responsible for the administration of the temple revenues, and they are in charge of maintaining the temple and its paraphernalia.[41]

A previous roster of Levitical personnel lists four families of gatekeepers returning from exile in Babylonia with a tally of 212 gatekeepers (9:17–27). By the time of Ezra and Nehemiah, depending on the register consulted, the temple gatekeepers numbered anywhere from 172 to 138 Levites (cf. Neh. 7:45; 11:19). The trend of diminishing numbers in the ranks of the Levitical gatekeepers, though inexplicable, continues into the era of the Chronicler, who tallies the corps of gatekeepers at 93 Levites (1 Chron. 26:8, 9, 11).

The divisions of gatekeepers (26:1–19). The first section of this chapter identifies two families of Levitical gatekeepers: Meshelemiah (26:1–3, 9) and Hosah (26:10–11). The family of Meshelemiah traces their heritage to the line of Korah through the family of Izhar and ultimately Kohath, one of the three sons of Levi (6:1–2, 22; 26:1).

The list of temple gatekeepers from the family of Obed-Edom (26:4–8) interrupts the register of the family of Meshelemiah. Obed-Edom has no direct Levitical connections, and the reason for the expansion of the register is unclear. Elsewhere in Chronicles he is identified as a musician (15:18, 24), and he is grouped with the family of Hosah among the temple gatekeepers (16:38). The report that God blessed Obed-Edom (26:5) may be a result of the fact that for a time the ark of the covenant was stored at his house (13:14). In addition, his large family is surely understood as the blessing of God (cf. Ps. 127:3–5).

The name Asaph (26:1) should be read as Ebiasaph as recorded in the earlier register of the gatekeepers (9:19; cf. the LXX of 26:1). Zechariah, the firstborn son of Meshelemiah (26:2) holds the important position of gatekeeper to the Tent of Meeting (cf. 9:21). The clause "capable men with the strength to do the work" (26:8) is not a reference to the military character

---

41. Thompson, *1, 2 Chronicles*, 180.

of these Levites (cf. "able men," 26:7, 9). Rather, it indicates that these individuals possess the physical strength demanded for the difficult task of opening, closing, and guarding the large doors or gates providing access to the temple precinct.[42]

The family of Hosah are descendants of Merari, another son of Levi (cf. Ex. 6:16–19). During the days of the tabernacle, the Gershonites and the Merarites were the porters of the structural materials of the tabernacle (Num. 4). Hosah is mentioned elsewhere as a gatekeeper in connection with the return of the ark of the covenant to Jerusalem by David (1 Chron. 16:38). Shimri has the distinction of preeminence among Hosah's sons, despite the fact he is not the firstborn son (26:10, a practice known elsewhere in the Old Testament; cf. Ephraim in Gen. 48:14).

The next unit (26:12–18) is a table of organization outlining the service assignments of the temple gatekeepers. The reference to the "families" (26:13) of the gatekeepers is an oblique reminder of the long and storied history of this Levitical office. Earlier in Chronicles we learned that during the days of the portable shrine or Mosaic tabernacle Phinehas was in charge of the gatekeepers (9:20; cf. Num. 25:10–13). Beyond that, the status and authority vested in the temple gatekeepers come about as a result of the role of King David and Samuel the seer in appointing the Levites "to their positions of trust" (1 Chron. 9:22).

Clearly, the Chronicler does not want this fact lost upon his audience. The essential purpose of the expansion to his record of temple gatekeepers is the recounting of the ceremony for the specific gatekeeper assignments. Lot-casting is used to determine gate assignments, as previously seen with the duty rosters for the priests and Levitical musicians (chs. 24–25). This method of selection for assignments precludes any partiality and places emphasis on the divine nature of the decision, since the outcome of a lot is from the Lord (Prov. 16:33). The expression "young and old alike" (26:13) stresses that the procedure covers everyone (cf. 24:31; 25:8).

The temple gates, corresponding to four compass points, are distributed among three Levitical families (26:14–16a; cf. Ezek. 40). The privilege of attending to the East Gate of the temple falls to (Me-)Shelemiah (26:14a, probably the "Shallum" of 1 Chron. 9:17). The East Gate was the most important of the temple gates because it was the orientation of the entrance to the tabernacle (Ex. 38:13). The glory of the Lord returned to the temple through the East Gate, according to Ezekiel's temple vision (Ezek. 43:1–12; note that cherubim guarded the east entrance to Eden after the expulsion of fallen humanity, Gen. 3:23).

---

42. See Japhet, *I and II Chronicles*, 457.

The North Gate is assigned to the second family of Korahites, Zechariah the firstborn of (Me-)Shelemiah (26:14b). Earlier Zechariah was described as "the gatekeeper at the entrance to the Tent of Meeting" (9:21). Here he has the reputation of "a wise counselor," although there is no indication as to the circumstance giving rise to the title.

The South Gate, including oversight of the temple storehouses, is assigned to the family of Obed-Edom (26:15).

The watch of the West Gate and the Shalleketh Gate fall to Shuppim and Hosah. The name Shuppim is unexpected and intrusive and is often deleted as an error of dittography (e.g., NEB).[43] The Shalleketh Gate is mentioned only here in the Old Testament, and its location on the western side of the temple precinct is unknown. This "gate" on the upper road (26:16a) may have been a checkpoint of some sort or the outer gate of a two-gate complex.

The final unit of this section enumerates a duty roster of sorts, indicating the number of Levites stationed at the various posts during the daily watches (26:16b–18). The temple gatekeepers serve two by two, and there are apparently twenty-four daily assignments, including a minimum of six on the east side, four each on the north and south sides (with a pair guarding the storehouses), and six on the west (four on the road and two at the court entrance). The duration of a shift or rotation of duty is unspecified, but the daily rotation may have included six shifts of four hours each, since the Hebrews divided the nighttime hours (6:00 P.M. to 6:00 A.M.) into three watches (cf. Ex. 14:24; Judg. 7:19).

The summary statement tracing the divisions of the temple gatekeepers to two of the sons of Levi, Kohath indirectly (from Izhar to Korah) and Merari (directly), legitimizes or sanctions these Levitical servants by means of their genealogy (26:19). The conclusion also attaches the family of Obed-Edom to the Kohathites through Korah (cf. 26:15, 19).

Treasurers and administrative officials (26:20–32). The second section of this chapter may be divided into two distinct units: the list of Levites who serve as treasurers (26:20–28) and those who hold administrative posts outside the temple precinct of Jerusalem (26:29–32). The two rosters complete the catalog of the various registers of Levites and their assigned duties (chs. 23–26). The unity of the two paragraphs is supplied by the genealogical framework of the four Kohathite families mentioned by the Chronicler (or his source, 26:23). The section contains a number of literary and historical difficulties that cannot be fully addressed.

Other Levites have supervision of the two temple treasuries: one identified as storage for the treasures of "the house of God" and the other for the

---

43. See further discussion in Braun, *1 Chronicles*, 246 n. 16.

storage of "dedicated things" (26:20).[44] Such duties are logical assignments for the Levites since the storehouses are located near the temple gates. Selman has distinguished the two treasuries as a "general account" for the regular support of the temple (tithes, offerings, etc.) and a "special account" for unusual gifts and dedications separate from the funds and goods required for the daily operation of the temple.[45] While the exact relationship of this passage to the earlier report concerning the tasks associated with the temple gatekeepers in unclear (9:22–32), the duties of the treasurers certainly include tracking the inventory of the treasuries, periodic accounting of the goods in storage, and the guarding of the repositories.

Amram was the father of Aaron, Miriam, and Moses; like the Izharites, the Amramites (26:23) were descendants of Levi through Kohath (Ex. 6:16–20). Shubael, who traces his pedigree to Moses, is the overseer of both treasuries (1 Chron. 26:24). The Ladanites are descendants of Levi through Gershon; they have charge of the temple treasury (26:21–22). It is possible that Ladan is another name for Libni since elsewhere Gershon's firstborn son has that name (cf. Ex. 6:17; 1 Chron. 6:17). Shelomith and his relatives have charge of the treasury for the "dedicated things"—the storage for the spoils of wars and special gifts (1 Chron. 26:26–28). The report of plunder dedicated to God by Samuel, Saul, Abner, and others may be a synopsis of an ancient booty list. The events behind the flow of the spoils of war by prominent Israelite kings are not referenced (except the booty from King Agag devoted to God by Saul, 1 Sam. 15:21).

Two special groups of Levites are placed in charge of public administration in regions west of the Jordan River (26:29–32). The passage has troubled commentators on three counts. (1) Civil-service assignments for the Levitical corps are usually understood as a postexilic development (cf. 2 Chron. 19:8–11; Neh. 11:16). (2) According to the Chronicler's tallies, there are more Levites in service east than west of the Jordan River. (3) Some biblical scholars have questioned whether the Israelites had political authority over the Transjordan between the united monarchy and the Maccabean period. It should be noted, however, that precursors of this type of civil service by the tribe of Levi may be found in the census-taking of Israel after the Exodus (cf. Num. 1:44) and in Samuel, the "circuit-riding" judge (cf. 1 Sam. 7:15–17). Selman has countered that the unusual geographical location and large number of the Levites employed as civil servants may be part of the "army of officials" commissioned by Solomon (cf. 1 Kings 4:7–19; 9:23).[46]

---

44. Here the NIV follows the LXX and reads "their brothers" for the MT "Ahijah."
45. Selman, *1 Chronicles*, 241.
46. Ibid., 242.

The two Levitical families singled out for civil service outside the environs of Jerusalem and among the Israelite tribes in the Transjordan are the Izharites (26:29) and the Hebronites (26:30–32). Thus, three of the four Levitical families mentioned earlier (26:23) are accounted for, namely, the Amramites, who serve as temple treasurers (26:24–28); the Izharites, who serve as "officials and judges" (26:29); and the Hebronites, who discharge duties related to the "work of the LORD" and the "king's service" (26:30–32). Though cited as one of the four Levitical families contributing to the civil-service work force (26:23), the Uzzielites are not mentioned.

The duties "away from the temple" performed by the Izharites is unspecified (26:29), other than being distinguished from "the work of the LORD" and "the king's service" (26:30). No doubt, these officials and judges from the Izharites correspond to the "officials and judges" among the four groups of Levites appointed for service by King David (i.e., temple servants, officials and judges, gatekeepers, and temple musicians, 23:4–5). According to Williamson, the expression "officials and judges" points to a judicial role, with the "official" working as a subordinate executive of the "judge."[47] Hashabiah (26:30) and Jeriah (26:31) have similar administrative duties on either side of the Jordan. The "work of the LORD" and the "king's service" (26:30, 32) may include responsibilities related to religious and civil taxation.

The date formula (26:31) suggests these Levitical assignments are made in the last year of David's reign (cf. 1 Kings 2:11; 1 Chron. 29:27). The Chronicler's purpose in reporting the Levitical presence in the public administration of the united monarchy is unclear. He may be attempting to legitimize the role of the Levites in offices of civil service at his own time or calling for their involvement in that role based on the earlier precedent.

Toward bridging contexts. King David's preparations for the building of the Jerusalem temple highlight two great theological continuities between the Old and New Testaments: the theme of leadership and the theme of worship. First Chronicles 26, reporting David's organization of the Levites as gatekeepers for the temple, points toward the contemporary significance of the larger literary unit (21:1–29:9) by reminding us that the lines between the ministry of spiritual service and the duties of civil service are fluid for God's people.

Military and Political Officials (27:1–34)

THE CHAPTER CONTAINS four (possibly unrelated) lists of military and political officials in the service of King David. This segment of the Chronicler's

---

47. Williamson, *1 and 2 Chronicles*, 173.

history has no formal parallels in 1–2 Kings. Like some of the previous chapters in this large pericope (esp. chs. 24–26), the genre is essentially one of register, including a rota (27:2–15) and three rosters (27:16–22a, 23–31, 32–34). Featured in the four lists comprising the unit are the military commanders who serve the king in a monthly rotation (27:1–15), the officers of the tribes of Israel (27:16–24), the stewards of the king's property (27:25–31), and David's personal advisers (27:32–34). The literary source for the rota and the first roster is cited as the "book of the annals of King David" (27:24).

Chapter 26 concluded with certain of the Levites assigned to combined religio-political duties. This chapter moves quite naturally to report the non-Levitical military and administrative personnel serving under King David. It has been noted that the contents of chapters 23–27 are basically outlined in reverse order to the groups David has called together as he transfers power to his son Solomon: "all the leaders of Israel, as well as the priests and Levites" (23:2). All this is in keeping with the Chronicler's theme of demonstrating the support of "all Israel" for Solomon as David's successor and as the one to build the Lord's temple.

The contemporary reader may question the Chronicler's tedious description of the governmental organization of David's monarchy. His own audience may have raised a similar cry for relevance, especially since the Persian overlords prohibited any organized military presence among their vassals. Certainly, the integration of Hebrew religious and political life is important to the Chronicler, and David's regime is seen as the exemplar of that philosophy, even into the restoration period. More important to the Chronicler, however, is the theological understanding of the God of David as "the LORD Almighty" (lit., "Yahweh of the armies [of heaven]"). Despite lack of political autonomy and the inability to raise a fighting force, God can still be trusted to be a "warrior" for Israel (cf. Ex. 15:3; Deut. 1:30: 3:22).

David's military commanders (27:1–15). The first verse ("This is the list of the Israelites ...") should be understood as the heading to the section treating the divisions of David's army (27:2–15), not the entire chapter. The terms "heads of families" or clan leaders, "commanders of hundreds," and "officers" have connotations associated with military administration in other contexts (cf. Num. 31:14; 1 Sam. 8:12).

The names of the twelve military commanders are listed among David's heroes (11:11–47; cf. 2 Sam. 23:8–39). Despite the clear literary interdependence between these lists of military leaders, numerous variations occur. For example, Jashobeam (27:2) is referred to as a Hacmonite (11:11), while Shammoth the Harorite (11:27) appears as Shamhuth the Izrahite (27:8).[48]

---

48. See the helpful comparative chart of David's tribal officers in Braun, *1 Chronicles*, 259.

Like the Levites, these military units "serve the king" (27:1; cf. 26:30, 32). The Chronicler includes this list of military commanders because these leaders are among the "officials" directly involved in preparations for the building of the temple (28:1).

Rather than a standing army, the military divisions described in 27:2–15 represent a militia or citizen army, perhaps akin to our National Guard. David carefully organizes his army in twelve divisions. Each one is commanded by a seasoned soldier from David's choice corps of "mighty warriors" and consists of 24,000 militia at full strength. Each division is obligated to serve the king's army for one month in a twelve-month relay. The permanent or professional Israelite army is comprised of the Three and the Thirty, along with the Kerethites, Pelethites, and the Gittites (cf. 2 Sam. 15:18; 23:23). The number 24,000 is probably an idealized number, projecting the divisions of the army at full strength (the number compares to that of the Levites assigned to the duties of the temple, 1 Chron. 23:4).

Tribal officers (27:16–24). The exact status of these tribal "officers" (*nagid*) is uncertain (typically tribal leaders were called "elders" [*zaqen*, cf. 11:3]). They are probably David's appointees, but their role in his political administration is unknown. Perhaps they assisted Joab in the census-taking (cf. 21:1–7), though Selman discounts the idea since Levi and Benjamin are included in the list even though they are excluded from the census (21:6).[49] Attempts to demonstrate that the Chronicler is seeking to connect David's census (27:23–24) with the Mosaic census of Israel in Numbers in order to show David's census in a better light are unconvincing.[50] This reference to "officers over the tribes" may indicate that the shift toward a centralized bureaucracy actually begins with David rather than with Solomon (cf. 1 Kings 4:7–28).

The brief but important paragraph explaining why no census statistics are recorded for the tribes of Israel in the book of the annals of King David (27:23–24) is significant for two reasons. (1) The report of Joab's failure to complete the census is not an effort by the Chronicler to transfer blame from David to Joab. Rather, the writer assumes the audience's knowledge of the parallel account in Samuel. The record notes Joab's aversion to the task and God's judgment against David and Israel for the king's presumption in equating political strength with the size of his military forces (2 Sam. 24:3, 10; cf. 1 Chron. 21:3, 7–8). Apparently Joab recognized more clearly than David that "no king is saved by the size of his army" (Ps. 33:16; cf. 147:10).

49. Selman, *1 Chronicles*, 246.
50. E.g., Williamson, *1 and 2 Chronicles*, 175–76; cf. the rebuttal by Selman, *1 Chronicles*, 246–47.

(2) Implicit in the reference to the Abrahamic covenant to make Israel as numerous as the stars in the sky is the sovereignty of God in "growing" Israel as a nation (cf. Gen. 12:2). David has compromised God's rule over Israel because, as Selman has observed, "any unauthorized census could limit Israel's faith and God's freedom."[51]

The order of the tribal list is unique in the Old Testament, although the register has some correspondence to previous enumeration of the Hebrew tribes (e.g., 2:1–2; cf. Num. 1:20–22). This list differs from the Chronicler's earlier tribal register in several respects: inserting the tribe of Levi and the tribe of Aaron (1 Chron. 27:17), placing Naphtali in Dan's position (27:19), substituting the half-tribes of Ephraim and Manasseh for Joseph (27:20–21a), and omitting the tribes of Gad and Asher (presumably to maintain the number of the Hebrew tribes at twelve).[52]

The reference to the tribe of Aaron headed by Zadok is an anomaly in the Old Testament. More than an attempt by the Chronicler to enhance the status of the tribe of Levi and the Aaronic family, this reference may represent developments in the counting of the tribes stemming from the Chronicler's own time as a result of the impact of the Babylonian exile on the Israelite tribal system. David has no brother named Elihu in the Chronicler's genealogy of Jesse's family (27:18; cf. 2:13–15). Either Elihu represents Eliab (as in the LXX) or Elihu is the eighth son of Jesse not mentioned in the Chronicler's genealogy (cf. 1 Sam. 16:10–11; 17:12).

The king's overseers (27:25–31). A portion of the revenue necessary to meet the expenses of the bureaucracy established by King David is generated by income from crown properties. These royal estates may have been acquired as a result of military conquest, appropriated through formal negotiation (e.g., David's purchase of Araunah's threshing floor, ch. 21), or in some cases even confiscated illegally (cf. Ahab and Naboth's garden, 1 Kings 21).

Material wealth is not only necessary to offset expenditures of the centralized government, but also it enhances the king's prestige. Generally, the Old Testament sees such wealth as a sign of God's blessing on the king's reign, although the Mosaic provision for kingship prohibited the amassing of large treasuries by the king (Deut. 17:17). Naturally these crown properties need responsible supervision, and the twelve officials named as overseers are in keeping with the pattern used by David in the administration of both the religious and the political sectors. With the exception of Azmaveth (1 Chron. 27:25; cf. 11:33), the twelve individuals named as overseers of crown properties are otherwise unknown in the Old Testament.

---

51. Selman, *1 Chronicles*, 247.

52. See the helpful comparative chart of Hebrew tribal lists in Braun, *1 Chronicles*, 260.

The "storehouses" or treasuries (cf. 26:15, 17, 20) are royal warehouses located in Jerusalem (implied in 27:25a) and in the outlying districts (27:25b). The phrase "towns, the villages and the watchtowers" (27:25) is unique in the Old Testament and indicates an intricate network of royal storage facilities moving outward from heavily populated areas to the open fields. No doubt the perishables are distributed or sold as necessary, while other goods may have been garnished against famine or military siege. David's wealth is apparently garnered from the breadth of his kingdom, from the Shephelah or "western foothills" (NIV, 27:28) to the plain of Sharon (27:29), perhaps as far north as Jezreel ("valleys," 27:29).

The diversified range of agricultural and pastoral activities sponsored by the king are striking and suggest a far more extensive administrative system in place under David than is sometimes recognized. The overseers may be distinguished in four categories: the treasurers (27:25), the overseer of agriculture (27:26), the overseers of wine and oil (27:27–28), and the overseers of livestock (27:29–31). It is unclear whether the duties of the treasurers include oversight of the taxes paid by the general populace to the crown.[53]

David's advisers (27:32–34). This list of David's personal advisers is usually contrasted with the registers delineating the king's public counselors and the official members of his royal cabinet (cf. 18:14–17; also 2 Sam. 8:15–18; 20:23–26). Although there is some overlap in the membership of the two groups of advisers, David's personal counselors are those "influential persons in the immediate entourage of the king."[54]

It seems clear that the contents of the roster spans the long reign of King David. Jonathan ("David's uncle") and Jehiel are otherwise unknown figures (27:32). Attempts to connect Jonathan with Saul's son Jonathan are unconvincing (this despite the fact that the Heb. word *"dod"* [NIV "uncle"] may be translated "friend"). Jonathan died before David became king, so there would be little point in including him in the list of royal personal advisers (cf. 2 Sam. 1:4). Ahithophel is mentioned as one of David's counselors (1 Chron 27:33; cf. 2 Sam. 15:31); he later defected to Absalom during his rebellion against David (2 Sam. 16:20). Ahithophel committed suicide when his counsel to pursue the retreating David was rejected by the usurper king (2 Sam. 17:23). Hushai remained loyal to David as a political adviser, and he is here called "the king's friend" (1 Chron. 27:33; cf. 2 Sam. 15:37; 16:16). This expression is probably a formal title for a trusted sage; the position has parallels in the Egyptian royal court.

---

53. Japhet, *I and II Chronicles*, 479.
54. Williamson, *1 and 2 Chronicles*, 177.

Jehoiada son of Benaiah is unknown (27:34), but Benaiah son of Jehoiada is known as one of the commanders of David's army (27:5; cf. 11:22–24; 18:17). It is possible that this Jehoiada is the son of Benaiah. Abiathar the priest had a long-standing reputation as David's close associate (1 Sam. 22:20–23), but he later fell out of favor with Solomon for his support of Adonijah as David's successor (cf. 1 Kings 1:7). Joab, the commander of David's army (1 Chron. 27:34), is a relative but not necessarily a friend of David (cf. 2 Sam. 2:18). David never forgave him for killing Abner and Absalom, yet he apparently needed the general's military leadership and advice (cf. 1 Kings 2:30–35).

The chapter concludes the description of the structure and key personnel of David's administration. Beyond the inauguration of governmental organization by David, the real purpose of chapters 23–27 for the Chronicler is the important message that "all Israel" is behind the king in his plans to build the temple.

Toward bridging contexts. King David's preparations for building the Jerusalem temple highlight two great theological continuities between the Old and New Testaments: the theme of leadership and the theme of worship. First Chronicles 27, delineating the military and political organization of David's kingdom, points toward the contemporary significance of the larger literary unit (21:1–29:9) by reiterating the importance of competent leadership in all domains of life—the religious, sociopolitical, and military. The Chronicler's focus on leadership in Israel anticipates the time when God will raise up a "righteous Branch" from David's line to do what is just and right as the Shepherd of Israel (Jer. 33:15; Ezek. 34:23–24).

Architectural Plans for the Temple (28:1–21)

THIS CHAPTER REPORTS three speeches by David: the summons to the officials of Israel (28:1–8), the formal transfer of power to Solomon (28:9–10), and instructions for building the temple (28:11–21). King David turns his attention to the issue of succession to the throne once he has finished organizing the Levites (chs. 23–26) and appointing military and administrative leaders (ch. 27). His earlier private charge to his son Solomon (22:6–16) is now made public.

The emphasis on the theme of obedience to God's law and the exhortation to "be strong and courageous" (28:20) echoes the commissioning of Joshua by Moses as his successor (cf. Deut. 31:7–9; 32:44–47). Two distinct threads tie the chapter together: (1) the stress placed on obedience by the leadership of Israel, both to God and to Solomon as David's successor (1 Chron. 28:7–8, 21), and (2) the understanding that the temple-building project is really a divine initiative (cf. 28:2, 10, 12, 19).

David's charge to the leaders of Israel (28:1–8). It is unclear exactly how this assembly of Israelite officials (28:1) compares with other reports of administrative personnel summoned to Jerusalem in this larger unit of the Chronicler's history (chs. 22–29). This congress of leaders is probably distinct from the "whole assembly" in 29:1 since the "people" were a part of that larger gathering (see 29:9). The summons to all the officials of Israel echoes the earlier call for the gathering of the priests and Levites and is a literary device intended to indicate the resumption of an earlier narrative (cf. 1 Chron. 23:2).[55] This may suggest that the leaders congregated here are the same officials mustered earlier to support Solomon in the building of the temple (22:17–19). The list of officials includes those leaders mentioned in chapter 27 as well as the king's sons and brave warriors (cf. 29:24).

The plural imperative verb forms encasing David's first address indicate that the speech is directed to all the "officials of Israel" (28:2–8; e.g., "listen to me," v. 2; "be careful to follow," v. 8). The pastoral heart of David as Israel's shepherd-king is seen in his appeal to the leaders of Israel as "my brothers" and the citizens of Israel as "my people" (28:2).

The opening lines of David's speech are a historical summary of sorts, outlining his aspirations for building Yahweh's temple (28:2–3). The expressions "house ... of rest" for the temple and "footstool" for the ark of the covenant are found only in Psalm 132 and Chronicles (though cf. also Isa. 66:1). Clearly, Psalm 132 is important to the Chronicler because it contains reflections about David's restless ambition to build a sanctuary for God. The addition of 132:8–9 to the end of Solomon's prayer of dedication for the temple (2 Chron. 6:41–42) is further evidence of the Chronicler's interest in this song of ascent.

The royal footstool (28:2) is a symbol of a king's authority, a symbol of the peaceful rest enjoyed by his kingdom, and a sign of humble loyalty to the monarch on the part of his subjects. By means of this symbol the Chronicler recognizes that Israel's "rest," whether in David's time or his own, is entwined with God's restful presence among his people. God's rejection of David as the builder of his temple because he is a warrior repeats information previously reported in David's private charge to Solomon as his successor (cf. 22:8–9). The temple will be built by a "man of peace and rest" (22:9).

It is widely agreed that the next segment of David's speech to the officials of Israel serves to legitimize his dynasty both retrospectively and prospectively. By way of the past, David traces his lineage to the tribe of Judah, the tribe given the "scepter" in Jacob's blessing of his sons (cf. Gen. 49:8–12). By

---

55. An example of what Williamson (*1 and 2 Chronicles*, 179) calls "repetitive resumption" (cf. 15:11).

way of the future, David points to the selection of Solomon as his successor (no doubt with allusions to the Davidic covenant announced by Nathan the prophet, 2 Sam. 7; 1 Chron. 17). Indeed, God's choice of Solomon from among David's many sons makes his divine election all the more remarkable (1 Chron. 28:5; David had nineteen sons, see 3:1–9).

The emphasis on Solomon as the "chosen ... son" among David's children leads naturally to the understanding that God's kingdom and David's kingdom are inseparably linked. In one sense, God "adopts" Solomon as his own son (28:6), and the Davidic throne is also the "throne of the kingdom of the LORD over Israel" (28:5). Hints of this relationship between God and the Israelite king are already embedded in Nathan's oracle establishing Davidic kingship (17:14). As Selman has observed, with the disappearance of the Davidic monarchy, the temple remains "the chief symbol of the continuing reality of the kingdom of the Lord" for the Chronicler and his audience—hence his emphasis on the personnel and the worship rituals associated with that institution.[56] Perhaps most important as David "passes the baton" to his son Solomon, he exhorts Israel to look to God for their hope and help—not to himself or even his dynasty (28:8).

David commissions Solomon (28:9–10). After his charge to all the "officials" of Israel, David shifts his attention to his son Solomon (28:9–10). The public transfer of power, accomplished "in the sight of all Israel" (28:8), completes the succession ritual begun with David's private charge to his son (22:11–13). Both admonitions link Solomon's success to his obedience to God's law, and both urge the new king to "be strong." The king's general exhortation to obedience continues that thematic emphasis in 28:9 and is followed by the specific command to build the Lord's temple (28:10).

The expression "God of your father" (singular in 28:9) is unusual (prompting the LXX to insert the plural "your fathers," in reference to the Hebrew patriarchs). The singular "your father" is preferable here because David's reference to himself probably alludes to the covenant of kingship God has granted him and his descendants. It seems only natural, as Solomon inaugurates that promised dynasty as David's successor, that the God of that covenant be acknowledged as well.

Selman has noted that God's "seeking" (28:9) may be understood in two different senses. (1) God "searches" (or "seeks," *drš*) every heart and tests human motives. (2) Beyond this, God "seeks" people so that he may be found by them. Rather than an invitation to repentance, Selman understands this as an invitation to action because Solomon will not be alone in his endeavor.[57]

---

56. Selman, *1 Chronicles*, 251.
57. Ibid., 252.

The Chronicler's understanding of Solomon's divine election to the Davidic throne is unusual in that he is the only Old Testament writer to apply the word "chosen" (*bḥr*) to Solomon (28:10). The repetition of God's prerogative in choosing Solomon is significant as it serves to validate the Davidic covenant (2 Sam. 7; 1 Chron. 17) and legitimize the new king's rule (28:5, 6, 10; 29:1). It has been noted that all those individuals "chosen" by God to fill leadership positions in the earlier Old Testament era did so by means other than those established by socially accepted convention—except Solomon.[58] There is a sense, however, in which Solomon's accession is also out of the ordinary in that he is not David's oldest living son and hence is not the logical heir to the throne (Adonijah is the natural successor, cf. 1 Kings 1:5).

We learn that Solomon is obedient to the command of building the Lord's temple. Regrettably, however, he is less than "wholehearted" in his devotion to God (cf. 1 Kings 11:4, 6). Ultimately it is his "divided heart" that leads to a "divided" Israelite monarchy.

Transfer of the temple plans (28:11–21). David's concluding speech in this chapter treating the issue of succession to the throne of Israel is addressed to Solomon. David's primary concern is the transfer of plans for the temple to its builder.

The detailed instructions handed over to Solomon deal with temple architecture (28:11–12), temple personnel (28:13), temple furnishings (28:14–19), and the final commissioning of Solomon as the crown prince (28:20–21). The influence of the tabernacle narrative is clearly evident in the vocabulary and theology of the passage. For example, the word "plan" (*tabnit*) is the term used to describe the pattern given by God for the construction of the tabernacle; it is found four times in the section (28:11, 12, 18, 19; cf. Ex. 25:9, 40). In fact, the word forms an inclusio or envelope as it begins and ends the passage outlining the transfer of plans for the temple (1 Chron. 28:11, 19). For the Chronicler, the temple is the continuation of all that the tabernacle represented in Israelite religion, and David plays a role similar to that of Moses as God's agent in establishing the institution.

The exact nature of the plans and instructions David gives to Solomon for the execution of the temple building project is unknown. It seems clear they are written plans, probably sketches or blueprints of sorts containing specific directions (28:19). Since the actual floor plan of the temple sanctuary proper is similar to the dimensions of the tabernacle, the plans most likely deal with issues related to the permanence of this structure in contrast to

58. According to one summary of the use of the term "election" in the Old Testament; see George E. Mendenhall, "Election," *IDB*, 2:76–82.

325

the portable tabernacle. In addition, the portico, the anterooms, and the courts are new elements in the construction plans, and they receive primary attention (28:11). The two treasuries are prominently featured in the plans (28:12), most likely because they were cited previously in connection with the duties of the Levites (26:22–28).

There is some question as to whether the "Spirit" (of God) inspires these plans (28:12, so NIV) or whether these are plans David had "in mind" (so NRSV, understanding "spirit" [*ruaḥ*] as "mind"). In either case, the plans have the imprint of God's revelation as they come "from the hand of the LORD" (28:19). In fact, that expression is a formula denoting divine revelation in prophetic contexts (e.g., Ezek. 1:3; 3:14). A second phrase, "the place of atonement," is used only here outside the Pentateuch. Not only is the temple a "house of prayer" (2 Chron. 6:21, 32), but also it is the place of the Lord's altar and ritual sacrifice (7:12). The temple is a place for forgiveness and healing (7:14), and as such it gives hope to all the guilty—king and nation— that they may be found innocent before the Lord (6:23).

Only one verse (1 Chron. 28:13) is devoted to the temple personnel by way of summary since the Chronicler has previously reported the reorganization of the priests and Levites in considerable detail (chs. 23–26).

The accessories important to the temple rituals include gold and silver vessels and implements (28:14–17). The inventory of gold vessels is listed in more detail in the list of temple furnishings (cf. 2 Chron. 4:7–8, 19–22). The number and type of silver vessels in the collection of temple service ware are unknown, although the items are mentioned generally as part of the booty the Babylonians plundered from the Jerusalem temple (cf. 2 Kings 25:15).

The gold and silver vessels are especially important to the Chronicler because they are among the goods the Persians restored to the Jews when they returned to the land after the Babylonian exile (cf. Ezra 1:7–11). Thus, they are tangible representations of the continuity of postexilic temple worship with preexilic temple worship. But more important, they are tokens of God's faithfulness in preserving and restoring his covenant people.

The table displaying the consecrated bread (28:16) is a notable feature of both the tabernacle and temple furnishings because it symbolizes God's constant presence and provision for his people. The "chariot" (28:18) is unmentioned elsewhere in the listings of tabernacle and temple furnishings. This may simply be a cryptic allusion to the cherubim on the lid of the ark of the covenant as a symbolic chariot of some sort. The idea of the chariot, whether real or symbolic, is the mobility of God's presence—he is always among his people (cf. Ezekiel's vision of God's throne mounted on a carriage or chariot, Ezek. 1).

The ark is given special emphasis in the inventory of temple furnishings by virtue of its placement at the end of the list (28:18). It was the symbol of God's presence with his people, and in its glorious uniqueness it embodied the nature and character of the special relationship he established with Israel through the mediator and lawgiver—his servant Moses.

David's final speech concludes with a third charge to Solomon as his successor to the throne of Israel (28:20–21). As in the case with the private commissioning of Solomon (22:11–13), the key elements of the so-called "induction into office formula" are also present in the public commissioning of King Solomon. Specifically, this formula contains a word of encouragement ("be strong," 28:20a), the promise of divine accompaniment ("my God is with you," 28:20b), and a description of the task at hand (i.e., building the Lord's temple, 28:20c). It is significant that the third and final charge to Solomon as he is inducted into office mentions a supporting cast that includes the religious leaders, the various guilds of craftsmen, the political leaders, and all the people (28:21). The temple is to be a national response to the God of Israel by his covenant people—not a monument to King David!

Toward bridging contexts. King David's preparations for building the Jerusalem temple highlight two great theological continuities between the Old and New Testaments: the theme of leadership and the theme of worship. This last full chapter outlining David's preparations for the temple points to the contemporary significance of the larger literary unit (21:1–29:9) by offering us the sober reminder that all human efforts expended to build the temple are designed to enthrone Yahweh on the praise of Israel (Ps. 22:3), not to build a monument to King David.

Gifts for Temple Construction (29:1–9)

KING DAVID'S THIRD and final speech to the "whole assembly" of Israel is similar in tone and theme to his earlier speeches reported by the Chronicler (22:2–19; 28:1–21). In terms of literary structure, David's speech comprises the first half of the unit (29:1–5) and the response of the people the second half (29:6–9). The event of David's farewell to Israel lasts two days (cf. 29:21), and the purpose of the assembly is to receive gifts for the temple and to ratify Solomon's succession to the throne.

In David's first two speeches the emphasis was placed on Solomon's divine election as the next king of Israel, while the theme of David's preparations for the temple was secondary (cf. 22:5–10; 28:4–5). The themes in this last speech are similar, but the emphasis changes. God's election of Solomon as Israel's king is now assumed, and the preparations for building the temple are now the focal point. Thus, David's final speech propels the narrative forward to the central thrust of the Chronicler's history: the reign of Solomon and the building of Yahweh's temple.

David's speech (29:1–5). David's exhortation to the people to fully support Solomon, given his youth and inexperience, echoes concerns in the king's first speech (cf. 22:5). The first speech contained a general call to the leaders and the people to support Solomon by devoting themselves to God (22:19). This third speech provides the tangible means to demonstrate their devotion to God and support for the crown prince Solomon—sacrificially giving of their material resources to the temple building fund.

The parallels between the giving of the Israelites for the building of the Mosaic tabernacle and the Solomonic temple are widely recognized. For example, Braun has noted that the lists of building materials secured for the building of the tabernacle and the temple are nearly identical (although the exact meaning of several of the terms for semiprecious and precious gemstones remains uncertain, cf. Ex. 25:3–7; 35:5–9, 22–28).[59] Selman, however, has effectively demonstrated that there are sufficient differences between the two events to clearly establish the independence of each account.[60] The identification of the gold given by David as "gold of Ophir" (29:4) probably refers as much to the quality of the gold as to its source of origin (note the parallelism with "refined silver"). As with the tabernacle, only the best of natural and human resources are to be given for the construction of Yahweh's earthly sanctuary.

David's speech includes several unusual terms, each one highlighting a theological truth important to the transition of power from father to son. The word translated "palatial structure" (*birah*, 29:1) is used to describe a citadel or a fortress elsewhere in the Old Testament (e.g., Neh. 2:8; Est. 1:2). Only the Chronicler uses the expression as a synonym for the temple (1 Chron. 29:1, 19). The word is an apt reminder to Solomon and the people that the kingdom belongs to God and that he is the one enthroned over Israel.

A second word, "personal treasures" (*segullah*, 29:3), is typically used to describe Israel as God's "special possession" (e.g., Ex. 19:5). This "treasure" is highly valued personal property of the king; this cache was extremely important to rulers in the biblical world because it was kept in reserve as insurance against unforeseen political misfortunes or natural calamities. David's example of selfless giving in the yielding of goods stored for his own personal security becomes the catalyst for the generous outpouring of gifts for the temple project from the leaders and the people. As McConville observes, "often the extent to which we are prepared to put at risk our material well-being is a measure of the seriousness with which we take our discipleship."[61]

---

59. Braun, *1 Chronicles*, 279–80.
60. Selman, *1 Chronicles*, 258–59.
61. McConville, *I and II Chronicles*, 103.

Last, the repetition of the verbal root meaning "to offer voluntarily" (*ndb*) introduces a key theme in the entire chapter (cf. 29:5, 6, 9, 14, 17). The word often denotes freewill gifts and offerings, giving that is not required but prompted by a willing heart or spirit (e.g., Ex. 25:2; 35:21). Here in David's speech, the idea of a voluntary offering is applied to the *giver* as an act of devotion and consecration to God—not *the gift* (1 Chron. 29:5). Much after the pattern of the Old Testament priesthood, David calls for the whole assembly, leaders and people alike, to freely offer themselves to God (cf. Ex. 28:41; 29:9). The issue is not the amassing of glittering jewels and precious metals, but the pouring of themselves as God's people into building the temple as a symbol of the wholehearted worship that will soon take place in that sanctuary. This is one way the Israelites can pledge themselves to God as a kingdom of priests (cf. Ex. 19:6).

The people's response (29:6–9). Several themes important to the Chronicler are knit together in the response of the Israelites to David's speech. The first is that of unity among the leadership of the various Hebrew administrative structures. The clan and tribal leaders, political officials, and military officers are of a single mind in responding to the king's challenge to give to the temple building fund (29:6a; the same leaders registered by name previously in ch. 27). A second emphasis is that of a charitable attitude—they "give willingly" (29:6b). It is a proven leadership principle that generosity needs an example (e.g., note how often the "matching gift" of a donor is used to spur philanthropic giving). The open-handed giving of Israelite leaders serves as an inducement for a similar response on the part of the people. Sadly, this kind of generosity is not always seen in later Hebrew kingship (e.g., Elijah rebuked King Ahab for his greed, 1 Kings 21:18–19; Micah condemned leaders who rendered judgment for a bribe, Mic. 3:11).

The quantities of precious metals given by the leaders of Israel are enormous (about 190 tons plus another 185 pounds of gold and about 375 tons of silver, cf. the NIV text notes). These contributions nearly double the gifts of gold and silver made by David (29:4), no doubt booty taken from his military campaigns (110 tons of gold and 260 tons of silver, cf. the NIV text notes). The precious metals are gathered for two purposes: to panel the interior walls of the temple and to provide raw materials for the implements cast by the craftsmen (29:4–5; cf. 1 Kings 6:20–22). Japhet dismisses the extravagant numbers as "typological," but Selman correctly cautions that it is impossible to fully understand the implications of the Chronicler's figures, given our historical distance from the event.[62] One thing is clear: The Israelites honor God with their wealth since it all belongs to him anyway (Prov. 3:9; cf. Job 41:11).

---

62. Japhet, *I and II Chronicles*, 507; Selman, *1 Chronicles*, 258.

The term *daric* (29:7) is a Persian loanword. The *daric* was a Persian coin in use at the time of the Chronicler's writing. The use of anachronism was an intentional practice at times on the part of ancient historians. This literary device allows the writer to bring greater clarity to a report by updating a later audience with contemporary equivalents. Today Bible translators often employ the same approach in expressing ancient measures in terms of modern equivalents. For example, the biblical measure of distances between sites is typically rendered in contemporary equivalents (cf. Luke 24:13 [NIV], where "sixty stadia" = "seven miles").

Jehiel (29:8) is a Levite of the clan of Gershon (23:8), whose family is linked to the temple treasuries (26:21). The significance of this reference to the temple treasurer should not be overlooked. The gift of administrative oversight, especially financial management, is an important service to the ongoing work of God—whether the temple in ancient Israel or the church in contemporary North America. The role requires scrupulous attention to detail and demands uncompromising integrity. One need only look to Judas, who as a "purser" of sorts stole from the "money bag" of the disciples (John 12:6), or the wave of financial scandals that rocked the "electronic church" during the 1980s. The sin of greed shows no partiality to historical era—the error of Balaam lurks wherever treasures of any sort begin to accumulate.

The voluntary generosity of leaders is contagious in a couple of ways (29:9). (1) The modeling of unselfish behavior prompts similar acts of generosity—reminding us of Paul's exhortation to "give generously ... to the needs of others" (Rom. 12:8). (2) The lavish gifts prompt both king and people to rejoice (1 Chron. 29:9a, c). This spirit of rejoicing characterizes the major religious events reported in Chronicles (cf. 12:40). In fact, the Chronicler has spliced together three closely related themes that are somewhat paradigmatic of Israel's relationship with God: a *pure heart* (cf. 28:9) that prompts *generous giving*, which in turn results in *joy*.

McConville associates the example of selfless giving with the image of God in humanity because "people are closest to God-likeness in self-giving, and the nearer they approach God-likeness the more genuinely and rightly they become capable of rejoicing."[63] The object of the giving must not be overlooked, as leaders and people alike give "to the LORD" (29:9b). The issue for most of us is not one of generosity but rather the direction of our giving—whether that be selfless giving to God and ultimately others or inward-focused self-gratification.

---

63. McConville, *I and II Chronicles*, 103.

Bridging Contexts

CONTINUITIES. One of the Chronicler's concerns is to demonstrate the continuity between the reigns of David and Solomon in the passing of the scepter from father to son. Among the "continuities" identified between the two Davidic generations are the imperative to seek God, the priority of obedience to the Torah of God, and the centrality of the worship of Yahweh alone for the well-being of God's people (cf. 22:11–13; 28:9–10).

What rationale motivates the Chronicler's search for continuity in the story of Solomon's succession to David's throne? Ultimately his interest lies in assuring his audience of the inherent authority, integrity, and goodness of God's sovereign rule of Israel and the nations for his redemptive purposes. This divine sanction was expressed in two forms: in the validation of the successor as God's agent to carry on the office and ministry of his predecessor, and in the authentication of that program of service as God's plan for his people. According to Allen, "the badge of authenticity which the new development must wear is an underlying consistency, whereby the old is not simply repeated but transmuted into the new."[64]

The question is how to illustrate this continuity in the transition from the "old" to the "new." One method the Chronicler uses involves the principle of typology, which "traces between the historical phases of God's revelations correspondences which serve to endorse them as the ongoing work of the same God."[65]

Intertestamental typology is a method of exegesis that establishes historical (and theological) correspondence between Old Testament events, persons, or objects and similar New Testament events, persons, or objects by way of foreshadowing or prototype. Typically, the Old Testament correspondent is identified as the "type"; the New Testament correspondent expressing the Old Testament truth in a greater way is regarded the "antitype." For example, the writer of Hebrews understands the priesthood of Melchizedek in the Old Testament (Gen. 14:17–24; Ps. 110:4) as the prototype of the superior priesthood of Jesus Christ (Heb. 7:1–22). In the same manner, the tabernacle (and later the temple) are symbols or types of the new covenant, foreshadowing Christ's eternal sacrifice for human sin (Heb. 9:6–14).

We might call the Chronicler's principle of typology "*intratestamental* typology," or an innerbiblical exegesis of the Old Testament documents. That is, the Chronicler demonstrates the underlying consistency of the "old" (i.e.,

---

64. Allen, *1, 2 Chronicles*, 186.
65. Ibid.

David's reign) and the "new" (i.e., Solomon's reign) by appealing to earlier precursors as exemplars. Especially striking here are the parallels drawn with the experiences of an earlier pair of Old Testament saints in the transition of leadership. Thus, in describing the preparations for and the construction of the temple of Yahweh, the Chronicler portrays David as a "second" Moses and Solomon as a "second" Joshua.

Specifically, David is prohibited from completing the temple just as Moses was denied the privilege of leading the Hebrews into the land of covenant promise (cf. Num. 20:2–12; 1 Chron. 22:8). Likewise, Solomon exemplifies Joshua in that he, like Joshua, is chosen as a successor privately and then given public acclaim; both are exalted by God, and both lead God's people into an era of "rest" and "blessing." Similarly, Joshua and Solomon both receive the same charge in assuming their leadership roles: "Be strong and courageous" (Deut. 31:7; cf. 1 Chron. 22:13) because "the LORD goes before you" (Deut. 31:8, 23; Josh. 1:5, 9; cf. 1 Chron. 22:11, 16), and "he will never leave you nor forsake you" (Deut. 31:8; Josh. 1:5, 9; cf. 1 Chron. 28:20). Naturally, the contemporary value of this charge for the commissioning of any servant of God entering a new work of ministry is self-evident.

Numerous continuities between the Chronicler's retelling of David's preparations for the building of Yahweh's temple and contemporary Christianity may be identified as well. The report of Satan's "inciting" David to take a census of Israel (1 Chron. 21:1) forces both the ancient and modern reader to consider the idea of theodicy, or the problem of evil and God's relationship to temptation, sin, pain, and suffering. Granted, dark theological mysteries swirl about this topic, yet a certain pattern in the human predicament emerges in the Old and New Testaments. Each individual is tempted when personal desires drag him or her into sin, and it is Satan who incites that evil desire into sin (1 Chron. 21:1; James 1:14–15). When human beings yield to their own sinful desires and succumb to the temptation of Satan, sin is birthed in wicked and godless behavior (cf. Rom. 1:18–25). God has no recourse but to punish evil—although in one sense sin punishes itself because when sin matures, it births death (James 1:15; cf. 1 Chron. 21:7). Like David, we are without excuse before God in our sin, because "God cannot be tempted by evil, nor does he tempt anyone" (James 1:13; cf. 1 Chron. 21:8).[66]

---

66. The Old Testament tends to use terminology that distinguishes "tempting" (Heb. *nasah;* Gk. *peirazo*) from "testing" (Heb. *bahan;* Gk. *dokimazo*). The first set of words tends to have a pejorative connotation in the sense that this tempting or testing is designed to disapprove and ruin one's faith in God. The second set of terms has a more positive connotation in the sense that this testing is designed to approve or build up one's faith in God. Typically, God does not engage in the former, but Satan does. In his providential rule of the created order God is able to overturn the tempting of Satan and use that experience to

A second link between the message of Chronicles and the teaching of the New Testament is the continuity of intercessory prayer resulting in atonement for sin against God and fellow human beings. After his sin of foolishly numbering the people of Israel, David first confesses his own guilt (21:8), and then he and the elders raise intercession for the people of Israel (21:16−17). David's intercession results in atoning for the sin of the census-taking, as evidenced by the staying of the plague of God's judgment against Israel.

There is a great legacy of intercessory prayer among God's people in the Old Testament, beginning with Abraham and continuing with Moses and the prophets (Gen. 18; Ex. 32:30; Dan. 9). That Old Testament heritage is embodied and ultimately realized in the priestly ministry of Jesus Christ (cf. John 17; Rom. 3:25; Heb. 2:17). As ambassadors of Christ, all Christians are encouraged to carry on this ministry of intercession for everyone (2 Cor. 5:20; 1 Tim. 2:1−2).

Both covenants admit no efficacy in the acts of ritual sacrifice accompanying intercessory prayer but regard them as merely external symbols of internal and spiritual realities (cf. Ps. 51:16−17; Heb. 10:3−7). The complex interplay of divine judgment and mercy is bound up in the holiness and righteousness of the character of God. This means God freely pardons sinners because he is gracious and compassionate and slow to anger (Isa. 55:7; cf. Ex. 34:6). Yet God declares he will not leave the guilty unpunished, for he will someday punish sinners (Ex. 34:7; cf. 32:34). This is why the Lord "is to be feared above all gods" (1 Chron. 16:25; Ps. 96:4).

Additional continuities may be found in the nature and character of priestly duty and Levitical ministry. The Chronicler's delineation of the differing tasks among the priests and Levites is not to establish a hierarchy of value in the types of temple service rendered. Rather, his intent is to underscore the dignity and equanimity of all the priestly and Levitical service offered to the Lord. As Allen has noted, a part of the Chronicler's purpose is to call for a "round of applause" for the labors of all the temple ministers.[67] McConville has cogently observed that "the readiness of small and great alike to be subject to the random decrees of the 'lot' (1 Chron. 25:8) is a testimony to a great humility."[68] The repeated emphasis on the organization of

---

encourage faith in the believer (e.g., the story of Job; cf. Jas. 1:12). The Bible admonishes the faithful not to "tempt" (Heb. *nasah*) God out of an unbelieving and rebellious heart (Deut. 6:16), although on occasion he may encourage the righteous to "test" (Heb. *bahan*) him with a view toward bolstering wavering faith (cf. Mal. 3:10). In a similar fashion, according to the book of James, God does not "tempt" anyone (Gk. *peirazo*), but he may use "testing" (Gk. *dokimazo*) to nurture and mature faith and godliness in the believer (James 1:3, 13).

67. Allen, *1, 2 Chronicles*, 158.
68. McConville, *I and II Chronicles*, 92.

the priestly and Levitical divisions and the orderliness of their temple ministry is noteworthy.

The Chronicler also reiterates the skill and ability with which the priests and Levites apply themselves to the tasks of temple service, especially the duties of Levitical singers and musicians. Such order and excellence are inherent to the proper worship of God, given the holiness that marks his impeccable character. Even the commendable trait of a cooperative spirit may be seen in the flexibility of the Levitical corps to adapt to new responsibilities in light of the new demands created by replacing the portable tent-shrine with a permanent sanctuary.

Each of these characteristics of priestly service and Levitical ministry in the Old Testament has its counterpart in the worship and spiritual life of the church. Though there are differing "gifts" yielding a diversity of functions or ministries in the church, all are bestowed by the same Spirit for the common good (1 Cor. 12:4–7). In a fashion somewhat akin to lot-casting, Paul reminds us that these gifts are distributed as God determines (12:11). This reality should prompt a like-minded humility in the Christian as each considers the manifold grace of God in equipping his church for worship and service to the world. His analogy of the interplay of the spiritual gifts in the life of the church to the interdependence of the parts of the body to the intricacies of bodily functions is well known (12:12–26).

In a related matter, Paul instructs the church that much like the temple worship of the Old Testament, the exercise of these gifts of the Holy Spirit in Christian worship must "be done in a fitting and orderly way" (1 Cor. 14:40). In imitation of the polished skill of priestly and Levitical service, Paul encourages the Christian to adopt "the most excellent way" in one's worship of God and service to others—the way of love (12:31b–13:13). Even the adaptability of ministry may be mirrored in the spontaneous prompting of the Spirit as the church gathers for worship, naturally tempered by a careful discerning of the spirits (14:26–28; cf. 1 John 4:1–3).

A final example of continuity between the messages of Chronicles and the New Testament is in David's private charge and public commission to Solomon as his successor to the throne. On both occasions, David admonishes his son to be careful to obey the commandments that the Lord God gave Moses (22:12–13; 28:8). Moses himself summarized the covenant demands of God in one great requirement: "to observe the LORD's commands and decrees" (Deut. 10:13). Here David uses the same verb as Moses, "to observe" (*šmr*), in the sense of guard or keep or pay strict attention to practicing God's decrees. The observance of Yahweh's covenant law is intertwined with other aspects of personal devotion for the Israelite, including repentance, drawing near to God, and the fear of the Lord (Deut. 4:6–8; 13:3–4).

More important, a lifestyle of covenant obedience was a sign of genuine love for the Lord God on the part of the righteous (Deut. 30:19–20). This willful submission to the authority of divine revelation is still an appropriate response of religious devotion to God. In a similar fashion Jesus challenges his own disciples: "If you love me, you will obey what I command" (John 14:15). This response of devotion is the litmus test for certifying the true children of God, for those who know Christ and live in him "obey his commands" (1 John 2:3; 3:24).

Beyond this, two exceptional continuities bridging the message of Chronicles to the message of the rest of the Old Testament and the New Testament require special attention. The theological center (and nearly the literary center) of 1–2 Chronicles is the lengthy reports rehearsing the kingships of David and Solomon. The defining achievement of the reigns of this father and son duo is the temple of Yahweh, with David as the planner and Solomon as the builder. Herein lies those two great theological themes that attract our attention: leadership and worship. We will now take a closer look at these two themes.

LEADERSHIP: A DAVIDIC PARADIGM. Leadership is a matter of universal importance, and effective supervision is essential to the survival of any social group, political organization, or religious institution. The impact of good or bad leadership has been felt by every generation of human history. The same is no less true today—and perhaps more so, given the "global village" that the new communications technologies have created. The challenges confronting effective leadership, however, are timeless because basic human needs remain essentially the same regardless of the historical period. Naturally, successful management principles discovered by leaders in bygone eras are often understood to be transferable as the plethora of self-help books appealing to historical figures as models for today's executives attest.

Biblical characters are frequently among the mix of past heroes and heroines to whom people look as exemplars of a successful leadership "profile." For example, Moses and Nehemiah from the Old Testament are often singled out as "case studies" of effective management styles.[69] The leadership

---

69. For example, see David Baron and Lynette Padwa, *The Management Methods of Moses: 50 Leadership Lessons from the Greatest Manager of All Time* (New York: Pocket Books, 2000); Donald K. Campbell, *Nehemiah: Man in Charge* (Wheaton, Ill.: Victor, 1979); J. I. Packer, *Nehemiah: A Passion for Faithfulness* (Wheaton, Ill.: Crossway, 1995), esp. 69–112 on "Man-Management."

techniques of Jesus himself have been the focus of recent works appealing to New Testament characters as role models for managers.[70]

But no biblical character is more prominent as an example of leadership than King David. In a previous essay, Gary Herion and I explored how the dynamic variable of individual faith in Yahweh confounded the management functions of planning, organization, direction, and control during David's reign.[71] Another study has examined the correlation between the modes of disclosure or "truth telling" and the shift in the social organization of Israel under the role of David and Solomon (as a monopoly of power and wealth emerged).[72] A third example has investigated David from the perspective of multicultural leadership, since he attempted "to balance native Hebrew cultural concepts of inspired religious authority with the more 'pagan' concepts of human political authority that pervaded the royal administration of Jerusalem."[73]

One example of such an appeal to the life of a biblical character for leadership principles is Calvin Miller's helpful, but perhaps forgotten, essay on Christian leadership based on the Old Testament story of King David.[74] Miller identified practical principles of leadership from the life of David based on the biblical records of Samuel and Kings. I have summarized the salient points of each of his leadership principles below.

(1) Leaders inherently possess strength of character and tend to be "omnicompetent" in terms of capabilities. The gifts of intellect, will, and skill innately possessed by these individuals are projected to others as a sort of "charisma." The term may be difficult to define, but people generally recognize charisma when they see and experience it. David had charisma. More important than his abilities, however, was the empowerment of the Holy Spirit in his life (1 Sam. 16:13). *Biblical leadership is "Spirit-led" leadership.* David

70. For example, Laurie Beth Jones, *Jesus, CEO: Using Ancient Wisdom for Visionary Leadership* (New York: Hyperion, 1995); Bob Briner, *The Management Methods of Jesus* (Nashville: Thomas Nelson, 1996).

71. Andrew E. Hill and Gary A. Herion, "Functional Yahwism and Social Control in the Early Israelite Monarchy," *JETS* 29 (1986): 277–84.

72. Walter Brueggemann, *David's Truth in Israel's Imagination and Memory* (Philadelphia: Fortress, 1985).

73. *Hartwick Classic Leadership Cases: King David* (Oneonta, N.Y.: Hartwick Humanities in Management Institute, 1994), 6. More generally on the life of David, see Gene Edwards, *A Tale of Three Kings* (Wheaton, Ill.: Tyndale, 1982); Eugene H. Peterson, *Leap Over a Wall: Earthy Spirituality for Everyday Christians* (New York: HarperCollins, 1998).

74. Calvin Miller, *Leadership* (Colorado Springs, Co.: NavPress, 1987); for a similar study stressing the importance of character formation among those in leadership positions, see Richard D. Phillips, *The Heart of an Executive: Lessons in Leadership from the Life of David* (New York: Doubleday, 1999).

knew this truth well, having seen the disintegration of Saul as king when the Spirit of the Lord left him (1 Sam. 16:14). This is why David pleaded with God to graciously permit the Holy Spirit to remain with him as Israel's leader when his sins concerning Uriah and Bathsheba were exposed by the prophet Nathan (Ps. 51:11; cf. 2 Sam 12:7).

(2) Leaders have a sense of self-esteem and self-confidence that enables them to deal with difficult circumstances and endure the criticism of others. Note David's persistence with his brother Eliab and other members of the Israelite militia in mounting some type of response to the taunts of the Philistine champion Goliath (1 Sam. 17:28–31). David's positive self-image was in effect a "God-competence," rooted in obedience to the word of the Lord (a lesson learned from the negative example of King Saul, cf. 15:22). This is why David's primary concern was God's reputation, not his own (cf. 17:46–47).

(3) Leaders develop a matrix of relationships that provide the array of "people resources" necessary for success. Miller identifies six categories of friends, each an important link in a leader's network of relationship. These categories of friendship include convenience friends, special-interest friends, historical friends, crossroads friends, cross-generational friends, and close friends.[75] Close friends are indispensable to leaders in times of crisis. David's covenant of friendship with Saul's son Jonathan is well known (1 Sam. 18:3–4; 20:8). What is impossible to assess is the course David's life may have taken had his covenant friend not died in battle against the Philistines on Mount Gilboa (31:2). As one reads the rest of the narrative of David's life, it appears that he never again had a "close friend" to rely on—a covenant friend like Jonathan.

(4) Leaders are men and women of vision, and where there is no vision people "cast off restraint" (NIV) or "perish" (KJV; Prov. 29:18). Often an idea or vision for future direction emerges from an "axial point," a crisis situation that opens a new vista and redefines a person's life. A personal dream or a national vision has the power to enthuse, and "enthusiasm is the energy that drives every successful idea."[76] The vision of leadership also unites people behind a common cause as well as provides a focus for leadership.

David well understood the importance of vision, as demonstrated in his conquest of Jerusalem (2 Sam. 5:6–10). That victory legitimized King David and propelled Israel into nationhood. It also became the impetus for David's lifelong quest to build a sanctuary for Yahweh in the very city that God helped him capture (cf. 1 Chron. 22:1).

---

75. Miller, *Leadership*, 32.
76. Ibid., 41.

1 Chronicles 21:1–29:9

(5) Leaders must be decisive. One example of this principle from the life of David is his decision to bring the ark of the covenant to Jerusalem (2 Sam. 6). That decision was the defining moment of David's kingship in one sense because it transformed Jerusalem from the city of David to the city inhabited by the living God (2 Sam. 5:9; cf. Ps. 48:1). Despite the initial setback in transporting the ark into Jerusalem, David persevered—a reminder that sometimes decisive leaders must be willing to postpone crucial decisions (cf. 2 Sam. 6:6–7, 12). The example of David teaches us that decision-making begins and ends with God because he relied on God's "good Spirit" to lead him on level ground as king of Israel (Ps. 143:10).

Organization is foundational to successful leadership. According to Miller, organizing for leadership requires the concepts of defining, structuring, and motivating.[77] *Defining* is formulating a plan for success or charting a course to move an entity from one level of achievement to a higher tier of performance. *Structuring* is presenting and enacting the project or idea, leading to completion. *Motivating* others to catch the vision or support the project is essential to successful leadership. There are numerous ways to motivate people to follow one's leadership, but affirmation, participation, and modeling are the most effective approaches to encourage others. This section of 1 Chronicles (21:1–29:9) offers an excellent illustration of David's ability to define the vision (i.e., build a house for Yahweh), structure the plan to accomplish the vision, and motivate others to implement and fulfill the vision.

(7) Miller reminds us that although "politics" are inevitably part of the leadership landscape, the word only secondarily emphasizes competition between groups or individuals for power and leadership.[78] Godly leadership practices the "politics of grace," as David demonstrated to the house of Saul in his treatment of Mephibosheth—the son of Jonathan (2 Sam. 9:7).

(8) Effective leadership shares the visibility and responsibility of governance through the delegation of workload to capable subordinates. Moses learned this principle from his father-in-law, Jethro (Ex. 18:21–22). David clearly understood the benefits of delegating authority to others as evidenced by his roster of cabinet appointees (2 Sam. 23:8–17; 1 Chron. 18:14–17). Paul applied this principle in his instructions to Timothy to entrust the message of Christ to others who were reliable (2 Tim. 2:2). Naturally, with the delegation of authority comes accountability—as we learn from Jesus' parable of the talents (Matt. 25:24–30).

(9) Leaders are prone to abuse their power, given the natural inclinations of fallen people in a fallen culture. David was no exception, as his sordid

---

77. Ibid., 60.
78. Ibid., 70.

338

affair with Bathsheba reveals (2 Sam. 11). Servant leaders must always be mindful that they are the beneficiaries of a gracious divine appointment. Would that David had recalled words similar to his later confession, "but who am I?" (29:14), on the fateful day he happened to spy Bathsheba. Yet, David shows us that a servant-leader can survive a grave mistake, an error of judgment, or a near fatal flaw because of God's mercy. The act of genuine repentance before God, the turning away from sin back to a habit of obedience to God in humility and contrition, results in restoration—even to a place of leadership (cf. Ps. 51). Here again, the words of Jesus remind us that leaders who demonstrate a spirit of forgiveness may receive a similar spirit of charity when they lapse (cf. Matt. 7:12; 18:28).

(10) Those who lead must learn to cope with difficult people—since people are people and nothing more. Fortunately, God is God and nothing less. The Gibeonites were "difficult people" for King David (2 Sam. 21:1–14). Their story reminds us that sometimes leadership must bury "ghosts of the past" created by the misdeeds of their predecessors, lest their "haunting" undo the work of the present and the plans for the future. All the more reason for leaders to have a "sense of history" as they discharge the duties of their position. According to Miller, the key to handing difficult people is twofold: (a) to understand the difference between *difficult people* and *people with difficulties;* (b) to respond to the difficult person in love and deal with him or her in private (rather than berating or rebuking in a public setting).[79]

(11) Effective leadership must be able to flex, adapt, and adjust because "change happens." Life, society, and organizations are not static. The ability of a leader to adapt to changing times and situations is a direct measure of the "currency" of his or her leadership. One example of adaptation in David's role as Israel's king was the shift from "participation" in battle as "commander-in-chief" to "modeling" his generalship behind the "front lines" (cf. 2 Sam. 11:1; 21:15, 17).

Some are quick to criticize David for remaining in Jerusalem and directing the military campaign from afar, since the move led to his adulterous affair with Bathsheba. Yet, David's wisdom in accepting the counsel of his senior military officer Joab to stay behind is evident. The nation of Israel is still in a formative stage, and the survival and long-term stability of the empire are dependent on David's leadership as the "lamp of Israel" (cf. 2 Sam. 21:17). The lack of an appropriate successor to carry on David's legacy at this time in his reign is even more crucial, as the subsequent narrative reveals.

Miller offers four practical suggestions helpful to a flexible management style: the need to address fatigue or burnout in a growing organization,

---

79. Ibid., 106.

identifying and/or grooming sources of good counsel in a growing organization, sharing the "giants to be killed" through strategic delegation of authority, and recognizing the importance for the leader of a growing organization to maintain vital family relationships.[80]

(12) Death is the ultimate "delete key." Miller aptly concludes that "death eliminates the future.... David died on the threshold of other people's futures."[81] Effective leadership must be a bridge-builder to the future for the sake of the future of others and of the survival of the organization, society, vision, or idea that the leader has championed. The final acts of David's kingship included naming his successor and providing that individual with all the resources needed to carry on David's vision for Israel (cf. 21:1–29:9). David built a bridge to the future through Solomon for all Israel for several centuries beyond his own death. Yahweh's temple in Jerusalem was a symbol of God's covenant faithfulness to Israel and a beacon of hope for the righteousness of God to one day overwhelm the world—as captive Daniel's prayer toward Jerusalem through those open windows in Babylon testified (Dan. 6:10).

Worship: A Davidic paradigm. King David's epitaph marks him as a worshiper of God par excellence—a person after God's own heart (1 Sam. 13:14; Acts 13:22). What was worship for David and how does he model worship for the Christian and for the church today? Let's take inventory of those items contributing to David's understanding of the proper worship of God as preserved in lyrics of his songs and hymns in the Psalter:

- based on a personal knowledge of God, his essential character, and his basic attributes (e.g., Ps. 23; 25)
- involved a whole-person response to God: mind, emotions, will, bodily movement (e.g., Ps. 35:10)
- reflected in a variety of moods, from joy to lament (e.g., Ps. 13:1–2, 5–6)
- sometimes a casual and spontaneous response and other times formal and planned response (e.g., Ps. 3; 63:2)
- sometimes a private response and sometimes a corporate response (e.g., Ps. 26:12; 63:6)
- ordered by a festival calendar (e.g., Ps. 55:17)
- represented and explained at times in symbols, images, and word pictures (e.g., Ps. 18:2)
- rooted in the revealed word of God (e.g., Ps. 18:30; 33:4; 56:4)
- integrated with music as part of the worship response (e.g., Ps. 33:2–3)

---

80. Ibid., 114–17.
81. Ibid., 120.

- preparation, including confession and repentance, as a prerequisite for worship (e.g., Ps. 15; 24; 51)
- primarily an internal issue, a matter of right heart, attitude, and motive (e.g., Ps. 51:6, 7, 10, 16–17)
- expressed in a variety of rituals, bodily movements, and external actions (e.g., Ps. 20:3; 30:11)

The point here is not to define worship, although David's worship reinforces the basic understanding of worship as a Spirit-led response to what we believe God has said and done. Nor is the intent to compile a comprehensive list of characteristics that present a complete profile of David as a worshiper of God. Rather, we seek to distill principles from the worship responses of David that will inform our own worship response to God and his mighty deeds of deliverance. As Marva Dawn reminds us, ultimately worship is all about God, as he is both the subject (i.e., our worship is for him and not ourselves) and the object (i.e., our worship is directed toward him) of right worship.[82] King David knew this well.

Robert Webber has argued that any historical or comparative study of the practice of Christian worship must take three essential factors into account: content, structure, and style.[83] Primary among the three is the *content* of Christian worship. The headwaters of Christian worship are found in the worship of the Israelites as recorded in the Old Testament. Hebrew worship and devotion were focused solely on the God of creation (Gen. 1:1–2), the God of covenant relationship (12:1–3), the God of redemptive acts in history (Ex. 12–13), and the God of sovereign rule over the nations (Dan. 2:20–21).

The Israelite exodus from Egypt is the redemptive event of the Old Testament because it was in this act that Yahweh "redeemed" his people (cf. Ex. 15:13; Deut. 7:8: 13:5). Throughout the rest of Old Testament history, Yahweh is known as the One who "brought" Israel out of Egypt (e.g., Ex. 12:51; 13:3; Ps. 80:8; Jer. 2:6). The Passover ritual connected with the Exodus foreshadowed the Christ-event of the New Testament, as Paul affirms that Jesus Christ is "our Passover lamb" (1 Cor. 5:7). More specifically, Christian worship remembers and celebrates the birth, life, death, resurrection, and ascension of Jesus Christ as recorded in the New Testament. The content of Christian worship is nonnegotiable, and Christian worship must be judged by its content, not by its structure or style.

---

82. Marva Dawn, *Reaching Out Without Dumbing Down* (Grand Rapids: Eerdmans, 1989), 76–82; on "David's Kind of Worship," see Sally Morgenthaler, *Worship Evangelism* (Grand Rapids: Zondervan, 1995), 37–38.
83. Robert E. Webber, *Worship Old and New*, rev. ed. (Grand Rapids: Zondervan, 1994), 149.

For more than twenty centuries the Christian church has raised the question of how to *structure* the content of worship. How is worship best ordered so that the story of God's saving work in history is clearly heard and experienced? This means we must deal with "liturgy" in some fashion. The term *liturgy* is an unsettling one for many evangelical Protestants, but this need not be the case. It simply means "the work or service of the people in public worship." All corporate Christian worship is liturgical in one sense in that it organizes the responses of the people to the Christ-event in an order of service. The Old Testament, the New Testament, and church history offer numerous models of worship structure, and human beings remain a vital part of the diverse Christian worship tradition.[84]

The *style* of Christian worship pertains to the atmosphere and environment in which the structure of worship is enacted. Worship style includes such things as the architecture of the worship space, aesthetic expression in art and music, the dress of worship leaders and the congregation, an active versus passive approach to congregational involvement (including the engagement of all the senses in worship), and the nature of the pulpit ministry. The style of Christian worship may be formal or casual, traditional or contemporary.

Worship style is the one aspect of Christian worship most easily influenced by popular culture. It is probably safe to say that most of the "worship wars" in the church today take place on this front—worship style. One helpful response to this struggle to achieve both substance and relevance in Christian worship today is the idea of "blended worship" or the "convergence of styles," in which an array of worship styles are incorporated into the worship experience.[85]

David's example as a worship leader has much to offer to those who minister in similar roles today.[86] The biblical psalms especially provide insight on David's approach to the worship of God. For our purposes, Psalm 62 may be

---

84. On the structure of worship see Andrew E. Hill, *Enter His Courts with Praise!* 50–51, 231–32; Barry Liesch, *The New Worship: Straight Talk on Music and the Church* (Grand Rapids: Baker, 1996), 47–74; Ralph P. Martin, *Worship in the Early Church* (Grand Rapids: Eerdmans, 1974), 130–39; Robert E. Webber, ed., *The Complete Library of Christian Worship;* vol. 1: *The Biblical Foundations of Christian Worship* (Nashville: StarSong, 1993), 123, 137–38; and vol. 2: *Twenty Centuries of Christian Worship* (Nashville: StarSong, 1994), 131–33, 247–48.

85. Robert E. Webber, *Blended Worship: Achieving Substance and Relevance in Worship* (Peabody, Mass.: Hendrickson, 1996).

86. I am indebted to two graduates of the Institute for Worship Studies, Eric Bolger and Heather Hood, for the impetus to explore David's role as a worship leader in ancient Israel (esp. Hood's unpublished paper: "Worship Leading in the New Millennium: Lessons from the Life of David," submitted in partial fulfillment of the requirements for DWS 501: Biblical Foundations and Historical Development of Worship).

effectively mined as a case study in worship leadership with the use of a little imagination.[87]

David understands that worship has a trajectory through two "audiences" before it reaches its primary "target audience"—God himself. This is implicit in his initial focus on himself (Ps. 62:1–7) before his attention shifts to calling the people to "pour out [their] hearts" in worship to God (62:8–10). Finally, God is the ultimate object of the adoration of David and the people (62:11–12). David knows that these steps in process of the worship response to God are vital to preventing worship from degenerating into heartless ritual or crass performance.

As a prelude to leading God's people in worship, the worship leader must first restore a right relationship with God as the exclusive spiritual resource for one's life (note that "salvation," "refuge," and "honor" are found "in God alone" (Ps. 62:1–2, 5–7). This instills confidence in God, not self (note the repetition of "I will never/not be shaken," 62:2, 6). The worship leader is thus enabled, indeed empowered, to exhort the congregation to do the same—thus rejecting society's reliance on status and wealth (62:9–10) for continual and unwavering "trust in him" (v. 8). Once both leader and people have recentered their lives in the absolute trust of God, they are capable of rendering proper worship to him, fully cognizant of his transcendence ("you, O God, are strong," 62:11) and his immanence ("you, O Lord, are loving," 62:12). The reminder that God is the supreme judge of all humanity (62:12) both seals and prompts the worshiper's commitment to "trust in [God] at all times" (62:8).

The worship leader, like a shepherd, knows the basic needs of her or his "flock." One need not be clairvoyant to determine these basic human needs since they are widely perceived as universal concerns.

Drawing from other resources, Marva Dawn has compiled a list of seven fundamental needs of our being: *identity* (i.e., who am I?), *master story* (i.e., how does it all fit together?), *loyalty* (i.e., to whom do I belong?), *values* (i.e., by what shall I live?), *power* (i.e., how can I protect myself?), *meaning* (i.e., what is the purpose of my life?), and *hope* (i.e., why should I go on?).[88] The experienced worship leader realizes that meeting human needs through the worship experience cannot be "canned" in some programmatic formula. Happily, the content and form of biblical worship inherently address life issues. When the redeemed creature properly worships the Creator and the Redeemer, the needs of our being are fully met. Meeting human need is *not the goal* of worship, but one of the *results* of true worship.

---

87. The idea for using Ps. 62 as a paradigm for worship leadership germinated from a sermon by John Casey, senior pastor at Blanchard Road Alliance Church (Wheaton, Ill.), entitled "How to Worship God in Trouble" and given on March 5, 2000.

88. Marva Dawn, *A Royal "Waste" of Time* (Grand Rapids: Eerdmans, 1999), 23–36.

An examination of Psalm 62 indicates that David intuitively deals with similar basic human needs in his song of trust. David's *identity* and confidence as a man (62:3) and a spiritual being (note the word "soul") is bound up in God alone (62:1, 5). The idea that David's "honor" or reputation (62:7) is tied to God's reputation casts David's identity as a creature of dignity made in God's image. That *imago Dei* built into our make-up as persons means we have divinely endowed capacities to worship God and enter into fellowship with him (Gen. 3:8; Isa. 43:7). Like God himself, the worship leader "shows no partiality" and views every individual as a person made in God's image and a potential worshiper of God (2 Chron. 19:7; Acts 10:34).

The *master story* that gives coherence to personal existence and human history is embedded in that word "salvation" (Ps. 62:1, 6). For David, salvation is the record of Israel's deliverance from Egypt and his personal deliverance from political enemies and his own moral failure—his own sin (cf. 3:8; 25:6–11). For the Christian salvation is the record of Christ's atoning work on the cross and personal deliverance from our moral failure by faith in God's effective but mysterious redemptive plan for fallen creation.

The master story is also implied in the fact that "God has spoken" (62:11). The spoken word of God has been inscripturated, and the master story of God is a matter of "public record" in the Bible. Worship celebrates the architect of the "master story"—the triune God. The worship leader, like David, loves God by loving his law (or revealed Word) and "stockpiling" it in his or her heart through reading, prayer, meditation, and memorization (18:1; 19:7–11; 40:8; cf. 119:9–16). The worship leader knows well both the *Master* and his *master story*.

David's *loyalty* is obvious. There is no question as to whom David belongs, as he takes his "rest" (Ps. 62:1) in God as his mighty rock and refuge (62:7). The emphasis on the personal pronoun "my" reinforces David's conviction that he indeed belongs to God (62:1–2, 5–7). David's loyalty to God grows out of his understanding of the idea of *covenant* in the biblical world. A covenant establishes an inviolable relationship between two parties (unlike a contractual relationship). God has pledged himself to be faithful in a covenant relationship, much like a bridegroom to a bride (Jer. 2:2). Both parties guard this sacred trust jealously (Deut. 5:9; Josh. 24:19; Ps. 18:21, 25). The worship leader facilitates the response of covenant loyalty by the worshiper as a part of the worship experience.[89]

David's *values* are exposed by way of negative example in his admonition against trusting in social status, unlawful activity, or wealth to secure iden-

---

89. For this reason the observance of the Lord's Table or the Eucharist is important to Christian worship. It is both a memorial of Christ's atoning work on the cross and an act of covenant renewal on the part of the believer, who rests in that relationship with God established by the cross.

tity and meaning in this life (Ps. 62:9–10). On the positive side, David's values may be seen in "honor" (or a reputation) that is dependent on God (62:7). I believe David understands the "greatest good" taught in the Bible, the *two great commandments*: to love God with our whole person and to love our neighbor as ourselves (Lev. 19:18; Deut. 6:5; cf. Ps. 18:1). The worship leader understands how to translate this into the *two great sacrifices* of the Bible (Heb. 13:15–16): the sacrifice of praise (i.e., worship) and the sacrifice of doing good (i.e., service to others).

David's need for protection against those who use *power* against him (Ps. 62:3–4) is fulfilled in the power or might of his "strong" God (62:11). David understands that worship is a form of spiritual warfare (4:2; 14:1–3; 40:4; 95:3; 96:4). The worship leader must be aware of this cosmic battle as well. Like David, we find empowerment for this "battle" in the ministry of the Holy Spirit (Ps. 51:11; 143:10).[90]

The destination of David's quest for *meaning* and purpose in life is found in a "loving" Lord who "rewards" each person according to the life he or she has lived (Ps. 62:12). What can make life any more meaningful than divine judgment of that life (cf. Eccl. 12:13–14)? David's approach to life anticipates the words of Christ, "Well done ... faithful servant" (Matt. 25:21), because he understood his life as a pilgrimage to "joy in [God's] presence" (Ps. 16:11) and everlasting life "in the house of the LORD" (23:6). The worship leader guides a band of "pilgrims" into the joy of God's presence.

Finally, David's *hope* is not something he manufactures by force of will or cleverness of imagination. Rather, his hope comes from God himself (Ps. 62:5) as a result of his relationship with Yahweh—the name of the covenant-making and covenant-keeping God. David's hope was rooted in his faithful God (25:10; 33:4). The worship leader's task is to help the worshiper encounter the faithful God in worship.

Like David, the worship leader ushers the faithful into the presence of God in corporate worship in order to gratefully respond to what we believe this one, triune God has said and done (as revealed in the Bible). In so doing, the worship leader discharges a high calling, because the act of worship touches the core of our humanity, fulfills the purpose for which we have been created, and prepares us for our "normal employment" in the next life—eternal worship in the heavenly realm.

---

90. On worship as "spiritual warfare" I am attracted to W. Brueggemann's contention that "the act of praise is indeed world-making for the community which takes the act of worship as serious and realistic ... worship is not only constitutive, but inevitably polemical. Praise (of Jesus) insists not only that this is the true world, but that other worlds are false.... The church sings praises not only toward God but against the gods" (*Israel's Praise: Doxology Against Idolatry and Ideology* [Philadelphia: Fortress, 1988], 26–27).

1 Chronicles 29:10–30

DAVID PRAISED THE LORD in the presence of the whole assembly, saying,

"Praise be to you, O LORD,
   God of our father Israel,
   from everlasting to everlasting.
¹¹ Yours, O LORD, is the greatness and the power
      and the glory and the majesty and the splendor,
      for everything in heaven and earth is yours.
   Yours, O LORD, is the kingdom;
      you are exalted as head over all.
¹² Wealth and honor come from you;
      you are the ruler of all things.
   In your hands are strength and power
      to exalt and give strength to all.
¹³ Now, our God, we give you thanks,
      and praise your glorious name.

¹⁴"But who am I, and who are my people, that we should be able to give as generously as this? Everything comes from you, and we have given you only what comes from your hand. ¹⁵We are aliens and strangers in your sight, as were all our forefathers. Our days on earth are like a shadow, without hope. ¹⁶O LORD our God, as for all this abundance that we have provided for building you a temple for your Holy Name, it comes from your hand, and all of it belongs to you. ¹⁷I know, my God, that you test the heart and are pleased with integrity. All these things have I given willingly and with honest intent. And now I have seen with joy how willingly your people who are here have given to you. ¹⁸O LORD, God of our fathers Abraham, Isaac and Israel, keep this desire in the hearts of your people forever, and keep their hearts loyal to you. ¹⁹And give my son Solomon the wholehearted devotion to keep your commands, requirements and decrees and to do everything to build the palatial structure for which I have provided."

²⁰Then David said to the whole assembly, "Praise the LORD your God." So they all praised the LORD, the God of their

fathers; they bowed low and fell prostrate before the LORD and the king.

²¹The next day they made sacrifices to the LORD and presented burnt offerings to him: a thousand bulls, a thousand rams and a thousand male lambs, together with their drink offerings, and other sacrifices in abundance for all Israel. ²²They ate and drank with great joy in the presence of the LORD that day.

Then they acknowledged Solomon son of David as king a second time, anointing him before the LORD to be ruler and Zadok to be priest. ²³So Solomon sat on the throne of the LORD as king in place of his father David. He prospered and all Israel obeyed him. ²⁴All the officers and mighty men, as well as all of King David's sons, pledged their submission to King Solomon.

²⁵The LORD highly exalted Solomon in the sight of all Israel and bestowed on him royal splendor such as no king over Israel ever had before.

²⁶David son of Jesse was king over all Israel. ²⁷He ruled over Israel forty years—seven in Hebron and thirty-three in Jerusalem. ²⁸He died at a good old age, having enjoyed long life, wealth and honor. His son Solomon succeeded him as king.

²⁹As for the events of King David's reign, from beginning to end, they are written in the records of Samuel the seer, the records of Nathan the prophet and the records of Gad the seer, ³⁰together with the details of his reign and power, and the circumstances that surrounded him and Israel and the kingdoms of all the other lands.

Original Meaning

TWO MAJOR PARALLELS in the second-Exodus motif typologically applied to the postexilic restoration of Judah surface in the concluding section of 1 Chronicles. (1) The first we have already examined in the previous chapter, namely, the gifts given by the Israelite community for the building of Yahweh's sanctuary (cf. 29:6–9), the temple eventually erected by Solomon—similar to the gifts given for the tabernacle of the Egyptian exodus (cf. Ex. 35:20–29). More than gifts of gold and silver, the Chronicler seeks to encourage the same "willing response" to God in the hearts of his audience (29:9; cf. Ex. 35:22, 29).

(2) The other parallel is that of divinely appointed succession in the leadership of the community. The Chronicler portrays David as a "second Moses" in that David is prohibited from building the temple, just as Moses was denied entry into the land of covenant promise (22:8; cf. Num. 20:2–12). Likewise, Solomon exemplifies Joshua in that both are given the same charge and each completes the task commissioned for him by his predecessor (1 Chron. 22:13; cf. Deut. 31:7). Theologically, the Chronicler assumes by analogy that the full measure of blessing Israel experiences under the guidance of past heroes such as Moses, Joshua, David, and Solomon can be shared by his audience because they worship the same Lord Almighty, the God of their ancestors (1 Chron. 29:10, 15, 18).

David's Prayer (29:10–20)

DAVID'S PRAYER OF thanks for God's enabling him to complete the necessary preparations to build the temple is one of ten royal prayers in Chronicles.[1] According to Throntveit, the royal prayers are an important vehicle for themes enhancing the Chronicler's theology of hope, especially the ideas of human inability, the power of God, and the effectiveness of prayer.[2]

The prayer divides naturally into three sections and blends three major psalmic types, the hymn, the song of thanksgiving, and the lament.[3] The three stanzas of the prayer include doxology (29:10–12), thanksgiving (29:13–16), and supplication (29:17–19). Thematically, David's prayer-poem has affinities to Psalm 145 as a psalm of the kingdom of God. Selman reminds us that "this magnificent prayer demonstrates beyond contradiction that Chronicles' priority is with the heart of worship rather than its form."[4]

By way of literary structure, the Chronicler sandwiches the account of David's life between two psalms or prayer-poems (16:7–36; 29:10–19), each commemorating momentous events in the worship life of Israel. The transfer of the ark of the covenant to Jerusalem centralizes the worship of Yahweh in that city and makes Mount Zion Yahweh's "home" in fulfillment of Moses' words that one day God will choose a place for his name (16:1–6; cf. Deut. 14:23–24; 16:2, 6). The building of the temple, God's "palatial" abode (1 Chron. 29:1), will establish a permanent structure for Israelite worship worthy of his holy name (29:16).

---

1. Mark A. Throntveit, *When Kings Speak: Royal Speech and Royal Prayer in Chronicles* (SBLDS 93; Atlanta: Scholars Press, 1987), 52.

2. Ibid., 63.

3. On psalmic types see Bernhard W. Anderson, *Out of the Depths: The Psalms Speak for Us Today*, 3d ed. (Philadelphia: Westminster, 2000).

4. Selman, *1 Chronicles*, 259.

Both events set the stage for the next major section of the Chronicler's history, the reign of King Solomon (2 Chron. 1–9). With the ascension of Solomon, God has made good his promise to build the "house of David" (1 Chron. 17:11–14; cf. 2 Sam. 7:16). With the construction and dedication of the temple, Solomon makes good on David's promise to build "God's house" (1 Chron. 17:1–2; cf. 2 Sam. 7:1–2).

Doxology (29:10–12). A hymn or doxology tends to offer praise to God in general terms for his greatness and faithfulness as Creator.[5] This doxology includes a stylistic device that multiplies adjectives describing the attributes of God in a connected series (29:11; cf. 16:25–27). According to Japhet, this technique, known as "accumulation," becomes a characteristic feature of postbiblical liturgy.[6] This liturgical feature influenced early Christian worship as the first portion of the verse was appended to the Lord's Prayer as a doxology (29:11a-b; cf. Matt. 6:13 [see NIV note]).

The repeated word "praise" (Heb. *baruk*, 29:10, 20) may be rendered alternately in English as "praise" (so NIV) or "bless" (so NRSV). Here David "blesses" God as an act of homage or reverence because God is the source of all blessing. To bless God in this context is to show gratitude for the bounty of God's provision, enabling the people to give generously to the temple "building fund." In blessing God, David also indirectly blesses the materials freely given and the people responsible for the outpouring of resources for the construction of the temple (cf. 29:16, 18). By his pronouncement of this liturgical formula, "blessed are you, O LORD," King David takes on a priestly role of sorts—a role connected with Davidic kingship (cf. Ps. 110:4).

The key theme of the doxology is the eternal kingdom of God (29:11d). David equates God's kingdom with the entirety of the created order (29:11c, 12a) and acknowledges that temporal human kingdoms (including his own) can only survive and thrive as they concede all power and strength and honor and wealth belong to God alone.

Thanksgiving (29:13–16). Typically, a song of thanksgiving opens with a statement of the worshiper's gratitude (29:13), moves to a narration of some past experience of God's gracious help in a time of need (29:14–15), and concludes by confessing Yahweh's graciousness and goodness (29:16). David continues his priestly role here, expressing the gratitude of the people in the collective "we" (29:13). The expression "aliens and strangers" (29:15; cf. Ps. 39:12) evokes the wanderings of the Hebrew patriarchs and matriarchs (cf. Heb. 11:13). The illustration has a parallel in the reference to the wandering of Abraham from "nation to nation" (1 Chron. 16:19–20). David

---

5. Anderson, *Out of the Depths*, 133.
6. Japhet, *I and II Chronicles*, 509; cf. Allen, *1, 2 Chronicles*, 191.

appeals to the imagery of the resident alien to remind his audience that they are little more than "widows and orphans," having no rights and utterly dependent on God for their security and physical well-being.[7] No doubt the Chronicler inveighs David's blessing for the purpose of inspiring this same attitude of humble faith in his own audience.

To reinforce the idea that God's people are "resident aliens" in this life, David offers the evidence of the brevity and frailty of human life ("our days ... are like a shadow," 29:15; perhaps a reference to Ps. 102:11). The concluding confession in 1 Chronicles 29:16 reiterates 29:12 in extolling God as the source of all gifts (cf. Deut. 8:18; James 1:17).

Supplication (29:17–19). David's blessing closes with a petition for the people of his realm: "Keep their hearts loyal to you" (29:18). The Chronicler can seek nothing more significant for his own audience. The "heart" is crucial to physical and spiritual life. David well knows that divine "cardiac stress tests" are essential to a healthy spiritual life (29:17). Moses also understood that God must test the heart to reveal motives for the sake of encouraging dependence on God and loyalty to him (cf. Deut. 8:2–3). This Old Testament principle of divine testing, including the complementary work of "self-testing," is affirmed in the New Testament (James 1:3–8; on self-assessment, cf. Lam. 3:40; 2 Cor. 13:5; Gal. 6:4).

Prominent on the "answer key" of the "divine testing" exam for David are two words, "integrity" and "honest intent" (29:17). These words are more than theological jargon for David, given the crucible of his own experience. As shepherd, poet and singer, loyal friend, warrior, king, repentant adulterer and murderer, and broken-hearted parent, David has learned the way of "integrity" (*mešarim;* cf. Ps. 9:8 [NIV = "justice"]) and honesty (*yošer;* cf. Ps. 25:21) through "trouble" (cf. Ps. 9:9; 22:11; 27:5).

Finally, David is sensitive to the need of a role model for the people, an individual who can foster honesty and integrity within the Israelite community by virtue of personal example. Hence, David petitions for his son Solomon, that he might exhibit "wholehearted devotion" through obedience to the law of God (29:19).

Response (29:20). The worship response of the people includes the recitation of a doxology and bodily prostration, a common worship posture in the Old Testament (cf. Ps. 95:6; 138:2). Though not mentioned in this context, on the basis of 1 Chronicles 16:36 it is possible that a congregational benediction is also recited. David mentions the "God of our fathers" in his prayer (29:18), and this phrase is repeated in the report of the people's worship response (29:20). Spiritual linkage to the past is a crucial element in the

---

7. Cf. Thompson, *1, 2 Chronicles,* 197; cf. Selman, *1 Chronicles,* 260.

Chronicler's theology of hope for the postexilic nation, demonstrated in the more than twenty-five occurrences of this phrase in Chronicles. It is important to the Chronicler that his audience understand that the God of Abraham, David, and Solomon is their God as well.

The report that the people do obeisance in reverence to "the LORD and the king" is both striking and theologically significant. The king of Israel is the anointed of God, and the occupant of the royal office is God's servant (cf. Ps. 45:6–7). The throne of Israel, however, belongs to Yahweh, and to bow to the king is ultimately to bow to God, who has installed the king as his agent of justice and righteousness (cf. Ps. 2:2, 6).[8]

Solomon Anointed a Second Time (29:21–25)

THE FIRST DAY of the "pre-groundbreaking" ceremony for the temple of the Lord is a celebration of Israel's God and his kingdom established through the family of David. The second day of the festival (29:21) is a celebration of God's provision of an heir to David's legacy. Solomon is anointed as the steward of the promises of the Davidic covenant, and the temple he will soon build symbolically embodies the theological tenets of God's treaty with David's descendants. The Chronicler indicates Solomon is anointed a "second time" (29:22). It seems likely this installation ceremony for King Solomon is the formal and public sequel to the hurried and private appointment of Solomon as David's successor (1 Kings 1:28–40), although apparently David has named Solomon coregent prior to his "first anointing" (cf. 1 Chron. 23:1).[9]

Zadok (29:22) was previously named as a priest in David's cabinet (18:16). The anointing of Zadok here probably refers to his promotion (or reappointment under a new king) to the office of high priest. According to 1 Kings 2:27, 35, the former high priest Abiathar was demoted for his role in the failed coup of Adonijah. Overall, the Chronicler largely ignores the palace intrigue surrounding the process of selecting David's successor reported in 1 Kings 1–2. For the Chronicler, the office of kingship transcends the person ruling as king. This explains his preoccupation with the outcome of the tangled succession story rather than the process.

The record of the pledge of loyalty by David's mercenary guard and the other princes (29:24) is a significant political datum. The stability of the Davidic throne was twice challenged by rivals within the royal family: by Absalom (2 Sam. 15–18) and by Adonijah (1 Kings 1). Solomon knows that such an oath of allegiance is crucial to the smooth transfer of power in the

---

8. See Japhet's comments on Ezra 6:10, *I and II Chronicles*, 512.
9. So Merrill, *1, 2 Chronicles*, 83.

aftermath of Adonijah's attempted coup. It is significant that the prince (i.e., Solomon), with the support of David's mercenary guard, is eventually installed as David's successor.

The changes introduced by the Chronicler in the citation of the parallel account from 1 Kings 2:12 are instructive of his theological agenda. According to 1 Kings 2:12a, "Solomon sat on the throne of his father David." The Chronicler, however, correctly recognizes that kingship in Israel belongs to God; thus, he writes: "Solomon sat on the throne of the LORD" as David's successor (1 Chron. 29:23a).

Even more significant for the Chronicler is the reality that the God of Israel reigns over all creation, regardless of whether there is a throne in Jerusalem. Rather than repeat 1 Kings 2:12b ("his rule was firmly established"), the Chronicler unpacks the theological meaning of that clause for his audience: King Solomon prospers because all Israel obeys him (1 Chron. 29:23b). The analogy is clear for postexilic Judah: They will prosper only as they remain unified in their loyalty to their historic roots, the God-given commandments of the Sinai covenant (cf. Deut. 28:2).

The summary statement touting the glory of Solomon's reign prior to the account of David's death is unusual. The alteration in the format calls attention to the place of "all Israel" (29:25) in this new regime, a key theme in Chronicles. In fact, the word of measure "all" occurs frequently in this literary unit. It expresses both the totality of God's rule and the unity of the Israelites as God's people. No doubt the Chronicler envisions a similar scenario: all Israel once again unified under a divinely ordained Davidic ruler.

David's Death (29:26–30)

THE NOTICE OF David's death finds its parallel in 1 Kings 2:10–11. Again the Chronicler has modified the earlier account for specific theological purposes. Unlike Kings, the Chronicler inserts the phrase "son of Jesse" (1 Chron. 29:26). The point is not to review David's family heritage, which has been done in a comprehensive way in the genealogical prologue. Rather, the Chronicler uses the name "Jesse" as a word prompt to remind his audience of the selection process by which David came to the throne of Israel (cf. 1 Sam. 16). I suspect the key episode in the whole narrative for the Chronicler is the criterion by which the prophet Samuel was instructed to make his choice among the sons of Jesse: "but the LORD looks at the heart" (1 Sam. 16:7; cf. David's concern for the "hearts" of his people in his prayer, 1 Chron. 29:18).

The role of David and Solomon in solidifying the tribes into a nation cannot be overlooked, given the repetition of the phrase "all Israel" for the fourth time (29:21, 23, 25, 26). Implicit in all this is God's faithfulness in making good on his promise to make Israel into a great nation (Gen. 12:2; 22:16–18). The tally of the length of David's reign agrees with that of 1 Kings 2:11, both rounding off David's seven and one-half year rule of Judah from Hebron to seven years (cf. 2 Sam. 5:5; 1 Chron. 3:4). Long life, wealth, and honor (1 Chron. 29:28) are blessings from God for those who walk in humility and who fear the Lord (Prov. 22:4). David has admitted as much in his prayer of thanksgiving (1 Chron. 29:14, 16).

The reference to Solomon as David's successor (29:28b) is both a statement of simple fact and a subtle reminder that in Solomon God has fulfilled his promise to the house of David through Nathan the prophet (2 Sam. 7; 1 Chron. 17). The Chronicler essentially tells two related stories in closing the book on David's career: the subplot of David's greatness as Israel's ideal king and the main plot of God faithfulness as Israel's "king maker."

The bibliographic citation to the records of the prophets Samuel, Nathan, and Gad (29:29) probably refers to the books of Samuel and Kings and perhaps an additional source available to the Chronicler. The writer is careful to inform his audience that his record of David's reign is based reliably on the authoritative word of God's prophets. Selman has observed that prophetic interventions by these three seers were pivotal in the life of David: Samuel anointed David king (1 Chron. 11:3; cf. 1 Sam. 16:13); Nathan mediated Yahweh's covenant with David for the building of a dynasty (1 Chron. 17); and through the prophet Gad the temple site was chosen (1 Chron. 21:9–13).[10] As noted earlier, the Chronicler's emphasis on the prophetic office is intended to present the priests and Levites as the legitimate heirs of that tradition to the postexilic community.

The interplay of the nation of Israel with the kingdoms of the other people groups surrounding the Hebrews is an important dimension of the Chronicler's history because God's sovereign hand is seen in that arena as well. Israel continually assessed her place among the nations in light of the Abrahamic covenant, the promise to make the people of God "a great nation" (Gen. 12:1–3). Myers is probably correct to identify "the kingdoms of all the other lands" (1 Chron. 29:30) with those sovereign states David subjugated during his reign (i.e., Philistia, Moab, Edom, Ammon, Aram, and Tyre).[11] Thus, the reference to "foreign policy" in this passage serves as a retrospective summary of the record of David's imperialistic expansion found in chapters 18–20. This phrase is prospective in that it anticipates Israel's interaction with the nations in 2 Chronicles, especially the ancient superpowers of Assyria and Babylonia.

---

10. Cf. Selman, *1 Chronicles*, 262–63.
11. Myers, *I Chronicles*, 200.

RECURRENT THEMES. The "bookends" of King David's life for the Chronicler are the two great events shaping the worship life of ancient Israel: the installation of the ark of the covenant in Jerusalem (chs. 15–16) and the preparations for the building of Yahweh's temple (chs. 28–29). Both accounts conclude with doxology and contribute purposefully to the recurrent themes of Chronicles as a "biography of God," a "theology of hope," a "call to worship," and "joy." Not surprisingly, all four remain timely topics for consideration in the church.

(1) David's prayer begins with the adoration of God, a recurring theme in Chronicles and an important component of the Chronicler's *biography of God* (see the introduction). Allen has identified four specific elaborations of God's greatness in David's prayer: God's ownership of creation by virtue of his role as Creator (29:11), God's rule as sovereign King over the world he created (29:11), God as the source of all human wealth (29:12), and God's providential endowment of human beings with power (29:12).[12] The first two reinforce the key theme in the Chronicler's biography of God, namely, his sovereignty (cf. 2 Chron. 20:6). The second two illustrate another central idea in the biography of God, his goodness (cf. 30:18–20).

(2) Both of these themes contribute to the Chronicler's development of a *theology of hope* because God is the Father of Israel "from everlasting to everlasting" (29:10). Even as God was sovereign in the life of Jacob and the other Hebrew forefathers, so God's sovereignty extends to the postexilic era and the audience of the Chronicler (note the emphasis on the ancestors of Israel in 29:10, 15, 18). By the same token, all that is good still comes from God. Much like the apostle Paul, the Chronicler has reminded the people that they can only give to God what they have already received from him (29:14; cf. 1 Cor. 4:7).

(3) All three sections of the verses under consideration form a *call to worship* God. David's praise-prayer (29:10–20) closes with the king's invoking the "whole assembly" to praise God. One senses that the Chronicler is issuing the same invitation to his audience through the declaration of David. The narrative preserving the second anointing of Solomon (29:21–25) climaxes with "all Israel" celebrating "in the presence of the LORD." No doubt, the Chronicler envisions a similar experience for the people of postexilic Judah. Even the eulogy of David (29:26–30) serves as an indirect call to worship because the king's long life, wealth, and honor are understood as gifts from God (cf. Prov. 22:4).

---

12. Allen, *1, 2 Chronicles*, 191.

This call to worship incisively supports Allen's observation that Chronicles may be considered a commentary on Psalm 84:4: "Blessed are those who dwell in your house; they are ever praising you."[13] It seems the Chronicler is inviting his audience, all of postexilic Judah, to share in the joy experienced daily by the priests and Levites in their service of worship to Yahweh in the Jerusalem temple.

David's invitation to share in the joy of worship represents a significant contribution to the role of a worship leader. As Israel's worship leader, David models and encourages the people to participate in worship "knowingly," "actively," and "fruitfully."[14] Or as Allen has rightly observed, "it must ever be the concern of the worship leader to ensure that the congregation does not lag behind as silent observers, but keeps pace with the leader as sincere participants."[15]

In a real sense, King David lays the foundation for participatory corporate worship in ancient Israel and later Judaism (esp. the synagogue tradition) in two dimensions. (a) The physical dimension of Israel's worship is secured in David's purchase of the property for a temple site and his preparation for building the edifice as a replacement for Yahweh's portable sanctuary and in his securing of the raw materials necessary for construction. The development of a permanent site for corporate worship localizes the notion of "sacred place" for the Hebrews.

(b) David reestablishes the elemental spiritual principle of Hebrew worship when he prays that an obedient heart might characterize the people and his son Solomon (29:18–19). Here David essentially echoes the sermon of Moses that called for absolute obedience to God's decrees because he alone is Israel's praise (Deut. 10:12–13, 21).

(4) Finally, Michael Wilcock offers insightful reflection on a subject of great importance in our section and one that has received scant attention in commentaries on Chronicles. This topic is a theme (though perhaps more minor) in the poems that commemorate the two "bookend" events of David's kingship mentioned previously. I speak of the term *joy* (cf. 16:27, 33; 29:17, 22). Wilcock notes that it is the inner principle of "the perennial joy that God's people should know" that binds the Hebrew people together through changing circumstances.[16] Praising God for his greatness, power, glory, majesty, and splendor (29:11) incites joy in his people

13. Leslie C. Allen, "הלל," *NIDOTTE*, 1:1037.
14. Craig D. Erickson, *Participating in Worship* (Louisville: Westminster John Knox, 1989), 5–9.
15. Allen, *1, 2 Chronicles*, 193.
16. Wilcock, *The Message of Chronicles*, 115.

because they celebrate the constant source of joy—God himself. According to Wilcock, the expression of joy as a responsive emotion "can be abiding only because God's bounty, which gives rise to it [i.e., joy], is itself an abiding thing."[17]

King David is fully aware of the secret to cultivating this attitude of joy as a characteristic or habit of the godly life. It is found in the word "alien," which he uses to identify himself and the Israelites and their relationship to God and the physical world (29:15). This term (Heb. *ger*) refers to a resident foreigner (or the "green-card holder" as a contemporary parallel). The Old Testament uses "alien" to distinguish the Hebrew (and heir of the covenant promises) from the non-Hebrew (those without entitlement to the promises of God but beneficiaries of his blessings because of the goodwill of the rightful title holders of the land of Canaan).[18] Isaiah likens the experience of the goodness of God to buying milk and wine without money (Isa. 55:1). Similarly, the apostle Paul marvels: "While we were still sinners, Christ died for us" (Rom. 5:8). Little wonder the early Christian apologist Tertullian proclaimed: "Sunday we give to joy!"[19]

Thus, perception of our "pilgrim" status as the faithful of God fans gratitude that expresses itself in continual praise as we become shareholders in the divine kingdom despite our lack of entitlement. David's insight comes from his firsthand experience as an "alien," first as a fugitive from King Saul (1 Sam. 21:10) and later as a fugitive from his own son Absalom (2 Sam. 15:14). The undeserved goodness of God not only sparks gratitude but also prompts the emotive response of joy. Joy, permitted its complete work, issues in loyalty or continued obedience to God. The Chronicler's "praise formula" may be diagrammed something like this:

"pilgrim" status → gratitude → joy → loyalty

This is not, however, a simplistic and mechanical cause-and-effect relationship between the Creator and his creatures. God cannot be manipulated in this way. Rather, it is the result of "wholehearted devotion" to God (29:19)—the mystery of a "synergistic" faith relationship between a people called to obey God and a God who keeps their hearts loyal to him (29:18).[20]

---

17. Ibid.
18. Cf. McConville, *I and II Chronicles*, 105.
19. Tertullian, *Ad Nationes*, 13.
20. Cf. C. G. Fry, "Synergism," in the *Evangelical Dictionary of Theology*, 2d ed., ed. W. A. Elwell (Grand Rapids: Baker, 2001), 1161–62.

VIRTUAL JOY. In his commentary on the message of Chronicles, Michael Wilcock (perhaps) unwittingly and (certainly) prophetically observed that the Christian subculture mirrors its secular counterpart in its penchant for a "virtual reality." By virtual reality we mean a simulated world of images (whether illusion, fantasy, feeling, etc.) created and manipulated by the individual for the sake of entertainment, as an experiment in detached and riskless life-simulation, or as an avenue of escape from the events and circumstances of life normally beyond the control of the individual.[21] In his discussion on "joy," Wilcock discerned that "we live in a time in the church's history which tends to value Christian experience more than the cause of that experience."[22] Or put another way, Christians today tend to value the circumstantial experience of joy more than the personal relationship with the God of joy.

In one sense, to divorce the God of joy from the emotive response of joy is to fabricate an alternate or virtual reality in which God becomes either the victim or the cause of any human circumstance that fails to match some preconceived or culturally conditioned ideal. This human tendency both to desire control over the events of our lives and to blame another when circumstances careen out of our control and render us powerless may be traced back to the first sin and its aftermath. That first human pair yielded to the temptation to be "like God" (Gen. 3:5) and then proceeded to blame God and each other when that decision went awry (3:12–13).

Dysfunctional behavior patterns associated with megalomania and displacement have been part of the human psyche ever since. Both psychological disorders encourage a virtual reality theologically speaking because they promote self-justification at the expense of divine justice (cf. Job. 40:8).[23] Whether God be indicted as loving but impotent or as omnipotent but unjust, given the fact that evil seemingly still overcomes good, he is effectively

---

21. While folklorist and literary constructions of an alternative reality have been with us ever since humankind began telling and writing stories, Neil Postman (*Technopoly: The Surrender of Culture to Technology* [New York: Knopf, 1992], 117) correctly associates Virtual Reality primarily with computer-generated images. He mused that VR may provide therapy of sorts for those who can no longer cope with the real world. Howard Rheingold (*Virtual Reality* [New York: Summit Books, 1991], 391) ventured that people will use cyberspace as a hybrid of entertainment, escape, and addiction because reality has always been too small for the human imagination.

22. Wilcock, *The Message of Chronicles*, 115.

23. Andrew W. Blackwood has traced every criticism of God to one unspoken assumption, "that God should have arranged the world so that man will be comfortable" (*Out of the Whirlwind: A Study of Job* [Grand Rapids: Baker, 1959], 151).

discounted as the sovereign Lord overruling events in a fallen world for good in the life of the Christian (cf. Gen. 50:20; Rom. 8:28).

Of course, the notion of putting God on trial for theological malpractice with respect to the problem of evil is not the exclusive property of modernism or postmodernism.[24] Well before the time of Moses a man named Job challenged the absolute goodness of God, actually naming God as the defendant in his lawsuit (Job 23:1–7; 31:35). The psalmists also lodged complaints against God for his apparent failure to keep his word concerning the blessing of the righteous and the cursing of the wicked in a psalmic form known as the "lament" (e.g., Ps. 10; 13; 22; cf. Deut. 28:2, 15). According to Anderson, the lament "is an appeal to God's compassion to intervene and change a desperate situation."[25] The lament is a legitimate vehicle for the believer's expression of honest doubt in the biblical tradition and an important testimony to God's power in answering prayer and meeting human need. There is always the danger, however, that theological truth may be misappropriated and enlisted for the purpose of manipulating God's intervention in the everyday course of human events for selfish reasons—another form of a virtual reality.[26]

The separation of the emotion of joy from the God of joy has led us to pawn satisfaction for gratification. The rise of the insidious contemporary idolatry of technology further demeans our humanness in the swapping of an abundant life lived in time and space for a virtual reality logged in cyberspace. Social critics have observed that the American right to "pursue happiness" in the form of instant emotional "fixes" has created a society addicted to fun but bereft of joy.

Interestingly, the thematic structure of the psalm of lament speaks to this dichotomy in that the lament typically concludes with a "vow of praise." The vow of praise, according to Anderson, is a vote of confidence in Yahweh as the God who hears and answers the prayers the needy.[27] It is testimony both to the sovereignty of God in human circumstance (i.e., affirmation of Yahweh's ability to change the situation if he wills to intervene) and to the goodness of God's character (i.e., the recognition that God is good whether

---

24. Cf. C. S. Lewis, *God in the Dock: Essays on Theology and Ethics* (Grand Rapids: Eerdmans, 1970).

25. Anderson, *Out of the Depths*, 76.

26. For example, the assumption of Job's friends that all human suffering is retributive (i.e., just punishment for sin; cf. Job 4:7–9; 8:20; etc.). Their skewed theology was inadequate for suffering that was necessarily mysterious, since God's character and plan are inscrutable (cf. 11:7; 42:3; see further R. B. Y. Scott, *The Way of Wisdom* [New York: Macmillan, 1971], 144–47).

27. Anderson, *Out of the Depths*, 62, 64–65.

or not he chooses to intervene and remedy a situation). This helps explain the Chronicler's report that the people of Israel "ate and drank with great joy in the presence of the LORD" at the coronation of King Solomon (29:22). He apprehends the theological truth that joy is connected to the person and presence of God (cf. 16:27).

C. S. Lewis made a similar discovery in his personal odyssey through atheism, theism, and pantheism to Christianity. Lewis came to understand that joy was a desire, but unlike pleasure, it is never experienced as a result of human power. Rather, as a desire joy "is turned not to itself but to its object."[28] Finally, Lewis realized that joy is something other, something that lies outside of himself. The ultimate question became not, "What is joy?" but, "Who is the desired?"[29] Much to his surprise, Lewis perceived a direct connection between God and joy. Joy is not a place but a Person, the very person of God revealed once for all in Jesus Christ. Much like Job, who no longer needed an answer to the question of why the righteous suffer after his encounter with God, Lewis wrote that he lost all interest in the topic of joy when he became a Christian and met the "God of Joy."[30]

---

28. C. S. Lewis, *Surprised by Joy* (New York: Harcourt Brace, 1955), 220.
29. Ibid., 221.
30. Ibid., 238.

2 Chronicles 1–9

SOLOMON SON OF David established himself firmly over his kingdom, for the LORD his God was with him and made him exceedingly great.

²Then Solomon spoke to all Israel—to the commanders of thousands and commanders of hundreds, to the judges and to all the leaders in Israel, the heads of families—³and Solomon and the whole assembly went to the high place at Gibeon, for God's Tent of Meeting was there, which Moses the LORD's servant had made in the desert. ⁴Now David had brought up the ark of God from Kiriath Jearim to the place he had prepared for it, because he had pitched a tent for it in Jerusalem. ⁵But the bronze altar that Bezalel son of Uri, the son of Hur, had made was in Gibeon in front of the tabernacle of the LORD; so Solomon and the assembly inquired of him there. ⁶Solomon went up to the bronze altar before the LORD in the Tent of Meeting and offered a thousand burnt offerings on it.

⁷That night God appeared to Solomon and said to him, "Ask for whatever you want me to give you."

⁸Solomon answered God, "You have shown great kindness to David my father and have made me king in his place. ⁹Now, LORD God, let your promise to my father David be confirmed, for you have made me king over a people who are as numerous as the dust of the earth. ¹⁰Give me wisdom and knowledge, that I may lead this people, for who is able to govern this great people of yours?"

¹¹God said to Solomon, "Since this is your heart's desire and you have not asked for wealth, riches or honor, nor for the death of your enemies, and since you have not asked for a long life but for wisdom and knowledge to govern my people over whom I have made you king, ¹²therefore wisdom and knowledge will be given you. And I will also give you wealth, riches and honor, such as no king who was before you ever had and none after you will have."

¹³Then Solomon went to Jerusalem from the high place at Gibeon, from before the Tent of Meeting. And he reigned over Israel.

[14]Solomon accumulated chariots and horses; he had four-teen hundred chariots and twelve thousand horses, which he kept in the chariot cities and also with him in Jerusalem. [15]The king made silver and gold as common in Jerusalem as stones, and cedar as plentiful as sycamore-fig trees in the foothills. [16]Solomon's horses were imported from Egypt and from Kue—the royal merchants purchased them from Kue. [17]They imported a chariot from Egypt for six hundred shekels of silver, and a horse for a hundred and fifty. They also exported them to all the kings of the Hittites and of the Arameans.

[2:1]Solomon gave orders to build a temple for the Name of the LORD and a royal palace for himself. [2]He conscripted seventy thousand men as carriers and eighty thousand as stonecutters in the hills and thirty-six hundred as foremen over them.

[3]Solomon sent this message to Hiram king of Tyre:

"Send me cedar logs as you did for my father David when you sent him cedar to build a palace to live in. [4]Now I am about to build a temple for the Name of the LORD my God and to dedicate it to him for burning fragrant incense before him, for setting out the consecrated bread regularly, and for making burnt offerings every morning and evening and on Sabbaths and New Moons and at the appointed feasts of the LORD our God. This is a lasting ordinance for Israel.

[5]"The temple I am going to build will be great, because our God is greater than all other gods. [6]But who is able to build a temple for him, since the heavens, even the highest heavens, cannot contain him? Who then am I to build a temple for him, except as a place to burn sacrifices before him?

[7]"Send me, therefore, a man skilled to work in gold and silver, bronze and iron, and in purple, crimson and blue yarn, and experienced in the art of engraving, to work in Judah and Jerusalem with my skilled craftsmen, whom my father David provided.

[8]"Send me also cedar, pine and algum logs from Lebanon, for I know that your men are skilled in cutting timber there. My men will work with yours [9]to provide me with plenty of lumber, because the temple I build must be large and magnificent. [10]I will give your servants, the woodsmen who cut the timber, twenty

thousand cors of ground wheat, twenty thousand cors of barley, twenty thousand baths of wine and twenty thousand baths of olive oil."

¹¹Hiram king of Tyre replied by letter to Solomon:

"Because the LORD loves his people, he has made you their king."

¹²And Hiram added:

"Praise be to the LORD, the God of Israel, who made heaven and earth! He has given King David a wise son, endowed with intelligence and discernment, who will build a temple for the LORD and a palace for himself. ¹³"I am sending you Huram-Abi, a man of great skill, ¹⁴whose mother was from Dan and whose father was from Tyre. He is trained to work in gold and silver, bronze and iron, stone and wood, and with purple and blue and crimson yarn and fine linen. He is experienced in all kinds of engraving and can execute any design given to him. He will work with your craftsmen and with those of my lord, David your father.

¹⁵"Now let my lord send his servants the wheat and barley and the olive oil and wine he promised, ¹⁶and we will cut all the logs from Lebanon that you need and will float them in rafts by sea down to Joppa. You can then take them up to Jerusalem."

¹⁷Solomon took a census of all the aliens who were in Israel, after the census his father David had taken; and they were found to be 153,600. ¹⁸He assigned 70,000 of them to be carriers and 80,000 to be stonecutters in the hills, with 3,600 foremen over them to keep the people working. ³:¹Then Solomon began to build the temple of the LORD in Jerusalem on Mount Moriah, where the LORD had appeared to his father David. It was on the threshing floor of Araunah the Jebusite, the place provided by David. ²He began building on the second day of the second month in the fourth year of his reign.

³The foundation Solomon laid for building the temple of God was sixty cubits long and twenty cubits wide (using the cubit of the old standard). ⁴The portico at the front of the temple was twenty cubits long across the width of the building and twenty cubits high.

He overlaid the inside with pure gold. ⁵He paneled the main hall with pine and covered it with fine gold and decorated it with palm tree and chain designs. ⁶He adorned the temple with precious stones. And the gold he used was gold of Parvaim. ⁷He overlaid the ceiling beams, doorframes, walls and doors of the temple with gold, and he carved cherubim on the walls.

⁸He built the Most Holy Place, its length corresponding to the width of the temple—twenty cubits long and twenty cubits wide. He overlaid the inside with six hundred talents of fine gold. ⁹The gold nails weighed fifty shekels. He also overlaid the upper parts with gold.

¹⁰In the Most Holy Place he made a pair of sculptured cherubim and overlaid them with gold. ¹¹The total wingspan of the cherubim was twenty cubits. One wing of the first cherub was five cubits long and touched the temple wall, while its other wing, also five cubits long, touched the wing of the other cherub. ¹²Similarly one wing of the second cherub was five cubits long and touched the other temple wall, and its other wing, also five cubits long, touched the wing of the first cherub. ¹³The wings of these cherubim extended twenty cubits. They stood on their feet, facing the main hall.

¹⁴He made the curtain of blue, purple and crimson yarn and fine linen, with cherubim worked into it.

¹⁵In the front of the temple he made two pillars, which together were thirty-five cubits long, each with a capital on top measuring five cubits. ¹⁶He made interwoven chains and put them on top of the pillars. He also made a hundred pomegranates and attached them to the chains. ¹⁷He erected the pillars in the front of the temple, one to the south and one to the north. The one to the south he named Jakin and the one to the north Boaz.

⁴:¹He made a bronze altar twenty cubits long, twenty cubits wide and ten cubits high. ²He made the Sea of cast metal, circular in shape, measuring ten cubits from rim to rim and five cubits high. It took a line of thirty cubits to measure around it. ³Below the rim, figures of bulls encircled it—ten to a cubit. The bulls were cast in two rows in one piece with the Sea.

⁴The Sea stood on twelve bulls, three facing north, three facing west, three facing south and three facing east. The Sea rested on top of them, and their hindquarters were toward the

center. ⁵It was a handbreadth in thickness, and its rim was like
the rim of a cup, like a lily blossom. It held three thousand
baths.

⁶He then made ten basins for washing and placed five on
the south side and five on the north. In them the things to be
used for the burnt offerings were rinsed, but the Sea was to be
used by the priests for washing.

⁷He made ten gold lampstands according to the specifica-
tions for them and placed them in the temple, five on the
south side and five on the north.

⁸He made ten tables and placed them in the temple, five on
the south side and five on the north. He also made a hundred
gold sprinkling bowls.

⁹He made the courtyard of the priests, and the large court
and the doors for the court, and overlaid the doors with
bronze. ¹⁰He placed the Sea on the south side, at the southeast corner.

¹¹He also made the pots and shovels and sprinkling bowls.

So Huram finished the work he had undertaken for King
Solomon in the temple of God:

¹²the two pillars;

the two bowl-shaped capitals on top of the pillars;
the two sets of network decorating the two bowl-shaped
capitals on top of the pillars;
¹³the four hundred pomegranates for the two sets of network
(two rows of pomegranates for each network, decorating the bowl-shaped capitals on top of the pillars);
¹⁴the stands with their basins;
¹⁵the Sea and the twelve bulls under it;
¹⁶the pots, shovels, meat forks and all related articles.

All the objects that Huram-Abi made for King Solomon for
the temple of the LORD were of polished bronze. ¹⁷The king
had them cast in clay molds in the plain of the Jordan between
Succoth and Zarethan. ¹⁸All these things that Solomon made
amounted to so much that the weight of the bronze was not
determined.

¹⁹Solomon also made all the furnishings that were in God's
temple:

the golden altar;
the tables on which was the bread of the Presence;

20 the lampstands of pure gold with their lamps, to burn in
    front of the inner sanctuary as prescribed;
21 the gold floral work and lamps and tongs (they were solid
    gold);
22 the pure gold wick trimmers, sprinkling bowls, dishes and
    censers; and the gold doors of the temple: the inner
    doors to the Most Holy Place and the doors of the main
    hall.

5:1 When all the work Solomon had done for the temple of
the LORD was finished, he brought in the things his father
David had dedicated—the silver and gold and all the furnishings—and he placed them in the treasuries of God's temple.

2 Then Solomon summoned to Jerusalem the elders of
Israel, all the heads of the tribes and the chiefs of the Israelite
families, to bring up the ark of the LORD's covenant from
Zion, the City of David. 3 And all the men of Israel came
together to the king at the time of the festival in the seventh
month.

4 When all the elders of Israel had arrived, the Levites took
up the ark, 5 and they brought up the ark and the Tent of
Meeting and all the sacred furnishings in it. The priests, who
were Levites, carried them up; 6 and King Solomon and the
entire assembly of Israel that had gathered about him were
before the ark, sacrificing so many sheep and cattle that they
could not be recorded or counted.

7 The priests then brought the ark of the LORD's covenant
to its place in the inner sanctuary of the temple, the Most
Holy Place, and put it beneath the wings of the cherubim.
8 The cherubim spread their wings over the place of the ark
and covered the ark and its carrying poles. 9 These poles were
so long that their ends, extending from the ark, could be seen
from in front of the inner sanctuary, but not from outside the
Holy Place; and they are still there today. 10 There was nothing
in the ark except the two tablets that Moses had placed in it at
Horeb, where the LORD made a covenant with the Israelites
after they came out of Egypt.

11 The priests then withdrew from the Holy Place. All the
priests who were there had consecrated themselves, regardless
of their divisions. 12 All the Levites who were musicians—
Asaph, Heman, Jeduthun and their sons and relatives—stood
on the east side of the altar, dressed in fine linen and playing

cymbals, harps and lyres. They were accompanied by 120 priests sounding trumpets. [13]The trumpeters and singers joined in unison, as with one voice, to give praise and thanks to the LORD. Accompanied by trumpets, cymbals and other instruments, they raised their voices in praise to the LORD and sang:

> "He is good;
>   his love endures forever."

Then the temple of the LORD was filled with a cloud, [14]and the priests could not perform their service because of the cloud, for the glory of the LORD filled the temple of God.

[6:1]Then Solomon said, "The LORD has said that he would dwell in a dark cloud; [2]I have built a magnificent temple for you, a place for you to dwell forever."

[3]While the whole assembly of Israel was standing there, the king turned around and blessed them. [4]Then he said:

> "Praise be to the LORD, the God of Israel, who with his hands has fulfilled what he promised with his mouth to my father David. For he said, [5]'Since the day I brought my people out of Egypt, I have not chosen a city in any tribe of Israel to have a temple built for my Name to be there, nor have I chosen anyone to be the leader over my people Israel. [6]But now I have chosen Jerusalem for my Name to be there, and I have chosen David to rule my people Israel.'
>
> [7]"My father David had it in his heart to build a temple for the Name of the LORD, the God of Israel. [8]But the LORD said to my father David, 'Because it was in your heart to build a temple for my Name, you did well to have this in your heart. [9]Nevertheless, you are not the one to build the temple, but your son, who is your own flesh and blood—he is the one who will build the temple for my Name.'
>
> [10]"The LORD has kept the promise he made. I have succeeded David my father and now I sit on the throne of Israel, just as the LORD promised, and I have built the temple for the Name of the LORD, the God of Israel. [11]There I have placed the ark, in which is the covenant of the LORD that he made with the people of Israel."

[12]Then Solomon stood before the altar of the LORD in front of the whole assembly of Israel and spread out his hands.

¹³Now he had made a bronze platform, five cubits long, five cubits wide and three cubits high, and had placed it in the center of the outer court. He stood on the platform and then knelt down before the whole assembly of Israel and spread out his hands toward heaven. ¹⁴He said:

"O LORD, God of Israel, there is no God like you in heaven or on earth—you who keep your covenant of love with your servants who continue wholeheartedly in your way. ¹⁵You have kept your promise to your servant David my father; with your mouth you have promised and with your hand you have fulfilled it—as it is today.

¹⁶"Now LORD, God of Israel, keep for your servant David my father the promises you made to him when you said, 'You shall never fail to have a man to sit before me on the throne of Israel, if only your sons are careful in all they do to walk before me according to my law, as you have done.' ¹⁷And now, O LORD, God of Israel, let your word that you promised your servant David come true.

¹⁸"But will God really dwell on earth with men? The heavens, even the highest heavens, cannot contain you. How much less this temple I have built! ¹⁹Yet give attention to your servant's prayer and his plea for mercy, O LORD my God. Hear the cry and the prayer that your servant is praying in your presence. ²⁰May your eyes be open toward this temple day and night, this place of which you said you would put your Name there. May you hear the prayer your servant prays toward this place. ²¹Hear the supplications of your servant and of your people Israel when they pray toward this place. Hear from heaven, your dwelling place; and when you hear, forgive.

²²"When a man wrongs his neighbor and is required to take an oath and he comes and swears the oath before your altar in this temple, ²³then hear from heaven and act. Judge between your servants, repaying the guilty by bringing down on his own head what he has done. Declare the innocent not guilty and so establish his innocence.

²⁴"When your people Israel have been defeated by an enemy because they have sinned against you and when they turn back and confess your name, praying and mak-

ing supplication before you in this temple, [25]then hear from heaven and forgive the sin of your people Israel and bring them back to the land you gave to them and their fathers.

[26]"When the heavens are shut up and there is no rain because your people have sinned against you, and when they pray toward this place and confess your name and turn from their sin because you have afflicted them, [27]then hear from heaven and forgive the sin of your servants, your people Israel. Teach them the right way to live, and send rain on the land you gave your people for an inheritance.

[28]"When famine or plague comes to the land, or blight or mildew, locusts or grasshoppers, or when enemies besiege them in any of their cities, whatever disaster or disease may come, [29]and when a prayer or plea is made by any of your people Israel—each one aware of his afflictions and pains, and spreading out his hands toward this temple—[30]then hear from heaven, your dwelling place. Forgive, and deal with each man according to all he does, since you know his heart (for you alone know the hearts of men), [31]so that they will fear you and walk in your ways all the time they live in the land you gave our fathers.

[32]"As for the foreigner who does not belong to your people Israel but has come from a distant land because of your great name and your mighty hand and your outstretched arm—when he comes and prays toward this temple, [33]then hear from heaven, your dwelling place, and do whatever the foreigner asks of you, so that all the peoples of the earth may know your name and fear you, as do your own people Israel, and may know that this house I have built bears your Name.

[34]"When your people go to war against their enemies, wherever you send them, and when they pray to you toward this city you have chosen and the temple I have built for your Name, [35]then hear from heaven their prayer and their plea, and uphold their cause.

[36]"When they sin against you—for there is no one who does not sin—and you become angry with them and give them over to the enemy, who takes them cap-

tive to a land far away or near; [37]and if they have a change of heart in the land where they are held captive, and repent and plead with you in the land of their captivity and say, 'We have sinned, we have done wrong and acted wickedly'; [38]and if they turn back to you with all their heart and soul in the land of their captivity where they were taken, and pray toward the land you gave their fathers, toward the city you have chosen and toward the temple I have built for your Name; [39]then from heaven, your dwelling place, hear their prayer and their pleas, and uphold their cause. And forgive your people, who have sinned against you.

[40]"Now, my God, may your eyes be open and your ears attentive to the prayers offered in this place.

[41]"Now arise, O LORD God, and come to your
resting place,
you and the ark of your might.
May your priests, O LORD God, be clothed
with salvation,
may your saints rejoice in your goodness.
[42]O LORD God, do not reject your anointed one.
Remember the great love promised to David
your servant."

[7:1]When Solomon finished praying, fire came down from heaven and consumed the burnt offering and the sacrifices, and the glory of the LORD filled the temple. [2]The priests could not enter the temple of the LORD because the glory of the LORD filled it. [3]When all the Israelites saw the fire coming down and the glory of the LORD above the temple, they knelt on the pavement with their faces to the ground, and they worshiped and gave thanks to the LORD, saying,

"He is good;
his love endures forever."

[4]Then the king and all the people offered sacrifices before the LORD. [5]And King Solomon offered a sacrifice of twenty-two thousand head of cattle and a hundred and twenty thousand sheep and goats. So the king and all the people dedicated the temple of God. [6]The priests took their positions, as did the Levites with the LORD's musical instruments, which King

David had made for praising the LORD and which were used when he gave thanks, saying, "His love endures forever." Opposite the Levites, the priests blew their trumpets, and all the Israelites were standing.

⁷Solomon consecrated the middle part of the courtyard in front of the temple of the LORD, and there he offered burnt offerings and the fat of the fellowship offerings, because the bronze altar he had made could not hold the burnt offerings, the grain offerings and the fat portions.

⁸So Solomon observed the festival at that time for seven days, and all Israel with him—a vast assembly, people from Lebo Hamath to the Wadi of Egypt. ⁹On the eighth day they held an assembly, for they had celebrated the dedication of the altar for seven days and the festival for seven days more. ¹⁰On the twenty-third day of the seventh month he sent the people to their homes, joyful and glad in heart for the good things the LORD had done for David and Solomon and for his people Israel.

¹¹When Solomon had finished the temple of the LORD and the royal palace, and had succeeded in carrying out all he had in mind to do in the temple of the LORD and in his own palace, ¹²the LORD appeared to him at night and said:

"I have heard your prayer and have chosen this place for myself as a temple for sacrifices.

¹³"When I shut up the heavens so that there is no rain, or command locusts to devour the land or send a plague among my people, ¹⁴if my people, who are called by my name, will humble themselves and pray and seek my face and turn from their wicked ways, then will I hear from heaven and will forgive their sin and will heal their land. ¹⁵Now my eyes will be open and my ears attentive to the prayers offered in this place. ¹⁶I have chosen and consecrated this temple so that my Name may be there forever. My eyes and my heart will always be there.

¹⁷"As for you, if you walk before me as David your father did, and do all I command, and observe my decrees and laws, ¹⁸I will establish your royal throne, as I covenanted with David your father when I said, 'You shall never fail to have a man to rule over Israel.'

¹⁹"But if you turn away and forsake the decrees and commands I have given you and go off to serve other

gods and worship them, ²⁰then I will uproot Israel from my land, which I have given them, and will reject this temple I have consecrated for my Name. I will make it a byword and an object of ridicule among all peoples. ²¹And though this temple is now so imposing, all who pass by will be appalled and say, 'Why has the LORD done such a thing to this land and to this temple?' ²²People will answer, 'Because they have forsaken the LORD, the God of their fathers, who brought them out of Egypt, and have embraced other gods, worshiping and serving them—that is why he brought all this disaster on them.'"

⁸:¹At the end of twenty years, during which Solomon built the temple of the LORD and his own palace, ²Solomon rebuilt the villages that Hiram had given him, and settled Israelites in them. ³Solomon then went to Hamath Zobah and captured it. ⁴He also built up Tadmor in the desert and all the store cities he had built in Hamath. ⁵He rebuilt Upper Beth Horon and Lower Beth Horon as fortified cities, with walls and with gates and bars, ⁶as well as Baalath and all his store cities, and all the cities for his chariots and for his horses—whatever he desired to build in Jerusalem, in Lebanon and throughout all the territory he ruled.

⁷All the people left from the Hittites, Amorites, Perizzites, Hivites and Jebusites (these peoples were not Israelites), ⁸that is, their descendants remaining in the land, whom the Israelites had not destroyed—these Solomon conscripted for his slave labor force, as it is to this day. ⁹But Solomon did not make slaves of the Israelites for his work; they were his fighting men, commanders of his captains, and commanders of his chariots and charioteers. ¹⁰They were also King Solomon's chief officials—two hundred and fifty officials supervising the men.

¹¹Solomon brought Pharaoh's daughter up from the City of David to the palace he had built for her, for he said, "My wife must not live in the palace of David king of Israel, because the places the ark of the LORD has entered are holy."

¹²On the altar of the LORD that he had built in front of the portico, Solomon sacrificed burnt offerings to the LORD, ¹³according to the daily requirement for offerings commanded by Moses for Sabbaths, New Moons and the three annual feasts—the Feast of Unleavened Bread, the Feast of Weeks

and the Feast of Tabernacles. [14]In keeping with the ordinance of his father David, he appointed the divisions of the priests for their duties, and the Levites to lead the praise and to assist the priests according to each day's requirement. He also appointed the gatekeepers by divisions for the various gates, because this was what David the man of God had ordered. [15]They did not deviate from the king's commands to the priests or to the Levites in any matter, including that of the treasuries.

[16]All Solomon's work was carried out, from the day the foundation of the temple of the LORD was laid until its completion. So the temple of the LORD was finished.

[17]Then Solomon went to Ezion Geber and Elath on the coast of Edom. [18]And Hiram sent him ships commanded by his own officers, men who knew the sea. These, with Solomon's men, sailed to Ophir and brought back four hundred and fifty talents of gold, which they delivered to King Solomon.

[9:1]When the queen of Sheba heard of Solomon's fame, she came to Jerusalem to test him with hard questions. Arriving with a very great caravan—with camels carrying spices, large quantities of gold, and precious stones—she came to Solomon and talked with him about all she had on her mind. [2]Solomon answered all her questions; nothing was too hard for him to explain to her. [3]When the queen of Sheba saw the wisdom of Solomon, as well as the palace he had built, [4]the food on his table, the seating of his officials, the attending servants in their robes, the cupbearers in their robes and the burnt offerings he made at the temple of the LORD, she was overwhelmed.

[5]She said to the king, "The report I heard in my own country about your achievements and your wisdom is true. [6]But I did not believe what they said until I came and saw with my own eyes. Indeed, not even half the greatness of your wisdom was told me; you have far exceeded the report I heard. [7]How happy your men must be! How happy your officials, who continually stand before you and hear your wisdom! [8]Praise be to the LORD your God, who has delighted in you and placed you on his throne as king to rule for the LORD your God. Because of the love of your God for Israel and his desire to uphold them forever, he has made you king over them, to maintain justice and righteousness."

⁹Then she gave the king 120 talents of gold, large quantities of spices, and precious stones. There had never been such spices as those the queen of Sheba gave to King Solomon.

¹⁰(The men of Hiram and the men of Solomon brought gold from Ophir; they also brought algumwood and precious stones. ¹¹The king used the algumwood to make steps for the temple of the LORD and for the royal palace, and to make harps and lyres for the musicians. Nothing like them had ever been seen in Judah.)

¹²King Solomon gave the queen of Sheba all she desired and asked for; he gave her more than she had brought to him. Then she left and returned with her retinue to her own country.

¹³The weight of the gold that Solomon received yearly was 666 talents, ¹⁴not including the revenues brought in by merchants and traders. Also all the kings of Arabia and the governors of the land brought gold and silver to Solomon.

¹⁵King Solomon made two hundred large shields of hammered gold; six hundred bekas of hammered gold went into each shield. ¹⁶He also made three hundred small shields of hammered gold, with three hundred bekas of gold in each shield. The king put them in the Palace of the Forest of Lebanon.

¹⁷Then the king made a great throne inlaid with ivory and overlaid with pure gold. ¹⁸The throne had six steps, and a footstool of gold was attached to it. On both sides of the seat were armrests, with a lion standing beside each of them. ¹⁹Twelve lions stood on the six steps, one at either end of each step. Nothing like it had ever been made for any other kingdom. ²⁰All King Solomon's goblets were gold, and all the household articles in the Palace of the Forest of Lebanon were pure gold. Nothing was made of silver, because silver was considered of little value in Solomon's day. ²¹The king had a fleet of trading ships manned by Hiram's men. Once every three years it returned, carrying gold, silver and ivory, and apes and baboons.

²²King Solomon was greater in riches and wisdom than all the other kings of the earth. ²³All the kings of the earth sought audience with Solomon to hear the wisdom God had put in his heart. ²⁴Year after year, everyone who came brought a gift—articles of silver and gold, and robes, weapons and spices, and horses and mules.

²⁵Solomon had four thousand stalls for horses and chariots, and twelve thousand horses, which he kept in the chariot cities and also with him in Jerusalem. ²⁶He ruled over all the kings from the River to the land of the Philistines, as far as the border of Egypt. ²⁷The king made silver as common in Jerusalem as stones, and cedar as plentiful as sycamore-fig trees in the foothills. ²⁸Solomon's horses were imported from Egypt and from all other countries.

²⁹As for the other events of Solomon's reign, from beginning to end, are they not written in the records of Nathan the prophet, in the prophecy of Ahijah the Shilonite and in the visions of Iddo the seer concerning Jeroboam son of Nebat? ³⁰Solomon reigned in Jerusalem over all Israel forty years. ³¹Then he rested with his fathers and was buried in the city of David his father. And Rehoboam his son succeeded him as king.

THE STORY OF SOLOMON'S reign is the second of three large blocks of connected narrative in Chronicles. The account of Solomon's building and dedication of the Jerusalem temple for Yahweh (chs. 2–7) is a companion volume to the one that discusses David's preparations for the structure (see 1 Chron. 21–29). Like the earlier literary unit, the genre of this composition is basically a combination of report and account.[1]

The account of Solomon's reign is drawn rather freely from the parallel in 1 Kings 2–11. At times the Chronicler drastically abridges the materials from 1 Kings, while at other times he omits portions of the earlier document altogether. The selective use of this material is not designed to misrepresent Solomon's life or ennoble his character, since the writer omits both positive and negative aspects of his reign (e.g., his sagacious judgment in the case of the two prostitutes, 1 Kings 3:16–28; his polygamy leading to his downfall, 11:1–13). The Chronicler assumes the audience's knowledge of the Kings record; his own selection and arrangement of the materials is best explained by the emphasis on themes germane to the Davidic covenant (1 Chron. 17). The contents of the section may be broadly outlined as follows:

---

1. As defined earlier, a *report* is a brief, self-contained prose narrative relating a single event, while the account is a narrative combining several reports organized around a major event or significant theme.

A. Solomon's Kingship (1:1–17)
B. Construction of the Temple (2:1–5:1)
C. Dedication of the Temple (5:2–7:22)
D. Solomon's Other Activities (8–9)

The repetition of the report of Solomon's wealth (from 1 Kings 10:26–29) at the beginning and the end of the literary unit form an inclusio or envelope construction for the passage (cf. 2 Chron. 1:14–17; 9:25–28). The recognition of this literary feature has led to the discovery of a chiastic arrangement of the narrative of Solomon's reign. Chiasm (or palistrophe) is a symmetrical literary device using the inverted parallelism of words or ideas around a central theme or event. The chiastic structure of 2 Chronicles 1–9 may be outlined as follows:

A Solomon's Wisdom and Wealth (1:1–17)
   B Solomon Prepares to Build the Temple (2:1–18)
      C Solomon Erects Yahweh's Temple (3:1–5:1)
      C' Solomon Dedicates Yahweh's Temple (5:2–7:22)
   B' Solomon Completes the Temple and Other Building Projects (8:1–16)
A' Solomon's Wisdom and Wealth (8:17–9:28)[2]

A quick reading of the Chronicler's retelling of King Solomon's reign yields numerous theological emphases. Chief among them is the building of the temple, an event that dominates six of the nine chapters (chs. 2–7). Lexical and thematic parallels to the construction of the tabernacle are also clear, with Solomon cast as a second Bezalel of sorts in applying his gift of wisdom to the building of a sanctuary for God (cf. Ex. 31:1–11). Selman notes the accent on the partnership of David and Solomon in establishing a Davidic dynasty in the linkage of father and son in several passages unique to Chronicles (e.g., 2 Chron. 2:3, 7; 3:1; 6:42; 7:10; 8:14).[3]

This partnership contributes to the ongoing development of the Davidic covenant. God has fulfilled the first stage of his promise to "build a house" for David by enabling Solomon to ascend the throne. The continuation of that covenant is contingent on the fulfillment of two conditions imposed by David on his successor: following through on David's desire to build a house for God by completing the Jerusalem temple (cf. 1 Chron. 28:6, 10), and an unswerving obedience to God's law (cf. 28:7–8).

---

2. This simple chiastic outline of 2 Chron. 1–9 follows the example of Selman, _1 Chronicles_, 285–86. For a more elaborate chiastic schema see Raymond B. Dillard, _2 Chronicles_ (WBC 15; Waco, Tex.: Word, 1987), 5–6.

3. M. J. Selman, _2 Chronicles_ (TOTC 10b; Downers Grove, Ill.: InterVarsity Press, 1994), 285.

Worship is also a topic of paramount importance for the Chronicler. His narrative of Solomon's reign underscores the purpose of the Jerusalem temple as both a place of prayer and ritual sacrifice (6:29, 40; 7:12). The king's own worship life illustrates the complementary nature of prayer and sacrifice, as Solomon began his rule by inquiring of the Lord and presenting burnt offerings to him (1:5–6). Beyond this, Solomon prays and God immediately and explicitly answers his requests (e.g., 1:8–10 [see 1:11–12]; 6:14–42 [see 7:12–22]). As David's son and successor, Solomon understands that only "wholehearted" worship is acceptable to God (6:14).

For the Chronicler prayer is the heart of worship, which ensures that ritual sacrifice is more than just the empty form of religion (6:21). Maintaining a proper relationship with God and restoring wholehearted worship is at times dependent on the forgiveness of God as a response to humble repentance (cf. 7:14). Yahweh is a merciful God (Deut. 4:31), and his compassions never fail (Lam. 3:22). No doubt, the Chronicler's "shorter catechism" for postexilic Judah includes these essential theological truths: Prayer still works, and there is always hope for the sinner![4]

Solomon's Kingship (1:1–17)

THE CHRONICLER RETURNS to the synoptic parallel found in 1 Kings as the historical source for retelling the story of Solomon's kingship after the account of David's preparations for the building of the temple. Specifically, the writer draws from three texts in presenting a prologue of sorts to Solomon's reign:

2 Chron. 1:2–13a = 1 Kings 3:4–15
2 Chron. 1:13b = 1 Kings 4:1
2 Chron. 1:14–17 = 1 Kings 10:26–29

The Chronicler's introduction, however, omits the palace intrigue found in 1 Kings 1–2. He undoubtedly assumes this background knowledge and commences his narrative with the king's petition to God for the gift of wisdom (2 Chron. 1:10).

Solomon's request for wisdom serves as a foil for the opening chapter and provides the framework for the entire literary unit (chs. 1–9). Instead of "wealth, riches or honor," Solomon entreats Yahweh for wisdom and knowledge to govern God's people effectively (1:11). Although he does not ask for these material blessings, God chooses to grant them to Solomon as a reward for his righteous prayer (1:12). The report of Solomon's wealth found in 1 Kings 10:26–29 are placed as bookends encasing the story of David's suc-

---

4. Ibid., 288.

cessor and the building of the Jerusalem temple (cf. 2 Chron. 1:14–17; 9:25–28). The emphasis of the opening chapter on wisdom and wealth as *divine* gifts mean they do not die with King Solomon. This is a cue to the postexilic Hebrew community that they too might acquire similar gifts from God through prayer.

Solomon's worship (1:1–6). It is important to keep in mind that 1–2 Chronicles is one book in the Hebrew Bible. This means links to preceding material are important to the original audience, who lack the benefit of "book, chapter, and verse." The Chronicler provides those narrative connectors as the story shifts from the rule of King David to King Solomon by means of intertextuality (i.e., the demonstration of a literary interdependence between texts or documents through the repetition of words, phrases, and ideas). For instance, the reference to "all Israel" (1:2) hearkens back to the unity of God's people under King David as Israel's divinely appointed leader (cf. 1 Chron. 28:4; 29:21, 23, 25).

Solomon's assembly at Gibeon (1:3) is clearly patterned after the account of David's plans to relocate the ark of the covenant in Jerusalem (including references to the same Hebrew officials, worship by means of the bronze altar and the Tent of Meeting, and the repetition of the verb "to inquire of" the Lord, cf. 1 Chron. 13:1–6). The word picture describing Israel as "a people who are as numerous as the dust of the earth" (2 Chron. 1:9) echoes promises made to the patriarchs and serves to bridge the history of Israel's monarchy with the story of those tribal ancestors (cf. Gen. 13:16; 28:14).

The Chronicler opens and closes his "photo album" of Solomon's reign with a similar "snapshot": the king firmly in control of the empire he has inherited from his father, David (1:1; cf. 9:26). The expression "established himself firmly" (Hithpael of *ḥzq*) may be an oblique reference to the steps taken by Solomon to secure the throne after his accession (including "showing kindness" to political assets and "striking down" political liabilities, cf. 1 Kings 2:5–46). The introductory verse also affirms Solomon as God's choice for governing his people. Much like his father, God is "with" Solomon (2 Chron. 1:1b; cf. 1 Chron. 11:9; 17:8).

In a fashion similar to both David and Joshua, God makes King Solomon "exceedingly great" (1:1c [*gdl*]; cf. 1 Chron. 29:25; Josh. 3:7; 4:14). Implicitly, Solomon's greatness is associated with the Jerusalem temple he will erect. Just as David desired to build a house for God and God instead "built" David's dynasty, so too Solomon's name is "exalted" in the process of establishing a sanctuary to exalt the name of Yahweh (cf. 2 Chron. 6:5, 7, 32–34). By more than coincidence, the Queen of Sheba confirms Solomon's divine appointment in her praise of the God of Israel at the conclusion of the Chronicler's review of Solomon's kingship (9:8).

Solomon begins his rule over Israel with an act of public worship (1:1–6). In terms of biblical chronology, Solomon's accession to David's throne occurs around 970 B.C. The prayer and ritual sacrifice offered at Gibeon is symbolic of the new king's primary task, as the acts of piety show Solomon to be a fitting candidate for building Yahweh's temple. The worshipers convene at Gibeon (or Gibeah of God), a town with an adjacent worship center some five miles northwest of Jerusalem (1:3a). The Chronicler reminds his audience (and us as later readers of his history) of the importance of Gibeon, a flashback to the account of David's transfer of the ark of the covenant to Jerusalem (1:3–5; cf. 1 Chron. 13–17). After a temporary shrine for the ark was established in Jerusalem, David appointed a group of priests and Levites to minister there before the Lord (1 Chron. 16:4–6). But the other priests and Levites remained stationed at Gibeon because "the tabernacle of the LORD [was located] at the high place" there (16:39).

The draw of Gibeon for the new king is more than simply its reputation as the site of the Mosaic portable shrine or "God's Tent of Meeting" and the original altar associated with Israelite sacrificial ritual. The pilgrimage to Gibeon is a return to first things for Solomon, a reconnection with the ancient Hebrew religious traditions. This report is in keeping with the Chronicler's interest in the theological principles informing Solomon's reign.

One important connection to the past is the recognition that the construction of shrines or sanctuaries for Yahweh require gifts of wisdom and knowledge, such as those bestowed on the tabernacle artisans like Bezalel (1:5; cf. Ex. 31:3). Solomon's petition for wisdom and knowledge (2 Chron. 1:10) is rooted in his worship experience before Bezalel's bronze altar (actually acacia wood overlaid with bronze; cf. Ex. 38:1–2). It is clear that in identifying Solomon as a "second Bezalel," the Chronicler understands the greatest demonstration of his wisdom to be the construction of the temple itself.

A second, more important touch point with the past is Solomon's adherence to the law of Moses as represented by the sacrificial ritual and symbolized in the institution of the Tent of Meeting (1:6). Solomon's worship at Gibeon is public testimony to the fact that the soon-to-be-built Jerusalem temple will carry on this ancient Mosaic tradition. The king's presentation of burnt offerings on the altar in Gibeon stands as a witness to his intentions to keep his father's charge to obey the laws of the Lord and thereby preserve the worship of his ancestors (cf. 1 Chron. 28:7–8). Interestingly, when God initiates a new phase of his redemptive plan for fallen creation, he sees to it that it is firmly grounded in the "ancient paths" of his revelation (Jer. 6:16).

The Chronicler's version of Solomon's worship at the high place of Gibeon (1:2–6) differs from that of the earlier parallel found in 1 Kings 3:4–5. Not only does Chronicles expand the report (from two to five verses), but the later version portrays the "high place" in a more favorable light than does Kings. The historian of 1–2 Kings takes a more pejorative view of high places theologically because they are associated with the false worship practices of the native Canaanites (cf. 1 Kings 3:3; 11:7). No doubt things have changed by the time of the Chronicler, which helps explain a differing theological perspective (idol worship at the high places is no longer a problem in postexilic Judah). Moreover, the Chronicler regards the high place of Gibeon as a legitimate worship center in its own right because the Tent of Meeting is located there (note 1 Kings 3:4, which identifies Gibeon as the "most important" high place for that reason).

Another contrast between the two narratives is the way in which Kings reports the event as if this were a private act of piety on Solomon's part (1 Kings 3:4, "the king went to Gibeon"). Chronicles, however, records the event as an act of public worship by the king witnessed by a national assembly (2 Chron. 1:2–3). Clearly nothing in the Kings narrative precludes harmonizing the two reports. The Kings' historian tended to focus his theological review on the character and deeds of the royal figure whereas the Chronicler's concern tends toward observing the relationship of "all Israel" to the royal figure.

Both sources agree on the purpose of Solomon's visit to Gibeon—the offering of ritual sacrifices as an act of worship to God (1:6; cf. 1 Kings 3:4). Chronicles includes the detail that "Solomon and the assembly inquired of him [i.e., the LORD] there" (2 Chron. 1:5). The verb "to inquire of [*drš*; lit., to seek] the LORD" is an important theme in Chronicles. It denotes an act of faith, and the goal or aim of this spiritual quest is generally to seek God's direction and help at a crucial moment in one's life (or even confirmation of an earlier divine word of instruction).[5]

The propensity "to inquire" of God is one measure of the faithfulness of the leaders of Israel (e.g., 1 Chron. 10:14; 2 Chron. 22:9). Curiously (and sadly) Selman observes that the term is not used of Solomon again, despite his exhortation in the prayer of dedication for the temple (2 Chron. 7:14).[6] Isaiah's admonition is still pertinent for the Chronicler's audience (and the church today)—"Seek [*drš*] the LORD while he may be found; call on him while he is near" (Isa. 55:6).

Solomon's wisdom (1:7–13). The story of Solomon's request for wisdom is more abbreviated than in 1 Kings 3:5–15. The "dream report" or "dream epiphany" is a new narrative subgenre in the Chronicler's history,

---

5. S. Wagner, "דָּרַשׁ," *TDOT*, 3:293–98.
6. Selman, *2 Chronicles*, 292.

although Chronicles itself omits the fact that God's appearance to Solomon occurs in a dream (cf. 1 Kings 3:5). The Chronicler seems to emphasize Solomon's recognition of the theocratic ideal, that he as the Davidic king is God's vice-regent because the people of Israel are "God's people" (2 Chron. 1:10). This is the gist of the Chronicler's message for his own audience. Israel is still God's people after the return from the Exile, and God is still the de facto sovereign of Israel. The Chronicler reminds his generation that God is enthroned in Israel through the worship of his people and that the Davidic kingdom (as the precursor of the kingdom of God) will be established through the prayers of the righteous.

Solomon seeks God by means of ritual sacrifice (1:6) and prayer (1:8–10). Interestingly, in response to Solomon's worship at Gibeon, God inquires of Solomon by asking him to request anything he wants—a blank check of sorts signed by God himself (1:7). This divine invitation prompts Solomon's petition for wisdom (1:10). We must realize that Solomon is not approaching God as if he were a genie in a bottle or a cosmic slot machine. The righteous are free to petition God for the desires of their hearts, assuming this is done in a posture of faith and not of doubt or selfish motives (Ps. 37:3–4; Mal. 3:10; cf. Deut. 6:16). The New Testament both expands and clarifies this invitation to the righteous to ask anything of God because Jesus expressly teaches that the faithful may ask, and seek, and knock—and it will be given, they will find, it will be opened to them (Matt. 7:7–8; John 15:7).

Here Solomon is a model of how the righteous should pray because he first inquires or seeks God (implying he approaches God in good faith, 1:5). He then couches his prayer in the history of God's "great kindness" to David (1:8), acknowledging that the Lord has indeed proven himself as a good God (cf. Ps. 25:7–8; 31:19; 34:8). Next, Solomon voices his humility and dependence on God in his rhetorical question, "Who is able to govern this great people of yours?" (2 Chron. 1:10). Beyond this, Solomon seeks spiritual blessing over material blessing in asking God for wisdom and knowledge to rule instead of personal wealth and riches (1:10–11).

Solomon responds to God's invitation by first acknowledging the covenant promise made to David (1:8–9; cf. 1 Chron. 17). The repetition of David's name indicates that he intends to continue that legacy. Solomon then rehearses God's faithfulness in fulfilling covenant promises to Abraham and Jacob in making Israel "a people who are as numerous as the dust of the earth" (2 Chron. 1:9; cf. Gen. 13:16; 28:14). This recitation of Yahweh's "covenant history" with Israel is a tacit declaration by Solomon that God indeed keeps his promises.

In his petition to "confirm" the promises made to his father (1:9), Solomon hearkens back to David's prayer and, like his father, enjoins God to "do as you promised" (1 Chron. 17:23–24). Here we must understand that Solomon is not placing demands on God in his arrogance as David's successor. Rather, he is simply asking God to be consistent with his character as one who "remembers his covenant forever" (cf. Ps. 111:5). With his request for "wisdom and knowledge" (2 Chron. 1:10), Solomon looks forward to the fulfillment of God's promise to David since it is tied to the completion of the temple (6:17).

The words "wisdom" and "knowledge" (1:10) have replaced the more expansive "a discerning heart to govern your people and to distinguish between right and wrong" found in 1 Kings 3:9. These terms are used in combination elsewhere only of the academic training of Daniel and his three companions (Dan. 1:4, 17). These two words are essentially an equivalent expression of the phrases found in the Kings' parallel since "wisdom" (ḥokmah) connotes both spiritual insight and moral discernment, and "knowledge" (maddaᶜ) relates to intellectual capacities. The Chronicler's use of a postexilic term for "knowledge" may be another example of his updating the earlier source with language that has greater currency for his audience.

Both Kings and Chronicles agree on the purpose of Solomon's request: able leadership "to govern" (špṭ; lit., "judge") the people of Israel (1:10; cf. 1 Kings 3:9). Solomon asks for wisdom and knowledge and receives wealth, riches, and honor as a bonus (2 Chron. 1:11–12). Selman cites God's gracious endowment of gifts on Solomon as an Old Testament example of God doing "immeasurably more than all we ask or imagine" (Eph. 3:20).[7]

After worshiping in Gibeon, Solomon returns to Jerusalem (1:13). The Chronicler omits Solomon's worship before the ark of the covenant in Jerusalem and the feast he prepares for the royal court (see 1 Kings 3:15). Presumably, the writer desires to associate the gift of Solomon's wisdom directly with the construction of the Jerusalem temple. The summary statement "and he reigned over Israel" (2 Chron. 1:13b) has its parallel in 1 Kings 4:1 and reconnects the Gibeon experience with Solomon's efforts to establish himself as king in Israel. Clearly the Chronicler wants his audience to understand a cause-and-effect relationship between Solomon's worship of God and his "firm rule" of Israel.

Solomon's wealth (1:14–17). The third defining characteristic of King Solomon's reign is his accumulation of unprecedented riches. The report of his wealth has its source in 1 Kings 10:26–29. As previously noted, this passage is repeated at the beginning and the end of the narrative summarizing Solomon's kingship and thus depicts the king as the epitome of piety, wisdom, and riches (cf. 2 Chron. 9:25, 27–28). Apparently the Chronicler's

---

7. Ibid., 295.

rationale for framing the story of Solomon with the description of the staggering wealth possessed by the king is to demonstrate God's faithfulness in fulfilling his promise cited in 1:12. Implicit in the reference to the size of Solomon's "bank account" is the idea of God's favor resting on a faithful king, since divine blessing results from obedience to the stipulations of the Mosaic covenant. In this way the Chronicler affirms God's "adoption" of the Davidic dynasty as "his son" (cf. 1 Chron. 17:13).

The Chronicler's citation of the Kings' parallel reveals a few changes from his source. For example, Chronicles adds "gold" (zahab) in 1:15 to complete the word pair with "silver" (kesep, although "gold" is found in the LXX and may suggest a different source behind the Chronicler's work). Here the literary device of hyperbole conveys the idea that these precious metals are as common as the stones littering the landscape of Palestine and the imported cedar lumber is as ordinary as the ubiquitous sycamore-fig tree indigenous to the region.

The threefold measure of Solomon's wealth includes "military hardware" (1:14), precious metals (1:15), and profits from international trade (1:16, of which horses and chariots are but one example). Solomon's merchants broker a lucrative import-export trade in chariots and chariot horses between the Egyptians, Hittites, and Arameans (1:16–17). It seems likely that Kue (1:16) denotes a region of Asia Minor, suggesting Solomon as the "middle man" for the trading of horses from Asia Minor for chariots from Egypt.[8]

The reference to chariots and horses (1:14) signals a new era in Israelite military history in that the chariot is now among the weapons of the Hebrew arsenal. (Note that prior to the reign of Solomon Israel's practice was to hamstring captured chariot horses and burn the chariots, indicating the Hebrews apparently possessed no "chariot technology"; cf. Josh. 11:9; 2 Sam. 8:4 = 1 Chron. 18:4. Although not discussed by the Chronicler, this would suggest David complied with the directive of Deut. 17:16, prohibiting the acquisition of great numbers of horses for military purposes, whereas Solomon was in violation of the Mosaic command.)[9]

Toward bridging contexts. King Solomon's construction and dedication of the Jerusalem temple highlight several important theological continuities between the Old and New Testaments: the appropriate understanding God's holiness and the liturgical use of "sacred space," the role of sacred space in mediating God's immanence and transcendence, the centrality of prayer in worship, the significance of "pilgrimage" in the life of faith, the relationship between the sacred place and religious instruction, and the idea that sacred

---

8. See Dillard, 2 Chronicles, 13–14.
9. See the discussion of the archaeological evidence for Solomon's chariot cities in ibid., 13.

space (and worship) brings order out of chaos. Second Chronicles 1, reporting Solomon's prayer for the gift of wisdom, points toward the contemporary significance of the larger literary unit (chs. 1–9) by calling attention to the act of prayer, to the Jerusalem temple as the house of prayer, and to God who hears and answers the prayers of his people.

Construction of the Temple (2:1–5:1)

SOLOMON'S PREPARATIONS for building the temple (2:1–18). Despite David's extensive preparations for the building of the Jerusalem temple (1 Chron. 21–29), the scope of the task still requires Solomon to supplant his father's work with preliminary efforts. The bulk of the present chapter is devoted to the exchange of correspondence between Solomon and Hiram, king of Tyre. Brief notes pertaining to the labor force for the temple project frame the negotiations of Solomon and Hiram (2:1–2, 17–18).

The Chronicler has drawn loosely from (and in some cases reordered) the contents of the Kings' version of the temple construction, given his exclusive focus on the building of Yahweh's temple (cf. 1 Kings 5:1–16). We should note that the Chronicler understands Solomon's building campaign as a two-phased undertaking—the "temple for the Name of the LORD" and his own royal palace (2 Chron. 2:1). This datum helps explain the timing of the Lord's appearance to Solomon, after both the temple and the palace complex have been completed (7:11). The actual construction of the temple begins in the fourth year of Solomon's reign (ca. 966 B.C.; cf. 1 Kings 6:1) and is completed six years later (960 B.C.).

Solomon makes three requests of Hiram: cedar logs, a skilled craftsman, and pine and algum logs (2:3–9). In return for these raw building materials Solomon will provide Hiram with supplies of wheat, barley, honey, and olive oil (2:10). The foodstuffs bartered for the lumber are sent overland to Tyre, while the timbers are floated down to Joppa from Tyre in rafts (2:16). The more interesting features of the correspondence are the synopsis of temple worship (2:4) and theological treatise (2:5–6) Solomon offers the Phoenician king.

The ritual observances cited by Solomon show a full knowledge of the Mosaic law: the daily altar of incense and bread of presence offerings (cf. Ex. 25:30; 30:7), the morning and evening burnt offerings (cf. 29:38–39), and the offerings pertaining to the ritual calendar (i.e., Sabbath, New Moon, and the pilgrimage festivals; cf. 23:14–19; 31:13; Num. 10:10). As to theology, Solomon underscores God's omnipotence and transcendence to his royal counterpart in Phoenicia—quite an apologetic to the Tyrian worshiper of Baal!

The census of Solomon's labor force (2:17–18) clarifies the earlier report of the numbers of workers conscripted for the temple and palace building projects (2:2). This census clearly followed the ill-fated numbering of Israel by David (2:17b). Here we learn that the 70,000 stone-haulers and 80,000 stone-cutters are aliens, that is, non-Israelites living within the borders of Israel (2:17a). Naturally, such a large work force needs supervision to maintain a construction timetable, hence the 3,600 foremen drawn from among the 153,600 workmen counted in the census (2:18). The parallel passage in Kings also mentions the formation of temporary labor gangs of 30,000 Israelites conscripted to cut and dress timber in Lebanon on a rotating basis in shifts of 10,000 under the supervision of Adoniram (1 Kings 5:13–18).

Solomon builds the temple (3:1–17). The Chronicler compresses the earlier version of the actual temple construction into fourteen verses (3:1–14; cf. 1 Kings 6:1–38). He completely omits the synchronization with the date of the Exodus in order to focus on the location of the temple instead (3:1–2; cf. 1 Kings 6:1). Explicitly, the building of Yahweh's temple at Mount Moriah fulfills the plans made by David for the structure in the purchase of Araunah's threshing floor (2 Chron. 3:1; cf. 1 Chron. 21:25–26).

The reference to Mount Moriah awakens memories of the Lord's appearance to Abraham at the near sacrifice of Isaac his son (cf. Gen. 22). The reminder of the Lord's appearances at this site earlier in Israelite history may be the Chronicler's attempt to encourage his own audience. Despite the fact the second temple is less glorious than Solomon's shrine, the great sense of history associated with the sacred site offers hope that God may yet appear again at his temple.

Selman comments that this chapter "provides a simple tour" through the temple building, beginning with the portico or porch (3:4), then moving through the sanctuary (3:5–7) and on to the Most Holy Place (3:8–13).[10] Rather than offer a description of the shape of the temple building, the Chronicler has placed the focus on the floor plan of the structure.

Ancient Israel used two different standards for measuring the cubit, although it is unclear what the Chronicler meant by "the old standard" (3:3). The short cubit (17.4 inches) and the long cubit (20.4 inches) were based on an Egyptian standard of six and seven palm lengths respectively (cf. Ezek. 40:5; 43:13). The dimensions of Solomon's temple rendered in contemporary equivalents (using the short cubit) compute as follows: The sanctuary proper is 90 feet long, 30 feet wide, and 45 feet high (with the Holy Place measuring 60' x 30' by 45' and the Most Holy Place measuring 30' x 30' x 45'); the porch or portico extends the temple by another 15 feet in length (i.e., 30' wide x 30' high). (See fig. 8: Solomon's Temple diagram.) The walls of the portico are overlaid with gold (3:4b), not only enhancing the beauty of the entrance but having the practical effect of reflecting light into the building.

10. Selman, 2 Chronicles, 304.

960-586 B.C.

The temple of Solomon, located adjacent to the king's palace, functioned as God's royal palace and Israel's national center of worship. The Lord said to Solomon, "I have consecrated this temple...by putting my Name there forever. My eyes and my heart will always be there" (1 Kings 9:3). By its cosmological and royal symbolism, the sanctuary taught the absolute sovereignty of the Lord over the whole creation and his special headship over Israel.

The floor plan is a type that has a long history in Semitic religion, particularly among the West Semites. An early example of the tripartite division into 'ulam, hekal, and debir (portico, main hall, and inner sanctuary) has been found at Syrian Ebla (c. 2300 B.C.) and, much later but more contemporaneous with Solomon, at Tell Tainat in the Orontes basin (c. 900 B.C.). Like Solomon's, the later temple has three divisions, contains two columns supporting the entrance, and is located adjacent to the royal palace.

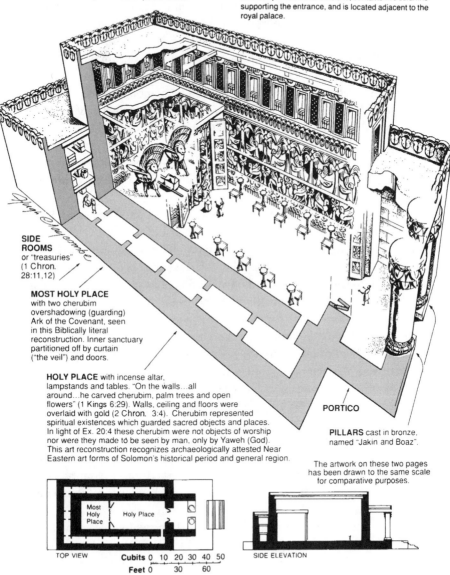

SIDE ROOMS or "treasuries" (1 Chron. 28:11,12)

MOST HOLY PLACE with two cherubim overshadowing (guarding) Ark of the Covenant, seen in this Biblically literal reconstruction. Inner sanctuary partitioned off by curtain ("the veil") and doors.

HOLY PLACE with incense altar, lampstands and tables. "On the walls...all around...he carved cherubim, palm trees and open flowers" (1 Kings 6:29). Walls, ceiling and floors were overlaid with gold (2 Chron. 3:4). Cherubim represented spiritual existences which guarded sacred objects and places. In light of Ex. 20:4 these cherubim were not objects of worship nor were they made to be seen by man, only by Yaweh (God). This art reconstruction recognizes archaeologically attested Near Eastern art forms of Solomon's historical period and general region.

PORTICO

PILLARS cast in bronze, named "Jakin and Boaz".

The artwork on these two pages has been drawn to the same scale for comparative purposes.

Most Holy Place | Holy Place

TOP VIEW

Cubits 0 10 20 30 40 50
Feet 0 30 60

SIDE ELEVATION

Fig 8. Solomon's Temple

385

The Chronicler next describes the sanctuary of the temple (3:5–7; cf. 1 Kings 6:20–22). The pinewood walls of the main hall are overlaid with gold and decorated with palm tree and chain motifs (2 Chron. 3:5). The precious stones collected by David also adorn the main hall in some unspecified way (cf. 1 Chron. 29:2). The rest of the interior is also overlaid with gold from Parvaim (an unknown site, 2 Chron. 3:6–7a).

Winged cherubim are also engraved on the gold overlay of the temple walls (3:7b). The cherubim of the Bible are angelic creatures combining numerous human and animal features (e.g., Ex. 37:7–9; Ezek. 41:18–19). According to Meyers, "these characteristics made them apt symbols for divine presence, since deities moved where humans could not and were something other than either animals or humans."[11] The combination of extensive gold overlay and the presence of the cherubim represent the beauty and majesty of a royal throne room, a fitting dwelling place for the Lord—the eternal King of glory (Ps. 10:16; 24:10). Two cherubim are fixed atop the cover of the ark of the covenant as well (Ex. 25:18–20). The repeated artistic motifs of the palm tree and the chain design may represent the ideas of life and eternality—the domains of God as Creator.

The extravagant use of gold overlay extends into the Most Holy Place (3:8–9). Much of the description of the Most Holy Place is devoted to the two massive sculptures of cherubim figures with outstretched wings that fill the room (3:10–13; cf. 1 Kings 6:23–27). Like the cherubim that guarded the entrance to the garden after the Fall (Gen. 3:24), these creatures guard the ark of the covenant eventually installed in the Most Holy Place (2 Chron. 5:7–8). We sometimes forget that this windowless room, the Most Holy Place, was enclosed with a veil and doors. Except for that one day in the year when the high priest entered the Most Holy Place to sprinkle the blood of the Day of Atonement sacrifice, this sacred space was pitch black. Yet, in terms of the symbolic divine presence resting there, the Hebrews know that "darkness is as light" to God (Ps. 139:12).

A veil woven of blue, purple, and scarlet yarn separated the Holy Place from the Most Holy Place in the Mosaic tabernacle or Tent of Meeting (Ex. 26:31–36). The veil of Solomon's temple replicates that tapestry, including the decorative embroidery of cherubim worked into the fabric (2 Chron. 3:14). The temple also has wooden doors overlaid with gold, including the inner doors to the Most Holy Place (4:22).

The Chronicler, then, understands Solomon's temple to possess both carved doors and a veil separating the Holy Place from the Most Holy Place. This fits well with the description of Herod's refurbished temple; according

---

11. Carol Meyers, "Cherubim," *ABD*, 1:900.

to Josephus that temple too had both a veil and doors at the entrance to the Most Holy Place (*Jewish War* 5.5). For the Chronicler, the veil represents continuity with the Mosaic tent and the Hebrew worship traditions established by the Sinaitic covenant. For Christians, the tearing of the veil at the death of Christ signified a glorious discontinuity with the "shadow" of greater realities (Matt. 27:51; cf. Heb. 10:1).

As with the veil, the bronze pillars in the front of the temple are given separate attention (3:15–17). Reconstructions prove difficult because it is unclear whether the two pillars are functional, load-bearing columns for the temple porch or free-standing fire cressets (columns or poles mounted with concave metal caps containing oil or pitch for burning to provide light).[12] Beyond the uncertainty of the origin and the function of pillars, they achieve additional notoriety because of the enigmatic names ascribed to each (Jakin and Boaz, 3:17). Jakin means "he establishes," and Boaz may mean "strength is in him." Selman's suggestion that these two named pillars signify the fact that Yahweh's covenant is confirmed through the temple is as good as any for understanding their symbolic value.[13] The NIV harmonizes the height of the pillars with the Kings' parallel by inserting the word "together" (i.e., the pillars are a combined thirty-five cubits; cf. eighteen cubits in height for each pillar, 1 Kings 7:15; see fig. 9 on the following page).

The temple furnishings (4:1–5:1). This section of 2 Chronicles repeats 1 Kings 7:23–51 with some variation. For instance, the Chronicler adds material in 2 Chronicles 4:1, 6–9 but omits the lengthy description of the ten water carts (cf. 1 Kings 7:27–37). The Kings' parallel fails to mention the bronze altar (2 Chron. 4:1), although it is referenced in the subsequent account of the temple dedication (1 Kings 8:64). The sizeable dimensions of the altar are usually understood to circumscribe the base of the structure, from which a staircase leads to the altar itself (cf. Ezek. 43:13–17).

The Sea of cast metal (4:2–5) replaces the laver of the Mosaic tabernacle (cf. Ex. 30:17–21). It holds 3,000 baths (a liquid measure in Old Testament times yielding a volume of about 17,500 gallons). The divergence of the Kings' parallel (where the Sea holds 2,000 baths, 1 Kings 7:26) may be explained by assuming that the larger total is based on a cylindrical shape for the Sea, while the smaller total is based on a hemispherical shape.[14] Whereas the Sea is for the ritual washing of the priests, the ten basins are for cleansing the utensils used for burnt offerings.

---

12. See discussion in Dillard, 2 *Chronicles*, 30. Descriptions of the two bronze pillars are found in 1 Kings 7:15–22; 2 Kings 25:17; 2 Chron. 3:15–17; and Jer. 52:21–22.

13. Selman, 2 *Chronicles*, 309.

14. Cf. Williamson, *1 and 2 Chronicles*, 210–11.

Harmonizing 1 Kings 7:15,16
with 2 Chronicles 3:15

The decorative 5 cubit capital (7 1/2') "in the shape of lilies" is shown (right) fitting down over the 17.5 cubit "pillar" described in 2 Chron.3:15. As hollow, with a 1/2 cubit (9") weight bearing surface at the top, a total pillar/capital unit of 18 cubits is created thus matching the "18 cubit pillar" recorded in 1 Kings 7:15. Some scholars have asserted that the books of 1 and 2 Chronicles are of secondary quality and are inaccurate regarding the portico and pillars in Solomon's Temple. Here we may lay that argument to rest.

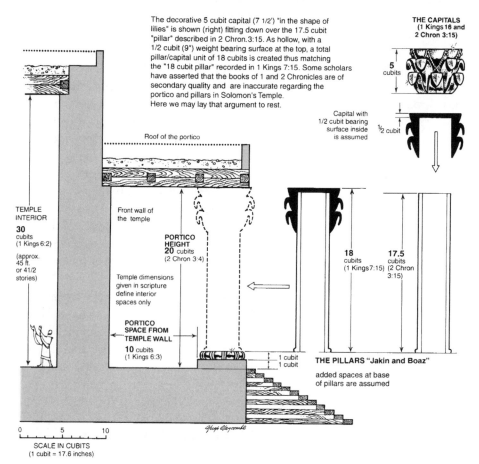

THE CAPITALS
(1 Kings 16 and 2 Chron 3:15)

5 cubits

Capital with 1/2 cubit bearing surface inside is assumed

1/2 cubit

Roof of the portico

TEMPLE INTERIOR
30 cubits
(1 Kings 6:2)
(approx. 45 ft. or 4 1/2 stories)

Front wall of the temple

PORTICO HEIGHT 20 cubits
(2 Chron 3:4)

Temple dimensions given in scripture define interior spaces only

PORTICO SPACE FROM TEMPLE WALL
10 cubits
(1 Kings 6:3)

1 cubit
1 cubit

18 cubits
(1 Kings 7:15)

17.5 cubits
(2 Chron 3:15)

THE PILLARS "Jakin and Boaz"

added spaces at base of pillars are assumed

0   5   10
SCALE IN CUBITS
(1 cubit = 17.6 inches)

"35 cubits" (2 Chron 3:15)

Were the pillars solid bronze? It is more likely that only the outer surface was metal, then highly polished.

"In the front of the temple he made two pillars, which together were thirty five cubits long,..." (2 Chron.3:15) This unusual way of expressing the 17.5 cubit length of each pillar may have occurred during the construction phase when the pillars were laying end to end. May we reconstruct a question that the writer may have asked: " How long are they?" Shown at the left is Huran, Solomon's bronze artisan correctly answering an unclear question.

Fig. 9. The Bronze Pillars

The ten golden lampstands replace the one lampstand featured in the Mosaic tabernacle (4:7; cf. Ex. 25:31–36). The ten tables are mentioned only here in the Old Testament descriptions of the Solomon's temple (2 Chron. 4:8). The Chronicler seems to assume that the ten lampstands rest on the ten tables. The insertion of the description of the courtyard of the priests completes the report of the Sea by noting its location in the southeast corner of the courtyard (4:9–10).

The summary of Huram-Abi's achievements (4:11–16) completes the record of the skilled smiths sent by King Hiram of Tyre to oversee the metal work and engraving for the temple (2:13–14). The added detail concerning the location of bronze casting (east of the Jordan River, halfway between the Dead Sea and the Sea of Galilee, 4:17) puts the process of metal casting a considerable distance from the source of copper used in the bronze casting if it was mined at Timnah. The "golden altar" is equivalent to the altar of incense in the Mosaic tabernacle (4:19a; cf. Ex. 30:1–10). The reference to "the tables" of the bread of the Presence is probably a scribal error since there is only one table for the showbread representing the twelve tribes (2 Chron. 4:19b; cf. Ex. 25:23–30). The Kings' parallel makes no mention of the temple doors or the set of doors protecting the entrance to the Most Holy Place (2 Chron. 4:22).

The reference to the deposit of David's war booty in the temple treasuries (5:1) serves as a transition to the account of the installation of the ark of the covenant. This verse also recalls the plunder taken from the Egyptians used in the construction of the Mosaic tabernacle (Ex. 12:36). In both cases, the wealth of the nations contributes to the building of God's sanctuaries. Finally, McConville has noted the Chronicler's wordplay on Solomon's name in the verb "finished" (both are related to the Heb. *šlm*, 5:1) as an apt conclusion to the narrative.[15]

Toward bridging contexts. King Solomon's construction and dedication of the Jerusalem temple highlight several important theological continuities between the Old and New Testaments: the appropriate understanding God's holiness and the liturgical use of "sacred space," the role of sacred space in mediating God's immanence and transcendence, the centrality of prayer in worship, the significance of "pilgrimage" in the life of faith, the relationship between the sacred place and religious instruction, and the idea that sacred space (and worship) brings order out of chaos. Second Chronicles 2:1–5:1, reporting the construction phase of the Jerusalem temple, points toward the contemporary significance of the larger literary unit (chs. 1–9) by calling attention to the association between the event of theophany and worship at a "sacred place" and the idea of pilgrimage to a sacred place.

---

15. McConville, *I and II Chronicles*, 125.

Dedication of the Temple (5:2–7:22)

THE REPORTS OF the installation of the ark of the covenant in the Most Holy Place and the dedication of the temple constitute the climax of the Chronicler's narrative of Israelite history. Historically, the reign of King Solomon was the zenith of Israelite political power and influence in the biblical world and the "golden age" of Israelite history culturally. The narrative reporting the events of the reign of Solomon, however, is important to the Chronicler for another reason. Theologically, this literary unit emphasizes the themes of the ark of the covenant, the temple, and the Davidic dynasty—the essential building blocks in the theology of hope he lays for his audience in the retelling of the history of Israelite kingship.

This section contains three distinct movements: the transfer and installation of the ark of the covenant (5:2–6:11), the dedicatory prayer for the temple (6:12–42), and the concluding ceremonies (7:1–11). Solomon's dream theophany (7:12–22), in which God voices his approval of the king's temple-related initiatives, provides a natural closure. The parallel that provides the primary historical source for this section of the Chronicler's narrative is 1 Kings 8:1–9:9.

The installation of the ark of the covenant (5:2–6:2). The transfer of the ark of the covenant comes almost verbatim from 1 Kings 8:1–13. The ark was the single most sacred object associated with the Mosaic tabernacle. It was a symbol of both God's presence in the midst of his people (1 Chron. 28:2) and his power among the nations (2 Chron. 6:41; see comments on 1 Chron. 13–17). Solomon gathers largely the same categories of political and religious leaders who helped David transfer the ark from Kiriath Jearim to Jerusalem (2 Chron. 5:2–3; cf. 1 Chron. 13:1–4). The Chronicler is careful to note that the Levites serve as porters for the ark while in transit, while the priests are required to station the ark in the Most Holy Place (2 Chron. 5:4, 7–8). The installation of the ark and the dedication of the temple are held in conjunction with the Feast of Tabernacles (5:3, see comments on 7:8–10; see fig. 7, the ark of the covenant diagram).

The rest of the sacred furniture from the Tent of Meeting, as well as the tent itself, is also transported to the temple precinct (5:4–5). Previously, the Tent of Meeting was located in Gibeon (cf. 1 Chron. 16:39). There is no mention of the Tent of Meeting being relocated in Jerusalem, so presumably these materials have been dismantled and transported from Gibeon to Jerusalem for the installation ceremony. The ark itself undoubtedly leads the procession from the temporary structure David erected in Zion to the Jerusalem temple (2 Chron. 5:2; cf. 1 Chron. 15:1–2).

Simultaneously with the installation of the ark, Solomon and the assembly of Israel offer sacrifices in the temple court (5:6). The reference to the tablets of Moses as the only contents of the ark of the covenant (5:10) indicates that the Chronicler is familiar with the tradition that the ark held additional contents at one time. For instance, Hebrews 9:4 records that a jar of manna and Aaron's rod were also in the ark of the covenant. The Old Testament, however, indicates that these items were placed in front of the ark (Ex. 16:32–34; Num. 17:10–11).

The reference to the Levitical musicians (5:11–13) in the final paragraph (5:11–6:2) is an addition to the Kings' version of the account and reflects the Chronicler's special interests in the musical tradition of the temple. The 120 priests are probably a group of ad hoc musicians who are off-duty from their usual service rotation (5:12). The hymnic refrain "he is good; his love endures forever" (5:13) is a liturgical response associated with other festal gatherings in Chronicles (e.g., 1 Chron. 16:34, 41; 2 Chron. 7:3, 6; 20:21; cf. Ps. 136:1 and the repeated refrain). The word "good" calls to mind God as Creator and the goodness of his creation, while "love" evokes the Mount Sinai experience and God's covenant relationship with Israel.

Following the pattern of the dedication of the tabernacle, the cloud of God's glory fills the temple after the priests install the ark in the Most Holy Place (5:14; cf. Ex. 40:34–35). This account of the event is told from a priestly perspective in terms of their service rendered in the temple. Later the event is retold from the perspective of Solomon and the assembly of Israel as the ceremonies for the temple dedication come to an end (7:1–2; see comments).

Solomon addresses the assembly of Israel (6:3–11). The report of Solomon's address to the assembly of Israel closely follows 1 Kings 8:14–21. Only two significant divergences may be noted. (1) The blessing is expanded to include Jerusalem as the site where God's "Name" will be established (6:6). (2) The reference to Israel's exodus from Egypt is omitted (6:11), since the Chronicler's emphasis is on the Davidic covenant. The reference to God's "promise" to David (6:4, 10) is not a precise quotation of any specific text but rather a conflation of several passages in order to present the gist of the Davidic covenant (cf. 1 Chron. 17:4–14; 22:7–10; 28:2–7).

After Solomon has turned from the dazzling spectacle of the cloud of Yahweh's glory filling the temple (5:14), he address the "whole assembly of Israel" (6:3). Like his father, David, Solomon assumes a priestly or pastoral role when addressing the nation of Israel (cf. 1 Chron. 16:43). The Chronicler, however, portrays Solomon as one who represents the interests of the people more than the office of the Levitical priesthood. He blessed the populace as one of them. The king's blessing underscores God's selection of David as Israel's ruler and the city of Jerusalem as the site for the temple (6:6). The succession of Solomon to David's throne and the completion of the temple inaugurate the Davidic covenant announced previously by the prophet Nathan (cf. 1 Chron. 17:3). The people are blessed by these developments because through the Davidic covenant God has made provision for righteous leadership over the people and established a national "house of prayer" for Israel. Through prayer (whether praise, confession, petition, or intercession) Israel will maintain her covenant relationship with Yahweh.

The contents of Solomon's blessing show him to be not only a pastor but also a theologian. Appropriately, the king begins his address with "praise" to God (Heb. *baruk*; lit., "blessed")—a blessing learned from his father (cf. Ps. 18:46; 26:12). The reference to the "God of Israel" (2 Chron. 6:4) and the repetition of the word "chosen" (6:5–6) allude to the Abrahamic covenant (Gen. 12:1–3; 15). The allusion to the Exodus (6:5) reveals that Solomon understands the historical and theological continuity between the Mosaic covenant and the Davidic covenant. Finally, the acknowledgment that Jerusalem is now the place identified with God's "Name" (6:6) demonstrates Solomon's awareness of the teaching of Deuteronomy concerning an eventual permanent worship site in Israel (cf. Deut. 12:11, 21).

Selman has noted that the anthropomorphisms (God's "hands" and "mouth," 6:4) indicate that "God's actions have confirmed his words."[16] The implicit exhortation embedded in the report of Solomon's blessing for the Chronicler's audience is the fact they are the heirs of these covenants made by the God of Israel.

The second half of Solomon's address to the people of Israel is basically a prayer of thanksgiving, acknowledging God as a "promise-keeper" (6:7–11). The king specifically cites his succession to David's throne (6:10a), the completion of the temple (6:10b), and the installation of the ark of the covenant (6:11) as proof positive that Yahweh is faithful to his word. The ark of the covenant is the symbol of God's presence among his people and a tangible witness of his special relationship with Israel. The installation of the ark in the Jerusalem temple signifies that these theological truths now undergird the Davidic covenant as well.

Solomon's prayer of dedication (6:12–42). The Chronicler's version of Solomon's prayer of dedication for the temple closely follows 1 Kings 8:22–53. The prayer may be outlined in four distinct units:

- the petition for posterity (6:14–17)
- principles of intercession (6:18–21)
- circumstances for intercession (6:22–39)
- the entrance hymn invoking God's presence (6:40–42)

---

16. Selman, *2 Chronicles*, 324.

Dillard observes that the Chronicler has given the prayer of dedication considerable prominence by virtue of its location at the heart of the chiastic structure of the narrative recounting Solomon's reign (see the outline above).[17] The fact that Solomon's prayer occupies more text than the actual construction of the temple further substantiates the argument that the Chronicler is making a theological statement to his own audience about the centrality of prayer in the life of the postexilic community. In fact, it seems as if the writer is calling for the "priests" and "saints" (or "loyal ones") among his contemporaries to reclaim the discipline of prayer, so that the second temple may become a house of prayer like the first temple and so that postexilic Israel may experience God's "salvation" and "goodness" (6:41). As McConville has summed up, "prayer is to be the essential instrument in the continuing relationship between God and his people. It is that which activates existing promises."[18]

The opening paragraph lists the preparations undertaken by Solomon for his dedicatory prayer for the Jerusalem temple (6:12–13). Chronicles expands the Kings' version by including details related to the bronze platform on which the king offers his prayer to the Lord God of Israel (6:13; cf. 1 Kings 8:22).

The bronze platform is most likely a temporary structure erected in the outer court of the temple precinct. Solomon's posture of standing before the altar and the assembly of Israel prior to praying suggests he has taken on a priestly role as a representative of the people (6:12). The backdrop of the bronze altar of burnt offering for the prayer of dedication points to the idea that prayer is also a form of "sacrifice" (cf. Ps. 141:2). Standing, kneeling, and spreading the hands are common prayer postures in biblical times. The description of Solomon kneeling (2 Chron. 6:13) calls to mind the psalmist's exhortation to "kneel before . . . our Maker" (Ps. 95:6). Bodily movement in worship generally, and posture in prayer specifically, are important parts of one's response to God because outward actions demonstrate and reinforce inward attitudes and beliefs. Typically, kneeling symbolizes reverence, even fear, before the deity, while spreading out raised hands is an act of veneration (i.e., blessing and praise) of the deity (cf. 1 Tim. 2:8).

The completion of the temple project has fulfilled a divine promise (6:15), but not exhausted the promises granted by God in conjunction with the Davidic covenant. Solomon first petitions God to bless him with a posterity so that the Davidic throne may be established forever (6:14–17; cf. 2 Sam. 7:13, 15). Solomon requests that Yahweh continue "building the house of

---

17. See Dillard, 2 *Chronicles*, 47.
18. McConville, *I and II Chronicles*, 129.

David" even though God's house now stands finished and ready for "occu-pation" (cf. 1 Chron 17:10–14). Note the biblical pattern of offering God praise before petition is raised (2 Chron. 6:14).

The threefold repetition of God's covenant name, "LORD, God of Israel" (6:14, 16, 17) addresses his majesty as Lord of creation (cf. 6:18), while the emphasis on his covenant love speaks to his uniqueness and incomparabil-ity as the one true God (6:14). As Wilcock admonishes us, "before we ask God for anything we remind ourselves of his character."[19] Solomon's prayer for the continuation of the Davidic dynasty is ultimately the Chronicler's prayer as well. The stylized retelling of the temple dedication ceremony is a call to prayer to the postexilic Jewish community with the hope that God will keep his promise to David and Solomon and reestablish the throne of David in Israel.

The bulk of the dedicatory prayer closely follows the Kings' version (6:18–39; cf. 1 Kings 8:27–50a). This section of Solomon's entreaty includes two distinct segments: the fundamental theological principles of intercessory prayer (2 Chron. 6:18–21) and the circumstances prompting intercession (6:22–39).

(1) To understand prayer is to acknowledge the paradoxical truth of God's simultaneous transcendence and immanence. Solomon recognizes that the vast expanse of the heavens cannot contain the unique "otherness" of the Creator, how much less a building like the temple (6:18; cf. Isa. 57:15). Yet somehow the Jerusalem shrine is the earthly interface of the Lord's divine presence and absolute holiness because it is at this place that God has cho-sen to set his Name (2 Chron. 6:20).

Solomon's temple becomes the symbolic focal point of God's interest in and care for humanity, for it is here that his "eyes" and "ears" are continually open to the supplications of both Israelite and foreigner alike (6:21; cf. 6:32–33). It is these qualities that differentiate God from the false gods of the nations, gods who have eyes but cannot see and ears but cannot hear (cf. Ps. 115:5; Isa. 44:18). God possesses the will, the power, and the compassion to respond to prayer and intervene in human crises just because he sees and hears (cf. Neh. 1:6, 11; Isa. 59:1).

Selman has identified a basic pattern for intercessory prayer in Solomon's plea:

- the idea that such prayer is characterized by sincerity and urgency (i.e., "plea for mercy," 6:19); it includes confession and repentance (6:26) and a change of heart (6:37)

---

19. Wilcock, *The Message of Chronicles*, 147.

- an appeal to God to "hear" (6:19) with "open eyes" (6:20); that is, praying in faith that because God hears and sees, he answers prayer
- offering prayer toward the temple as the symbol of God's presence and authority, since praying in that manner is praying in the Name of the One to whom the temple belongs (6:21)
- the truth that God is accessible by anyone who acknowledges Yahweh as "my God" (6:19, 22)
- the purpose of such prayer, namely, the forgiveness of sins for the sake of restoration, healing, and blessing (6:21).[20]

Above all else, Solomon learned a lesson from his father, David, that was later crystallized by Isaiah the prophet. It is not that "the arm of the LORD is . . . too short to save, nor his ear to dull to hear. But your iniquities have separated you from your God" (Isa. 59:1; cf. Ps. 51:1–3). The temple as a "house of prayer" serves to bridge the gap between God and his people caused by their sins, because God is a "forgiving" God (2 Chron. 6:21, 25, 27, 30, 39).

(2) The list of circumstances prompting intercessory prayer should be regarded as representative and not comprehensive (6:22–39). The examples of personal injustices (6:22–23), warfare (6:24–25, 34–39), and natural calamities and disasters affecting the land (6:26–31) are universal experiences in the agrarian society of biblical times. We forget that life in biblical times was lived on the "ragged edge" of survival most of the time. The event of childbirth was often fatal to child or mother or both. A simple infection was potentially lethal. The essential point seems to be the reminder to the faithful of Israel to bring all the "stuff of life" to God in penitential prayer— lest national or personal sin be the cause of the affliction.

The most extensive alterations of the earlier version of Solomon's prayer of dedication for the temple occur in the final section (6:40–42), suggesting that this portion of the prayer is especially important to the Chronicler. The parallel in 1 Kings 8:50b–53 grounds the expectation for God's favorable response to the prayer in the special relationship between Yahweh and Israel established by the Mosaic covenant. By contrast, the Chronicler omits the reference to Moses and the Exodus and grounds this expectation in God's promises to David (6:41–42). The so-called entrance hymn is an adaptation of Psalm 132:1, 8–10, inviting the Lord to enter his temple and emphasizing the Davidic covenant.

The repetition of God's "great love" (ḥesed) and the phrase "David your servant" in the final verse (6:42) has the effect of forming an inclusio or envelope construction with the opening petition of Solomon's prayer (6:14–17;

---

20. Selman, 2 Chronicles, 327–28.

see esp. "covenant of love" in 6:14 and "your servant David" in 6:16). McConville has noted that "the basis of any relationship between God and Israel can only ultimately be God's keeping covenant and showing steadfast love. God's action in establishing the relationship must precede any obedience on Israel's part."[21]

The Chronicler is fully aware of this theological truth, given his knowledge of Israel's history. It is his own historical context of Second Temple Jerusalem during the postexilic era that prompts his insertion of portions of the entrance hymn for two specific reasons. (1) The invitation to Yahweh to arise and enter his "resting place" (6:41) anticipates the Lord's return to his temple as prophesied by Zechariah (Zech. 1:16). The postexilic community is still awaiting the revisitation of God's glory to his temple (cf. Hag. 2:7).

(2) As Williamson has recognized, the temple building only "confirms, not absorbs," the hope that God will restore the vitality of the Davidic kingship in keeping with his promise (6:15; cf. Ps. 132:11).[22] This reality explains the Chronicler's reordering and change of wording in his appropriation of Psalm 132:10 in 2 Chronicles 6:42 as an allusion to the "everlasting covenant ... promised to David" (cf. Isa. 55:3). Both Psalm 132:10–11 and Isaiah 55:3 stress the Lord's promise to continue David's dynasty—a message the Chronicler's audience needs to hear!

Dedication of the temple (7:1–10). The circumstantial clause denoting the cause-and-effect relationship between Solomon's prayer and God's response clearly marks the beginning of a new section of the narrative. This portion of the Chronicler's story of Solomon's reign contains two major units: the dedication of the temple (7:1–10) and the report of the Lord's appearance to Solomon (7:11–22). Each section in chapter 7 begins with the name "Solomon" since he is credited as the builder of Yahweh's temple (7:1, 5, 7, 8, 11). The chiastic structure of the narrative recounting Solomon's reign (chs. 1–9) is further enhanced by the inclusio formed by the repetition of the hymn of thanksgiving (5:13 and 7:3). This section of the narrative corresponds to 1 Kings 8:54–9:9 (2 Chron. 7:4–9//1 Kings 8:62–66 with some modification, and 2 Chron. 7:1–2, 17–22//1 Kings 9:1, 3, 4–9 with some modification).

The opening paragraph (7:1–3) shares but one clause with 1 Kings 8:54 ("when Solomon finished praying"). The Chronicler omits Solomon's blessing of the assembly (1 Kings 8:55–61) and instead inserts the report of fire raining down from heaven and consuming the burnt offerings and sacrifices (2 Chron. 7:1b–3). The account of the fire from heaven completes the twofold response of God to the temple dedication ceremony begun earlier

21. McConville, *I and II Chronicles*, 132.
22. Williamson, *1 and 2 Chronicles*, 221.

in the narrative recording the installation of the ark of the covenant (5:13–14). The simultaneous events of fire from heaven falling on the bronze altar and the cloud of Yahweh's glory filling the temple prompt a predictable reaction from the people—prostration in worship (7:3).

The dramatic depiction of God's issuing fire from heaven on an altar is a familiar motif in the Old Testament. For example, fire from the Lord's presence consumed the burnt offerings on the altar as the priests began their ministry in the Mosaic tabernacle (Lev. 9:23–24). Later, fire from heaven licked up David's offering on the altar at the threshing floor of Araunah as a testimony to God's decision to stay the plague against Israel for the king's foolish census (1 Chron. 21:26). In both cases, the fire from heaven indicates God accepts these acts of worship.

In a similar manner, each aspect of the divine response to the temple dedication ceremonies orchestrated by Solomon is crucial to the inauguration of the new sanctuary as the central Israelite worship center. (1) The fire from heaven that engulfs the sacrifices on the bronze altar affirms that the Lord God has accepted the work of Solomon in building the temple and the worship of the priests and people in dedicating the edifice to the service of Yahweh. (2) The cloud of glory that fills the temple and prevents the priests from entering the structure signals God's approval of this new "house of prayer" as his abode among his people.

National unity is a recurring theme for the Chronicler, and it resurfaces in the report that the king, the people, and the priests and Levites all join in the ceremony of dedication for the new temple (7:4–6). Critics have questioned the large number of sacrifices offered at the dedication, since the slaughter of 142,000 animals would require twenty sacrifices per minute for ten hours a day for twelve straight days.[23] This fact has led some to suggest that the numbers represent a hyperbole of some sort.[24] Others remain more open-minded about the enormous number of sacrifices and point to the use of the courtyard as additional "altar space" as an argument for the plausibility of the Chronicler's rendition of the event.[25] Regardless of whether one understands the tally of animals sacrificed in a symbolic or a literal fashion, the point is that the magnitude of this worship response to God makes Solomon's new bronze altar inadequate for the task (cf. 7:7). The insertion of the reference to the temple musicians (7:6) is a stylistic feature further enhancing the chiastic structure of Solomon's kingship narrative (cf. 5:12–13).

---

23. See John. W. Wenham, "Large Numbers in the Old Testament," *TynBul* 19 (1967): 49–53.

24. So Thompson, *1, 2 Chronicles*, 234.

25. E.g., Selman, *2 Chronicles*, 335.

Solomon had a new bronze altar cast for the temple courtyard (2 Chron. 4:1). Presumably, this altar replaces the bronze altar located at the tabernacle site in Gibeon (cf. 1 Chron. 16:40). This being the case, the sign of the fire from heaven also represents a divine validation of this altar as a substitute for the altar associated with the Mosaic tabernacle in Gibeon. This parenthetical note explaining why burnt offerings are also made in the courtyard reflects the Chronicler's concern for propriety in ritual procedures (cf. also the writer's report that Solomon consecrates the area prior to offering the sacrifices). Typically, burnt offerings addressed issues of sin as well as dedication to the Lord; grain or meal offerings symbolized thanksgiving (Lev. 2); and the fat portions of the peace offerings connoted fellowship with God (Lev. 3).

The Chronicler clarifies the Kings' parallel on the chronological details associated with the temple dedication (see 1 Kings 8:65–66). The week-long dedication of the temple actually precedes the week-long Feast of Tabernacles celebration (this latter celebration began on the fifteenth day of the seventh month; see Lev. 23:34–36, 39–43; Deut. 16:13–15). Solomon holds a sacred assembly on the eighth day (2 Chron. 7:9; this would be the twenty-second day; cf. Lev. 23:36). The Feast of Tabernacles (or Ingathering) was a pilgrimage festival, thus explaining the large assembly in Jerusalem (Ex. 23:16). A similar two-festival event was held in conjunction with Passover during the reign of King Hezekiah (cf. 2 Chron. 30:23).

The reference to "Lebo Hamath to the Wadi of Egypt" constitutes the ideal boundaries of ancient Israel, the possession promised to the patriarchs (cf. Gen. 15:18; Num. 34:5, 8). The Chronicler adds the clause "for they had celebrated the dedication of the altar" (2 Chron. 7:9), since the temple was both a house of prayer and a house of sacrifice (7:12). The act of dedication was a formal initiation of something or someone for a divinely ordained role—in this case, the bronze altar for burnt offerings (cf. Num. 7:10–11).

The Chronicler also adds the phrase "and Solomon" to "the good things the LORD had done for David," in order to give the sense that the reigns of these two kings are complementary, almost presenting a seamless narrative of a single episode in the history of Israel. The Chronicler is careful to note that the people are blessed through David and Solomon as divine agents— it is the Lord himself who has done the "good things" for Israel (7:10). The report of the temple dedication is sometimes understood as an example of the festal schema. This literary form is a formulaic summary of joyful worship that includes a chronological statement, a list of the participants, and the ceremonial rituals observed (cf. 2 Chron. 15:9–15; 30:13–27; 35:1–19).[26]

---

26. De Vries, 1 and 2 Chronicles, 264–65.

The Lord appears to Solomon (7:11–22). The second half of chapter 7 describes the Lord's appearance to Solomon "at night" (7:11). This unit is a confirmatory dream report since the theophany repeats the pattern of the Lord's first appearance to Solomon at Gibeon (cf. 1 Kings 3:5). Despite the juxtaposition of the accounts of the temple dedication and the second appearance of the Lord to Solomon, the two dream events occur thirteen years apart (i.e., after the completion of the temple and Solomon's palace, 2 Chron. 7:11b; cf. 1 Kings 7:1; 9:10).

The dream report may be divided into two uneven segments: an introduction (7:11–12a) and the divine address (7:12b–22). The introductory remarks roughly parallel 1 Kings 9:1–3, while the last portion of the divine address (2 Chron. 7:17–22) is a more faithful rendering of the Kings' parallel (1 Kings 9:4–9). (1) The notation that Solomon "finished the temple of the LORD" (2 Chron. 7:11) sets up the inclusion or envelope construction begun earlier (2:1, with the commencement of the temple building project) and completed in 8:16 with the statement "so the temple of the LORD was finished."

(2) The Lord's speech to Solomon on the occasion of his second dream theophany may be outlined in three distinct parts: the Lord's acceptance of Solomon's prayer of dedication and his approval of the Jerusalem temple as the place for his Name to dwell (7:12b), the Lord's promise to Solomon and the people he shepherds (7:13–18), and the Lord's threat of punishment for disobedience (7:19–22). (a) The divine affirmation calls attention to the temple as a place for "sacrifices" and emphasizes the word "chosen" (bḥr, 7:12b). This term is loaded with "theological freight" for the Hebrew, most notably the election of Israel as God's people from all the nations of the earth (Deut. 7:6). Divine approval is reiterated with the repetition of the word "chosen" (2 Chron. 7:16), coupled with the declaration that the "consecration" of the temple is really an act of Yahweh himself in response to Solomon's dedicatory sacrifices and prayer.

(b) The Lord's promise to Solomon confers the right to rule to the household or dynasty of King David (7:13–18). This theological truth is reinforced by the Chronicler's insertion of the word "covenanted" for the word promised in the divine charge to Solomon (7:18; cf. 1 Kings 9:5). The fulfillment of the promise, however, is conditioned by two separate but related factors. The first is the obedience of the people to the laws of God (7:13–16); the second is the obedience of the king to those same divine decrees and laws (7:17–18). Little has changed in the theological progression from the Mosaic covenant to the Davidic covenant—the blessing of God still requires the response of faith acted out in loving obedience to God's revelation. As a further aside to progressive revelation, biblical commentators see an allusion by the Chronicler to the messianic hope offered in Micah 5:2 in the sentence "a man to rule over Israel."

The paragraph of the Lord's speech to Solomon addressing the call to repentance and the promise of forgiveness is unique to Chronicles (7:13–16). In one sense, this passage is the answer to the king's prayer of dedication for the temple in which he calls for Yahweh to be attentive to the prayers of petition and repentance offered by the people in the new constructed sanctuary (see esp. 6:22–40). The activities of "humbling, praying, seeking, and turning" should be understood as four facets or aspects of the act (or even process) of biblical repentance (7:14).

Each of these words is theologically charged. The word "humble" (kn^c) means to subdue one's pride and submit in self-denying loyalty to God and his will (cf. Lev. 26:41). "Pray" (pll) in this context is a shameless acknowledgment of personal sin and a plea for God's mercy, much like that of David's prayer of repentance (cf. Ps. 51:1–2). "Seek" ($bq\check{s}$) is often used in desperate situations in which God is the only possible hope for deliverance (cf. Deut. 4:29–30). "Turn" ($\check{s}wb$) is the Old Testament term for repentance and signifies a complete change of direction away from sin and toward God (or an "about-face" in military parlance; cf. Ezek. 18:30, 32).

Verse 14 is a theological digest of the rest of the Chronicler's narrative. The history of the monarchy demonstrates how both the kings and the people "humble" themselves before God (e.g., Rehoboam, 12:6–7), "pray" to God in repentance (e.g., Hezekiah, 32:20), "seek" God's face for restoration (e.g., Jehoshaphat and the people of Judah, 20:3–4), and "turn" from sin to obey God's commands (e.g., Asa and the people, 15:4). Such behavior will ensure that God's "Name" or presence will remain associated with the Jerusalem temple (7:16a).

The reference to the "eyes" and the "heart" of Yahweh being connected to the temple (7:16b) is an unusual expression for the idea of the divine presence in the Old Testament. The eyes and heart of God symbolize his concerned watch-care for humanity in that he sees people in distress and has a compassionate heart for their plight, and he has the power to intervene and deliver his people. One cannot reflect on the association of the "eyes and heart" of God with the Jerusalem temple and not have inklings about the incarnation of Jesus Christ.

The call to repentance and the promise of forgiveness in verse 14 is also the Chronicler's sermon to his own audience. The postexilic Jewish community needs the reminder that God's choice of Jerusalem as the place to set his Name is still valid. De Vries correctly observes that the Chronicler's descriptions of the temple dedication and great pilgrimage festivals are prescriptive; that is, "Israel's greatest joy ought ever to be to journey to the temple and take part in the sacred festivals."27 More important for the Chronicler is the theology symbolized in the second temple, for, like Solomon's sanctuary, it embodies the truth that God will forgive the repentant sinner.

(c) The Chronicler omits the reference to Solomon's descendants (7:19; cf. 1 Kings 9:6), though the plural pronouns have been retained. Although contextually the Lord's threat (2 Chron. 7:19–22) is addressed to Solomon and the people of Israel, the Chronicler clearly understands that the threat of divine punishment is still in force for his own audience. The question-and-answer schema couched in the conversation of the casual stranger passing by the rejected temple (7:21–22) is a literary form often found in prophetic literature (e.g., Deut. 29:24–25; Jer. 22:8-9; cf. Jer. 24:9; Ezek. 14:8). This device emphasizes the sin and guilt of the people precipitating such calamity. The words are no doubt a grim reminder to the Chronicler's audience of what once did happen, and could happen again, to the temple. Whether or not Yahweh's temple becomes the moral of a proverb (i.e., "byword," *mašal;* 2 Chron. 7:20) ever again or the object of taunting and ridicule is dependent on the people's response to God's call to repentance and his promise to forgive.

Toward bridging contexts. King Solomon's construction and dedication of the Jerusalem temple highlight several important theological continuities between the Old and New Testaments: the appropriate understanding of God's holiness and the liturgical use of "sacred space," the role of sacred space in mediating God's immanence and transcendence, the centrality of prayer in worship, the significance of "pilgrimage" in the life of faith, the relationship between the sacred place and religious instruction, and the idea that sacred space (and worship) brings order out of chaos. Second Chronicles 5:2–7:22, recounting the dedication of the Jerusalem temple, points toward the contemporary significance of the larger literary unit (chs. 1–9) by emphasizing the priority of intercessory prayer. The account of the glory of God entering the temple furthers the topic of "sacred space" that mediates God's immanence and transcendence and ultimately foreshadows the incarnation of Jesus Christ (John 1:14).

Solomon's Other Activities (8:1–9:31)

THE CONCLUDING SECTION of the Chronicler's report summarizing Solomon's reign finds its parallel in 1 Kings 9:10–28; 10:1–13. The overarching theme of each element of this literary unit is clear. The emphasis of 2 Chronicles 8 is Solomon's faithfulness in following through on all of David's preparations and seeing the temple building project to completion (cf. 8:16). Chapter 9 praises God for his faithfulness in making good on his covenant promise to

27. Ibid., 265.

"build David's house" and to bless his successor with wisdom (cf. 9:8). The divine pledge granting Solomon wisdom (1:11–12), wealth, and honor is realized in 9:13–28, suggesting an overall design for the entire section (chs. 1–9). More than the achievements of the king, the last segment of the Chronicler's review of Solomon celebrates what God has achieved through this Davidic king.

Additional building projects (8:1–6). The Chronicler appeals rather erratically to 1 Kings 9:10–14 here. The twin priorities of erecting a temple for the worship of Yahweh and Solomon's establishing his own administrative center require twenty years of building activity (2 Chron. 8:1). The report of the cities given by Hiram of Tyre to Solomon seems to reverse the report found in the Kings' parallel, in which Solomon gives the Phoenician city-state king twenty towns (towns restored to Solomon because Hiram is "unhappy" with them, 1 Kings 9:10–12).

Rather than assume the Chronicler has rewritten the story in Kings out of embarrassment, it may be possible to harmonize the reports in one of two ways. (1) Perhaps Kings and Chronicles refer to two different occasions in which cities are exchanged as a part of agreements arranged between Hiram and Solomon. (2) Chronicles may be the sequel to the Kings' account in that Hiram held the twenty cities temporarily as collateral for the timber supplied to Solomon until such time as a "cash" payment (of gold) could be made.[28]

The site of Hamath Zobah, an Aramean city, is uncertain (8:3). The capture of Hamath is the only reference to military campaign by King Solomon, a man of peace (1 Chron. 22:9), in all of Chronicles. The oasis and caravan stop of Tadmor (Palmyra of Greek sources) affords a shortcut along the desert trade route into Mesopotamia some 120 miles northeast of Damascus. The writer seems to be calling attention to the extent of the ideal borders of Israel achieved under David and Solomon ("from Lebo Hamath to the Wadi of Egypt," 2 Chron. 7:8; cf. 1 Chron. 13:5). Possession of Hamath and Tadmor means Solomon controls the major overland trade routes with Mesopotamia, another reason for his vast wealth.[29] Despite the fortification of the cities, Solomon is unable to maintain control of these northern holdings (cf. 1 Kings 11:23–25).

The twin towns of Upper and Lower Beth Horon were about two miles apart and located twelve miles northwest of Jerusalem. The two cities were strategically located on a ridge guarding the approach to Jerusalem from the coastal plain along the road linking the interior with the coastal highway. The

---

28. Jacob M. Myers, *II Chronicles* (AB 13; Garden City, N.Y.: Doubleday, 1965), 47.

29. See Carl G. Rasmussen, *NIV Atlas of the Bible* (Grand Rapids: Zondervan, 1989), 123.

location of Baalath (8:6) is uncertain, although the site was originally allocated to the tribe of Dan (Josh. 19:44). According to Thompson, context places the city along the Gezer-Beth Horon-Jerusalem road.[30] The emphasis on store cites and chariot cities (1 Chron. 8:6) highlights the priority Solomon gives to the related activities of trade and military defense. The summary statement (8:6c) lauding Solomon's achievements indicates he has both the political power and the economic resources to build at will throughout his empire.

Slave labor force (8:7–10). The report of Solomon's forced labor levy closely follows 1 Kings 9:20–23. This passage distinguishes clearly between Solomon's treatment of his own countrymen and the subjugated non-Israelite people groups (8:8). Vanquished and disposed peoples were commonly used as slave labor for building projects in the ancient Near East. The writer emphasizes how Solomon puts fellow countrymen in positions of leadership (2 Chron. 8:9–10). The writer of Kings mentions that Solomon also conscripts Israelites as part of the forced labor levy (1 Kings 5:13). These workers are apparently considered another category of "civil servant" since they work only one month in three and are classified as "conscripted laborers" (*mas*), whereas non-Israelite laborers are classified as "state slaves" (*mas ʿobed*).

The tally of Solomon's chief officials differs in the two reports (250 in 8:10 versus 550 in 1 Kings 9:23). Wenham has noted a similar overage in 2 Chronicles 2:18 (3,600 foremen) and 1 Kings 5:16 (3,300 foremen). Since the totals of 3,850 "chief officials" are consistent in the two accounts, it seems likely that the number of overseers is the same but somehow reckoned differently (perhaps by task specialization?).[31]

The removal of Pharaoh's daughter (8:11). The Chronicler assumes his audience's knowledge of Solomon's political marriage to a daughter of Pharaoh (unnamed) and the fact that she lived in the city of David (i.e., the former Jebusite citadel complex of Jerusalem, including David's palace) until Solomon's palace was completed (1 Kings 3:1). The parallel passage in 1 Kings 9:24 concurs with the report in Chronicles that Solomon relocates this unnamed Egyptian princess in her own special quarters once that structure is completed. Chronicles clearly intimates that the building of the temple and Solomon's palace take precedence over constructing quarters for the Egyptian queen.

Only Chronicles records the rationale for the displacement of Solomon's Egyptian wife, ostensibly because of issues of ritual purity ("because the places the ark of the LORD has entered are holy"). The city of David was

30. Thompson, *1, 2 Chronicles*, 239.
31. Wenham, "Large Numbers," 49.

considered a "sanctified" place because of the installation of the ark of the covenant in a temporary shelter erected by David and attended by a select group of priests and Levites (1 Chron. 15:2; 16:37–38).

Dillard speculates that later Second Temple practices restricting women to the "court of women" may already have been enacted.[32] But the issue here is not one of gender so much as it is ethnicity, in that this Egyptian woman is a "foreigner." Israelite women were not required to leave the city of David because of purity laws, but the "foreigner" (nekar) was prohibited from entering Yahweh's sanctuary (Ezek. 44:7–9). There is a certain irony in this report of Solomon's fastidious concern for ritual purity (at least during the first twenty years of his reign) because he later profanes Jerusalem by building places of worship for the gods of all his foreign wives (1 Kings 11:5–8). Then, as now, ritual purity was not a one-time event (e.g., the ark entering Jerusalem) but an ongoing process of applying the biblical teaching about God's holiness to daily living (cf. Lev. 11:44; Matt. 5:48).

The altar of the Lord (8:12–15). The report of the perpetual offerings made to Yahweh as part of the worship of the Jerusalem temple expands the reference to Solomon's observance of the pilgrimage festivals three times a year (cf. 1 Kings 9:25). The Torah required a burnt offering morning and evening with incense (Num. 28:1–8). The burnt offering symbolized God's gift of atonement for sin and the consecration of Israel wholly to God. Burning incense represented the prayers of God's people (Ps. 141:2; Rev. 5:8). Solomon's obedience to the law of Moses legitimizes the Jerusalem temple and the new altar opposite its portico as the primary location for the worship of Yahweh (as was the case formerly for the altar in Gibeon, cf. 2 Chron. 1:3–5).

Not only does King Solomon obey the law of Moses, but he is also careful to implement his father's instructions (without deviation!) concerning the reorganization of the priests and Levites (8:14–15; cf. 1 Chron. 23–26). As the juxtaposition of the preceding report of Solomon's success in a range of activities verifies (2 Chron. 8:1–11), obedience to God's word as well as his instructions of the previous generation is the key to success. It seems reasonable to conclude that this lesson is not lost on the Chronicler's audience, given the recent memories of the Babylonian exile. Things have changed little as the Old Testament gives way to the New, for "success" among God's saints still hinges on obedience to his commands (cf. John 14–15; Rev. 14:12).

Summary statements (8:16–18). The review of Solomon's other significant royal activities concludes with a summary statement concerning the completion of the Jerusalem temple (8:16) and a synopsis of the coop-

32. Dillard, 2 Chronicles, 65.

erative maritime operations Solomon negotiated with Hiram, the Phoenician king of Tyre (8:17). Rhetorically, 8:17 (along with 8:18) belongs with the chapter recounting Solomon's splendor (ch. 9), since other details of the shipping arrangements are recorded in 9:10, 21. De Vries has noted that the final clause of 8:16 contains a pun on Solomon's name (the name "Solomon" and the verb "finished" derive from the same Heb. root, šlm).[33] Technically, 8:16 is an "epitome" or a distinct distillation and summation through authoritative interpretation usually found at the end of a perciope.[34] In this case, the summary statement works together in a literary manner with Solomon's directive to begin building the temple in 2:1 to form an inclusio or envelope for the section detailing the construction and the dedication of the temple (2:1–8:16).

The summary statement that Solomon perseveres in the task of building the temple from the foundation to its completion expands the final clause of the Kings' parallel (8:16a; cf. 1 Kings 9:25). This emphasis on beginning to end conveys the idea that Solomon "cuts no corners" and "spares no expense" in getting the job done. For the Chronicler, Solomon's role as king is summed up in his work of completing the temple. He also makes it clear that this is "the temple of the LORD," not Solomon's temple (2 Chron. 8:16b). Thus Solomon fulfills the commission he received from his father, David (cf. 1 Chron. 28:20). McConville, however, has aptly commented that in another sense, the temple is "completed" only after he demonstrated its lasting purpose as a place of prayer and worship—hence the emphasis on the dedication of the temple.[35]

The report of the joint venture in maritime trade to the south of Israel with Hiram, king of Tyre, concludes chapter 8. As noted above, however, this passage structurally fits better as the beginning of the section treating select international relationships entertained by King Solomon (2 Chron. 8:17–9:12). The repetition of Hiram and gold from Ophir (9:10) forms a natural inclusio with the earlier report of the sea trade agreement with the Phoenician king (8:17–18). The divergences between the Chronicler's version and the parallel in 1 Kings 9:26–28 are easily harmonized, in that the ships Solomon's men build are assembled from timbers imported from Tyre on vessels manned by Phoenician sailors. The difference in the tally of the quantity of gold on the ships and successfully delivered to Solomon may be attributed to a copyist's error in the transmission of the text (e.g., 420 talents in 1 Kings 9:28 versus 450 talents in 2 Chron. 8:18).

33. De Vries, *1 and 2 Chronicles*, 268.
34. Ibid., 430.
35. McConville, *I and II Chronicles*, 143.

The port of Ezion Geber may have been located on an island south of the town of Elath (located on the mainland at the north end of the Gulf of Aqabah [8:17], an island today known as Jezirat Farun). The Chronicler's report suggests that Solomon goes down to the coast to oversee the operation himself. The exact location of Ophir is uncertain. The shipping lane from Elath and Ezion Geber passes through the Gulf of Aqabah and into the Red Sea and then into the Indian Ocean. Scholarly speculation concerning the land of Ophir includes the southern end of the Arabian peninsula, the horn of Africa (e.g., Punt), or even India.

The Phoenicians were well known in the ancient world for their ship-building technology and seamanship, so Solomon's alliance with Hiram of Tyre for the purpose of maritime trade is a natural one (cf. Isa. 23:1–4; Ezek. 27:4, 8–9). These joint Israelite-Phoenician maritime expeditions are three-year trading junkets; in addition to the gold, algumwood (ebony?), gem-stones, silver, ivory, and exotic animals are among the goods returned to port at Ezion Geber (cf. 2 Chron. 9:10, 21). It is unclear what Solomon's merchants trade for the gold and other products, but cedar timber from Phoenicia was always in demand for royal building projects, and the Israelites probably traded surplus grain, olive oil, and other foodstuffs (since famine and crop failure has always been a part of the lifecycle on the fringes of the Mediterranean basin).

Queen of Sheba visits Solomon (9:1–12). The story of the Queen of Sheba's visit to Jerusalem to "verify" Solomon's wisdom and wealth closely follows 1 Kings 10:1–13. This entire chapter (ch. 9) balances the opening chapter (ch. 1) in that God has honored Solomon's obedience in giving the wealth accumulated by David to the building of the temple by restoring wealth to the monarchy through trade and gifts from other nations.

The story also illustrates the key themes of the larger literary unit (chs. 1–9), namely, Solomon's wisdom, wealth, and fame—all gifts from God. For example, Solomon petitioned God for wisdom and was blessed with promises of wealth and fame as well (1:11–12). As a result of her visit with King Solomon, the Queen of Sheba testifies of Solomon's unsurpassed wisdom (9:5) and contributes to Solomon's wealth with lavish gifts of gold, spices, and gemstones (9:9). Beyond this, the queen bears witness to the fact that Solomon's wisdom and wealth are the result of God's blessing on the king and his love for the nation of Israel (9:8).

The actual name of the Queen of Sheba is unknown. Later legends romanticize the encounter between Solomon and the Queen of Sheba, but these traditions are unfounded. The place name "Sheba" is usually equated with ancient Saba, commonly identified with modern-day Yemen in the southern

Arabian peninsula. According to Dillard, we should not be surprised at the queen's active role in her nation's foreign policy, as there is a strong tradition of female leadership in pre-Islamic Arabic society.[36]

It seems likely that the queen's 1,400-mile trek to Israel is motivated by economic interests as much as curiosity about the reports of Solomon's wisdom. Solomon and the nation of Israel control overland trade routes linking Arabia, Africa, and regions to the north such as Aram and Anatolia (most notably the King's Highway, a major north-south road connecting Damascus and the Gulf of Aqabah). Israel's recent alliance with Hiram of Tyre for the purpose of a joint venture in maritime trade may also have prompted the queen's visit (cf. 8:17–18; 9:10–11). The economy of ancient Saba was based on spice trade, and these developments may have affected that commercial enterprise in some way.

The spices in question are most likely frankincense and myrrh (9:1, 9). Frankincense is extracted from the resin of certain species of trees from the genus *Boswellia* of the family *Burseraceae*, which grow almost exclusively in southern Arabia. Myrrh is a fragrant gum extracted from several different shrubs and trees, especially the *Commiphora myrrha* (a thorny tree peculiar to southern Arabia).

These aromatic resins (whether in the form of powder, solid sticks, or oil) were prized possessions and enjoyed wide use in the biblical world in cosmetics, embalming, religious offerings, and pharmacopeia. Frankincense was an ingredient in the mixture of spices burned on the altar of incense in worship (Ex. 30:34); it accompanied the grain offerings (Lev. 2:1–2, 15–16) and was placed with the loaves on the table of the Presence as well (Lev. 24:7). Myrrh was an essential ingredient in the sacred anointing oil used to sanctify objects and persons in Hebrew worship (Ex. 30:23). The pleasant odor, high demand, and restricted sources of these perfumes made them expensive commodities in the ancient times. Myrrh was also used in burial (cf. Mark 16:1; John 19:39). The value of these ointments, often classified with gemstones and gold, made them appropriate gifts for royalty—including the infant Jesus (Matt. 2:11).

God's covenant with Abraham and Sarah included a clause that their descendants, the nation of Israel, would be a blessing to the nations (Gen. 12:3). Declaring the glory of God among the nations is a minor theme in Chronicles, and the report of the Queen of Sheba's visit to Jerusalem contributes to Asaph's exhortation to "make God known among the nations" (1 Chron. 16:8, 24). Selman has noted that the Hebrew words for " true" (ʾemet, 2 Chron. 9:5) and "believe" (ʾaman, 9:6) are related, and they prove

---

36. Dillard, 2 *Chronicles*, 71.

important to the story because the demonstration of fulfilled promises promotes God's glory among the nations.[37]

The Queen of Sheba's testimony about Yahweh (9:8) echoes other aspects of Old Testament "covenant theology" in the reference to God's "love" (i.e., election; cf. Mal. 1:2) of Israel and the duty of the king to "maintain justice and righteousness" (as the demonstration of divine wisdom and the embodiment of kingdom rule on earth, cf. 1 Kings 3:28; Isa. 9:7; 33:5). The reference to Solomon as a vice-regent on God's "throne" (2 Chron. 9:8) alludes to the kingdom of God, a distinctive concept in Chronicles.[38] It is unclear whether the queen's affirmation is simply an example of a non-Hebrew acknowledging the Israelite God as a "local deity" or if it represents a deeper faith commitment to the one true and universal God. Either way, McConville reminds us that "the impression made upon the Queen of Sheba shows the power that belongs to the children of God to bring God to those who are, figuratively speaking, 'far off.'"[39]

The Gospel writers appeal to the Queen of Sheba story as both a sign of judgment against unbelief and as a typological foreshadowing of Jesus Christ as the greater king (Matt 12:42; Luke 11:31). More than this, Jesus taught that God's goodness to Solomon should not be viewed as an invitation to materialism but rather as an invitation to seek God's kingdom and his righteousness above all else—trusting that "these [material] things" will be given to us as well (Matt. 6:28–34).

Solomon's splendor (9:13–21). The Chronicler includes a collection of related materials reporting Solomon's great wealth as a summary statement asserting the incomparability of his riches and wisdom (cf. 9:22). The review of the opulence of Solomon's kingdom further enhanced the king's (and Israel's) reputation among all the other kingdoms (9:19). The objects of his splendor are organized in three categories: gold and its abundant use (9:13–16), the ivory throne (9:17–19), and the king's "household articles" (9:20–21). The account corresponds loosely to 1 Kings 10:14–28. Theologically, it stands as a testimony to God's faithfulness in keeping his promise to give Solomon unsurpassed wealth and honor (cf. 2 Chron. 1:11–12).

Israel's strategic location connecting the continents of Africa and Asia and Solomon's control of the trade routes transversing that corridor generates enormous wealth (9:13–14). The 666 talents of gold that Solomon receives annually is approximately twenty tons in modern-day equivalents (9:13). The annual tribute is most likely composed of tariff and tax revenues. The unspecified

---

37. Selman, *2 Chronicles*, 335.
38. Ibid.
39. McConville, *I and II Chronicles*, 148.

sum of Solomon's gross yearly income includes both the tribute money and the profits from his own capital ventures (primarily international trade, 9:14).

The Chronicler assumes his audience's knowledge of the "Palace of the Forest of Lebanon" (9:16). According to the writer of Kings, this is the name given to Solomon's palatial home (presumably because of the vast amount of cedar timber from Lebanon required to build the royal palace complex, cf. 1 Kings 7:1–12). The five hundred shields hammered from gold adorning the palace eventually become booty for Pharaoh Shishak as a result of Rehoboam's disobedience to the law of the Lord (2 Chron. 12:1, 9–11).

The royal throne is made of wood, inset with ivory plaques and overlaid with gold (9:17).[40] Perhaps the twelve tribes of Israel are represented in the twelve lions that flank the six steps on either side leading up to the throne platform (9:19). The lion is a universal symbol of kingship in the ancient world and may have been the symbol for the Davidic line of Israelite kingship, given David's reputation as a shepherd who rescued his sheep from the paws of the lion (cf. 1 Sam. 17:34–37).

The Chronicler calls attention to the footstool attached to the throne, whereas 1 Kings 10:19 places emphasis on the rounded top of the throne. The Hebrew phrase in question may also be translated "calf-head" ("at the back of the throne was the head of a calf," so NEB), prompting some commentators to suggest the Chronicler simply omits the reference, given the associations of the calf with false worship in preexilic Israel.[41] The significance of the footstool, a symbol of royal authority, has been discussed previously (see the Original Meaning at 1 Chron. 28:1–8).

Solomon's commercial alliance with Hiram of Tyre results in a merchant fleet of Israelite ships manned by Phoenician sailors (9:21). The literal "ships that went to Tarshish" has been rendered "trading ships" in the NIV (also NLT). Tarshish is commonly identified with Tartessus in Spain, but this is more likely an example of a place name becoming a descriptor of a quality, that is, ships capable of distant sea travel. Dillard observes that commodities of trade often represent "alien lexical items" in any given language.[42] This explains the

---

40. See the discussion in J. A. Montgomery and H. S. Gehman, *The Books of Kings* (ICC; London: T. & T. Clark, 1951), 221–22; for examples of throne ornamentation (including ivory insets) see Andre Parrot, *The Arts of Assyria* (New York: Golden Press, 1961), 155–57; J. W. and G. M. Crowfoot, *Early Ivories from Samaria* (London: Palestine Exploration Fund, 1938), pl. 9, fig. 1; G. Loud, *The Megiddo Ivories* (Chicago: Univ. of Chicago Press, 1939), pl. 4, figs. 2a, 2b. Finally, note the depictions of the Phoenician King Ahiram on a sphinx throne with footstool and the Aramean King Bar Rakab seated on a throne with footstool in *ANEP*, no. 458 and no. 460.

41. Williamson, *1 and 2 Chronicles*, 235.

42. Dillard, *2 Chronicles*, 73.

various renderings of the terms translated in the NIV as "ivory, and apes and baboons" (9:21; e.g., "ivory, apes, and peacocks," NLT and NRSV; "monkeys and peacocks," CEV).

Encomium on Solomon's glory (9:22–28). By way of literary form, this passage is an encomium adulating the wisdom and wealth of King Solomon. The encomium is an extended (in this case, prose) lyric praising an abstract quality or general character type.[43] This encomium combines both features as it is the abstract quality of wisdom that defines the character type of King Solomon. The Chronicler also includes a statement of incomparability (a declaration using the syntax of the superlative to the effect that the subject is beyond comparison with anything in its category) to further emphasize the literary device of the encomium.[44]

By way of literary structure, 9:22–28 completes the envelope construction introduced in 1:14–17. The two texts recite the symbols of Solomon's great wealth (silver and gold, cedar lumber, and horses and chariots), and in so doing frame the entire literary unit (chs. 1–9). The Chronicler reminds us, however, that these dividends of Solomon's riches result from the investment of his wisdom and wealth with building Yahweh's temple.

Theologically, chapters 1–9 complete the idealized biographies of King David and his son and successor, King Solomon. These biographies represent the fulfillment of the Davidic covenant in that God has built David's "house" (i.e., dynasty) in establishing Solomon as king, and Solomon has fulfilled the commission of his father to build Yahweh's "house" (i.e., the temple). Of special import is the declaration that Solomon's wisdom and wealth are the result of God's favor, since foreign potentates come to Jerusalem from all over the world to hear "the wisdom God had put in his heart" (9:23). Dillard reminds us, however, that the Chronicler is not simply revisiting the "good old days" of the Israelite monarchy. Rather, the biographies of David and Solomon "represent an eschatological program and give expression to the fondest hopes of many in the restoration community for the day that a David/Solomon redivivus would again in righteousness lead Israel to glory among the nations."[45]

Concluding regnal résumé (9:29–31). The regnal résumé of Solomon's reign essentially repeats the summary found in 1 Kings 11:41–43. The typical formulas are intact, including the citation of historical source(s), length of reign, death and burial, and succession. Solomon's reign is variously dated between 975 and 922 B.C., depending on the source. Our study dates Solomon's forty-year rule from 970–930 B.C.

---

43. Ryken, *How to Read the Bible As Literature*, 119.
44. De Vries, *1 and 2 Chronicles*, 431.
45. Dillard, *2 Chronicles*, 73.

There are two notable variations.(1) The phrase "from beginning to end" (9:29) is a characteristic of the Chronicler's style in the regnal résumés (cf. 1 Chron. 29:29; 2 Chron. 12:15). (2) The Chronicler cites three prophetic records as the historical sources for Solomon's kingship (2 Chron. 9:29). De Vries considers the references to the "records of Nathan the prophet," "the prophecy of Ahijah," and the "visions of Iddo the seer" as a fictitious device the Chronicler uses "to gain credence for his own writing."[46] Both Kings and Chronicles, however, emphasize the prophetic "voice" or perspective in their narratives of Israelite royal history. These "prophetic sources" are probably sections contained within other documents (e.g., the Elijah and Elijah stories of Kings) or an even larger compendium of monarchic records.

The phrase "rested with his fathers" (or better "ancestors," 9:31) signifies both a peaceful death and a long and prosperous life. The Chronicler omits altogether the unfavorable theological review of Solomon's idolatry-tainted reign found in 1 Kings 11:1–13 as well as the opposition recorded in 11:14–40.

IN THE LAST CHAPTER we learned that one of the Chronicler's concerns was to demonstrate the continuity between the reigns of King David and King Solomon. His purpose was not to celebrate human achievement in the building of the Jerusalem temple. Rather, he sought to glorify God by accenting both divine sovereignty and divine faithfulness in fulfilling promises made to David (cf. 1 Chron. 17:10–12). This was an important reminder to a community that only a generation or two earlier had responded to Yahweh's prophets with skepticism and contempt (cf. Mal. 1:1; 3:13–14). Yet, the more cynical living in postexilic Jerusalem might be less than impressed with this rehearsal of united kingdom history—that was then. The more pertinent question for the Chronicler's audience may have been one along the lines of "what about God's faithfulness to Israel—now?"

For this reason, the Chronicler is keen to display the theological continuity between David and Solomon and his own time. It is one thing for God to prove himself faithful to the ancestors of a bygone era, but quite another for him to make good on "Davidic covenant" and "new covenant" promises that at best lay dormant in the rubble of prophetic rhetoric or at worst were rendered null and void by the Babylonian exile. Surely God appeared to David and Solomon. But the Chronicler's challenge is to illustrate that God's faithfulness spans the intervening five centuries from the "golden age" of

---

46. De Vries, 1 and 2 Chronicles, 273.

Israel to his own "tarnished" era. Yet, in the second temple, God has accomplished that very feat!

The historical transition from the first temple to the second temple provides numerous theological touchstones for the Chronicler. Three specific examples will be examined: the idea of sacred space, the polarity of divine immanence and divine transcendence, and the ancient Near Eastern motif of restoring order out of chaos by means of temple building. We must not lose sight of the fact that the Chronicler is both a historian and a preacher. This means Chronicles is both report and sermon. There is virtue in retelling the history of Israelite kingship for the Chronicler primarily as a "historian" rather than a "preacher." This permits him to accomplish his agenda as a "meddling preacher" much more subtly by simply describing selectively the "facts" about Israel's past in his effort to instruct, exhort, and admonish postexilic Judah. Given the emphasis on "story" and narrative theology in postmodern thought, we do well to learn a lesson from the Chronicler with respect to effective pulpit communication in the twenty-first century.

Sacred space. The story of Moses at the burning bush near Horeb, the mountain of God, is well known (Ex. 3:1–6). God himself visited this place in the form of the angel of the Lord, and because of Yahweh's holy presence Moses was instructed to remove his sandals and to keep his distance. Terrified, Moses tried to hide his face from God—not an uncommon response to the divine presence of the Almighty (even the seraphs hid their face in God's presence, Isa. 6:2). The story of Moses' close encounter of the first kind with the God of his ancestors introduces us to the idea of "sacred space" in the Old Testament.

The theological concept of sacred space was not peculiar to the Hebrews in the ancient world. The Canaanites and other people groups also worshiped their deities at particular holy sites (Num. 21:28; 1 Kings 11:5–8). These sacrosanct locations were often associated with mountainous or elevated regions because the gods were believed to gather and hold sessions on the summit of the great mountain of assembly. By analogy, then, the Canaanite shrines were situated in the high places, above ordinary life and nearer the dwelling of the gods. The Chronicler's retelling of the construction of Solomon's temple, built on a "high place" (Mount Zion), gives us pause to consider the ancient Hebrew understanding of "sacred space."

As the dramatic story of salvation history unfolds in the Old Testament, God at times chose to make himself known in special ways to those who seek him. Since human beings are finite, God accommodates this human limitation by disclosing features of his divine character and aspects of his divine will for humanity at specific geographical locations. Naturally, the creation story in Genesis offers a glimpse of this idealized relationship between the

Creator and his creatures in their direct communication in the Garden of Eden (Gen. 3:8).

Sadly, those first humans doubted God's goodness and succumbed to the tempter (Gen. 3:1–13). God's judgment of their disobedience included curses making life more difficult and banishment from the Garden of Eden—the very presence of God (3:14–24). Yet in his mercy, God opted to overcome the sin barrier and restore the fractured relationship with humanity by occasionally revealing himself in a visible and/or auditory manner to his fallen creatures.

Such a divine manifestation initiated by God is called a *theophany*. These revelatory events took on a variety of forms, such as a voice (Gen. 4:9; 6:13), a dream (15:12), a flame in a bush (Ex. 3:2–6), the lightning and thunder on Mount Sinai (19:18–20), the pillar of cloud and fire in the desert wandering (40:34–38), and even the angel of the Lord in human form (Judg. 13:8–20). Typically, the actual physical and external details of these divine manifestations are somewhat obscure because the emphasis is on the person and character of God and his message to the ones who experience the visitation (e.g., Gen. 12:1–3).

The locations associated with the theophany were usually identified with a landmark denoting them as a sacred site because of God's manifestation there. For example, altars built for worship at the places where God appeared served as landmarks (Gen. 12:8; 22:9). Other times stone pillars and stelae, or engraved standing stones, were erected to commemorate a place of divine revelation (e.g., Jacob's stone pillar at Bethel, Gen. 35:14; the cairn of twelve stones at Gilgal, Josh 4:1–9; the plastered stela of the Ebal ceremony, Josh. 8:32). In some cases natural geographical features functioned as the landmark signifying the sacred site, as in the case of the oak trees at Shechem and Mamre (near Hebron, Gen. 12:6; 18:1).

The purpose of these landmarks designating a particular geographical location as sacred or holy was threefold. (1) The establishment of a permanent marker at the place of divine visitation served as both a worship response to God and a tangible witness confirming the theophany for the recipient. (2) Marking the site provided a geographical point of reference permitting a later return or pilgrimage to the place of divine revelation. (3) The landmark often became a teaching memorial by which the Israelites instructed successive generations in the knowledge of Yahweh's covenant (e.g., Ex. 3:12; Josh. 4:20–24).

The most visibly dramatic and time-sustained theophany was the Israelite experience at Mount Sinai after the exodus from Egypt (Ex. 19–24). After the covenant ceremony enacted there, Mount Sinai (or Mount Horeb) became revered as the holy of mountain of God (19:9–25). This sacred place was associated with the awesome presence of God, seismic disturbances, and covenant lawgiving. Later, the Old Testament venerates the Lord God as the "One of Sinai" (Ps. 68:8) and commemorates the mountain site as the place where the earth shook during God's initial visitation to Israel after the Exodus (Deut. 33:2).

The divine revelation delivered at Mount Sinai also included the provision of a permanent holy place or sacred space within the camp of the Israelites (Ex. 25–40). The tabernacle or Tent of Meeting was designed to be the very precinct where God would symbolically live with his people (25:8). His holy presence was associated specifically with the ark of the covenant (37:1–9). The cloud of glory and pillar of fire were visible symbols representing Yahweh's sacred presence among his people (40:34–38). Since the tabernacle and the ark of the covenant were portable, the sacred place of the Lord's presence could travel with the Hebrews on their desert trek to the land of covenant promise—Canaan.

Later divine revelation given at the covenant-renewal ceremony in Moab prior to the conquest of Canaan indicated that the sacred place of divine presence would not always be mobile. God announced clearly through Moses that once the Israelites possessed the land of the promise, he would choose a place where his Name would be permanently established in the midst of his people (Deut. 12:5, 11, 21). The sacred space associated with this future site was to be the place of worship for all the tribes of Israel. Until such time as the permanent location for Yahweh's name had been secured, the travels of the tabernacle eventually gave sacred-space status to several sites: Mount Ebal and Mount Gerezim (Deut. 27:1–14), Shechem (Josh. 24:1), Shiloh (Judg. 18:31), and Gibeon (1 Chron. 16:39).

Finally, as we learn from the Chronicler's retelling of David's kingship, that permanent site for establishing the sacred place for Yahweh's name was the threshing floor of Araunah the Jebusite (1 Chron. 21:18–26; cf. 2 Sam. 24:18–25). In keeping with the custom of erecting a landmark at the site of a theophany, an altar was built to respond to the visitation of the angel of the Lord (1 Chron. 21:18–19, 25–26). Fittingly, the characteristic of God revealed at the threshing floor became the hallmark of Solomon's temple— the abode of Yahweh, who in mercy forgives sin. According to Allen, the theology of the temple is a "pastoral theology, for it comes to where people so often are and compassionately points the way back from failure."[47] The divine character trait portrayed in Solomon's temple is that of God who takes sinners back and restores them.

The implications of the idea of sacred space for Hebrew worship may be as numerous as the list of holy sites that emerge from Old Testament religious

---

47. Allen, 1, 2 Chronicles, 239–40.

history. Given the Chronicler's attention to certain details in recounting the festival worship at Solomon's temple, however, it seems that at least these five theological emphases constitute both instruction and exhortation to his own audience on the matter of "sacred space."

(1) Inherent in the idea of sacred space is the reality of God's holiness. Even as the visitation or manifestation of God to the righteous sanctified a particular location as sacred or holy, so too the worshiper was obligated to sanctify himself or herself in order to enter the presence of God. In some cases this preparation included physical activity (e.g., ritual washing, changing garments, animal sacrifice; cf. Ex. 19:9–16). But in every case this preparation was spiritual, hence the entrance psalms admonish that only those who have a pure heart (Ps. 24:3–6) and a blameless lifestyle (15:1–5) may stand in the sacred place. The Chronicler knows that right worship demands right preparation. Little has changed in the new covenant, as we are warned that without "holiness no one will see the Lord" (Heb. 12:14).

(2) The experience of the divine presence in time and space made pilgrimage a part of Israel's religious life from the beginning, attested by the patriarchal journeys to holy sites like Bethel (Gen. 12:8; 31:13; 35:1, 8). A pilgrimage is defined as "a journey made to a sacred place as an act of devotion." The pilgrimage as an act of worship was actually built into the Hebrew religious calendar in the form of the three annual festivals, when "all Israel" was to appear before the Lord (Ex. 23:17). The pilgrimage festivals were events of great joy and celebration in homage to the living God. They afforded an opportunity for the community to renew covenant vows, teach the next generation, and affirm the unity of the twelve tribes as the people of God.

In fact, it was the recollection of past pilgrimages to Zion's temple with the faithful of Israel that helped renew the psalmist's faith in the midst of deep distress (Ps. 42:4). The pilgrimage festivals were also designed to instill an attitude toward time and develop a worldview toward life that recognized every aspect of the human experience as a journey into God's eschatological presence (Ps. 84:5, 10).

(3) The Hebrew practice of commemorating sacred places with landmarks contributed greatly to the covenant catechism of the next generation. These tangible markers affirmed the historical reality of God's intervention in the natural order and functioned as teaching memorials for successive Israelite generations.

Unlike the religious myths of Israel's neighbors, Yahweh of the Hebrews had disclosed covenant revelation and performed mighty acts of redemption for his people in history (e.g., the exodus from Egypt, Ex. 13:14–16; the entrance into Canaan, Josh. 4:4–7). The rehearsal of God's work in history at designated sacred places taught essential truths about God (e.g., his holiness, his power; cf. Josh. 24:1–15) and the promises and obligations of his covenant relationship with Israel (Gen. 35:1–15). The active participation in the remembrance of Yahweh's past words and deeds at the sacred site was intended to foster covenant obedience and instill a sense of loyalty in the community to its spiritual heritage.

(4) The idea of sacred space gave currency to site-specific worship because Israelite worship at these holy places fostered attitudes and responses of faithfulness on two difference planes. On the vertical level, individual and corporate worship at the sacred place encouraged loyalty to God. The act of worship at that location served as a reminder that God in his grace had met with his people on their terms—in time and space. The carefully preserved tradition of those past visitations encouraged obedience to God's revelation and offered hope for yet another manifestation of the divine presence (cf. Deut. 4:21–40).

On the horizontal level, the act of worship at the sacred place strengthened the covenant bonding of the religious community. The corporate and public identification with Yahweh at the sacred place heightened awareness of the obligations for loyalty and service to each other as common members of the covenant community (cf. Ex. 23:1–9). If the Chronicler addresses an audience similar to that of Malachi (people breaking faith with God and each other, Mal. 1:13–14; 2:15–16), then his emphasis on place-specific worship (i.e., the Jerusalem temple) makes good sense as a component of his subtle catechism couched in the history of Israel.

(5) Perhaps most important, the idea of sacred space in the Old Testament restored the possibility of intimate fellowship once enjoyed by God and human beings. A key outcome of the covenant agreement between Yahweh and Israel and later between Yahweh and David was the presence of God "dwelling in the midst of his people" (Ex. 25:8; 2 Chron. 5:14). That presence first associated with the portable shrine of Moses and then housed in the permanent temple of Solomon was an important theological foreshadowing of that day when "Immanuel" himself would appear (Isa. 7:14; 9:7; 11:9). Through the incarnation of Jesus Christ, God ultimately reestablished his presence among the faithful of Israel, all nations, and all creation (John 1:14).

Divine immanence and transcendence. A second theological touchstone for the Chronicler in demonstrating God's faithfulness to postexilic Judah is grounded in the mystery of God as both a transcendent and immanent deity. The prophet Isaiah captured the gist of this paradox when he affirmed in Isaiah 57:15:

> For this is what the high and lofty One says—
> he who lives forever, whose name is holy:
> "I live in a high and holy place,
> but also with him who is contrite and lowly in spirit,
> to revive the spirit of the lowly
> and to revive the heart of the contrite."

This text harmoniously blends two opposite and distinct attributes of the Godhead. (1) God is "high and holy," or transcendent. This means God is detached and self-existent from his creation. He is far removed from his creatures, including humanity, in his essential being. (2) Yet God is also immanent. This means he is near to and pervasively indwells everything he has created— the world, its creatures, and its processes. God is at one and the same time the external sovereign Creator and Judge of his world and the intimate indwelling One, holding all things together (Acts 17:24–28; Col. 1:15–17). As an aside, it is actually the divine attribute of God's immanence discussed above that gives rise to the notion of "sacred place" in Old Testament.

Theologically, the visible symbol of sacred or holy space as represented by Solomon's temple holds great value in mediating the paradox of divine immanence and divine transcendence to the community of faith. On the one hand, as Solomon himself prays, God is unique and immense so that the highest heavens cannot contain him (7:14, 18). The awesome holiness of God demands that the nation, the Levitical priesthood, and the objects that contribute to the worship of Yahweh be consecrated or sanctified for service (Lev. 11:44–45; 19:2). But on the other hand, Yahweh is not a distant and uncaring God, remotely stationed in the heavens. Rather, Yahweh is a most personal deity, who not only registers the birth and birthplace of all the peoples (Ps. 87:5–6) but also is the God of heaven who stoops down to help the poor and bring aid to the needy (Ps. 113:6–8).

These spiritual truths have profound implications for Israelite worship. Since God is everywhere present, the spontaneous and informal worship of the Lord of heaven knows no restriction of space or time. The righteous may rejoice in his presence continually (Ps. 16:8; 34:1). Such praise is infectious— as praising the splendor of the God of heaven generates hope that in turn elicits even more praise (71:8, 14–15). In fact, this continual praise and worship of God is the whole purpose of life (63:4; 119:175). This was the implicit exhortation in the Chronicler's retelling of the story of Solomon's temple: "This is the day the LORD has made; let us rejoice and be glad in it" (118:24).

Another point of contact between the first temple of Solomon and the second temple of postexilic Jerusalem for the Chronicler is the hazard of exchanging loyalty to Yahweh for loyalty to a sacred place. As Dyrness has observed, "the danger was always present that Israel would believe that God was limited to these [sacred] places."[48] God's people had to learn continually and relearn that there is no necessary connection between Yahweh and the places where he revealed himself to his people. This meant that the holy or sanctified place of God's visitation can never serve as a talisman or good-luck charm to avert either evil or divine judgment.

The prophet Jeremiah attacked the "temple theology" pedaled by the deluded priesthood and national leaders who understood God's temple to guarantee Judah's inviolability, regardless of the lives of the people. Jeremiah merely had to review Israelite history to substantiate his argument. God could dispense with the temple in Jerusalem as easily as he ruined Shiloh because of the wickedness of his people (Jer. 7:8–15; cf. 1 Sam. 4:1–11).

The prophet Ezekiel also countermanded this fallacious notion of sacred space in his chariot vision (Ezek. 1–3). There he disclosed that the very throne of God rested on a magnificent carriage, signifying his presence was not restricted to any one location (1:15–28). At the time, this was a vital message of encouragement to the captives in Babylonia because they needed to know that Yahweh was not "parked" in Jerusalem.

Whether Israelite theology in the Old Testament or Christian theology in light of the New Testament, the idea of sanctified or holy space can only be a vehicle for the demonstration of the divine mystery of God's nearness and hiddenness. It can never serve as a visible or concrete reality of God's revelation since that would make the sacred place (or sacred artifact) an object of reverence and worship—and an end in itself and thus a form of idolatry. R. K. Harrison comments that God demands conversion of mind and heart and actions as the basis of spiritual peace and security, not superstitious veneration of a stone building or a traditionally sacred site.[49] This warning to those worshiping in the second temple is implicit in the Chronicler's "sermonic" retelling of the story of Solomon's temple.

Restoring order out of chaos. The initiative taken by David to build a temple for Yahweh and its completion by his successor Solomon fit a pattern of temple building by kings in the ancient world. Kapelrud has illustrated that elements of the temple-building motif in ancient Near Eastern literature have parallels in the biblical narratives treating the construction of the Mosaic tabernacle and the Solomonic temple (see the chart below).[50]

---

48. William Dyrness, *Themes in Old Testament Theology* (Downers Grove, Ill.: InterVarsity Press, 1979), 148.

49. R. K. Harrison, *Jeremiah and Lamentations* (TOTC; London: Tyndale, 1973), 85–86.

50. A. Kapelrud, "Temple Building: A Task for Gods and Kings," *Orientalia* 32 (1963): 56–62.

Temple Building Motif	Mosaic Tabernacle	Solomonic Temple
1. A sanctuary is to be built	Ex. 25:1–8	1 Chron. 28:11–21
2. The king visits a temple overnight	Ex. 24:12–18	2 Chron. 1:2–7
3. The deity reveals the temple plans	Ex. 25:8–30:38	1 Chron. 28:2–3, 11–19; 2 Chron. 1:7–12
4. The king announces intentions to build	Ex. 35:4–10; 36:2–35	2 Chron. 2:1–10
5. A master builder and materials secured	Ex. 31:1–6; 35:4–29	1 Chron. 22:14–15; 29:1–9; 2 Chron. 2:7–14
6. Sanctuary is finished according to plan	Ex. 39:42–43	2 Chron. 5:1; 6:10
7. Offerings and dedication occur	Ex. 40:9–11	2 Chron. 6:12–42; 7:4–7
8. The people assemble	Ex. 39:32–33, 42–43	2 Chron. 5:2–13
9. The deity enters the sanctuary	Ex. 40:34–35	2 Chron. 5:13–14; 7:1–3
10. The king is blessed and promised dominion	—	2 Chron. 7:12–18

Royal protocol in the ancient Near East required that a king newly ascended to power build a temple to his patron deity as an expression of thanksgiving for the role that deity played in installing him on the throne. Typically, the temple-building initiative was also seen as an opportunity for the king to invoke the blessing of the deity for a long and prosperous dynasty. Kapelrud's study proves interesting because it provides yet another example of how the ancient Israelites were a product of their literary and cultural context. The custom of royal temple building in the ancient world as reported in the Bible is also a reminder of the complexities associated with the interface of divine revelation and human culture.

In this case, we have an illustration of God's intracultural revelation (i.e., God's choice to accommodate aspects of his revelation to the Israelites within the cultural conventions of their day), in contradistinction to his supracultural revelation (i.e., God's choice to convey aspects of his divine revelation outside of cultural norms), such as the "cities of refuge" (a unique institution in the ancient world created for those guilty of accidental manslaughter, Num. 35:9–28; Josh. 20). More directly, the adaptation of Kapelrud's study in the chart above indicates the interdependence of the tabernacle and temple-building narratives in the Old Testament.

Although Kapelrud's essay provides helpful literary and historical background to the Chronicler's temple-building narrative, it fails to address the theological purpose tied to the construction of a "sacred space" in the cultural context of the ancient world. In his analysis of ritual in the sociocultural context of the ancient world, Gorman has argued that "rituals serve as one means to effect restoration" when inappropriate actions have disrupted the world order of a given society.[51] By ritual he means "a complex performance of symbolic acts, characterized by its formality, order, and sequence, which tends to take place in specific situations, and has as one of its central goals the regulation of the social order."[52] The "disruption of world order" in a society occurs when individual or group conduct violates established rules and norms for appropriate meaning and existence in that given cultural context. That is, the disruption of social order represents some sort of incongruity between the ideal defined by the society's worldview and the reality of current behavior by one or more of the group members.

More concretely, the Israelites had a worldview or world order established by the principles and legislation codified in the Mosaic covenant ratified at Mount Sinai. Violations of the covenant stipulations were regarded as disruptions of the social order and were dealt with by rituals that both punished the offender and cleansed the community. This permitted the full restoration of the relationship between the Israelite people and their God, Yahweh. In terms of the Mosaic covenant, for instance, the ritual of the burnt offering addressed the disruption of the social order by atoning for sinful conduct by a member of the community (cf. Lev. 4:1–12). The ritual of the morning and evening sacrifices were essential acts of obedience for maintaining the community's ongoing relationship with God (cf. Ex. 29:38–41).

By applying Gorman's analysis to the cosmological level, we understand that God established a social order for the world in original creation that was disrupted by the fall of humanity. By enacting a series of covenants with humanity (each typically including legislation designed to shape worldview and ritual intended to maintain the covenant relationship), God graciously and systematically responded to the problem of human sin in order to redeem his fallen creation and restore order out of chaos. This divine reclamation program culminated in the person and work of Jesus Christ as the "Lamb of God, who takes away the sin of the word" (John 1:29). The restoration of God's created order de facto coincides with the second advent of Jesus, when everything is made new (Rev. 21:5).

---

51. Frank H. Gorman, *The Ideology of Ritual: Space, Time and Status in the Priestly Theology* (JSOTSup 91; Sheffield: Sheffield Academic Press, 1990), 18.
52. Ibid., 19.

Thus, according to Gorman, ritual becomes one means of regulating social order, which may be done in one of two ways.[53] (1) Ritual provides a means for maintaining the structures, processes, and relations of an already-existing sociocultural system. (2) Ritual serves to regulate the societal order when the normative structures, processes, and relations have been broken or ruptured. In other words, ritual may serve to either maintain or restore societal order. Ritual action in the Israelite society was centered in the tabernacle (and later the temple) and orchestrated by the Levitical priesthood. The priestly ritual system communicated theological truth about the state of being or status with reference to four interrelated areas of Hebrew society: the individual, the community or society, the cosmos or created order, and God himself.[54]

The ministry of the Levitical priesthood was vital to the health of the community because through their instruction and ritual actions the people were led into righteousness and away from sin (Mal. 2:5–9; cf. Deut. 33:10). In this way, covenant relationship with Yahweh was maintained and the community of God's people enjoyed peace and the prosperity of his blessing.

As we recall from Gorman's definition of ritual cited above, ritual is a complex performance of symbolic actions, and one of its chief goals is the regulation of social order. Furthermore, ritual is comprised of several basic elements, like ritual space and time, ritual objects and roles, ritual actions, and even ritual sounds and language. But how did the enactment of ritual actually maintain or restore societal order?

By analogy to the movement from chaos to cosmos in the creation account of Genesis 1–2, Gorman posits that ritual brings order to sociocultural systems by a similar principle. The "creation principle" facilitating the movement from chaos to cosmos in Genesis 1–2 is that of "order through separation."[55] The Bible depicts God's creative activity as that of dividing between the various elements of creation and thereby prescribing order through a system of classification (e.g., God "separated" [bdl] the light from the darkness, 1:4).

The biblical worldview recognizes three distinct but interrelated orders of creation, each established by the speech of God: the cosmological (reflecting a system of identification), the societal (reflecting a system of meaning and value), and the religious (or the "cultic" for Gorman, reflecting a system of praxis). "Just as the cosmological order is achieved by acts of separation— the establishing of boundaries between different categories of created

53. Ibid., 28.
54. Ibid., 37–38.
55. Ibid., 44.

things—so also the societal and cultic orders achieve order through categorical distinctions."[56]

God instructed the Israelite priesthood to maintain (or restore) societal and religious order by establishing boundaries or separating elements of creation in a similar fashion. Specifically, the priests were charged to "divide" or "distinguish" (*bdl*) between the holy and the common, between the clean and the unclean (Lev. 10:10–11). Applying the concepts of the holy, common, clean, and unclean to the physical, moral, and spiritual realms of life was basic to the ancient Israelite worldview. The purpose of these theological categories for ritual purity allowed the people to order their relationship to the natural world in such a way that they might fulfill the mandate to be "holy" as God is holy (Lev. 11:44–45). In fact, the basic intention of the book of Leviticus was to provide instruction for the community in "holy worship" (2 Chron. 1–10) and "holy living" (chs. 11–27) so that as the covenant people they might enjoy the blessing of Yahweh's presence (cf. Lev. 26:1–13). The relationship of these concepts is illustrated in the chart below:

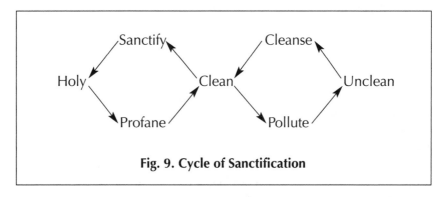

Fig. 9. Cycle of Sanctification

On the basis of Levitical law, everything in life was either holy or common for the Israelites. Those things determined common were subdivided into categories of clean and unclean. Clean things might become holy through the ritual of sanctification or unclean through the pollution of sin. Holy things could be profaned and become common or even unclean through sin. Unclean things could be cleansed and then consecrated or sanctified to be made holy through prescribed rituals.

As the central worship center for the nation of Israel, Solomon's temple was an integral part of God's design for maintaining order and/or restoring order in the social and religious life of his people. This was accomplished primarily in one of two ways, since the temple was the place for sacrifices (2 Chron.

---

56. Ibid.

2:6; 7:12) and a house of prayer (Isa. 56:7). In the next section we will examine how individual Christians and the Christian church corporately might learn how to "restore order out of chaos" in our contemporary context on the basis of the principles and practices associated with Solomon's temple.

RESTORING ORDER OUT OF CHAOS. Recovering order out of chaos is still an issue in our society. You may be familiar with the expression "twenty-four–seven." No, the numbers do not represent a new chain of convenience stores. They are not even a formula for a new household cleaner. The numerical phrase "twenty-four–seven" refers to the work schedule for many in the business world today. Whether to achieve status or remain competitive, many Americans are overworked and stressed to the point of exhaustion. Two-career families, jobs with long hours, greater responsibilities with less control, and technological advances that extend work into supposedly leisure time all contribute to the nationwide burnout.[57] Given the globalization of the economy, some have expanded the formula to "twenty-four–seven–three-sixty-five" because staying in business or keeping up with the markets means there is no longer any "down time."

The frenetic pace of American life has made all sorts of stress therapies fashionable, if not effective. Exotic remedies advertised as the answer to stress run the gamut from "A to Z," from aroma therapy to zodiac analysis. Fantastic new products or highly specialized programs for coping with the stress of North American life are made available almost weekly. Regrettably, these ads promise more than they can deliver, and as a result the destructive consequences of our chaotic pace of life provide the sorry fodder for the daily newscasts. The broadcasters in our news media never lack for tragic stories of abuse, rape, aggravated assault, suicide, and murder caused by the venting of rage from pent-up stress. In fact, "rage" has now become part of our hyphenated vocabulary in America, be it "road-rage," or "employee-rage," or "classroom-rage," or even "voter-rage."[58] Sadly, the Christian subculture has not escaped the curses that result from life spent on the "24x7 treadmill." But the church possesses the key to unlock the shackles that bind humanity in service to the gods of time, production, and efficiency rather than to God.

---

57. See the cover story by LyNell Hancock, "Breaking Point," *Newsweek* (March 6, 1995), 56–63.

58. For example, see Andrew Stephen, "Bigger and Better Here: Road Rage," *New Statesman* (April 2, 1999), 24–26; Timothy Roche et al., "Voices from the Cell" (on School Rage), *Time* (May 28, 2001), 32–38.

The implicit and explicit biblical theology associated with Solomon's temple provides helpful principles for restoring "order from chaos," for recovering God's design for "making the most of every opportunity" in these evil days (Eph. 5:16). We will examine three ways the "temple theology" of the Solomonic era might serve the church (individually and corporately) as an instrument for overturning the chaos of sin and reordering the world according to God's ideal. (1) We will explore the relationship between the temple as "sacred space" and the importance of prayer in maintaining a vital relationship with God. (2) We will probe the idea of "sacred time" and "reset" our watches and clocks theologically speaking. (3) Finally, we will investigate how the "sacred actions" of worship help reorient us in the journey of life.

Sacred space: The daily office of prayer. The establishment of Solomon's temple in Jerusalem brings a renewed emphasis on prayer to Israelite religious thought and life. Solomon's prayer of dedication for the temple places great importance on prayer in maintaining Israel's covenant relationship with God (cf. 1 Kings 8; 2 Chron. 6). Specific circumstances mentioned by Solomon providing the impetus for prayer either to maintain or to repair relationship with Yahweh include: prayers of personal supplication (2 Chron. 6:21), prayers of confession and repentance for sin (6:24, 26), petitions and intercessions concerning natural disasters and health afflictions (6:29), prayers of homage offered by the foreigner (6:32), petitions and intercessions offered during times of national emergency (e.g., war; 6:34), and prayers seeking restoration should sin cause Israel to be exiled from the land of covenant promise (6:39). Practically speaking, this made the temple a "house of prayer" for King Solomon (cf. 6:40).

Later Old Testament writers formalized this understanding of the temple as a "house of prayer for all nations," not just for Israel (Isa. 56:7). Jesus himself recognized the temple as both his "Father's house" (John 2:16) and a "house of prayer for all nations" when he cleared the temple of those who turned the sanctuary into a merchandise mart (Mark 11:17). Right relationship with God, whether Old or New Testament, is rooted in prayer prompted implicitly and explicitly by the revelation of God's nature, character, and activity in history. Prayer is effective, not because of the righteousness of the suppliant (James 5:16) but because of the power possessed by the One to whom prayer is offered (cf. 5:15).

The prayers of the righteous in the Old Testament are not to be equated with the superstitious incantations and magical chants of Israel's pagan neighbors (e.g., the prayers of the priests of Baal in 1 Kings 18:20–29). For the ancient Israelites prayer is always a personal encounter with God rooted in his divine self-revelation and covenant relationship with them as his people. Whether audible (Dan. 9:4) or silent (1 Sam. 1:13), prayer is direct communication with a responsive deity—a God in Zion who hears and answers prayers (Ps. 65:1–2). The teachings of Jesus on prayer to God as a loving Father in the Gospels confirm this Old Testament theology of prayer (cf. Matt. 6:6, 18, 30; 7:11).

Walter Leifeld is correct when he identifies the several aspects of prayer as overlapping with worship because they lead to the glory of God.[59] Whether one expresses homage to God or discloses a need, both types of prayer demonstrate dependence on God and glorify him as the One who has either answered prayer in the past or has the compassion and ability to do so in the future. The distinct but related expressions of prayer may be delineated as follows:

- worship—ascribing God the glory due his name (Ps. 29:1–2)
- praise—preoccupation with who God is and what he has done (Ps. 135:1–7)
- thanksgiving—specifically acknowledging the goodness of God (Ps. 136:1)
- adoration—personal, loving worship (Ps. 73:25)
- devotion—prayer resulting in a vow (1 Sam. 1:11)
- communion—emphasizing relationship with God and two-way communication and fellowship in prayer (Ps. 5:3; 42:8; 94:19)
- confession—admitting sin and guilt individually or corporately before God, a necessary prerequisite for prayer and worship (Ezra 9:6–15; Neh. 9:1–3)
- petition or supplication—presenting personal needs, concerns, cares, complaints to God (1 Sam. 1:17; Ps. 20:5)
- intercession—petitioning for another individual or group (Ex. 32:11; 2 Sam. 12:16)
- imprecation—invoking the application of divine justice against God's enemies in the form of a curse (Ps. 137:8)

The Old Testament mentions appointed times for prayer. Specifically, the Psalms speak of the faithful praying in the morning (Ps. 5:3), even before dawn (119:147). Elsewhere the psalmists utter prayers of lament in the morning, at noon, and in the evening (55:17). Perhaps this text served as Daniel's inspiration for praying three times a day facing Jerusalem (Dan. 6:10). Also, it seems morning and evening prayers were common, patterned after the morning and evening sacrifices of the temple liturgy (1 Chron. 23:30; cf. 16:40). Finally, much like the apostle Paul's injunction to "pray continually" (1 Thess. 5:17), the psalmist encouraged praying continually (Ps. 72:15; 105:4).

---

59. Walter Liefeld, "Prayer," ISBE, 3:937.

Several different prayer postures are mentioned in the Old Testament: standing (2 Chron. 20:5), kneeling with arms outstretched (1 Kings 8:54; note that Solomon begins his prayer in a standing position, 8:22), kneeling (Ezra 9:5), head bowed (Neh. 8:6), prostrate (Josh. 7:6), with uplifted hands (Ps. 28:2), and bowing with the face between the knees (1 Kings 18:42). As a result of Solomon's prayer of dedication for Yahweh's permanent sanctuary, the Temple Mount became the direction for prayer for the faithful outside Jerusalem (cf. 2 Chron. 6:20, 21, 26, 29).

Of particular interest to our study are the appointed prayer times or prayer cycles observed in Scripture. Prayer was no less important in maintaining a right relationship with God in the New Testament than it was in the Old Testament. The early church certainly understood this, so much so that prayer was one of the staples of early Christian worship (Acts 2:24). In fact, many of the Jewish Christians continued the discipline of attending daily prayers at the temple (e.g., Peter and John, Acts 3:1). During New Testament times, prayer services accompanied the morning and evening sacrificial rituals. This practice, in part, gave rise to the prayer-book tradition of morning and evening prayer.

In the fourth century, Basil of Caesarea drew up a set of monastic rules for Eastern Christianity that included eight daily appointments for prayer. Later Benedict of Nursia (ca. A.D. 530) developed a similar daily office of prayer for Western Christianity. The term *daily office* "refers to a variety of services of set prayers and readings that are said together through the day."[60] The daily cycle of prayer, whether in the early church or later monastic practice, was an attempt to heed the admonition of Scripture to "pray continually" (1 Thess. 5:17). Eventually a standardized observance of a daily cycle of prayer emerged in the tradition of the Christian church. The eightfold Western monastic cycle of the daily office (or liturgy of the hours), one example of this standardized prayer format, may be outlined as follows:

- vespers (at the end of the working day)
- compline (before bedtime)
- nocturns or vigils or matins (during the middle of the night)
- lauds (at daybreak)
- prime (shortly thereafter)
- terce (during the middle of the morning)
- sext (at noon)
- none (during the middle of the afternoon)

---

60. Arthur P. Boers, "Learning the Ancient Rhythms of Prayer," *Christianity Today* 41 (Jan. 8, 2001): 38.

Both the prayers of the Eastern and Western monastic daily offices relied heavily on the Psalter. As Christianity gained respectability in the Constantinian world, monasticism replaced martyrdom as one means of separating true Christianity from the "christianized culture" of the Roman world. Unfortunately, monasticism began to set the tone for spiritual life and formation in the church. Most Christians were unable to devote themselves to lengthy services of communal daily prayer like the monastic orders. According to White, the people's office of prayer in popular Christianity slipped out of sight during the medieval era, and daily prayer office became professionalized with the monks taking it over.[61]

Later, the idea of the daily prayer office was pared down to morning and evening prayer or rejected altogether by the Protestant Reformers. Interestingly, the Book of Common Prayer is a vestige of the morning and evening daily office, and it had the practical effect of guiding the laity in personal daily prayer as the complexities of English life (in 1545!) often prevented attendance at the communal prayer services held each day in the local churches.

Given the renewed interest in church history and liturgical worship, however, the daily prayer office is finding its way back into the life of the church.[62] I believe the Chronicler would approve of the observance of the daily office in the Christian church since he was accustomed to the daily cycle of temple worship. I too would advocate a return to the daily office of prayer in some form. We must concede that the logistical problems associated with the implementation of the corporate approach to the daily office by a local church on a sustained basis proves more problematic many times over in comparison to sixteenth-century England. But surprisingly, many local churches are now observing certain hours of the daily office on a weekly basis, especially the hours of vespers and compline.

Following the example of the prayer-book tradition, some kind of personal or familial adaptation of morning and evening prayers can easily be developed as one type of spiritual discipline. The special seasons of the church year also lend themselves readily to the hours of the daily office with certain modifications (e.g., some variation on lauds for the Easter Sunday sunrise service).

The call for a return to some form of the daily prayer office is not necessarily a call to monasticism, although monastic retreats are gaining in popularity in Christian circles. Neither is the corporate or personal observance of the daily office of prayer encouraged simply because "more is better" or

---

61. James F. White, *A Brief History of Christian Worship* (Nashville: Abingdon, 1993), 55.

62. See Boers, "Learning the Ancient Rhythms of Prayer," 38–45; esp. the bibliography cited addressing the "daily office," 38–39.

because formality is more effective. Christian prayer is first and foremost a matter of heart and attitude, not vain repetitions (Ps. 25:4–7; cf. Matt. 6:5–6). Nor should the daily prayer office be construed as an attempt to achieve righteousness by works of human effort. The current "fashionablility" of pre-Reformation spirituality is also an insufficient reason for praying according to the daily office. Finally, praying according to the hours of the daily office should not be mistaken as some sort of badge of superspirituality.

Rather, exploring the Christian tradition of the daily office permits the Christian and the local Christian church to learn the ancient rhythm of prayer. Participation in the daily cycle of prayer hearkens back to the temple as the house of prayer and the idea that prayer is one means for recovering order out of chaos. Numerous reasons for a return to the daily office of prayer in some form may be advanced:

(1) Boers finds the daily office helpful as a "counterculture" discipline for Christians in a society "where many are formed by a weekly average of twenty-eight hours of television."[63]
(2) The practice of the daily office in some form encourages Christians to pray more often and with greater regimen and organization.
(3) The daily office is another way for Christians to reconnect with the rich heritage of prayer in the Christian tradition. Praying the prayers of saints who have gone on before us deepens faith and adds to a sense of awe and wonder at the mystery of Christ and the gospel.
(4) Whether observed in a corporate or private setting, there is a certain communal aspect to the daily office because the Christian stands in solidarity with others who are praying at that same time.
(5) The daily office also has the practical effect of teaching the worshiper Scripture, since the prayers and readings of the liturgy of the hours are taken directly from the Old and New Testaments.

St. Benedict wrote of "singing Psalms in such a way that our minds are in harmony with our voices." According to Boers, "the daily office can integrate life and prayer in just this way."[64] This kind of holistic spirituality is essential to the process of restoring God's order in the midst of the chaos of our fallen world.

Sacred time: The church year. Solomon's temple was a lavish reminder that God, through the Mosaic law, ordered Hebrew worship according to set times and seasons. In fact, Solomon's letter to Hiram king of Tyre, requesting building materials and a master builder to supervise the construction pro-

63. Ibid., 40.
64. Ibid., 45.

ject, mentions the four cycles of time appointed for Hebrew worship (2:4). Israelite personal and corporate worship was organized around a daily sequence (e.g., the morning and evening sacrifices, Ex. 29:39), a weekly sequence (e.g., the Sabbath, Ex. 20:8–11), a monthly sequence (e.g., the New Moon, Num. 10:10), and an annual sequence (e.g., the pilgrimage festivals, Ex. 23:14–19). Since the early church was comprised largely of Jewish Christians, these time cycles of Jewish worship naturally became a part of the New Testament record of Christian worship (e.g., Acts 2:46; 3:1; 13:14; 20:7).

Over the course of several centuries the Christian church has also ordered worship according to set cycles of time by developing a "church year" or liturgical calendar. The expression *church year* refers to the regular sequence of cycles, seasons, festivals, and fasts observed in the calendar of the Christian church. The succession of events is ordered independently from the civil calendar, although the church-year dates are reckoned according to the Julian calendar for the sake of convenience.[65] The beginnings of a liturgical calendar in the Christian church can be traced to the third century A.D. The church year was largely patterned after the Jewish religious calendar, with the key events of Jesus Christ's life and redemptive ministry replacing the Exodus and the Passover of Old Testament salvation history. Eventually the church year grew by accretion to include a complex rotation of church seasons and festivals.

The purpose of the church year is to sanctify time within the yearly experience of church life. The celebration of Christ's life, teaching, death, resurrection, ascension, and sending of the Holy Spirit is intended to bring spiritual renewal to the church through "a vibrant reliving of the paschal mysteries."[66] Due to abuses that crept into the observance of the church year during the medieval period, the Reformers abandoned the practice. Today, the idea of a church year is foreign to many Protestant worshipers.

Naturally, abuse remains a potential in the celebration of the church year. The most common problem associated with the liturgical calendar is the dichotomy it invites between "sacred" and "secular" time. For example, the periods of time between the festival cycles in the church year are usually referred to as "ordinary time" or nonfestive time. These intervals are not considered special, nor do they demand the same intensity of spiritual participation. Here Jacques Ellul has addressed the gist of the problem: "Very

65. See Peter G. Cobb, "The History of the Christian Year," in *The Study of Liturgy*, ed. C. Jones, G. Wainwright, and E. Yarnold (New York: Oxford Univ. Press, 1978), 403–19.
66. Terrence J. German, "Christian Year," in *Evangelical Dictionary of Theology*, 2d ed., ed. Walter A. Elwell (Grand Rapids: Baker, 2001), 237.

quickly some days of the week ... come to rank as sacred"[67]—and soon sacred-versus-secular distinctions blur the perception of time.

The Old Testament, however, knows no such distinction between sacred and secular time. All time is God's gift to humanity (Ps. 31:15; 139:16; Isa. 60:22), and each season or cycle of time has its appropriate place within the divinely ordered sphere of human experience in time (Eccl. 3:1–9; Song 2:12; Hos. 10:12). For the ancient Israelite, in one sense each day was a special or sacred day because it could be used to fulfill creation's purpose of worshiping and praising God (Ps. 34:11; 118:24; Isa. 43:7).

The Hebrew religious calendar did not mark special festival days and seasons in order to separate them as sacred from ordinary or nonfestive time. Rather, the Hebrew liturgical year marked all time in the annual cycle as sacred, with the special festival days and seasons celebrated as suprafestive times. The annual cycle of festivals in that religious calendar was a type of "time insurance," guaranteeing the daily celebration of all time as God's gift and the arena of divine activity.

Of special interest to this study is the idea of "festival time." The divine mandate for the seasonal festivals is found in Leviticus 23 and 25. This Mosaic legislation actually constitutes ancient Israel's religious calendar, bringing time under the domain of God's rule. The major festivals appointed for celebration by special worship ceremonies included the Sabbath, the Passover and Feast of Unleavened Bread, the Offering of Firstfruits, the Festival of Weeks (or Pentecost), the Festival of Trumpets (or New Year's Day), the Day of Atonement, the Festival of Booths (or Tabernacles), Sabbath Year, and the Year of Jubilee (see Appendix B: The Hebrew Religious Calendar).

The order of major festival times observed in the Israelite religious calendar reflects the seasonal rhythms of nature, since most of the ancient calendars were originally based on the agricultural cycles of planting and harvesting. Unlike their Canaanite counterparts, however, the Hebrew religious festivals and appointed sacred times "have been historicized—

---

67. Jacques Ellul, *The Subversion of Christianity*, trans. G. W. Bromiley (Grand Rapids: Eerdmans, 1986), 63. One example of this application of the notion of "sacred time" to specific days of the week is the "Christian Sabbath" (i.e., the equation of Sunday as the Old Testament Sabbath). For a historical and theological discussion of the issue, see D. A. Carson, ed., *From Sabbath to Lord's Day* (Grand Rapids: Zondervan, 1982). Although the Chronicler places more emphasis on "festival time," the topic of "Sabbath time" offers another fruitful area of study for contemporary application to the theme of recovering order from chaos. See further Abraham J. Heschel's classic essay, *The Sabbath: Its Meaning for Modern Man* (Philadelphia: Jewish Publication Society, 1952); cf. Marva Dawn, *Keeping the Sabbath Wholly* (Grand Rapids: Eerdmans, 1989).

that is, they have received their content and meaning from the history of redemption."[68] In other words, the Hebrew religious calendar was not bound inextricably with the annual cycle of the agricultural seasons. Instead, it was linked to redemptive events in Israelite history, especially those connected with the Exodus.

The essential purpose of this religious calendar for ancient Israel was "a dramatic replay of [redemptive] history, done every year to bring home its meaning for the present."[69] It was designed both to instill and to affirm faith in God within the covenant community. This annual cycle reminded all Israel that it was the Lord God who delivered them from Egypt and established his covenant with them (Lev. 23:43).

Dyrness has identified additional purposes for the seasons of the Hebrew religious calendar:

- the annual reminder that all time belongs to God and all good gifts come from him
- the practice of obedience to God as Creator and Redeemer by acknowledging his good gifts in the rhythm of nature and the cycle of redemptive history
- the recognition of God's dominion over nature and the demonstration (by reenactment) that God worked within time and history by means of specific events and the natural process to reveal his goodness and to deliver his people
- the expression of confidence in God that Israel's life possessed a divine order, direction, and purpose
- the assurance that God would continue to show his goodness and deliver his people in the future[70]

The common denominator between the Christian church year and the Hebrew religious calendar is the ordering of time according to a redemptive schema. Here is yet another way in which "temple theology" informs Christian theology on the matter of restoring "order out of chaos." This is especially true for the annual cycle of "festival time" in the two liturgical calendars, because the "feast" conquers *chaos* (the disorder and upheaval of the fallen world) and recovers *kosmos* (the divine order established in creation). There is a real sense in which the festival cycle of time overturns the world and re-creates it according to the model of God's original creation. There are several

68. E. H. Van Olst, *The Bible and Liturgy*, trans. J. Vriend (Grand Rapids: Eerdmans, 1991), 38.
69. Ibid., 39.
70. Dyrness, *Themes in Old Testament Theology*, 148–51.

theological principles associated with festival time that contribute to this "re-creating" of the world order:

- celebrating God's redemptive intervention in human history, so that the "feast" is a conscious rejection of all that is negative, an act of rebellion against the perverse and destructive power of evil and against death and the evil one
- emphasizing rejoicing and sharing and thus asserting the dignity and goodness of life bestowed on humanity as God's gift and the value of the community of the faithful in the journey of life
- publicly affirming a higher order—God, good, and meaning and purpose in life as a result of God's redemptive acts in history through Jesus Christ, so that festival time is a bold witness of hope to a hopeless world that the divine order will be restored and God's righteousness will one day prevail

This being the case, I can only offer an "Amen!" to Robert Webber's prophetic plea to the church (esp. the free-church movement in Protestantism) to find a place for "commemorative time" by observing the Christian year in some fashion. Webber's apologetic is threefold: (1) the historical dimension of remaining faithful to the church's long tradition of observing the Christian year; (2) the theological dimension of participating in commemorative time so that the power of the Christ-event is remembered, proclaimed, enacted, and celebrated in the worshiping community; and (3) the evangelistic dimension of governing time in the worshiping community by the birth, life, death, and resurrection of Jesus Christ in opposition to the secular community and its practice of observing time.[71]

I would simply add that experiencing commemorative time by observance of the church year brings perspective and synthesis to "clock time" (i.e., *chronos*) through the celebration of "event time" (i.e., *kairos*, i.e., moments of time and special occasions). What better way to restore order from chaos than to cease "serving time" in the enemy's domain and to start "celebrating time" in God's domain?

Sacred actions: The pilgrimage. One of the theological emphases derived from the idea of the temple as "sacred space" was that of the "pilgrimage." In the Bridging Contexts section, we defined pilgrimage as "a journey made to a sacred place as an act of devotion." The practice of journeying to sacred places by God's faithful people was not limited to the Hebrew religion of Old Testament times. By the second century A.D. Christian pilgrimages to the Holy Land were popular. Retracing Jesus' movements during his last week of

---

71. Webber, *Worship Old and New*, 225–26.

life on earth (his Passion Week) by walking the Via Dolorosa in Jerusalem became especially significant. Later, travels to the graves of martyrs and saints, sites where miracles had been performed, and other holy cities (e.g., Rome, Canterbury) were added to the Christian tradition of pilgrimages.

The church encouraged pilgrimages as a means of penance, since travel in the ancient world was undertaken with considerable risk of hardship and personal sacrifice. The significance of the pilgrimage for Christianity was (unfortunately) demonstrated militarily with the medieval Crusades, ordered by the church to make the Holy Land free and safe for pilgrim travels.

Despite the views of prominent critics over the centuries of church history (e.g., John Chrysostom, Jerome [who made a pilgrimage to Jerusalem, by the way], and Erasmus), pilgrimages to the Holy Land and elsewhere remained an important feature of personal spirituality in many Christian traditions. Alternatives to these treks to specific sacred sites of Christianity have gained in popularity recently. These mock pilgrimages may include the re-creation of the Bethlehem advent scene or the stations of the Way of the Cross during the Easter season. The more liturgical Christian traditions view the worship processional as a reenactment of the pilgrimage to the temple on Mount Zion, while some Christians understand their weekly journey to their local church as a type of pilgrimage. In other instances, travels to local church reunions, anniversaries, baby dedications, or baptisms, or revisiting the site of one's conversion or baptism prompts the same spiritual reflection and renewal associated with the more traditional pilgrimage experience.

More important to the New Testament writers is the equation of the Christian life with the pilgrimage of the Hebrew tradition. Even as Jacob considered his life a "sojourn" of 130 years (Gen. 47:9), so the life of faith is a pilgrimage to the heavenly country (Heb. 11:13–16). For this reason, the New Testament refers to Christians as "aliens and strangers" (1 Peter 2:11), whose citizenship is in heaven (Phil. 3:20). The psalmist had a similar understanding of the life of faith when he blessed all who set their hearts on the pilgrimage—literally in the celebration of the Hebrew festivals and metaphorically by embracing the hardships of daily living in the strength God provides (Ps. 84:5). Likewise, the Christian's earthly life is but a long pilgrimage to that city whose maker and architect is God himself (Heb. 11:10).

Thus, Paul compares this spiritual pilgrimage of the Christian life to that of a soldier on a mission, who refuses to entangle himself in civilian affairs (2 Tim. 2:3–4). As a pilgrim or alien in this life, the Christian is called to be separated from the corruption of the world in order to live a righteous life before the ungodly to the glory of God (1 Peter 2:12).

In light of our study of Solomon's temple, Paul's rhetorical question to the Corinthians takes on new meaning: "Or didn't you realize that your body is a sacred place, the place of the Holy Spirit?" (1 Cor. 6:19a, *The Message*). This is especially true when we recognize that Paul's term for "temple" (Gk. *naos*) refers to the niche where the idol was displayed in the pagan Greek temples. Thus, Paul is essentially telling the Corinthians (and the contemporary reader of his letter) that the Christian is the "most holy place" in the "sacred space" of the temple sanctuary. For this reason, he asks:

> Don't you see that you can't live however you please, squandering what God paid such a high price for? The physical part of you is not some piece of property that belongs to the spiritual part of you. God owns the whole works. So let people see God in and through your body. (1 Cor. 6:19b–20, *The Message*)

2 Chronicles 10:1–21:3

REHOBOAM WENT TO Shechem, for all the Israelites had gone there to make him king. ²When Jeroboam son of Nebat heard this (he was in Egypt, where he had fled from King Solomon), he returned from Egypt. ³So they sent for Jeroboam, and he and all Israel went to Rehoboam and said to him: ⁴"Your father put a heavy yoke on us, but now lighten the harsh labor and the heavy yoke he put on us, and we will serve you."

⁵Rehoboam answered, "Come back to me in three days." So the people went away.

⁶Then King Rehoboam consulted the elders who had served his father Solomon during his lifetime. "How would you advise me to answer these people?" he asked.

⁷They replied, "If you will be kind to these people and please them and give them a favorable answer, they will always be your servants."

⁸But Rehoboam rejected the advice the elders gave him and consulted the young men who had grown up with him and were serving him. ⁹He asked them, "What is your advice? How should we answer these people who say to me, 'Lighten the yoke your father put on us'?"

¹⁰The young men who had grown up with him replied, "Tell the people who have said to you, 'Your father put a heavy yoke on us, but make our yoke lighter'—tell them, 'My little finger is thicker than my father's waist. ¹¹My father laid on you a heavy yoke; I will make it even heavier. My father scourged you with whips; I will scourge you with scorpions.'"

¹²Three days later Jeroboam and all the people returned to Rehoboam, as the king had said, "Come back to me in three days." ¹³The king answered them harshly. Rejecting the advice of the elders, ¹⁴he followed the advice of the young men and said, "My father made your yoke heavy; I will make it even heavier. My father scourged you with whips; I will scourge you with scorpions." ¹⁵So the king did not listen to the people, for this turn of events was from God, to fulfill the word the LORD had spoken to Jeroboam son of Nebat through Ahijah the Shilonite.

¹⁶When all Israel saw that the king refused to listen to them, they answered the king:

> "What share do we have in David,
>> what part in Jesse's son?
> To your tents, O Israel!
>> Look after your own house, O David!"

So all the Israelites went home. ¹⁷But as for the Israelites who were living in the towns of Judah, Rehoboam still ruled over them.

¹⁸King Rehoboam sent out Adoniram, who was in charge of forced labor, but the Israelites stoned him to death. King Rehoboam, however, managed to get into his chariot and escape to Jerusalem. ¹⁹So Israel has been in rebellion against the house of David to this day.

¹¹:¹When Rehoboam arrived in Jerusalem, he mustered the house of Judah and Benjamin—a hundred and eighty thousand fighting men—to make war against Israel and to regain the kingdom for Rehoboam.

²But this word of the LORD came to Shemaiah the man of God: ³"Say to Rehoboam son of Solomon king of Judah and to all the Israelites in Judah and Benjamin, ⁴'This is what the LORD says: Do not go up to fight against your brothers. Go home, every one of you, for this is my doing.'" So they obeyed the words of the LORD and turned back from marching against Jeroboam.

⁵Rehoboam lived in Jerusalem and built up towns for defense in Judah: ⁶Bethlehem, Etam, Tekoa, ⁷Beth Zur, Soco, Adullam, ⁸Gath, Mareshah, Ziph, ⁹Adoraim, Lachish, Azekah, ¹⁰Zorah, Aijalon and Hebron. These were fortified cities in Judah and Benjamin. ¹¹He strengthened their defenses and put commanders in them, with supplies of food, olive oil and wine. ¹²He put shields and spears in all the cities, and made them very strong. So Judah and Benjamin were his.

¹³The priests and Levites from all their districts throughout Israel sided with him. ¹⁴The Levites even abandoned their pasturelands and property, and came to Judah and Jerusalem because Jeroboam and his sons had rejected them as priests of the LORD. ¹⁵And he appointed his own priests for the high places and for the goat and calf idols he had made. ¹⁶Those from every tribe of Israel who set their hearts on seeking the LORD, the God of Israel, followed the Levites to Jerusalem to

offer sacrifices to the LORD, the God of their fathers. [17]They strengthened the kingdom of Judah and supported Rehoboam son of Solomon three years, walking in the ways of David and Solomon during this time.

[18]Rehoboam married Mahalath, who was the daughter of David's son Jerimoth and of Abihail, the daughter of Jesse's son Eliab. [19]She bore him sons: Jeush, Shemariah and Zaham. [20]Then he married Maacah daughter of Absalom, who bore him Abijah, Attai, Ziza and Shelomith. [21]Rehoboam loved Maacah daughter of Absalom more than any of his other wives and concubines. In all, he had eighteen wives and sixty concubines, twenty-eight sons and sixty daughters.

[22]Rehoboam appointed Abijah son of Maacah to be the chief prince among his brothers, in order to make him king. [23]He acted wisely, dispersing some of his sons throughout the districts of Judah and Benjamin, and to all the fortified cities. He gave them abundant provisions and took many wives for them.

[12:1]After Rehoboam's position as king was established and he had become strong, he and all Israel with him abandoned the law of the LORD. [2]Because they had been unfaithful to the LORD, Shishak king of Egypt attacked Jerusalem in the fifth year of King Rehoboam. [3]With twelve hundred chariots and sixty thousand horsemen and the innumerable troops of Libyans, Sukkites and Cushites that came with him from Egypt, [4]he captured the fortified cities of Judah and came as far as Jerusalem.

[5]Then the prophet Shemaiah came to Rehoboam and to the leaders of Judah who had assembled in Jerusalem for fear of Shishak, and he said to them, "This is what the LORD says, 'You have abandoned me; therefore, I now abandon you to Shishak.'"

[6]The leaders of Israel and the king humbled themselves and said, "The LORD is just."

[7]When the LORD saw that they humbled themselves, this word of the LORD came to Shemaiah: "Since they have humbled themselves, I will not destroy them but will soon give them deliverance. My wrath will not be poured out on Jerusalem through Shishak. [8]They will, however, become subject to him, so that they may learn the difference between serving me and serving the kings of other lands."

[9]When Shishak king of Egypt attacked Jerusalem, he carried off the treasures of the temple of the LORD and the

treasures of the royal palace. He took everything, including the gold shields Solomon had made. ¹⁰So King Rehoboam made bronze shields to replace them and assigned these to the commanders of the guard on duty at the entrance to the royal palace. ¹¹Whenever the king went to the LORD's temple, the guards went with him, bearing the shields, and afterward they returned them to the guardroom.

¹²Because Rehoboam humbled himself, the LORD's anger turned from him, and he was not totally destroyed. Indeed, there was some good in Judah.

¹³King Rehoboam established himself firmly in Jerusalem and continued as king. He was forty-one years old when he became king, and he reigned seventeen years in Jerusalem, the city the LORD had chosen out of all the tribes of Israel in which to put his Name. His mother's name was Naamah; she was an Ammonite. ¹⁴He did evil because he had not set his heart on seeking the LORD.

¹⁵As for the events of Rehoboam's reign, from beginning to end, are they not written in the records of Shemaiah the prophet and of Iddo the seer that deal with genealogies? There was continual warfare between Rehoboam and Jeroboam. ¹⁶Rehoboam rested with his fathers and was buried in the City of David. And Abijah his son succeeded him as king.

¹³:¹In the eighteenth year of the reign of Jeroboam, Abijah became king of Judah, ²and he reigned in Jerusalem three years. His mother's name was Maacah, a daughter of Uriel of Gibeah.

There was war between Abijah and Jeroboam. ³Abijah went into battle with a force of four hundred thousand able fighting men, and Jeroboam drew up a battle line against him with eight hundred thousand able troops.

⁴Abijah stood on Mount Zemaraim, in the hill country of Ephraim, and said, "Jeroboam and all Israel, listen to me! ⁵Don't you know that the LORD, the God of Israel, has given the kingship of Israel to David and his descendants forever by a covenant of salt? ⁶Yet Jeroboam son of Nebat, an official of Solomon son of David, rebelled against his master. ⁷Some worthless scoundrels gathered around him and opposed Rehoboam son of Solomon when he was young and indecisive and not strong enough to resist them.

⁸"And now you plan to resist the kingdom of the LORD, which is in the hands of David's descendants. You are indeed a

vast army and have with you the golden calves that Jeroboam made to be your gods. ⁹But didn't you drive out the priests of the LORD, the sons of Aaron, and the Levites, and make priests of your own as the peoples of other lands do? Whoever comes to consecrate himself with a young bull and seven rams may become a priest of what are not gods.

¹⁰"As for us, the LORD is our God, and we have not forsaken him. The priests who serve the LORD are sons of Aaron, and the Levites assist them. ¹¹Every morning and evening they present burnt offerings and fragrant incense to the LORD. They set out the bread on the ceremonially clean table and light the lamps on the gold lampstand every evening. We are observing the requirements of the LORD our God. But you have forsaken him. ¹²God is with us; he is our leader. His priests with their trumpets will sound the battle cry against you. Men of Israel, do not fight against the LORD, the God of your fathers, for you will not succeed."

¹³Now Jeroboam had sent troops around to the rear, so that while he was in front of Judah the ambush was behind them. ¹⁴Judah turned and saw that they were being attacked at both front and rear. Then they cried out to the LORD. The priests blew their trumpets ¹⁵and the men of Judah raised the battle cry. At the sound of their battle cry, God routed Jeroboam and all Israel before Abijah and Judah. ¹⁶The Israelites fled before Judah, and God delivered them into their hands. ¹⁷Abijah and his men inflicted heavy losses on them, so that there were five hundred thousand casualties among Israel's able men. ¹⁸The men of Israel were subdued on that occasion, and the men of Judah were victorious because they relied on the LORD, the God of their fathers.

¹⁹Abijah pursued Jeroboam and took from him the towns of Bethel, Jeshanah and Ephron, with their surrounding villages. ²⁰Jeroboam did not regain power during the time of Abijah. And the LORD struck him down and he died.

²¹But Abijah grew in strength. He married fourteen wives and had twenty-two sons and sixteen daughters.

²²The other events of Abijah's reign, what he did and what he said, are written in the annotations of the prophet Iddo.

¹⁴:¹And Abijah rested with his fathers and was buried in the City of David. Asa his son succeeded him as king, and in his days the country was at peace for ten years.

²Asa did what was good and right in the eyes of the LORD his God. ³He removed the foreign altars and the high places, smashed the sacred stones and cut down the Asherah poles. ⁴He commanded Judah to seek the LORD, the God of their fathers, and to obey his laws and commands. ⁵He removed the high places and incense altars in every town in Judah, and the kingdom was at peace under him. ⁶He built up the fortified cities of Judah, since the land was at peace. No one was at war with him during those years, for the LORD gave him rest.

⁷"Let us build up these towns," he said to Judah, "and put walls around them, with towers, gates and bars. The land is still ours, because we have sought the LORD our God; we sought him and he has given us rest on every side." So they built and prospered.

⁸Asa had an army of three hundred thousand men from Judah, equipped with large shields and with spears, and two hundred and eighty thousand from Benjamin, armed with small shields and with bows. All these were brave fighting men.

⁹Zerah the Cushite marched out against them with a vast army and three hundred chariots, and came as far as Mareshah. ¹⁰Asa went out to meet him, and they took up battle positions in the Valley of Zephathah near Mareshah.

¹¹Then Asa called to the LORD his God and said, "LORD, there is no one like you to help the powerless against the mighty. Help us, O LORD our God, for we rely on you, and in your name we have come against this vast army. O LORD, you are our God; do not let man prevail against you."

¹²The LORD struck down the Cushites before Asa and Judah. The Cushites fled, ¹³and Asa and his army pursued them as far as Gerar. Such a great number of Cushites fell that they could not recover; they were crushed before the LORD and his forces. The men of Judah carried off a large amount of plunder. ¹⁴They destroyed all the villages around Gerar, for the terror of the LORD had fallen upon them. They plundered all these villages, since there was much booty there. ¹⁵They also attacked the camps of the herdsmen and carried off droves of sheep and goats and camels. Then they returned to Jerusalem.

¹⁵:¹The Spirit of God came upon Azariah son of Oded. ²He went out to meet Asa and said to him, "Listen to me, Asa and all Judah and Benjamin. The LORD is with you when you are

with him. If you seek him, he will be found by you, but if you forsake him, he will forsake you. ³For a long time Israel was without the true God, without a priest to teach and without the law. ⁴But in their distress they turned to the LORD, the God of Israel, and sought him, and he was found by them. ⁵In those days it was not safe to travel about, for all the inhabitants of the lands were in great turmoil. ⁶One nation was being crushed by another and one city by another, because God was troubling them with every kind of distress. ⁷But as for you, be strong and do not give up, for your work will be rewarded."

⁸When Asa heard these words and the prophecy of Azariah son of Oded the prophet, he took courage. He removed the detestable idols from the whole land of Judah and Benjamin and from the towns he had captured in the hills of Ephraim. He repaired the altar of the LORD that was in front of the portico of the LORD's temple.

⁹Then he assembled all Judah and Benjamin and the people from Ephraim, Manasseh and Simeon who had settled among them, for large numbers had come over to him from Israel when they saw that the LORD his God was with him.

¹⁰They assembled at Jerusalem in the third month of the fifteenth year of Asa's reign. ¹¹At that time they sacrificed to the LORD seven hundred head of cattle and seven thousand sheep and goats from the plunder they had brought back. ¹²They entered into a covenant to seek the LORD, the God of their fathers, with all their heart and soul. ¹³All who would not seek the LORD, the God of Israel, were to be put to death, whether small or great, man or woman. ¹⁴They took an oath to the LORD with loud acclamation, with shouting and with trumpets and horns. ¹⁵All Judah rejoiced about the oath because they had sworn it wholeheartedly. They sought God eagerly, and he was found by them. So the LORD gave them rest on every side.

¹⁶King Asa also deposed his grandmother Maacah from her position as queen mother, because she had made a repulsive Asherah pole. Asa cut the pole down, broke it up and burned it in the Kidron Valley. ¹⁷Although he did not remove the high places from Israel, Asa's heart was fully committed to the LORD all his life. ¹⁸He brought into the temple of God the silver and gold and the articles that he and his father had dedicated.

¹⁹There was no more war until the thirty-fifth year of Asa's reign.

^{16:1}In the thirty-sixth year of Asa's reign Baasha king of Israel went up against Judah and fortified Ramah to prevent anyone from leaving or entering the territory of Asa king of Judah.

²Asa then took the silver and gold out of the treasuries of the LORD's temple and of his own palace and sent it to Ben-Hadad king of Aram, who was ruling in Damascus. ³"Let there be a treaty between me and you," he said, "as there was between my father and your father. See, I am sending you silver and gold. Now break your treaty with Baasha king of Israel so he will withdraw from me."

⁴Ben-Hadad agreed with King Asa and sent the commanders of his forces against the towns of Israel. They conquered Ijon, Dan, Abel Maim and all the store cities of Naphtali. ⁵When Baasha heard this, he stopped building Ramah and abandoned his work. ⁶Then King Asa brought all the men of Judah, and they carried away from Ramah the stones and timber Baasha had been using. With them he built up Geba and Mizpah.

⁷At that time Hanani the seer came to Asa king of Judah and said to him: "Because you relied on the king of Aram and not on the LORD your God, the army of the king of Aram has escaped from your hand. ⁸Were not the Cushites and Libyans a mighty army with great numbers of chariots and horsemen? Yet when you relied on the LORD, he delivered them into your hand. ⁹For the eyes of the LORD range throughout the earth to strengthen those whose hearts are fully committed to him. You have done a foolish thing, and from now on you will be at war."

¹⁰Asa was angry with the seer because of this; he was so enraged that he put him in prison. At the same time Asa brutally oppressed some of the people.

¹¹The events of Asa's reign, from beginning to end, are written in the book of the kings of Judah and Israel. ¹²In the thirty-ninth year of his reign Asa was afflicted with a disease in his feet. Though his disease was severe, even in his illness he did not seek help from the LORD, but only from the physicians. ¹³Then in the forty-first year of his reign Asa died and rested with his fathers. ¹⁴They buried him in the tomb that he had cut out for himself in the City of David. They laid him on a bier covered with spices and various blended perfumes, and they made a huge fire in his honor.

^{17:1}Jehoshaphat his son succeeded him as king and strength-
ened himself against Israel. ²He stationed troops in all the fortified cities of Judah and put garrisons in Judah and in the
towns of Ephraim that his father Asa had captured.

³The LORD was with Jehoshaphat because in his early years
he walked in the ways his father David had followed. He did
not consult the Baals ⁴but sought the God of his father and
followed his commands rather than the practices of Israel.
⁵The LORD established the kingdom under his control; and all
Judah brought gifts to Jehoshaphat, so that he had great
wealth and honor. ⁶His heart was devoted to the ways of the
LORD; furthermore, he removed the high places and the
Asherah poles from Judah.

⁷In the third year of his reign he sent his officials Ben-Hail,
Obadiah, Zechariah, Nethanel and Micaiah to teach in the
towns of Judah. ⁸With them were certain Levites—Shemaiah,
Nethaniah, Zebadiah, Asahel, Shemiramoth, Jehonathan,
Adonijah, Tobijah and Tob-Adonijah—and the priests
Elishama and Jehoram. ⁹They taught throughout Judah, taking
with them the Book of the Law of the LORD; they went
around to all the towns of Judah and taught the people.

¹⁰The fear of the LORD fell on all the kingdoms of the lands
surrounding Judah, so that they did not make war with
Jehoshaphat. ¹¹Some Philistines brought Jehoshaphat gifts and
silver as tribute, and the Arabs brought him flocks: seven
thousand seven hundred rams and seven thousand seven hundred goats.

¹²Jehoshaphat became more and more powerful; he built
forts and store cities in Judah ¹³and had large supplies in the
towns of Judah. He also kept experienced fighting men in
Jerusalem. ¹⁴Their enrollment by families was as follows:

> From Judah, commanders of units of 1,000:
>> Adnah the commander, with 300,000 fighting men;
> ¹⁵next, Jehohanan the commander, with 280,000;
> ¹⁶next, Amasiah son of Zicri, who volunteered himself for
>> the service of the LORD, with 200,000.
> ¹⁷From Benjamin:
>> Eliada, a valiant soldier, with 200,000 men armed with
>> bows and shields;
> ¹⁸next, Jehozabad, with 180,000 men armed for battle.

¹⁹These were the men who served the king, besides those he stationed in the fortified cities throughout Judah.

¹⁸:¹Now Jehoshaphat had great wealth and honor, and he allied himself with Ahab by marriage. ²Some years later he went down to visit Ahab in Samaria. Ahab slaughtered many sheep and cattle for him and the people with him and urged him to attack Ramoth Gilead. ³Ahab king of Israel asked Jehoshaphat king of Judah, "Will you go with me against Ramoth Gilead?"

Jehoshaphat replied, "I am as you are, and my people as your people; we will join you in the war." ⁴But Jehoshaphat also said to the king of Israel, "First seek the counsel of the LORD."

⁵So the king of Israel brought together the prophets—four hundred men—and asked them, "Shall we go to war against Ramoth Gilead, or shall I refrain?"

"Go," they answered, "for God will give it into the king's hand."

⁶But Jehoshaphat asked, "Is there not a prophet of the LORD here whom we can inquire of?"

⁷The king of Israel answered Jehoshaphat, "There is still one man through whom we can inquire of the LORD, but I hate him because he never prophesies anything good about me, but always bad. He is Micaiah son of Imlah."

"The king should not say that," Jehoshaphat replied.

⁸So the king of Israel called one of his officials and said, "Bring Micaiah son of Imlah at once."

⁹Dressed in their royal robes, the king of Israel and Jehoshaphat king of Judah were sitting on their thrones at the threshing floor by the entrance to the gate of Samaria, with all the prophets prophesying before them. ¹⁰Now Zedekiah son of Kenaanah had made iron horns, and he declared, "This is what the LORD says: 'With these you will gore the Arameans until they are destroyed.'"

¹¹All the other prophets were prophesying the same thing. "Attack Ramoth Gilead and be victorious," they said, "for the LORD will give it into the king's hand."

¹²The messenger who had gone to summon Micaiah said to him, "Look, as one man the other prophets are predicting success for the king. Let your word agree with theirs, and speak favorably."

¹³But Micaiah said, "As surely as the LORD lives, I can tell him only what my God says."

¹⁴When he arrived, the king asked him, "Micaiah, shall we go to war against Ramoth Gilead, or shall I refrain?"

"Attack and be victorious," he answered, "for they will be given into your hand."

¹⁵The king said to him, "How many times must I make you swear to tell me nothing but the truth in the name of the LORD?"

¹⁶Then Micaiah answered, "I saw all Israel scattered on the hills like sheep without a shepherd, and the LORD said, 'These people have no master. Let each one go home in peace.'"

¹⁷The king of Israel said to Jehoshaphat, "Didn't I tell you that he never prophesies anything good about me, but only bad?"

¹⁸Micaiah continued, "Therefore hear the word of the LORD: I saw the LORD sitting on his throne with all the host of heaven standing on his right and on his left. ¹⁹And the LORD said, 'Who will entice Ahab king of Israel into attacking Ramoth Gilead and going to his death there?'

"One suggested this, and another that. ²⁰Finally, a spirit came forward, stood before the LORD and said, 'I will entice him.'

"'By what means?' the LORD asked.

²¹"'I will go and be a lying spirit in the mouths of all his prophets,' he said.

"'You will succeed in enticing him,' said the LORD. 'Go and do it.'

²²"So now the LORD has put a lying spirit in the mouths of these prophets of yours. The LORD has decreed disaster for you."

²³Then Zedekiah son of Kenaanah went up and slapped Micaiah in the face. "Which way did the spirit from the LORD go when he went from me to speak to you?" he asked.

²⁴Micaiah replied, "You will find out on the day you go to hide in an inner room."

²⁵The king of Israel then ordered, "Take Micaiah and send him back to Amon the ruler of the city and to Joash the king's son, ²⁶and say, 'This is what the king says: Put this fellow in prison and give him nothing but bread and water until I return safely.'"

27Micaiah declared, "If you ever return safely, the LORD has not spoken through me." Then he added, "Mark my words, all you people!"

28So the king of Israel and Jehoshaphat king of Judah went up to Ramoth Gilead. 29The king of Israel said to Jehoshaphat, "I will enter the battle in disguise, but you wear your royal robes." So the king of Israel disguised himself and went into battle.

30Now the king of Aram had ordered his chariot commanders, "Do not fight with anyone, small or great, except the king of Israel." 31When the chariot commanders saw Jehoshaphat, they thought, "This is the king of Israel." So they turned to attack him, but Jehoshaphat cried out, and the LORD helped him. God drew them away from him, 32for when the chariot commanders saw that he was not the king of Israel, they stopped pursuing him.

33But someone drew his bow at random and hit the king of Israel between the sections of his armor. The king told the chariot driver, "Wheel around and get me out of the fighting. I've been wounded." 34All day long the battle raged, and the king of Israel propped himself up in his chariot facing the Arameans until evening. Then at sunset he died.

19:1When Jehoshaphat king of Judah returned safely to his palace in Jerusalem, 2Jehu the seer, the son of Hanani, went out to meet him and said to the king, "Should you help the wicked and love those who hate the LORD? Because of this, the wrath of the LORD is upon you. 3There is, however, some good in you, for you have rid the land of the Asherah poles and have set your heart on seeking God."

4Jehoshaphat lived in Jerusalem, and he went out again among the people from Beersheba to the hill country of Ephraim and turned them back to the LORD, the God of their fathers. 5He appointed judges in the land, in each of the fortified cities of Judah. 6He told them, "Consider carefully what you do, because you are not judging for man but for the LORD, who is with you whenever you give a verdict. 7Now let the fear of the LORD be upon you. Judge carefully, for with the LORD our God there is no injustice or partiality or bribery."

8In Jerusalem also, Jehoshaphat appointed some of the Levites, priests and heads of Israelite families to administer the law of the LORD and to settle disputes. And they lived in Jerusalem. 9He gave them these orders: "You must serve faithfully and wholeheartedly in the fear of the LORD. ¹⁰In every case that comes before you from your fellow countrymen who live in the cities—whether bloodshed or other concerns of the law, commands, decrees or ordinances—you are to warn them not to sin against the LORD; otherwise his wrath will come on you and your brothers. Do this, and you will not sin.

¹¹"Amariah the chief priest will be over you in any matter concerning the LORD, and Zebadiah son of Ishmael, the leader of the tribe of Judah, will be over you in any matter concerning the king, and the Levites will serve as officials before you. Act with courage, and may the LORD be with those who do well."

²⁰:¹After this, the Moabites and Ammonites with some of the Meunites came to make war on Jehoshaphat.

²Some men came and told Jehoshaphat, "A vast army is coming against you from Edom, from the other side of the Sea. It is already in Hazazon Tamar" (that is, En Gedi). ³Alarmed, Jehoshaphat resolved to inquire of the LORD, and he proclaimed a fast for all Judah. ⁴The people of Judah came together to seek help from the LORD; indeed, they came from every town in Judah to seek him.

⁵Then Jehoshaphat stood up in the assembly of Judah and Jerusalem at the temple of the LORD in the front of the new courtyard ⁶and said:

"O LORD, God of our fathers, are you not the God who is in heaven? You rule over all the kingdoms of the nations. Power and might are in your hand, and no one can withstand you. ⁷O our God, did you not drive out the inhabitants of this land before your people Israel and give it forever to the descendants of Abraham your friend? ⁸They have lived in it and have built in it a sanctuary for your Name, saying, ⁹'If calamity comes upon us, whether the sword of judgment, or plague or famine, we will stand in your presence before this temple that bears your Name and will cry out to you in our distress, and you will hear us and save us.'

¹⁰"But now here are men from Ammon, Moab and Mount Seir, whose territory you would not allow Israel to invade when they came from Egypt; so they turned away from them and did not destroy them. ¹¹See how they are repaying us by coming to drive us out of the

possession you gave us as an inheritance. ¹²O our God, will you not judge them? For we have no power to face this vast army that is attacking us. We do not know what to do, but our eyes are upon you."

¹³All the men of Judah, with their wives and children and little ones, stood there before the LORD.

¹⁴Then the Spirit of the LORD came upon Jahaziel son of Zechariah, the son of Benaiah, the son of Jeiel, the son of Mattaniah, a Levite and descendant of Asaph, as he stood in the assembly.

¹⁵He said: "Listen, King Jehoshaphat and all who live in Judah and Jerusalem! This is what the LORD says to you: 'Do not be afraid or discouraged because of this vast army. For the battle is not yours, but God's. ¹⁶Tomorrow march down against them. They will be climbing up by the Pass of Ziz, and you will find them at the end of the gorge in the Desert of Jeruel. ¹⁷You will not have to fight this battle. Take up your positions; stand firm and see the deliverance the LORD will give you, O Judah and Jerusalem. Do not be afraid; do not be discouraged. Go out to face them tomorrow, and the LORD will be with you.'"

¹⁸Jehoshaphat bowed with his face to the ground, and all the people of Judah and Jerusalem fell down in worship before the LORD. ¹⁹Then some Levites from the Kohathites and Korahites stood up and praised the LORD, the God of Israel, with very loud voice.

²⁰Early in the morning they left for the Desert of Tekoa. As they set out, Jehoshaphat stood and said, "Listen to me, Judah and people of Jerusalem! Have faith in the LORD your God and you will be upheld; have faith in his prophets and you will be successful." ²¹After consulting the people, Jehoshaphat appointed men to sing to the LORD and to praise him for the splendor of his holiness as they went out at the head of the army, saying:

"Give thanks to the LORD,
    for his love endures forever."

²²As they began to sing and praise, the LORD set ambushes against the men of Ammon and Moab and Mount Seir who were invading Judah, and they were defeated. ²³The men of

Ammon and Moab rose up against the men from Mount Seir to destroy and annihilate them. After they finished slaughtering the men from Seir, they helped to destroy one another.

²⁴When the men of Judah came to the place that overlooks the desert and looked toward the vast army, they saw only dead bodies lying on the ground; no one had escaped. ²⁵So Jehoshaphat and his men went to carry off their plunder, and they found among them a great amount of equipment and clothing and also articles of value—more than they could take away. There was so much plunder that it took three days to collect it. ²⁶On the fourth day they assembled in the Valley of Beracah, where they praised the LORD. This is why it is called the Valley of Beracah to this day.

²⁷Then, led by Jehoshaphat, all the men of Judah and Jerusalem returned joyfully to Jerusalem, for the LORD had given them cause to rejoice over their enemies. ²⁸They entered Jerusalem and went to the temple of the LORD with harps and lutes and trumpets.

²⁹The fear of God came upon all the kingdoms of the countries when they heard how the LORD had fought against the enemies of Israel. ³⁰And the kingdom of Jehoshaphat was at peace, for his God had given him rest on every side.

³¹So Jehoshaphat reigned over Judah. He was thirty-five years old when he became king of Judah, and he reigned in Jerusalem twenty-five years. His mother's name was Azubah daughter of Shilhi. ³²He walked in the ways of his father Asa and did not stray from them; he did what was right in the eyes of the LORD. ³³The high places, however, were not removed, and the people still had not set their hearts on the God of their fathers.

³⁴The other events of Jehoshaphat's reign, from beginning to end, are written in the annals of Jehu son of Hanani, which are recorded in the book of the kings of Israel.

³⁵Later, Jehoshaphat king of Judah made an alliance with Ahaziah king of Israel, who was guilty of wickedness. ³⁶He agreed with him to construct a fleet of trading ships. After these were built at Ezion Geber, ³⁷Eliezer son of Dodavahu of Mareshah prophesied against Jehoshaphat, saying, "Because you have made an alliance with Ahaziah, the LORD will destroy what you have made." The ships were wrecked and were not able to set sail to trade.

²¹:¹Then Jehoshaphat rested with his fathers and was buried with them in the City of David. And Jehoram his son succeeded him as king. ²Jehoram's brothers, the sons of Jehoshaphat, were Azariah, Jehiel, Zechariah, Azariahu, Michael and Shephatiah. All these were sons of Jehoshaphat king of Israel. ³Their father had given them many gifts of silver and gold and articles of value, as well as fortified cities in Judah, but he had given the kingdom to Jehoram because he was his firstborn son.

THE EARLY HISTORY of Judah comprises the third of three large blocks of related narrative material in Chronicles. The theme of establishing Israel as Yahweh's nation and the Jerusalem temple as Yahweh's sanctuary is central to Chronicles and occupies the bulk of the material in the two books (1 Chron. 10—2 Chron. 9). The rest of Chronicles, a narrative of the kingdom of Judah during the period of the divided monarchy (2 Chron. 10–36), is the story of God's bringing wrath or blessing on his nation and his temple. This divine punishment or favor is meted out in accordance with the inclination of the heart of the Judahite king to the commandments of the Sinai covenant—whether for disobedience or for obedience.

A subplot in this pericope and the entire narrative of the divided monarchy is God's faithfulness to the Davidic covenant—his promise to establish the throne of David forever (1 Chron. 17:12; 2 Chron. 7:18). This promise is the foundation on which the Chronicler builds his theology of hope for postexilic Judah—God will reestablish the throne of David.

Unifying factors in this section treating the early history of the divided monarchy include warfare, whether internal (i.e., civil war between the northern kingdom of Israel and the southern kingdom of Judah) or external (i.e., international war with aggressor nations on the borders of the northern or southern kingdoms and beyond). For instance, Rehoboam faces the challenge of an invasion by Pharaoh Shishak of Egypt (ch. 12), Asa battles the Cushites (ch. 14), Abijah has to fend off Jeroboam and the northern kingdom (ch. 13), and Jehoshaphat is tested by a coalition of Transjordanian armies that include the Moabites and the Ammonites (ch. 20). In each case, relying on Yahweh rather than alliances with other nations is the formula for victory.

A second unifying factor in this portion of the Chronicler's narrative is the role of God's prophet as a force that impacts the kings of Judah and shapes the history of the divided monarchy. Specifically, three of the four kings of

Judah portrayed in this segment of the story have encounters with Yahweh's prophets: Shemaiah confronts Rehoboam (ch. 12), Azariah challenges King Asa (ch. 15), and Micaiah, Jehu, and Jahaziel all prophesy to Jehoshaphat (chs. 18–20). In one sense, King Abijah functions as Yahweh's prophet in his speech to Jeroboam and the kingdom of Israel (ch. 13). In each case, the Spirit-induced message of the prophet affects the king's heart and prompts repentance and/or a response of obedience to God's commandments.

In a literary sense, all of 2 Chronicles 10–36 is anticlimactic, since the climax of history for the Chronicler is the building and dedication of Yahweh's temple under the direction of Solomon. Thematically, the accounts of David and Solomon are the historical and theological ideal for the Chronicler—his "new" (or perhaps better "retro") paradigm for postexilic Judah.

The source for this section of Chronicles is the Kings' version of the history of the divided monarchy. The Chronicler makes selective use of 2 Kings 12–22, borrows from other historical sources (typically cited in the regnal résumés), and on occasion inserts his own commentary. The basic genre of chapters 10–21 is that of account, containing primarily historical stories, reports, and regnal résumés.

The theological motif of reward for faith and punishment for apostasy dominates the divided monarchy narrative (chs. 10–36). The Chronicler not only applies the retribution principle to the good and evil kings of Judah but also to the good kings who backslide and the evil kings who repent. At times God's will for the king and the people of Judah is found in speeches of prophets (e.g., ch. 18); at other times God reveals his will for the king and the nation through the king's own sermons and prayers (e.g., ch. 20). The Chronicler's message for his own audience seems to be found in the repetition of the retribution principle (i.e., reward for obedience and punishment for apostasy) and in the warnings against foreign alliances. God will rebuild postexilic Judah through the unswerving faith of his people!

This portion of the narrative may be outlined accordingly:

A. **Rehoboam** (10:1–12:16)
   1. Israel Rejects Davidic Dynasty (10:1–11:4)
   2. Judah Supports Rehoboam (11:5–17)
   3. Rehoboam's Family (11:18–23)
   4. Pharaoh Shishak Raids Judah (12:1–12)
   5. Concluding Regnal Résumé (12:13–16)

B. **Abijah** (13:1–14:1)
   1. Opening Regnal Résumé (13:1–2a)
   2. War with Israel (13:2b–21)
   3. Concluding Regnal Résumé (13:22–14:1)

King Rehoboam (10:1–12:16)

THE SUMMARY OF REHOBOAM'S reign in Chronicles is three times longer than the version found in 1 Kings 12:1–24 and 14:21–31. By way of literary subgenres, the narrative account of Rehoboam's reign is comprised of historical story (2 Chron. 10:1–19), two reports (Rehoboam's early success, 11:1–23; Shishak's punitive raid, 12:1–12), and a concluding regnal résumé (12:13–16). Irony runs thick in the story, as seen in the emphasis on Rehoboam's "rejection" of the advice he seeks (as a courtesy?) from the council of the elders and his "rejection" by his own people. According to Williamson, the account is structured according to a thematic pattern that begins with failure, is followed by success through obedience, is then undone as a result of disobedience, and finally is climaxed by a partial restoration through self-humbling.[1]

The story of Rehoboam's foolish decision documents the shattering of the ideal of "all Israel" and concludes with the thought that the people of Israel now exist as a house divided. Sadly, this state of affairs will remain as such until both northern and southern kingdoms are swallowed up by the ancient superpowers of Assyria and Babylonia respectively.

Israel rejects the Davidic dynasty (10:1–11:4). The opening section of Rehoboam's reign describes the split of Solomon's kingdom into the rival northern and southern monarchies of Israel and Judah respectively. The event sets the stage not only for the reign of Rehoboam but also for the rest of 2 Chronicles. The Chronicler's version closely follows 1 Kings 12:1–24. His omission of the material in 1 Kings 11 helps explain the abrupt change in the political climate of the united monarchy at Rehoboam's succession. He assumes his audience's knowledge of such earlier events as these: Solomon's decline as a result of idolatry (11:1–13), Ahijah's prophecy against the Davidic

---

1. Williamson, *1 and 2 Chronicles*, 238.

dynasty and the divine appointment of Jeroboam as a rival king (11:26–39), and Jeroboam's asylum in Egypt as a fugitive (11:40).

The genre of the literary unit may be termed "historical story," that is, a self-contained narrative recounting a particular event and how it happens.[2] The historical story tends to demonstrate considerable literary sophistication, including the development of a plot (the continuation of the Davidic monarchy), conflict (the threat to the unity of Israel), characterization or character development (as seen in Rehoboam's interaction with the two groups of advisers), and even subplots (the intervention by prophets of God, e.g., Ahijah [10:15] and Shemaiah [11:1–4]).

At the risk of oversimplifying a complex sociopolitical situation, a combination of interrelated factors make taxation an issue. The loss of revenue from satellite states that regained their autonomy during the latter years of Solomon's decline deplete the royal treasuries (1 Kings 11:14–25). The support of the multilayered bureaucracy of Solomon's administration suck vast amounts of resources from the general populace (4:20–28). Finally, all this is compounded by the extravagance and waste characteristic of Solomon's social and economic policies (10:14–22).

By definition, centralized government is parasitic; that is, it must exist off the revenues it collects from the people governed. When faced with a budget crisis, any centralized government has but two options: raise taxes or reduce spending. But as Selman reminds us, when read as complementary records of the division of the united monarchy, both sources concur that Solomon, Rehoboam, and Jeroboam all share in the blame: Solomon does impose a "heavy yoke" on Israel (2 Chron. 10:4, 9–11, 14), Jeroboam does lead the northern tribes of Israel in revolt (10:19; cf. 13:6–7), and Rehoboam does reject the wise advice of the elders (10:6–8, 13).[3]

The Israelite tribes assemble at Shechem (10:1–4). It was customary for a new Israelite king to receive the formal approval of the people at a national assembly. David was acknowledged as king by "all Israel" at Hebron after Saul's death (1 Chron. 11:1). Solomon was anointed and installed as king by the assemby of "all Israel" in Jerusalem (28:1, 8; 29:22–23). Here Rehoboam travels for his public coronation to Shechem (2 Chron. 10:1)—a strategic military, political, and religious center for Israel from ancient times. Both Abraham and Jacob built altars there (Gen. 12:6–7; 33:18–20), and Joshua enacted a covenant-renewal ceremony there after the initial victories of the Canaanite conquest (Josh. 24).

Sensing possible unrest during his transition to power, Rehoboam may be hoping the long Israelite tradition associated with this site will contribute to

2. De Vries, *1 and 2 Chronicles*, 280.
3. Selman, *2 Chronicles*, 359.

easing political tensions. The reference to "all Israel" in this context signifies the full number of the tribes. Clearly the Chronicler has telescoped the sequence of events resulting in Jeroboam's presence at the assembly for the public coronation of Rehoboam. No doubt Jeroboam was monitoring the situation from afar (whether by means of formal channels through Pharaoh Shishak or informally by sympathetic Israelite couriers) and so makes his way to Shechem during the interim period between the national mourning over Solomon's death and the installation of Rehoboam as his successor.

Because of his earlier commissioning by the prophet Ahijah, Jeroboam is dubbed as spokesman for "all Israel" (10:3, here the phrase refers to the northern tribes that will soon constitute the northern kingdom). Two issues of primary concern must be settled in order for the northern tribes to guarantee loyalty to the new king: "harsh labor" (i.e., forced labor gangs) and a "heavy yoke" (i.e., taxation, 10:4). The request is not unreasonable, as the terms used to describe the "harsh labor" and the "heavy yoke" are the same as those used to depict the oppression the Hebrews experienced under the Egyptian pharaoh prior to the Exodus (cf. Ex. 5:9; 6:6–7, 9).

A logistical survey also supports the complaint of the northern tribes, since for ten months of every year the northern administrative districts supplied the tons of provisions needed to sustain the centralized bureaucracy (located in the south; cf. 1 Kings 4:22–28). Obviously, the northern administrative districts have tired of a one-way flow of resources that has only led to greater impoverishment. (As an aside, the situation is not unlike that of my own state of Illinois, where the down-state taxpayers frequently complain that they see little benefit in their districts from state taxation because the lion's share of their tax dollars end up in the budgetary column of the "money-pit" known as Chicago.)

God had built the release of debt and servitude into the calendar through his law (the sabbatical and Jubilee years, cf. Lev. 25). Curiously, however, the number of years decreed for the "Sabbath rest" of the land suggests that neither of these were ever practiced by the kings of Israel or Judah (cf. 2 Chron. 36:21; i.e., the seventy years of Hebrew exile from the land of covenant promise implies that sabbatical year had not been kept for nearly five centuries—coinciding roughly with the beginning of the monarchy in Israel).

Rehoboam consults with his advisers (10:5–11). The story of Rehoboam's consultation with his royal advisers is well known. The northern tribes demand some modification of the king's forced labor requirements and a reduction in taxes as a condition for fealty to the Davidic monarchy. The conditional nature of the proposal from the tribal representatives indicates they are looking for more than words—they seek a diplomatic solution resulting in a pact.

The three-day delay (10:5) buys time for Rehoboam to consider his options and provides a "cooling off" period for the party bringing the grievance.

Rehoboam consults two groups of royal advisers. The first is a cohort of elders left over from Solomon's reign (10:6). These men held official positions in the cabinet of the royal court as sages, an office that was highly respected in the political circles of the ancient world. They achieved status by virtue of their age and years of civil service. The "young men who had grown up" with Rehoboam comprise the second advisory council. These men are contemporaries of the king, perhaps other royal princes, half-brothers of Rehoboam, or "junior-level" civil servants. Some see a bicameral system of authority operative in the monarchy, whose counsel to the king shapes government policy, although this remains speculative.

The advice of Solomon's elders is conciliatory—win their approval and earn their support by "doing good" or "being kind" (10:7). A "favorable answer" to the assembly at Shechem would be a wise move, a gracious gesture, and a culturally appropriate response for the new king. The advice of Rehoboam's cronies (10:8–9), by contrast, threatens the implementation of an even more severe corvée and taxation policy against the northern tribes— a policy that is carefully recorded and includes much repetition, suggesting thoughtful deliberation rather than a casual "coin flip" (10:8b–11). A certain irony or even contempt may be seen in the advice of the "young men," since wisdom is found among the aged (Job 12:12).

Rehoboam is not so young as inexperienced (he is forty-one years old at his accession; 12:13). Nothing in chapter 10 suggests that he is especially malicious or cruel—only foolish. Whether out of fear that he may appear weak or for the sake of pragmatism, given the need to keep the machinery of the bureaucracy humming, he rejects the good advice of the elders and follows the bad advice (10:14). Thus, he answers his northern kinsmen harshly (10:13). The yoke, a symbol of servitude, will be made heavier (10:14a); the scourge or whip, a goad for lazy animals and a symbol of punishment for stubbornness and rebellion, will inflict even greater pain (10:14b). The representatives of the northern tribes need to hear no more.

The division of Israel and Judah (10:12–19). After the three days specified for reaching a decision have elapsed, Jeroboam and his retinue and Rehoboam and his entourage reconvene the assembly of "all Israel" at Shechem (10:12). It is interesting to note that David's coronation lasts three days and the celebration includes feasting as part of a covenant meal, sealing a pact or treaty between the tribes (cf. 1 Chron. 12:39). This lends further support to the idea that the three-day delay by Rehoboam in responding to the complaints of the northern tribes is meant to salvage a pact or treaty formalizing the loyalty of all the tribes to the new king.

Twice we are told that Rehoboam rejects the counsel of the elders to show leniency and to honor the demands of the disgruntled workers in the labor corvées (10:8, 13). Instead, he utters the advice offered by his contemporaries and venomously threatens even harsher treatment than the workers knew under his father—the sting of his whip will seem like that of the scorpion.

A key theological interpretation of developments resulting in the "meltdown" of the united monarchy is found in the Kings' parallel and is repeated by the Chronicler. The biblical historians note that this "turn of events was from God" (10:15a; cf. 1 Kings 12:15). The Chronicler connects his commentary to Ahijah's prophecy predicting the split of Solomon's kingdom as punishment for his sin of idolatry—thus assuming his audience's knowledge of the story (2 Chron. 10:15b; cf. 1 Kings 11:29–40). This approach fits a pattern in Chronicles that associates crucial moments in Israel's history with what God has said through his prophets in an effort to demonstrate his absolute sovereignty as the Lord of history (cf. 1 Chron. 11:2; 17:13–15; 2 Chron. 36:22–23).[4]

In light of theological review provided by the biblical historian, we can rightly conclude that the northern tribes are not reprehensible in their role in splitting the united monarchy. Rather, they become odious to God and the biblical historians because of their subsequent sin—idol worship. In view of Ahijah's prophecy to Jeroboam, the division of Solomon's kingdom may be inevitable, but it is certainly not irreversible—the rival kingdom is designed to punish the house of David only temporarily (cf. 1 Kings 11:39).

The repetition of Rehoboam's refusal to "listen" to the people further underscores the intransigence of the king (10:15–16). The poetic fragment that commemorates the split of the united monarchy is the traditional rallying cry of the northern tribes (cf. 2 Sam. 20:1). What a stark contrast between the taunt tossed at Rehoboam, "What share do we have in David?" and the vote of confidence King David received earlier from defectors to his band of mercenaries from the northern tribes, "We are yours, O David!" (1 Chron. 12:18).

The clause "so all the Israelites went home" signifies both the rejection of Rehoboam in the act of dismissal and also the finality of the decision—the negotiations are over (10:16d). The identification of both the northern and the southern tribes as "Israelites" is significant (10:16–17). They are all still the "one people" of God despite the rift between the "house of David" and the "house of Israel" (i.e., the northern tribes). This fact is important to the Chronicler's message of hope for God's restoration of postexilic Judah because it is dependent on the unity of all the Israelites living in the land.

---

4. Ibid., 363.

Adoniram (10:18)—or Adoram, as he is known from the Kings' parallel (1 Kings 12:18)—is one of Jeroboam's successors as an overseer of the forced labor gangs established by Solomon (cf. 1 Kings 11:28). Selman has critiqued Rehoboam's effort to make amends and restore tribal unity as "pathetic."[5] Knowing full well that the patience of the northern tribes has worn on the issue of forced labor, the king sends the cabinet official in charge of the forced labor gangs on a mission of reconciliation (10:18a). The "secretary of labor" is promptly stoned to death by the "civil servants" under his charge (10:18b). Apparently Rehoboam has accompanied Adoniram on the peace initiative because he barely escapes with his life from the unspecified location of the meeting (10:18c).

The term "rebellion" ($p\check{s}^c$, 10:19) may not be simply a neutral term describing the separation of the northern and southern tribes. Jeroboam and the northern tribes are in rebellion against Yahweh in the sense that they have rejected the divinely ordained Davidic covenant. The phrase "to this day" (10:19) is copied from 1 Kings 12:19 and basically means "from then on," given the historian's chronological perspective. This is one of the few instances where the expression is still applicable to the Chronicler's time (cf. also 1 Chron. 5:26).

Shemaiah brokers peace between Israel and Judah (11:1–4). The Chronicler omits the reference to the coronation of Jeroboam as king of "all Israel" (i.e., the ten northern Hebrew tribes, 1 Kings 12:20), although this is implicit in the expression "to regain the kingdom for Rehoboam" (2 Chron. 11:1). Apart from this, Chronicles closely adheres to 1 Kings 12:21–24. The civil war that later characterizes the first fifty years of coexistence of the divided kingdoms of Israel and Judah is averted early on by prophetic intervention (2 Chron. 11:2–4, though see 12:15, which reports "continual warfare between Rehoboam and Jeroboam").

Shemaiah is one of several preclassical prophets mentioned briefly in the Old Testament historical books. No collections of their oracles have been preserved, only extracts of sermons and prophecies—as in the case of Shemaiah's message to Rehoboam (11:3–4; note the reference to "the records of Shemaiah the prophet" cited in the concluding regnal résumé, 12:15). This time Rehoboam heeds the advice offered, without asking for a "second opinion." It is unclear what motivates his receptivity to the prophetic message—whether the ominous threat of Egyptian invasion prompting his fortification of strategic cities in Judah (11:5), the pang of conscience in the admonition not to wage war against "brothers" (11:4; cf. 28:11), or, most likely, the realization that the split of the united monarchy is the Lord's "doing" (11:4;

5. Ibid., 364.

cf. 10:15). The kingdom is God's to grant to whom he wills, not Rehoboam's to regain by force. Clearly God's will for the divided kingdom is peace because the northern tribes are as capable of repentance as the southern tribes are of apostasy.[6]

Rehoboam's impetuous response to muster troops and wage war to counter Jeroboam's coup calls to mind nuggets of Solomonic wisdom. Earlier Rehoboam sought advice but listened to foolish counsel (10:5–11). Here Rehoboam seeks no advice but plans his own course—only to have the Lord "determine his steps" (Prov. 16:9). But in heeding Shemaiah's word, Rehoboam begins to act wisely by listening to advice and accepting instruction (Prov. 12:15; 19:20).

The references to "Judah and Benjamin" are both tribal (11:1) and geographical (11:3). The accuracy of the tally of troops mustered in Judah (180,000 militia) is sometimes challenged. The number, however, does not appear unreasonable, given the muster of 470,000 militia in Judah according to David's ill-advised census (1 Chron. 21:5) or the 580,000 militia assembled by King Asa (2 Chron. 14:8). The call "to your tents" is a declaration of rebellion by the northern tribes against Rehoboam (10:16). Shemaiah's call to "go home" is an appeal to Judah to abandon the plans for war against Israel (11:4a). Rehoboam and Judah accept God's will as spoken by his prophet and turn back from the campaign against their northern tribesmen (11:4b).

Judah supports Rehoboam (11:5–17). The passage divides neatly into two sections, a summary of Rehoboam's defensive measures against foreign invasion (11:5–12) and the support Rehoboam received from the northern tribes after the split of the united monarchy (11:13–17). The unit continues the emphasis on God's reward for faithfulness and introduces for the first time the religious apostasy of Jeroboam (perpetuated by all the rulers of the northern kingdom).

Dillard notes that Jeroboam's return from asylum in Egypt under Pharaoh Shishak's protection "would be ample enough stimulus for a fortification program."[7] The list of cities reinforced as military outposts and stocked with provisions and weapons are strategically located, each defending important routes into the heart of Judah. Yet the line of fortresses enclose a rather limited defensive perimeter, suggesting that Rehoboam is confident of holding only the Shephelah and the Judean hill country—"a de facto concession of territory and the demise of the Solomonic empire."[8] Shishak's invasion of Judah via the coastal highway and the Negev confirm the weakness of Rehoboam's position, for he captures the fortified cities of Judah (12:4).

---

6. Dillard, 2 Chronicles, 95.
7. Ibid.
8. Ibid., 96.

The report of priests and Levites migrating from Israel to Judah after the split of the united monarchy offers a southern kingdom perspective on the false worship centers established in the northern kingdom by Jeroboam (11:13–17; cf. 1 Kings 12:26–33). These priests and Levites find themselves "disenfranchised" as a result of the alternative shrines erected by Jeroboam in Dan and Bethel. The reference to the "goat and calf" idols recalls the golden calf episode after the Exodus (Ex. 32:1–10; Deut. 9:16). Jeroboam's calf gods probably represent the syncretism of the Egyptian Apis (bull god) and Hathor (cow goddess) cults and Canaanite religion, which often depict deities standing on calves or bulls as symbols of their power and fertility. The goat idols are probably demons or satyrs in the form of male goats; such worship was expressly forbidden in the law of Moses (Lev. 17:7; cf. Deut. 32:16–17).

The Levites are probably rejected as candidates for religious service in Jeroboam's "calf cult" because they remain loyal to the Jerusalem temple as the legitimate worship center for all Israelites. It remains unclear if these "defectors" from Jeroboam's idol worship abandon their properties in Israel and take up permanent residency in Judah or simply observe the pilgrimage festivals in Jerusalem (11:14). Their example prompts other Israelites from the northern tribes to join them in worshiping the Lord in Jerusalem (11:16). Interestingly, these Israelites have "set their hearts on seeking the LORD," something King Rehoboam ultimately refuses to do (12:14).

The phrase "the God of their fathers" (11:16) is suggestive, almost an implicit censure of Jeroboam's gods because they have no standing in Israel's history. The influx of loyal priests and Levites and faithful Israelites from the northern tribal districts strengthens Rehoboam's rule and bolsters morale in Judah (11:17a). For a brief time, unfortunately only three years, the kingdom of Judah demonstrates faith in God and obedience to his commandments after the manner modeled by David and Solomon (11:17b).

Rehoboam's family (11:18–23). The report concerning the family of Rehoboam is unique to Chronicles. The insertion of the genealogical material may explain the cryptic reference to the records of Iddo the seer "that deal with genealogies" in the regnal résumé (12:15). Most biblical scholars recognize Mahalath (11:18) as a second cousin to Rehoboam. Since her father, Jerimoth, is nowhere mentioned as a son of David, presumably his mother is one of David's concubines (cf. 1 Chron. 3:9). Mahalath's mother, Abihail (2 Chron. 11:18), is the daughter of David's oldest brother, Eliab (cf. 1 Chron. 2:13). This means her own parents are also second cousins within the family of Jesse.[9] Nothing is known of Mahalath's three sons (2 Chron. 11:19).

9. Williamson, *1 and 2 Chronicles*, 244.

There is some question as to the identity of Maacah, Rehoboam's beloved wife (11:21). It seems likely that she is the granddaughter of David's son Absalom by his daughter Tamar (given Absalom's untimely death, cf. 2 Sam. 14:27). A quick recall of Absalom's own parentage reveals his mother's name was Maacah as well, a princess from Geshur whom David married to seal an alliance with King Talmai (1 Chron. 3:2). The Chronicler reports the practice of polygamy in the Davidic dynasty as a matter of fact—apparently accepting the cultural convention (despite the Mosaic prohibition against kings taking many wives, Deut. 17:17). Thompson appropriately reminds us of the tragic aspect of polygamy in the inevitable favoritism shown to a particular wife in the harem.[10] Typically in such marriages in the Old Testament, favoritism bred jealousy, jealousy hatred, and hatred too often resulted in destructive behavior patterns.

It should be noted, in addition to his own eighteen wives and sixty concubines (11:21), Rehoboam is responsible for supporting his father Solomon's harem (since royal women were "property" of the state in perpetuity). This obligation may have had something to do with his decision to levy a tax hike on his subjects. Nothing is known of Maacah's sons (11:20) except for Abijah, Rehoboam's successor (12:16). Perhaps the Chronicler intends this "genealogical sidebar" as an apology of sorts, explaining why Abijah (the oldest son of Rehoboam's favored wife) ascends to the throne. The appointment of Abijah as "chief prince among his brothers" (11:22) is tantamount to implementing a coregency for the purpose of guaranteeing an orderly transition of power when Rehoboam dies.

The concluding verse of the regnal résumé lauds Rehoboam's wisdom in "dispersing some of his sons throughout the districts of Judah" (11:23). Rehoboam apparently imitates his father's practice of delegation of royal authority by means of district governors (cf. 1 Kings 4:7—19), but he makes those appointments from princes within the royal household rather than from tribal leaders. The policy yields practical benefits: preventing the infighting experienced in David's royal household by prospective successors to the throne, solidifying the king's position, guarding against disloyalty in the form of an Absalom-like coup, ensuring an heir for the continuation of the dynasty (since housing the royal family in one location makes it easier for a usurper to execute all rivals), and extending the influence of the royal family to outlying districts.

Pharaoh Shishak raids Judah (12:1—12). The Chronicler's report of the Egyptian invasion of Judah is based on the parallel in 1 Kings 14:21—28. The details concerning the size of Shishak's army (12:3—4) and the speech

---

10. Thompson, *1, 2 Chronicles*, 256.

of Shemaiah the prophet (12:5–8) have no parallel and represent an unknown source (perhaps "the records of Shemaiah" mentioned in 12:15). Pharaoh Shishak or Sheshonq I was the founder of the Twenty-Second Dynasty, and he reunified Upper and Lower Egypt. He ruled from 945–924 B.C., and his campaign into Palestine takes place during the fifth year of Rehoboam (925 B.C.). His own account of the campaign is inscribed on the walls of the temple of Karnak, according to which he sweeps through Judah and Israel as far north as the Valley of Jezreel and Megiddo, capturing more than 150 towns and villages along the way.[11]

The Chronicler understands Shishak's invasion of Judah as punishment for sin, in that Rehoboam and all Israel have "abandoned the law of the LORD" (12:1). By "all Israel" the Chronicler means all the Israelites living in Judah (the "true" Israel), whether from northern or southern Hebrew tribal stock. The Chronicler assigns this breach of Judah's faithfulness to Yahweh and the Egyptian raid into Palestine a cause-and-effect relationship, a clear indication of his acknowledgment of the God of the Hebrews as the sovereign Lord of history (12:2).

The reason for the lapse in Judah's loyalty to Yahweh after three years of walking faithfully in the ways of David and Solomon is unclear (cf. 11:17). The phrase "he had become strong" (12:1) suggests that pride and self-reliance have replaced Rehoboam's dependence on God. Perhaps Rehoboam has taken his initiatives to fortify the cities guarding Jerusalem too seriously (cf. 11:5–12), trusting in his own defensive measures rather than on God.

The expression "the law of the LORD" is usually understood to refer to a canonical corpus fixed by the time of the Chronicler (perhaps the Torah or law of Moses). In this case, being "unfaithful to the LORD" (12:2) has covenantal implications, thus explaining the enforcement of the curse formulas of the Mosaic law (cf. Deut. 28:45–52). The Chronicler's inclusion of the "Sukkites" among the allies of Shishak attests to the antiquity of the sources for the report of Shishak's campaign, since these Libyan warriors from the oases of the western desert are known primarily from Egyptian records of the thirteenth and twelfth centuries B.C.[12]

Shemaiah the prophet (12:5) is known as a "man of God" (11:2) and earlier warned Rehoboam not to wage war against the northern tribes of Israel after the split of Solomon's kingdom (11:4). He now brings a message of both judgment (12:5) and mercy to Rehoboam and the leaders of Judah (12:7–8). The principle that God "abandons" those who "abandon" him is

---

11. Dillard, 2 *Chronicles*, 99–100.

12. Ibid., 100; for more on Pharaoh Shishak and his Palestinian campaign see F. Clancy, "Shishak/Shoshenq's Travels," *JSOT* 86 (1999): 2–23; K. A. Kitchen, "The Sheshonqs of Egypt and Palestine," *JSOT* 93 (2001): 3–12.

candidly presented and basic to the Chronicler's theology (cf. 1 Chron. 28:9, 20; 2 Chron. 15:2; 24:20). The response by Rehoboam and the leaders of Judah that "the LORD is just" (2 Chron. 12:6) is essentially a confession of sin—an acknowledgment that God is in the right (cf. Dan. 9:14). God accepts this confession as an act of "humbling oneself" (2 Chron. 12:6–7), a form of repentance that brings the sinner back to God.

God mercifully decrees that Judah will experience a "qualified" deliverance from Shishak (12:7b), but they will not escape the consequences of their disobedience—they will "become subject to him [i.e., Shishak]" for a time (12:8). The so-called "school of hard knocks" is a trying way to learn that it is better to serve the Lord than to be subjects of a foreign king (12:8). At times God uses whatever means are necessary to teach his people important lessons about the nature of his covenant relationship with them (in this case "fearing" God and not Shishak, 12:5).

The report of the "treasures" of the Jerusalem temple and royal palace "carried off" by Shishak suggests the loot is given as tribute to "buy off" Shishak rather than taken as booty through war (12:9–11). It is even possible that an unhealthy fixation on these "treasures" may have been connected to Rehoboam's unfaithfulness (since Israel's kings were not to accumulate large amounts of silver and gold, cf. Deut 17:17). Beyond the fact that Judah is a diminished nation politically and economically after Shishak's invasion, the reference to the confiscation of Solomon's gold shields, subsequently replaced by bronze replicas, emphasizes the loss of Israel's splendor (cf. 1 Kings 10:16–17; 2 Chron. 9:15–16).

The split of Solomon's kingdom signals the end of Israel's "golden age" both figuratively and literally. The harsh consequences of divine retribution for disobedience to Yahweh's covenant is no doubt meant as a "wake-up" call to both the kingdoms of Israel and Judah. The Shishak episode illustrates what can (and sadly does) happen again in Israelite history. The message has currency for the Chronicler's audience as well since God is still the sovereign Lord of history, and postexilic Israel is still bound to him in covenant relationship.

Selman regards the last verse of the report of Shishak's raid into Judah (12:12) as a summary of the Chronicler's review of Rehoboam's entire reign.[13] The act of Rehoboam's humbling himself before God recalls events associated with the Egyptian invasion of Judah (esp. Rehoboam's response to the speech of the prophet Shemaiah, 12:6–7). The ambiguous phrase "there was some good in Judah" seems to look back to those three years when Rehoboam and Judah imitated the faithfulness of David and Solomon (esp. 11:13–17).

---

13. Selman, 2 *Chronicles*, 375.

The word "humbled himself" (Niphal of *knᶜ*, 12:12) means to forsake one's pride and yield in self-denying loyalty to God. This action appeases God's wrath and spares Rehoboam and Judah from total destruction. God delivers on his promise to respond with forgiveness and healing to those who humble themselves before him in prayer (7:14). The message of "humbling oneself" before God and receiving forgiveness and healing remains pertinent for the Chronicler and his audience. This will become the gist of John the Baptist's preaching (cf. Luke 3:2—9).

Concluding regnal résumé (12:13—16). The regnal résumé of King Rehoboam's reign repeats the summary found in 1 Kings 14:21—22, 29—31. The Chronicler reorders the material by combining the opening and closing résumés of the Kings' narrative into one concluding résumé. The typical formulas are intact: the length of reign, accession age, mother's name, citation of historical source(s), death and burial, and succession. Rehoboam's reign is dated variously between 937 and 913 B.C. Our study dates his seventeen-year rule from 930—913 B.C.

There are two notable variations in Chronicles, one theological and one bibliographic. (1) The theological review in 1 Kings 14:22 indicts the people of Judah for the blatant religious apostasy during Rehoboam's reign. By contrast, the Chronicler places blame for idolatry directly on Rehoboam, even adding the commentary that the king "had not set his heart on seeking the LORD" (2 Chron. 12:14). The spiritual posture of setting one's heart on seeking the Lord is a theme in this literary unit, with Rehoboam serving as a foil for both Asa and Jehoshaphat, whose hearts are fully devoted to the Lord (see 15:17; 17:6). The expression "to seek [*drš*] the LORD" in Chronicles refers to one's overall inclination and habits for spiritual things, whether faith in God or self-reliance. Implicit in the Chronicler's commentary on Rehoboam is the call for his audience to take inventory so as to set their hearts on seeking the Lord.

(2) The Chronicler substitutes two prophetic sources in his citation of the historical formula for "the book of the annals of the kings of Judah" found in 1 Kings 14:29 (see 2 Chron. 12:15). The "records of Shemaiah the prophet and of Iddo the seer" may have been sections contained in other documents (like "the annals of the kings of Judah") or an even larger compendium of the monarchy's archival materials. The Chronicler's citation of additional historical sources may help explain why his account of Rehoboam's reign is three times longer than the parallel in 1 Kings. Moreover, these references indicate the breadth of historical sources available to the Chronicler as well as a concern for accuracy in his reporting.

The regnal résumé in Chronicles omits the second reference to Rehoboam's Ammonite mother, Naamah (12:13; cf. 1 Kings 14:21, 31). This is likely for stylistic reasons, although the Chronicler's understanding of any direct relationship between Rehoboam's evil ways and the influence of his non-Hebrew mother is unclear. Given the importance the Chronicler attaches to the death and burial formula, however, Selman views the omission of the fact that Rehoboam is buried with his ancestors as a negative assessment of the king (2 Chron. 12:16; cf. 1 Kings 14:31, "buried with his ancestors," so NRSV; NIV reads "buried with them" [i.e., "his fathers"]).[14]

Toward bridging contexts. The Chronicles are all about the relevance of earlier Israelite history for the writer's generation. That relevance is demonstrated by the example of God's people of a bygone era and includes especially the relevance of obedience to God's Word, the relevance of prayer to the God of heaven, and the relevance of proper worship at Yahweh's temple. For the Chronicler, the applicability of earlier Israelite history for postexilic Judah includes the currency of the prophetic voice for the spiritual and moral well-being of God's people, despite the fact that the voice of God's prophets and prophetesses has not been heard for perhaps a century or more by the time the Chronicler retells the story of Israel's kingship. Second Chronicles 10–12, summarizing the reign of Rehoboam, points toward the contemporary significance of the larger literary unit (10:1–21:3) by calling attention to the negative example of Solomon's son in his inability to "listen" to advice (10:8, 13, 15, 16). Rejecting the message of God's sage or the prophet quickly makes a relevant word irrelevant!

King Abijah (13:1–14:1)

THE CHRONICLER'S VERSION of Abijah's reign is more than twice as long as its precursor in 1 Kings 15:1–8. The parallel accounts share only portions of four verses in common (the opening and closing regnal résumés). Critics are quick to point out that the theological review in 1 Kings paints Abijah as a failure because "his heart was not fully devoted to the LORD" (15:3). We must remember, however, that Chronicles records but a single event of Abijah's three-year reign. McConville rightly notes, then, that the Chronicler's "treatment of Abijah is less a character-portrait than a record of a particular confrontation with Jeroboam and the northerners designed to illuminate the true condition of the latter."[15]

Furthermore, a careful reading of Chronicles reveals there is no formal theological review of Abijah's reign. The harmonization of the two versions is rather straightforward in that Chronicles reports one of those instances when Abijah's heart is devoted to the Lord even though overall this posture

---

14. Ibid., 377.
15. McConville, *I and II Chronicles*, 163.

toward God is uncharacteristic of the monarch. The story plot is larger than Abijah versus Jeroboam. It is a test of the resolve between the two kingdoms over the issue of the Davidic covenant and the question of vindication on the part of the Lord.[16] The genre of the story of Abijah's "holy war" is identified as report, and the contents of the story may be outlined as follows: prelude to war (13:2b–3), Abijah's speech (13:4–12), and the battle report (13:13–21). The story is framed by opening and closing regnal résumés (13:1–2a; 13:22–14:1).

Opening regnal résumé (13:1–2a). The opening regnal résumé is based on 1 Kings 15:1–2. The citation to the eighteenth year of Jeroboam (2 Chron. 13:1) is the only synchronism with the northern kingdom in all of Chronicles. Jeroboam ruled as king of Israel for twenty-two years (930–909 B.C.). Abijah's three-year reign over Judah is thus fixed from 913–910 B.C. The name Abijah is consistently rendered Abijam in the Kings' narrative (whether this is an issue of orthography or perhaps the difference between his given name and throne name is unclear).

The Hebrew name of Abijah's mother (lit., Micaiah) is a scribal variant for Maacah (cf. 1 Kings 15:2; note the NIV harmonizes the name with Kings' account [see text note]). Maacah is named as the wife of Rehoboam (2 Chron. 11:20), the mother of Abijah (13:2), and the mother of Asa (15:16). Either the various reports refer to a different woman with same name or Maacah must be understood as the grandmother of King Asa (cf. NIV). The world "daughter" (*bat*) may be translated precisely as "daughter" or more generally as "female descendant" (e.g., "granddaughter"). The most likely reconstruction, then, identifies Maacah as the granddaughter of Absalom (Abishalom in 1 Kings 15:2) by his daughter Tamar and her husband Uriel of Gibeah (2 Chron. 13:2; cf. 2 Sam. 14:27). This means that Maacah is King Asa's grandmother.

War with Israel (13:2b–21). *Setting the stage (13:2b–3).* The story begins with a blunt announcement that civil war has erupted between the kingdom of Israel (led by Jeroboam) and the kingdom of Judah (led by Abijah). This statement repeats 1 Kings 15:7, but in that context the conflict seems to be a continuation of the civil war that waged between Jeroboam and Rehoboam during Abijah's formative years as Judah's crown prince (cf. 1 Kings 15:6). There is no direct indication as to which party has declared war, although according to Selman Jeroboam is likely the aggressor in an attempt to reunite the twelve tribes under a single monarch. He bases his conjecture on the defensive posture of Abijah's speech (esp. 2 Chron. 13:8) and Jeroboam's military strategy relying on the surprise attack of an ambush (13:13–14).[17]

---

16. Ibid.
17. Selman, 2 *Chronicles*, 379.

The Chronicler's report of the size of the two opposing armies proves troublesome for some commentators. Various interpretive approaches have been suggested: taking the numbers at face value since the writer seems to intend them as literal, understanding the numbers as somehow symbolic or a form of hyperbole, or assigning a more technical meaning to the word "thousand" ('elep; e.g., "chieftain" or a military "cohort" of an unspecified number of soldiers). However one chooses to understand the numbers, the basic meaning of the tallies is clear—the troops of Israel outnumber the troops of Judah two to one.

Abijah's speech (13:4–12). King Abijah of Judah addresses his rival Jeroboam and the vast Israelite army from Mount Zemaraim (13:4). The location of this mountain is uncertain, but presumably it is situated somewhere in the hill country of Ephraim on the northern border of Benjamite territory—perhaps near Bethel (cf. Josh. 18:22). Abijah's speech is propagandistic, given the military context of the address; "psychological warfare" is not a modern development. His address is also sermonic in that it is hortatory in nature. Indirectly, the king appeals to the northern tribes to reunify under Davidic rule because the kingdom of the Lord has been given to David and his descendants (13:5, 8a). Abijah also directly challenges the Israelite army to give up the fight because God's covenant of kingship with the house of David is a perpetual one, as signified by the reference to "a covenant of salt" (13:5; cf. Lev. 2:13; Num. 18:19 on the connotations of eternality associated with the "covenant of salt").

The speech contrasts the faithfulness and loyalty of Abijah with the rebellion and disloyalty of Jeroboam in two issues: the Davidic covenant (13:4–8a) and God's temple in Jerusalem (13:8b–12). In order to create dissension and separate Jeroboam from his troops, Abijah refers to his northern counterpart in the third person and characterizes his leadership as "rebellion" against Solomon (13:6), since he was formerly a court official under David's successor (1 Kings 11:26). Implicitly, Jeroboam has rebelled against God since God has given the kingdom to David and his descendants (2 Chron. 13:5).

Abijah goes on to defend his father's role in the split of the monarchy, acknowledging he was "young and indecisive" at the time (13:7). Meanwhile, Jeroboam has surrounded himself with "scoundrels," who aided and abetted him as the mastermind of the coup (13:7, although Williamson understands the "scoundrels" gathered around "him" to be Rehoboam; i.e., his young advisers).[18] Williamson has observed that pinning blame on Rehoboam for the schism will make it easier for members of the northern tribes to defect to Judah.[19]

---

18. Williamson, *1 and 2 Chronicles*, 252–53.
19. Ibid., 252.

The second half of Abijah's speech contrasts Jeroboam's forsaking of the Lord's temple and his banishment of the Levitical priesthood with Abijah's compliance with the Mosaic law related to the proper worship of God (13:8b–12). Like the first half of the address, this segment includes a rhetorical question based on the conviction that Israel ought to know they are the party in the wrong (13:9).[20] The installment of a pseudo-priesthood aside (13:9b), the most damning indictment against the northern tribes are "the golden calves that Jeroboam made to be your gods" (13:8b).

The punch line of Abijah's oration is eminently theological and decidedly practical: "God is with us" (13:12a). What kind of folly is it to "fight against the LORD" (13:12b)? Allen has penetrated to the heart of Abijah's appeal in his insight that the king's speech is ultimately all about "self-determination."[21] Israel can choose not to fight against the Lord. The Chronicler holds out that same option for his own audience. They too can bury the tribal schisms of the past and in self-determination pursue an agenda of reconciliation and unity for the good of all the Israelites in postexilic Judah. This is the only way the "restoration" of Israel will succeed.

The battle at Mount Zemaraim (13:13–19). The battle report is a stylized account of the conflict containing several elements familiar to Old Testament warfare narratives: the strategy of an ambush (13:13; cf. Josh. 8:2), waging battle on two fronts (before and behind them, 2 Chron. 13:13; cf. 2 Sam. 10:9), and the sound of trumpets and shouting to signal the troops into action (2 Chron. 13:14–15; cf. Josh. 6:16). These motifs fit the pattern of "holy war" ideology, although Selman prefers the term "Yahweh war" because the emphasis is correctly placed on God as a divine warrior siding with his people as an instrument of his righteousness and justice.[22]

The battle report is presented in four stages: Jeroboam's tactic of an ambush (13:13–14a), Judah's prayers for divine help (13:14b–15a), God's granting victory to Judah (13:15b–16), and details concerning the outcome of the battle (13:17–19). The realization that Jeroboam's troops catch Judah in ambush, resulting in a pincers-type attack that force the action at the front and the rear of Abijah's army, causes them to cry out to God for divine intervention. This battle shout is "an act of faith" that God's swift and dramatic involvement will ensue (reminiscent of the battle shout that brought down Jericho, Josh. 6:20).[23]

God responds by allying himself to the army of Judah and routing the forces of the northern kingdom (13:15). The divine-warrior motif is revisited

---

20. McConville, *I and II Chronicles,* 164.
21. Allen, *1, 2 Chronicles,* 272.
22. Selman, *2 Chronicles,* 382.
23. McConville, *I and II Chronicles,* 165.

in that overwhelming odds present no problem when his people rely on him (13:18). Though Judah is outnumbered two to one and outflanked on the battlefield, Israel loses more than half its military force, and the remainder flee in panic (13:16).

The entire battle report turns on a key verb—the men of Judah are victorious "because they *relied on* the LORD" (13:18). The word "rely" (*šʿn*) means to lean on something or someone in the sense of trust; it is used later of King Asa (14:11; 16:7–8).[24] The significance of the attached phrase "God of their fathers" should not be lost—God has done this kind of thing before! The capture of Bethel is significant because it means the cessation of the calf-cult worship there for a time (13:19). Selman notes that the retaking of Bethel provides ironic commentary on the calf-cult of Jeroboam, since the bovine images used as a battle palladium (much like the ark of the covenant at Shiloh) are unable to protect their own sanctuary (cf. 13:8).[25] By the time of Jehu, the calf-cult has been reestablished in Bethel (2 Kings 10:29), perhaps as a result of King Baasha's Ramah campaign (2 Chron. 16:1).

The aftermath (13:20–21). The heavy losses sustained by Jeroboam at the battle of Mount Zemaraim cripple his capacities for further aggression against the southern kingdom. In that sense, Jeroboam does "not regain power" (13:20a) during Abijah's reign (remember that Abijah only rules for three years). The report of Jeroboam's death (13:20b) is telescoped for the sake of the Chronicler's theological emphasis, since Jeroboam actually outlives Abijah (cf. 1 Kings 15:9). The Chronicler understands Jeroboam's eventual death as an act of divine judgment ("the LORD struck him down," 2 Chron. 13:20b).

The verb "strike down" (*ngp*) is the same verb translated "routed" in the report of God's deliverance of Jeroboam and his army into the hands of Judah (13:15). The term often denotes a divine plague or blow executed by God as a divine warrior, who brings judgment on rebellious and sinful people.[26] The Chronicler's insertion that Abijah "grew in strength" and married fourteen wives and fathered thirty-eight children is usually taken as a statement of God's blessing on the king (13:21). The information concerning the size of the royal harem, however, seems to stand in contradiction to the legislation of the Mosaic law, which prohibits the king from taking many wives (Deut. 17:17), as well as the Genesis ideal of heterosexual monogamy (Gen. 2:24).

Concluding regnal résumé (13:22–14:1). The concluding résumé for Abijah excerpts with modification the summary contained in the earlier parallel source (13:22–14:1//1 Kings 15:7–8). The typical expressions of sum-

---

24. A. M. Harmon, "שָׁעַן," *NIDOTTE*, 4:202.
25. Selman, *2 Chronicles*, 383.
26. I. Swart, "נגף," *NIDOTTE*, 3:26.

mation are intact, including the citation of historical source (2 Chron. 13:22), death and burial, and succession formulas (13:22–14:1). Two divergences may be noted. The Chronicler cites a different historical source for the verification of his record ("the annotations of the prophet Iddo" instead of "the annals of the kings of Judah" [1 Kings 15:7]). In addition, the report of war between Abijah and Jeroboam has been moved from the concluding résumé to the beginning of the narrative (2 Chron. 13:2b; cf. 1 Kings 15:7).

Toward bridging contexts. The Chronicles are all about the relevance of earlier Israelite history for the writer's generation. That relevance is demonstrated by the example of God's people of a bygone era and includes especially the relevance of obedience to God's Word, the relevance of prayer to the God of heaven, and the relevance of proper worship at Yahweh's temple. For the Chronicler, the applicability of earlier Israelite history for postexilic Judah includes the currency of the prophetic voice for the spiritual and moral well-being of God's people, despite the fact that the voice of God's prophets and prophetesses has not been heard for perhaps a century or more by the time the Chronicler retells the story of Israel's kingship. Second Chronicles 13:1–14:1, summarizing the reign of Abijah, points toward the contemporary significance of the larger literary unit (2 Chron. 10:1–21:3) by emphasizing the fact that the relevance of the prophetic message is rooted in the faithfulness of God and his power to deliver his people from their enemies (13:18).

King Asa (14:2–16:14)

EARLY YEARS (14:2–15). This first unit summarizing Asa's reign consists of two literary subunits: a lengthy (and favorable) theological review of the king (14:2–7) and the record of Judah's victory over Zerah and the Cushites (14:8–15). The two reports work together to support the writer's theological declaration that Asa is a good and upright king (14:2). That he does "what was good and right in the eyes of the LORD" (14:2) agrees with 1 Kings 15:11. The Chronicler's version of Asa's cleansing of false worship in Judah expands the Kings' version but omits the reference to the removal of the male cult prostitutes and the idols "his fathers" made (1 Kings 15:12). Asa's obedience to the Mosaic law is seen in the fact that Deuteronomy 7:5; 12:2 prescribe removing heathen altars, smashing the sacred stones, cutting down the Asherah poles, and destroying the Canaanite high places (2 Chron. 14:5).

In summary, King Asa is a religious reformer (14:3–5) and a builder of fortifications for the defense of Judah's perimeter (14:7). The repetition of "seeking the LORD" in 14:4, 7 (2x)—an expression that occurs nine times in the three chapters recounting Asa's kingship (see also 15:2, 4, 12, 13, 15; 16:12)—sets the theme for the entire section. The "rest" (14:5, 6, 7) or peace that Judah enjoys under Asa is due in part to Abijah's victory over Jeroboam (13:19–20) but is also a reward for Asa's faithfulness to God (14:7). This accords well with the Chronicler's emphasis on the retribution principle in Israelite history; that is, obedience to God's commands results in reward whereas disobedience brings punishment. "Rest" in the land is the fulfillment of God's covenant promise to give Canaan to the Israelites as their "inheritance" (Deut. 12:8—10).

The story of Zerah the Cushite's march against Judah (14:8—15) has no parallel in the Kings' version of Asa's reign. There is some question as to the identity of the Cushites, whether they are Ethiopians (cf. 16:8, where the Cushites and Libyans are paired) or part of a bedouin group of the Sinai peninsula associated with the Midianites (cf. Num. 12:1). The decisive battle takes place at Mareshah (14:10), a town of the Shephelah allotted to Judah, some thirteen miles northwest of Hebron (cf. Josh. 15:44), and one of the cities of Judah's defense perimeter fortified by Rehoboam (2 Chron. 11:8). The Valley of Zephathah has not been identified (14:10). Asa has a large and well-equipped army (14:8). In addition he has fortified several border cities (14:7)—both characteristics of a good king (see 17:14—19; 26:11—15).

But Zerah's army is "vast" (lit., "a thousand thousands" or "beyond counting," 14:9). In addition, he has chariot forces (the equivalent of the modern-day tank) and allies among the pastoral clans from the villages near Gerar, who are apparently in league with him (14:14—15). The record of Judah's plundering the enemy after the battle (14:12—15) is probably included because some of these spoils are offered as sacrifices as a part of Asa's covenant-renewal ceremony (15:11).

The story turns on Asa's prayer for "help" from the Lord (14:11). His prayer seems to be modeled on Solomon's exhortation for the Israelites to pray toward the temple and God will hear from heaven and "uphold their cause" (6:34—35). As in the report of Abijah's war with Jeroboam (ch. 13), Yahweh-war motifs flavor this story: the overwhelming numbers of the enemy army (14:9; cf. 13:3), a prebattle speech or prayer invoking God to be a warrior for Israel (14:11—12; cf. 13:5—11), Yahweh's striking down the enemy for the king of Judah (14:12—13; cf. 13:15—16), and the fear of Yahweh falling on the enemy (14:13; cf. 13:16).

The Chronicler includes this story of Judah's victory over Zerah and the Cushites as evidence of the king's faithfulness and reliance on God. Despite Asa's defensive strategy and military resources (14:7—8), he acknowledges powerlessness before the foe and pleads for divine deliverance (14:11). McConville observes that events like this one are recorded in the Bible "precisely to encourage faith that can hold in the face of such (overwhelming) odds."[27] Allen goes further, first by outlining the beautiful structure of Asa's

---

27. McConville, *I and II Chronicles*, 171.

prayer, "beginning and ending with appeals to God and setting human faith in the middle, surrounded by the protective power of the covenant God," and second by noting that "God's help is triggered by prayer, prayer which admits to human helplessness and lays claim to God's patronage."[28] Such prayer is exemplary, whether for the Chronicler's time or our own!

Reforms (15:1–19). The second self-contained report of Asa's reign divides neatly into three sections: Azariah's sermon (15:1–7), Asa's reforms and covenant-renewal ceremony (15:8–15), and the deposing of the queen mother, Maacah (15:16–19). The report of Azariah's prophecy and the covenant ceremony are unique to Chronicles. The only date formula in the chapter places the assembly in Jerusalem for enacting the covenant with Yahweh in the fifteenth year of Asa's reign (15:10; i.e., 895 B.C.).

The prophet's sermon (15:1–7) explains the occasion of King's Asa's reforms (cf. 14:3). Azariah is unknown in the Old Testament apart from this one episode. The expression "the Spirit of God came upon" (15:1) is typically used in the Old Testament to signify divine empowerment for some specific task, often prophetic inspiration for delivering oracles from God (e.g., 20:14; 24:20). A direct commission of some sort usually accompanies the work of God's Spirit; in this case Azariah is charged to go and find King Asa (15:2a). God's prophet serves as the conscience of the divided monarchies, so it is appropriate that Azariah's message is delivered to the king and the people of Judah and Benjamin (15:2b).

Commentators try to identify the historical circumstances depicted by the "distress" Israel experiences in "those days" (15:3–5). It seems the writer is intentionally ambiguous because cycles of apostasy and deliverance characterize all of Israelite history. The constant in that story line is the deliverance God provides for those who seek his help. These are the themes highlighted in the prophet's message: God is with those who side with him, and he rewards obedience (15:2, 7); God will be found by those who seek him but forsakes those who abandon him (15:2). In good homiletical style, the sermon ends with an exhortation to continue the good work already begun because God will honor it (15:7). The prophet's speech also has currency for the Chronicler's audience, for it summarizes the three essentials for sustaining the faith of the restoration community in postexilic Judah: the true God, the teaching priest, and the law (15:3).

The king's obedience to God's word through the prophet Azariah launches sweeping religious reforms in Judah (continuing perhaps for ten years). The report of Asa's reform and covenant renewal ceremony (15:8–15) expands the earlier summary statement of the king's eradication of false worship in Judah

---

28. Allen, *1, 2 Chronicles*, 282.

(cf. 14:3) and should be understood as parallel accounts. As with later religious reforms, the initiatives include purging false worship and repairing Yahweh's temple precincts (15:8; cf. 24:4). The true Davidic king is the shepherd of all Israel (cf. 1 Chron 17:6), an idea that stands behind the assembly of Judah, Benjamin, and large numbers of defectors from Ephraim, Manasseh, and Simeon who settle in Judah (2 Chron. 15:9).

The covenant ceremony may have been associated with the Feast of Weeks or Pentecost, as the spring pilgrimage festival would have naturally necessitated the gathering of all Israel in Jerusalem at that time of year (15:10). It also appears that the victory over Zerah the Cushite (cf. 14:9–15) was incorporated into the festival since some of the animals taken as plunder from that battle are included in the sacrificial offerings to the Lord (15:11).

The "covenant to seek the LORD" (15:12) is presumably an outworking of the call to seek the Lord embedded in God's response to Solomon's prayer of dedication for the Jerusalem temple (cf. 7:14). The word "seek" (*drš*) in this context means to vow an allegiance to God that results in obedience to his commands. The phrase "all their heart and soul" (15:12), coupled with the emphasis on the death penalty for those who violate the pact (15:13), suggest that this covenant is based on the tradition of the Sinai covenant (cf. Deut. 6:5; 10:12; 13:6–10; 17:2–7). Though seemingly harsh, the death penalty for breach of covenant underscores the solemnity of the event and the mutually binding nature of the covenant agreement. The swearing of an oath of allegiance means the people are accountable to God and to each other to uphold the agreement.

For the Chronicler acts of obedience to God (like swearing the covenant oath) are also acts of worship, and worship erupts in "rejoicing" (15:15; cf. 23:13, 21; 30:21, 25). The shouts of the people and the blasts of trumpets and horns (15:14) are external expression of an internal reality, echoing Asaph's psalm of thanksgiving in celebration of the transfer of the ark of the covenant to Jerusalem (cf. 1 Chron. 16:10). As Allen has remarked, for the Chronicler "this was a model of temple worship, a scene of spiritual commitment in which religious forms reflected the worship of the heart."[29]

The covenant ceremony marks the beginning of a twenty-year period of peace under King Asa (cf. 15:19). The word "rest" (*nwḥ*) occurs three times in the review of Asa's reign (14:6, 7; 15:15) and signifies the blessing of God for a peaceful and prosperous life as a reward for covenant obedience. Selman's observation that opportunities for unification of the tribes always arise in the context of worship (not coercion through military force) is cogent.[30]

29. Ibid., 285.
30. Selman, 2 *Chronicles*, 393.

The Chronicler's emphasis on temple worship in the retelling of Israelite history is a "call to worship" for his own audience for the purpose of reestablishing the unity of the restoration community in the aftermath of the Babylonian exile.

The deposing of Maacah, Asa's grandmother, continues the king's reform initiatives (15:16–19). The report is taken almost verbatim from 1 Kings 15:13–15. The queen mother played an influential role in the royal court, both as an adviser to the king and teacher of the children born into the royal harem.[31] Maacah is removed from her position of authority as queen mother because of her idolatry (15:16).

The Asherah pole was a cultic symbol of the Canaanite fertility goddess Asherah in the form of a tree or tree trunk. The pole represented the tree of life in Canaanite religion, and the fertility cult associations of the symbol made the object "repulsive" or even "obscene" (NEB). It was among the objects of false worship under the ban of holy war for the Israelites at the time of the conquest of Canaan (Deut. 7:5). The raising of an Asherah pole is expressly forbidden in Mosaic law as an act that God hates (Deut. 16:21; cf. 2 Kings 23:6). Asa smashes this pole and burns it in the Kidron Valley southeast of Jerusalem, a garbage pit and refuse dump sometimes used for the disposal of such religious objects (cf. 2 Chron. 29:16; 30:14).

Nevertheless, Asa fails to remove the high places from Israel. Rather than see this as a contradiction to the record of the king's reforms (15:17; cf. 14:2), it is probably better to assume that the writer distinguishes between the high places of Judah and Israel, or perhaps the two statements are but "evidence of the persistence of the indigenous cults over several years."[32] The theological review that Asa's "heart was fully committed to the LORD all his life" (15:17) is difficult to harmonize with the details of chapter 16. This statement should be read as an overall assessment of his life, recognizing that the argument from silence does not preclude Asa's eventual repentance as a result of the rebuke of Hanani the seer (16:7).

Later years (16:1–10). After two decades of peace, conflict once again breaks out between the kingdoms of Israel and Judah (16:1). King Baasha of Israel is the aggressor in that the defensive measures he takes to fortify Ramah also threaten the territory of Judah economically and militarily. The town of Ramah (or er-Ram, a site some five miles north of Jerusalem) is strategically located on the major north-south ridge route that bypasses Jerusalem (cf. Judg. 19:10–13). According to Dillard, control of Ramah is also close enough

---

31. See N. Andreasen, "The Role of the Queen Mother in Israelite Society," *CBQ* 45 (1983): 179–94.

32. Thompson, *1, 2 Chronicles*, 272.

to the Beth-Horon ridge to menace the east-west traffic traversing the central Benjamin plateau. From this choke point, Baasha can control traffic flow in and out of northern Judah—trade caravans, Israelite defectors heading south, or pious Hebrews journeying to the temple to celebrate the pilgrimage festivals.[33]

The date formula ("thirty-sixth year of Asa's reign," 16:1) is problematic because according to 1 Kings 15:33 and 16:8, King Baasha is already dead. Williamson's proposal for the harmonization of the data proves as helpful as any of the several options offered by commentators. He suggests that the date formulas in 15:19 ("the thirty-fifth year of Asa's reign") and 16:1 ("the thirty-sixth year . . .") actually refer to the split of the monarchy. This means these two date formulas correspond to the fifteenth and sixteenth years of King Asa's reign.[34]

The Chronicler's report of Baasha's activity at Ramah and Asa's response is based on 1 Kings 15:17–22. Asa resorts to the oft-used political ploy of paying tribute to a third party for the purpose of engaging an aggressor nation on a second front (2 Chron. 16:3–4). The cost of contracting Ben-Hadad king of Aram to wage war against Israel is apparently steep, because Asa has to siphon monies from two treasuries (the temple and the palace, 15:6) to seal the pact. This is probably due to the fact that Aram and Israel are already partners in an alliance, and Ben-Hadad will need a greater offer to break his treaty with Baasha (16:3b).

The Arameans were irrepressible foes of Israel throughout the history of the northern kingdom, so there is doubtless little reservation about reneging on a treaty with Baasha as long as the price is right. The Arameans invade Israelite cities along the northeastern border between the two nations (16:4). When Baasha hears the news that several important cities have fallen to Ben-Hadad, he has to abandon his plan to fortify Ramah and divert his attention to the war with Aram in the northern extremities of his territory (16:5). After Baasha withdraws from Ramah, Judah destroys the fortifications under construction and reuses the stones and timber to fortify Geba (modern day Jeba, a town of Benjamin some six miles northeast of Jerusalem) and Mizpah, thus extending Judah's defensive perimeter north of Ramah (16:6, assuming this is the Mizpah of Benjamin or Tell en-Nasbeh, nearly eight miles northeast of Jerusalem; cf. Josh. 18:24, 26).

God responds to Asa through Hanani the seer (16:7–9). Nothing is known of this prophet apart from the sermon recorded here. His son Jehu, also a seer, prophesies to Jehoshaphat on one occasion (19:2) and is credited

---

33. Dillard, *2 Chronicles*, 125.
34. Williamson, *1 and 2 Chronicles*, 255–58.

as one of the historiographers of Israelite kingship (20:34). The word "seer" (*ro'eh*) is an older term for a prophet of God, associated with the era of Samuel (1 Sam. 9:9, 19). Typically, the "seer" is a prophet who experiences the act of seeing God's message by means of a dream or a vision. Unlike the prophet Azariah's sermon of exhortation and challenge (15:1–7), Hanani sees a message of rebuke and judgment for Asa (cf. Amos. 1:1).

The key word in the prophet's speech is "rely" (*š'n*). Earlier in his reign, Asa "relied" on God, and Judah prevailed over the Cushites who mustered a vast army against them (14:11). History should have been Asa's teacher (16:8). Yet, instead of relying on God when threatened by the Israelite king Baasha, Asa "relies" on Ben-Hadad and the kingdom of Aram. Previously Asa asked for divine help because he recognized he was powerless to remedy the situation (14:11). Here in this crisis, Asa shuns divine aid and trusts in his own power—his political savvy and human instincts to deliver Judah.

The consequences of Asa's unbelief are immediate and far-reaching. (1) Judah loses the opportunity to defeat Ben-Hadad and the Arameans (16:7). (2) War will now plague the nation of Judah (16:9). Surprisingly, God intended to grant Judah victory over both Aram and Israel, had Asa trusted God for deliverance (note 16:7, "the king of Aram has escaped"). Somehow Asa has foolishly lost sight of God's sovereignty—hence the reminder that "the eyes of the LORD range throughout the earth" (16:9; cf. Zech. 4:10). The heart fully committed to God demonstrates such allegiance by relying on the Lord in all things—and God himself works in the faithful to strengthen that resolve. Asa's "anger" (2 Chron. 16:10) is a sure sign that Hanani's words are true and have hit their mark.

Asa's response to Hanani constitutes the first incident of royal persecution of a prophet of God recorded in the Old Testament (16:10). Hanani is imprisoned (lit., placed in "a house of stocks," *bet mahpeket*; cf. Jer. 20:2). Sadly, this is a portent for the future of the relationship between God's prophet and the reigning king. Often in fulfilling his divine commission to confront the king with a contrary word from God, the prophet risks persecution and even death (cf. 1 Kings 19:14; Neh. 9:26; Amos 2:12). Naturally, this gives rise to a movement of "false prophets," who are paid to tell the king what he wants to hear (cf. Mic. 2:11; 3:5).

Concluding regnal résumé (16:11–14). The Chronicler has omitted the opening regnal résumé from the parallel in 1 Kings 15:9–10 and rewritten a closing regnal résumé (based on 15:23–24). The citation formula in both versions of Asa's résumé refer to the same historical source, "the book of the kings of Judah and Israel" (2 Chron. 16:11; cf. the variation in 1 Kings 15:23, "the book of the annals of the kings of Judah"). This is the first of several citations by the Chronicler of the Israelite royal annals. Curiously he does not refer to the annals by the title "the book ... of the kings of Judah" (as does 1 Kings). According to Thompson, evidently the writer "wished to insist that Judah was part of the inclusive Israel."[35]

The Chronicles version of the regnal résumé expands the report of King Asa's foot disease with theological commentary (16:12; cf. 1 Kings 15:23b). The speculation as to the exact nature of this disease is unproductive.[36] The Chronicler's point is that at times divine judgment takes the form of illness (e.g., 2 Chron. 21:16–20; 26:16–23). The writer implies that the sickness is an unheeded warning from God, expressing his displeasure over Asa's response to recent events.[37] The statement that Asa seeks human help in the form of physicians rather than divine help for healing (16:12b) impugns his faith in God, not ancient medical practitioners.

King Asa's forty-one-year reign may be dated from 910 to 869 B.C. It seems his demise began with the attack against Judah by King Baasha of Israel in 874 B.C. (Asa's thirty-sixth year, 16:1).[38] Asa's decline was further compounded by his foot disease (his thirty-ninth year [871 B.C.], 16:11). The expansion of the death and burial formula is unique to Chronicles (cf. 1 Kings 15:24). The Chronicler adds the detail of the king's commissioning the digging of his own tomb, presumably in the royal tomb complex of Jerusalem. The spices and blended perfumes lavished on Asa's bier are tokens of affection for the dead king (2 Chron. 16:14b). The great fire mentioned is not cremation but an honor accorded some kings (cf. 21:19; Jer. 34:5). This is yet another example of the esteem the general populace hold for King Asa. Despite his "backsliding" during the last years of his reign, the people love the king.

Toward bridging contexts. The Chronicles are all about the relevance of earlier Israelite history for the writer's generation. That relevance is demonstrated by the example of God's people of a bygone era and includes especially the relevance of obedience to God's Word, the relevance of prayer to the God of heaven, and the relevance of proper worship at Yahweh's temple. For the Chronicler, the applicability of earlier Israelite history for postexilic Judah includes the currency of the prophetic voice for the spiritual and moral well-being of God's people, despite the fact that the voice of God's prophets and prophetesses has not been heard for perhaps a century or more by the time the Chronicler retells the story of Israel's kingship. Second Chronicles 14:2–16:14, summarizing the reign of Asa, points toward the contemporary

35. Thompson, *1, 2 Chronicles*, 275.
36. See the protracted discussion of the diagnoses of Asa's malady in Williamson, *1 and 2 Chronicles*, 276.
37. Thompson, *1, 2 Chronicles*, 276.
38. E.g., Selman, *2 Chronicles*, 404.

significance of the larger literary unit (10:1–21:3) by underscoring the perpetual relevance of seeking help from the Lord (20:4).

King Jehoshaphat (17:1–21:3)

ALONG WITH KINGS Hezekiah and Josiah, Jehoshaphat ranks as one of the Chronicler's favorite kings of the divided monarchy. This is attested not only by the volume of material devoted to his reign (four chapters), but also among the kings of Judah only Jehoshaphat (17:3), Hezekiah (29:2), and Josiah (34:2) are likened to King David. Chronicles expands the Kings' version of Jehoshaphat's rule over Judah (50 verses in Kings compared to 103 verses in Chronicles) and shifts the focus of attention from King Ahab of Israel to Jehoshaphat.

Jehoshaphat is portrayed favorably as a man of faith and prayer and a religious reformer. The narrative in Chronicles is apparently intentionally shaped to demonstrate the parallels between the reigns of Jehoshaphat and his father Asa. His rule is not without problems, however, and like all the kings of Judah he receives a "mixed" theological review from the biblical historian (cf. 17:3–4, 6; 19:3; 20:33). Although the narrative summarizing Jehoshaphat's kingship lacks a rigid chronological framework, the dates for his twenty-five-year reign are between 872 and 848 B.C. On the basis of comparative analysis of the date formulas for Jehoshaphat's length of reign, it is generally understood he rules for three years as a coregent with his father prior to his own twenty-two-year tenure on the throne (from 869–848 B.C.; cf. 2 Kings 3:1; 8:16; 2 Chron. 20:31).

The account of King Jehoshaphat may be outlined as follows: the character of his reign (17:1–19), his alliance with King Ahab of Israel (18:1–19:3), his judicial reforms (19:4–11), the war with Moab and Ammon (20:1–30), and concluding regnal résumé (20:31–21:3).

Character of his reign (17:1–19). The opening chapter of the account of Jehoshaphat's reign over Judah portrays the king in an entirely favorable manner. This does not mean that the writer is blind to the king's faults. Two prophetic speeches critical of Jehoshaphat's tendency for political compromise with the northern kingdom of Israel, nearly his fatal flaw, are included (19:1–3; 20:37). Like all the good kings of Judah during the divided monarchy, Jehoshaphat's reign receives a mixed review in the end. Especially important to the Chronicler is the reciprocal nature of the king's relationship to God: "The LORD was with Jehoshaphat" (17:3) because he "sought the God of his father and followed his commands" (17:4).

This portion of the narrative has no parallel in the Kings' version of Jehoshaphat's rule (except for the succession formula 17:1a = 1 Kings 15:24b, and possibly a loose paraphrase of 1 Kings 22:41–44 in 2 Chron. 17:3–6). The contents of the chapter may be divided into three subunits: the theological review of the king (17:1–6), his program of religious instruction for Judah (17:7–9), and his military prowess (17:10–19).

Chapter 17 introduces topics that will be addressed in more detail later. For example, the promulgation of the king's example of personal faith and obedience to the Mosaic tradition by the Levitical corps (17:7–9) is developed more fully in chapter 19, and the subject of his military might (17:10–19) is expanded in chapters 18 and 20 (although ironically it is God's intervention as the divine warrior, not Jehoshaphat's extensive fortifications and massive army, that carries the day in battle).

Theological review (17:1–6). The theological review discusses Jehoshaphat's military activity (17:1–2) and his religious activity (17:3–6). The clause that he "strengthened himself *against* Israel" (17:1, NIV) is problematic. This may refer to the defensive measures taken by Jehoshaphat to secure his kingdom against aggression from the north in the sporadic civil wars that marked the coexistence of Israel and Judah (17:2, 12–13). Typically, however, the verb "strengthened himself" (Hithpael of *ḥzq*) denotes a king's consolidation of power internally upon ascending to the throne (e.g., 1:1; 12:13; 13:21; 21:4). Some commentators, then, understand that Jehoshaphat "strengthened himself *over* Israel" (with Israel representing the kingdom of Judah as the true or spiritual Israel).[39]

Several times in this opening section of the summary of Jehoshaphat's reign the Chronicler establishes direct or indirect continuity with King Asa (e.g., by noting the towns of Ephraim captured by Asa, 17:2; by indicating that he follows the God of his father and commands of his father, 17:4; and by his removal of the high places, 17:6). The purpose is to present Jehoshaphat as a good and upright king like his father Asa (cf. 14:2). It is important for the Chronicler to highlight the spiritual continuity from one generation to the next because the Lord is with his people (17:3) to the extent that they seek him and follow his commands (17:4).

The kings of the divided monarchy (2 Chron. 10–36) are evaluated against the "gold standard" of kingship, King David himself. Jehoshaphat is compared favorably to David because he is single-minded in his obedience to God (17:3). In contrast to the kings of Israel, Jehoshaphat seeks God, not the Baals (17:3). Consulting the Baals was the snare of kingship in Israel (17:4), and the writer may have had Ahab in mind since he is a contemporary of Jehoshaphat (cf. 18:1). The kings of Judah are not immune from the seductions of this insidious counterfeit religion, however, as the accounts of

39. Thompson, *1, 2 Chronicles*, 278.

Jehoram and Ahaziah testify (cf. 21:6; 22:3). This is why the theological review for the biblical historians is a "litmus test" of the "heart" (17:6).

Both the Old and New Testaments teach that the righteous are to love God and obey his commandments with a whole heart (Deut. 6:5; 11:13; 26:16; Matt. 22:37; Rom. 1:9; Eph. 6:6). Jehoshaphat's "heart was devoted to the ways of the LORD" (2 Chron. 17:6, at least "in his early years," 17:3). The demonstration of wholehearted devotion to God is the removal of the symbols and practices of false worship so that the "high places and the Asherah poles" are purged from the land (17:6). Thus, "the LORD was with Jehoshaphat" (17:3), just as he was with Solomon (1:1), Abijah (13:12), and Asa (15:9). No doubt the Chronicler hopes his own audience will see the obvious pattern of divine presence and blessing conditioned by obedience to God's law.

Finally, echoes of the Davidic prayer of dedication of the gifts for the temple may be seen in the statement "the LORD established the kingdom under his control" and in the "wealth and honor" that come to Jehoshaphat (17:5). The kingdom is the Lord's, and it is his to grant and establish as he wills; likewise, wealth and honor come from God as tokens of his own power and greatness (1 Chron. 29:11–12).

There are also overtones of the Davidic covenant in the theological review of King Jehoshaphat. Not to be lost on the Chronicler or his audience is the fact that God has maintained his covenant with the house of David (cf. Ps. 89). The evidence of God's faithfulness to his word is seen in the succession of Jehoshaphat and the continuation of the Davidic dynasty (2 Chron. 17:1; cf. 1 Chron. 17:10–11), in the fact that God has cut off the enemies of Judah (2 Chron. 17:2; 20:27; cf. 1 Chron. 17:8–10), and in Jehoshaphat's leadership in shepherding the people into the way of God through his religious reforms (2 Chron. 17:6; cf. 1 Chron. 17:6–7).

Religious instruction for Judah (17:7–9). The reference to the "third year" of Jehoshaphat's reign is significant, if the historical reconstruction understanding a three-year coregency between Asa and his son Jehoshaphat is correct (perhaps coinciding with Asa's affliction in his feet, cf. 16:12). This means that Jehoshaphat marks the beginning of his own independent rule over Judah with an initiative aimed at spiritual reform. The king's religious instruction program is supervised by five civil officials (17:7) and ten Levitical officials (eight Levites and two priests, 17:8). This "theological faculty" engages in "distance learning" of sorts, in that they launch an itinerant teaching ministry throughout the towns of Judah (17:9).

The curriculum consists of "the Book of the Law," presumably some form of the Pentateuch—perhaps more specifically the Covenant Code (Ex. 19–24) or even what we now know as the book of Deuteronomy. This type of teaching ministry is in keeping with Moses' charge to the tribe of Levi: "He teaches your precepts to Jacob and your law to Israel" (Deut. 33:10). The verb "to teach" (*lmd*; 2 Chron. 17:7, 9) is a common word for instruction in the Old Testament (cf. Deut. 4:10; 5:1).[40] It implies that education is a process of assimilation, not the dumping of information. The teacher stimulates the learner to imitate the desired action or behavioral response by word and example. The program appears to have been one of unrestricted access to religious education, as the "people" of Judah are the target audience of this "tuition-free" instruction (2 Chron. 17:9).

Military organization (17:10–19). God's blessing rests on Jehoshaphat's reign; as a result, "the fear of the LORD" falls on Judah's neighbors (17:10). The writer's ordering of the material is significant insofar as the details concerning the organization and size of Jehoshaphat's army follows the report about the dread Judah inspires among the surrounding nations (17:14–19). Clearly this is a deliberate ploy, lest anyone mistakenly equate the king's military might with the Lord's work in establishing Jehoshaphat's kingdom (cf. 17:5). Respect for Judah's political clout results in the payment of tribute from peoples to the west and south (17:11).

Often the historical events of a king's reign are telescoped in the Chronicler's sweeping summaries of the Judahite rulers of the divided monarchy. Perhaps the tribute from the Philistines and Arabs is the unsolicited by-product of the defeat of Moab and Ammon to the east (ch. 20). The payment of tribute to Judah is seen as a judicious precautionary measure against experiencing a similar fate. The flow of wealth into Judah permits the building of fortifications and store cities (17:12–13). Such defensive precautions are necessary because Judah is always in a precarious political, economic, and military position, situated on the land bridge buffering the ebb and flow of the hegemonic designs of the super-empires in Egypt and Mesopotamia.

This is the second of four enumerations of Judah's army in Chronicles (17:14–19; cf. also 14:8; 25:5; 26:11–15). Jehoshaphat's army is comprised of the standing army or professional military and the conscript army or the militia. The experienced soldiers are strategically stationed in Jerusalem (those who serve the king, 17:19, and the four commanders of the units of a thousand, 17:14–18). The professional military personnel protect the capital city from foreign invasion and protect the king in the case of internal political unrest. Extensive building programs and mustering large armies are evidence of divine favor for the Chronicler.

According to the tallies of the tribal muster rolls, Jehoshaphat's army totals 1,160,000 soldiers (17:14–18). As we have already noted elsewhere,

---

40. Ronald P. Chadwick, *Teaching and Learning: An Integrated Approach to Christian Education* (Old Tappan, N.J.: Revell, 1982), 27–28.

our understanding of numerical data must take into consideration the range of possible meanings for the word "thousand" (*'elep*) in context, whether a "chieftain," a "military cohort" of some size, or a literal "thousand."

Alliance with Ahab (18:1–19:3). Micaiah's prophecy against King Ahab of Israel is the longest prophetic narrative in Chronicles. The Chronicler has borrowed the prophetic battle story from 1 Kings 22:1–35, with only minor modifications. That version of the battle at Ramoth Gilead ends with the report of Ahab's death and the fulfillment of the word of the Lord concerning the dogs lapping his blood (22:36–40). The Chronicler omits this passage and adds his own conclusion to the story in the form of Jehu the seer's prophetic rebuke of Jehoshaphat (2 Chron. 19:1–3). The change in the ending of the battle story shifts the moral of the narrative from an emphasis on the fulfillment of the word of God's prophets in 1 Kings to one of warning that righteous kings must trust Yahweh and avoid entangling foreign alliances and religions.

Proposal for war (18:1–4). The gist of the opening report is King Jehoshaphat's consent to partner with King Ahab in a war against Ramoth Gilead (18:3). Ramoth Gilead is a city of the Transjordan located southeast of the Sea of Galilee (perhaps Tell Ramith, not far from the modern Jordanian city of Ramtha). Originally it was one of the cities of refuge established by Moses for the tribe of Gad (Deut. 4:43). Later it became an important border city between Israel and Aram or Syria (cf. 2 Kings 9:14). Sometime during the reign of Ben-Hadad (ca. 860–843 B.C.), the Arameans took possession of Ramoth Gilead. Ben-Hadad besieged Samaria twice as well but was repulsed by Ahab's troops (cf. 1 Kings 20:1–21, 22–34). Ahab's design in waging war with Aram is to recapture former Israelite territory. Perhaps his motivation for war is triggered by Ben-Hadad's treachery in breaking an earlier treaty (cf. 1 Kings 20:34).

Jehoshaphat consents to enter a coalition with Ahab (2 Chron. 18:3), but he then requests Ahab to "seek the counsel of the LORD" (18:4). Consulting the Lord seems to be Jehoshaphat's concern, not Ahab's, as the king from Judah requests to inquire of a prophet two times (18:4, 6). The word "to seek" (*drš*) is used here in the sense of seeking guidance or direction for a course of action from the prophets (cf. 1 Kings 14:5). Naturally, the king is looking for some kind of divine assurance that the military campaign will be successful.

The introduction of the story in Chronicles differs at three points from that of the parallel in 1 Kings 22:1–4. (1) First Chronicles 18:1a accents Jehoshaphat's wealth and honor. (2) Then it records his alliance to King Ahab of Israel by marriage (18:1b). (3) The Chronicler reports how the king from Judah is "dazzled by the extravagance of his state visit to Samaria . . .

swept off his feet and falls an ingenuous victim to Ahab's wishes."[41] His reshaping of this introduction implicitly indicts Jehoshaphat on three counts: his marriage alliance with the northern kingdom of Israel, his pride (incited by the lavish reception he receives in Samaria), which clouds his sensibilities for decision-making, and his agreement to participate in a military campaign with King Ahab. This introduction anticipates the prophetic condemnations of Jehoshaphat for his foolishness in allying himself with the apostate Ahab (cf. 19:1−3).

Prophetic counsel (18:5−27). The passage largely consists of dialogue between the kings of Israel and Judah and several prophets. Kings in the ancient world often sought a word of favor from the deities or a sign from the gods before embarking on a military campaign. Jehoshaphat's request to "seek the counsel of the LORD" is an example (18:4; cf. David's seeking direction from the Lord against the Philistines, 1 Chron. 14:10; the king of Babylon's seeking an omen against Judah, Ezek. 21:21). Ahab obliges his counterpart from Judah by assembling four hundred prophets, all of whom predict victory for Ahab and Israel (2 Chron. 18:5).

Jehoshaphat remains unpersuaded, perhaps even suspicious, since he knows that the true prophets are often dissenters in the face of popular opinion, and he requests yet another prophetic judgment (18:6). Micaiah son of Imlah is summoned, but Ahab remonstrates that this prophet only speaks "bad" about him (18:7). By this he means that Micaiah never agrees with the plans of the king by simply telling him what he wants to hear. While the royal parties await the arrival of Micaiah, Ahab's prophets continue to forecast victory for Israel (18:9−11). One of the prophets, Zedekiah, even dramatizes Ahab's success with iron horns he has made and proclaims that Ahab will "gore the Arameans until they are destroyed" (18:10; cf. Deut. 33:17).

Apart from his confrontation with Ahab and Jehoshaphat (18:12−24), nothing else is known of Micaiah. The king's envoy attempts to "coach" Micaiah as he enters the situation, informing him that the other prophets have spoken favorably about the campaign against Ramoth Gilead and he should do the same (18:12). But Micaiah staunchly refuses to compromise any message from the Lord (18:13). His response to Ahab's initial inquiry must have been sarcastic, a parody of the king's four hundred "yes men" (18:14). Exasperated, Ahab ironically demands the truth from the Lord's prophet—if only to prove to Jehoshaphat that Micaiah only speaks "bad" about him (18:15).

Micaiah's prophecy takes the form of two visions. The first depicts a scene of sheep without a shepherd on the hills (18:16−17). Ahab presumes the prophet portends his death in battle, which he does (18:17). But Micaiah's

---

41. Allen, *1, 2 Chronicles*, 298.

message has a double meaning, in that the people of Israel currently "have no master" (18:16b). Ahab's corrupt rule has led the people far from God—how sardonic that the sheep will have "peace" (18:16c) when the shepherd is gone! Selman notes that the tragedy of this kind of leadership is "neither new nor unrepeatable" (cf. Num. 27:16—17; Ezek. 34:5—6; Zech. 10:2); it is a situation for which God is deeply concerned and leads ultimately to the coming of the Good Shepherd (cf. Matt. 9:36; Mark 6:34).[42]

Micaiah's second vision offers a window into the throne room of God, where the divine council discusses the battle of Ramoth Gilead and the fate of King Ahab (18:18—22). Typically, the role of divine council in Israel's warfare is mustering the heavenly army to fight on behalf of Israel, but here the council plots the death of Ahab and the defeat of the combined armies of Israel and Judah.[43] McConville puts the ethical conundrum of God's perpetuating a falsehood in perspective by helping us appreciate the fact that "the issue of falsehood is raised long before v. 19. The whole reign of Ahab and the constitution of Israel is a falsehood."[44]

Micaiah's message about the "lying spirit" sent from God unmasks the fraudulent prophets of Ahab (18:20—22). No doubt this is something Ahab already knows, given his encounters with the prophet Elijah—but this exchange leaves him without excuse before God. We must remember that "the 'spirit of falsehood' sent by God *actually deceives no-one*. It is sent . . . to those who recognize the truth and suppress it."[45] The enraged Zedekiah, exposed as a lying prophet in front of his own king, slaps Micaiah's face and challenges the source of the spirit that has led him to pronounce a contrary prophecy (18:23). Micaiah responds with a pun, mocking Zedekiah as a "seer" who cannot "see" ("you will find out [r^3h, lit., see]," 18:24).

Ahab accents his rejection of Micaiah's message by having the prophet thrown in prison in Samaria (18:25—26; cf. v. 9). Amon must have held a position in the city of Samaria similar to that of mayor. The phrase "king's son" may be a title for Joash, someone with royal authority in overseeing the palace prison (18:26). Much like the prophet Jeremiah at a later time period, Micaiah is imprisoned as a traitor because his prophecy undermines the authority of the king and demoralizes the troops (cf. Jer. 38:1—6). Meager rations were standard fare for those incarcerated (cf. Isa. 30:20; Jer. 38:9).

Micaiah responds to Ahab's "in your face" declaration that he will return safely (18:26b) with a death threat (18:27). The king's death in battle will

---

42. Selman, *2 Chronicles*, 411.

43. Cf. Patrick Miller, "The Divine Council and the Prophetic Call to War," *VT* 18 (1968): 100—107.

44. McConville, *I and II Chronicles*, 183.

45. Ibid., 186.

vindicate Micaiah and verify the truth of his message. Jeremiah made a similar pronouncement to the false prophet Hananiah during the reign of Zedekiah, and Hananiah died "in the seventh month of that same year" (Jer. 28:15–17). The king's strategy to confine Micaiah rather than execute him is a wise one. By keeping him alive, the king leaves open the option of publicly shaming the prophet and disgracing his message after his safe return. To kill the prophet might make him a martyr, should his message be accurate.

Battle of Ramoth Gilead (18:28–34). By engaging in the battle against the Arameans at Ramoth Gilead (18:28), Ahab fulfills Micaiah's prophecy about the king being lured to his own destruction (cf. 18:20–22). Ahab's ploy to disguise himself is perhaps an attempt to thwart the word of the prophet that the king fears may be true (18:29), even as later Josiah king of Judah tried to nullify the prophetic word by means of disguise (35:22). It is also possible that Ahab is simply anticipating a known military tactic of the Arameans, assigning the charioteers the sole mission of killing the enemy king (18:30; cf. 2 Kings 3:26, where the king of Moab employed the same strategy against the king of Edom).

Who, then, becomes the target of the Aramean charioteers? King Jehoshaphat of Judah, dressed in his royal robes (18:31—causing one to wonder about the motive behind Ahab's earlier directive to Jehoshaphat, 18:29). The Chronicler interprets Jehoshaphat's cry as a prayer and adds the clause "and the LORD helped him" (18:31). Allen quips: "The S.O.S. prayer of this believer, although he is in trouble of his own making, is charitably answered with divine help."[46] The "random" arrow that pierces a chink in Ahab's armor is certainly God's arrow (18:33), verifying that God has indeed spoken through Micaiah the prophet (18:27). Ahab's heroic effort to prop himself up in his chariot to sustain the morale of his troops and continue to press the battle is of no avail (18:34). He dies that evening, and the army of Israel withdraws from Ramoth Gilead in defeat—details ignored by the Chronicler (see 1 Kings 22:35–36).

Jehu's prophecy (19:1–3). The Chronicler inserts the report of Jehu's prophetic condemnation of King Jehoshaphat as an alternative conclusion to the Ramoth Gilead battle report. The passage has no parallel in the Kings' version of the story. Jehu the seer (19:2) is the son of Hanani the seer, who rebuked King Asa of Judah for entering into a foreign alliance with Ben-Hadad of Aram (16:1–9). By allying himself with King Ahab of Israel, Jehoshaphat is a partner to "the wicked" and an accomplice of "those who hate the LORD"—offenses deserving of the "wrath of the LORD" (19:2). Jehoshaphat's "mixed review" from Jehu ("there is ... some good in you") is

46. Allen, *1, 2 Chronicles,* 299–300.

based on the king's religious reforms—purging the land of false worship (19:3). The conflicting reports that Jehoshaphat has removed the "Asherah poles" (19:3) but does not remove the "high places" (20:33) may be harmonized in such a way that the king removes the objects of false worship but permits the shrines to remain. This may be a compromise decision by the king since the people "had not set their hearts on the God of their fathers" (20:33).

According to Dillard, the inclusion of the Ahab narrative is a conscious effort by the Chronicler "to model Jehoshaphat in Asa's image," since both kings are condemned for entering alliances with "foreign" nations.[47] The change in the ending of the battle story shifts the moral of the narrative from an emphasis on the fulfillment of the word of God's prophets in 1 Kings 22:38 to a warning "that righteous kings must trust Yahweh and avoid entangling foreign alliances." The evil of *alliances* with foreign nations in lieu of *reliance* on God is a repeated theme in Chronicles (cf. Asa, 2 Chron. 16:1−9; Jehoshaphat, 20:35−37; Amaziah, 25:6−8; Ahaz, 28:16−23). The moral still has currency for the Chronicler's audience, for the full restoration of Judah will be accomplished by trust in God, not by brokering alliances with foreign nations.

Judicial reform (19:4−11). It is only fitting that Jehoshaphat appoints judges throughout Judah since his name means "Yahweh has judged." The directive to appoint judges in the land (19:5) and the admonitions against distorting justice by taking bribes or showing favoritism (19:7, 9−10) find their source in the Mosaic law (Deut. 1:16−17; 10:17; 16:18−20). A detailed discussion of the questions related to the sources used by the Chronicler for his report of Jehoshaphat's reform of the judicial system in Judah and the historicity of that account lie outside the scope of this commentary.[48] This unit discusses Jehoshaphat's revival (19:4), Jehoshaphat's appointment of judges, (19:5−11c), and Jehoshaphat's final admonition (19:11d).

Jehoshaphat's revival (19:4). The section opens with a brief account of Jehoshaphat's activity as an "evangelist" throughout Judah after the debacle at Ramoth Gilead (19:4; cf. 18:26−34). The phrase "he went out again" probably implies the king's earlier teaching mission through his emissaries (17:7− 9). The king's spiritual fervor seems to be motivated by the curse of "God's wrath" placed on him by Jehu the seer (19:1−3). The expression "and turned them back [*šwb*] to the LORD" (19:4b) is in keeping with God's response to Solomon's dedication of the temple to forgive the sin of those who "turn [*šwb*] from their wicked ways" (7:14). The prominent feature of Jehoshaphat's revival is the reform of the judicial system. Most commentators take the

---

47. Dillard, 2 *Chronicles*, 139.
48. Ibid., 147−48.

clause "Jehoshaphat lived in Jerusalem" (19:4a) to mean he stays in Jerusalem and makes no more dubious excursions to the northern kingdom to make alliances against rival kings.

Jehoshaphat's appointment of judges (19:5–11c). The appointment of judges in the cities of Canaan given by God to his people was mandated in the law of Moses (Deut. 16:18). Jehoshaphat's decision to place judges and establish forums for legal proceedings in the "fortified cities" is a logical one (2 Chron. 19:5). These cities are royal command centers and part of a network of defensive posts ringing Jerusalem. The cities house royal storehouses and have a garrison of royal troops stationed there. The strategic location of these fortified cities makes them accessible for the general population.

The role of the judge is that of an agent for God, not the king (19:6). As Thompson has summarized, "judicial authority depended upon the rule of the Lord and was to reflect his own attributes of righteousness, justice, and fairness."[49] The injunction against showing favoritism or bribery (19:7) was a foundational judicial principle in the Mosaic legal tradition (Deut. 1:17; 16:19). The numerous prohibitions against bribery in the Old Testament indicate the pervasiveness of the problem (cf. Prov. 17:23; Isa. 1:21–23; Mic. 3:11).

Showing partiality in judgment or taking a bribe distorts justice in at least two ways. (1) It puts the poor at a disadvantage for a fair hearing because they are typically unable to afford the bribe to sway a judge's decision. (2) Moreover any deviation from justice in the courts results in injustice, and injustice in any society is the seedbed of social unrest. The association of the king's admonition with the "fear of the LORD" suggests that the judges take a vow to uphold the king's charge as an oath of office of sorts (19:7; cf. v. 9).

Unlike the provincial courts of the outlying districts of Judah, Jehoshaphat appoints judges who represent both religious and civil leadership in Jerusalem (presumably because the Levitical priesthood holds jurisdiction over the temple precinct, 19:8). Apparently the priests and Levites assigned to judicial offices are required to live in Jerusalem rather than in one of the Levitical cities, serving in Jerusalem on an annual rotation (19:8b).

In addition to hearing cases and rendering fair verdicts, the judge must also warn (or instruct) the citizenry who come before the bench not to commit further sin against the Lord, lest the "wrath" of God come against them and their family (19:9–10). This "fear of the LORD" is understood as a deterrent to further criminal activity (19:9); it permits all the citizens of Judah to enjoy the protection afforded by the law. In addition, the just application of the law to everyday life will lead to an equitable society—the ideal social dynamic of the covenant community.

---

49. See Thompson, *1, 2 Chronicles*, 289.

The clause "in every case that comes before you from your fellow countrymen who live in the cities" suggests that the judges in Jerusalem act as a court of appeals for the provincial courts in the outlying districts of Judah (19:10). Dillard is probably correct in his assumption that there is also a lower court in Jerusalem so that the appeals court is not the court of original jurisdiction for the citizens of Jerusalem.[50] The right to an appeal is rooted in the Sinai tradition of Moses hearing the cases that were too difficult for the appointed judges (cf. Ex. 18:17–26; Deut. 1:17–18). Apparently at the time of the Hebrew monarchy, the king is the "supreme court" for those appealing legal decisions (cf. 2 Sam. 15:2–4). The main purpose of setting up an appeals court system is to prevent "sin against the LORD" so as to avoid "his wrath" (2 Chron. 19:10).[51] Certainly the Chronicler believes such a goal for the Hebrew judicial system is still germane for the application of Mosaic law to society in the courts of postexilic Judah.

Jehoshaphat's appointment of dual "attorneys general" serves as a sober reminder that the tensions between "church" and "state" in the administration of public policy has a long history (19:11). To ensure some separation of power and introduce a check-and-balance mechanism into the judicial organization, the king gives the chief priest Amariah jurisdiction over religious matters (19:11a). He then grants jurisdiction in all crown or civil matters to Zebadiah, the leader of the tribe of Judah (19:11b). Dillard speculates this joint oversight may be due, in part, to the need to control the revenues accruing to the temple and palace treasuries.[52] The Levites serve as "officials" and assist the courts as clerks and bailiffs (19:11c).

Jehoshaphat's final admonition (19:11d). Unlike his earlier two charges, Jehoshaphat's final admonition is more positive. Instead of warning the judicial appointees not to sin (19:7, 10), the king exhorts them to "act with courage" and invokes the Lord's presence with them as they discharge their duties (19:11d).

War with Moab and Ammon (20:1–30). Judah's victory over the Moabites and the Ammonites has no parallel in 1 Kings. The passage is usually described as a "holy war" or "Yahweh war" story. The chapter may be outlined as follows:

A. Preparations for war in Jerusalem (20:1–19)
    1. Fasting and seeking God (20:1–4)
    2. Jehoshaphat's prayer (20:5–12)
    3. Report of a prophetic oracle (20:13–17)
    4. Liturgical response by the king and all the people (20:18–19)

---

50. Dillard, 2 *Chronicles*, 149.
51. Selman, 2 *Chronicles*, 419.
52. Dillard, 2 *Chronicles*, 149–50.

B. Yahweh war (20:20−30)
1. Yahweh's victory (20:20−26)
2. March of triumph to Jerusalem (20:27−28)
3. Aftermath of Yahweh war (20:29−30)

This Yahweh-war story is one of the great stories in the Bible. Its literary purpose is to contrast Jehoshaphat's *reliance* on God when threatened by an enemy with his *alliance* with Ahab of Israel when faced with a similar situation (ch. 18). Theologically, the story is another example of "seeking God" (20:4), a major theme in Chronicles. For Selman, the story of Judah's victory over Moab and Ammon is the "showpiece" of the Chronicler's account of the divided monarchy (chs. 10−36).[53] To humble oneself before God in the face of insurmountable odds humanly speaking and to trust him fully for deliverance are the essence of biblical faith. As Jehoshaphat exhorts his people: "Have faith in the LORD your God and you will be upheld" (20:20)—that is, have faith in your God and you will find him faithful! The other key verses of this Yahweh-war story convey the same theology that the church clings to today: "We do not know what to do, but our eyes are upon you" (20:12); and "the battle is not yours, but God's" (20:15).

Judah prepares for war (20:1−4). The phrase "after this" (20:1) refers to the revival among the people of Judah after the debacle at Ramoth Gilead (19:4) and presumes a chronological ordering of the Jehoshaphat narrative. A coalition of three nations invades Judah (20:1). Two of the three peoples assembled for war are known from previous conflicts. Earlier during Jehoshaphat's reign, the Moabites under King Mesha rebelled against King Jehoram (or Joram) of Israel after his succession of Ahab (2 Kings 3:4−27). The Moabites were attempting to break their vassalage to Israel and free themselves from the annual tribute of sheep and wool paid to the kingdom. Even earlier, David's general, Joab, led a successful campaign against the Ammonites (1 Chron. 19).

The third member of the alliance is somewhat uncertain, given the textual problems in the opening verse. The Hebrew text simply has "other Ammonites" as part of the coalition. The NIV agrees with the majority of English versions and follows the LXX by reading "Meunites" (20:1, see text note). The Meunites are among the subjugated peoples who bring tribute to King Hezekiah a century later (26:7). In this story they are equated with the "people of Seir" (cf. 20:22−23). They reside somewhere on Mount Seir (a mountain range running the length of Edom), though the exact location of Meunite territory remains a question.

It seems likely that revenge motivates the pact of aggression against Judah between Moab and Ammon. Selman may be correct in his assumption that

---

53. Selman, 2 *Chronicles,* 419.

the coalition chooses to attack Judah as the weaker partner in the alliance Jehoshaphat has with the northern kingdom of Israel (first with Ahab, 18:1–3; then with Ahaziah, 20:35–37; then renewed with Jehoram, 2 Kings 3:7).[54]

The expression "vast army" (*hamon rab*) is the Chronicler's way of describing the overwhelming numerical superiority of the invaders (20:2). The attacking armies come across the Dead Sea ("the Sea," 20:2), probably at a shallow ford across the Lisan (or jut of land protruding into the sea from the eastern side). When the report reaches King Jehoshaphat, the Transjordan coalition has already arrived at En Gedi, only twenty-five miles southeast of Jerusalem (20:2). This explains the king's "alarm" (20:3).

After Jehoshaphat's initial panic has subsided, he inquires of the Lord with deep resolve and proclaims a national fast (20:3). In the Old Testament, fasting was usually directed toward securing direction or deliverance from God in times of national crisis (like war) or natural disaster (like famine). The fact that people from "every town" (20:4) in Judah rally together to seek the Lord indicates the lasting spiritual impact Jehoshaphat's revival has upon the nation.

Jehoshaphat's prayer (20:5–12). The assembly of Judah and Jerusalem gather at the "new courtyard" of the temple (20:5), possibly the "great court" (cf. 4:9). The emphasis on the "assembly" (20:5, 14, 26) stresses the unity of the people as they face this dire circumstance. This is one of the Chronicler's sermon points in his retelling of Israel's history, an exhortation to unity in the postexilic community as they seek to rebuild the nation spiritually.

Jehoshaphat's prayer takes the form of a community or national lament (cf. Ps. 12; 44; 58). Certain features characterize this literary form: an address to God (cf. 20:6), a recitation of past favors (cf. 20:7–8), a protestation of innocence, a confession of trust (cf. 20:9), a complaint (cf. 20:10–11), and a plea for deliverance (cf. 20:12).[55]

Jehoshaphat's prayer-speech appeals widely to other Old Testament texts. For example, his address to God, "O LORD, God of our fathers" (2 Chron. 20:6), echoes David's prayer before the assembly of Israel after the gifts for the temple were collected (1 Chron. 29:10; cf. 12:17); likewise, the phrase "power and might are in your hand" (2 Chron. 20:6; cf. 1 Chron. 29:12). To acknowledge God "who is in heaven" is to extol his greatness (2 Chron. 2:5; 6:18) and to testify to him as a God who hears prayers (6:21). The literary device of rhetorical questions (20:6–7) is a poetic method for expressing the absolute certainty about something (e.g., 32:13–14).

---

54. Ibid., 422.

55. See David L. Petersen, *Late Israelite Prophecy: Studies in Deutero-Prophetic Literature in Chronicles* (SBLMS 23; Missoula, Mont.: Scholars Press, 1977), 72; Anderson, *Out of the Depths,* 49–76.

The expression "Abraham your friend" (20:7) hearkens back to Genesis 18:17−19 (cf. Isa. 41:8). The reference to driving out the inhabitants of the land "before your people Israel" (2 Chron. 20:7) recalls Moses' historical sermon prior to the covenant-renewal ceremony at Mount Nebo prior to the invasion of Canaan (Deut. 4:38). Finally, the king repeats the idea from Solomon's temple dedication prayer that God will hear his people when they pray before they go to war—and he will uphold their cause (2 Chron. 20:9; cf. 6:34−35).

Jehoshaphat's prayer makes allusions to three important Old Testament covenants in a few short sentences: the Abrahamic covenant, the Mosaic covenant, and the Davidic covenant. This pattern of appealing to God's earlier covenant promises is clear in other prayers in Chronicles (e.g., 1 Chron. 17:21−22; 2 Chron. 6:15−17). Here the reference to the covenants provides a context for the king's complaint, namely, the injustice of nations repaying "evil for good" (revisiting the post-Exodus sojourn and the reprieve granted Moab and Ammon while Israel trekked toward Canaan through those eastern territories, cf. Deut 2:1−19). God had promised to defeat the enemies who would rise up against Israel (Deut. 28:7)—Jehoshaphat asks for God to make good on that pledge now! The king's plea for deliverance (20:12), couched in the frank admission of Judah's helplessness, calls for God to judge the enemies of his people.

Jahaziel's salvation oracle (20:13−17). Jehoshaphat's prayer of lament is answered by a salvation oracle. As is typical in this speech form, it begins with the admonition "do not be afraid" (20:15) and concludes with a promise of "deliverance" (20:17; Heb. *yešuʿah*). The specific form of Jahaziel's speech seems to blend the salvation oracle and the priestly address prescribed by the law of Moses to be delivered to the army before a battle (cf. Deut. 20:2−4).

God's answer to Jehoshaphat's prayer comes immediately, perhaps from an unexpected source. Jahaziel the Levite is empowered by God's Spirit to deliver a word of knowledge to the king and the people of Judah (20:14). During Old Testament times the prophetic gifts of God's Spirit were given to prophets and nonprophets alike (cf. 1 Chron. 12:18; 2 Chron. 15:1; 18:23). The Chronicler's special interest in the Levites is shown in the recital of Jahaziel's impressive pedigree, tracing his lineage back to Asaph of King David's era (20:14).

A number of the Yahweh-war motifs are continued in the prophetic speech of Jahaziel: the exhortation to take courage and stand firm (20:15, 17), the numerical superiority of the enemy armies ("vast army," 20:15), the Israelites not having to fight because Yahweh will wage war for them (20:15, 17), and the promise of certain victory because God will sustain his people with his presence (20:16−17). Jahaziel even identifies the location for

Yahweh's victory, although the "Desert of Jeruel" cannot be identified with certainty (20:16). The prediction that the people of Judah will see God's victory "tomorrow" (20:17) is a reminder of the urgency of the situation, as the coalition armies are only a day's march from Jerusalem!

Liturgical response (20:18–19). The response of Jehoshaphat and all the people of Judah and Jerusalem to the prophetic oracle of Jahaziel has affinities to both covenant-renewal liturgy and the temple liturgy in Old Testament corporate worship: worship proper (demonstrated by prostration before God) followed by enthusiastic praise (20:18–19; cf. Neh. 9–10; Ps. 95).

We would do well to imitate the liturgical response reported by the Chronicler because "real worship is something you do—not something you watch."[56] This is especially true of "bowing down" or prostration (20:18). Lying on the ground or bowed with bent knees is a symbol of humility. This posture is both an act of repentance (Ps. 38:6) and worship (138:2). Erickson calls us to relearn liturgical gestures and postures as "nonverbal communicators that give rich expression to, intensify, and provoke the deepest religious instincts. They give to the liturgy a power to prompt the human spirit to an awareness of the presence of God."[57] Jehoshaphat and the people of Judah are fully aware of the presence of God.

Yahweh's victory (20:20–26). The army of Judah sets out "early in the morning" for the Desert of Tekoa (20:20), suggesting a sense of expectation and confidence in what God is about to do in achieving deliverance for his people. Jehoshaphat fulfills the role of the priest charged to address the troops before entering a battle (Deut. 20:1–4). He paraphrases the priestly exhortation and adds the words "have faith in his prophets and you will be successful" (2 Chron. 20:20). This statement affirms the efficacy of the prophetic word prompted by the Spirit of God and may even signify canonical prophetic literature by this time. The more immediate reference, of course, is the salvation oracle uttered by Jahaziel as God's answer to Jehoshaphat's prayer (20:15–17).

Williamson, almost humorously, has commented that the battle cry has been replaced by the Levitical chorale.[58] The report of an army going into battle singing the praises of God is unique in the Bible, although music accompanies the appearance of the divine warrior when he executes judgment on the earth (Ps. 47; 96; 98). The event gives new meaning to the psalmist's declaration that God's "pleasure is not in the strength of the horse, nor his delight in the legs of a man; the LORD delights in those who fear him, who put their hope in his unfailing love" (147:10–11).

---

56. Hill, *Enter His Courts with Praise!* 133.
57. See ibid., 135.
58. Williamson, *1 and 2 Chronicles,* 300.

The text the Levites sing in praise of Yahweh was Psalm 136:1, an often-repeated refrain in Chronicles (2 Chron. 20:21; cf. 5:13; 7:3; 1 Chron. 16:34). Interestingly, the Levitical chorus initiates God's battle strategy against the enemy coalition (2 Chron. 20:22). Whether God terrifies the coalition armies with the appearance of his heavenly army (as in 2 Sam. 5:24; 2 Kings 7:5–7) or sends a spirit of confusion and mistrust among the allies (as in Judg. 7:22; 2 Kings 3:23) is unclear. What is clear is that God stirs the Transjordan armies into a spirit of frenzied self-destruction (20:22–23). First, the armies of Moab and Ammon slaughter the soldiers from Seir, perhaps out of distrust (20:23a). Then the Moabites and the Ammonites destroy each other so that no one escapes (20:23b–24a).

Amazingly, scouts on a natural lookout point over the valley behold a battlefield strewn with corpses—in a battle Judah does not have to fight (cf. 20:17). It takes the army of Judah three days to plunder the spoils from the battlefield, one day for each army of the coalition (20:25). The fourth day is devoted to worship in praise of God's victory; the name given to the valley where the Lord upheld his people is the Valley of Beracah (i.e., Praise, 20:26; cf. v. 20).

March of triumph to Jerusalem (20:27–28). Fittingly, the story of the Yahweh war against the Transjordan coalition ends where it began—at the temple of the Lord God of Israel. The march of triumph from the battle site to the Jerusalem sanctuary confirms God's answer to the king's prayer—the battle was indeed God's (20:15). The atmosphere of the march of triumph is depicted almost as a festival worship processional; the musical instruments that accompanied the singing of the Levites in battle (20:21) are now employed in the joyful celebration of the victory God has given them over their enemies (20:27–28).

The aftermath (20:29–30). Characteristically, Yahweh war leaves in its wake "the fear of God" among the nations (20:29) and the "peace" and "rest" of God for his faithful community (20:30). Such was the case after the Exodus and the initial phases of the Hebrew conquest of Canaan (Ex. 12:30–36; Josh. 21:44). Similarly, the first advent of Jesus Christ brought "peace" and "rest" to those willing to believe in his gospel as the power of God unto salvation (Matt. 11:28–29; John 14:27). It also brought "the fear of God" among the nations in the form of persecution of the Christian church (cf. John 15:20). The second advent of Jesus Christ will result in the "fear of God" among the nations in the form of abject submission to Christ and a perfect peace and rest for God's faithful in a new heaven and earth (Phil. 2:10–11; Rev. 21).

Concluding regnal résumé (20:31–21:3). Jehoshaphat's concluding résumé follows the Kings' parallel with some modification (e.g., Chronicles omits the usual synchronism with the northern kingdom, 1 Kings 22:41; the later version also fails to include the statement of Jehoshaphat's peace with the king of Israel and his purging of the male cult prostitutes from the land, 1 Kings 22:44, 46). Beyond that, the résumé contains the standard formulas: the accession age (2 Chron. 20:31a), length of reign (20:31b), mother's name (20:31c), theological review (20:32), historical source citation (20:34), and death and burial and succession formulas (21:1). In keeping with 1 Kings 22:48−49, Jehoshaphat's death and burial formula is interrupted by the report of his disastrous shipping venture with Ahaziah king of Israel (2 Chron. 20:35−37).

King Jehoshaphat's twenty-five-year reign may be dated between 872 and 848 B.C. (20:31). According to 2 Kings 3:1, Jehoshaphat ruled for twenty-two years plus an additional four years (8:16). Most commentators harmonize the additional data by assuming Jehoshaphat had a three-year coregency with his father Asa (872−869 B.C.) before he ascended to the throne of Judah (coinciding with Asa's foot disease, cf. 2 Chron. 16:12).

Jehoshaphat is likened to his father, Asa, as a king who did "what was right in the eyes of the LORD" (20:32). He receives a favorable but not unqualified theological review from the biblical historians. Much like his father, Jehoshaphat was rebuked by God's prophet for entering into foreign political alliances (19:1−3; cf. 16:7−9), and he failed to remove completely the high places—vestiges of Canaanite worship still infecting Hebrew religion (20:33; cf. 15:17). Although Jehoshaphat "walked in the ways of his father Asa" (20:32), neither Asa nor Jehoshaphat is given the epitaph of Hezekiah and Josiah as one who "walked in the ways of his father David" (29:2; 34:2),[59] although Jehoshaphat did receive this accolade for the early years of his reign (see comments on 17:3).

The writer calls attention to the fickleness of the people, whose hearts are not fully set on God (20:33; cf. 1 Kings 22:43). The Chronicler's commentary here seems to be directed at his own audience as much as it reports Judah's history. Whether for Jehoshaphat's generation or his own, the need for unswerving faithfulness to God and constant vigilance to his commandments must be set before God's people on a continual basis.

Jehu's father, Hanani the seer, rebuked King Asa for his alliance with Ben-Hadad, king of Aram (16:7−9). The "annals of Jehu" are part of larger historical materials documenting the Israelite monarchies (20:34). The title of the historical source cited by the Chronicler has been changed from "the book of the annals of the kings of Judah" (1 Kings 22:45) to "the book of the kings of

---

59. On the seeming contradiction of Jehoshaphat removing the high places (17:6) but not removing the high places (20:33), see comments on the similar report for Asa's reforms in 15:1−19 .

Israel." Either the writer understands the kingdom of Judah as the "true Israel," or he simply recognizes postexilic Judah as the current representative of "all Israel" and updates the title of the bibliographic resource accordingly.

Like the commentary that calls attention to the incomplete religious reforms of Jehoshaphat (20:33), the insertion of the failed maritime venture in partnership with Ahaziah, king of Israel, appears to be yet another qualification of the "good" king's reign (20:35–37). The prophecy from Eliezer predicting catastrophe for Jehoshaphat's fleet (20:37) fits a pattern of prophetic rebuke and divine judgment of the king of Judah for entering into political and commercial alliances with the northern kingdom of Israel or other foreign nations. Biblical historians are careful to portray the full humanity of the characters on stage in the Old Testament, so that God is praised as the key actor in the drama of history, not "supersaints." No doubt, the story is an important reminder to each generation of hearers and readers about Israelite history as well about the moral and spiritual dangers associated with such entanglements.

The addendum to the succession formula (21:1) naming the seven sons of Jehoshaphat (21:2) and providing rationale for the succession of Jehoram as the firstborn son (21:3) serves both as a prelude to the report of King Jehoram's reign and as a memorial to those sons murdered by their brother Jehoram (21:4).

RELEVANCE OF THE PROPHETS. The Chronicles are all about the relevance of the example of God's people of a bygone era for the writer's generation. That relevance includes especially obedience to God's word, prayer to the God of heaven, and proper worship at Yahweh's temple. For the Chronicler, the applicability of earlier history for postexilic Judah includes the currency of the prophetic voice for the spiritual and moral well-being of God's people—despite the fact that the voice of God's prophets and prophetesses has not been heard for perhaps a century by his time. The profound relevance of the prophetic voice for the Chronicler's audience is captured in Jehoshaphat's exhortation to Judah before engaging the Moabite and Ammonite coalition in battle: "Have faith in his prophets and you will be successful" (20:20).

But who are the Israelite prophets and prophetesses? In many ways, the ranks of the prophetic corps in the Old Testament are filled with ordinary men and women. Many are anonymous figures, nameless voices faithfully proclaiming a message from God. Often these individuals appear only briefly in the biblical narrative, "on stage" for but a few lines. Yet at times they "steal the show" with a rhetorical question, a homespun parable, a dramatic object lesson, or even an outrageous claim challenging the status quo.

The prophets represent a cross-section of Israelite society, whether a farmer like Amos or a "blue-blood" like Isaiah. But blue-collar and white-collar prophet alike, these ordinary individuals exhibit an extraordinary faith in God and an unswerving faithfulness to the proclamation of his word. Oftentimes they speak to their own peril (as Jeremiah could attest). But they are truly human too, as their ministries are not without lapses of doubt and fits of disobedience (as Jonah could attest).

Jewish scholar Rabbi Heschel raises the question: "What manner of person is the prophet of God?" Part of his answer includes the following list of prophetic characteristics. It is offered here as an example for Christians because that is how the Chronicler portrays the prophets for his audience— exemplary figures of faith in God:

- a spirit scandalized by evil because of their keen sensitivity to holiness (Hab. 1:3)
- a consuming passion with the "trivialities" of life because everything related to the plight of humanity is important (Amos 2:7)
- a sometimes "explosive" and volatile personality—a sharp sword and a polished arrow (Hos. 6:5)
- the pursuit of the highest good—love, justice, and righteousness (Jer. 9:23–24; Zech. 4:6)
- an iconoclastic posture—a willingness to challenge the apparently holy, the seemingly sacred, the patently traditional (Jer. 7:4)
- a burden for people arising out of divinely motivated compassion (Hos. 1–3)
- a life of paradox blending loneliness and misery with joy and elation (Jer. 15:16; 20:9)
- the courage to confront God with honest doubt (Hab. 1:2–3, 12)
- a willingness to wait on God in prayer (Hab. 2:1–2).[60]

What role does the prophetic voice play in Old Testament times? The functions of God's prophet or prophetess in Hebrew society vary somewhat, depending on the time frame of that individual's ministry. (1) The prophetic voice prior to the beginning of the monarchy is represented by figures like Moses, Deborah, and even Samuel, each of whom served as a spokesperson for God and as a leader for his people, often in the office of judge. The Hebrew judge frequently filled duties in multiple roles, including that of legal magistrate, military general, civil leader, and spiritual overseer.

60. Abraham J. Heschel, *The Prophets* (New York: Harper & Row, 1962), 1:3–26.

(2) The preclassical or nonwriting prophets ministered to both the kings and the people during the united and divided monarchies as spokespersons for God and as political and spiritual advisers. Representative examples of the preclassical prophetic voice include individuals like Nathan, Elijah, and Micaiah the son of Imlah from this very unit (cf. 18:8). The prophetic speeches recorded in Chronicles, with a single exception (24:20–22), portray the prophets and Huldah the prophetess primarily as advisers to the king (see fig. 2 in the introduction).

(3) The classical or writing prophets stood watch during the eras of the divided monarchies (e.g., Hosea, Amos, Isaiah), the Exile (e.g., Jeremiah and Ezekiel), and the early postexilic periods (e.g., Haggai and Zechariah). They too were spokespersons for God and acted primarily as social and spiritual commentators.

What is the form of the prophetic message? Broadly understood, three types of speech are identifiable in the prophetic books of the Old Testament: historical accounts, prophetic utterances, and prayers. The prophetic speeches of the classical or writing prophets are often separated into two basic types of oracles: the judgment oracle and the salvation oracle.[61] The judgment-oracle category may be further subdivided into indictment and judgment oracles, and the salvation-oracle category may be subdivided into instruction and aftermath oracles.[62] The *indictment oracle* rehearses the offenses of the guilty party (whether an individual or a nation), and the *judgment oracle* cites the divine punishment to be meted out. The *instruction oracle* exhorts the guilty to respond to the threat of divine judgment, often a call to repentance. The *aftermath oracle* offers the promise of future hope in the form of deliverance from an enemy and restoration after destruction.

The four oracle categories are foundational as a basic outline of the message of many of the writing prophets. For example, this oracle pattern undergirds the macrostructure of Hosea: account of Hosea's marriage (Hos. 1–3), indictment (chs. 4–5), instruction (ch. 6), judgment (chs. 7–13), and aftermath (ch. 14). Also in Amos we have indictment (Amos 1–4), instruction (ch. 5), judgment (chs. 6–8), and aftermath (ch. 9). The essential idea of the judgment and salvation oracles may be seen in the prophetic speeches recorded in Chronicles, whether defeat for the king (i.e., judgment oracle; e.g., 12:5–8; 18:12–22) or success for the king (i.e., salvation oracle; e.g., 15:1–7; 16:7–9).

The Old Testament prophets are typically associated with prediction, foretelling the future of Israel and the nations by means of cryptic apocalyptic

---

61. Cf. Claus Westermann, *Basic Forms of Prophetic Speech*, trans. H. C. White (Louisville: Westminster John Knox, 1991), 90–98.

62. Hill and Walton, *A Survey of the Old Testament*, 409.

visions. It is true that at times the Hebrew prophets pronounce oracles forecasting both near and distant future events of Israelite history. This type of prophetic speech is often couched in phrases like "the day of the LORD"—examples include Elijah's forecast of drought in Israel (1 Kings 17:1) and Isaiah's promise of Jerusalem's restoration under Yahweh's servant King Cyrus (Isa. 45:1). Among the key themes of prophetic foretelling are the promises of future deliverance and restoration of Israel, the judgment of the wicked, the new covenant, a coming messiah-king like David who will rule in righteousness, and the hope of a new creation.

Prognostication, however, is not the primary emphasis of the ministry of the prophets as only 20 percent or so of prophetic speech in the Old Testament is predictive. The bulk of prophetic speech is forthtelling or interpretive exposition. This type of prophetic speech consists of instruction, admonition, and exhortation based on Mosaic law. The prophets not only serve as expositors of the Mosaic tradition, but they are also social and political commentators. King Ahab called Elijah the prophet a "troubler" of Israel (1 Kings 18:17)—and indeed the title is fitting because the prophets were the "conscience" of both Israelite kings and society. The repeated themes of prophetic speech include the call to repentance and a return to true worship, the practice of social justice, the rejection of immorality, and reliance on Yahweh rather than on false gods and foreign alliances.

There are seventeen prophetic speeches in Chronicles made by fourteen named prophets, one named prophetess, and two unnamed prophets. Fourteen of the prophetic speeches are directed to kings, one to the Israelite army, and two to the general populace of Judah. Apart from Nathan's oracle concerning the Davidic covenant (1 Chron. 17), the predominant message of these speeches is one of either the proclamation of success and deliverance or warning and judgment for the kings. Their primary purpose is to demonstrate God's faithfulness to the Davidic covenant and his concern for the success of Davidic rule in Judah.

But why would Jehoshaphat encourage his people to "have faith" in God's prophets? For the simple fact that the word of prophets is inextricably bound to God himself, as the full quotation of Jehoshaphat's exhortation reveals: "Have faith in the LORD your God and you will be upheld; have faith in his prophets and you will be successful" (20:20). To have faith in God's prophets is tantamount to having faith in God because they are commissioned as his servants to speak his word to Israel and the nations. Support for this understanding is found in two related biblical ideas, that of the divine assembly and the form of prophetic speech patterns.

The concept of a *divine assembly* is found in the religious literature of the ancient Near East. In Mesopotamian literature the divine assembly is comprised of the gods and goddesses of the pantheon and their angelic attendants. This assembly met, often after feasting, to discuss and determine the fate of the course of human events. Their decision was then duly pronounced and executed on earth. In Mesopotamian religion the executor of the will of the divine council was the storm god Enlil.[63]

A similar notion may be found in the Hebrew understanding of the heavenly realm. Cryptic references in the Psalms mention the assembly of the holy ones who surround God (Ps. 29:1; 89:5, 7). The abode of Yahweh is depicted as a heavenly throne room; in addition to the Godhead this divine council is comprised of his angelic attendants, including the four living creatures and angels of other ranks and descriptions (cf. Isa. 6:1–3; Ezek. 1:4–10). The council of Yahweh makes and enforces decrees concerning the operation of the cosmos. The angelic members of the council are often sent as envoys of God to deliver his messages and his decrees (e.g., "the angel of the LORD" [*mal'ak yhwh*] in Ex. 3:2; Judg. 13:13, 15; angels [*mal'ak*] like Gabriel, Dan. 8:16).

Micaiah is an example of God's prophet invited by means of a vision to observe the divine assembly in action and who then reports the message of the "lying prophets" to Ahab and Jehoshaphat (18:18–22). In fact, the most frequently used term for the "prophet" (*nabi'*) denotes this idea of the messenger from the divine council since it essentially means "one who speaks for another" as a representative of that authority. The Israelite prophet, then, in one sense stood in the divine assembly as a messenger of the council, heard God's word, and was then commissioned to deliver it to his people. This explains why their oracles are usually delivered in the past tense—it is a message they have already heard, and because it was spoken by God himself, it would assuredly come to pass.

Typically the speech patterns of the Old Testament prophets are characterized by highly repetitive formulaic language. These stock phrases and expressions are cues to the audience as to the divine source and authority of their message and to the authenticity and integrity of the divine messenger. Here are the more prominent formulas of the prophetic speech pattern:

- the messenger formula (lit., "thus says Yahweh"; NIV = "this is what the LORD says," 2 Chron. 20:15)
- the prophetic word formula ("the word of the LORD came to me," e.g., 1 Chron. 17:3; 2 Chron. 12:7)
- the divine utterance formula ("declares the LORD," e.g., 2 Chron. 34:27)

---

63. E. T. Mullen Jr., "Divine Assembly," *ABD*, 2:214–17.

- the revelation formula ("the LORD showed" or "the LORD spoke," e.g., 1 Chron. 21:27; 2 Chron. 33:10; cf. 36:12)
- the proclamation formula ("hear the word of the LORD," e.g., 18:18).[64]

The idea of a messenger sent from the divine council to relay God's word heard in the assembly of the holy ones culminates in Jesus Christ. The prophet Malachi foretold of a day when God would send a "messenger" (mal'ak) before his appearance at the Jerusalem temple (Mal. 3:1). Jesus identified John the Baptist as that messenger or prophetic forerunner of Messiah (Matt. 11:10–14). Beyond this, Jesus claims a position in the Godhead when he announces that the temple is indeed *his* Father's house (John 2:16). Later Peter ascribes the prophetic office to Jesus when he recognizes him as "a prophet" like Moses to the onlookers after the healing of the crippled beggar (Acts 3:22; cf. Deut. 18:18). Finally, Jesus indicates on several occasions that he was sent from the heavenly realm by his Father, that he spoke only what he heard from the Father, and that he did only what his Father commanded him (John 5:30, 36–38; 6:33, 38). As the ultimate messenger of God's "divine assembly," Jesus Christ ("who is at the Father's side") not only makes known the decrees of God but reveals God himself (1:18).

The relevance of the story of the prophets' interface with the kings of Israel and Judah for the Chronicler's audience is in the response to their message. From King Saul to King Zedekiah, the story of the kingship is one of either faith or unbelief in the message of God's prophets. In the end, the sorry epitaph for each of the divided kingdoms includes a fatal byline referencing the fact that the people ignore "his prophets" to their own destruction (2 Kings 17:23; 2 Chron. 36:16). Nehemiah sternly reminds postexilic Judah of the suicidal stubbornness of their ancestors as an admonition or warning of his own, lest history be repeated (Neh. 9:30).

The Chronicler must have shared the same concern, since the response to God's prophets by both king and people sets the tone for the latter portion of his history (2 Chron. 10–36). Now the people must heed God's prophets by obeying their word as inscripturated in the corpus of the Hebrew canon. Thus, the relevance of the prophets for postexilic Judah becomes associated with responding to God's messages as preserved in the prophetic writings and taught to the people. For the Chronicler, the exhortation to "have faith in his prophets" (20:20) is a "wake-up" call to prevent the neglect of the prophetic writings found in the Scriptures. Jesus told his own audience as much in their clamor for convincing signs, even resurrection from the dead: "They have Moses and the Prophets; let them listen to them" (Luke 16:29).

---

64. De Vries, *1 and 2 Chronicles*, 437–39.

BELIEVING THE PROPHETS. One of the "buzz words" in contemporary culture is "relevance." Whether education, politics, or even religion, people are looking for relevance. This is cultural, in part due to American pragmatism. The demand for productivity and efficiency driven by technological advances contributes to the quest for relevance as well. Finally, the high value placed on "relevance" is in some measure a reaction to modernity by a culture drifting with a postmodern current. Modernism's irrelevance stems from its tendency to define a person as a rational human being. Postmodernity prefers to define a person in terms of emotional and spiritual qualities. In either case, however, the emphasis is still largely on the individual, and in that sense the postmodern desire for personal relevance is a carryover from the modernist culture of narcissism.

But what is meant by the term *relevance?* It denotes "direct relationship to the matter at hand, practicality, pertinence, currency, and applicability." The connotation of relevance in today's society is informed not by the dictionary definition but by the entrepreneurial culture of the business and marketing sector of American life. Relevance in the business world is defined by degrees in terms of "customer satisfaction." The success or failure of any business is dependent on its responsiveness to the consumer. A business can only be as responsive as it is effective in discerning perceived customer needs and articulating those needs through the various levels of the corporate hierarchy. In both cases success is contingent on relevant communication, first in accurate polling of consumer demand and second in efficient dissemination of that information up the organizational ladder.[65]

The notion of relevance is extremely important to the Christian subculture as well. For some time now the Christian church has struggled to retain its distinctive identity as the people of God, all the while attempting to keep the pews filled with "satisfied customers."[66] Beyond this, church-growth gurus identify a vibrant pulpit ministry as a high priority item on the checklist of the "church consumer." Not surprisingly, a quick review of any of the numerous guides to preaching available reveals that "relevance" is vital to effective pulpit communication.

---

65. See, e.g., H. Thomas Johnson, *Relevance Regained: From Top-Down Control to Bottom-Up Empowerment* (New York: Free Press, 1992).

66. On how the Christian church might respond to the influence of consumerism, see Rodney Clapp, ed., *The Consuming Passion: Christianity and the Consumer Culture* (Downers Grove, Ill.: InterVarsity Press, 1998).

Haddon Robinson, for instance, insists that "apart from *life-related*, biblical content we have nothing worth communicating" (italics added).[67] The continuing success of the "life-application" type of study Bible is another indicator of the value the Christian community places on relevance, in this case the immediate practicality of biblical truth to the individual's life situation. The influence of postmodernism thought has even generated a demand for more relevance in corporate worship experiences in our Christian churches. What is meant by relevant worship is worship that is more in step with the contemporary culture, worship that fosters the experience of mystery, worship that is participatory, worship that appreciates the inter-relatedness of all things, and worship that communicates through the visual.[68]

The idea of relevance is not a recent cultural invention. People, whether living in an ancient, modern, or postmodern society, seek relevance because at some level "theory" and "practice" must overlap for life to have meaning and purpose. For instance, the psalmist Asaph laments the seeming incongruity between the "theory" (or theology) of the Mosaic law that obedience to God's commandments results in divine blessing and disobedience yields divine punishment (e.g., Ps. 73:13–14; cf. Deut. 28). He questions the relevance (or practicality) of punishment "every morning" as his reward for the life of "innocence" and purity that he seeks to live in adherence to Yahweh's covenant commands. The prophet Malachi's audience registers a similar complaint when they challenge the relevance of a theology that "blesses" the arrogant while the righteous languish in futility (Mal. 3:14–15). Much later, the apostle Peter anticipates the relevance question when he warns Christians against siding with the scoffers who find no pertinence in the teaching of Jesus' second coming (2 Peter 3:3–4).

In fact, if Chronicles is indeed a "theology of hope" for postexilic Judah, then in one sense the two books are all about the relevance of earlier Hebrew history for the contemporary generation. For the Chronicler, that relevance or applicability is found in things like the example of humble obedience to the commandments found in God's Word, the efficacy of heartfelt prayer to the Lord God of heaven when trouble looms large on the horizon, or the experience of joy associated with the proper worship of Yahweh at his temple. There is even relevance in listening to the prophetic voice: "Have faith in his prophets and you will be successful" (2 Chron. 20:20c). This is so because to "have faith in his prophets" is to "have faith in the LORD your

---

67. Haddon W. Robinson, *Biblical Preaching*, 2d ed. (Grand Rapids: Baker, 2001), 201; cf. Keith Willhite, *Preaching with Relevance: Without Dumbing Down* (Grand Rapids: Kregel, 2001), who offers ten "how-to steps" on relevant pulpit communication.

68. Webber, *Blended Worship*, 27.

God" (20:20b). Faith in God is always relevant because true and purposeful life can only be found by believing God—taking him at his word (Gen. 15:6; Hab. 2:4).

The word "success" communicates in any age. The context of Jehoshaphat's prayer is that of success in a military battle (20:20). The Chronicler understands, however, that it is God alone who grants success to individuals and nations.[69] Here I suggest that the oracles of the Old Testament prophets are always relevant or continually have currency for the life of faith in God. This is true not because they predict "success," but because like Jehoshaphat's exhortation they call to people to "have faith in the LORD . . . God" (20:20). This is hardly a new concept. R. B. Y. Scott was touting the relevance of the Old Testament prophets five decades ago in what might now be considered his "minor classic" by that title.[70]

But why are the Old Testament prophets relevant, and what makes their message spoken to ancient Israel more than twenty-five centuries ago applicable to contemporary culture? According to Scott, the remarkable contemporaneity of these ancient figures and the perennial freshness of their message spring from several distinctive characteristics:

- their power to penetrate past the maze of appearances to identify the essential underlying human and theological facts of a given circumstance or historical situation
- their ability to define essential justice and essential religion amid moral confusion, secular influence, and human waywardness
- their shrewd understanding of human nature and the human predicament as a result of their suffering (what at times is called the "prophetic pathos")
- their sensitivity to the urgent meaning of history as the sphere of humanity's moral decisions and God's preemptory intervention
- their knowledge of God as the fountainhead of ultimate meaning and purpose in the context of everyday life
- their intuitive comprehension of the reality of God's presence in the inner world of their own heart and spirit
- their capacity to communicate concretely, in universal terms, and with both passion and conviction—to speak with divine authority by the power of God's Spirit as choice servants commissioned by God— unlike their rivals, who told "fortunes for money" (Mic. 3:11; cf. Amos 3:8; Mic. 3:8)[71]

---

69. Alex Luc, "צלח," NIDOTTE, 3:804.
70. R. B. Y. Scott, The Relevance of the Prophets (New York: Macmillan, 1953).
71. Ibid., 204–5.

Scott has also provided numerous categories for the contemporary application of the message of the Old Testament prophets:

- history: The key ideas here include the sovereignty of God as the one who "sets up kings and deposes them" (Dan. 2:21), God's redemptive purpose in human history for both judgment and salvation (cf. Isa. 52:7; Jer. 51:29), and the notion that biblical history is both cyclical (cf. Eccl. 3:1–8) and linear (the terminus of human history is implicit in the phrase "the day of the LORD," cf. Isa. 65:17).

- social order: Individual behavior matters—the prophetic voice held people accountable for their deeds and espoused an agenda for social justice rooted in the teachings of the Sinai covenant (e.g., Jer. 11:4–5; Amos 4:1; 5:11).

- religion: Essential religion in the Old Testament was personal and communal (exemplified in the lives and ministries of prophets like Jeremiah and Hosea) and covenantal (cf. Jer. 31:31–33); it emphasized the knowledge of God and personal holiness (cf. Isa. 29:23; 35:8), demanded a whole-person response of love and obedience in worship (cf. 1:10–20), and issued in actions that promoted social justice (cf. Amos 5:23–24; Mic. 6:6–8).

- theology: For the Old Testament prophetess or prophet, theology was all about the "knowledge" of God (Hos. 6:3), and they knew God as an immanent and transcendent deity (cf. Isa. 57:15: 66:2), as a consuming fire in his holiness (cf. 30:27), and as a refuge in his goodness (cf. Nah. 1:7); his revelation was rooted in historical reality (as seen in the date formulas introducing prophetic oracles, e.g., Isa. 6:1), the prophetic ministry was a call to spiritual warfare (cf. 1 Kings 18), and both divine punishment for sin and divine mercy as a means of grace were realities in God's providential rule of creation (cf. Isa. 54:7).

- preaching: The authority of prophetic preaching resides in the faithful proclamation of the word of the Lord (validated in the messenger formula, such as "this is what the LORD says," Jer. 2:5); the essential message of prophetic preaching is repentance (e.g., Joel 2:12–13); the medium of prophetic preaching is both word and image (as seen in the object lesson of Jeremiah's linen belt [Jer. 13:1–11] or the example of the "living parable" of Hosea's marriage to Gomer as the illustration of God's call of repentance to Israel [Hos. 1–3]).

- culture: The prophetic school was called to "contextualize" their message from God by means of incarnational preaching, teaching, and confirming miraculous signs—living in and ministering to people in their cultural setting (as seen in the example of Elijah's living among the indigenous Canaanite peoples and demonstrating Yahweh's supremacy over Baal in his supposed domains of fire, food, and life itself, cf. 1 Kings 17–18).

- politics: The prophets of God were called at times to an "iconoclastic" ministry with respect to the religious and political offices and institutions of Hebrew society; they were also the "conscience" of both priest and king as they decried the exercise of social power without social responsibility—religion and government must serve the common welfare (Hos. 4:1–3; Amos 2:6–7; cf. Jas. 1:27).[72]

A word of caution is in order here before we rush off to apply the message of the Old Testament prophets to our contemporary setting. We are well served by Scott's admonition that it is presumptuous to speak of the relevance of the prophets apart from the knowledge of their message.[73] They do not speak *of* our age but *to* it because the word of Yahweh is in their mouths as his messengers.

But here is the rub: I fear we do not know the message of the prophets. Granted, my perceptions are based largely on two decades of service as a professor of Old Testament studies at three different Christian liberal arts colleges. Yet, I am inclined to surmise that many of our Protestant "free church" traditions perpetuate a "practical Marcionism" because they send students to college who have little or no acquaintance with the Old Testament story. Naturally, the home and the church must work together in the biblical education of Christian young people, and the impact of Christian "home schooling" and Christian elementary and high school education is encouraging. But the general lack of Old Testament knowledge among students entering Christian colleges is a disturbing trend. Most students in an entry-level Old Testament class cannot find the book of Habakkuk in their Bible, let alone articulate its message. Yet the message of this prophet was foundational to the Protestant Reformation (cf. Hab. 2:4).

Perhaps the significance of the "prophetic voices" in this section of Chronicles is not the application of their message to our times but an exhortation to find out what that message was so we can then make contemporary application. King Jehoshaphat's charge to "have faith in his prophets" (20:20) is still our directive in the sense that we too accept the Old Testament prophets as Yahweh's clarions, trumpeting his Word to God's faithful across the generations. The Chronicler would call us to "have faith" in God's prophets to the point where we indeed believe that they were divinely commissioned messengers who spoke the very words of God. Scott has ably demonstrated that

72. Ibid., 206–27.
73. Ibid., 204.

the Old Testament prophetic voice is still relevant to the Christian life so that like Ezekiel's countrymen, we should "gather around" the prophet to hear "the message that has come from the LORD" (cf. Ezek. 33:30). Unlike Ezekiel's audience, however, who only listened to the words of God's prophets as a form of entertainment, we must be willing to "put them into practice" (33:31).

One way for the Christian church to "gather around" the Hebrew prophets is to utilize the prophetic books of the Old Testament on a regular basis—thus giving credence to Paul's instruction to be devoted "to the public reading of Scripture, to preaching and to teaching" (1 Tim. 4:13). Adopting the tradition of the more liturgical Christian churches of including both Old and New Testament readings in a systematic way is one helpful approach to ensuring some balance in the use of Scripture in corporate worship. In fact, Robert Webber encourages more public reading of Scripture as one way to renew the service of the Word in corporate worship.[74]

The Christological focus of worship may be recovered through the reenactment of the Christ-event by means of recitation (the reading and preaching of Scripture) and drama (gathering at the table of the Lord's Supper). The Old Testament must be included in this recitation of God's work through Christ because we learn that the things written in the Law, the Prophets, and the Psalms were about Jesus Christ (cf. Luke 24:44). I concur with Webber when he says, "I want someone to read [i.e., Scripture] who knows how to read, and I want the person who preaches to communicate to me."[75] The church is slowly learning how to implement the "lively reading" of Scripture in corporate worship by taking a page out of the Chronicler's "handbook" for Levitical ministry. This is being accomplished, in part, by utilizing the gifts of those individuals who have capacities to memorize biblical passages and deliver them as dramatic presentations, by "reader's theater" approaches that incorporate people who "know how to read," and by the antiphonal singing and chanting of biblical texts.

In addition to the public reading of the Old Testament as a part of the Scripture lessons in the service of the Word in corporate worship, the corpus of the Old Testament prophets must also be a resource for Christian preaching. Again, according to Webber, "people need to experience the immediacy of the Word of God. They need to know that the God who acted in history can be active now, touching their lives, healing their hurts, and giving them a vision for the future."[76] Since all Scripture is "God-breathed" (2 Tim. 3:16, in context a reference to the Old Testament) and since those

---

74. Webber, *Worship Old and New* (1994), 170.
75. Webber, *Blended Worship*, 45.
76. Ibid.

things "written in the past" were written to "teach" (Rom. 15:4) and "warn" (1 Cor. 10:11) us, clearly Christians can experience the "immediacy" of God's Word from the preaching of the Old Testament as well as the New. As John Bright has cogently argued,

> the normative element in the Old Testament, and its abiding authority as the Word of God, rests not in its laws and customs, its institutions and ancient patterns of thinking, nor yet in the characters and events of which its history tell, but in that structure of theology which undergirds each of its texts and which is caught up in the New Testament and announced as fulfilled in Jesus Christ.[77]

More specifically, Duduit has suggested the following reasons for preaching the Old Testament as part of a balanced and effective pulpit ministry:

- It aids us in understanding the New Testament (indeed, one-third of the New Testament is Old Testament quotation or allusion or explication).
- It is vital for a balanced understanding of biblical theology.
- It offers practical insights for Christian living.
- It deals with life's great questions.
- It leads us to Jesus Christ.[78]

The Word of God, including the Old Testament prophets, remains "living and active.... It penetrates even to dividing soul and spirit, joints and marrow; it judges the thoughts and attitudes of the heart" (Heb. 4:12). The Word of God has a "prophetic ministry" in the heart of its hearer or reader; how much more does the "sharpened sword" and "polished arrow" (Isa. 49:2) of Old Testament prophets enhance that "prophetic ministry."

The practical benefits of exploring the relevance of the Old Testament prophets for the Christian church are timely, even crucial as modernity gives way to postmodernity. This is true primarily because the ideology of religious pluralism is the shared common denominator between the cultural contexts of the biblical prophets and contemporary North American society. Reclaiming the prophetic mantle is relevant for the church in at least three important ways:

(1) Our acquaintance with the Old Testament prophets will help raise awareness and appreciation for the message of their contemporary

---

77. John Bright, *The Authority of the Old Testament* (Grand Rapids: Baker, repr., 1975), 156.

78. Michael Duduit, "The Church's Need for Old Testament Preaching," in *Reclaiming the Prophetic Mantle: Preaching the Old Testament Faithfully*, ed. George L. Klein (Nashville: Broadman, 1992), 9–16.

counterparts—men and women who stand in their tradition of pro-claiming God's Word of admonition and exhortation to the right-eous and repentance to the unrighteous (cf. 2 Peter 1:12–21).

(2) Sound instruction in the Spirit-spawned message of the Old Testa-ment prophets contributes to the cultivation of the spiritual disci-pline of testing or discerning the spirits for the purpose of exposing false teachers and false teaching (cf. 1 John 4:1–3).

(3) The preaching and teaching of the Old Testament prophets as part of the "whole counsel of God" may encourage a new generation of "prophets" and "prophetesses" to take on the mantle of calling peo-ple to repentance and serving as the moral conscience of the sur-rounding culture (cf. Eph. 4:11). Jehoshaphat's charge to Judah before going to battle against the Moabite and Ammonite coalition still has relevance for God's people: "Have faith in the LORD your God and you will be upheld; have faith in his prophets and you will be suc-cessful" (20:20).

2 Chronicles 21:4–23:21

WHEN JEHORAM ESTABLISHED himself firmly over his father's kingdom, he put all his brothers to the sword along with some of the princes of Israel. ⁵Jehoram was thirty-two years old when he became king, and he reigned in Jerusalem eight years. ⁶He walked in the ways of the kings of Israel, as the house of Ahab had done, for he married a daughter of Ahab. He did evil in the eyes of the LORD. ⁷Nevertheless, because of the covenant the LORD had made with David, the LORD was not willing to destroy the house of David. He had promised to maintain a lamp for him and his descendants forever.

⁸In the time of Jehoram, Edom rebelled against Judah and set up its own king. ⁹So Jehoram went there with his officers and all his chariots. The Edomites surrounded him and his chariot commanders, but he rose up and broke through by night. ¹⁰To this day Edom has been in rebellion against Judah.

Libnah revolted at the same time, because Jehoram had forsaken the LORD, the God of his fathers. ¹¹He had also built high places on the hills of Judah and had caused the people of Jerusalem to prostitute themselves and had led Judah astray.

¹²Jehoram received a letter from Elijah the prophet, which said:

"This is what the LORD, the God of your father David, says: 'You have not walked in the ways of your father Jehoshaphat or of Asa king of Judah. ¹³But you have walked in the ways of the kings of Israel, and you have led Judah and the people of Jerusalem to prostitute themselves, just as the house of Ahab did. You have also murdered your own brothers, members of your father's house, men who were better than you. ¹⁴So now the LORD is about to strike your people, your sons, your wives and everything that is yours, with a heavy blow. ¹⁵You yourself will be very ill with a lingering disease of the bowels, until the disease causes your bowels to come out.'"

¹⁶The LORD aroused against Jehoram the hostility of the Philistines and of the Arabs who lived near the Cushites.

¹⁷They attacked Judah, invaded it and carried off all the goods found in the king's palace, together with his sons and wives. Not a son was left to him except Ahaziah, the youngest.

¹⁸After all this, the LORD afflicted Jehoram with an incurable disease of the bowels. ¹⁹In the course of time, at the end of the second year, his bowels came out because of the disease, and he died in great pain. His people made no fire in his honor, as they had for his fathers.

²⁰Jehoram was thirty-two years old when he became king, and he reigned in Jerusalem eight years. He passed away, to no one's regret, and was buried in the City of David, but not in the tombs of the kings.

²²:¹The people of Jerusalem made Ahaziah, Jehoram's youngest son, king in his place, since the raiders, who came with the Arabs into the camp, had killed all the older sons. So Ahaziah son of Jehoram king of Judah began to reign.

²Ahaziah was twenty-two years old when he became king, and he reigned in Jerusalem one year. His mother's name was Athaliah, a granddaughter of Omri.

³He too walked in the ways of the house of Ahab, for his mother encouraged him in doing wrong. ⁴He did evil in the eyes of the LORD, as the house of Ahab had done, for after his father's death they became his advisers, to his undoing. ⁵He also followed their counsel when he went with Joram son of Ahab king of Israel to war against Hazael king of Aram at Ramoth Gilead. The Arameans wounded Joram; ⁶so he returned to Jezreel to recover from the wounds they had inflicted on him at Ramoth in his battle with Hazael king of Aram.

Then Ahaziah son of Jehoram king of Judah went down to Jezreel to see Joram son of Ahab because he had been wounded.

⁷Through Ahaziah's visit to Joram, God brought about Ahaziah's downfall. When Ahaziah arrived, he went out with Joram to meet Jehu son of Nimshi, whom the LORD had anointed to destroy the house of Ahab. ⁸While Jehu was executing judgment on the house of Ahab, he found the princes of Judah and the sons of Ahaziah's relatives, who had been attending Ahaziah, and he killed them. ⁹He then went in search of Ahaziah, and his men captured him while he was hiding in Samaria. He was brought to Jehu and put to death. They buried him, for they said, "He was a son of Jehoshaphat, who

sought the LORD with all his heart." So there was no one in the house of Ahaziah powerful enough to retain the kingdom.

¹⁰When Athaliah the mother of Ahaziah saw that her son was dead, she proceeded to destroy the whole royal family of the house of Judah. ¹¹But Jehosheba, the daughter of King Jehoram, took Joash son of Ahaziah and stole him away from among the royal princes who were about to be murdered and put him and his nurse in a bedroom. Because Jehosheba, the daughter of King Jehoram and wife of the priest Jehoiada, was Ahaziah's sister, she hid the child from Athaliah so she could not kill him. ¹²He remained hidden with them at the temple of God for six years while Athaliah ruled the land.

²³:¹In the seventh year Jehoiada showed his strength. He made a covenant with the commanders of units of a hundred: Azariah son of Jeroham, Ishmael son of Jehohanan, Azariah son of Obed, Maaseiah son of Adaiah, and Elishaphat son of Zicri. ²They went throughout Judah and gathered the Levites and the heads of Israelite families from all the towns. When they came to Jerusalem, ³the whole assembly made a covenant with the king at the temple of God.

Jehoiada said to them, "The king's son shall reign, as the LORD promised concerning the descendants of David. ⁴Now this is what you are to do: A third of you priests and Levites who are going on duty on the Sabbath are to keep watch at the doors, ⁵a third of you at the royal palace and a third at the Foundation Gate, and all the other men are to be in the courtyards of the temple of the LORD. ⁶No one is to enter the temple of the LORD except the priests and Levites on duty; they may enter because they are consecrated, but all the other men are to guard what the LORD has assigned to them. ⁷The Levites are to station themselves around the king, each man with his weapons in his hand. Anyone who enters the temple must be put to death. Stay close to the king wherever he goes."

⁸The Levites and all the men of Judah did just as Jehoiada the priest ordered. Each one took his men—those who were going on duty on the Sabbath and those who were going off duty—for Jehoiada the priest had not released any of the divisions. ⁹Then he gave the commanders of units of a hundred the spears and the large and small shields that had belonged to King David and that were in the temple of God. ¹⁰He

stationed all the men, each with his weapon in his hand, around the king—near the altar and the temple, from the south side to the north side of the temple.

¹¹Jehoiada and his sons brought out the king's son and put the crown on him; they presented him with a copy of the covenant and proclaimed him king. They anointed him and shouted, "Long live the king!"

¹²When Athaliah heard the noise of the people running and cheering the king, she went to them at the temple of the LORD. ¹³She looked, and there was the king, standing by his pillar at the entrance. The officers and the trumpeters were beside the king, and all the people of the land were rejoicing and blowing trumpets, and singers with musical instruments were leading the praises. Then Athaliah tore her robes and shouted, "Treason! Treason!"

¹⁴Jehoiada the priest sent out the commanders of units of a hundred, who were in charge of the troops, and said to them: "Bring her out between the ranks and put to the sword anyone who follows her." For the priest had said, "Do not put her to death at the temple of the LORD." ¹⁵So they seized her as she reached the entrance of the Horse Gate on the palace grounds, and there they put her to death.

¹⁶Jehoiada then made a covenant that he and the people and the king would be the LORD's people. ¹⁷All the people went to the temple of Baal and tore it down. They smashed the altars and idols and killed Mattan the priest of Baal in front of the altars.

¹⁸Then Jehoiada placed the oversight of the temple of the LORD in the hands of the priests, who were Levites, to whom David had made assignments in the temple, to present the burnt offerings of the LORD as written in the Law of Moses, with rejoicing and singing, as David had ordered. ¹⁹He also stationed doorkeepers at the gates of the LORD's temple so that no one who was in any way unclean might enter.

²⁰He took with him the commanders of hundreds, the nobles, the rulers of the people and all the people of the land and brought the king down from the temple of the LORD. They went into the palace through the Upper Gate and seated the king on the royal throne, ²¹and all the people of the land rejoiced. And the city was quiet, because Athaliah had been slain with the sword.

THIS SECTION OF CHRONICLES taps into a theme common in the wisdom tradition of the Old Testament. In fact, the Bible knows only two "paths" or "ways" of life. In the book of Proverbs the sage contrasts the "way of the wisdom" (Prov. 4:11) with the "way of the fool" (12:15).

For the psalmist, the two ways are identified with the "righteous" and the "wicked" (Ps. 1:6). While there may be alternative descriptive terms for representing the two paths in life, the destination of each path is unalterably fixed. One path, the way of the wise or the righteous, leads to life—even immortality (cf. Prov. 4:18; 12:28). The other path, the way of the fool or the wicked, leads to death (cf. 4:19; 12:26; 14:12). Jesus himself affirmed this basic understanding of the course of life as a choice between "the narrow way" and "the broad way" (Matt. 7:13; 12:30).

The Old Testament historians have equated the "two paths" of the wisdom tradition with the dynasties of the divided monarchies. Thus, the "way of the house of David" is contrasted with the ways of "the house of Ahab" (2 Chron. 21:6; cf. 2 Kings 8:27; 22:2; 2 Chron. 11:17; 22:3). The house of David is characterized as a good way, marked by loyalty to God, obedience to his Word, and righteousness in royal rule (cf. 1 Kings 3:6; 1 Chron. 29:18–19). Conversely, the house of Ahab is characterized as an evil way, given to economic oppression, social injustice, idolatry, and witchcraft (cf. 1 Kings 16:30; 21:19; 2 Kings 9:22).

All this confirms the fact that true wisdom is not so much about knowledge and intellect as it is about character and behavior (cf. Prov. 1:3; 2:9). In the end, only one house will survive—for the Lord's curse rests on the house of the wicked, but his blessing rests on the home of the righteous (3:33). The Chronicler "spoils" the story of the near annihilation of the Davidic family for his audience by disclosing the resolution of the plot's conflict at the very beginning of his narrative: "The LORD was not willing to destroy the house of David. He had promised to maintain a lamp for him" (2 Chron. 21:7). The outcome of the rival house is equally assured, as we learn that God had anointed Jehu "to destroy the house of Ahab" (22:7).

To tell the ending of the story at the onset of the narrative is not necessarily bad storytelling. The storyteller can encourage, affirm, and instill confidence in the audience in this way. The Chronicler's audience knows the "story" anyway, since they have the legacy of the monarchies preserved already in the books of Kings. That may have been the very point for the Chronicler. This section of Chronicles is all about God, who keeps his promises and preserves his people facing the threat of destruction. This message is always timely for the faithful of God!

Jehoram (21:4–20)

THE CHRONICLER'S ACCOUNT of King Jehoram's reign is unusual in that reg-nal résumés frame the narrative like bookends (21:4–7, 20). As in the case with the previous royal summaries of Asa and Jehoshaphat, Chronicles more than doubles the parallel in 2 Kings 8:16–24.

Jehoram is the first king to receive an entirely negative review by the Chronicler. As Japhet has observed, this is especially noticeable in the dark tone set for his reign by an emphasis on his fratricide at the onset of his rule (21:4) and his fatal illness cutting short his tenure on Judah's throne (21:19).[1] Two recurring themes are dominant in this entire unit: Judah's affiliation with Baal because of the alliance with the "house of Ahab" (21:6; 22:3, 4, 7, 8), and the threat to the survival of the royal line of King David (21:7; 22:10).

The literary genre of the section is identified as "report," including an uncommon report of a prophetic oracle in the form of Elijah's letter to King Jehoram (21:12–15). Dillard's suggestion that the writer has shaped the nar-rative in the form of a palistrophe (i.e., a chiastic literary structure that coun-terbalances key theological themes focused on one fundamental teaching) has merit.[2] The key theme or idea is the atrocity of Jehoram's fratricide. Elijah's letter serves as the hinge or midpoint of a larger inverted thematic structure:

A Chronology (21:5)
   B Wrongdoing (royal sons) (21:4, 6–7)
      C Rebellion of Edom and Libnah (21:8–11)
         D Letter from Elijah (royal sons) (21:12–15)
      C′ Rebellion of Philistines and Arabs (21:16–17)
   B′ Punishment for wrongdoing (royal sons) (21:17–19)
A′ Chronology (21:20)

Introducing the kings of Judah with a regnal résumé and theological review is typical of the Chronicler's narrative style. The accession age formula and length of reign formula (21:5) date Jehoram's eight-year rule to 848–841 B.C. The writer assumes the audience's knowledge of the parallel in 2 Kings. What is atypical in this section of the Chronicler's narrative is the report of a crime prefaced to the résumé, namely, Jehoram's fratricide (21:4).

The execution of political rivals, even family members, is not unprece-dented in the Old Testament (e.g., Judg. 9:5; 2 Kings 10:11; 11:1). The prac-tice was common in the biblical world and especially in Canaanite culture. The custom was probably imported into the monarchy of Judah by the coun-sel of Jehoram's wife Athaliah, since her mother, Jezebel, was a Phoenician

---

1. Japhet, *I and II Chronicles*, 806.
2. Dillard, *2 Chronicles*, 164.

princess who worshiped the god Baal. No doubt this influence contributed to Athaliah's vendetta against the family of David (2 Chron. 22:10). The Chronicler uses the earlier name list of Jehoram's brothers to foreground his crime of fratricide (21:2). What a difference one's perspective brings to a situation, whether theological or political (as here).

The numerous sons born to King Jehoshaphat were a sign of God's favor to a ruler who sought to do what was right in the eyes of the Lord (20:32). Yet, for wicked Jehoram (needled by a power-crazed wife) his brothers were but potential rivals and a threat to the stability and longevity of his kingship.

Jehoram's crime of fratricide is the first of four acts of violence against the house of David in this narrative unit (21:4, 17; 22:8–9, 10–11). The Chronicler traces the wickedness of Jehoram directly to his marriage to "a daughter of Ahab" (21:6). Tragically, the corruption of godly kingship through intermarriage is a repeated theme in the history of the Israelite monarchy (e.g., 1 Kings 11:3; 16:31). According to the indictment of King Ahab by Jehu, the ways of the house of Ahab were idolatry and witchcraft—the antithesis of the code of conduct that the Israelites received at Mount Sinai (2 Kings 9:22; cf. Ex. 20:4; Deut. 18:10). In the present case, the affiliation of the house of Judah with the house of Ahab through the marriage of Jehoram and Athaliah is a recipe for self-destruction. The Hebrew sage knows there can be no other outcome, for the house of the wicked will be destroyed (Prov. 14:11). This explains why Jehoram is tagged with the same negative theological review given to the rulers of the northern kingdom of Israel (2 Chron. 21:6b; cf. 2 Kings 13:2, 11).

The ray of hope in this black history gleams from the "lamp" of David, maintained by the promise of God (21:7). The faithfulness of God to the Davidic covenant sets up the conflict that carries the plot of the biblical story from the Israelite monarchy right on through to the Gospels and the book of Revelation, namely, the continuation of the line of David and the fulfillment of the divine promise in the face of great wickedness poised to destroy that family. The truth that God is eternally faithful to the word of his covenant as demonstrated throughout the history of the Davidic monarchy is also a message of hope for the Chronicler's audience (cf. Ps. 111:5, 9). His retelling of Israel's history is a reminder that God's promise remains operative and that the lamp of David still burns. That truth is no less important for the New Testament writers as Israel awaits the coming of David's kingdom and the triumph of his root (Mark 11:10; Rev. 5:5).

The report of rebellions against Jehoram and Judah by Edom and Libnah (21:8–10a) closely follows 2 Kings 8:20–22. David had conquered Edom, and the territory was a satellite state during Solomon's reign (2 Sam. 8:13–14; 1 Kings 11:15–17). Judah's hegemony over Edom was apparently reestablished during the reign of Asa or Jehoshaphat; once again the region was a vassal nation to the Davidic dynasty.

Libnah was a city of the western foothills of Palestine allotted to the tribe of Judah (Josh. 15:42). The town is also identified as a Levitical city in the Judah-Simeon list of allotments (21:13). The exact location of this city is disputed by archaeologists, but the site was clearly a border town between Judah and Philistia on the western boundary shared by the two kingdoms.

According to the Chronicler's theology of immediate retribution, there is direct correspondence between a king's political power and his faithfulness to the tenets of Yahweh's covenant. Jehoram's political weakness is attested by his failure to control former Judean satellite states and cities. The author's theological commentary on the two revolts against Jehoram places blame directly on the king's sin of idolatry, implied in the references to the "high places" and the activity of the people in "prostituting themselves" (21:10b–11). By way of personal example and public policy, Jehoram is held responsible for leading God's people astray in their worship.

Thus, the rebellion of Jehoram becomes another example in the history of the Davidic monarchy of a successor undoing the work of his predecessor. In this case, the internal decay associated with Jehoram's apostasy not only nullifies the reforms of his father, Jehoshaphat, but also leads to the loss of gains made in foreign policy by both Asa and Jehoshaphat.

Along with royal speeches and prayers, the report of Elijah's letter to King Jehoram is typical of the kinds of material peculiar to the Chronicler in the nonsynoptic portions of his history. Critics have challenged the letter's authenticity, contending it is the creation of the Chronicler. Primary among the reasons for this is the omission of the letter in the Kings parallel, the northern kingdom focus of Elijah's prophetic ministry, and the fact that Elijah was not alive during the reign of Jehoram.

Selman, however, has cogently responded that although the presence of a letter from Elijah is unexpected, its authenticity need not be questioned.[3] For instance, Elijah was alive during part of Jehoram's reign since he was apparently a coregent with Jehoshaphat as early as 853 B.C. Prophetic documents like letters and written oracles are known at the same time period (cf. 1 Chron. 29:29; 2 Chron. 20:34). Finally, 2 Kings suggests that Elijah and Elisha were complementary prophets at least for a time and that Elijah's letter may have been written during this period of his old age before his translation into heaven (cf. 2 Kings 2:1–2).

The letter's contents reflect Elijah's confrontation with the house of Ahab in both subject matter and tone. Although the other features of ancient letters

3. Selman, 2 *Chronicles*, 435.

are lacking, the body of Elijah's letter is characteristic of Old Testament prophetic speech. The messenger formula ("this is what the LORD ... says," 21:12) identifies the source and authority of the message. The pattern of indictment followed by the pronouncement of judgment is typical of the structure of preexilic prophetic oracles. Jehoram's crimes are twofold: adhering to the ways of the kings of the rival northern kingdom and murdering his own brothers (21:13). The phrase "the ways of the kings of Israel" refers to Jeroboam's sin of idolatry, perpetuated by all his successors in Israel (1 Kings 14:9; cf. 15:34).

The expression "prostitute themselves" (21:13; Hiphil of *znb*) connotes spiritual harlotry—the worship of the Canaanite deities instead of God (1 Chron. 5:25; 2 Chron. 21:11, 13). According to Elijah's letter, God's judgment will reach as far as Jehoram's sin, impacting in reverse order the royal family and the people of Judah (2 Chron. 21:14). The king's punishment, a hideous and lingering disease (21:15), strikes at the heart of Jehoram's sin— his failure to recognize that kingship belongs to God and not to any human being. The humiliating malady exposes his mortality and mocks his dignity as royalty, calling to mind the admonition of the psalmist: "Do not put your trust in princes, in mortal men, who cannot save" (Ps. 146:3).

The Chronicler understands Jehoram's punishment as the work of God, the Lord of the nations and the Lord of history (2 Sam. 22:48; 2 Chron. 20:6; Ps. 33:10–11). The report of the revolt on the part of the Philistines and Arabs (2 Chron. 21:16b) validates the prophecy of Elijah against the royal household (21:14) and underscores the theme of immediate divine retribution in Chronicles. The capture (and eventual execution) of the royal family and the plundering of royal spoils (21:17) strikes a telling blow at the core values of kingship, humanly speaking. As Dillard has observed, "if progeny is a measure of divine favor, their loss shows divine anger."[4]

The reference to "the king's palace" (21:17) presupposes the knowledge that members of the royal family have been stationed in royal quarters in various fortified cities throughout the kingdom (cf. 21:3). Ironically, the purpose behind this maneuver was to prevent the massacre of the entire royal family in a single attack against Jerusalem. We must assume Ahaziah and his mother, Athaliah, remain in Jerusalem, thus explaining their survival of the invasion.[5]

The focus of the report of divine judgment against the house of Jehoram shifts to the king himself (21:18–19). Again, God is identified as the agent of justice in the punishment of Jehoram's sin (21:18; cf. v. 10). Selman observes

---

4. Dillard, *2 Chronicles*, 164; cf. Dennis Pardee, "Ancient Hebrew Epistolography," *JBL* 97 (1978): 322.

5. The NIV inserts "Ahaziah" for the variant form "Jehoahaz" found in the MT.

the language of Chronicles is reminiscent of the "Yahweh war" motif (i.e., God "aroused . . . the hostility of," 21:16), indicating the gravity of the sin of idolatry and justifying the severity of God's response.[6] The "aroused nations of the earth are Yahweh's servants for weal or woe."[7]

God is a jealous God, who will not share his glory with idols (Isa. 42:8). As in the case of Asa (16:12–14) and Uzziah (26:16–19), disobedience to God results in immediate punishment in the form of some serious physical ailment. Jehoram is afflicted with a humiliating and an incurable illness, described only as an excruciatingly painful disease of the bowels (21:14, 18).[8] Tragically, this descendant of David dies ignominiously, and even his own people refuse to honor him in death with the customary royal funeral fire (21:19; cf. 16:14).

The concluding regnal résumé (21:20) repeats information from the beginning résumé (21:5). The report shares in common with 2 Kings 8:23–24 only the fact that Jehoram is buried in the city of David. Sadly, his unpopularity is broadcast in the epitaph that Jehoram dies "to no one's regret" (2 Chron. 21:20b). Thompson has noted that the Chronicler's contempt for Jehoram extends even to the omission of the historical citation formula, thus preventing the consultation of sources for further information about the king (cf. 2 Kings 8:23).[9] The last words concerning Jehoram are both a parting insult of his person and a final assessment of his reign—he is denied burial in the royal tomb complex of the Davidic family (2 Chron. 21:20d). This is a fitting end for Jehoram, since he has walked in the ways of the house of Ahab, not David.

King Ahaziah (22:1–9)

THE CHRONICLER HURRIES to tell the story of Jehoram's son Ahaziah. His version abridges the fifty-six verses of 2 Kings 8:25–10:14 in just nine verses. The broad relationship of the two accounts may be represented as follows:

2 Chron. 22:1–6 = 2 Kings 8:25–29
2 Chron. 22:7 = 2 Kings 9:21
2 Chron. 22:8 = 2 Kings 10:13–14
2 Chron. 22:9 = 2 Kings 9:28

6. Selman, 2 Chronicles, 436.
7. Victor P. Hamilton, "עור," NIDOTTE, 3:358.
8. Along with the NEB, NKJV, and NRSV, the NIV understands the MT "two days" as an idiom for "two years," in keeping with the context, which suggests the protracted nature of the king's illness.
9. Thompson, 1, 2 Chronicles, 301.

Ahaziah's reign is treated almost like an extension of Jehoram's rule. The subject of the section is not so much the reigns of Jehoram, Ahaziah, and Athaliah but the "house of Ahab" and the threat it poses to the "house of Judah" and the Davidic dynasty (21:6; 22:3, 7, 10).

The parallel accounts are not without variations. For example, the Chronicler's historical interests primarily lie with the kingdom of Judah. Thus, the writer assumes some knowledge of the coup of Jehu in Israel as found in 2 Kings 9. The subtle addition of "he too" (2 Chron. 22:3) links the reigns of Kings Jehoram and Ahaziah, whom the Chronicler regards as an evil duo. The insertion that Ahaziah takes counsel from the "house of Ahab" (22:4) again signals the Chronicler's concern over the impact political alliances have on the history of the two monarchies.

The parallel accounts are not without problems. According to Dillard, the divergences between the two reports concerning the death of Ahaziah is one of the most difficult historical questions in the Old Testament.[10] The three essential differences usually cited by biblical commentators are the timing of the slaughter of the princes of Judah (whether before or after the death of Ahaziah, 22:8; cf. 2 Kings 10:12–14), the place of Ahaziah's death (2 Chron. 22:9; cf. 2 Kings 9:27), and the place of Ahaziah's burial (2 Chron. 22:9; cf. 2 Kings 9:28). Harmonizing the reports of Chronicles in detail with the synoptic parallels in Kings lies outside the scope of this commentary. It should be noted, however, in reference to the execution of the princes of Judah that the outline showing the relationship between the accounts of Kings and Chronicles clearly indicates the interests of the Chronicler are theological, not chronological. Likewise, note that Chronicles does not specify the place of Ahaziah's death or burial (2 Chron. 22:9). The argument from silence does not necessarily imply a conflict of fact in the two sources.

The account of King Ahaziah's reign consists of three brief reports: the regnal résumé and theological review (22:1–4), the alliance with Joram of Israel (22:5–6a), and the death report (22:6b–9). The one-year reign of Ahaziah is dated anywhere from 845–841 B.C., depending on the source. His brief tenure in the royal office is best placed in 842 or 841 B.C.

The Chronicler's résumé for Ahaziah (22:1–4) includes the succession and accession age formulas found in 2 Kings 8:25–27 but omits the corresponding date formula to the reign of the king of Israel. The expression "the people of Jerusalem" (2 Chron. 22:1) is difficult to interpret. The phrase may be a reference to the "people of the land," religious and political power brokers who installed kings during times of dynastic crisis. It is even possible that this expression should be understood exclusively as a group distinct from

10. Dillard, 2 *Chronicles*, 172.

the populace of the rest of Judah. This prompts Dillard to suggest that perhaps the installation of Ahaziah as king of Judah takes place without consultation or participation by the people of the outlying districts.[11]

The raiders in league with the Arabs who are responsible for slaying the older princes of Judah are probably Philistines (22:1; cf. 21:16–17). Ahaziah is thus the sole surviving heir of Jehoram and the Davidic line (21:17). This motif both begins and ends the literary unit, as Joash emerges as the sole survivor of Athaliah's murderous coup against the family of her own son (22:11). The reference to the killing of Ahaziah's older sons by marauders is another example of the theme of immediate divine retribution against a wicked king of Judah.

The name of Ahaziah's mother, Athaliah, is included in the regnal résumé for two reasons (22:2). (1) Her relationship to the dynasty of Omri as daughter of Ahab and Jezebel explains the influence of the "house of Ahab" on the kingdom of Judah. The author accents the negative theological review of the king's brief reign by associating him with his father in following the ways of "the house of Ahab" (22:3). (2) As a member of Ahab's family, Athaliah takes it upon herself to destroy the royal family of Judah (22:10). By virtue of her role as queen mother, she holds the important position of royal adviser, thus poisoning the counsel received by both her husband Jehoram and her son Ahaziah (cf. 1 Kings 15:13; 2 Kings 24:15).[12] The status and authority she enjoys as queen mother also enables her to fill the power vacuum left by the death of her son and to usurp the throne of David (cf. 2 Chron. 22:9).[13]

The Chronicler offers one example of such lethal counsel in the decision of Ahaziah to join forces with King Joram of the rival Israelite kingdom against a common enemy, Hazael king of Aram (22:5–6a). Such an alliance with the apostate state of Israel is doomed to failure, as the unfolding story demonstrates. Ramoth Gilead was a Levitical city of refuge in the eastern or Transjordan territory of the tribe of Gad (Deut. 4:43; Josh. 21:38). The city commanded a strategic location along the King's Highway. This made the site a frequent battleground for the armies of Israel and Aram as each nation sought to control the commerce along the trade route. Joram's father, Ahab, was killed in battle at Ramoth Gilead attempting to wrest by force what Ben-Hadad of Aram had ceded to Israel in a treaty after his defeat at Aphek (1 Kings 20:34).

We learn from the narrative that King Joram is wounded in battle at Ramoth Gilead by the Arameans (22:6a). Hoping to speed the healing of his injuries, Joram retreats to the safety of Jezreel (cf. 2 Kings 9:14–15). Jezreel

---

11. Ibid., 173.

12. See Andreasen, "The Role of the Queen Mother," 179–94.

13. The NIV reads "twenty-two" for the accession age of Ahaziah, following the Greek and Syriac versions, instead of the number "forty-two" in the MT.

was a town allotted to the tribe of Issachar and lay at the foot of Mount Gilboa on the plain of Jezreel (Josh. 19:18). Later, the summer palace of the Israelite kings was located there (1 Kings 18:45–46; 21:1). Jehu's purge of the house of Ahab was completed at Jezreel (2 Kings 10:6–11). It is there that Ahaziah visits his recuperating ally, only to meet his end (2 Chron. 22:6b). One cannot help but recall the long shadow Mount Gilboa casts on Israelite kingship, dating back to the death of King Saul (cf. 1 Chron. 10:1, 8).

The Chroniclers' theological commentary bluntly states that God "brought about Ahaziah's downfall" (22:7). Wilcock notes three reasons for Ahaziah's downfall: foreign influence in the form of false religion, family inheritance (with respect to the alliance by marriage of Judah and Israel), and personal responsibility (because neither true spirituality nor impiety is hereditary).[14] Jehu son of Nimshi becomes God's agent of justice in punishing the evil of both Joram of Israel and Ahaziah of Judah (22:7–8; cf. 2 Kings 9:24–29). While 2 Kings 9 relates the parallel destruction of "two houses" (Judah and Israel), the focus of Chronicles is exclusively on the "house of Judah." The message of the passage is alarmingly clear: God repays evil for evil almost immediately on those who fail to emulate David's example of righteous rule.

Although the sins of the house of Ahab perpetuated by King Ahaziah are unnamed in Chronicles, it seems they include idolatry, witchcraft, and a failure to trust in God as the Sovereign of Judah, as evidenced by "unholy" political alliances (cf. 2 Kings 9:22).[15] The Chronicler's emphasis on the divine judgment of the kings of Judah for trusting in diplomacy instead of God may serve as a subtle affirmation of the exclusivist and isolationist policies promoted during the reforms of Ezra and Nehemiah (cf. Ezra 9:1–2; Neh. 9).

Unlike King Joram, whose corpse is left exposed on the field of Naboth (2 Kings 9:26), Ahaziah is given a proper burial in the royal tomb complex of King David. This is due to a lingering respect for his grandfather Jehoshaphat (22:9b; cf. 2 Kings 9:28). The death of Ahaziah returns us to the theme of this section of the narrative: the conflict between God's promise to David of a dynasty forever and the apparent lack of an heir to the throne. The house of David has been purged of sin, but the end result seems worse than the combined reigns of Jehoram and Ahaziah. The "lamp" of David (2 Chron. 21:7) is in jeopardy of being extinguished by powerful Athaliah (22:9c). Dillard aptly notes that this lesson is not lost on the Chronicler's audience. Even as Davidic hopes were not doused by Ahaziah's sin or Athaliah's reign of terror, so too the Davidic hope remains alive in the postexilic period despite all appearances to the contrary.[16]

14. Wilcock, *The Message of Chronicles*, 202–7.
15. Dillard, *2 Chronicles*, 175.
16. Ibid.

The Interregnum of Athaliah (22:10–23:21)

THE STORY OF ATHALIAH and Joash follows 2 Kings 11:1–20 in large measure. The majority of the divergences are the result of the Chronicler's interest in accenting the role of the priests and Levites in the history of the Davidic monarchy. According to Selman, the differences between Chronicles and the parallel in 1 Kings permit three themes submerged in that earlier text to become central in the later version.[17] (1) The temple is a sacred place. It is the visible projection of the character of God and must be kept holy and clean (2 Chron. 23:6, 19). (2) God is faithful in fulfilling his promise made to maintain "a lamp" for the house of David (23:7; cf. 21:7). (3) "All the people" play an important role in installing Joash as king and in renewing Yahweh's covenant. This section includes five reports: the asylum of Joash with Jehosheba's help (22:10–12); the accession of Joash with Jehoaida's help (23:1–11); the execution of Athaliah (23:12–15); covenant renewal in Judah (23:16–19); the installation of King Joash (23:20–21).

The asylum of Joash with Jehosheba's help (22:10–12). Athaliah seizes the Davidic throne (cf. 2 Kings 11:1–3). The lack of opening and closing regnal résumés for her indicates neither historian considers Athaliah's reign legitimate. Rather, she is regarded as a usurper of royal power, and her tenure in office is deemed an interregnum. It seems likely that Athaliah is the daughter of the Phoenician princess Jezebel and King Ahab of Israel (2 Kings 8:18, 26).[18] Like her mother she worships the Canaanite fertility god Baal and foists Baal worship on the citizenry of the kingdom through manipulation of the king.

Athaliah tyrannizes Judah for six years (the dates assigned to her rule are typically within a year or two of 842–837 B.C.). She attempts to do what God himself will not do—completely destroy the house of David (22:10; cf. 21:7). The term "destroy" (Piel of *dbr*) has the sense "obliterate" or "exterminate" here. Whatever her motivation, Athaliah seeks to eliminate all rivals to the throne of David. According to Gray, much like Jehoram she seeks to quell any nationalist uprising under a prince from the royal family by massacring the Davidic line.[19]

In one sense, the report of Athaliah's usurpation of the Judean throne may be described as a tale of two women. Indeed, Allen has observed that the narrative "presents contrasted cameos of self-seeking exploitation and unselfish heroism."[20] One woman, Athaliah, seeks to destroy the family of David and rules the land for six years. The other, Jehosheba, works

---

17. Selman, 2 *Chronicles*, 444.
18. See Winfried Theil, "Athaliah," *ABD*, 1:511–12.
19. John Gray, *I and II Kings* (OTL, 2d ed.; Philadelphia: Westminster, 1970), 565.
20. Allen, *1, 2 Chronicles*, 323.

courageously and covertly to preserve the family of David during those same six years (22:11). Jehosheba is the daughter of Jehoram and probably the step-sister of Ahaziah. She is also the wife of the priest Jehoiada, who plays a prominent role in the rest of the narrative. This insertion by the Chronicler explains how the child comes to have asylum in the temple for six years. Thus, Joash becomes another in a series of vulnerable infants through whom God achieves his covenant purposes (cf. Ex. 2:1–10; 1 Sam. 1:24–28).

The name Jehosheba (Chronicles actually uses Jehoshabeath, a variant form of the name) means "Yahweh vows." Fittingly, God uses this faithful woman to keep his oath to maintain the lamp of David (cf. 21:7). No matter how gloomy the prospects, the destiny of the nation is secure in God's hands. The Chronicler's audience needs that reminder too!

The accession of Joash with Jehoiada's help (23:1–11). The coup led by Jehoiada the priest occurs during the seventh year of Athaliah's rule (or about 837 B.C.; 23:1). The parallel in 2 Kings 11:4 reports that Jehoiada makes a pact with military commanders and the Carites (mercenary soldiers who serve as royal bodyguards) to install Joash as the rightful heir to the Davidic throne. The Chronicler's account includes the Levites and the clan leaders of Judah in the conspiracy against Athaliah (2 Chron. 23:1–2). The conflation of the two narratives suggests that the revolt against Athaliah is carried out by a coalition of military and religious leaders in Judah. Jehoiada is not driven by selfish motives; rather, he appeals to the promise of God anchored in the Davidic covenant (23:3b; cf. 1 Chron. 17; 2 Chron. 21:7).

Jehoiada the priest is a clever strategist, planning his coup in three stages: first assembling a coalition of conspirators (23:1–3a), then strategically deploying armed guards to ensure the safety of the king (23:3b–7), and finally presenting Joash for public installation as king of Judah (23:8–11). Dillard's reminder that the history of Israel reveals that the Levites were acquainted with military procedures and warfare is helpful.[21] This would serve to strengthen the hand of the coalition of religious and military personnel against any attempts by the palace guards of Athaliah to quell the coup. It also helps explain Jehoiada's restrictions on the type of armed personnel permitted in the temple courtyard (23:5–6). The precise location where each unit of the armed guard is stationed is difficult to reconstruct, given the divergences between 2 Chronicles 23:4–6 and 2 Kings 11:5–8.[22] Suffice to say, the armed guards are given two orders: (1) slay anyone who enters the temple complex during the installation ceremony, and (2) stay close to the king at all times (2 Chron. 23:6–7).

Jehoiada's coup is a well-planned and carefully orchestrated event. There is no dissension in the ranks, as everyone does as he is ordered (23:8). The

---

21. Dillard, 2 *Chronicles*, 182.
22. Ibid.

conspiracy is shrewdly coordinated with the Sabbath observance (23:8b). The commotion of an assembly at the temple would have been in character with the Hebrew religious calendar. The Chronicler takes pains to note that the priests and Levites rotating off-duty for the Sabbath remain in the temple area as a show of solidarity for the new king.

The distribution of weapons is a precautionary measure (23:9). The spears and shields are probably ceremonial weapons (cf. 1 Chron. 18:7). The strategic deployment of armed guards completely encircle the child-king as he is presented to the public for installation (i.e., with men positioned behind the king between the pillars of the temple and the temple building proper and additional sentinels flanking Joash on the right and left in closed ranks extending to the entrance of the inner court of the temple precinct, 23:10). The installation of a king includes a coronation (a "crown" or diadem placed on the head of Joash, 23:11), anointing with oil (not mentioned here but known from the installation of David, 1 Chron. 11:3), and the presentation of a covenant document (2 Chron. 23:11b, probably a copy of the agreement mentioned previously [23:3]).

The execution of Athaliah (23:12–15). The enthusiastic tumult centered at the temple attracts Athaliah's attention—to the degree she goes to investigate for herself rather than send a royal servant (23:12). She is abruptly greeted by the sight of a coronation, that of a child-king wearing a crown and standing by his pillar at the entrance to the temple (23:13). The scene is reminiscent of the noise over Solomon's coronation that startled the usurper Adonijah and ultimately dashed all hope he held for ascending to David's throne (cf. 1 Kings 1:39–41).

According to 2 Kings 11:14, it was customary for the king to take a position near one of the two great pillars flanking the entrance from the city plaza to the inner court of the temple. King Solomon had the two bronze pillars cast and named them Jakin and Boaz (1 Kings 7:21). The origin of the Hebrew custom calling for the king to stand by one of the pillars is unspecified. In characteristic fashion, the Chronicler singles out the singers and the musicians for the role they play in the coronation of Joash (2 Chron. 23:13).

Commentators are quick to note the irony in the usurper Athaliah's cry of treason upon witnessing the coronation of Joash (23:13). Although for all she knows, this child-king is simply a puppet usurper installed by the religious aristocracy—since to her mind the Davidic line has been exterminated. Yet McConville points out that by her own standards, "there can be no treason, since . . . power is rightly held by those who can hold it."[23] Interestingly, Athaliah's long-awaited exposure and censure as an illegitimate ruler affords

---

23. McConville, *I and II Chronicles*, 206.

the occasion for a public test of loyalty to the new regime. Jehoiada the priest orders that any who follow Athaliah from the ranks are to be executed as well (23:14).

The cooperation of the priests with army commanders suggests that a coalition of religious and military leaders is responsible for the coup that elevates Joash to the throne. Jehoiada the priest also decrees that Athaliah is be executed outside temple precincts, so not to defile the sacred site (23:14). Unfortunately, Jehoiada's directive cannot deliver his own son Zechariah from a similar fate later in Joash's reign (24:21). The site of Athaliah's execution, the Horse Gate of the palace, is not to be confused with the Horse Gate of the city wall of Jerusalem (23:15; cf. Neh. 3:28; Jer. 31:40).

Covenant renewal in Judah (23:16–19). The coronation of Joash climaxes with a covenant-renewal ceremony led by Jehoiada the priest (23:16). Two distinct but related covenants are enacted in the aftermath of the coup against Athaliah. The first covenant is ratified by the king and the people of Jerusalem, reestablishing the authority of Davidic kingship in Judah (23:3, 11; cf. 2 Kings 11:17b). The second pact is a covenant-renewal ceremony binding king and people in obedience to the law of Moses (2 Chron. 23:16; cf. 2 Kings 11:17a).

The covenant renewal with Yahweh prompts the reform of religious practice in Judah. False worship is purged from the land by destroying the temple of Baal in Jerusalem and executing the priest of Baal, Mattan (23:17; cf. Deut. 13:5–10). Little is known about the temple of Baal in Jerusalem, but it may have been built as part of a marriage contract between Jehoram and Athaliah (cf. 2 Kings 11:1–8). The first covenant rids the land of Athaliah, the illegitimate usurper of the Davidic throne, and reinstates Davidic kingship in Judah. The second covenant renews Yahweh's relationship with Judah as God's people and reorganizes temple worship according to the law of Moses. The destruction of the Baal temple in Jerusalem and the purification of temple worship mirrors similar reforms taking place in the northern kingdom at the same time under the leadership of Jehu (cf. 2 Kings 9). For the Chronicler, the restoration of proper temple worship is no less important than the reestablishment of Davidic kingship in Judah.

The report of Jehoiada's appointment of guards or doorkeepers at the gates of the temple (23:19) is shared with 2 Kings 11:18c, but 2 Chronicles 23:18 is unique to Chronicles. The Chronicler's expansion of the events surrounding the coronation of Joash and the covenant ceremonies emphasizes the role of the priests in overseeing the temple ritual, the restructuring of sacrificial worship according to the law of Moses, and the role of the third division of the Levites as gatekeepers in maintaining the sanctity of the temple precinct (2 Chron. 23:18–19).

The installation of King Joash (23:20–21). The Chronicles narrative recounting the installation of Joash returns to the parallel of 2 Kings 11:19–20 with minor variations. For instance, the processional includes "the nobles" and "the rulers of the people" instead of the "Carites" and "the guards" (probably an updating of terminology for the audience). The processional leading Joash from the temple to the palace is symbolic, because in one sense Yahweh is returning to the throne of Judah along with the Davidic descendant.

The installation of Joash on the royal throne (2 Chron. 23:20) marks the end of the interregnum under Athaliah. Thanks to Jehosheba and Jehoiada, there has been, in one sense, no interruption of Davidic kingship in Judah— Joash has been there all along. Typically, the Chronicler employs the expression the people "rejoiced" (*śmḥ*) to signify the fact that the will of God is now being observed (23:21; cf. 1 Chron. 29:9; 2 Chron. 15:15; 29:36). A second idiom using the word "quiet" (*šqṭ*) is often found in Chronicles to denote divine blessing on those who are obedient to God's word (cf. 1 Chron. 4:40; 22:9; 2 Chron. 13:23; 14:4–5). The biblical adages hold true: The violence of the wicked returns to them (Ps. 7:15–16; Prov. 26:27; Eccl. 10:8), and the judgment of the Lord leads to "quietness" in the land (Ps. 76:8).

THE ONE AND THE MANY. One of the fascinating aspects of the cultural context of the biblical world is the relationship of the "one" (i.e., a person) to the "many" (i.e., the clan, tribe, or nation). In sociological terms we are referring to the interface of the individual with the group. Biblical scholars have described the predominance of the "many" or national identity in the worldview of the ancients as "corporate personality" or "group solidarity."[24]

The basic concept of corporate personality means that the whole group may function as a single individual or, alternately, a single individual may represent the group. Characteristically in a group-centric society, the individual submits personal rights to the collective good of the group, seeks to conform to group norms, and promotes the interdependence of the group.[25] Typically, group membership among the societies of the ancient world

---

24. See, e.g., H. Wheeler Robinson, *Corporate Personality in Ancient Israel*, rev. ed. (Philadelphia: Fortress, 1980); John J. Pilch, *Introducing the Cultural Context of the Old Testament* (New York: Paulist, 1991), 95–116; Joel Kaminsky, *Corporate Responsibility in the Hebrew Bible* (JSOTSup 196; Sheffield: Sheffield Academic Press, 1995).

25. On the traits of "group solidarity," see Pilch, *Introducing the Cultural Context*, 97–98.

included both dead ancestors and the unborn. In one sense, then, "the group could be conceived as living forever" since its corporate identity extended beyond the present to the both the past and the future.[26]

This dynamic relationship of the "one" to the "many" in group solidarity is readily seen in the story of Achan's sin following the battle of Jericho and its impact on the nation of Israel and his family (Josh. 7). Achan's sins of covetousness, theft, and false testimony for failing to confess his transgression when given ample opportunity compromised the holiness of the whole nation as God's covenant community (7:11). Not only was Achan put to death for his own sin, but also his family was stoned for presumed complicity in their father's crime (7:25; cf. Ex. 20:5; Deut. 24:16). Furthermore, Achan's violation of Yahweh's taboo on the plunder of Jericho had ramifications for the entire nation insofar as the rout of the Hebrews in the first battle at Ai occurred because "Israel" had sinned (Josh. 7:5, 11).

The idea of group solidarity, however, does pose certain theological problems heard especially in the complaints and laments of the righteous concerning God's justice. The destruction and exile of both the divided kingdoms of Israel and Judah forecast by the prophets of God meant that the so-called "righteous remnant" suffered the same fate as those who had abandoned Yahweh's covenant (cf. Hab. 1:13). Thus, in the aftermath of the horrors of the Babylonian exile, the Jews raised the "sour grapes" parable in protest of the principle that one generation should bear the punishment for the sin of another (Jer. 31:29; Ezek. 18:2). In response, both Jeremiah and Ezekiel predicted a redefinition of the relationship of the "one" to the "many" in the new covenant, which would bring an even greater degree of individual responsibility and personal accountability before God (Jer. 31:30; Ezek. 18:4, 30). As late as Malachi's preaching, the Israelites raised the lingering question of the merit of covenant obedience to Yahweh when it appeared that God punished the righteous for the deeds of the wicked (Mal. 3:14–15).

Even into the New Testament period, Jesus is questioned as to the cause of divine judgment in an individual's life, whether it should be attributed to that person's sin or the parents' sin (John 9:2). Jesus' response is interesting because it asserts that the principle of divine retribution cannot be applied wholesale to individual misfortune (cf. Luke 13:4–5). Paul too recognized that vestiges of corporate personality remain in the new covenant since the sin of an individual put the entire church or community of faith at risk of divine judgment (1 Cor. 5:6).

We have already observed that the theme of "all Israel" is foundational to the Chronicler's retelling of Hebrew history (see "Audience" in the intro-

26. Robinson, *Corporate Personality*, 27.

duction). The widespread use of this phrase in Chronicles suggests the writer has in mind the citizenry of the entire nation, including the political leadership, the religious leadership, and the general populace. The intentional reference to "all Israel" in the context of the divided monarchies indicates that the writer is attempting to heal wounds of schism among the tribes as a result of the rift caused by the competing kingdoms of Israel and Judah. Moreover, the emphasis on the dual theological themes of the Davidic covenant and temple worship in Chronicles serves to remind the postexilic community that their unity is assured by divine promise and exhibited in their common worship of Yahweh, the God of the covenant. Finally, the Chronicler's representation of the nation by appealing to an outstanding personality like Abraham or David illustrates that the nation of Israel as a group includes its past, present, and future members.

Yet as important as the corporate identity of "all Israel" is for the Chronicler, he does not overlook the strategic role of the "one" in relationship to the "many." He betrays his interest in the individual almost immediately in the anecdotal stories and heroic acts inserted within the tribal genealogies. In point of fact, the "two ways" by which the writer characterizes the Israelite kings are identified with individuals: the way of David and the way of Ahab. Even this section of Chronicles is less about the Judean monarchy and more about two contrasting individuals: "one" Athaliah acting for the "many" for evil purposes, and "one" Jehoiada acting for the "many" for good purposes.

As a perceptive historian the Chronicler is careful to recognize and document the strategic role of certain individuals in the ebb and flow of Israel's history. As a clever writer he helps us appreciate the vital sociological relationship between the "one" and the "many" in his retelling the story of Davidic kingship. As an insightful theologian, he anticipates the New Testament theology of the "one" acting for the "many" in Paul's teaching of human sin and divine redemption rooted in Adam and in Jesus Christ as the "second Adam" (Rom. 5:12–17).

INDIVIDUAL AND COMMUNITY. The current cultural transition from a somewhat monolithic modernist worldview to eclectic postmodernist worldviews has witnessed paradigm transformations in several sociological and anthropological categories.[27] One of these philosophical shifts has occurred along the "fault line" of the "one" and the "many" in contemporary sociology. There appears to a growing trend toward

---

27. Charles Jencks, ed., *A Post-Modern Reader* (New York: St. Martin's, 1992), 10–39.

the rejection of the "individualism" of modernism and the acceptance of the notion of "community" embraced by postmodernism.[28] Individualism or the autonomy of self is a by-product of Enlightenment rationalism and may be defined as the conception that all values, rights, and duties originate in the individual—that is, an idolatry of self and self-interest.

The ideological countercurrent of postmodernism places a renewed emphasis on group identity and communal relationships. This has been stirred, in part, by an increasing awareness of the "global village" concept as a result of the rapid growth and spread of communications technology and the interdependence of national economies. This movement to "relocate" in a community is also sparked by a resurgence of historical memory in our society. This postmodern "classicism" seeks to transcend the modern paradigm by looking to the past, especially the ancient and medieval periods of Western history. In keeping with its heterotopian and pluralistic underpinnings, postmodernism also continues to dismantle traditional cultural paradigms by celebrating all that is non-Western and all that is representative of the "marginalized" and "victimized" populations of the world. Naturally in this model there is the danger of what Veith calls the "new tribalism," in which segmented and isolated communities replace the individual as "islands" in culture.[29]

The same trend toward relocation in community may be observed in the Christian subculture, especially with respect to worship. The historical understanding of the church as the community of God's presence in the world is reemerging today. The "lone ranger" faith of the modernist paradigm is giving way to the idea of the celebration of mystery and the discovery of knowledge with the people of God in a faith community.[30] The peril of the pendulum, however, is ever present. In the discarding of enlightenment "individualism," we must be careful not to deny or neglect our "individuality," by which we mean one's total character and personality, those attributes and abilities that distinguish a particular human being as unique from all others.

Walter Brueggemann has forwarded a thoughtful and compelling thesis that the image of God in the human person is essentially relational and that the individual is a "covenant partner" with Yahweh.[31] According to him, the characteristic markings of our covenantal humanness are commensurate with attributes of God's nature and person: Yahweh is sovereign, Yahweh is faithful, and Yahweh is covenantal in the enactment of his sovereignty in that he authorizes the human person to represent him as a transactional partner in

---

28. See ibid., 34–39; Webber, *Ancient Future Faith*, 37.

29. Veith, *PostModern Times*, 143–56.

30. Cf. Webber, *Ancient Future Faith*, 34–37, 78–83.

31. Walter Brueggemann, *Theology of the Old Testament* (Minneapolis: Fortress, 1997), 453–54.

accomplishing God's purposes for creation.[32] He has identified a triad of disciplines of our humanness that facilitate this "partnering" with God in the promotion of justice and well-being in the world, such as listening, discerning, and trusting.

The individual who listens to God obeys his Word. The discerning person manages the generous mystery of God's goodness in respectful and constructive ways for the benefit of creation and human society. The trusting human being has unshakable confidence in the reliability of Yahweh and his Word. One of the merits of Brueggemann's model of the person as Yahweh's partner is that it respects the tension between God's sovereignty and human freedom. It also affirms the value of the individual in community and recognizes the importance of individuality in the divine scheme for restoring all creation. Only such an approach can explain the "venturesome initiative" of a spunky teenager who accepts Goliath's challenge to engage in a seemingly one-sided duel (1 Sam. 17:32), a brash adviser whose counsel thwarts the preeminent political adviser of the day (2 Sam. 17:14), or even an insubordinate princess who betrays her own parents by kidnapping a child from the royal nursery (2 Chron. 22:11—12).

The books of Chronicles afford ample opportunity to preach and teach these disciplines of our humanness through character studies—both positive and negative. For example, Jehoiada the priest is a study in courageous "listening (obedience)" to the word of Yahweh when he "showed his strength" (23:1) and set events in motion to honor the "promise of God" concerning Davidic kingship (23:3). Heroic Jehosheba is a marvelous example of "discernment" in her well-managed and carefully guarded decision to "kidnap" Joash and hide him away "for the sake of the community in the service of Yahweh's will for justice."[33]

By way of negative example, the usurper Athaliah illustrates the discipline of trust gone awry in her unchecked willingness to "assert" her power for the destruction of the family of David (22:10). As Brueggemann has noted, the courage to assert oneself in "venturesome initiative" must be tempered by the "confidence to yield" in faith to the sovereignty to God.[34] One without the other dissolves the partnership with God to which the person is called and overturns the justice and well-being God intends to promote in creation through that partnership.

Brueggemann introduces another set of markings of our humanness made necessary by the Fall and the onset of human sinfulness. This second grouping

32. Ibid., 459.
33. Ibid., 464.
34. Ibid., 459.

of disciplines "emerges when the individual is left in 'the Pit.'"[35] Trouble happens in our fallen world. It comes to human beings in many hideous forms: illness, injustice, oppression, isolation, and inevitably death. A life in crisis often compels the individual to seek God in prayer, specifically in the disciplines of complaint, petition, and thanksgiving.[36] The complaint or lament is the personal expression of honest doubt to God about his goodness given in a particular situation of distress in the life circumstance of that individual. The petition is an act of self-insistence in which the individual presents personal needs, cares, and concerns to God (e.g., 1 Sam. 1:17; Ps. 20:5). The response of thanksgiving specifically acknowledges the goodness of God in transforming the situation prompting the complaint (e.g., Ps. 30:10–12).

The purpose of the prayer sequence is to invoke divine intervention, appealing to the power, goodness, and mercy of God to change the circumstance that has the person in the "pit." The result of this sequence of complaint, petition, and thanksgiving is restored relationship with God—a rehabilitation of the individual as Yahweh's partner. Ultimately, according to Brueggemann, this relocation of the person in covenant partnership with God gives rise to praise and hope[37]—praise because only God can redeem a person's life from the pit (Ps. 40:2), and hope because God's effective intervention dispels human fear (42:5, 11; 56:3, 11).[38]

As modernism gives way to postmodernism and both secular society and the Christian church recover a new sense of collective identity in their denial of "individualism" and rediscovery of "community," let us not forget the Chronicler's affirmation of human "individuality." His emphasis on named individuals in the genealogical prologue and the narrative history of the Israelite monarchies reminds each of us of our uniqueness and importance as Yahweh's "listening, discerning, and trusting partner" in the ever-unfolding drama of redemption. In the stories of a man like Jehoiada and a woman like Jehosheba, the Chronicler proclaims that each person is indeed fearfully and wonderfully made in the image of our God (Ps. 139). More than this, the Chronicler reminds us that each person of faith in the God of the Bible becomes an integral player on the stage of redemptive history as he or she steps out and "shows strength" with the help of the Holy Spirit (2 Chron. 23:1). His record of Hebrew history becomes an invitation and exhortation to renew our partnership with Yahweh in the making of "His-story" as Jesus Christ continues to build his church in the world!

---

35. Ibid., 470.
36. Ibid., 470–74.
37. Ibid., 476.
38. On the structure of the psalmic lament form, see Anderson, *Out of the Depths*, 60–62.

JOASH WAS SEVEN years old when he became king, and he reigned in Jerusalem forty years. His mother's name was Zibiah; she was from Beersheba. ²Joash did what was right in the eyes of the LORD all the years of Jehoiada the priest. ³Jehoiada chose two wives for him, and he had sons and daughters.

⁴Some time later Joash decided to restore the temple of the LORD. ⁵He called together the priests and Levites and said to them, "Go to the towns of Judah and collect the money due annually from all Israel, to repair the temple of your God. Do it now." But the Levites did not act at once.

⁶Therefore the king summoned Jehoiada the chief priest and said to him, "Why haven't you required the Levites to bring in from Judah and Jerusalem the tax imposed by Moses the servant of the LORD and by the assembly of Israel for the Tent of the Testimony?"

⁷Now the sons of that wicked woman Athaliah had broken into the temple of God and had used even its sacred objects for the Baals.

⁸At the king's command, a chest was made and placed outside, at the gate of the temple of the LORD. ⁹A proclamation was then issued in Judah and Jerusalem that they should bring to the LORD the tax that Moses the servant of God had required of Israel in the desert. ¹⁰All the officials and all the people brought their contributions gladly, dropping them into the chest until it was full. ¹¹Whenever the chest was brought in by the Levites to the king's officials and they saw that there was a large amount of money, the royal secretary and the officer of the chief priest would come and empty the chest and carry it back to its place. They did this regularly and collected a great amount of money. ¹²The king and Jehoiada gave it to the men who carried out the work required for the temple of the LORD. They hired masons and carpenters to restore the LORD's temple, and also workers in iron and bronze to repair the temple.

¹³The men in charge of the work were diligent, and the repairs progressed under them. They rebuilt the temple of

God according to its original design and reinforced it. ¹⁴When they had finished, they brought the rest of the money to the king and Jehoiada, and with it were made articles for the LORD's temple: articles for the service and for the burnt offerings, and also dishes and other objects of gold and silver. As long as Jehoiada lived, burnt offerings were presented continually in the temple of the LORD.

¹⁵Now Jehoiada was old and full of years, and he died at the age of a hundred and thirty. ¹⁶He was buried with the kings in the City of David, because of the good he had done in Israel for God and his temple.

¹⁷After the death of Jehoiada, the officials of Judah came and paid homage to the king, and he listened to them. ¹⁸They abandoned the temple of the LORD, the God of their fathers, and worshiped Asherah poles and idols. Because of their guilt, God's anger came upon Judah and Jerusalem. ¹⁹Although the LORD sent prophets to the people to bring them back to him, and though they testified against them, they would not listen.

²⁰Then the Spirit of God came upon Zechariah son of Jehoiada the priest. He stood before the people and said, "This is what God says: 'Why do you disobey the LORD's commands? You will not prosper. Because you have forsaken the LORD, he has forsaken you.'"

²¹But they plotted against him, and by order of the king they stoned him to death in the courtyard of the LORD's temple. ²²King Joash did not remember the kindness Zechariah's father Jehoiada had shown him but killed his son, who said as he lay dying, "May the LORD see this and call you to account."

²³At the turn of the year, the army of Aram marched against Joash; it invaded Judah and Jerusalem and killed all the leaders of the people. They sent all the plunder to their king in Damascus. ²⁴Although the Aramean army had come with only a few men, the LORD delivered into their hands a much larger army. Because Judah had forsaken the LORD, the God of their fathers, judgment was executed on Joash. ²⁵When the Arameans withdrew, they left Joash severely wounded. His officials conspired against him for murdering the son of Jehoiada the priest, and they killed him in his bed. So he died and was buried in the City of David, but not in the tombs of the kings.

²⁶Those who conspired against him were Zabad, son of Shimeath an Ammonite woman, and Jehozabad, son of Shimrith a Moabite woman. ²⁷The account of his sons, the many prophecies about him, and the record of the restoration of the temple of God are written in the annotations on the book of the kings. And Amaziah his son succeeded him as king.

²⁵:¹Amaziah was twenty-five years old when he became king, and he reigned in Jerusalem twenty-nine years. His mother's name was Jehoaddin; she was from Jerusalem. ²He did what was right in the eyes of the LORD, but not wholeheartedly. ³After the kingdom was firmly in his control, he executed the officials who had murdered his father the king. ⁴Yet he did not put their sons to death, but acted in accordance with what is written in the Law, in the Book of Moses, where the LORD commanded: "Fathers shall not be put to death for their children, nor children put to death for their fathers; each is to die for his own sins."

⁵Amaziah called the people of Judah together and assigned them according to their families to commanders of thousands and commanders of hundreds for all Judah and Benjamin. He then mustered those twenty years old or more and found that there were three hundred thousand men ready for military service, able to handle the spear and shield. ⁶He also hired a hundred thousand fighting men from Israel for a hundred talents of silver.

⁷But a man of God came to him and said, "O king, these troops from Israel must not march with you, for the LORD is not with Israel—not with any of the people of Ephraim. ⁸Even if you go and fight courageously in battle, God will overthrow you before the enemy, for God has the power to help or to overthrow."

⁹Amaziah asked the man of God, "But what about the hundred talents I paid for these Israelite troops?"

The man of God replied, "The LORD can give you much more than that."

¹⁰So Amaziah dismissed the troops who had come to him from Ephraim and sent them home. They were furious with Judah and left for home in a great rage.

¹¹Amaziah then marshaled his strength and led his army to the Valley of Salt, where he killed ten thousand men of Seir. ¹²The army of Judah also captured ten thousand men alive,

took them to the top of a cliff and threw them down so that all were dashed to pieces.

¹³Meanwhile the troops that Amaziah had sent back and had not allowed to take part in the war raided Judean towns from Samaria to Beth Horon. They killed three thousand people and carried off great quantities of plunder.

¹⁴When Amaziah returned from slaughtering the Edomites, he brought back the gods of the people of Seir. He set them up as his own gods, bowed down to them and burned sacrifices to them. ¹⁵The anger of the LORD burned against Amaziah, and he sent a prophet to him, who said, "Why do you consult this people's gods, which could not save their own people from your hand?"

¹⁶While he was still speaking, the king said to him, "Have we appointed you an adviser to the king? Stop! Why be struck down?"

So the prophet stopped but said, "I know that God has determined to destroy you, because you have done this and have not listened to my counsel."

¹⁷After Amaziah king of Judah consulted his advisers, he sent this challenge to Jehoash son of Jehoahaz, the son of Jehu, king of Israel: "Come, meet me face to face."

¹⁸But Jehoash king of Israel replied to Amaziah king of Judah: "A thistle in Lebanon sent a message to a cedar in Lebanon, 'Give your daughter to my son in marriage.' Then a wild beast in Lebanon came along and trampled the thistle underfoot. ¹⁹You say to yourself that you have defeated Edom, and now you are arrogant and proud. But stay at home! Why ask for trouble and cause your own downfall and that of Judah also?"

²⁰Amaziah, however, would not listen, for God so worked that he might hand them over to Jehoash, because they sought the gods of Edom. ²¹So Jehoash king of Israel attacked. He and Amaziah king of Judah faced each other at Beth Shemesh in Judah. ²²Judah was routed by Israel, and every man fled to his home. ²³Jehoash king of Israel captured Amaziah king of Judah, the son of Joash, the son of Ahaziah, at Beth Shemesh. Then Jehoash brought him to Jerusalem and broke down the wall of Jerusalem from the Ephraim Gate to the Corner Gate—a section about six hundred feet long. ²⁴He took all the gold and silver and all the articles found in the temple of

God that had been in the care of Obed-Edom, together with the palace treasures and the hostages, and returned to Samaria.

²⁵Amaziah son of Joash king of Judah lived for fifteen years after the death of Jehoash son of Jehoahaz king of Israel. ²⁶As for the other events of Amaziah's reign, from beginning to end, are they not written in the book of the kings of Judah and Israel? ²⁷From the time that Amaziah turned away from following the LORD, they conspired against him in Jerusalem and he fled to Lachish, but they sent men after him to Lachish and killed him there. ²⁸He was brought back by horse and was buried with his fathers in the City of Judah.

^{26:1}Then all the people of Judah took Uzziah, who was sixteen years old, and made him king in place of his father Amaziah. ²He was the one who rebuilt Elath and restored it to Judah after Amaziah rested with his fathers.

³Uzziah was sixteen years old when he became king, and he reigned in Jerusalem fifty-two years. His mother's name was Jecoliah; she was from Jerusalem. ⁴He did what was right in the eyes of the LORD, just as his father Amaziah had done. ⁵He sought God during the days of Zechariah, who instructed him in the fear of God. As long as he sought the LORD, God gave him success.

⁶He went to war against the Philistines and broke down the walls of Gath, Jabneh and Ashdod. He then rebuilt towns near Ashdod and elsewhere among the Philistines. ⁷God helped him against the Philistines and against the Arabs who lived in Gur Baal and against the Meunites. ⁸The Ammonites brought tribute to Uzziah, and his fame spread as far as the border of Egypt, because he had become very powerful.

⁹Uzziah built towers in Jerusalem at the Corner Gate, at the Valley Gate and at the angle of the wall, and he fortified them. ¹⁰He also built towers in the desert and dug many cisterns, because he had much livestock in the foothills and in the plain. He had people working his fields and vineyards in the hills and in the fertile lands, for he loved the soil.

¹¹Uzziah had a well-trained army, ready to go out by divisions according to their numbers as mustered by Jeiel the secretary and Maaseiah the officer under the direction of Hananiah, one of the royal officials. ¹²The total number of family leaders over the fighting men was 2,600. ¹³Under their

command was an army of 307,500 men trained for war, a powerful force to support the king against his enemies. [14]Uzziah provided shields, spears, helmets, coats of armor, bows and slingstones for the entire army. [15]In Jerusalem he made machines designed by skillful men for use on the towers and on the corner defenses to shoot arrows and hurl large stones. His fame spread far and wide, for he was greatly helped until he became powerful.

[16]But after Uzziah became powerful, his pride led to his downfall. He was unfaithful to the LORD his God, and entered the temple of the LORD to burn incense on the altar of incense. [17]Azariah the priest with eighty other courageous priests of the LORD followed him in. [18]They confronted him and said, "It is not right for you, Uzziah, to burn incense to the LORD. That is for the priests, the descendants of Aaron, who have been consecrated to burn incense. Leave the sanctuary, for you have been unfaithful; and you will not be honored by the LORD God."

[19]Uzziah, who had a censer in his hand ready to burn incense, became angry. While he was raging at the priests in their presence before the incense altar in the LORD's temple, leprosy broke out on his forehead. [20]When Azariah the chief priest and all the other priests looked at him, they saw that he had leprosy on his forehead, so they hurried him out. Indeed, he himself was eager to leave, because the LORD had afflicted him.

[21]King Uzziah had leprosy until the day he died. He lived in a separate house—leprous, and excluded from the temple of the LORD. Jotham his son had charge of the palace and governed the people of the land.

[22]The other events of Uzziah's reign, from beginning to end, are recorded by the prophet Isaiah son of Amoz. [23]Uzziah rested with his fathers and was buried near them in a field for burial that belonged to the kings, for people said, "He had leprosy." And Jotham his son succeeded him as king.

As in the preceding section (21:4–23:21), the main genre of this literary unit of Chronicles is report. The Chronicler features the reigns of three kings following the execution of the usurper Athaliah: the child-king Joash, his son and successor Amaziah, and his son and successor Uzziah (also known as Azariah, 2 Kings 15:1). The narrative continues a pattern introduced with King Jehoram, that of framing each royal record with an opening and closing regnal résumé. Typically, the opening résumé consists of formulaic expressions containing basic information: the accession age, the length and place of reign, the identification of the queen mother, and a theological review. Likewise, the closing résumé usually includes a citation of source formula, a succession formula, and a notice of death and burial formula.

The Chronicler's account of King Joash (24:1–27) roughly parallels 2 Kings 12:1–21. The same is true for the reign of King Amaziah (2 Chron. 25:1–28//2 Kings 14:1–20). The Chronicler, however, greatly expands his review of King Uzziah from the parallel in Kings (2 Chron. 26:1–4, 21–23//2 Kings 14:21–15:3, 5–7; 2 Chron. 26:5–20 is essentially unique to Chronicles). The divergences between these two texts are attributed to differing sources and the peculiar methods and pointed theological interests of the Chronicler when compared to the writer of Kings.[1]

Theme and structure are intertwined in this section. The pattern of early success contrasted with later failure ties the records of Joash, Amaziah, and Uzziah as a literary unit. This is in keeping with the Chronicler's keen interest in the theology of divine retribution, especially the immediate impact of reward and punishment in the king's reign. Thus, each royal record consists of two parts: a rehearsal of blessing and prosperity as a result of the king's obedience to God, followed by a report of his apostasy and its detrimental religious and political consequences. This motif is not new, as the same literary pattern characterized Rehoboam (chs. 11–12) and Asa (chs. 14–16). But sadly, something has changed in these royal reports, as Selman carefully observes: "Positive balancing factors at the end of these reigns are no longer to be found."[2]

In great hope and faith for his dynasty, David prayed that his successor(s) would serve God with "wholehearted devotion" (1 Chron. 29:19). Tragically, each of these kings fails to maintain covenant loyalty with Yahweh and falls into apostasy. Thus, we read about Joash, who "abandoned . . . the LORD . . . and worshiped . . . idols" (24:18); about Amaziah, who "turned

---

1. See the discussions in Dillard, 2 Chronicles, 187–88; Williamson, 1 and 2 Chronicles, 318–19.
2. Selman, 2 Chronicles, 450.

away from following the LORD" (25:27); and about Uzziah, who "was unfaithful to the LORD his God" (26:16).

Like the previous narrative unit, this section also incorporates a theme common to the Hebrew wisdom tradition. According to the proverbs of Solomon, "the way of a fool seems right to him, but a wise man listens to advice" (Prov. 12:15). Unfortunately, Joash, Amaziah, and Uzziah all spurn advice to their own demise (cf. 2 Chron. 24:20–21; 25:15–16; 26:18–19). This unwise behavior is not unrelated to their negative theological review, since "the advice of the wicked is deceitful" (Prov. 12:5). Either by rejecting wise counsel or by endorsing poor counsel, each of the three kings is foolishly led astray—with predictable results!

Joash (24:1–27)

OPENING REGNAL RÉSUMÉ (24:1–3). The opening résumé for the most part repeats the information found in 2 Kings 12:1–2. Given his almost exclusive focus on the kingdom of Judah, the Chronicler characteristically omits the synchronism to the king of Israel (i.e., the seventh year of Jehu). He also fails to mention the "instruction" (*yarah*) of the priest Jehoiada that keeps Joash faithful to Yahweh's covenant (cf. 2 Kings 12:2). The forty-year reign of Joash is dated variously between 840 and 796 B.C. The Old Testament chronology informing this study dates his rule from about 835 to 796 B.C.

The Chronicler divides the reign of Joash into two distinct and contrasting periods: the good years of his early rule under the tutelage of Jehoiada and the later years of apostasy. For this reason, the reference to the "high places" in the regnal résumé of 2 Kings 12:3 is lumped together with the events associated with Joash's unfaithfulness (cf. 2 Chron. 24:18). Instead, the Chronicler refers to the progeny of Joash (24:3), perhaps using the source mentioned in the closing résumé (24:27). This information is unique to Chronicles, and one assumes it is registered as part of the king's favorable theological review since children are a sign of divine blessing (cf. 11:18–21; 13:21). The arrangement of two marriages for Joash by the priest Jehoida (24:3) is in keeping with the Mosaic law (cf. Ex. 21:10–11). It is probably an attempt to ensure the viability of the Davidic line, given the recent episodes of fratricide and infanticide against the royal family.

Jehoiada and Joash (24:4–16). The favorable report concerning Joash's reign centers on the dual themes of the renovation of Yahweh's temple and the figure of Jehoiada as the ideal high priest. The temple of Solomon has apparently fallen into a general state of disrepair. In addition, Athaliah not only usurped the Davidic throne but also seized the temple and implemented Baal worship there. The desecration of the sanctuary included structural damage as well (24:7). The reference to the "sons of ... Athaliah" (24:7) is puzzling, since she had them murdered. Perhaps the expression is used figuratively to denote her followers or adherents, or perhaps her sons conspired in the desecration of the temple before their own deaths.

This portion of Chronicles is only loosely tied to the parallel in 2 Kings 12:4–16, making the reconstruction of the events related to the royal initiative for fund raising and the eventual temple repair difficult to piece together. The lack of specific chronological referents compounds the ambiguity (cf. 2 Kings 12:6, where we learn that the compromise hammered out between the king and the priests takes place in the twenty-third year of Joash's reign). The sequence of events recorded in Kings and Chronicles resulting in the renovation of Yahweh's temple in Jerusalem may be harmonized as follows:

- Joash orders the priests to go to the people town by town and solicit money for the renovation of the temple (2 Kings 12:4–5; 2 Chron. 24:4–5).
- Kings mentions three sources of revenue (2 Kings 12:4), but Chronicles highlights only one—the annual tax imposed by Moses for the construction and maintenance of the tabernacle (2 Chron. 24:5–6; cf. Ex. 30:12–16). The description of the Mosiac tabernacle as the "Tent of the Testimony" (Heb. ʾedut) is unique in Chronicles and occurs elsewhere only in Numbers 9:15; 17:7, 8; 18:2.
- The priests and Levites stall in obeying the king's command—perhaps balking at the idea of reallocating funds intended for the support of temple staff (2 Kings 12:6; 2 Chron. 24:5). (This report of insubordination on the part of priests and Levites is a rare negative review of Levitical behavior in Chronicles.) Joash may also be attempting to reassert royal authority over an area that Jehoiada assumed responsibility for while the king was still the ward of the high priest. It is even possible that the royal coffers are empty as a result of Athaliah's mismanagement (or Joash is simply hoarding royal funds for other purposes). The insertion concerning the desecration of the temple by Athaliah's sons (2 Chron. 24:7) is perhaps instructive. In view of recent precedent, the priests and the people may be skeptical of royal intentions for the temple.
- Joash brokers a compromise with the priests to the effect that the people will bring their taxes and offerings to the temple rather than contribute to Levitical "collection agents" (2 Kings 12:6–8; 2 Chron. 24:8–11). In addition, laborers are contracted to do the repair work instead of using the Levites as construction workers.

- The Chronicler reports that both people and officials give joyously and generously, furthering his theme of tabernacle-temple typology (2 Chron. 24:10; cf. Ex. 36:4–7).
- A chest or collection box is stationed near the altar (in the courtyard) outside the gate of the temple building (2 Kings 12:9; 2 Chron. 24:8). Joint oversight of the funds deposited in the chest is provided by a royal and priestly official (2 Kings 12:10; 2 Chron. 24:11).
- Workers, including carpenters, masons, and smiths, are hired and paid directly from the funds deposited in the temple collection box (2 Kings 12:10–12; 2 Chron. 24:12–13). Presumably these funds include the three types of revenues specified by Joash: the annual tax, personal vows, and freewill offerings (2 Kings 12:4).
- The temple repairs are made according to the original architectural design and completed under budget (2 Chron. 24:14).
- Surplus funds are used to make the implements necessary for the temple rituals (2 Kings 12:13–16; 2 Chron. 24:14).

Jehoiada is the model high priest for the Chronicler because of his role as royal guardian and adviser. The ideal of shared power between the civil and religious sectors in the oversight of Israel can be traced back to the leadership of Moses and Aaron after the Exodus. In one sense Jehoiada is a prototype for the high priests of the later postexilic period since he wields considerable civil authority. Unlike those priests of the later period, however, Jehoiada shows great concern for the preservation of legitimate kingship in Israel.

The expression "old and full of years" is an idiom signifying honor and respect, and Jehoiada's longevity is a sign of divine favor (24:15). Jehoiada (who dies at the age of 130) actually outlives several prominent Old Testament figures, such as Sarah (127, Gen. 23:1), Joseph (110, Gen. 50:26), Moses (120, Deut. 34:7), Aaron (110, Num. 33:39), and Joshua (110, Josh. 24:29). Jehoiada is remembered especially for two things: leading Israel in covenant faithfulness (2 Chron. 24:16; cf. the reference to the continual maintenance of the burnt offerings during his tenure as high priest, 24:14), and leading in the initiative to refurbish the temple (24:16). Ironically, Jehoiada is accorded a better burial than Joash eventually receives ("buried with the kings," 24:16; cf. v. 25).

Joash's apostasy (24:17–26). Joash's apostasy is recounted in the second half of his royal review. The Chronicler informs us that the king is led astray by the counsel of the officials of Judah (24:17). The expression "paid homage" (*ḥwh*; lit., "do obeisance") may suggest that the leaders of the clans of Judah exploit a character weakness in Joash through flattery. The elders prefer to return to the policies of Joash's father, Ahaziah, for unspecified reasons. Perhaps the "old ways" are now custom in Judah, or such religious policy is advantageous socially and economically. For the Chronicler, however, to abandon the temple is to abandon God (24:18).

Asherah was a Canaanite fertility cult goddess whose symbol was a tree represented by an upright wooden pole. She was the wife of El and the mother of the gods in Canaanite mythology. Like the Baal fertility cult, the worship of idols accompanied the veneration of Asherah (cf. 2 Kings 23:4). God voices his displeasure with Judah through the message of an unspecified number of prophets—but to no avail, as the people will "not listen" (24:19).

One of those divine messengers is the priest Zechariah, son of Jehoiada (24:20), the priest who earlier showed "kindness" (ḥesed) to King Joash by installing him on the throne of Judah as rightful heir of David's dynasty (24:22). The phrase "the Spirit [of God/the LORD] came upon" (24:20; Heb. *lbš*, lit., "clothed") occurs elsewhere only in Judges 6:34 and 1 Chronicles 12:18 (the expression connotes a gift of prophecy similar to that found in 2 Chron. 15:1 and 20:14).

Zechariah's message is delivered in two parts typical of prophetic speech: an indictment followed by a pronouncement of judgment. The indictment is posed in the form of a rhetorical question, rebuking the king's disobedience to divine commands, presumably the Mosaic injunctions concerning the worship of Yahweh only (24:20b; cf. Ex. 20:3–4; Deut. 16:21–22). The pronouncement of judgment is built on the wordplay of "abandon" (ʿzb; NIV "forsake") and echoes the retribution theme: Even as God returns to those who return to him, he also abandons those who abandon him (2 Chron. 24:20c; cf. Zech. 1:3).

Ironically, Joash has Zechariah murdered in the courtyard of the temple, the very site where "Jehoiada and his sons" anointed Joash as king of Judah (24:21; cf. 23:11). Zechariah's dying words (24:22b) should not be regarded as a plea for vengeance. Rather, it is a petition for God to mete out divine justice according to his righteousness. Zechariah's prayer includes a haunting wordplay on the Hebrew word *drš* ("seek"), in that God will "call to account" (*drš*) for judgment since the king does not seek (*drš*) God. Zechariah's words soon come to pass with the assassination of Joash (24: 25). This may be the same Zechariah mentioned by Jesus in reference to the martyrs of the Old Testament era ("from Abel to Zechariah," Matt. 23:35; Luke 11:51).[3]

---

3. Matthew, however, identifies Zechariah as the son of "Berekiah" rather than the son of Jehoiada. It is unclear whether Berekiah is an alternate family name or a priestly title for Jehoiada.

The reference to the "turn of the year" probably indicates the spring season. This is the time for military campaigns in the ancient world since the dry season is beginning and agricultural activity slackens (24:23a; cf. 2 Sam. 11:1; 1 Chron. 20:1). The kingdom of Aram occupied the region north and northeast of Israel, including the territory around the capital city of Damascus. King Hazael of Aram (and his son Ben-hadad) sporadically oppressed both the kingdoms of Israel and Judah during the ninth century B.C. (cf. 2 Kings 12:17–18; 13:4–7, 22; etc.). Since the Chronicler's account of Aram's invasion of Judah differs at several points from 2 Kings 12:17–18, it is assumed that the Chronicler relies on an alternative historical source.[4]

As the prophet Habakkuk learned just prior to the Babylonian exile, God often accomplishes the judgment of sin among his people by means of foreign invasion (cf. Hab. 1:6–11). Such is the case here, including the slaying of Judean officials and the plundering of Jerusalem (2 Chron. 24:23b-c). The motif of "tit for tat" retribution is seen again in the killing of the Judean leaders, most likely the same individuals who led King Joash into apostasy after the death of Jehoiada (24:23b; cf. v. 17).

To remove any doubt that the Aramean invasion is divinely ordained as punishment for Joash and Judah, the Chronicler reports that the small contingent of Aramean soldiers is victorious because "the LORD delivered" the larger army of Judah into the hands of the Arameans (24:24a). The sovereignty of God as just judge and Lord of history is further highlighted in the extensive wordplay in the Chronicler's account. For example, King Joash is gravely wounded by the Aramean invaders and is subsequently assassinated by members of his cabinet while recovering in bed (24:25a). The same Hebrew verb (*hrg*) is used to describe the killing of Zechariah (24:22) and Joash (24:25). Even as Joash has abandoned God (24:20), so the Arameans "leave" or abandon the king for dead (24:25). All of this comes about because Judah has "forsaken" or abandoned the Lord (24:24). In each case, the same word is employed (*czb*).

According to the Chronicler, Joash's officials conspire against him in retaliation for the murder of Zechariah (24:25b). Interestingly, the writer is careful to note that prominent among the conspirators are Zabad and Jehozabad—both sons of non-Hebrew women (24:26). It is as if the Chronicler seeks to emphasize the irony of the situation since these "mixed-blood" Israelites have a greater sense of justice than the king and citizens of Judah.

Concluding regnal résumé (24:27). The closing regnal résumé combines information taken from 2 Kings 12:19, 21. The citation of source formula differs from that of Kings—one clear example of additional documents

---

4. Dillard, 2 *Chronicles*, 193.

available to the Chronicler. The reference to the children of Joash and other details unique to Chronicles may be attributable to that now lost source. The word "annotations" (midraš) occurs elsewhere only in 13:22, where the historical source is associated with Iddo the prophet. Presumably the idea of "midrash" here is theological commentary on the annals of the monarchy. If the prophetic oracles or burdens (maśśa᾿; NIV "prophecies") mentioned in this concluding résumé refer to the prophetic ministry of 24:19, then the rendering "prophecies about him" is perhaps a charitable reading. The translation "oracles *against* him" (e.g., NRSV) may be closer to the Chronicler's intended meaning.

Amaziah (25:1–28)

THE REPORT OF King Amaziah's reign follows the pattern established with Joash: an early period of rule assessed more or less favorably, contrasted with the negative theological review of the latter years of the king. Biblical commentators rightly raise the question as to whether Amaziah's reign should be characterized as one of decline from "good to bad" or from "bad to worse." I am inclined to agree with McConville and Selman, who view Amaziah's reign as one of weakness and steady degeneration.[5] The report, however, still fits the Chronicler's theme for this unit of the history of the Judean monarchy of kings who start their reigns relatively well but finish poorly. The Chronicler follows 2 Kings 14:1–20 rather closely, except for the expansion of Amaziah's war with Edom. Sandwiched between the opening (2 Chron. 25:1–4) and closing (25:25–28) résumés are the main sections of the chapter: Amaziah's Edomite campaign (25:5–13), his apostasy (25:14–16), and his campaign against Jehoash of Israel (25:17–24).

Opening regnal résumé (25:1–4). The opening résumé (25:1–2) repeats the age of accession, length of reign, and name of mother formulas found in 2 Kings 14:2. In typical fashion, the Chronicler omits the synchronism with King Jehoash of Israel (2 Kings 14:1). According to the biblical data, Amaziah seems to share a lengthy coregency with his son Uzziah (twenty-four years of his twenty-nine-year reign, cf. 2 Kings 14:23; 15:1). The capture of Amaziah by Jehoash of Israel may have necessitated the extended period of coregency (cf. 2 Chron. 25:23).[6] Amaziah rules the kingdom of Judah from approximately 796 to 767 B.C.

As in 2 Kings 14:3–4, the initial résumé also includes a theological review of the king's reign. The record in 2 Kings qualifies Amaziah's righteousness as a ruler by reporting that he follows his father Joash's example rather than

5. McConville, *I and II Chronicles*, 214–15; Selman, *2 Chronicles*, 458.
6. Dillard, *2 Chronicles*, 198.

David as the ideal king. The report that Amaziah fails to remove the idolatrous "high places" serves as evidence against his complete loyalty to God (14:4). The Chronicler offers the same assessment of Amaziah's reign but omits the report of worship in the high places (2 Chron. 25:2–3). Instead, he inserts the report about Amaziah's execution of the assassins responsible for murdering his father (25:3–4; cf. 2 Kings 14:5–6).

Both Kings and Chronicles take pains to demonstrate Amaziah's strict adherence to the prescriptions of Mosaic law in not executing the sons of the conspirators by quoting the legal code verbatim (cf. Deut. 24:16). Assuming a knowledge of the parallel in 2 Kings, the Chronicler's indictment of Amaziah for failing to serve God "wholeheartedly" (25:2) becomes patently clear. Amaziah obeys the law of Moses selectively, bringing just punishment against the conspirators responsible for his father's murder (and solidifying his own rule in the process) but ignoring the injunctions against false worship in the Canaanite high places (cf. Deut. 7:5; 12:2).

The campaign against Edom (25:5–13). The military campaign against Seir or Edom is summarized in a single verse in 2 Kings 14:7 (cf. 2 Chron. 25:11). The battle report of the war with the Edomites is likely pulled from those other historical sources to which the Chronicler often makes appeal. There are two reasons for an expanded account of the Edomite campaign in Chronicles: (1) The ill-fated hiring of Israelite mercenaries (25:6, 10, 13) helps explain Amaziah's later challenge and subsequent war with Jehoash king of Israel (25:17); (2) Amaziah's apostasy (25:27) is directly related to the aftermath of his resounding victory over Edom when he worships the Edomite gods (25:14).

The mustering of militia along tribal subdivisions follows the pattern of previous kings, including David (1 Chron. 21:5–6), Asa (2 Chron. 14:8), and Jehoshaphat (15:9; 17:14–19). Conscripting males aged twenty and older for military service goes back to the census of the Israelites taken by Moses after the Exodus (cf. Num. 1:18–19). The fact that the tribe of Benjamin is explicitly mentioned in the muster roll suggests that Judah still controls that region, which buffered the kingdoms of Judah and Israel. The actual size of Amaziah's army is dependent on whether the word for "thousand" (*'elep*) is taken in a literal sense or as a military unit of a specified number of soldiers. Regardless of how the figures are assessed, Amaziah's army of 300,000 militia is smaller than the armies of Asa (580,000; see 14:8) and Jehoshaphat (1,160,000; see 17:14–18). This probably explains his felt need to hire 100,000 Israelite mercenaries (25:6).

The expression "man of God" (25:7) is often a title for a prophetic figure (e.g., 1 Kings 13:1; 17:18; 2 Kings 1:9). This unnamed individual is one of two anonymous prophets who approach King Amaziah with a message from

God. He heeds the instruction of the first but rejects the counsel of the second to his own demise (cf. 2 Chron. 25:15–16). At times God's prophets remain unnamed so as to highlight the message rather than the messenger. The first prophet advises the king to reject the help of mercenaries from the kingdom of Israel because "the LORD is not with Israel" (25:7). God's abandonment of the kingdom of Israel for the persistent sin of idolatry related to the calf-cult of King Jeroboam I assures military failure. In other words, Judah's association with Israel means that God will side with the Edomites against Amaziah.

More than this, Amaziah needs to be reminded that God rules the nations and determines the outcome of wars. Judah's power and might reside in God as her ally, not in the sheer number of soldiers marshaled for battle (cf. Ps. 118:9; 146:3; 147:10). Dillard aptly reminds us that the man of God's encounter with Amaziah accents two prominent themes in the Old Testament: trusting God rather than foreign political and military alliances, and the few winning the victory against the many, provided the Lord goes into battle before them.[7]

Amaziah's question to this man of God about the lost wages paid to the Israelite mercenaries may reveal something about his motives and true loyalties (25:9). If so, the king has forgotten that God's resources are inexhaustible. The Lord will see to it that Amaziah and the nation of Judah suffer no measurable loss if they trust God for victory, not the help of soldiers of fortune.

Amaziah's decision to dismiss the Israelite mercenaries (25:10), however, is not risk free. The man of God makes no promises that the campaign against Edom will be completely void of trouble. The king's "severance package" with mercenaries means each soldier goes back to Israel with three shekels (or about three months of wages) for sidestepping the battlefield. Perhaps not bad pay for "no work," but what an insult to the professional solider! Beyond this, the Israelite mercenaries also lose any share of the spoils that might be taken from the Edomites. Their "great rage" (25:10) portends evil for Judah, as the Chronicler reports (25:13).

The battle report (25:11–12) is based in part on the brief account found in 2 Kings 14:7. Judah's defeat of Edom is both decisive and bloodthirsty, with 10,000 Edomite soldiers killed in battle and another 10,000 prisoners of war marched to a brutal death off a cliff (2 Chron. 25:12). According to 2 Kings 14:7, King Amaziah captures Sela and renames the place Joktheel (or "God destroyed"). It is unclear whether Sela (lit., "rock") is a city or the rock-cliff over which the Edomite prisoners are thrown to their deaths. According to

---

7. Ibid., 199.

Dillard, Sela may be identified with the site of Es-Sela located some two and a half miles northwest of Bozrah (Sela should not be equated with the city of Petra).[8] The Valley of Salt (2 Chron. 25:11) is the location of an earlier victory over the Edomites by David (1 Chron. 18:12–13). The area is identified generally with the depression of the Arabah south of the Dead Sea (or possibly the Wadi el-Milh, east of Beersheba).

It is to his credit that Amaziah responds favorably to the word of the man of God in the matter of the Israelite mercenaries (25:10). But the same cannot be said for the enraged soldiers who are dismissed and sent back to Samaria. Their fury against Amaziah and the kingdom of Judah is vented in a raid staged from Samaria that targets villages along the coastal route to Beth Horon (a border town between Ephraim and Benjamin some twelve miles northwest of Jerusalem, 25:13). The attack yields much booty for the mercenaries but leaves three thousand citizens of Judah dead. No doubt, the mercenaries feel justified in plundering these villages as compensation for their "lost revenue" in terms of the victory spoils they are denied in the campaign against Edom. The savage killing of civilians is presumably retaliation for their "wounded pride" as professional soldiers. This event prompts Amaziah to "challenge" King Jehoash of Israel (25:17).

Amaziah's apostasy (25:14–16). The plundering of an enemy's temples and the carrying off of their idols as trophies of war were common to the practice of warfare in the ancient Near East (25:14a). Note, for example, the display of the ark of the covenant in the temple of Dagon by the Philistines after the fall of Shiloh (1 Sam. 5:1–2). The act symbolized the deity's abandonment of the vanquished people and the supremacy of the victor's deity in the war of "local deities."[9] Worship of these subjugated deities by the conquering nation is attested in the biblical world, but rather infrequently (25:14b). Perhaps Amaziah assumes that Judah's defeat of Edom is due in part to a shift in loyalty of the Edomite deities to the cause of Judah. This would explain his need to placate these gods in some way. The words "bow down" (*ḥwḥ*) and "burn sacrifices" (*qṭr*, "burn incense") are terms signifying acts of worship reserved solely for Yahweh according to the Mosaic law (cf. Ex. 20:5; 23:24; Jer. 1:16).

A second nameless prophet is commissioned by God to rebuke Amaziah (25:15). His worship of the Edomite gods is utter folly on two counts. (1) These gods have failed to deliver their own people in a time of crisis— the essential test of any deity. (2) The Mosaic injunction against idolatry has been firmly in place for centuries (Ex. 20:4–5). The expression "the anger of the LORD burned" (2 Chron. 25:15a) is typically found in contexts where

---

8. Ibid., 200.

9. Morton Cogan, *Imperialism and Religion: Assyria, Judah, and Israel in the Eighth and Seventh Centuries B.C.* (SBLMS 19; Missoula, Mont.: Scholars Press, 1974), 9–21.

God's jealousy has been provoked by idolatry on the part of the Israelites (e.g., Deut. 7:4; Judg. 3:8; 2 Kings 13:3). According to the sanctions of the Davidic covenant, idolatry by the royal family puts the whole nation at risk of being exiled from the land (cf. 2 Chron. 7:19–22).

The petulant Amaziah interrupts the prophet mid-sentence and commands him to desist in his indictment, upon threat of death (25:16). The prophet obeys the edict as a subject of the king and stops his denouncement. No doubt the earlier murder of Zechariah by Joash under similar circumstances is still fresh in the memory of Judah (cf. 24:22). Although the prophet stops his oracle, God's message cannot be stopped—to reject the counsel of God's prophet is to reject God himself. Amaziah is doomed to destruction by a righteous God. Not to be overlooked is the clever play of the writer on the word "counsel" (y's, 25:16, 17). The course of events will soon demonstrate that Amaziah can ignore the prophet's counsel—but not God's!

As aptly noted by Selman, Amaziah's worship of the Edomite gods reveals his true character.[10] His lapse into idolatry sets a course of self-destruction that eventually leads to the persecution of God's prophets (25:16), taking revenge against the kingdom of Israel (25:17), prideful revelry in his military achievements (25:19), open rebellion against God's word (25:20), and apostasy that proves fatal (25:27).

The campaign against Israel (25:17–24). The account of Amaziah's campaign against Jehoash[11] of Israel is drawn from 2 Kings 14:8–14. The Chronicler has inserted the introductory statement concerning the king's "counsel" with his advisers. As just noted, the opening remark features a forceful wordplay with the Hebrew word y's ("counsel") and links the pericope recording Amaziah's apostasy (2 Chron. 25:14–16) with the report of his war with the rival northern kingdom. It is unclear whether Amaziah's invitation to meet Jehoash "face to face" (25:17) is an act of diplomacy for the purpose of arranging a political marriage between the northern and southern kingdoms (25:18) or a veiled challenge to "cross swords" in a military engagement in order to seek revenge against the Israelite mercenaries who have raided towns in Judah (cf. 25:13). King Jehoash of Israel clearly interprets the initiative as the latter.

Jehoash responds to Amaziah's challenge with a fable about a thistle trampled by a wild beast (25:18). The story is reminiscent of Jotham's fable about the bramble and the trees (Judg. 9:8–15), and both are equally insulting— the whole point of the indirect response. The king of Israel speaks almost prophetically for God in this context, much like Pharaoh Neco's later speech

---

10. Selman, 2 Chronicles, 462.

11. The NIV reads Jehoash for the related Hebrew name Joash (25:17, 18, 21, 23, 25) to avoid confusion with King Joash of Judah (24:1).

to King Josiah (2 Chron. 35:21). Jehoash identifies the motivation behind Amaziah's challenge, pride, and arrogance as a result of his success against the Edomites (25:19a). His warning threatens doom not only on Amaziah but also puts the entire nation of Judah at risk (25:19b).

The Chronicler again emphasizes the rule of God behind the scenes of history in his acknowledgment that Yahweh is sovereign (25:16, 20). God utilizes Amaziah's pride and obstinacy to accomplish his purposes of judging the king's sin and punishing the nation of Judah for their breach of covenant loyalty (cf. 1 Kings 12:15). Regrettably, one of the tragic results of Israel's request for a king during the judgeship of Samuel was that many others would often suffer the consequences of a king's disobedience (cf. 1 Sam. 8:10–18). According to the battle report (2 Chron. 25:21–24), King Jehoash goes on the offensive in response to Amaziah's challenge and routs Judah at Beth Shemesh (25:21–22).

Beth Shemesh is situated some fifteen miles southwest of Jerusalem. According to Selman, the battle site suggests a westerly attack on Jerusalem motivated by Jehoash's desire to control trade routes.[12] King Amaziah is captured and eventually deported to Samaria (25:23–24). It is possible that Amaziah's son Uzziah is made a coregent over Judah at the time since it is impossible for his father to rule in absentia.

In a further show of force and as an added measure of humiliation heaped on King Amaziah and Judah, Jehoash batters down a lengthy section of the wall of Jerusalem and plunders the temple of its gold and silver (25:24). The Chronicler added the detail that the temple articles confiscated by Jehoash were under the care of Obed-Edom, a Levitical singer and gatekeeper (1 Chron. 15:18; 26:15). The taking of hostages (after the pillaging of the royal palace) may have been a precautionary move by Jehoash to prevent retaliation by Judah once the shock of their defeat has worn off. The word of the Lord through the unnamed prophet (25:15) and King Jehoash (25:19) promising "trouble" for Judah has come to pass.

Concluding regnal résumé (25:25–28). The closing résumé summarizing Amaziah's reign follows 2 Kings 14:17–20 verbatim, including the citation of historical source formula (2 Chron. 25:26) and the death report (25:27–28). The lone exception is the Chronicler's insertion of a negative theological review: "from the time that Amaziah turned away from serving the LORD" (25:27a). The indictment of apostasy may be traced to the worship of Edomite idols captured in battle (25:14).

It is likely that Amaziah's false worship is the catalyst that bonds a group of conspirators from Judah to plot Amaziah's assassination for some fifteen

---

12. Ibid., 463.

years.[13] It is unclear as to who these men of Judah are, but most likely it is a coalition of priests along with civil and military leaders similar to the one that elevated Joash to the throne of Judah. The report of Amaziah's assassination includes his flight to Lachish for asylum—but to no avail. Assassins from Jerusalem hunt him down there, execute him, and convey his corpse back to Jerusalem for burial in the royal tomb complex (25:27–28).

Selman's comments on the value of reading yet another depressing story of a wayward king merit consideration at this juncture:

- The repeated stories of sinful political leaders are a testimony to God's patience with fallen humanity.
- Such stories are not restricted to the Old Testament, as the New Testament too has examples of those who fall away after receiving God's grace (e.g., 1 Cor. 5:1–3; 2 Tim. 2:16–18; Rev. 2:4–6).
- Such stories serve both to instruct and to warn so that others may avoid falling into the same snare (cf. 1 Cor. 10:11–13).
- Belonging to the people of God entails more than genealogical pedigree or socialization in the traditions of the Hebrews; belonging to God's people is a matter of the heart (cf. Rom. 2:28).[14]

Uzziah (26:1–23)

OPENING REGNAL RÉSUMÉ (26:1–5). The introductory information cited for King Uzziah essentially repeats 2 Kings 14:21–22; 15:2–3. The writer of Kings prefers the name Azariah, apparently a variant of Uzziah. Perhaps the Chronicler's preference for Uzziah is a deliberate attempt to avoid confusion with Azariah the priest (2 Chron. 26:17–20). In typical fashion, the Chronicler omits the synchronism to the king of the northern kingdom of Israel. This résumé contains the usual formulas: accession age and length of reign (26:3ab), identification of his mother (26:3c), and theological review (26:4–5). The Chronicler's assessment of Uzziah as one who does "right in the eyes of the LORD, just as his father Amaziah had done" (26:4) is hardly a ringing endorsement, since in the end Amaziah was an apostate king (25:27). Uzziah rules the kingdom of Judah for fifty-five years, from approximately 792 to 740 B.C. (ruling as coregent with his father from 792–767).

Uzziah's fame (26:6–15). The report of Uzziah's prosperity (26:6–15) has no parallel in 2 Kings. The litany of achievements attesting divine favor include military victory over Judah's archenemies (26:6–8), extensive building activity and agricultural bounty (26:9–10), and the marshalling of a large,

---

13. Cf. Thompson, *1, 2 Chronicles*, 325.
14. Selman, *2 Chronicles*, 458.

well-trained, and well-equipped army (26:11–15). The unit is framed by a formula of prosperity that highlights Uzziah's "fame" and "power" (26:8, 15). In combination these two epithets are a recipe for pride and eventual self-destruction, since a proud heart tends to "forget the LORD" (Deut. 8:14).

The Chronicler summarizes Uzziah's foreign policy by reporting his military campaigns against the Philistines, Arabs, and Ammonites (26:6–8). The expansion of Judah's influence to the west, south, and southeast accords well with that fact that the strength of Israel under Jeroboam II made territorial annexation to the north and northwest impossible. It appears that economic concerns motivate King Uzziah's imperialistic agenda. Wresting control of the coastal highway from the Philistines and the recapture of Elath (26:1–2) have significant implications for Judah's role in international commerce. Lest this important truth be overlooked, the Chronicler reminds his audience of a direct correlation between God's help and Uzziah's success (26:7). The fame he garners for his military exploits echoes that lavished on King David (cf. 1 Chron. 14:17).

King Uzziah's domestic policy is characterized by building achievements and agricultural prosperity (26:9–10). Both are typically understood as signs of divine favor in the Old Testament world. No doubt, some of the construction is to repair the damage done by King Jehoash of Israel in his assault on Jerusalem (25:23). It also seems likely that some of the building activity is related to the restoration of destruction caused by the well-known earthquake during Uzziah's reign (cf. Amos 1:1; Zech. 14:5). The Corner Gate is located at the northwest angle of Jerusalem (cf. Zech. 14:10), while the Valley Gate and "the angle" cannot be precisely identified (cf. Neh. 3:13, 19, 24; these texts suggest they are located along the southeastern section of the Jerusalem wall).

A considerable amount of archaeological data supports the biblical account of Uzziah's building activity, especially the reference to towers and cisterns (26:10).[15] Dillard has remarked that Uzziah's love of the soil (26:10) justifies identifying him as "the patron saint of farming" among the kings of Judah.[16] Not since Solomon has there been a king with such agrarian interests (cf. 1 Kings 4:33).

The muster roll of Uzziah's army (26:11–15) is the last of several such reports in Chronicles, all associated with righteous kings of Judah (cf. 1 Chron. 12:23–40; 21; 27; 2 Chron. 13:3–4, 17; 17:12–19; 25:5–6). The

---

15. See Alfred J. Hoerth, *Archaeology and The Old Testament* (Grand Rapids: Baker, 1998), 329–31, 336–38; on the historical grounding of the figure of King Uzziah, see Japhet, *I and II Chronicles*, 883–84.

16. Dillard, *2 Chronicles*, 209; see esp. his discussion of "crown lands."

Chronicler regards the maintenance of a large army by the king of Judah as a sign of God's blessing. In addition to the militia levied by tribe and led by tribal chieftain or clan elder, Uzziah's army includes another layer of leadership in the royal officials who function like chiefs of staff in today's military parlance (2 Chron. 26:11). The organization of the militia into "divisions" (26:11) represents a new development in Israel's military structure. The same is true for the armaments provided for the soldiers (26:14), since in earlier times the conscript was required to provide his own weapons (cf. Judg. 20:16–17; 1 Chron. 12:2, 8, 24). Thus, the reign of Uzziah witnesses the increasing sophistication of warfare as practiced by the Israelites.

The repetition of "help" (or "support," 26:13; Heb. ʿzr) frames the beginning and the end of the section (26:7, 15) and compares Uzziah favorably to kings like David (1 Chron. 12:1, 18, 21–22), Solomon (22:17), and Hezekiah (2 Chron. 32:3). The Chronicler suggests that Uzziah is an inventor of sorts, designing "machines" (26:15; or "inventions," from the Heb. ḥšb, "to think") for use in combat. The immediate context suggests that this new offensive weapon is a type of catapult.[17] Dillard (following Yadin), however, prefers to identify this new military technology as defensive constructions erected on the city walls and towers to offer some protection to troops stationed on the ramparts.[18]

Uzziah's pride and God's judgment (26:16–21). This segment of Uzziah's royal annals is based on the terse report of the king's affliction with leprosy found in 2 Kings 15:5. The Chronicler provides the explanation for Uzziah's malady by noting, as with the two other kings of this literary unit, his fatal flaw (26:16). In this case, much like his father, Amaziah (cf. 25:16, 19), the sin of pride (Heb. *gobah* + *leb*; lit., "high heart" or "haughtiness") brings divine judgment and Uzziah's eventual destruction. Try as he might, Uzziah is unable to escape the truth of the sage's wisdom: "Pride goes before destruction" (Prov. 16:18).

The report of Uzziah's pride is the focal point of the Chronicler's review of his reign. The ominous words, when the king "became powerful" (26:16a), link the commentary on the two phases of Uzziah's rule: the early years of God's blessing (26:5–15) and the later years of divine judgment (26:16–21). Ironically, Uzziah's success leads to his downfall because the pride that swells out of his many achievements is the cause of his failure.

This pride results in his unfaithfulness to the Lord (26:16b). The expression "was unfaithful" (mʿl) is used in Chronicles to describe various violations of covenant loyalty with Yahweh. As Selman has noted, this word is the

---

17. Williamson, *1, 2 Chronicles*, 337–38.
18. Dillard, *2 Chronicles*, 209–10; cf. the discussion in Japhet, *I and II Chronicles*, 883.

single most important term for sin in Chronicles, and it may topple a dynasty (1 Chron. 10:13) or sweep a nation away into exile (5:25; 2 Chron. 36:14).[19] From this point on, this word becomes a regular theme in the Chronicler's retelling of the history of Davidic kingship (cf. 2 Chron. 28:19, 22; 29:6, 19; 30:7; 33:19).

Uzziah's haughtiness so impairs his judgment that he attempts to enter the temple and burn incense to the Lord, thus usurping the role of the priests (26:17). The altar of incense symbolized the prayers of Israel rising continually before God (cf. Ps. 141:2). Only the Aaronic priesthood was allowed to attend to the altar and burn incense there (cf. Ex. 30:1–10).

Like Kings Saul (1 Sam. 13:9) and Jeroboam I (1 Kings 12:32–13:1), who also sought to assume the priestly role, Uzziah is rebuked by a priest (2 Chron. 26:17–18). Azariah the priest is not mentioned elsewhere, although two priests by that name are mentioned in the genealogy of Kohath (1 Chron. 6:9, 13). More important to the Chronicler is the courage he and eighty other priests show in confronting the king over the issue of ritual protocol (2 Chron. 26:17). This challenge to royal authority is done at great risk, given the distant memory of Saul's massacre of the priests at Nob (cf. 1 Sam. 22:17–19) and the more recent horror of Joash's murder of the priest Zechariah (cf. 2 Chron. 24:22).

Azariah identifies the key issue in the conflict with Uzziah by appealing to the special divine anointing or consecration of the priesthood for the specific task of offering such sacrifices (26:18; cf. Ps. 133). Even as the Davidic king is anointed to shepherd the Israelite nation, so the Aaronic priest is anointed to serve God and the people through the ministry of ritual sacrifice. This divinely ordained division of labor and service is also designed to separate political power from religious authority in Israelite society in order to prevent abuse of one office by the other. Azariah's threat to Uzziah is cast generally as a censure of divine honor for the king (2 Chron. 26:18).

The king does not have to wait long before the priestly threat becomes a divine curse. Enraged at the priests for intercepting him in the temple and thwarting his attempt to burn incense on the altar, Uzziah is afflicted by God (26:20). It is important to notice that God's anger breaks out against Uzziah only after he has vented his anger against the priests (26:19). The king was warned to leave, but he ignored that warning. His disregard for the Lord's priests and the Lord's sanctuary implicitly signals a disregard for God himself. God will not stand idly by when his holiness has been violated by ritual impropriety (cf. Aaron's sons, Lev. 10:1–2; the men of Korah, Num. 16:35).

---

19. Selman, 2 Chronicles, 470.

Uzziah thus joins the ignominious list of other kings afflicted by God with a disease as punishment for unfaithfulness to God's covenant (e.g., Asa, 16:12–13; Jehoram, 21:12–19). According to Dillard, the rash that breaks out on Uzziah's forehead is not leprosy but an infectious skin disease of an unknown sort (the Heb. *sara*ᶜ denotes a variety of skin diseases, including forms of psoriasis and diverse fungal infections).[20]

Such an infectious skin disease renders the king ritually impure and socially unclean, as one afflicted with a communicable disease. For this reason, King Uzziah lives in quarantine in a separate house (26:21a; Chronicles here rejoins the account of the parallel in 2 Kings 15:5). Uzziah's "dishonor" certainly includes his banishment and isolation from society. More significant for the Chronicler is the dishonor of being excluded from worship in the temple of the Lord (2 Chron. 26:21). Uzziah's son Jotham assumes the role of coregent, takes charge of the palace, and has the oversight of the affairs of the kingdom of Judah (26:21c).

Concluding regnal résumé (26:22–23). The summary résumé features the standard formulas: the citation of historical source, the death and place of burial, and the succession formulas. The report contains two significant divergences from 2 Kings 15:6–7. (1) The Chronicler's historical source is identified as a document written by Isaiah the prophet, whereas the Kings' account is taken from "the annals of the kings of Judah" (15:6). The record of Isaiah son of Amoz is one of several prophetic resources in the Chronicler's bibliography (cf. 1 Chron. 29:29; 2 Chron. 9:29). The appeal to the royal annals shaped by the prophetic tradition may explain why the reigns of certain kings of Judah juxtapose a period of divine blessing with a period of divine judgment.

The Chronicler expands the death and place of burial formula to include the detail that King Uzziah is buried in a field adjacent to the royal tombs of Judah because of his leprosy-like infection. The stigma of disease follows him even in death. The details concerning his skin disease and his place of burial are important to the Chronicler for two reasons: (1) The Chronicler is a priest, and ritual purity is paramount for his fellow members of the Levitical orders; (2) preservation of Uzziah's banishment from the royal tomb complex serves to further the legitimation of the priestly hierocracy in Judah during the postexilic period.

20. Dillard, 2 *Chronicles*, 211.

Bridging Contexts

FEAR THE LORD AND LISTEN. We have already noted affinities between Chronicles and Old Testament wisdom literature, especially Proverbs, in our study of kingship during the united and divided monarchies. Themes or characteristics shared by the two books include the retribution principle (i.e., God rewards faithfulness and punishes apostasy), the idea of the twofold path of wickedness versus righteousness as seen in the evil and good behavior of the Israelite kings, the wisdom of obeying God's commandments, and the testing of motive and the evaluation of the heart—whether or not the heart of the people or the king is fully committed to the Lord.

To this list we may add another feature of wisdom literature that Chronicles and Proverbs have in common: one's capacity to receive instruction and accept wise counsel. According to Proverbs, those who "listen to advice and accept instruction . . . will be wise" (Prov. 19:20); those who are wise will "listen to advice" (12:15) and to "a life-giving rebuke" (15:31).

Tragically, one of the distinguishing behavioral traits unifying the accounts of the reigns of Joash, Amaziah, and Uzziah is their failure to receive instruction and accept wise counsel. In the case of King Joash, not only does he listen to bad advice (24:17), but he also refuses to receive a Spirit-prompted, "life-giving rebuke" from Zechariah the priest (24:20–21). This happens, according to the Chronicler, because Joash "did not remember the kindness Zechariah's father Jehoiada had shown him but killed his son" (24:22).

In similar fashion, King Amaziah refuses to listen to the counsel of God's prophet warning him against the folly of idolatry (25:15–16). Not long after, Amaziah does not listen to the "life-giving rebuke" of King Jehoash of Israel when he advises the king of Judah against going to war with their rival kingdom to the north (25:19–20). Jehoash rightly observes that Amaziah's success against Edom incited a blinding arrogance and pride in him that proves self-destructive (25:19).

Last, but in like manner, King Uzziah rejects the counsel of the priests who advise him to leave the temple and not commit the sacrilege of offering incense to the Lord (26:16–20). Uzziah's failure to heed this "life-giving rebuke" from the eighty priests who courageously confront him results in divine judgment in the form of leprosy—a stigma he carries to his grave (26:19–20; cf. 26:23). Sadly, Uzziah "inherits" the same character flaw that compromised his father's reign—the sin of pride spawned by fame and power (26:15–16).

Biblical scholars have suggested that the wisdom literature of Proverbs was in effect a school textbook for the royal family and the elite of society. The youth of these social strata were trained in the ways of wisdom so that in the future they might be wise and productive leaders of the next generation of Israelites. Ironically, the instruction of Proverbs not only addresses the subject of receiving instruction and accepting counsel but also treats topics like the dangers in listening to bad advice (Prov. 12:5; 17:4; 21:28) and the folly of pride (8:13; 11:2; 16:18). Obviously, this practical teaching proves ineffective in the lives of the three kings featured in this section. When kings are directed to "take pleasure in honest lips" and to "value a man who speaks the truth" (16:13), why do Joash, Amaziah, and Uzziah spurn the wise and true counsel of God's spokesmen?

The answer to this question is found in the wisdom concept of the "fear of the LORD"—the first step toward the "knowledge of God" (Prov. 1:7; 2:5). The fear of the Lord is a complex idea comprised of interrelated attitudes, actions, and outcomes:

- the desire to get understanding that arises from a decision grounded in the human will (Prov. 1:29–30; 2:5)
- faith and trust in God's plan for human life and a rejection of self-reliance (Prov. 3:5–6)
- a proactive righteousness that hates and avoids evil and refuses to envy sinners (Prov. 3:7; 9:13; 16:6)
- a posture of awe and reverence for the God of creation and redemption that elicits genuine worship and willing obedience to his commands (Prov. 24:21)

Hence, it is the "fear of the LORD" that enables one to "listen to advice and accept instruction" for the sake of becoming wise (Prov. 19:20). The story of Uzziah bears out this truth because he "sought God," and "God gave him success" during the days he was mentored in the "fear of God" by one (otherwise unknown) Zechariah (2 Chron. 26:5). If one does not have the fear of the Lord, kings and people alike turn in self-reliance to their "own wisdom" (Prov. 3:5, 7; 18:2; 26:12). Although this "way" of one's own wisdom seems right, it leads to death in the end (14:12; 16:25). This too is confirmed by Uzziah's example. The king is "unfaithful to the LORD his God" because after he becomes powerful, "his pride led to his downfall" (2 Chron. 26:16).

Perhaps the more important question for us is how to develop the capacity to "fear the LORD" so that we may receive sound instruction and accept wise counsel. The key to answering this question is found in the word "listen," since it is the wise who "listen and add to their learning" (Prov. 1:5). In fact, the exhortation to "listen" to the instruction of the biblical wisdom tradition is repeated more than a dozen times in Proverbs (e.g., 1:8; 4:1, 10). We take up that discussion in the application section that follows.

ON ACCEPTING WISE COUNSEL. A plethora of "how-to" books have been written on every subject imaginable. Typically one or more books of this genre will appear on bestseller lists at any given time. One highly successful example is Stephen Covey's *The 7 Habits of Highly Effective People*.[21] The book offers principles for the development of personal and interpersonal effectiveness and has sold more than twelve million copies in thirty-two languages. The *7 Habits* are especially popular with the business sector of society, since effective management and organization are essential to profit margins. It has spawned a couple of sequels and a collection of testimonials from people who have successfully applied the seven principles to the problems and challenges of real-life experiences.[22] Naturally, the book's popularity has generated numerous "effective habits" spinoffs aimed at the Christian subculture.[23] Covey advocates a personal philosophy of life that moves from dependence to independence and culminates in interdependence.

Of special interest to our study is his chapter entitled "Principles of Empathic Communication."[24] There are four basic types of communication: reading, writing, speaking, and listening. Covey has correctly observed that most of us have had little, if any, training in the communication skill of listening. To counter this deficiency, he promotes what he calls "empathic listening." By this he means an approach to communication that seeks first to understand rather than to be understood. "Most people do not listen with the intent to understand; they listen with the intent to reply. They're either speaking or preparing to speak. They're filtering everything through their own paradigms, reading their autobiography into other people's lives."[25] Empathic listening does not necessarily mean agreement with the speaker, but it does seek to truly understand the verbal communication of another individual by getting inside the speaker's frame of reference. "The essence of empathic listening is not that you agree with someone; it's that you fully, deeply, understand that person, emotionally as well as intellectually."[26]

21. Stephen R. Covey, *The 7 Habits of Highly Effective People* (New York: Simon & Schuster, 1989).

22. Sean Covey, *The 7 Habits of Highly Effective Teens* (New York: Simon & Schuster, 1998); Sandra and Stephen Covey, *The 7 Habits of Highly Effective Families* (New York: Simon & Schuster, 1998); Stephen R. Covey, *Living the 7 Habits* (New York: Simon & Schuster, 1999).

23. See, e.g., Lowell O. Erdahl, *10 Habits for Effective Ministry* (Minneapolis: Fortress, 1996); George Barna, *The Habits of Highly Effective Churches* (Ventura, Calif.: Regal, 2000).

24. Covey, *7 Habits of Highly Effective People*, 236–60.

25. Ibid., 239.

26. Ibid., 240.

I find it interesting, if not amusing, when pop-culture or pop-psychology catches up with biblical teaching. What the popular media may describe as "penetrating truth," "profound principles," and "fresh insights" are often not that fresh or that profound. The Bible has usually "been there and done that" centuries earlier.

Take, for instance, the teaching of James, a book that in many ways is the New Testament counterpart to the Old Testament book of Proverbs. James exhorts the Christian to "be quick to listen, slow to speak and slow to become angry" (James 1:19). The Greek verb "to listen" (*akouo*) means not only to hear with reference to sense perception but also to listen with understanding—as Ropes summarizes, "Let your aim be not speech, but attentive hearing."[27] Unlike *The 7 Habits*, however, the goal or outcome of listening in the biblical tradition is "the righteous life that God desires" (James 1:20), not effectiveness in managing one's personal life or successful management of business enterprises.

We have already learned from the lives of kings Joash, Amaziah, and Uzziah that receiving instruction and accepting counsel demand listening skills and that such skills are directly related to "the fear of the LORD." It is the biblical notion of the fear of the Lord that fosters reliance on God and receptivity to divine wisdom, in contrast to self-reliance and dependence on one's own understanding. But how do we as Christians learn to listen attentively to God and to others with empathy and understanding as the apostle James or a self-help guru like Covey suggests? By what strategies or techniques or formulas do we develop the communication skill of attentive listening?

According to Richard Foster, "Jesus calls us from loneliness to solitude."[28] The discipline of *solitude* that Foster encourages is a state of mind and heart that is dependent on *silence*. For Foster "though silence sometimes involves the absence of speech it always involves the act of listening," and the purpose of silence and solitude is to be able to see clearly and hear truly, especially God but others as well.[29]

The Bible shows awareness of the importance of solitude and silence in attentive listening to others and to God. We have the example of Job, who understood that grasping instruction requires silence or "quiet" for "attentive listening" (Job 6:24). In another instance, Job reminisced about his own role as an elder when "men listened to me expectantly, waiting in silence for my counsel" (29:21). We also have the example of Jesus, who often retreated

---

27. James H. Ropes, *A Critical and Exegetical Commentary on the Epistle of St. James* (ICC; Edinburgh: T. & T. Clark, 1973), 168.

28. Richard J. Foster, *Celebration of Discipline* (New York: Harper & Row, 1978), 84.

29. Ibid., 86.

to "lonely places," seeking solitude and silence for prayer (Luke 5:16). It seems certain that Jesus sought solitude and silence both to pray and to listen to his Father, since he only did exactly what the Father had commanded him (John 14:31).

The spiritual disciplines of solitude and silence are not an end in themselves but a means to the greater goal of the life of righteousness God desires for each Christian. Solitude and silence ready the heart and open the mind, so that like Samuel we may say, "Speak, LORD, for your servant is listening" *attentively* (1 Sam. 3:9). As we have already discovered, one outcome of solitude and silence is attentive listening. In the discomfort of our quietness God's Spirit has an opportunity to do the preparatory work necessary for us to receive instruction and accept counsel from God and from the godly men and women who serve as "his voice" in our lives from time to time.

Another outcome of the disciplines of solitude and silence is freedom, for "silence frees us from the need to control others."[30] As Foster so painfully reminds us, "we are accustomed to relying upon words to manage and control others," but "when we become quiet enough to let go of people, we learn compassion for them."[31]

Like any of the other spiritual disciplines, solitude and silence are activities, things we must do or practice. Foster offers several helpful suggestions as the first steps for entering the realms of solitude and silence:

- taking advantage of the "little solitudes" that fill each day
- finding or developing a "quiet place" designed for solitude and silence in the home
- finding places outside the home designated specifically as "quite places" that may be visited regularly (e.g., a park or a chapel)
- learning to control our speech patterns after the counsel of Proverbs, which says, "a [person] of knowledge uses words with restraint" (Prov. 17:27)
- taking time to withdraw four times a year for three to four hours for the purpose of reorienting your life goals
- taking a retreat of two or three days once a year for no other purpose but solitude and silence.[32]

According to the teachings of the New Testament, a vital component of our Christian religion is "to look after orphans and widows in their distress" (James 1:27). Put another way, we are to continually offer the sacrifice of

---

30. Richard J. Foster, *Freedom of Simplicity* (New York: Harper & Row, 1981), 57.
31. Ibid., 57–58.
32. Foster, *Celebration of Discipline*, 92–95.

doing good and sharing with others (Heb. 13:15–16). In either case, such Christian behavior must be motivated by compassion for others. The fruit of solitude and silence is just that—an increased sensitivity and compassion for others, a "new attentiveness to their needs, new responsiveness to their hurts."[33] May we, like Thomas Merton, learn that "it is in deep solitude that I find the gentleness with which I can truly love my brothers [and sisters]. Solitude and silence teach me to love my brothers [and sisters] for what they are, not for what they say."[34]

The same might be said for our relationship to God because in solitude and silence we learn to love God and attentively listen to his voice *for who he is* as Creator, Redeemer, and Sustainer of all things, *not for what he might do for us*. Unlike stubborn Israel, who so often rejected God's instruction, may we attentively listen to his divine counsel and learn that

> in repentance and rest is [our] salvation,
> in quietness and trust is [our] strength. (Isa. 30:15)

---

33. Ibid., 95.
34. Thomas Merton, *The Sign of Jonas* (New York: Harcourt, Brace & Co., 1953), 261.

2 Chronicles 27–32

JOTHAM WAS TWENTY-FIVE years old when he became king, and he reigned in Jerusalem sixteen years. His mother's name was Jerusha daughter of Zadok. ²He did what was right in the eyes of the LORD, just as his father Uzziah had done, but unlike him he did not enter the temple of the LORD. The people, however, continued their corrupt practices. ³Jotham rebuilt the Upper Gate of the temple of the LORD and did extensive work on the wall at the hill of Ophel. ⁴He built towns in the Judean hills and forts and towers in the wooded areas.

⁵Jotham made war on the king of the Ammonites and conquered them. That year the Ammonites paid him a hundred talents of silver, ten thousand cors of wheat and ten thousand cors of barley. The Ammonites brought him the same amount also in the second and third years.

⁶Jotham grew powerful because he walked steadfastly before the LORD his God.

⁷The other events in Jotham's reign, including all his wars and the other things he did, are written in the book of the kings of Israel and Judah. ⁸He was twenty-five years old when he became king, and he reigned in Jerusalem sixteen years. ⁹Jotham rested with his fathers and was buried in the City of David. And Ahaz his son succeeded him as king.

²⁸:¹Ahaz was twenty years old when he became king, and he reigned in Jerusalem sixteen years. Unlike David his father, he did not do what was right in the eyes of the LORD. ²He walked in the ways of the kings of Israel and also made cast idols for worshiping the Baals. ³He burned sacrifices in the Valley of Ben Hinnom and sacrificed his sons in the fire, following the detestable ways of the nations the LORD had driven out before the Israelites. ⁴He offered sacrifices and burned incense at the high places, on the hilltops and under every spreading tree.

⁵Therefore the LORD his God handed him over to the king of Aram. The Arameans defeated him and took many of his people as prisoners and brought them to Damascus.

He was also given into the hands of the king of Israel, who inflicted heavy casualties on him. ⁶In one day Pekah son of

Remaliah killed a hundred and twenty thousand soldiers in Judah—because Judah had forsaken the LORD, the God of their fathers. ⁷Zicri, an Ephraimite warrior, killed Maaseiah the king's son, Azrikam the officer in charge of the palace, and Elkanah, second to the king. ⁸The Israelites took captive from their kinsmen two hundred thousand wives, sons and daughters. They also took a great deal of plunder, which they carried back to Samaria.

⁹But a prophet of the LORD named Oded was there, and he went out to meet the army when it returned to Samaria. He said to them, "Because the LORD, the God of your fathers, was angry with Judah, he gave them into your hand. But you have slaughtered them in a rage that reaches to heaven. ¹⁰And now you intend to make the men and women of Judah and Jerusalem your slaves. But aren't you also guilty of sins against the LORD your God? ¹¹Now listen to me! Send back your fellow countrymen you have taken as prisoners, for the LORD's fierce anger rests on you."

¹²Then some of the leaders in Ephraim—Azariah son of Jehohanan, Berekiah son of Meshillemoth, Jehizkiah son of Shallum, and Amasa son of Hadlai—confronted those who were arriving from the war. ¹³"You must not bring those prisoners here," they said, "or we will be guilty before the LORD. Do you intend to add to our sin and guilt? For our guilt is already great, and his fierce anger rests on Israel."

¹⁴So the soldiers gave up the prisoners and plunder in the presence of the officials and all the assembly. ¹⁵The men designated by name took the prisoners, and from the plunder they clothed all who were naked. They provided them with clothes and sandals, food and drink, and healing balm. All those who were weak they put on donkeys. So they took them back to their fellow countrymen at Jericho, the City of Palms, and returned to Samaria.

¹⁶At that time King Ahaz sent to the king of Assyria for help. ¹⁷The Edomites had again come and attacked Judah and carried away prisoners, ¹⁸while the Philistines had raided towns in the foothills and in the Negev of Judah. They captured and occupied Beth Shemesh, Aijalon and Gederoth, as well as Soco, Timnah and Gimzo, with their surrounding villages. ¹⁹The LORD had humbled Judah because of Ahaz king of Israel, for he had promoted wickedness in Judah and had

been most unfaithful to the LORD. ²⁰Tiglath-Pileser king of Assyria came to him, but he gave him trouble instead of help. ²¹Ahaz took some of the things from the temple of the LORD and from the royal palace and from the princes and presented them to the king of Assyria, but that did not help him.

²²In his time of trouble King Ahaz became even more unfaithful to the LORD. ²³He offered sacrifices to the gods of Damascus, who had defeated him; for he thought, "Since the gods of the kings of Aram have helped them, I will sacrifice to them so they will help me." But they were his downfall and the downfall of all Israel.

²⁴Ahaz gathered together the furnishings from the temple of God and took them away. He shut the doors of the LORD's temple and set up altars at every street corner in Jerusalem. ²⁵In every town in Judah he built high places to burn sacrifices to other gods and provoked the LORD, the God of his fathers, to anger.

²⁶The other events of his reign and all his ways, from beginning to end, are written in the book of the kings of Judah and Israel. ²⁷Ahaz rested with his fathers and was buried in the city of Jerusalem, but he was not placed in the tombs of the kings of Israel. And Hezekiah his son succeeded him as king.

²⁹:¹Hezekiah was twenty-five years old when he became king, and he reigned in Jerusalem twenty-nine years. His mother's name was Abijah daughter of Zechariah. ²He did what was right in the eyes of the LORD, just as his father David had done.

³In the first month of the first year of his reign, he opened the doors of the temple of the LORD and repaired them. ⁴He brought in the priests and the Levites, assembled them in the square on the east side ⁵and said: "Listen to me, Levites! Consecrate yourselves now and consecrate the temple of the LORD, the God of your fathers. Remove all defilement from the sanctuary. ⁶Our fathers were unfaithful; they did evil in the eyes of the LORD our God and forsook him. They turned their faces away from the LORD's dwelling place and turned their backs on him. ⁷They also shut the doors of the portico and put out the lamps. They did not burn incense or present any burnt offerings at the sanctuary to the God of Israel. ⁸Therefore, the anger of the LORD has fallen on Judah and Jerusalem; he has made them an object of dread and horror

and scorn, as you can see with your own eyes. ⁹This is why our fathers have fallen by the sword and why our sons and daughters and our wives are in captivity. ¹⁰Now I intend to make a covenant with the LORD, the God of Israel, so that his fierce anger will turn away from us. ¹¹My sons, do not be negligent now, for the LORD has chosen you to stand before him and serve him, to minister before him and to burn incense."

¹²Then these Levites set to work:

from the Kohathites,
  Mahath son of Amasai and Joel son of Azariah;
from the Merarites,
  Kish son of Abdi and Azariah son of Jehallelel;
from the Gershonites,
  Joah son of Zimmah and Eden son of Joah;
¹³from the descendants of Elizaphan,
  Shimri and Jeiel;
from the descendants of Asaph,
  Zechariah and Mattaniah;
¹⁴from the descendants of Heman,
  Jehiel and Shimei;
from the descendants of Jeduthun,
  Shemaiah and Uzziel.

¹⁵When they had assembled their brothers and consecrated themselves, they went in to purify the temple of the LORD, as the king had ordered, following the word of the LORD. ¹⁶The priests went into the sanctuary of the LORD to purify it. They brought out to the courtyard of the LORD's temple everything unclean that they found in the temple of the LORD. The Levites took it and carried it out to the Kidron Valley. ¹⁷They began the consecration on the first day of the first month, and by the eighth day of the month they reached the portico of the LORD. For eight more days they consecrated the temple of the LORD itself, finishing on the sixteenth day of the first month.

¹⁸Then they went in to King Hezekiah and reported: "We have purified the entire temple of the LORD, the altar of burnt offering with all its utensils, and the table for setting out the consecrated bread, with all its articles. ¹⁹We have prepared and consecrated all the articles that King Ahaz removed in his unfaithfulness while he was king. They are now in front of the LORD's altar."

²⁰Early the next morning King Hezekiah gathered the city officials together and went up to the temple of the LORD. ²¹They brought seven bulls, seven rams, seven male lambs and seven male goats as a sin offering for the kingdom, for the sanctuary and for Judah. The king commanded the priests, the descendants of Aaron, to offer these on the altar of the LORD. ²²So they slaughtered the bulls, and the priests took the blood and sprinkled it on the altar; next they slaughtered the rams and sprinkled their blood on the altar; then they slaughtered the lambs and sprinkled their blood on the altar. ²³The goats for the sin offering were brought before the king and the assembly, and they laid their hands on them. ²⁴The priests then slaughtered the goats and presented their blood on the altar for a sin offering to atone for all Israel, because the king had ordered the burnt offering and the sin offering for all Israel.

²⁵He stationed the Levites in the temple of the LORD with cymbals, harps and lyres in the way prescribed by David and Gad the king's seer and Nathan the prophet; this was commanded by the LORD through his prophets. ²⁶So the Levites stood ready with David's instruments, and the priests with their trumpets.

²⁷Hezekiah gave the order to sacrifice the burnt offering on the altar. As the offering began, singing to the LORD began also, accompanied by trumpets and the instruments of David king of Israel. ²⁸The whole assembly bowed in worship, while the singers sang and the trumpeters played. All this continued until the sacrifice of the burnt offering was completed.

²⁹When the offerings were finished, the king and everyone present with him knelt down and worshiped. ³⁰King Hezekiah and his officials ordered the Levites to praise the LORD with the words of David and of Asaph the seer. So they sang praises with gladness and bowed their heads and worshiped.

³¹Then Hezekiah said, "You have now dedicated yourselves to the LORD. Come and bring sacrifices and thank offerings to the temple of the LORD." So the assembly brought sacrifices and thank offerings, and all whose hearts were willing brought burnt offerings.

³²The number of burnt offerings the assembly brought was seventy bulls, a hundred rams and two hundred male lambs— all of them for burnt offerings to the LORD. ³³The animals

consecrated as sacrifices amounted to six hundred bulls and three thousand sheep and goats. ³⁴The priests, however, were too few to skin all the burnt offerings; so their kinsmen the Levites helped them until the task was finished and until other priests had been consecrated, for the Levites had been more conscientious in consecrating themselves than the priests had been. ³⁵There were burnt offerings in abundance, together with the fat of the fellowship offerings and the drink offerings that accompanied the burnt offerings.

So the service of the temple of the LORD was reestablished. ³⁶Hezekiah and all the people rejoiced at what God had brought about for his people, because it was done so quickly.

³⁰:¹Hezekiah sent word to all Israel and Judah and also wrote letters to Ephraim and Manasseh, inviting them to come to the temple of the LORD in Jerusalem and celebrate the Passover to the LORD, the God of Israel. ²The king and his officials and the whole assembly in Jerusalem decided to celebrate the Passover in the second month. ³They had not been able to celebrate it at the regular time because not enough priests had consecrated themselves and the people had not assembled in Jerusalem. ⁴The plan seemed right both to the king and to the whole assembly. ⁵They decided to send a proclamation throughout Israel, from Beersheba to Dan, calling the people to come to Jerusalem and celebrate the Passover to the LORD, the God of Israel. It had not been celebrated in large numbers according to what was written.

⁶At the king's command, couriers went throughout Israel and Judah with letters from the king and from his officials, which read:

"People of Israel, return to the LORD, the God of Abraham, Isaac and Israel, that he may return to you who are left, who have escaped from the hand of the kings of Assyria. ⁷Do not be like your fathers and brothers, who were unfaithful to the LORD, the God of their fathers, so that he made them an object of horror, as you see. ⁸Do not be stiff-necked, as your fathers were; submit to the LORD. Come to the sanctuary, which he has consecrated forever. Serve the LORD your God, so that his fierce anger will turn away from you. ⁹If you return to the LORD, then your brothers and your children will be shown compassion by their captors and will come back to this land, for the LORD your God is gracious and compassionate. He will not turn his face from you if you return to him."

¹⁰The couriers went from town to town in Ephraim and Manasseh, as far as Zebulun, but the people scorned and ridiculed them. ¹¹Nevertheless, some men of Asher, Manasseh and Zebulun humbled themselves and went to Jerusalem. ¹²Also in Judah the hand of God was on the people to give them unity of mind to carry out what the king and his officials had ordered, following the word of the LORD.

¹³A very large crowd of people assembled in Jerusalem to celebrate the Feast of Unleavened Bread in the second month. ¹⁴They removed the altars in Jerusalem and cleared away the incense altars and threw them into the Kidron Valley.

¹⁵They slaughtered the Passover lamb on the fourteenth day of the second month. The priests and the Levites were ashamed and consecrated themselves and brought burnt offerings to the temple of the LORD. ¹⁶Then they took up their regular positions as prescribed in the Law of Moses the man of God. The priests sprinkled the blood handed to them by the Levites. ¹⁷Since many in the crowd had not consecrated themselves, the Levites had to kill the Passover lambs for all those who were not ceremonially clean and could not consecrate their lambs to the LORD. ¹⁸Although most of the many people who came from Ephraim, Manasseh, Issachar and Zebulun had not purified themselves, yet they ate the Passover, contrary to what was written. But Hezekiah prayed for them, saying, "May the LORD, who is good, pardon everyone ¹⁹who sets his heart on seeking God—the LORD, the God of his fathers— even if he is not clean according to the rules of the sanctuary." ²⁰And the LORD heard Hezekiah and healed the people.

²¹The Israelites who were present in Jerusalem celebrated the Feast of Unleavened Bread for seven days with great rejoicing, while the Levites and priests sang to the LORD every day, accompanied by the LORD's instruments of praise.

²²Hezekiah spoke encouragingly to all the Levites, who showed good understanding of the service of the LORD. For the seven days they ate their assigned portion and offered fellowship offerings and praised the LORD, the God of their fathers.

²³The whole assembly then agreed to celebrate the festival seven more days; so for another seven days they celebrated joyfully. ²⁴Hezekiah king of Judah provided a thousand bulls and seven thousand sheep and goats for the assembly, and the officials provided them with a thousand bulls and ten thousand sheep and goats. A great number of priests consecrated themselves. ²⁵The entire assembly of Judah rejoiced, along with the priests and Levites and all who had assembled from Israel, including the aliens who had come from Israel and those who lived in Judah. ²⁶There was great joy in Jerusalem, for since the days of Solomon son of David king of Israel there had been nothing like this in Jerusalem. ²⁷The priests and the Levites stood to bless the people, and God heard them, for their prayer reached heaven, his holy dwelling place.

³¹:¹When all this had ended, the Israelites who were there went out to the towns of Judah, smashed the sacred stones and cut down the Asherah poles. They destroyed the high places and the altars throughout Judah and Benjamin and in Ephraim and Manasseh. After they had destroyed all of them, the Israelites returned to their own towns and to their own property.

²Hezekiah assigned the priests and Levites to divisions—each of them according to their duties as priests or Levites—to offer burnt offerings and fellowship offerings, to minister, to give thanks and to sing praises at the gates of the LORD's dwelling. ³The king contributed from his own possessions for the morning and evening burnt offerings and for the burnt offerings on the Sabbaths, New Moons and appointed feasts as written in the Law of the LORD. ⁴He ordered the people living in Jerusalem to give the portion due the priests and Levites so they could devote themselves to the Law of the LORD. ⁵As soon as the order went out, the Israelites generously gave the firstfruits of their grain, new wine, oil and honey and all that the fields produced. They brought a great amount, a tithe of everything. ⁶The men of Israel and Judah who lived in the towns of Judah also brought a tithe of their herds and flocks and a tithe of the holy things dedicated to the LORD their God, and they piled them in heaps. ⁷They began doing this in the third month and finished in the seventh month. ⁸When Hezekiah and his officials came and saw the heaps, they praised the LORD and blessed his people Israel.

⁹Hezekiah asked the priests and Levites about the heaps;
¹⁰and Azariah the chief priest, from the family of Zadok,
answered, "Since the people began to bring their contributions to the temple of the LORD, we have had enough to eat
and plenty to spare, because the LORD has blessed his people,
and this great amount is left over."

¹¹Hezekiah gave orders to prepare storerooms in the temple of the LORD, and this was done. ¹²Then they faithfully
brought in the contributions, tithes and dedicated gifts. Conaniah, a Levite, was in charge of these things, and his brother
Shimei was next in rank. ¹³Jehiel, Azaziah, Nahath, Asahel, Jerimoth, Jozabad, Eliel, Ismakiah, Mahath and Benaiah were
supervisors under Conaniah and Shimei his brother, by
appointment of King Hezekiah and Azariah the official in
charge of the temple of God.

¹⁴Kore son of Imnah the Levite, keeper of the East Gate,
was in charge of the freewill offerings given to God, distributing the contributions made to the LORD and also the consecrated gifts. ¹⁵Eden, Miniamin, Jeshua, Shemaiah, Amariah and
Shecaniah assisted him faithfully in the towns of the priests,
distributing to their fellow priests according to their divisions,
old and young alike.

¹⁶In addition, they distributed to the males three years old
or more whose names were in the genealogical records—all
who would enter the temple of the LORD to perform the daily
duties of their various tasks, according to their responsibilities
and their divisions. ¹⁷And they distributed to the priests
enrolled by their families in the genealogical records and likewise to the Levites twenty years old or more, according to
their responsibilities and their divisions. ¹⁸They included all
the little ones, the wives, and the sons and daughters of the
whole community listed in these genealogical records. For
they were faithful in consecrating themselves.

¹⁹As for the priests, the descendants of Aaron, who lived on
the farm lands around their towns or in any other towns, men
were designated by name to distribute portions to every male
among them and to all who were recorded in the genealogies
of the Levites.

²⁰This is what Hezekiah did throughout Judah, doing what
was good and right and faithful before the LORD his God. ²¹In
everything that he undertook in the service of God's temple

and in obedience to the law and the commands, he sought his God and worked wholeheartedly. And so he prospered.

³²:¹After all that Hezekiah had so faithfully done, Sennacherib king of Assyria came and invaded Judah. He laid siege to the fortified cities, thinking to conquer them for himself. ²When Hezekiah saw that Sennacherib had come and that he intended to make war on Jerusalem, ³he consulted with his officials and military staff about blocking off the water from the springs outside the city, and they helped him. ⁴A large force of men assembled, and they blocked all the springs and the stream that flowed through the land. "Why should the kings of Assyria come and find plenty of water?" they said. ⁵Then he worked hard repairing all the broken sections of the wall and building towers on it. He built another wall outside that one and reinforced the supporting terraces of the City of David. He also made large numbers of weapons and shields.

⁶He appointed military officers over the people and assembled them before him in the square at the city gate and encouraged them with these words: ⁷"Be strong and courageous. Do not be afraid or discouraged because of the king of Assyria and the vast army with him, for there is a greater power with us than with him. ⁸With him is only the arm of flesh, but with us is the LORD our God to help us and to fight our battles." And the people gained confidence from what Hezekiah the king of Judah said.

⁹Later, when Sennacherib king of Assyria and all his forces were laying siege to Lachish, he sent his officers to Jerusalem with this message for Hezekiah king of Judah and for all the people of Judah who were there:

¹⁰"This is what Sennacherib king of Assyria says: On what are you basing your confidence, that you remain in Jerusalem under siege? ¹¹When Hezekiah says, 'The LORD our God will save us from the hand of the king of Assyria,' he is misleading you, to let you die of hunger and thirst. ¹²Did not Hezekiah himself remove this god's high places and altars, saying to Judah and Jerusalem, 'You must worship before one altar and burn sacrifices on it'?

¹³"Do you not know what I and my fathers have done to all the peoples of the other lands? Were the gods of

those nations ever able to deliver their land from my hand? [14]Who of all the gods of these nations that my fathers destroyed has been able to save his people from me? How then can your god deliver you from my hand? [15]Now do not let Hezekiah deceive you and mislead you like this. Do not believe him, for no god of any nation or kingdom has been able to deliver his people from my hand or the hand of my fathers. How much less will your god deliver you from my hand!"

[16]Sennacherib's officers spoke further against the LORD God and against his servant Hezekiah. [17]The king also wrote letters insulting the LORD, the God of Israel, and saying this against him: "Just as the gods of the peoples of the other lands did not rescue their people from my hand, so the god of Hezekiah will not rescue his people from my hand." [18]Then they called out in Hebrew to the people of Jerusalem who were on the wall, to terrify them and make them afraid in order to capture the city. [19]They spoke about the God of Jerusalem as they did about the gods of the other peoples of the world—the work of men's hands.

[20]King Hezekiah and the prophet Isaiah son of Amoz cried out in prayer to heaven about this. [21]And the LORD sent an angel, who annihilated all the fighting men and the leaders and officers in the camp of the Assyrian king. So he withdrew to his own land in disgrace. And when he went into the temple of his god, some of his sons cut him down with the sword.

[22]So the LORD saved Hezekiah and the people of Jerusalem from the hand of Sennacherib king of Assyria and from the hand of all others. He took care of them on every side. [23]Many brought offerings to Jerusalem for the LORD and valuable gifts for Hezekiah king of Judah. From then on he was highly regarded by all the nations.

[24]In those days Hezekiah became ill and was at the point of death. He prayed to the LORD, who answered him and gave him a miraculous sign. [25]But Hezekiah's heart was proud and he did not respond to the kindness shown him; therefore the LORD's wrath was on him and on Judah and Jerusalem. [26]Then Hezekiah repented of the pride of his heart, as did the people of Jerusalem; therefore the LORD's wrath did not come upon them during the days of Hezekiah.

²⁷Hezekiah had very great riches and honor, and he made treasuries for his silver and gold and for his precious stones, spices, shields and all kinds of valuables. ²⁸He also made buildings to store the harvest of grain, new wine and oil; and he made stalls for various kinds of cattle, and pens for the flocks. ²⁹He built villages and acquired great numbers of flocks and herds, for God had given him very great riches.

³⁰It was Hezekiah who blocked the upper outlet of the Gihon spring and channeled the water down to the west side of the City of David. He succeeded in everything he undertook. ³¹But when envoys were sent by the rulers of Babylon to ask him about the miraculous sign that had occurred in the land, God left him to test him and to know everything that was in his heart.

The other events of Hezekiah's reign and his acts of devotion are written in the vision of the prophet Isaiah son of Amoz in the book of the kings of Judah and Israel. ³³Hezekiah rested with his fathers and was buried on the hill where the tombs of David's descendants are. All Judah and the people of Jerusalem honored him when he died. And Manasseh his son succeeded him as king.

THE CHRONICLER SLIGHTLY expands the synoptic portions of Kings in his accounts of the reigns of Jotham (cf. 2 Kings 15:32–38) and Ahaz (cf. 2 Kings 16:1–20). His retelling of Hezekiah's reign, however, stands almost completely independent of 2 Kings 18–20. The essential literary form of the unit remains the report. The pattern of encasing the review of each king's rule with opening and closing regnal résumés begun with King Jehoram continues as well.

This section of the Chronicler's retelling of the story of the Davidic monarchy interrupts the pattern of the previous literary unit. There the historian contrasted the obedience of each king early on during his reign with his later apostasy. Here theme and structure are intertwined in a different way as each king's reign is measured against a single theme—faithfulness to God. The result is an alternating pattern of faithfulness (with Kings Jotham and Hezekiah) and unfaithfulness (with King Ahaz sandwiched between the two).

Selman has suggested that this three-generation sequence of a faithful father followed by a wicked son and a faithful grandson is based on the situation described by Ezekiel in his oracle on individual responsibility before

God (Ezek. 18:1–20).[1] The stories of Jotham, Ahaz, and Hezekiah carry an important message for the Chronicler's audience—each person and every generation is responsible to God for their behavior. The reigns of Jotham and Hezekiah are instrumental in demonstrating that a new generation need not be held hostage to the ungodliness they inherit from their predecessors.

The combined tenure of Jotham, Ahaz, and Hezekiah on the throne of Judah extend from about 750 to 686 B.C. This means all three kings rule under the mighty shadow cast by the Neo-Assyrian empire (ca. 750–650 B.C.). The brutal grip of Assyria on Israel and Judah was first felt during the second western campaign of Tiglath-Pileser III (734–732 B.C.), when Pekah was replaced by Hoshea on the throne of the northern kingdom of Israel as an Assyrian puppet king (cf. 2 Kings 15:29–30). For all practical purposes Israel was annexed into the Assyrian Empire, and it is at this time that King Ahaz of Judah becomes an Assyrian vassal king (2 Kings 16:8).

Not long thereafter, Shalmaneser V (and his successor Sargon II, who completed the campaign) invades Israel in order to punish the rebellion of Hoshea (cf. 2 Kings 17:1–6). After a three-year siege, the city of Samaria was destroyed, survivors were deported to Assyria, and the entire northern kingdom was formally annexed into the Assyrian Empire (722 B.C.). Some time later, during the reign of Hezekiah, the Assyrian overlord Sennacherib launches a western campaign (701 B.C.). The Assyrians subdue the coastal plain of Syria-Palestine from Phoenicia to Philistia and then turn full attention to Judah. They pillage the outlying regions of Judah but are thwarted in their siege of Jerusalem by a disastrous plague attributed to divine intervention as a result of prayers offered by Hezekiah and the prophet Isaiah (2 Kings 18:17–19:36). The Assyrian annals do not report the outcome of Sennacherib's siege of Jerusalem.

Jotham (27:1–9)

THE BRIEF REPORT of King Jotham's reign is little more than a postscript to King Uzziah's tenure on the throne of Judah. The beginning regnal résumé (27:1–2) includes the expected formulaic information (age of accession, length of reign, and name of mother). In keeping with his emphasis on the Davidic monarchy, the Chronicler characteristically omits the synchronism to Pekah king of Israel (cf. 2 Kings 15:33–35). McConville treats the Chronicler's refusal to recognize the independent status of Israel as a type of "denial"— that is, he considers the northern kingdom to be "in rebellion against the house of David" (cf. 2 Chron. 10:19).[2]

---

1. Selman, *2 Chronicles*, 473.
2. McConville, *I and II Chronicles*, 225.

Harmonizing the chronological data for Jotham's reign proves challenging. Typically, his sixteen-year rule is dated from 750–735 B.C. It appears that Jotham serves as a coregent with his father Uzziah for the first ten years of his kingship (750–740 B.C.). The reference to the twentieth year of King Jotham (2 Kings 15:30) is usually understood to mean that Jotham's reign also overlaps with that of his son Ahaz. If so, then Ahaz is coregent and junior partner with his father Jotham commencing in 735 B.C. Jotham probably dies in 732 B.C.

Jotham is the first king of Judah since Abijah to receive an unqualified theological review from the Chronicler (27:2; cf. 13:1–22). Jotham's righteousness is illustrated by both a positive and negative analogy to his father Uzziah. (1) He is compared favorably to his father in that he does "right in the eyes of the LORD"; that is, he is obedient to God's law (27:2a). (2) But in contrast with his father, Jotham does not violate the temple precincts by attempting to usurp the priestly role (27:2b). The theme of individual responsibility reappears in the Chronicler's report in that Jotham's reign has little impact on the corrupt practices of the citizenry of Judah (27:2c). Unlike kingship at an early period (e.g., David), a righteous king on the Davidic throne is no guarantee that his subjects will behave in like manner.

The Chronicler's review of Jotham's reign applauds achievements on three fronts: his building program, his military success, and his consolidation of political power (27:3–6). The report represents an expansion of the parallel in 2 Kings 15:32–38. The Upper Gate of the temple (2 Chron. 27:3) was located on the northern side of the structure (cf. Ezek. 9:2), and Selman suggests the area was in need of repair because of the earlier attack against Jerusalem by King Jehoash of Israel (25:24).[3] The hill of Ophel (27:3) is equated with the southeastern hill of Jerusalem at southern end of the temple precinct. The building of "towns ... and forts and towers" in the outlying regions of Judah serves as testimony to the prosperity and growth achieved under Jotham. These installations are probably defensive measures as well, designed to buffer Jerusalem from direct attack by invading enemies.

Jotham's war with Ammonites (27:5) is not mentioned elsewhere in the Old Testament, but the campaign extends his father's military expansion from areas southwest of Judah to the east. According to modern-day equivalents, the amount of tribute received from the Ammonites is staggering—more than three tons of silver and approximately 62,000 bushels of barley. The reference to Jotham's becoming "powerful" is instructive. The same expression was used to characterize Uzziah's earlier reign (Heb. *ḥzq*; cf. 26:16). But unlike his father, Jotham does not fall prey to the temptation of

---

3. Selman, 2 *Chronicles*, 474.

pride and turn away from God. His success is attributed directly to the fact that he "walked steadfastly before the LORD" (27:6). This unique expression is generally understood to be synonymous with the phrase "to set one's heart on God" (cf. 1 Chron. 22:19; 28:9; 2 Chron. 30:19).

With the concluding regnal résumé (27:7–9), the writer returns to the parallel in 2 Kings 15:36–38. The reference to "all his wars" (2 Chron. 27:7) is an addition by the Chronicler and may refer to initial stages of conflict with the Syro-Ephraimite coalition (cf. 2 Kings 15:37; 16:5–6).[4] The repetition of age of accession and length of reign from the opening résumé is unusual. The resulting inclusio or envelope construction serves to emphasize the significant accomplishments of a youthful king in a comparatively brief period of time. In contrast to his father Uzziah, Jotham is buried in the city of David in the royal tomb complex (27:9; cf. 26:23).

Ahaz (28:1–27)

APART FROM THE opening and closing regnal résumés, the report of Ahaz's reign in Chronicles has little in common with 2 Kings 16. Specifically, the Chronicler expands the battle report of the Syro-Ephraimite war (2 Chron. 28:5–15) and the report of Assyrian intervention (28:16–21), along with the insertion of further commentary on Ahaz's apostasy (28:22–25). Ahaz rules Judah for sixteen years, from about 732 to 715 B.C. Presumably the Chronicler has omitted referencing the four-year coregency of Ahaz with his father Jotham (see comments on ch. 27).

Opening regnal résumé (28:1–4). The opening résumé contains the typical formulas: accession age, length of reign, and theological review (28:1). The Chronicler also omits, as usual, the synchronism with King Pekah of Israel (cf. 2 Kings 16:1). The negative theological review of Ahaz is uniquely phrased in that he is measured against King David and then indicted for not doing "what was right in the eyes of the LORD" (cf. 2 Kings 16:2; 2 Chron. 28:2).

The negative theological review is supported by a shocking list of covenant violations, such as idolatry (28:2), child sacrifice (28:3), and participation in the false worship associated with the Canaanite high places (28:4). The Valley of Ben Hinnom (28:3) was located immediately south of the Temple Mount and was the site of the city dump, where fires continually burned dead animals and garbage. The ritual of human sacrifice is associated with this valley elsewhere in the Old Testament (cf. 2 Kings 23:10; 2 Chron. 33:6; Jer. 7:31–32).

Perhaps the most striking comment in this résumé is the observation that King Ahaz is guilty of perpetuating the very sins for which God previously

---

4. So ibid., 475.

judged the indigenous Canaanites (28:3; cf. Deut. 18:9–13). The remark foreshadows the Babylonian exile, given the threat attached to the so-called "vomit theology" of the Mosaic code. Imitating the abominable practices of Canaanite religion will put Israel at risk of divine judgment and jeopardize their claim to the land of covenant promise (cf. Lev. 18:24–28).

Defeat by Syria (Aram) and Israel (28:5–15). The defining event of King Ahaz's reign is the so-called Syro-Ephraimite war. The conflict is so named because it pits the coalition kingdoms of Israel (or Ephraim) and Syria (or Aram) against Judah. The Old Testament accounts of this war are numerous (cf. 2 Kings 16:5–9; Isa. 7:1–9:6; Hos. 5:8–6:6). It seems likely that the Syro-Ephraimite alliance invades Judah in order to coerce it to join their anti-Assyrian coalition. Ahaz appeals to the Assyrians for help, it is granted, and the anti-Assyrian alliance is defeated.

The account of the Syro-Ephraimite war in Chronicles differs from that in 2 Kings 16 by downplaying the coalition of Syria (or Aram) and Israel and stressing instead the extent of Judah's defeat. Dillard suggests that the Chronicler's desire to cast Israel in a favorable light prompts him to present the invasion of Judah almost as if it were two separate campaigns—one by the Arameans (2 Chron. 28:5) and one by the Israelites (28:6–8).[5] This not only allows the writer to extricate the northern kingdom from an unsavory political alliance but also highlights more directly the reversal of roles recorded in Abijah's defeat of Jeroboam (13:13–18).

The large numbers of casualties and captives reported by the Chronicler (28:6, 8) have troubled biblical commentators. Rather than assume hyperbole on the writer's part, Selman posits understanding the fatalities as the equivalent of 120 "military units" and the captives as coming from 200 separate "families" or "clans" (i.e., understanding the Heb. term *ʾelep* as a "military unit" or "clan" instead of the literal number 1,000).[6]

Beyond the sheer totals, the devastating losses to Judah are compounded by the deaths of key officials, namely, "the king's son," the overseer of the palace, and the leader who is "second to the king" (28:7). The expression "the king's son" may be a title for a high-ranking officer, or the person named Maaseiah may be one of the royal princes.[7] The title "second to the king" occurs elsewhere in the Old Testament only in Esther 10:3, where context suggests it is the office held by the senior political adviser. In any case, the deaths of three members of Ahaz's "cabinet" would have had a crippling effect in the administration of political and military affairs in Judah. The

5. Dillard, 2 Chronicles, 220–21.
6. Selman, 2 Chronicles, 479.
7. Williamson, 1 and 2 Chronicles, 345–46.

reference to the "kinsmen" (lit., "brothers"; *aḥim*) may be another deliberate ploy on the part of the Chronicler to affirm the unity of the Israelite tribes despite the political schism that resulted in the northern and southern kingdoms (cf. "fellow countrymen," 2 Chron. 28:11, 15).

The Chronicler often uses prophetic intervention and oracular speech as a vehicle for his theology of immediate retribution. Interestingly, Oded is a prophet of Yahweh from Israel, whose ministry is centered in Samaria; clearly God still has a voice in the northern kingdom (28:9). Oded is not mentioned anywhere else in the Old Testament. His indictment of Israel serves as the source for the Chronicler's interpretation of the events of Ahaz's reign, as it is God who hands over Judah to Aram and Israel (28:9; cf. v. 5). According to Dillard, Israel oversteps its bounds in the excessive zeal shown in the wanton slaughter of the Judahites (28:9).[8] Beyond this, enslaving fellow Hebrews was forbidden by law of Moses; thus, Israel adds to its guilt and risks divine wrath (28:10–11; cf. Lev. 25:39–55). The Chronicler's positive portrayal of the northern kingdom should not go unnoticed, as he links both Israel and Judah to the same God (Yahweh [NIV LORD], 2 Chron. 28:10) and identifies the citizenry of each as "fellow countrymen" (28:11).

Unlike King Ahaz and their Judean counterparts, the leadership of Israel responds to the word of God through the prophet Oded and repents of their actions (28:12–13). The response of the Ephraimite leaders in releasing the prisoners of war to return to Judah and restoring the booty plundered in battle is tantamount to an admission of being "guilty . . . against the LORD" (28:10).[9] They are not guilty for the mistreatment of fellow Hebrews but guilty for rejecting Yahweh and worshiping idols (cf. 13:4–12). The care given to the former prisoners of war in providing food, clothing, and medical aid is reminiscent of the command to "love your neighbor as yourself" (Lev. 19:18). It has also been suggested that this story is the source for Jesus' parable of the good Samaritan (Luke 10:25–37).[10]

Further defeats of Judah (28:16–21). King Ahaz faces enemy aggression on two fronts, the Syro-Ephraimite coalition in the north and the alliance of the Philistines and Edomites in the south. The heavy losses suffered at the hands of the invading Israelites and Arameans (28:5–15) forces Ahaz to seek the "help" (28:16; Heb. *ʿzr*) of Tiglath-Pileser III, king of Assyria (745–727 B.C.). This dangerous diplomacy of playing one ancient superpower (i.e., Assyria) against another (i.e., Egypt) as an ally in petty border wars with neighboring nations was a ploy of the northern kingdom of Israel

---

8. Dillard, 2 *Chronicles*, 222.

9. Williamson, *1 and 2 Chronicles*, 347.

10. Dillard, 2 *Chronicles*, 223.

during the reign of Jeroboam II—a tactic soundly condemned by Hosea the prophet (Hos. 7:11).

In one sense, Ahaz is paying for the success of his predecessors since the Edomites seek retaliation against King Amaziah (cf. 25:14) and the Philistines seek to recoup earlier losses to King Uzziah (cf. 26:6). Given his predicament, Ahaz seeks help from the Assyrians despite the fact that God helped faithful kings of Judah in times past (cf. 1 Chron. 5:20; 2 Chron. 14:11; 18:31; 25:8; 26:7, 15; 32:8). According to the Chronicler, all this comes about to "humble Judah" because of the wickedness of Ahaz (2 Chron. 28:19). The reference to Ahaz as the "king of Israel" (28:19) serves as a stern reminder that the responsibility for Judah's plight lies with Ahaz as the Davidic shepherd of the people.

Tiglath-Pileser is only too happy to oblige Ahaz and interpose. In his campaign of 734 B.C. the Assyrian king overruns the Philistine cities of the coastal plain, sweeps over the Israelite kingdom, and carves up the territories into three Assyrian provinces. Finally, he sacks Damascus, executes King Rezin, and reorganizes the Aramean kingdom into four Assyrian provinces.[11] The intervention is costly to Judah, however, in the form of vassalage to Assyria for the next thirty years. Rather than "help," Ahaz receives "trouble" from the Assyrians (28:20). Judah not only suffers depleted economic resources because of the imposition of annual Assyrian tribute (28:21), but also loses its political autonomy—as Judah, Ammon, Moab, Ashkelon, Edom, and Gaza are all subordinated to Assyria as vassal states.[12] The punishment inflicted on Judah as divine judgment that Isaiah the prophet forecast is fulfilled (cf. Isa. 7:17).

Ahaz's apostasy (28:22–25). The Chronicler's account of King Ahaz's "paganization" of the kingdom of Judah is loosely based on 2 Kings 16:10–18. Ahaz's "time of trouble" (2 Chron. 28:22) affords the king the opportunity to seek the Lord in penitent prayer—a providential act of divine grace, in a way. But instead of turning to God and heeding Isaiah's injunction to fear the Lord (Isa. 7:13), he strays even further from Yahweh's covenant moorings by worshiping the gods of the victorious Syrians or Arameans (2 Chron. 28:23).

There is a sad irony in the wordplay emphasizing "help" (ʿzr), in that Ahaz first seeks help from the king of Assyria against the Arameans (28:16) and then from the gods of the Arameans after they have defeated Israel (28:23). Yet, it is Yahweh who "hands" Israel over to the king of Aram (28:5). By failing to acknowledge the God of Israel as sovereign Lord, Ahaz rejects the one source from which he may have received the help he so desperately pursues.

---

11. Ibid.

12. See Donald J. Wiseman, *1 and 2 Kings* (TOTC 9; Downers Grove, Ill.: InterVarsity Press, 1993), 261–62.

The parallel in 2 Kings 16:17–18 reports that Ahaz plunders the temple, presumably in order to pay the tribute demanded by Tiglath-Pileser. The Chronicler understands the act of stripping the temple of its furnishings as desecration of the holy sanctuary (2 Chron. 28:24). He does not report the meeting in Damascus between Ahaz and Tiglath-Pileser or the casting of a substitute altar for the Jerusalem temple after an Aramean or Syrian proto-type (2 Kings 16:10–16). Rather than Assyrian religious sanctions imposed on Ahaz as a vassal, it seems likely that the new altar and ritual sacrifices in Judah are the result of local Canaanite cultic influence.[13]

The cessation of ritual sacrifice presumed by the closing of the temple (28:24) does not stand in contradiction to the preceding reference to the offering of sacrifices (28:23) because the sacrificial altar is located in the court-yard outside of the temple proper. According to 2 Kings 16:16, the Levitical priesthood complies with the demands of Ahaz without resistance.

The proliferation of false worship under King Ahaz (28:24–25) echoes the apostasy of Jeroboam I at the time of the schism (cf. 13:8–9). The idol-atry of Ahaz has even greater affinities to the reign of King Ahab of Israel, however, in that both Ahaz and Ahab "institutionalize" the worship of false gods as the state religion of their respective kingdoms. In each case, the kings "provoke the anger of the LORD" and set in motion a course of events that inevitably culminates in exile (note 28:9, 11, 13 on "the anger of the LORD;" cf. 1 Kings 16:32–33; 2 Chron. 36:16).

Concluding regnal résumé (28:26–27). The closing résumé repeats 2 Kings 16:19–20 with some variation. For instance, the citation of source formula adds "and Israel" to the title of "the annals of the kings of Judah" (2 Chron. 28:26), and "Jerusalem" is substituted for the "City of David" (28:27). More notably, the Chronicler expands the summary statement of what Ahaz did according to 2 Kings 16:19 with "all his ways, from beginning to end" (2 Chron. 28:26). In so doing, the Chronicler implicitly calls atten-tion to the persistently wicked character of Ahaz rather than any heroic deeds that may have been attributed to him. Like King Uzziah before him (26:23), Ahaz is denied the honor of proper burial "in the tombs of the kings of Israel"—the ultimate negative theological review for the Chronicler.

Hezekiah (29:1–32:33)

KING HEZEKIAH RECEIVES more attention in the Chronicler's retelling of Israel's history than any other kings except David and Solomon. The account of

---

13. See the discussions in Cogan, *Imperialism and Religion*, 73–77; J. McKay, *Religion in Judah and Israel Under the Assyrians* (SBT, 2d series; Naperville, Ill.: Allenson, 1973), 5–12.

his reign in Chronicles is almost entirely independent of the parallel in 2 Kings 18–20. For example, the Kings narrative devotes but a single verse to Hezekiah's religious reforms whereas Chronicles spends three chapters elaborating on the cleansing and rededication of the temple and the restoration of the Passover festival (2 Chron. 29–31). Hezekiah's reign is usually dated from about 715 to 687 B.C.

The Chronicler's theological review of Hezekiah is almost entirely a favorable one—save a bout of pride from which he repents (2 Chron. 32:24–26). His reordering of the reports in 2 Kings and his inversion of the political and religious emphases is designed to portray Hezekiah as a "second" Solomon. Thus, even as Solomon erected the temple for Yahweh and established proper worship in Jerusalem (2 Chron. 3–7), so Hezekiah is unswerving in his restoration of proper worship in the Jerusalem temple (chs. 29–31). Likewise, just as God blessed Solomon with peace, prosperity, and military success as a result of his religious initiatives, so too Hezekiah's prosperity and military success follow upon his religious reforms.

McConville has noted that the closing chapters of Chronicles are not so much an end as they are an arrival—the conclusion of a long preamble that brings the audience to their own day under the rule of the Persian Empire.[14] The Chronicler holds out hope for a united Israel under a Davidic king overseeing the true worship of God in the Jerusalem temple. For him Hezekiah and Josiah are the prototypes of such kingship, hence their elevation as parade examples of "worshiping kings" at the end of the book. Dillard has observed that this lesson is not lost on the Chronicler's audience since "the path to the reunification of Israel and the fulfillment of prophetic hopes was the path of cultic fidelity."[15]

Invitation to purify the temple (29:1–11). The Chronicler's account of King Hezekiah's reign is framed by the customary regnal résumés. The opening résumé is the only citation of the synoptic parallel in this chapter (see 2 Kings 18:1b–3). In keeping with his standard practice the writer omits the synchronism with Hoshea king of Israel. The genre of report comprises all of chapters 29–31, which document Hezekiah's temple reforms and festival keeping. Unlike Jehoshaphat, who was likened to King David during the early years of his reign (2 Chron. 17:3), King Hezekiah is fully compared to David (29:2). In fact, the reference to David foreshadows several direct analogies between that ideal king and Hezekiah later in the narrative.

---

14. McConville, *I and II Chronicles*, 230.

15. Dillard, *2 Chronicles*, 228. On Hezekiah's religious reforms, and specifically his appeal to the northern tribes of Israel, see Andrew G. Vaughn, *Theology, History, and Archaeology in the Chronicler's Account of Hezekiah* (Atlanta: Scholars Press, 1999), 169–81.

Hezekiah's invitation to purify the temple (29:3–11) is dominated by a royal speech (29:5–11) directed to the priests and Levites (29:4). Like King Solomon (cf. 2:1), the proper worship of Yahweh is an immediate priority for Hezekiah as he initiates the cleansing of the temple in his first month of rule and celebrates the religious festivals in his second (cf. 30:2). The act of reopening the temple doors shut up by King Ahaz (28:24) and repairing them is a symbolic gesture indicating the temple is once again serviceable for worship (29:3). Hezekiah assembles the priests and Levites outside the still defiled sanctuary in a square to the east of the temple precinct (29:4)—perhaps the square adjacent the Water Gate (cf. Neh. 8:1).

The king's speech to the priests and Levites contains two injunctions: a call to the religious leadership to "consecrate" themselves and an instruction to them to "remove all defilement from the sanctuary" (29:5). The term "consecrate" (*qdš*) means to make holy by setting apart someone or something exclusively for the service for God (cf. Ex. 28:41; 29:1; 30:30). The word "defilement" (*niddah*) is used generally of ritual impurity, although here the writer probably has the pollution of idol worship in mind.

The rest of the royal address rehearses the neglect of the temple by Hezekiah's predecessors (29:6–8). The depth of Judah's apostasy under Ahaz is underscored in the fivefold emphasis on their wicked deeds: faithlessness, doing evil, forsaking God, turning their faces away from the temple, and turning their backs on Yahweh (29:6). It is for this reason that Yahweh's wrath fell on Judah, resulting in costly losses in battle and the exile of many citizens of Judah (29:9; cf. 28:5–8).

The dire nature of the situation facing Hezekiah is seen in the descriptors applied to Judah and Jerusalem: "an object of dread and horror and scorn"— words used to depict the aftermath of the Babylonian exile by the prophets Jeremiah and Ezekiel (cf. Jer. 25:9, 18; Ezek. 23:46). In advocating covenant renewal, Hezekiah is almost a Moses-type figure, acting as intercessor for the nation (2 Chron. 29:10). Hezekiah adjures the priests and Levites against continued apathy and dereliction of duty (29:11). By appealing to them as "sons," the king acknowledges their key role and encourages their renewed participation in the religious life of the Hebrew community. The litany of verbs ("stand," "serve," "minister," "burn incense," 29:11) describes the liturgical duties of the priests and Levites and reminds them of their unique status as a tribe "set apart ... to stand ... [and] minister" before the Lord (cf. Deut. 10:8; 18:5).

Renewing temple worship (29:12–36). According to Selman, nothing is more important to the central message of Chronicles than the proper worship of God.[16] This section along with chapters 30–31 is devoted to that very

---

16. Selman, 2 *Chronicles*, 484.

topic. In fact, it is the purification and consecration of the temple and its precincts by the Levitical corps that make renewed temple worship possible. The report describing the restoration of temple worship contains two main sections: the purification of temple (29:12–19) and the consecration of the temple and the reestablishment of sacrificial rituals (29:20–36).

The purification of the temple (29:12–19). It is standard practice for Chronicles to list the names of those involved in particular activities related to the liturgical life of the nation. The name list serves both to memorialize the contributions of key leaders in Israelite history and to remind the present audience that God's work is accomplished through the cooperative efforts of faithful individuals. The Chronicler records the names of fourteen individuals (29:12–14) who serve as the leaders of the purification ritual of the temple (29:15–19).

The basic organizational structure of Levitical leadership is similar to that in the list of Levites who assisted David in bringing the ark of the covenant to Jerusalem (cf. 1 Chron. 15:4–10). The first four groups are identical, the clans of Kohath, Merari, and Gershon, and the family of Elizaphan (2 Chron. 29:12–13a; cf. 1 Chron. 15:5–8). The family of Elizaphan has apparently risen to such prominence it is almost accorded the status of a fourth Levitical clan, although the family is a subclan of Kohath. By the time of Hezekiah, the three guilds of Levitical musicians (Asaph, Heman, and Jeduthun, 2 Chron. 29:13b–14) have replaced the two subclans of Levites (Hebron and Uzziel, cf. 1 Chron. 15:9–10). This suggests a gradual expansion in the influence of musical families in the Levitical hierarchy.

The actual cleansing of the temple takes two weeks, one week for the outer courts and another week to purge the sanctuary itself (29:15–17). The Chronicler is careful to indicate the work is done in accordance with the "the word of the LORD" (cf. Deut. 12:2–4). The work of cleansing the temple involved a two-stage process: (1) the purification of the temple and its courts by the removal of everything "unclean" (2 Chron. 29:16), and (2) the consecration of the temple structure and its furnishings and implements by ritual sacrifice (29:20–36). The word "unclean" (*ṭumʾah*) specifies those objects rendered ceremonial impure and hence unfit for use by virtue of their contact with other unclean objects or personnel (in this case, all that went along with the idolatry sanctioned under King Ahaz). Although not mentioned, all the trappings of false worship are removed to the Kidron Valley for burning (29:16; cf. 15:16; 30:14).

We learn elsewhere that the Levites were responsible for maintaining a careful inventory of the temple furnishings and implements (1 Chron. 9:28). No doubt that tradition persists, since the report presented to King Hezekiah includes the fact that all the temple utensils have been recovered and cleansed

(2 Chron. 29:18–19). Presumably they were stored or simply discarded in one of the anterooms of the temple during the reign of "unfaithful" Ahaz (29:19). Ackroyd notes that the emphasis on the recovery and cleansing of the temple implements constitutes an important bridge to the past for the restoration community, since these implements are of Solomonic origin (4:19–22).[17] The purified temple implements are arrayed before the altar of burnt offering, thus setting the stage for the report of the ritual sacrifices necessary for the consecration of the priests, Levites, and temple furnishings and implements and the resumption of the temple liturgy (29:20–36).

The consecration of the temple (29:20–36). The ceremony for the consecration of the temple is a multifaceted event. (1) The initial phase addresses the issues of sin and purification in the community (29:20–24). (2) The next phase features burnt offerings signifying the dedication of the religious and civic leaders and the sanctuary to the service of God (29:25–30). The burnt-offering ritual is accompanied by instrumental and choral music from the Levitical musicians and concludes with prostration in reverent worship (29:29–30). There is some question as to whether the sin offering and burnt offering are sequential or simultaneous events. (3) The final stage includes participation by the assembly of people from Jerusalem and Judah (representing "all Israel") through additional burnt offerings and thank offerings (29:31–36).

The Chronicler's emphasis on Hezekiah's orchestration of the consecration ceremony is unmistakable as the king "gathers" the civic leaders (29:20a), "commands" the priests to perform the ritual sacrifice (29:21b), and "gives orders" for the proceedings to begin (29:24). The multiples of seven in the list of sacrificial animals suggest the completeness of both the extent and the degree to which the sin offering is to be applied to the nation of Judah (29:21).

The "burnt offering" was an atoning sacrifice for the suppliant who participated vicariously in the ritual by laying his hand on the animal victim (Lev. 1:3–9). The "sin offering" of seven goats was specifically designated for the atonement and purification of "the kingdom, for the sanctuary and for Judah" (29:21). The phrase "for the kingdom" (29:21) is puzzling and may refer to the dynasty of David or the rule of God over the earth (cf. 1 Chron. 29:11).[18] The laying on of hands on the goat sacrifices calls to mind the Day of Atonement ceremony, the national day of purification for God's people (2 Chron. 29:23; cf. Lev. 16). The combination of sin and burnt offerings

17. See Peter Ackroyd, "The Temple Vessels—A Continuity Theme," in *Studies in the Religion of Ancient Israel,* ed. P. de Boer (VTSup 23; Leiden: Brill, 1972), 166–81.
18. Selman, *2 Chronicles,* 489.

is comprehensive in the sense that every sin is to be sacrificially atoned for so as to remove all forms of evil from Hezekiah's realm. The multiple sin offerings are also inclusive in the sense that they atone for the sins of "all Israel" (2 Chron. 29:24).

The consecration ceremony next emphasizes the dedication of the purified religious and civic leaders and the temple structure to the service of Yahweh (29:25–30). The Chronicler takes great pains to demonstrate the legitimacy of the rituals associated with the consecration ceremony by establishing direct connections to earlier traditions originating with David and sanctioned by God's word through the prophets (29:25–26). Even the detailed report that the priests are the ones blowing the trumpets is in keeping with the law of Moses (cf. Num. 10:8). In this stage of the consecration ceremony, the sacrificing of animals and the musical accompaniment of the Levitical musicians occur simultaneously (2 Chron. 29:27).

According to Selman, burnt offerings are sacrificed at every stage of the consecration ceremony, so the burnt offering here (29:27) need not be equated with the burnt offering mentioned earlier (29:24).[19] At the beginning and conclusion of the dedicatory portion of the ceremony, the whole assembly bows in reverence to God—a formal act of worship (29:28–29; cf. Ps. 95). It is clear to all that Yahweh is King in Israel, not Hezekiah, for he too bows before the Lord with the assembly (2 Chron. 29:29). The blending of joy in the singing of praises and reverence in bowing down are significant. The atonement ritual is not perceived as an end in itself but rather as a necessary preparation for the responses of praise and thanksgiving to God. The reference to Asaph the seer (29:30) recalls the commissioning of certain members of the Levitical musical guilds for the ministry of prophesying (cf. 1 Chron. 25:1–3).

During the final phase of the consecration ceremony (29:31–36) the rites of purification and dedication are extended to the "assembly" (29:31) and "all the people" of Judah (29:36). Unlike the public sacrifices atoning for the sin of the civic and religious leaders, the sacrifices of this final stage are freewill offerings presented by individuals "whose hearts were willing" (29:31). At least that much has not changed from King David's time—right attitudes must accompany the right acts of worship (cf. Ps. 51:16–17).

A variety of sacrifices is performed during the last stage of the consecration ceremony: burnt offerings, symbolizing the selfless worship of God, since the entire animal is consumed by fire (29:32); fellowship or peace offerings, symbolizing an intimate relationship with God, since the worshiper shares a portion of the sacrifice in a ritual meal (29:35; cf. Lev. 3); and drink

---

19. Ibid., 490.

offerings or libations of oil or wine poured onto the ground or sacred objects, in thanksgiving for God's goodness (2 Chron. 29:35; cf. Lev. 23:13, 18, 37).

The Chronicler commends the spirit of the Levites in assisting the priests in flaying the animals for sacrifice (29:34a). Apparently a spirit of apathy still plagues the priesthood, since some are slow to respond to Hezekiah's reforms (29:34b). Obviously the reign of Ahaz has cast a long shadow over temple worship and the priestly corps who serve there. According to Leviticus 1:6, the worshiper was to skin the sacrificial animal, but the Chronicler reports that the priests and Levites do all the flaying for the burnt offerings (2 Chron. 29:34). Rather than contradicting the Mosaic code, it is possible that skinning the sacrificial animals is among the additional duties David assigned to the Levites when he reorganized Israelite worship (cf. 1 Chron. 23:28, 32).

The rejoicing reported by the Chronicler celebrates the rescue of the people of Judah by God, since they now realize they had come perilously close to sharing the fate of the northern kingdom. That the restoration of temple worship is truly an act of God is seen in the fact that it is accomplished so quickly (29:36).

Invitation to celebrate the Passover (30:1–12). Biblical scholars who are skeptical of the reliability of Chronicles continue to cast suspicion on the historicity of Hezekiah's Passover. The quibble is over the exact nature of the relationship of the Feast of Unleavened Bread to Passover in the praxis of Hezekiah's Passover and the seeming variance in the reporting of the scope of the event when compared to Josiah's Passover (see 30:26; cf. 35:18).[20]

A detailed analysis of the objections raised against the historicity of the Chronicler's report of Hezekiah's Passover lies outside the scope of this commentary. The issues, however, are not insurmountable when evaluated against the Chronicler's distinctive purposes. For example, the emphasis on the Feast of Unleavened Bread in this Passover is to be clearly distinguished from a similar deemphasis on the Feast of Unleavened Bread in Josiah's Passover. Hezekiah's accent on the Feast of Unleavened Bread is designed to focus on the themes of fellowship and unity as he seeks to reunite the tribes after the fall of Israel to Assyria.

The introductory section of the chapter recounts the decision to celebrate the Passover in Jerusalem at the reopened temple (30:1–5). King Hezekiah and the "assembly" make this decision; the latter is apparently an advisory council comprised of ordinary citizens, tribal leaders, and royal officials (cf. 1 Chron. 13:1–2; Neh. 8:2). The "assembly" figures prominently in the Chronicler's narrative of Hezekiah's Passover (2 Chron. 30:2, 4, 13, 17, 23,

---

20. See Williamson, *1 and 2 Chronicles*, 361–62.

24, 25) and provides yet another link between this king and the "populist" reigns of David and Solomon (cf. 1 Chron. 29:1, 10; 2 Chron. 1:3–5).

The first verse of the introductory section serves as a header for 30:1–12. The actual text of Hezekiah's letter is summarized in the second section of the unit (30:6–9). Curiously, the letter itself does not mention the Passover celebration—although this is the theme of the entire pericope. The so-called "Passover letter" is sent "throughout Israel and Judah" as Hezekiah seeks to reunite the tribes in the aftermath of the Assyrian conquest and annexation of the northern kingdom. The reference to "Ephraim and Manasseh" (a word pair often used for the northern kingdom of Israel, cf. 34:9) is inserted almost as a point of clarification or special emphasis.

The Passover commemorated the Exodus from Egypt and was typically observed on the fourteenth day of Abib, the first month of the Hebrew calendar (cf. Ex. 23:14–15). The rationale for celebrating the Passover two weeks late includes the fact that time is needed for the priests to consecrate themselves as well as to allow for the people to make the pilgrimage to Jerusalem. Thompson suggests the delay may have also been precipitated by King Jeroboam's tampering with the religious calendar, setting the northern kingdom one month behind Judah (cf. 1 Kings 12:32–33).[21] Though irregular, observing the Passover in the second month is not without legal precedent. According to the Mosaic law, those ceremonially unclean or those absent because of a distant journey were permitted to celebrate the Passover on the fourteenth day of the second month (Num. 9:9–12). Here that principle is applied to whole community.

The phrase from "Beersheba to Dan" (30:5) represents the ideal geographical boundaries of Israel (cf. 1 Chron. 21:2). The idea here seems to be that of tribal representation; that is, Israelites who live anywhere from Beersheba to Dan are invited to the Passover. The reference to "according to what was written" (30:5c) is somewhat cryptic. It may be an acknowledgment of the restoration of Jerusalem as the place of centralized worship or, more likely, an inference to prescriptions for the Passover found in Deuteronomy 16:1–8.

The Chronicler's report (30:6–12) continues to emphasize King Hezekiah's role in the initiative to reunite Israel and Judah through worship at the site chosen and consecrated by God (30:8). The king's couriers also function as heralds, presumably proclaiming the contents of the letters to the local officials and reading the letters aloud in public forums. The letters are addressed to "all Israel and Judah" (30:6 NRSV), signifying Hezekiah's concern to rejoin the tribes after the collapse of the northern kingdom in the Assyrian onslaught.

---

21. Thompson, 1, 2 Chronicles, 352.

The text of the letter has affinities to the Levitical sermons and prophetic speeches of Chronicles. It is framed by the echo of Zechariah's call for the Israelites to "return to the LORD" or repent because God returns to those who return to him (šwb, 30:6, 9 [2x]; cf. Zech. 1:3). The series of imperative verbs within the body of the letter (e.g., "return," 30:6, 9; "submit," v. 8; "come," v. 8; "serve," v. 8) recalls God's answer to Solomon's prayer of dedication for the temple to forgive and heal those who turn to him (cf. 7:14).

In addition to calling the people to repentance, Hezekiah's letter admonishes the Israelites to cease being "unfaithful" (30:7) and "stiff-necked" (30:8) like their ancestors. The time to break with the past is long overdue. Hezekiah's letter holds out hope to those who have escaped the wrath of God meted out through Assyrian kings by offering them the possibility of reunion with those exiled in Mesopotamia to return to the worship of God in the Jerusalem sanctuary (30:9). The appeal to the Lord, who "is gracious and compassionate" (30:9), seems to allude once again to Solomon's dedicatory prayer, beseeching God to induce Israel's conquerors to show mercy on his people should they sin and be overtaken by their enemies (cf. 1 Kings 8:50).

Predictably, Hezekiah's invitation to renew festival worship in the reopened Jerusalem temple receives a mixed response (30:10–12). The scornful reception given to his couriers may have been life-threatening, perhaps explaining why the heralds do not traverse the entire northern kingdom with their message (cf. 30:5). The majority of Israelites in the regions of Ephraim, Manasseh, and Zebulun spurn the invitation, while others from Asher, Manasseh, and Zebulun humble themselves before the Lord and make the pilgrimage to Jerusalem (30:10–11). The overwhelming response of those in the kingdom of Judah to obey the king is a remarkable demonstration of solidarity and is attributed to the "hand of God" on the people (30:12).

Celebrating the Passover and the Feast of Unleavened Bread (30:13–31:1). The Passover was one of the three pilgrimage festivals observed in the Hebrew religious calendar, along with the Feast of Pentecost and the Feast of Tabernacles (Ex. 23:14–17; Deut. 16:16–17). The Passover and the Feast of Unleavened Bread were closely associated since the latter began the day after Passover and continued for seven days (Ex. 23:15; Deut. 16:3). The Chronicler's report alternates between the description of the Feast of Unleavened Bread (2 Chron. 30:13–14, 21–27) and the Passover (30:15–20). While some scholars argue that the shift in emphasis signals the writer's appeal to divergent sources, it seems more likely the Chronicler's interest in the themes of reestablished tribal unity and joy in corporate worship account for the prominence of the Feast of Unleavened Bread in the narrative.[22]

---

22. Cf. Dillard, *2 Chronicles*, 245; Thompson, *1, 2 Chronicles*, 355.

Hezekiah's festival may be outlined in three broad movements: the assembling of large numbers of Israelites making the pilgrimage to Jerusalem (30:13, 17–18), the cleansing and consecration rituals (30:14–16, 19), and the "sacrifice" of joyful praise extended over a two-week period (30:21–27). The reference to the size of the crowd gathered in Jerusalem for the festival is significant not so much for the sake of the sheer numbers as its composition of people from all over Judah and Israel (30:13). The inclusion of worshipers from the northern tribes speaks to the theme of "reunification" under King Hezekiah (cf. 30:18).

Previously the priests and Levites cleansed the temple precincts (29:15–17). Now the people participate in the religious reforms by ridding the city and the surrounding countryside of the vestiges of false worship perpetuated by King Ahaz (30:14). As in the case with the ritually unclean "debris" removed from the temple, the paraphernalia associated with false worship ends up in the Kidron Valley, the garbage dump of ancient Jerusalem (cf. 29:16).

The rituals associated with the Passover are the focus of the Chronicler's report in 30:15–20. The Passover animals are killed by the worshipers in keeping with the prescriptions for the feast in Exodus, except for those who are ritually impure and hence unfit to perform the task (30:15, 17; cf. Ex. 12:21). The zeal coupled with the appropriate actions of the people in observing the Passover shame the priests and Levites. The religious leaders in charge of instructing the people in the law of Moses and in mediating the sacrificial worship of Israel are outdone by a righteous laity (who presumably have not been taught the Torah for some time by a negligent and corrupt priesthood under King Ahaz). Shortly thereafter the priests and the Levites are consecrated, so they too are careful to follow the prescriptions of the Mosaic law in discharging their duties as mediators of the Passover (2 Chron. 30:16).

The Chronicler makes an important theological observation that intent of heart and acts of repentance, when combined with intercessory prayer, override the letter of the law when it comes to the worship of God (30:18–19; cf. Isa. 1:15–19; Mic. 6:8). Williamson aptly observes that the report of Hezekiah's Passover (esp. 2 Chron. 30:18–20) completes the allusion to a key portion of Solomon's prayer of dedication for the temple (7:14).[23] The leaders and the people have "returned" to God (30:9) and "humbled" themselves (30:11), and King Hezekiah himself has "prayed" for God's forgiveness. The result is answered prayer in the form of God's "healing" of the people (30:20). The "healing" in this context should be understood as spiritual restoration and social reconciliation, as the covenant relationship with God has been renewed and elements of the northern and southern tribes are reunited in true worship.

---

23. Williamson, *1 and 2 Chronicles*, 361–62.

The "great rejoicing" (30:21) celebrates God's grace in the pardon for sin and the cleansing from ritual impurity because this results in restoration of fellowship in covenant relationship with God. Earlier the Levites were central figures in the sacrificial ritual of the Passover in the slaughtering of animals and the handling of the blood for sprinkling by the priests (30:16–17). Now they return to center stage through their ministry of praise music during the week-long festival (30:21–22). Hezekiah's affirmation of the Levites is a poignant personal touch preserved by the Chronicler (30:22). Despite the fact that the tradition of the pilgrimage festivals had been neglected for years under the rule of evil King Ahaz, the religious personnel receive commendation for the knowledge and professional skill they demonstrate in the execution of their duties. "How good is a timely word!" (Prov. 15:23).

The seven-day extension of Hezekiah's Passover and Unleavened Bread festivals (30:23–27) has its precedent in the protraction of the ceremonies accompanying Solomon's dedication of the temple (cf. 7:8–10). The "whole assembly" (30:23) includes the people of Judah, the priests and Levites, and even "aliens" (i.e., resident non-Israelites) from the areas in the former northern kingdom (30:25). Some commentators understand the donations of thousands of animals by the king and other royal officials as additional victims for ritual sacrifice, while others assume that the animals are provided as food for the crowds of people staying on in Jerusalem.[24] It is likely a matter of "both-and" rather than "either-or," since worshipers could eat portions of the thanksgiving offerings.

Thompson has quipped that the size of the crowd and the length of the festival necessitate the participation of additional cultic personnel so that "more priests consecrated themselves and thus made amends for earlier dilatoriness."[25] The joy experienced by those participating in the festival affords the Chronicler a further opportunity to compare King Hezekiah with the Davidic and Solomonic ideal (30:26). No doubt, there is a less than subtle message about the relationship between right worship and answered prayer for the Chronicler's audience (30:27). The NIV inserts the conjunction "and" between priests and Levites (30:27), though it is not a part of the Hebrew text. It is probably more correct to read "Levitical priests" following Dillard and others, since the priests are the cultic officials charged with "blessing" the people (cf. Num. 6:22–27).[26]

---

24. On the former position see Williamson, *1 and 2 Chronicles*, 371; on the latter position see Thompson, *1, 2 Chronicles*, 356.

25. Thompson, *1, 2 Chronicles*, 356.

26. Dillard, *2 Chronicles*, 245.

The purging of idolatry and the destruction of false worship centers in the aftermath of Hezekiah's Passover and Unleavened Bread celebration (31:1) is loosely based on the parallel in 2 Kings 18:4. The Chronicler omits the reference to the smashing of the bronze snake, Nehushtan, a symbol from the Exodus wanderings that apparently became an object of worship in Judah (cf. Num. 21:8–9). The Chronicler adds specific details to the geographical extent of the reforms, including the regions of Judah, Benjamin, and territories in the former northern kingdom. The abrupt shift from King Hezekiah to the people as agents of the religious reforms is instructive. As Selman has noted, this is yet another lesson in worship renewal designed to encourage the Chronicler's audience "to restore faithful patterns of worship for themselves."[27]

Hezekiah's further reforms (31:2–21). The cleansing and reopening of the temple brings about the restoration of the temple liturgy. This means, in turn, that the sacrificial and musical guilds of the priests and Levites must be reorganized so they can adequately service the temple liturgy. Naturally, this calls for the reinstitution of the regular tithes and offerings prescribed by the law of Moses in order to support the temple personnel. This section of the Chronicler's report of Hezekiah's reign addresses the reordering of Levitical corps (31:2–3) and the reestablishment of the Mosaic tithes and offerings (31:4–19).

Hezekiah reinstates the system of tithes and offerings designed to both worship God and financially underwrite the ministry of the priests and Levites (30:2–3; cf. Lev. 6:14–7:36; Num. 18:8–32; Deut. 14:27–29). These reforms are necessary because presumably the priestly orders devoted to the sacrificial liturgy and the Levitical divisions assigned to various ministries were abolished when Ahaz closed Yahweh's temple (2 Chron. 29:24).

The reference to the Lord's "dwelling" (31:2; lit., "camp," Heb. *mahaneh*) may be a nostalgic allusion to the tabernacle, signifying faithfulness to Mosaic principles. The parallels to ancient ideals persist in the reorganization of the Levitical corps since the report indicates that Hezekiah restores the divisions of the priests and Levites implemented by Solomon (8:14). In fact, Thompson lists three ways in which Hezekiah may be likened to Solomon: giving generously of his own wealth for the support of the temple (31:3; cf. 9:10–11), overseeing the duties of the temple personnel as previously noted (31:3; cf. 8:14), and manifesting concern for abiding by the law of Moses (31:3).[28]

Dillard has noticed that the Chronicler delights in demonstrating that "faithful and generous kings prompt similar generosity in the population

---

27. Selman, 2 *Chronicles*, 501.
28. Thompson, 1, 2 *Chronicles*, 357.

(1 Chron. 29:6–9; 2 Chron. 24:8–14; 31:5–10)."[29] The Old Testament is unapologetic about the daily provisions secured for the priests and Levites by means of the tithes and offerings brought to the temple by the citizenry. The priests and Levites were to live on a portion of those offerings as part of their inheritance since they were allotted no land as a tribe (Deut. 18:1–2). This enabled the temple personnel to devote themselves to the study and teaching of "the Law of the LORD" (2 Chron. 31:4).

The rest of the section (31:5–19) links the regular giving of the tithes and offerings to the vitality of temple worship. The response to the king's command to bring the firstfruits of the produce of the field and tithe of the herds and flocks is overwhelming (31:5–8). No doubt, the Chronicler understands these actions as signifying the genuineness of the people's repentance. The offerings of grain, wine, and oil are designated for the priests (cf. Num. 18:12–13), while the Levites receive the tithe (cf. Num. 18:21). The contributions come from all Israel, including the citizens of Jerusalem as well as the residents of Judah and the Israelites from the northern tribes who have emigrated to Judah (2 Chron. 31:4, 6). The ingathering of both food stuffs and animals (31:7) lasts from the grain harvest of the third month (the Feast of Pentecost [May/June]) to the fruit and vine harvests of the seventh month (the Feast of Tabernacles [Sept/Oct]).

The Chronicler continues his pattern of relating the events of Hezekiah's reign to an earlier ideal. (1) He associates the king's blessing with those of Kings David and Solomon (31:8; cf. 1 Chron. 16:2; 2 Chron. 6:3). (2) He equates the people's abundant giving with the overflow of contributions collected for the building of the tabernacle and the temple (cf. Ex. 36:2–7; 1 Chron. 29:6–9). (3) Finally, the Chronicler carefully reports that the bounty of goods received is inventoried, properly stored and maintained, and distributed with equity among the families of the priests and Levites (2 Chron. 31:11–19).

The concluding theological review (31:20–21) may be a paraphrase of the parallel in 2 Kings 18:5–7a.[30] In any case, the positive evaluation of Hezekiah is an extension of the favorable assessment found in the opening regnal résumé (2 Chron. 29:1–2). The review also links Hezekiah with David in his wholehearted devotion to God and with Solomon in his concern for the Lord's temple, ranking him among the great kings of Israel (cf. 7:11).

Williamson notes that the theological review also stands as a literary marker of sorts, a signal that the Chronicler's independent account of Hezekiah's reign has ended and the narrative now returns to the synoptic

---

29. Dillard, 2 *Chronicles*, 249
30. See ibid., 251.

parallel of Kings.[31] Hezekiah's sterling record of obedience and faithfulness to Yahweh elevates him as parade example of the Chronicler's "retribution theology" (see 31:21) and foreshadows the providential turn of events reported next.

Sennacherib besieges Jerusalem (32:1–23). Along with the building of Solomon's temple and the fall of Samaria, Sennacherib's invasion of Judah is one of the most important events in the history of the southern kingdom. The Assyrian campaign is dated to 701 B.C., during the fourteenth year of Hezekiah (2 Kings 18:13). The Chronicler assumes a thorough knowledge on the part of his audience of the earlier parallel accounts (2 Kings 18–19; Isa. 36–37). Further, he ignores the problems of harmonizing posed by the conflicting details of the invasion reported in the Kings version. As Selman notes, the Chronicler has edited the earlier sources in such a way that the conflict becomes largely a "war of words."[32]

The Chronicler's summary of the event largely consists of two speech acts: one by Hezekiah (32:6–8) and one by an officer of Sennacherib's army (32:10–15). This is followed by the report of a prayer by Hezekiah and Isaiah the prophet (32:20). The repetition of the Hebrew verb *nṣl* (NIV "save" [32:11, 14], "deliver" [vv. 13, 14, 15], and "rescue" [v. 17]) identifies the question that is central to the plot of the story: Can Yahweh deliver his people from the Assyrian onslaught?

The relationships between the three accounts of the Assyrian invasion of Judah may be outlined as follows:

2 Chronicles	2 Kings	Isaiah
32:1	18:13	36:1
32:9–10	18:17–19	36:2–4
32:12	18:22	36:7
32:13–14	18:35	36:20
32:15	18:29	36:14
32:16	18:27–28a	36:12–13a
32:17	18:33, 35	36:18, 20
32:18	18:28a	36:13a
32:19	19:18	37:19
32:20	19:15a	37:15
32:24	20:1–2	38:1–2
32:32–33	20:20–21	

---

31. Williamson, *1 and 2 Chronicles*, 377.
32. Selman, *2 Chronicles*, 508.

Hezekiah's defensive preparations (32:1–8). The opening verse of the report of Sennacherib's invasion of Judah is modified in two significant ways when compared to the earlier parallels. (1) The Chronicler ignores the chronological aspect of the event (which takes place in the fourteenth year of Hezekiah). (2) He juxtaposes the pious acts of King Hezekiah with the arrogant thoughts of King Sennacherib (32:1b). Beyond this, the Chronicler also omits the Assyrian capture of the towns and villages surrounding Jerusalem, the siege of the city itself, and the tribute Hezekiah pays to induce Sennacherib to call an end to his campaign and withdraw from Judah (cf. 2 Kings 18:13–16). Instead, in keeping with his theological agenda, the writer emphasizes that the Assyrian invasion occurs "after all that Hezekiah had so faithfully done." No doubt this refers to the extensive religious reforms implemented by Hezekiah documented in chapter 31. The key to the divine deliverance of Jerusalem from the Assyrian assault is the king's faithfulness to God in restoring proper temple worship.

The Chronicler's report of Hezekiah's efforts to make ready for an Assyrian siege against Jerusalem has no parallel in the synoptic accounts (32:2–5). Hezekiah's defensive precautions should not be interpreted as a lack of faith in God but rather as an example of prudence on the part of a wise king who understands there is "a time for war and a time for peace" and prepares accordingly (cf. Eccl. 3:8). In addition, the Chronicler understands success in building projects by faithful kings as a sign of divine favor (e.g., 2 Chron. 26:9–10; 27:3–4).

The defensive measures Hezekiah uses to thwart the Assyrian army include the stoppage of springs supplying fresh water around the environs of Jerusalem (32:3–4), repairing the walls and towers of Jerusalem and fortifying this reconstruction with a second "wall outside" (32:5a), and stockpiling an arsenal by making weapons and shields (32:5b). It is unclear as to whether Hezekiah's water tunnel linking the Gihon spring with the Pool of Siloam is engineered at this time. Likewise, the location of the springs and the identity of the "stream that flowed through land" is a matter of speculation.[33] Despite the uncertainty related to the water systems of ancient Jerusalem, we should not lose sight of Hezekiah's leadership skills, first in seeking wise counsel (32:3) and then in mobilizing the people to accomplish the tasks (32:4).

Finally, Hezekiah organizes the citizens of Jerusalem into a militia of sorts with oversight by select military personnel (32:6). As "commander-in-chief" he encourages the people with a motivational speech patterned after the charge to Joshua as he succeeded Moses before the conquest of Canaan (32:6b–8a; cf. Deut. 31:8; Josh. 1:9). The king's appeal to the people is a the-

---

33. Japhet, *I and II Chronicles*, 982–83.

ological treatise, not a nationalistic or patriotic rally cry. Despite the overwhelming odds stacked against Hezekiah and Jerusalem numerically speaking, victory is assured because it is God himself who is fighting for Judah (Ex. 14:14; Deut. 1:30; 20:4; cf. Deut. 17:16).

The reality of Yahweh as a "strong tower" of safety for his people was proven throughout the course of Hebrew history—as recently as Asa's defeat of Zerah the Cushite (14:11; cf. Prov. 18:10). As the psalmist observes, "no king is saved by the size of his army.... The LORD ... is our help and our shield" (Ps. 33:16, 20). Perhaps more significant for the terrified people of Jerusalem "caged" within their own walls by the Assyrian besiegers is the promise of God's presence in the midst of the conflict (2 Chron. 32:8; cf. Deut. 20:1).

The people take heart from the king's words and gain confidence to face the crisis because Hezekiah is able to articulate that his confidence is deeply rooted in the Lord their God. For the Hebrews, that epithet "the LORD our God" (32:8) is a reminder of God's election of the nation of Israel and his mighty deliverance of his people from Egyptian oppression at the Exodus (cf. Ex. 8:10).

Sennacherib's invasion of Judah (32:9–19). The Chronicler's account of Sennacherib's invasion of Judah and siege of Jerusalem abridges 2 Kings 18:17–19:13. The introductory adverb "later" (2 Chron. 32:9) and the omission of the reference to the "large army" against them (cf. 2 Kings 18:17) suggest the writer also assumes the audience's knowledge of the Assyrian siege of Lachish (cf. 2 Kings 18:13–16). The Assyrian annals claim that Sennacherib swept through Judah and ransacked forty-six towns and villages on his third campaign, taking more than 200,000 captives and locking up Hezekiah in Jerusalem "like a bird in a cage."[34] The biblical record in 2 Kings 18:14 reports that the Assyrians attack Judah during the fourteenth year of Hezekiah (701 B.C.) and that he pays tribute to Sennacherib as an inducement to withdraw his troops from the Judean territory. Yet this narrative in Kings abruptly shifts to the Assyrian siege of Jerusalem (18:17–37). This has led some scholars to postulate that Sennacherib's siege of Jerusalem is actually an event during his second campaign against Judah a decade later.

As Wiseman has noted, however, it seems better to understand one Assyrian invasion of Judah since there is nothing in the biblical accounts "which cannot be reconciled with the Assyrian annals, which refer to one attack on the city and make no reference to any capture of it."[35] It is likely that Sennacherib's Judean campaign unfolds in two stages. The first phase includes

---

34. William W. Hallo, gen. ed., *The Context of Scripture: Monumental Inscriptions from the Biblical World* (Leiden: Brill, 2000), 2:303.

35. Wiseman, *1 and 2 Kings*, 276. Moreover, extant Assyrian annals make no reference to a second Judean campaign by Sennacherib.

the capture of the environs of Jerusalem and the second siege of the city itself. The reason for Sennacherib's failure to withdraw from Judah after receiving Hezekiah's tribute is unclear, although the Assyrian king is no doubt motivated by greed to possess all the wealth of the Jerusalem temple— not just a portion of it.

The message delivered to King Hezekiah by the officers of Sennacherib (32:10–15) is a cleverly arranged summary of several speeches found in 2 Kings 18:19–25, 27–35; 19:9–13. The key element of the passage is the question posed by the Assyrian officers: "On what are you basing your confidence...?" (2 Chron. 32:10). That question remains as pertinent for today's reader of the story of Sennacherib's invasion of Judah as it is for the Chronicler's audience some three centuries after the fact.

The gist of the Assyrian message is a call to surrender the city of Jerusalem or die in the siege. King Sennacherib's emissaries offer two logical reasons for Judah's capitulation to the invading army. (1) The success of the Assyrian campaign in the outlying regions of Judah is interpreted as necessary retribution against Hezekiah because he has offended the gods in his purge of the "high places" (32:11–12). (2) Recent history has shown that none of the gods of the other nations was able to deliver their people from the Assyrian juggernaut (32:13–15).

The final section of the Assyrian message to Hezekiah and the citizens of Jerusalem is a taunt against the God of Israel, mocking his impotence in the current crisis (32:16–19). The gibes are delivered in the form of "insulting" letters written by Sennacherib himself (32:17). According to 2 Kings 18:28, the Rabshakeh (or the "field commander" of King Sennacherib) announces the message in Hebrew so that those along the walls and in the towers might overhear the Assyrian threats.[36] The Assyrians were masters of psychological warfare, and this is but another example of their practice of conquest by intimidating and terrifying the enemy with religious and military propaganda (note the earlier reference to the "hunger and thirst" by which the people of Jerusalem would die as a result of a protracted siege of the city, 2 Chron. 32:11).

According to Selman, the Assyrians "dealt Yahweh the final insult" by ignominiously comparing the God of Israel with the idols of the nations— "the work of men's hands" (32:19).[37] Sennacherib and the Assyrians will soon experience the dire consequences of putting God to the test by profaning his name in this manner (cf. Deut. 5:11; 6:14–16).

---

36. Note that this is the only direct reference to the Hebrew language in the Old Testament, cf. Isa. 19:18.
37. Selman, *2 Chronicles*, 513.

God defends Judah (32:20–23). God's deliverance of Hezekiah and the people of Judah is achieved through prayer, perhaps another allusion to Solomon's paradigmatic prayer of dedication for the temple (7:13–16). Curiously, the Chronicler omits any reference to the temple in the report of the prayer offered by Hezekiah and the prophet Isaiah (32:20; cf. 2 Kings 19:14). Williamson has suggested this is a deliberate effort on the part of the writer to remove a "particularity" that might prohibit the application of the power of prayer by his audience.[38]

The Chronicler also heightens the direct intervention of God against the Assyrians by reporting that "the LORD sent an angel" into the enemy camp (32:21; cf. 2 Kings 19:35). The "death angel" annihilates the Assyrian army, including officers and troops. It is suggested that God's angel afflicts the Assyrians with some kind of disease or plague (cf. the plague brought against Israel as a result of David's census, 1 Chron. 21:12–15). Sennacherib withdraws from Jerusalem in disgrace and returns to Assyria with the remnants of his decimated army.

No doubt the Chronicler has certain psalms in mind in which the enemies of the righteous are turned back in shame and disgrace (cf. Ps. 6:10; 40:14; 70:2). His account compresses time in such a way to suggest that Sennacherib is assassinated immediately upon his return to Nineveh, perhaps to accent the retribution principle for his audience. In actuality, Sennacherib is murdered by his son Adrammelech while worshiping in the temple of Nisroch some twenty years later (ca. 681 B.C.).[39]

Far more important to the Chronicler is God's deliverance of Hezekiah and Judah from the superior forces of the Assyrians (32:22). The key question of the story line has been answered: God has "saved" the king and the nation. Interestingly, the writer uses another Hebrew word (*yšʿ*, "to save, deliver") instead of the term *nṣl* to report that "the LORD saved Hezekiah and the people of Jerusalem." This may simply reflect the reliance of Chronicles on the Isaiah version of the story (cf. Isa. 37:20, 35), or it may be a deliberate attempt to equate the deliverance from the Assyrians with the exodus from Egypt (cf. Ex. 14:30).

The words of Hezekiah's speech have proven true: God's power is greater than that of the Assyrians, and he indeed fought the battle for Judah (32:8). The expression "he [Yahweh] took care of them on every side" (lit., "and he gave them *rest* round about") is "a blessing enjoyed as a reward for faithfulness" in Chronicles (cf. 15:15; 20:30). The "offerings" brought to the Lord (32:23) are probably thank offerings (made for an unexpected blessing) or

---

38. Williamson, *1 and 2 Chronicles*, 385.
39. Wiseman, *1 and 2 Kings*, 285.

vow (votive) offerings (presented for deliverance when a vow is made on that condition, cf. Lev. 22:18–30). The exaltation of Hezekiah in the eyes of the nations parallels that of King Solomon (2 Chron. 9:23–24).

Hezekiah's pride and death (32:24–33). The expression "in those days" (32:24) is intended to closely link Hezekiah's illness with the Assyrian invasion in a chronological sense. The actual healing of Hezekiah's life-threatening ailment is reported briefly, as the Chronicler apparently assumes his audience's knowledge of 2 Kings 20:1–11. Unlike the account in Kings, however, the Chronicler uses the sign of miraculous healing to establish a cause-and-effect relationship with the visit of Babylonian envoys (cf. 2 Chron. 32:31). The emphasis in the opening paragraph (32:24–26) is on Hezekiah's prayer and his repentance of the sin of pride in the aftermath of his remarkable cure. These "acts of devotion" (32:32) are no doubt offered to the Chronicler's audience as a model of virtuous behavior to be emulated.

The direct relationship between divine blessing and God's forgiveness recorded in 32:27–31 repeats a motif associated with righteous kings (e.g., David, Solomon, Jehoshaphat, Uzziah). The reference to Hezekiah's "great riches and honor" is another parallel the Chronicler draws between this king and Solomon (cf. 1:12; 9:22). Among Hezekiah's numerous achievements as a builder is the digging of a tunnel to channel water from the Gihon spring into the city of Jerusalem (32:30; cf. 2 Kings 20:20). The hewing of Hezekiah's water shaft is a remarkable engineering feat, and the now-famous Siloam inscription commemorates the event.[40]

Hezekiah's "success" (32:30) may be viewed as God's reward for overcoming the circumstances of God's testing in his life (32:31). Divine testing is a recurring Old Testament theme, not because God needs to know the intents of the human heart, but rather because the Lord tests the hearts of his servants so that they might respond to him in complete faith as a result of the discernment that emerges from this kind of self-knowledge (cf. Deut. 8:2–3).

The concluding regnal résumé (32:32–33) repeats, with some variation, 2 Kings 20:20–21). For instance, the historical citation formula (2 Chron. 32:32) references the "vision of the prophet Isaiah" as the source of the Chronicler's information. The association of this source as a special literary collection within the "book of the kings of Judah and Israel" militates against equating the "vision of the prophet Isaiah" with the prophetic book of Isaiah. The burial formula is expanded to include a more detailed description of Hezekiah's tomb and the honor accorded him by the general populace at his death (cf. 16:14; 21:19). The phrase "on the hill" (32:33) may refer liter-

---

40. Hallo, *The Context of Scripture*, 2:145–46.

ally to an elevated or prominent location in the royal tomb complex (so NIV), or it may be an idiom for "a place of privilege" in the royal cemetery.[41]

 HEADLINES. The headlines characteristic of the print media are "attention-getters" or "hooks," designed to draw the reader into "the rest of the story" or to entice a consumer into purchasing a product. Leslie Allen has noted that the Chronicler helps draw his audience into his retelling of Hebrew history by providing cues or "headlines" that highlight key aspects of his message before illustrating them or elaborating on them in detail.[42]

One example of a headline from the reign of King Jotham is the statement that he "grew powerful because he walked steadfastly before the LORD his God" (27:6). The cause-and-effect relationship between the king's success as a ruler and his obedience to the word of the Lord cannot be missed—even by the casual reader of the Chronicler's history. The simple lesson to be learned, whether or not one reads past the headline, is that obedience to God pays dividends—be they spiritual or material. This message is sorely needed for those inhabiting postexilic Jerusalem at the time of the Chronicler, especially if the attitude expressed by the people living at the time of Malachi the prophet still prevails. They challenge God and his prophet with this question: "What did we gain by carrying out his requirements?" (Mal. 3:14).

The counterpoint to this example is a tragic headline from the story of King Ahaz, who "in his time of trouble . . . became even more unfaithful to the LORD" (28:22). Once again, the gist of this story is encapsulated in this "one-liner," apart from a further careful reading of the narrative. The depth of Ahaz's rebellion against God and the perverseness of his evil ways are accentuated by his failure to seek God in a situation when any other ordinary human being would implore divine help—a time of severe personal and/or national crisis. Like all master teachers, the Chronicler recognizes that learning takes place through both negative and positive examples.

Hezekiah is the prominent character in this section of the Chronicler's retelling of Israelite history. He is featured primarily for restoring the appropriate worship of Yahweh in the Jerusalem temple and for modeling courageous faith in the throes of the Assyrian crisis. It is widely recognized that the writer of Chronicles emphasizes the reigns of Kings Hezekiah and Josiah because they represent important links to the ideal of Hebrew kingship

---

41. Williamson, *1 and 2 Chronicles*, 388.
42. Allen, *1, 2 Chronicles*, 366.

embodied in David and Solomon. In so doing, the Chronicler makes the heroic, even legendary figures, of Israel's glorious past more accessible to his own audience living in an ignoble present.

Especially important is the portrayal of the exemplary personal qualities and character traits of these ancestral stalwarts in the narrative of the Chronicler. He presents characterizations in such a way that the common person can readily aspire to imitate them—with the conviction that these aspirations are realistic and attainable. The "headlines" from Hezekiah's reign offer several such patterns of godly behavior, which ordinary folk might take to heart, copy, and benefit from.

- Hezekiah **"opened the doors of the temple"** (29:3). An open door is an invitation—in this case, an invitation to encounter the divine presence through corporate worship. This invitation is supremely valuable because it permits human beings to fulfill their purpose as creatures made in God's image, reflecting the praise of his glory (Isa. 43:7). What's more, worship of God is the integrating principle of human life. It removes the artificial "sacred-versus-secular" dichotomy usually applied to time and vocation. Worship also brings proper perspective to the issue of theodicy (i.e., the problem of evil in the world), for it is only after the psalmist enters the sanctuary that he understands why the wicked seem to prosper while the righteous seem to suffer unjustly (cf. Ps. 73:12–17). It is the experience of worship that assures the psalmist of the ultimate vindication of the righteous.
- **"Now I intend to make a covenant with the LORD"** (29:10). Hezekiah's declaration to make a covenant with the Lord is more than political rhetoric or religious showmanship. The expression "to make a covenant" takes the people back to their roots, back to "first things"— the Israelites' experience at Mount Sinai. This reflection on "first things" is important both for an individual and for a nation, because it permits a recentering of priorities and a refocusing of perspective. No doubt, the Chronicler believes such an occasion motivating a recentering and refocusing of one's life is essential for his own audience.

  The term *covenant* is a callout of sorts because it signifies the reciprocal obligations of the parties involved in sealing the agreement. Covenant renewal was an essential feature of Israelite religious practice because it is the covenant itself that establishes direct relationship with God. The act of will on Hezekiah's part ("I intend") is a reminder of the importance of human responsibility in maintaining that relationship with God. Each generation must renew or personalize and revitalize that relationship with God (cf. Josh. 24:15).

- King Hezekiah sends word to all Israel: "**Return to the LORD, the God of Abraham, Isaac and Israel, that he may return to you**" (30:1, 6). The great prophetic cry of the Old Testament is to "turn to God and live" (Ezek. 18:23, 32). As we have learned elsewhere in our discussion of the Chronicler's message, the word "return" (šwb) is essentially a call to repentance—a total change of heart, mind, and direction in life away from sin and toward God, an "about face," to borrow a military command. This word is important to a biblical understanding of theology proper, that is, the knowledge of God. The word "return" reminds us that the Lord is a "compassionate and gracious God, slow to anger, abounding in love and faithfulness . . . and forgiving wickedness, rebellion and sin" (Ex. 34:6–7a). The word carries a stern warning as well because the Lord "does not leave the guilty unpunished" (34:7b).

  According to one rabbi, "no word is God's final word."[43] That is, beware of divine silence because when God stops speaking to his people, judgment is imminent. Clearly, the full import of the word "return" is still available for the Chronicler's audience if they are willing to hear and respond—God is still speaking!

- "**But Hezekiah prayed for them**" (30:18; cf. 32:20). The power of prayer in petition for oneself and intercession for others is attested time and again in the Old Testament. Unlike the false gods who have ears but are deaf (Ps. 115:6), prayer to the God of Israel is effective because he is a God who hears and answers prayer. Compare, for example the words of the psalmist whose testimony is repeated over and over by the Old Testament faithful: "When I called, you answered me" (Ps. 138:3). The Jews of the Chronicler's day have no Davidic king ruling over them, no army to protect them, and no political leverage within the bureaucratic structures of the Persian Empire—but they still have prayer and a God who hears and answers!

- Hezekiah "**sought his God and worked wholeheartedly**" (31:21). Whether king or peasant, scribe or farmer, man or woman, adult or child, all can apply themselves to seeking God and doing his work wholeheartedly. God shows no partiality, but his eyes range throughout the earth to search out those who are fully committed to seeking him (16:9; cf. 19:7; 2 Sam. 14:14; Rom. 2:11). Seeking God is not our natural inclination as fallen people in a fallen world (cf. Ps. 14:2; Rom. 3:11). Yet, as a contemporary of the prophet Isaiah, Hezekiah knows the importance of seeking God while he may be found (Isa. 55:6). He also knows that there are great benefits attached to this quest for God,

43. Heschel, *The Prophets*, 1:194.

including spiritual life and those good things God provides for sustaining physical life (cf. Ps. 34:10; 69:32). What better quest can the Chronicler offer his audience than to seek God with all their heart (119:2)?

- "So the LORD saved Hezekiah and the people of Jerusalem" (32:22a). The Chronicler understands the simple truth that people are people, nothing more, and that God is God, nothing less. A faithful God delivers his faithful people. The mere presence of the Jews back in Jerusalem after the Babylonian exile is testimony to this fact. This alone leads the Chronicler to summon his audience to renew their worship of the Lord, the God of heaven, who appointed King Cyrus of Persia to rebuild his holy temple in Jerusalem (36:23).

- Perhaps the most significant headline posted by the Chronicler in his retelling of Hezekiah's reign is the banner line: "He took care of them on every side" (32:22b). The overt reference in this verse is to the Lord, who delivered Hezekiah and the people of Judah from Assyrian aggression (32:22a). But the header is implicitly true of King Hezekiah as well, since he did what was "good and right and faithful" throughout Judah (31:20).

    The record of Chronicles provides numerous "snapshots" of Hezekiah tending to the needs of his people. For example, he attends to the spiritual welfare of his people in the rehabilitation of the priesthood and the restoration of temple worship (29:3). His care for the physical needs of his people is manifested in the building of storehouses for stockpiling surplus foodstuffs against future famine or siege and in the provision of a reliable fresh water supply for the inhabitants of Jerusalem (32:28, 30). Finally, Hezekiah's concern for social and political stability in his realm may be seen in his desire to reunite the remnants of the kingdom of Israel with the kingdom of Judah in his great Passover celebration (30:5).

To compare human leaders as shepherds is a natural metaphor for writers in a pastoral community. The Old Testament portrayal of Israelite authority figures like kings as shepherds is based on the analogy of God as Shepherd for his people, especially in the depiction of leading his flock to safe pastures in the Exodus (Ex. 15:13, 17; cf. Ps. 78:52–55; 80:1).[44] The idea of the king as a shepherd or guide for his people is also a common motif in the ancient Near East.[45]

---

44. Louis Jonker, "רעה," *NIDOTTE*, 3:141–42.

45. See, e.g., H. W. F. Saggs, *The Greatness That Was Babylon* (New York: New American Library, 1968), 353.

An important subtext in the Chronicler's retelling of the history of the Israelite monarchies is the conviction that God will once again restore Davidic kingship over his people. The Chronicler has not given up on Ezekiel's promise that the Sovereign Lord will place a "shepherd" over his people like his servant David, who will tend to their needs (Ezek. 34:23–24). The New Testament writers are not slow to pick up on applying this motif to Jesus—the "good shepherd" according to John's Gospel (John 10:11) and that "great Shepherd of the sheep" from the familiar benediction in the letter to the Hebrews (Heb. 13:20).

HEZEKIAH THE ENCOURAGER. The members of the clergy of the Christian church have been recognized as "pastors" (lit., "herdsman" in Latin) from the apostolic age to the present, largely on the basis of Peter's exhortation to the elders to be "shepherds of God's flock that is under your care" (1 Peter 5:2). Michael Wilcock has compared Hezekiah with "the pastor coping with crisis" in his handling of the Assyrian invasion of Judah.[46] He offers four principles for the Christian leader facing such crossroads in ministry: looking up to God (i.e., worship and obey God first of all), looking around at the church (i.e., focus on the needs of God's people as a whole), looking into the heart (i.e., emphasize the inward response of genuine devotion and true spirituality), and looking out at the enemy (i.e., fully trust God for deliverance).

This advice is still valid for the pastor or Christian leader facing a crisis situation, especially the prominence given to the place of worship at critical moments in one's life (cf. Ps. 73:16–17). Yet, striking in its absence from Wilcock's list is Hezekiah's role as an encourager—a key duty of the pastor or Christian leader. Three times the Chronicler conspicuously reports how Hezekiah speaks words of encouragement to the people, affirming their service to God and instilling confidence in them despite the dire circumstances portended by Sennacherib's invasion of the southern kingdom (cf. 30:22; 32:6–7, 8).

The repetition of this character trait in the king of Judah seemingly makes the topic an obvious one for a contemporary application of this passage. Much to my surprise, however, an investigation of several recent books on the subject of pastoral theology have turned up little on the importance of the "Barnabas-principle" (or the gift of encouragement) in pastoral ministry. Undaunted, I probed books that catalogue exemplary human virtues, certain

---

46. Wilcock, *The Message of Chronicles*, 245–55.

that the attribute of encouragement would be rostered among those highly esteemed personal traits of the morally educated person. Once again, I was confounded because the virtue of encouragement is missing in the honor roles of desirable human qualities.[47]

Naturally this raises the question of exactly what a "virtue" is. Perhaps I was mistaken about encouragement as a virtue. Are virtues only "inner-directed" qualities and traits that define human goodness and morality? Is there an equal place for "outer-directed" characteristics of human goodness? I discovered that very early the Christian church recognized four "cardinal virtues" because of the promotion of Plato's ethical teaching by Ambrose of Milan (A.D. 340–397): wisdom, courage, temperance, and justice. Later the church added the theological virtues of faith, hope, and charity (or love), so that seven virtues might be contraposed to the seven deadly sins in catechetical teaching. In its simplest form, a virtue is defined as "a commendable quality or trait." Given this understanding of virtue, Hezekiah's ability to encourage others is indeed a "commendable trait"— and one worth emulating!

In fact, there is a biblical mandate to be a "Hezekiah" of sorts, as the New Testament itself *encourages* Christians, whether pastors or not, to be *encouragers*. The apostle Paul actually identifies the ability to encourage others as a spiritual gift and a manifestation of God's grace in a Christian's life (Rom. 12:8). Beyond this, he links "encouragement" (*paraklesis*, from the Gk. word *parakaleo*, lit., "to call to one's side" [i.e., "to encourage"]) to the edification of other Christians and instructs believers in Christ to take on encouraging the saints as a sort of spiritual discipline (cf. 1 Thess. 5:11, 14). Paul knew the benefit of encouragement because he himself had been helped both by the responsiveness to spiritual things among those he encouraged (e.g., 2 Cor. 7:13) and by the encouragement he received from fellow Christians (e.g., Acts 28:15).

There is a sense in which encouragement may be viewed as an extension of the virtue of courage. Courage is "a settled disposition to feel appropriate degrees of fear and confidence in challenging situations.... It is also a settled disposition to stand one's ground, to advance or retreat as wisdom dictates"; more simply stated, courage is "*acting* bravely when we don't really *feel* brave."[48] The attributes of courage and encouragement are related in that a timid or fearful person is more susceptible to the encouragement of example than the rash or reckless person. The former may be inspired to act courageously while the latter's overconfidence may do more harm than good in a crisis situation.

---

47. For example, Bennett, *The Book of Virtues*.

48. Ibid., 442. To be fair to Bennett, it is possible to understand "encouragement" as a subcategory of "compassion" (pp. 105–82) or "courage" (pp. 439–524).

To encourage, then, is to embolden another to overcome a paralyzing fear or deep-seated reluctance. To encourage is to inspire, to hearten, and to offer hope to another through word or deed. The New Testament values encouragement as a Christian virtue because it serves to embolden the timid in the service of Christ (1 Thess. 5:14). The encourager also contributes to the righteous endurance of the Christian in that daily mutual encouragement prevents the heart from being hardened by sin's deceitfulness (Heb. 3:13; cf. 10:25). The encourager thus helps build the kingdom of God because those who endure "will . . . reign with him [i.e., Christ]" (2 Tim. 2:12).

Few will dispute the need for the gift of encouragement as part of the daily Christian experience in our fallen world. The need was so apparent for the apostle Paul that the ministry of encouragement carried the force of an imperative in his counsel to the young pastors under his tutelage (2 Tim. 4:2; Titus 1:9). Clearly, encouraging people is one of the vital tasks of a pastor as "shepherd of God's flock." The greater question is one of implementation: How do I become an encourager? No doubt there are numerous ways in which one might fulfill Paul's charge to "encourage—with great patience and careful instruction" (2 Tim. 4:2). Here are three specific suggestions aimed at cultivating the virtue of encouragement as an aspect of Christian character.

(1) Be a disciplined student of the Bible—God's Word. We are equally well-served by Paul's reminder to the Roman church that "everything that was written in the past was written to teach us, so that through endurance and the encouragement of the Scriptures we might have hope" (Rom. 15:4). Naturally, as a professor of Old Testament studies I am partial to this text because the Scriptures for Paul at this time were the books of the Old Testament. Whether it be the Old or New Testament, however, the Scriptures reveal Jesus Christ, in whom we have *eternal encouragement* by the grace of God (2 Thess. 2:16).

Pastor Wiersbe offers us one practical example of the encouragement and hope found in the Scriptures when he informs us that despite the fact we are "troubled" like those believers in the Corinthian church (2 Cor. 4:8–9), "we don't have to fail."[49] The Christian possesses a conquering faith because "our competence comes from God" (3:5). Beyond this, the Christian has access to extraordinary resources—a divine "treasure in jars of clay to show that this all-surpassing power is from God" (4:7). So then, we enjoy *eternal encouragement*, knowing that "if God is for us, who can be against us?" (Rom. 8:31).

49. Warren W. Wiersbe, *Be Encouraged* (Wheaton, Ill.: Victor, 1984), 23–34.

(2) Be a discerning student of human behavior. We have noted in our study that the Chronicler is well-acquainted with the Hebrew wisdom tradition. Wisdom is practical knowledge garnered from experience and observation and then applied to the circumstances of life. As a "pastor," King Hezekiah is able to speak encouragingly to his people because he knows them intimately through shared experiences of war and worship and through the careful observation of their life situations as their ruler. The beauty, goodness, and vigor of a well-timed word is an enduring maxim in the book of Proverbs (Prov. 15:23; 25:11). There is great power in our words, for "the tongue has the power of life and death" (18:21). This Old Testament teaching is not lost on James in the writing of his letter, for he too recognizes that "out of the same mouth come praise and cursing" (James 3:10). What Larry Crabb calls "life words" must spring out of the compassion and wisdom of the encourager's heart.[50]

Ultimately, words that encourage are motivated by love and are directed toward the target of fear. This means "encouragement depends on loving motivation in the encourager as well as wisdom to discern the needs of the other person accurately."[51]

(3) The ministry of encouragement has parallels to coaching. According to Leonard Sweet, "one test of a healthy soul is whether or not it can cheer a rival from the bench."[52] Our highly individualistic culture has created a social environment that fosters a fierce competition in all areas of life—vocational, recreational, political, commercial, and so on. This competitive spirit leads to rivalry, which in turn promotes feelings and attitudes of professional jealousy.

Sadly, the Christian subculture is not immune to this insidious disease. Probably each of us has witnessed, experienced, or in weaker moments even been overtaken by the symptoms of envy, resentment, and critical spirit that often mark one who begrudges the achievement of another. Professional jealousy is but one aspect of the dark side of Christian ministry, be it among the professionals in the church and the academy, the paraprofessionals in church-related ministry, or the laity. But it need not afflict the Christian community. There is a ready remedy. The godly encourager has learned how to avoid the snare of

---

50. Larry J. Crabb and Dan B. Allender, *Encouragement: The Key to Caring* (Grand Rapids: Zondervan, 1984), 23–25; cf. David G. Peterson, "The Ministry of Encouragement," in P. T. O'Brien and D. G. Peterson, eds., *God Who Is Rich in Mercy* (Grand Rapids: Baker, 1986), 235–53.

51. Crabb and Allender, *Encouragement*, 79.

52. Leonard Sweet, *Soul Salsa* (Grand Rapids: Zondervan, 2000), 104.

professional jealousy because he or she esteems others as "better" individuals and continually looks to the interests of others rather than to one's own (Phil. 2:3–4).

Such an approach to the ministry of encouragement outstrips Sweet's culturally conditioned exhortation to "cheer a rival from the bench" because it acknowledges no rivals. The humble encourager is free to come alongside and "rejoice with those who rejoice" or "mourn with those who mourn," without the excess baggage of pride and conceit that an emphasis on competition tends to carry (Rom. 12:15–16). So with God's help and the Spirit's prompting, learn to be an encourager. Take a page from Hezekiah's "pastoral manual" and bolster confidence in others!

MANASSEH WAS TWELVE years old when he became king, and he reigned in Jerusalem fifty-five years. ²He did evil in the eyes of the LORD, following the detestable practices of the nations the LORD had driven out before the Israelites. ³He rebuilt the high places his father Hezekiah had demolished; he also erected altars to the Baals and made Asherah poles. He bowed down to all the starry hosts and worshiped them. ⁴He built altars in the temple of the LORD, of which the LORD had said, "My Name will remain in Jerusalem forever." ⁵In both courts of the temple of the LORD, he built altars to all the starry hosts. ⁶He sacrificed his sons in the fire in the Valley of Ben Hinnom, practiced sorcery, divination and witchcraft, and consulted mediums and spiritists. He did much evil in the eyes of the LORD, provoking him to anger.

⁷He took the carved image he had made and put it in God's temple, of which God had said to David and to his son Solomon, "In this temple and in Jerusalem, which I have chosen out of all the tribes of Israel, I will put my Name forever. ⁸I will not again make the feet of the Israelites leave the land I assigned to your forefathers, if only they will be careful to do everything I commanded them concerning all the laws, decrees and ordinances given through Moses." ⁹But Manasseh led Judah and the people of Jerusalem astray, so that they did more evil than the nations the LORD had destroyed before the Israelites.

¹⁰The LORD spoke to Manasseh and his people, but they paid no attention. ¹¹So the LORD brought against them the army commanders of the king of Assyria, who took Manasseh prisoner, put a hook in his nose, bound him with bronze shackles and took him to Babylon. ¹²In his distress he sought the favor of the LORD his God and humbled himself greatly before the God of his fathers. ¹³And when he prayed to him, the LORD was moved by his entreaty and listened to his plea; so he brought him back to Jerusalem and to his kingdom. Then Manasseh knew that the LORD is God.

¹⁴Afterward he rebuilt the outer wall of the City of David, west of the Gihon spring in the valley, as far as the entrance of

the Fish Gate and encircling the hill of Ophel; he also made it much higher. He stationed military commanders in all the fortified cities in Judah.

¹⁵He got rid of the foreign gods and removed the image from the temple of the LORD, as well as all the altars he had built on the temple hill and in Jerusalem; and he threw them out of the city. ¹⁶Then he restored the altar of the LORD and sacrificed fellowship offerings and thank offerings on it, and told Judah to serve the LORD, the God of Israel. ¹⁷The people, however, continued to sacrifice at the high places, but only to the LORD their God.

¹⁸The other events of Manasseh's reign, including his prayer to his God and the words the seers spoke to him in the name of the LORD, the God of Israel, are written in the annals of the kings of Israel. ¹⁹His prayer and how God was moved by his entreaty, as well as all his sins and unfaithfulness, and the sites where he built high places and set up Asherah poles and idols before he humbled himself—all are written in the records of the seers. ²⁰Manasseh rested with his fathers and was buried in his palace. And Amon his son succeeded him as king.

²¹Amon was twenty-two years old when he became king, and he reigned in Jerusalem two years. ²²He did evil in the eyes of the LORD, as his father Manasseh had done. Amon worshiped and offered sacrifices to all the idols Manasseh had made. ²³But unlike his father Manasseh, he did not humble himself before the LORD; Amon increased his guilt.

²⁴Amon's officials conspired against him and assassinated him in his palace. ²⁵Then the people of the land killed all who had plotted against King Amon, and they made Josiah his son king in his place.

^{34:1}Josiah was eight years old when he became king, and he reigned in Jerusalem thirty-one years. ²He did what was right in the eyes of the LORD and walked in the ways of his father David, not turning aside to the right or to the left.

³In the eighth year of his reign, while he was still young, he began to seek the God of his father David. In his twelfth year he began to purge Judah and Jerusalem of high places, Asherah poles, carved idols and cast images. ⁴Under his direction the altars of the Baals were torn down; he cut to pieces the incense altars that were above them, and smashed the

Asherah poles, the idols and the images. These he broke to pieces and scattered over the graves of those who had sacrificed to them. ⁵He burned the bones of the priests on their altars, and so he purged Judah and Jerusalem. ⁶In the towns of Manasseh, Ephraim and Simeon, as far as Naphtali, and in the ruins around them, ⁷he tore down the altars and the Asherah poles and crushed the idols to powder and cut to pieces all the incense altars throughout Israel. Then he went back to Jerusalem.

⁸In the eighteenth year of Josiah's reign, to purify the land and the temple, he sent Shaphan son of Azaliah and Maaseiah the ruler of the city, with Joah son of Joahaz, the recorder, to repair the temple of the LORD his God.

⁹They went to Hilkiah the high priest and gave him the money that had been brought into the temple of God, which the Levites who were the doorkeepers had collected from the people of Manasseh, Ephraim and the entire remnant of Israel and from all the people of Judah and Benjamin and the inhabitants of Jerusalem. ¹⁰Then they entrusted it to the men appointed to supervise the work on the LORD's temple. These men paid the workers who repaired and restored the temple. ¹¹They also gave money to the carpenters and builders to purchase dressed stone, and timber for joists and beams for the buildings that the kings of Judah had allowed to fall into ruin.

¹²The men did the work faithfully. Over them to direct them were Jahath and Obadiah, Levites descended from Merari, and Zechariah and Meshullam, descended from Kohath. The Levites—all who were skilled in playing musical instruments—¹³had charge of the laborers and supervised all the workers from job to job. Some of the Levites were secretaries, scribes and doorkeepers.

¹⁴While they were bringing out the money that had been taken into the temple of the LORD, Hilkiah the priest found the Book of the Law of the LORD that had been given through Moses. ¹⁵Hilkiah said to Shaphan the secretary, "I have found the Book of the Law in the temple of the LORD." He gave it to Shaphan.

¹⁶Then Shaphan took the book to the king and reported to him: "Your officials are doing everything that has been committed to them. ¹⁷They have paid out the money that was in the temple of the LORD and have entrusted it to the supervi-

sors and workers." ¹⁸Then Shaphan the secretary informed the king, "Hilkiah the priest has given me a book." And Shaphan read from it in the presence of the king.

¹⁹When the king heard the words of the Law, he tore his robes. ²⁰He gave these orders to Hilkiah, Ahikam son of Shaphan, Abdon son of Micah, Shaphan the secretary and Asaiah the king's attendant: ²¹"Go and inquire of the LORD for me and for the remnant in Israel and Judah about what is written in this book that has been found. Great is the LORD's anger that is poured out on us because our fathers have not kept the word of the LORD; they have not acted in accordance with all that is written in this book."

²²Hilkiah and those the king had sent with him went to speak to the prophetess Huldah, who was the wife of Shallum son of Tokhath, the son of Hasrah, keeper of the wardrobe. She lived in Jerusalem, in the Second District.

²³She said to them, "This is what the LORD, the God of Israel, says: Tell the man who sent you to me, ²⁴'This is what the LORD says: I am going to bring disaster on this place and its people—all the curses written in the book that has been read in the presence of the king of Judah. ²⁵Because they have forsaken me and burned incense to other gods and provoked me to anger by all that their hands have made, my anger will be poured out on this place and will not be quenched.' ²⁶Tell the king of Judah, who sent you to inquire of the LORD, 'This is what the LORD, the God of Israel, says concerning the words you heard: ²⁷Because your heart was responsive and you humbled yourself before God when you heard what he spoke against this place and its people, and because you humbled yourself before me and tore your robes and wept in my presence, I have heard you, declares the LORD. ²⁸Now I will gather you to your fathers, and you will be buried in peace. Your eyes will not see all the disaster I am going to bring on this place and on those who live here.'"

So they took her answer back to the king.

²⁹Then the king called together all the elders of Judah and Jerusalem. ³⁰He went up to the temple of the LORD with the men of Judah, the people of Jerusalem, the priests and the Levites—all the people from the least to the greatest. He read in their hearing all the words of the Book of the Covenant, which had been found in the temple of the LORD. ³¹The king

stood by his pillar and renewed the covenant in the presence of the LORD—to follow the LORD and keep his commands, regulations and decrees with all his heart and all his soul, and to obey the words of the covenant written in this book.

³²Then he had everyone in Jerusalem and Benjamin pledge themselves to it; the people of Jerusalem did this in accordance with the covenant of God, the God of their fathers.

³³Josiah removed all the detestable idols from all the territory belonging to the Israelites, and he had all who were present in Israel serve the LORD their God. As long as he lived, they did not fail to follow the LORD, the God of their fathers.

³⁵:¹Josiah celebrated the Passover to the LORD in Jerusalem, and the Passover lamb was slaughtered on the fourteenth day of the first month. ²He appointed the priests to their duties and encouraged them in the service of the LORD's temple. ³He said to the Levites, who instructed all Israel and who had been consecrated to the LORD: "Put the sacred ark in the temple that Solomon son of David king of Israel built. It is not to be carried about on your shoulders. Now serve the LORD your God and his people Israel. ⁴Prepare yourselves by families in your divisions, according to the directions written by David king of Israel and by his son Solomon.

⁵"Stand in the holy place with a group of Levites for each subdivision of the families of your fellow countrymen, the lay people. ⁶Slaughter the Passover lambs, consecrate yourselves and prepare the lambs for your fellow countrymen, doing what the LORD commanded through Moses."

⁷Josiah provided for all the lay people who were there a total of thirty thousand sheep and goats for the Passover offerings, and also three thousand cattle—all from the king's own possessions.

⁸His officials also contributed voluntarily to the people and the priests and Levites. Hilkiah, Zechariah and Jehiel, the administrators of God's temple, gave the priests twenty-six hundred Passover offerings and three hundred cattle. ⁹Also Conaniah along with Shemaiah and Nethanel, his brothers, and Hashabiah, Jeiel and Jozabad, the leaders of the Levites, provided five thousand Passover offerings and five hundred head of cattle for the Levites.

¹⁰The service was arranged and the priests stood in their places with the Levites in their divisions as the king had

ordered. ¹¹The Passover lambs were slaughtered, and the priests sprinkled the blood handed to them, while the Levites skinned the animals. ¹²They set aside the burnt offerings to give them to the subdivisions of the families of the people to offer to the LORD, as is written in the Book of Moses. They did the same with the cattle. ¹³They roasted the Passover animals over the fire as prescribed, and boiled the holy offerings in pots, caldrons and pans and served them quickly to all the people. ¹⁴After this, they made preparations for themselves and for the priests, because the priests, the descendants of Aaron, were sacrificing the burnt offerings and the fat portions until nightfall. So the Levites made preparations for themselves and for the Aaronic priests.

¹⁵The musicians, the descendants of Asaph, were in the places prescribed by David, Asaph, Heman and Jeduthun the king's seer. The gatekeepers at each gate did not need to leave their posts, because their fellow Levites made the preparations for them.

¹⁶So at that time the entire service of the LORD was carried out for the celebration of the Passover and the offering of burnt offerings on the altar of the LORD, as King Josiah had ordered. ¹⁷The Israelites who were present celebrated the Passover at that time and observed the Feast of Unleavened Bread for seven days. ¹⁸The Passover had not been observed like this in Israel since the days of the prophet Samuel; and none of the kings of Israel had ever celebrated such a Passover as did Josiah, with the priests, the Levites and all Judah and Israel who were there with the people of Jerusalem. ¹⁹This Passover was celebrated in the eighteenth year of Josiah's reign.

²⁰After all this, when Josiah had set the temple in order, Neco king of Egypt went up to fight at Carchemish on the Euphrates, and Josiah marched out to meet him in battle. ²¹But Neco sent messengers to him, saying, "What quarrel is there between you and me, O king of Judah? It is not you I am attacking at this time, but the house with which I am at war. God has told me to hurry; so stop opposing God, who is with me, or he will destroy you."

²²Josiah, however, would not turn away from him, but disguised himself to engage him in battle. He would not listen to what Neco had said at God's command but went to fight him on the plain of Megiddo.

²³Archers shot King Josiah, and he told his officers, "Take me away; I am badly wounded." ²⁴So they took him out of his chariot, put him in the other chariot he had and brought him to Jerusalem, where he died. He was buried in the tombs of his fathers, and all Judah and Jerusalem mourned for him.

²⁵Jeremiah composed laments for Josiah, and to this day all the men and women singers commemorate Josiah in the laments. These became a tradition in Israel and are written in the Laments.

²⁶The other events of Josiah's reign and his acts of devotion, according to what is written in the Law of the LORD— ²⁷all the events, from beginning to end, are written in the book of the kings of Israel and Judah. ³⁶:¹And the people of the land took Jehoahaz son of Josiah and made him king in Jerusalem in place of his father.

Original Meaning

THE CHRONICLER'S RETELLING of the reigns of Kings Manasseh, Amon, and Josiah represents a selective appeal to the earlier parallels in 2 Kings 21–23. The broad parallels may be outlined accordingly:

King Manasseh = 2 Kings 21:1–18//2 Chron. 33:1–20
King Amon = 2 Kings 21:19–26//2 Chron. 33:21–25
King Josiah = 2 Kings 22:1–23:30//2 Chron. 34:1–36:1

Specifically, Chronicles expands the record of Kings to include the temporary exile and "deathbed" repentance of King Manasseh (33:11–16). It also expands the report of Josiah's reforms (34:3–7) and Josiah's Passover celebration (35:2–17). Finally, it omits the report of Yahweh's anger against Judah (2 Kings 23:24–27). The Chronicler's omissions and expansions in appealing to the Kings' history are striking but certainly in keeping with his theological emphases of repentance and true worship in this section .

The theme of repentance binds the trio of seventh-century Judahite kings into a logical literary unit. Both Manasseh and Josiah "humbled" themselves (Niphal of kn^c) before God (33:12, 19; 34:27), while tragically Amon refused to humble himself before the Lord (33:23). The report of Amon's rule thus serves as a foil of sorts to the "bookend" structure of the accounts of Manasseh and Josiah.

Like much of chapters 27–32, this unit is considered "report" (i.e., a brief, self-contained prose narrative that concentrates on a single event or situation).[1] Critical scholars have challenged the historicity of the Chronicler's reporting of Manasseh since the parallel source in Kings does not mention his Assyrian captivity or his "foxhole" conversion at the end of his reign. Thompson has noted, however, that King Manasseh is numbered among those kings listed as vassals of the Assyrians in extrabiblical documents.[2] Moreover, numerous rebellions by Assyrian vassals are known to have occurred during the reigns of both Esarhaddon and Ashurbanipal.[3] So even though the biblical account of Manasseh's exile is unattested in Kings and the extrabiblical records, the Chronicler's report is certainly within the realm of plausibility.

King Manasseh (33:1–20)

THE RECORD ON Manasseh's reign may be divided into four reports: Judah's relapse into false worship under Manasseh (33:1–10), Manasseh's exile and repentance (33:11–13), Manasseh's infrastructural repairs and spiritual reforms (33:14–17), and the concluding regnal résumé (33:18–20). The most significant divergence from 2 Kings 21 is the report of Manasseh's repentance during his exile in Assyria. No doubt the Prayer of Manasseh in the Apocrypha was inspired by the Chronicler's cryptic allusion to the king's pleas for divine mercy.[4]

Judah's relapse into false worship (33:1–10). This section repeats 2 Kings 21:1–9 with some minor variations, such as the omission of Manasseh's mother's name (Hephzibah). In fact, Chronicles leaves off the queen mother of the Judahite kings after the reign of Hezekiah—perhaps because of a shift in the source material or the deliberate expunging of these women's names as a result of their Arabian origin.[5] The Chronicler also avoids comparing Manasseh to King Ahab of Israel (cf. 2 Kings 21:3).

Manasseh rules longer than any other Israelite king. His fifty-five-year reign probably includes a coregency of several years with his father, Hezekiah. The dates of his reign extend from about 696 to 642 B.C. As an aside, it bears mention that Manasseh was probably born into the royal family during the fifteen-year extension of Hezekiah's life granted by God in response to his prayer for healing from a fatal disease (cf. 2 Kings 20:1–6).

This entire section turns on the juxtaposition of the evil deeds of Manasseh and the identification of God's "Name" with the Jerusalem temple (33:4–5, 7).

---

1. De Vries, *1 and 2 Chronicles*, 434.

2. Thompson, *1, 2 Chronicles*, 366–67.

3. See Myers, *I Chronicles*, 198–99; Dillard, *2 Chronicles*, 264–65.

4. Bruce M. Metzger and Roland E. Murphy, eds., *The Oxford Annotated Apocrypha* (NRSV; New York: Oxford, 1991), 281–82.

5. Cf. Williamson, *1 and 2 Chronicles*, 390.

The litany of the king's detestable practices possibly represents the conflation of two independent sources (i.e., 33:3–6 and 33:7–9), given the repetition of the desecration of the temple precincts. The specific catalog of abominations promoted by Manasseh as "alternative religion" for the kingdom of Judah invites comparison with the Mosaic prohibitions against false worship (Deut. 16:21–17:7; 18:9–13). Among the taboos borrowed wholesale from Canaanite culture are idolatry associated with the fertility cult deities Asherah and Baal, astral worship, infanticide, and the occult (2 Chron. 33:3–6).

According to 2 Kings 17:7–13, 16–20, these are the very sins that incited God's wrath against the northern kingdom of Israel and brought about the Assyrian exile. Note too how centuries earlier the theocratic kingdom of Israel under Joshua's leadership waged war against the indigenous populations of Canaan as divine judgment for the same list of abominations (Lev. 18:24–28). The narrative in 2 Kings 24:3–4 ascribes blame directly to King Manasseh for the Babylonian exile of the southern kingdom. Like matter reaching an irreversible energy state of critical mass in the science of physics, the course charted by the political and religious policies of Manasseh lead irrevocably to the Exile.

The Chronicler hints at Manasseh's role in Judah's exile by referring to the "nations" driven out by the Lord when Israel entered the land of Canaan (33:2). Manasseh's responsibility for the welfare of Judah is made more clear in the Chronicler's allusion to the Davidic covenant and Israel's security in the land of covenant promise (33:7; cf. 2 Sam. 7:10). The king leads the people astray by breaking the first commandment (2 Chron. 33:7; cf. Ex. 20:3–4). The carved image he erects in God's temple symbolizes his rejection of God's rule at both the personal and the national level. King Manasseh's arrogance breeds the evil of idolatry and poisons his subjects with the sin of idolatry (1 Sam. 15:23; cf. Ex. 20:3–4).

Once the Israelites renounce their covenant loyalty to Yahweh and become more evil than the nations he destroyed in the land of Canaan, God has no choice but to invoke the covenant curses on his people (cf. Deut. 28:36–37). The conclusion of the first report (2 Chron. 33:10), however, shifts some of the responsibility for the Babylonian exile to the people of Judah as well. They shoulder blame for the catastrophe because they refuse to heed the word of the Lord through his prophets.

Manasseh's exile and repentance (33:11–13). While Manasseh's exile has no parallel in 2 Kings and is uncorroborated by extant Assyrian sources, it seems likely that he is a coconspirator with the Babylonians in the revolt against Shamash-shum-ukin in Babylon.[6] Shamash-shum-ukin was the brother

6. See Dillard, *2 Chronicles*, 265.

of the Assyrian king Ashurbanipal and the appointed king of Babylon. The nose "hook" and "bronze shackles" (33:11) are typical of the humiliation inflicted on captives in the biblical world (cf. Isa. 37:29; Amos 4:2; Hab. 1:15).

God often brings trouble against his people in the Old Testament to punish and to purify them. The psalmist recognizes that God is a refuge for those in distress (cf. Ps. 20:1; 41:1; 46:1). Unlike King Ahaz, Manasseh turns to God in his distress and finds favor with the Almighty (2 Chron. 33:12; cf. 28:22). The expression "seek the favor" (lit., "soften [ḥlh] the face") is found in the intercessory prayers of Moses, Hezekiah, and Daniel; it connotes an appeal to the mercy of God (cf. Ex. 32:11; Jer. 26:19; Dan. 9:13).

Manasseh's plea issues from a contrite heart, for he "humbled himself [knʿ] greatly" (33:12). This word signifies true repentance, demonstrated by a broken spirit coupled with acts of penance (e.g., tearing of garments and weeping) for personal sin and disobedience to God (cf. 2 Kings 22:19). For this reason, the report of Manasseh's repentance and prayer of forgiveness is reminiscent of the language of God's promise to King Solomon to restore those who "humble themselves and pray" (2 Chron. 7:14).

The expression "the LORD was moved" (33:13) is unusual and marks a theological distinctive of the God of the Bible. Unlike the deaf Baals after which the Israelites continually strayed, the God of Israel is not only approachable, but he listens to prayer and is capable of responding with empathy toward those in dire need (Ex. 22:27; 2 Chron. 30:9; cf. 1 Kings 18:26; Isa. 44:18; Hab. 2:18). The stark contrast between God who listens to the plea of Manasseh (2 Chron. 33:13) and the people who pay no attention to God (33:10) would not be lost on the Chronicler's audience. The episode foreshadows the hallmark attribute of Jesus Christ as the great high priest, who is moved to grant mercy because he sympathizes with human weakness, having experienced it himself (Heb. 4:14–16).

According to Selman, the conversion of King Manasseh ranks second in dramatic impact only to the experience of Saul of Tarsus on the Damascus road (Acts 9:3–6).[7] God is always faithful in returning to those who return to him (Jer. 3:22; Zech. 1:3; Mal. 3:7). In fact, this is how Manasseh knows that "the LORD is God"—not only because he is restored to the throne out of exile but because "who is a God like you, who pardons sin and forgives the transgression ... of his inheritance?" (Mic. 7:18).

Manasseh's infrastructural repairs and spiritual reforms (33:14–17). This next report emphasizes Manasseh's political and religious reforms. Usually this is construed as the "healing of the land," the natural aftermath of prayer and repentance according to God's promise in 7:14. The Chronicler

---

7. Selman, 2 *Chronicles*, 522.

sees royal building projects as an indication of divine blessing for obedience.[8] Manasseh's reforms are both political and religious in nature, suggesting God's acceptance of the king's prayer of repentance. The rebuilding of the city wall of Jerusalem (33:14) may refer to repairs made necessary when Manasseh was taken captive by the Assyrians or to the continuation of the expansion of Jerusalem begun under Hezekiah (cf. Isa. 22:10–11; 2 Chron. 32:5). Strengthening the military presence in the fortified cities of Judah (33:14) is almost routine for kings ruling in Jerusalem, since these cities form a shield against foreign invaders (cf. 2 Kings 18:13; 2 Chron. 14:6; 17:2; 26:9). Assuming Manasseh's renewed loyalty as an Assyrian vassal after his release from exile, both initiatives may have been encouraged by the Assyrians as defensive measures aimed at discouraging an Egyptian military campaign into Judah.

Curiously, the religious reforms of Manasseh are unsupported by other biblical passages (33:15–17). This should not discount the historical validity of the Chronicler's report (as some critics contend). Numerous biblical events receive only single citations. For example, Elijah's contest with the prophets of Baal lacks parallels as well (1 Kings 18). Specifically, Manasseh orders the direct reversal of previous policies he implemented with respect to temple worship (2 Chron. 33:15; cf. vv. 3, 7).

Yet the depth, extent, and duration of Manasseh's religious reforms remain an open question. Clearly, the temple is purified and proper worship is restored at least for a short time. We are told, however, that false worship is pervasive during the reigns of the next two kings of Judah (33:22; 34:3–7). The impact of Manasseh's religious reforms seems restricted to Jerusalem and its immediate environs, given the Chronicler's reference to ongoing worship in the high places (33:17). The worship associated with the Canaanite high places proves a snare for the Israelites throughout the history of the monarchies (cf. the theological commentary on the reigns of Asa in 15:17 and Jehoshaphat in 20:33).

Of course, the chief architect of the religious syncretism in Israel was King Solomon, who promoted the worship of Yahweh in Canaanite high places (1 Kings 3:3). Unfortunately, as Selman has rightly observed, too often the reform of the ritual of Israelite worship has little impact on the heart of the majority of the people, given the irresistible sensual appeal of Canaanite religious practice (cf. Isa. 29:13; Jer. 3:10).[9] As another commentator has noted, "it is easier to lead a people into sin than to lead them back out of it."[10]

---

8. Williamson, *1 and 2 Chronicles*, 240.
9. Selman, *2 Chronicles*, 524.
10. Thompson, *1, 2 Chronicles*, 371.

Concluding regnal résumé (33:18–20). The summaries of both Man-asseh's and Josiah's reigns contain introductory and concluding regnal résumés (33:1–2, 18–20; 34:1–2; 35:24–36:1). Typically, the introductory résumé includes various formulas announcing the king's age at accession, the length and location of the king's reign, the king's mother, and the theological review. The concluding one usually includes the historical source citation formula, the death and burial formula, and the succession formula. Manasseh's concluding résumé is significant theologically because of the emphasis on the king's prayer of entreaty and God's response to his repentance (33:18–19). Selman reminds us that "the Bible consistently affirms that God's door remains open to any-one, even after what should have been closing time."[11] Apparently the Chron-icler desires to remind his postexilic audience of this timeless truth as well!

King Amon (33:21–25)

THE CHRONICLER OFFERS a condensed version of Amon's reign as found in 2 Kings 21:19–26. Concluding the report of Amon's reign by referring to Josiah's succession, however, provides a natural lead into the account of Josiah (2 Chron. 33:25; cf. 2 Kings 21:24b, 26).

The Chronicler's theological assessment of Amon expands the Kings par-allel on two key points. (1) Amon differs from his father, Manasseh, in that he refuses to humble himself and repent of his sin (33:23a). (2) As a result of this behavior, Amon increases his guilt before God (33:23b). The Old Tes-tament prophets promise restoration to those who turn to God in repen-tance (cf. Isa. 59:20; Jer. 15:19), while those who spurn God's mercy and reject his forgiveness experience judgment (Jer. 5:3–6). There is a foreshad-owing of later New Testament teaching when we consider the judgment Jesus pronounced on Korazin and Bethsaida for their failure to turn to God in repentance despite the miracles they witnessed (Matt. 11:20–24).

Amon's rule lasts only two years (642–640 B.C., 33:21). He is judged an evil king because he perpetuates the false worship established in Judah by his father (33:22). The reason behind his assassination is unspecified (33:24). Clearly the general populace is not in sympathy with the coup since they exe-cute those palace officials party to the conspiracy (33:25a). Selman notes that reports of such treachery in Chronicles are interpreted as divine judgment, and such may be the case here (cf. 24:25; 25:27).[12] The expression "people of the land" (33:25a) may be an idiom for a coalition of religious and polit-ical leadership centered in Jerusalem since they also function as "king mak-ers" in other succession crises (cf. 22:1; 26:1; 36:1).

---

11. Selman, 2 *Chronicles*, 519.
12. Ibid., 525.

Josiah (34:1–36:1)

BOTH THE HISTORIES of Kings and Chronicles review King Josiah's reign in a positive light by associating him with King David (34:2; cf. 2 Kings 22:2). Josiah's link to David extends beyond his genealogical pedigree to a similar heart for worship, as Josiah begins to "seek" (*drš*) the Lord at an early age (2 Chron. 34:3). The Chronicler summarizes Josiah's rule with four reports: Josiah's religious reform (34:1–7), the temple repairs and finding of the law scroll (34:8–33), the celebration of the Passover (35:1–19), the battle report of Josiah's death (35:20–25). It concludes with a regnal résumé (35:26–36:1). De Vries offers a helpful two-point distillation of the Chronicler's purpose concerning the account of King Josiah: all his good deeds cannot save him from an ignominious death or the nation from exile, and Josiah is memorialized for his promulgation of the law by which the nation will one day live again.[13]

One of the Chronicler's characteristic literary techniques reemerges in this section, that of framing the narrative structure by means of sequential chronological notes (e.g., 34:3, 8).[14] The theme of humbling oneself before God prominent in chapter 33 persists in this pericope (34:27; cf. 2 Kings 22:19). Also, the theme of "seeking the Lord" is introduced in order to demonstrate Josiah's single-minded devotion to the things of God (2 Chron. 34:3, 21, 26). Williamson has correctly recognized that the biography of Josiah does not mark a particular turning point in the Chronicler's narrative, but rather he is the last of a series of key figures in the story of the rise and fall of Davidic kingship in Israel.[15]

Josiah's religious reform (34:1–7). The Chronicler begins by essentially repeating the regnal résumé of 2 Kings 22:1–2, minus the reference to Josiah's mother, Jedidah. The rest of the report is a digest of 2 Kings 23:4–20 about Josiah's comprehensive cleansing of the temple and purification of temple worship. His reign can be dated with confidence to 640–609 B.C.

According to 34:3, Josiah begins his reform initiatives at age twenty, while 2 Kings 22:3 indicates the reform coincides with the finding of the law scroll when he is twenty-six years old. The age of twenty was the age of majority in Hebrew culture and, more than coincidentally for the Chronicler, the age when the Levite began his service to Yahweh (cf. Num. 1:3; 1 Chron. 23:24). The decline of Assyrian empire after the death of Ashurbanipal in 627 B.C. affords Judah an opportunity to reassert its own political and religious agenda after languishing as a vassal state since the time of King

13. De Vries, *1 and 2 Chronicles*, 402.
14. Cf. Dillard, *2 Chronicles*, 276.
15. Williamson, *1 and 2 Chronicles*, 396.

Ahaz. There is a growing consensus among scholars that Josiah's reform movement predates the finding of the law book by Hilkiah the priest.[16] It seems we can speak of Josiah's early reforms prior to the discovery of the law scroll in 622 B.C. and his later reforms associated with the temple renovation and eradication of false worship centers.

Temple repair and finding of the law scroll (34:8−33). The account of Josiah's campaign to refurbish the temple and the subsequent finding of the "Book of the Law" has it parallel in 2 Kings 22:3−23:3. The Chronicler adds material promoting the participation of the Levites in the temple restoration (2 Chron. 34:12−13). Otherwise, this report represents an essentially faithful citation of the parallel text in 2 Kings.

The narrative neatly divides into four literary units: the restoration of the temple (34:8−13), the discovery and then the interpretation of the law scroll (34:14−28), and the covenant renewal ceremony (34:29−33). Curiously, the religious reforms prompted by the finding of the law scroll are treated almost incidentally (see comments above on 34:1−7). For the Chronicler, the important story is the discovery of the scroll and its interpretation, whereas in Kings the finding of the law scroll is merely a prerequisite for the religious reforms of King Josiah. The genre of the section is identified as report, with the exception of Huldah's prophetic speech (34:23−28a). The repetition of the date formula ("the eighteenth year of Josiah's reign," 34:8; 35:19) forms an inclusio or envelope construction, indicating the religious reforms associated with the finding of the law scroll and the Passover celebration are to be understood as a chain of related events.

The eighteenth year of Josiah's reign is 622 B.C., and the king is twenty-six years old (34:8). The ministries of Jeremiah and Zephaniah are concurrent with the religious reforms and temple repair initiative of Josiah (Jer. 1:2; Zeph. 1:1). Josiah's campaign to restore the dilapidated temple in Jerusalem is one of a series of royal renovation projects aimed at repairing the sanctuary of Yahweh. More than a century prior (ca. 812 B.C.), King Joash undertook a similar enterprise (cf. 2 Kings 12:1−21; 2 Chron. 24:1−14). As recently as King Hezekiah, the doors of the temple were repaired and made serviceable again (2 Chron. 29:3).

Josiah's temple renovation (34:8−13). The report of Josiah's restoration of the temple is based on 2 Kings 22:3−7. Josiah's plans to repair the temple serve as the setting in that Kings narrative for the discovery of the law scroll and the subsequent sweeping religious reforms in Judah. The report of Josiah's renovation of the temple in Chronicles is linked to the early reforms of the king by the insertion of the clause "to purify the land and the temple" (2 Chron.

---

16. E.g., see Dillard, *2 Chronicles*, 276−77; Thompson, *1, 2 Chronicles*, 374−75.

34:8; cf. v. 3). Thus the Chronicler understands the report of the temple repair as one episode in a series of related events in Josiah's comprehensive reform movement.

Shaphan the scribe (probably a state scribe who also serves as a royal messenger) is the only character the two accounts have in common. The Chronicler adds the name of "the ruler of the city," Maaseiah, along with the name of the court recorder Joah. The office of ruler or governor of Jerusalem is mentioned in 2 Kings 23:8 and attested by archaeological discovery.[17] The office of recorder or secretary to the king (2 Kings 22:8) was a cabinet post established by David (cf. 2 Sam. 8:16). The reference to the people from the northern kingdom as the "remnant of Israel" may suggest that the Chronicler understands the reunification of "all Israel" as already having begun during the reign of Josiah (2 Chron. 34:9).

The need for skilled craftsmen such as carpenters and masons indicates the temple is in a serious state of disrepair (34:10–11). Unlike 2 Kings 22:5–6, Chronicles places blame for the "ruin" of the temple on the kings of Judah. No doubt the negligent kings the writer has in mind included Manasseh and Amon, perhaps going as far back as Ahaz. The Chronicler connects the success of the temple repairs to the faithfulness of the workers and effective supervision by the Levites (2 Chron. 34:12–13). Though not mentioned in the parallel text, the several roles filled by the Levites in the renovation project (e.g., temple-tax collectors, doorkeepers [i.e., security], accompanying musicians pacing the workers [?], treasurers, crew foreman, site supervisors, etc.) are in keeping with the wide-ranging duties David assigned to the Levites (1 Chron. 25–26).

Discovery of the law scroll (34:14–18). The Chronicler's account of the discovery of the law scroll faithfully follows 2 Kings 22:8–20 except for certain details added to Hilkiah's finding of the document (2 Chron. 34:14, 17). This portion of Josiah's reign divides into two units—the discovery of the scroll and then its interpretation—and combines the genres of report (34:14–22, 29b) and prophetic speech (34:23–28a). Huldah's speech contains a prophecy of punishment (34:24–25) and a prophecy of salvation (34:26–28a), introduced by the messenger formula ("this is what the LORD says," 34:24, 26) and confirmed by the emphatic prophetic utterance formula ("declares the LORD," 34:27b).

The reference to the money collected by the Levites for renovating the temple links the previous section with this segment of the story (cf. 34:9, 14). Surprisingly, while the discovery of the law scroll is the key event of the chapter and the turning point of Josiah's reign, its actual uncovering is

---

17. Williamson, *1 and 2 Chronicles*, 400.

mentioned only briefly (34:14b–15a). The Chronicler's expansion of Hilkiah's role in the discovery of the law scroll (34:14, 17) accents the find as the by-product of the initiative to repair the temple. In this way, its discovery becomes a reward of sorts for Josiah's faithfulness in attending to God's sanctuary.

The scroll is given two titles in the narrative: "the Book of the Law" (34:15) and "the Book of the Covenant" (34:30). The puzzling question for biblical scholars has been the identity of this book. The general consensus favors the book of Deuteronomy or an earlier version of that book.[18] We can only speculate as to why the law scroll disappeared from the collection of Hebrew religious documents. Was it suppressed, or lost, or hidden? Presumably the scroll fell out of circulation because of the need to hide it for the sake of preservation at the threat of military invasion (e.g., the Assyrian campaign against Hezekiah); or else it was censored by rulers and/or concealed by the priests during one of the lapses of Israel into religious apostasy (e.g., the reigns of Athaliah, Ahaz, Amon, Manasseh).

Interpretation of the scroll (34:19–28). Josiah's twofold response to Shaphan's reading of the scroll is immediate and decisive. Recognizing the message of the scroll as the very word of God, Josiah tears his clothes (34:19)—a tangible expression of grief in response to personal or national crises (cf. 1 Kings 21:27; 2 Kings 19:1; Ezra 9:3). The prophetess Huldah clearly understands the action as symbolic of repentance, since the expression "humble oneself" (34:27) is applied to Josiah's self-abasement and weeping.

The king perceives that the message of the law scroll has profound implications for both him and his subjects ("the remnant in Israel and Judah" [34:21] is another instance of the Chronicler's emphasis on the unity of Israel). This explains Josiah's decision to appoint envoys to seek an interpretation of the scroll and to ask for counsel in addressing the disturbing news about God's anger revealed in the law scroll. The theme of God's anger incited by the disloyalty of the people of Israel is prominent in 2 Chronicles (e.g., 28:9; 29:8; 32:25). The king's reference to the sins of the "fathers" (34:21) implies some knowledge of the potential impact of the retribution principle across successive generations (cf. Ex. 20:5).

Hilkiah's visit to Huldah seems to be based on his relationship with Shallum, her husband. Shallum is "keeper of the wardrobe" (34:22) for the priests and the Levites, which means he has oversight of the production and maintenance of the vestments and robes of Levites. Thus, Hilkiah is in regular contact with Shallum. Huldah is not mentioned elsewhere in the Old Testament,

18. Cf. Dillard, 2 *Chronicles*, 280, who outlines seven reasons why the general consensus favors the identification of the law scroll with the book of Deuteronomy.

although she is among a handful of Hebrew women titled as a prophetess (e.g., Miriam, Ex. 15:20; Deborah, Judg. 4:4). She is respected as a servant of Yahweh because she is consulted and her interpretation of the law scroll is received as a word from God. The exact location of the "Second District" in preexilic Jerusalem is unknown (cf. Zeph. 1:10).

That interpretation is delivered to Hilkiah, Shaphan, and the others in a two-part message. (1) An oracle of punishment (34:24−25) assumes the curses of Deuteronomy 28. They will be inflicted on Jerusalem and the people of Judah as divine judgment for sins associated with idolatry (a veiled reference to the apostasy of Manasseh?). Though not specifically mentioned by the prophetess, the repetition of the verb "pour out" (*ntk*, 2 Chron. 34:21, 25) and the allusion to the curses of Deuteronomy strongly hint at the impending Babylonian invasion and exile.

(2) An oracle of salvation (34:26−28a) is prompted by Josiah's repentance as demonstrated in his acts of humility and contrition. The idea of repentance in the form of "humbling oneself" before the Lord is the dominant theological theme of this section of Chronicles (33:12, 19, 23; 34:27; cf. 29:10; 30:8). According to Williamson, the repetition of the king's "humbling himself" in repentance (34:27) is the Chronicler's way of offering Josiah's actions as an example to be emulated by his own audience.[19] The postscript recounting how Josiah pressures his subjects to serve the Lord (34:33) seems to confirm Williamson's contention that the Chronicler desires the experience of Josiah's repentance for his own audience.

There is some question as to Huldah's pronouncement of a peaceful burial for Josiah (34:28a), given his violent death in battle against the Egyptians. We should note, however, that Josiah is promised a peaceful burial, not death, and this honor is accorded to him (35:24). Beyond this, the assurance that Josiah will not see the disaster of the Babylonian exile is another way in which the king ends his life peacefully, comparatively speaking.

Covenant-renewal ceremony (34:29−33). The report of Josiah's covenant renewal ceremony closely follows 2 Kings 23:1−3. Certain significant changes are commonly noted. For example, the phrase "the priests and the Levites" (2 Chron. 34:30) is substituted for "the priests and the prophets" (2 Kings 23:2). For the Chronicler, the Levites now stand in the tradition of the prophets as preachers and teachers of the law of Moses. Also the king stands "in his place" (NRSV) (2 Chron. 34:31) rather than "by the pillar" (2 Kings 23:3), which perhaps suggests the absence of the pillars Jakin and Boaz in the second temple (cf. 2 Chron. 3:17).[20]

---

19. Williamson, *1 and 2 Chronicles*, 402.
20. See Selman, *2 Chronicles*, 535.

Finally, Chronicles 34:32 paraphrases the response of the people in pledging their loyalty to the covenant agreement (cf. 2 Kings 23:3b). The Chronicler's version stresses that Josiah imposes the pledge of obedience on the assembly, suggesting that the people do not fully share the king's faith or convictions about the covenant relationship with Yahweh. Or, as McConville comments, King Josiah "determined that the people shall be worthy of the mercy received."[21] This is borne out by the fact that Josiah's religious reforms died with him at Megiddo (cf. 2 Chron. 36:8, 14; Jer. 3:10).[22]

The expression "the Book of the Covenant" is a rarely used technical term for the entire Pentateuch in later Judaism (34:30; cf. Sir. 24:23). Thus, this book title likely refers to the core of the Sinai covenant code, Exodus 19–24 (cf. Ex. 24:7), or perhaps the book of Deuteronomy. More important is the theological significance of the term *covenant*, which denotes an agreement that creates new relationships in accordance with stipulations outlined in advance. The Old Testament recognizes two types of covenants. The *treaty* or *obligatory covenant* creates a relationship between unequal parties (i.e., God and Israel) and obligates the servant or vassal to serve the master or suzerain by means of specific regulations (e.g., Mosaic law). The *grant* or *promissory covenant* obligates the master to the vassal, who is rewarded for past loyalty (e.g., God's promise of a dynasty for David). Divine punishment in the form of curses may be invoked for violation of the agreement in both cases.

The key issue for our study is the creation of relationships by means of a covenant ritual, and this through the voluntary act of the individual (or community). Hence Joshua's challenge, "choose for yourselves this day whom you will serve" (Josh. 24:15). Covenant renewal for ancient Israel was repairing or restoring a relationship with God broken because of their willful violation of the stipulations regulating the relationship. Repentance or humbling oneself is the first step in renewing a covenant relationship with God, as King David well knew (cf. Ps. 51:17).

Josiah's covenant-renewal ceremony combines elements of the Mosaic covenant (esp. seen in the terms "commands, regulations and decrees," 34:31; cf. Deut. 4:40; 6:1) and of the Davidic covenant (esp. seen in the leadership of the king and the temple site, 2 Chron. 34:29, 31; cf. 7:13–14, 17–18). Beyond treaty definition and form, the idea of covenant combines both judgment and hope for Israel: judgment in the form of divine curse for disloyalty to the treaty demands and hope in the form of divine blessing for loyalty to

21. McConville, *I and II Chronicles*, 258.
22. On this reality Michael Wilcock laments that Josiah is a "pastor alone" in that the people are not with him (*The Message of Chronicles*, 269–70).

the treaty demands (cf. Lev. 26; Deut. 28). By God's design, almost frighteningly so, Israel's destiny lies in the decision of the people to choose "life and prosperity" or "death and destruction" (Deut. 30:15). Thankfully in this instance, because of the strong leadership of Josiah, the people chose life— for a time.

In keeping with the prescription of the Mosaic law, all the people gather for the reading of the law scroll and the covenant-ratification ceremony (34:29–30; cf. Deut. 31:11). The precedent for involving the entire community in covenant renewal was already established by Asa (2 Chron. 15:1– 15) and Hezekiah (29:10; 30:1). Theologically, the idea of God's grace extended to the disobedient people of God is not lost on the Chronicler. What God did in Israel by way of religious reform and spiritual renewal through the covenant-renewal ceremonies of Asa, Hezekiah, and Josiah is "repeatable" history for the Jews living in postexilic Judah—if they too humble themselves and pray and pledge covenant loyalty to Yahweh.

Thompson's reminder that the "Book of the Covenant" does not in and of itself create the change in the corporate religious life of Israel is timely.[23] Then, as now, spiritual renewal and true transformation must begin at the individual level, and it only comes by the power of the Holy Spirit—as the postexilic prophets Haggai and Zechariah well understand (Hag. 2:5; Zech. 4:6; 12:10).

The final verse of this section (34:33) summarizes the impact of the discovery of the law scroll and the covenant-renewal ceremony on Josiah's reign by means of allusion to the extensive religious reforms carried out in Judah (cf. 2 Kings 23:4–20). The Chronicler emphasizes how Josiah purges false religion "from all the territory belonging to the Israelites." The conclusion also echoes the expurgation of the early reforms of Josiah outlined in 2 Chronicles 34:6–7, thus forming an envelope construction thematically linking 34:1–7 with 34:8–33. Dillard has even suggested that the lengthy summary statement is a literary signal that the writer has turned to another source for the next episode of the narrative.[24]

Josiah's Passover (35:1–19). The Chronicler frames the report of Josiah's Passover with the brief version of the event from 2 Kings 23:21– 23. The source for the expanded account of the festival is unknown but presumably is a priestly or temple record since the text gives primacy to the role of the Levites. The attention given to their service in leading worship and the detail spent on sacrificial ritual are in keeping with priestly motifs important to the Chronicler.

---

23. Thompson, *1, 2 Chronicles*, 379.
24. Dillard, *2 Chronicles*, 282.

The Passover is the preeminent religious festival for postexilic Judah and the apex of temple worship for the Chronicler. The reason for the prominence of this feast in the Jewish restoration community stems from the Passover observed after the completion of the second temple in 516 B.C. and the understanding that the return from Babylonian captivity is a "second exodus" for God's people (cf. Ezra 6:19–22). The Passover, more than any other Hebrew religious festival, drew the nation of Israel back to her roots since it was at Mount Sinai that the former Hebrew slaves were constituted as the people of God.

The version of Josiah's Passover in 2 Kings 23:19–20, 24–25 is set in the context of religious reform. By contrast, the Chronicler's purpose in relating the Passover observance is to encourage "the right use of the temple, its service, and its offerings."[25] The account of Josiah's Passover may be outlined in four sections: the preparations for the festival (2 Chron. 35:1–6), the provision of sacrificial animals (35:7–10), the ritual service of the offerings (35:11–15), and the epilogue affirming the fulfillment of Josiah's orders (35:16–19). Interestingly, the first two sections begin with a focus on the role of Josiah as the organizer of the feast (35:1, 7), while in the last two sections the service of the Passover ritual itself is highlighted (35:10, 16).

The preparations for the festival (35:1–6). The Chronicler specifies the precise date for the observance of the Passover (35:1) in order to demonstrate that Josiah is in compliance with Mosaic law (cf. Lev. 23:5; Num. 28:16), perhaps in contrast to the delayed Passover celebration of Hezekiah (2 Chron. 30:2–3). Like Hezekiah, Josiah is also an "encourager" (35:2; cf. 30:22; 32:6). In each case his encouragement takes the form of a series of imperative verbs designed to guide behavior. The ethical aspects of this speech form (i.e., the imperative verb) connect the Hebrew wisdom and prophetic traditions to the moral codes of Hebrew law and extend throughout biblical literature to the teachings of Jesus and Paul (e.g., Matt. 5–7; Rom. 12:9–21).[26] The importance of religious instruction by the Levites is no doubt heightened during reform movements of the righteous kings of Judah (e.g., 2 Chron. 17:7–8; cf. Neh. 8:7–9).

The reference to transfering the ark of the covenant back to the temple is obscure (35:3), since there is no record that it was moved from the sanctuary.[27] McConville's suggestion that Josiah deliberately reenacts the installation of the ark of the covenant as a symbolic gesture has merit.[28] The

25. Selman, *2 Chronicles*, 536.

26. On the pedagogical role of the Levites in ancient Israel see comments on 1 Chron. 6.

27. See Dillard's helpful discussion of scholarly conjecture on the transfer of the ark of the covenant (*2 Chronicles*, 284 n. 3.c-d).

28. McConville, *I and II Chronicles*, 262.

authority behind the specific instructions for the change in the ritual duties of the Levites is based on the decrees of Kings David and Solomon in recognition of the shift from portable sanctuary to permanent temple (35:4) .

The appeal to the authority of Moses (35:6) refers more generally to Passover legislation in the Pentateuch (e.g., Ex. 12–13; Deut. 16:1–8). According to law, the Passover animal was to be slaughtered and offered for sacrifice by the suppliant, not the Levitical priesthood (cf. Ex. 12:3–6; Deut. 16:5–6). The procedural change in the ritual of sacrifice to the priesthood was first implemented as an emergency of circumstance by Hezekiah, because of ritual impurity among the people (2 Chron. 30:17). By the time of Josiah, this practice has become standard, perhaps as a pragmatic response to the size of the population at this time (note "all the people" in 35:13, 18).

Quite apart from the technicalities of sacrificial worship, we cannot overlook the essential calling of the Levitical priesthood as mediators (note the repeated phrases "serve ... his people," 35:3, and "your fellow countrymen," 35:5–6). The Levitical priests are to mediate the holy presence of God in Israel by making atonement first for their own sins and then for the sins of the people (Lev. 9:7). Hence the Levites must first prepare themselves (2 Chron. 35:4) before they can serve the people in the ministry of sacrificial worship (35:5–6).

The provision of sacrificial animals (35:7–10). The key piece of information in this section is the report of the generosity of the king in providing the sacrificial animals for the Passover. In addition to the sheep and goats from Josiah's personal flocks (35:7), his royal officials and the administrators of the temple also contribute animals for the Passover offerings (35:8–9). The royal "officials" are probably members of Josiah's "cabinet," including princes and appointees to posts such as the recorder, secretary, chief of staff over the army, and advisers (cf. the list of David's officials, 2 Sam. 8:15–18). The temple administrators are senior priests in charge of the Levitical divisions and the musical and service guilds.

The Chronicler notes that the civil and religious leaders of Judah are not only generous but also willing (35:8). This precedent was set by David (1 Chron. 29:2–5) and later by Hezekiah, who provided one thousand bulls and seven thousand sheep and goats for his Passover feast (2 Chron. 30:24). Such benevolence was not always the case during the history of the monarchies in Israel and Judah. The story of Ahab's annexation of Naboth's vineyard (1 Kings 21) and the indictments of the prophets against royal policies that trampled the poor and oppressed the righteous (e.g., Mic. 3:1–7) are sad testimony to the darker side of Israel's kingship.

No doubt the Chronicler seeks to impress the importance of the virtue of generosity on his audience as well. In terms of the sheer numbers of animals to be sacrificed, Josiah's celebration doubles the size of Hezekiah's Passover (2,000 bulls and 17,000 sheep and goats were offered for Hezekiah's Passover [30:24]; 3,800 bulls and 37,600 sheep and goats are offered for this Passover [35:7–9]).

The ritual service of the offerings (35:11–15). This third unit describes the actual Passover ceremony. The ritual consists of two segments: offering the animal sacrifices (35:11–12) and eating the Passover meal (35:13–15). The shift in the locus of the Passover from the home to the temple as the central shrine radically alters the ritual character of the Passover. The priests are now responsible for slaughtering the Passover lambs (35:6, 11), sprinkling the blood of the slain animal on the altar of burnt offering (35:11; cf. 29:22; 30:16), and then skinning the animal for cooking (35:11; cf. 29:34). Moreover, the priests and attending Levites supervise the roasting of the sacrificial animals and serve the Passover meal to the assembly (35:13).

The term "roasted" (*bšl*, 35:13a) is a general word for cooking food either by boiling or by roasting. The original Passover meal was cooked by roasting (Ex. 12:8; Deut. 16:7). Certain other types of offerings included in fellowship meals were boiled in clay pots (e.g., Ex. 29:31; Lev. 6:28). It seems the Passover celebration combined both types of cooked food offerings.

The presentation of burnt offerings along with the Passover offering has puzzled biblical scholars (2 Chron. 35:12, 14). One approach assumes these burnt offerings are merely portions of the Passover sacrifices burnt on the altar.[29] Another explanation identifies these burnt offerings as separate holocaust sacrifices complementing the Passover offerings (cf. Lev. 1:3–9).[30] The reference to "fat portions" (2 Chron. 35:14) clearly indicates that some assimilation of the peace offering with the Passover offering has taken place by the time of Hezekiah and Josiah (a logical association, since both offerings included a fellowship meal, cf. Lev. 3:9–17).

The Chronicler emphasizes how the priests and Levites fulfill all the requirements of the ceremony demanded by the king and the law of Moses (note "the service was arranged" [*kun* + *ᶜabodah*], 35:10; "the entire service ... was carried out," 35:16). In fact, the eager ministry of the Levites supersedes the requirements of the ceremony. They not only serve the people "quickly" as a reminder of the hasty meal eaten at the first Passover (35:13), but they also are a model of servanthood at the communal meal by making additional preparations for their fellow priests, musicians, and gatekeepers, who remain on duty at their posts for the entire day (35:14–15).

---

29. E.g., Williamson, *1 and 2 Chronicles*, 406–7; Dillard, *2 Chronicles*, 291.
30. E.g., Selman, *2 Chronicles*, 539–40.

The epilogue (35:16–19). The Chronicler reiterates the detailed diligence of the priests and Levites in carrying out the instructions of the king and the law of Moses. The declaration that Josiah's Passover is unrivaled as a religious festival in Israel anticipates a comparison with Hezekiah's Passover celebration (cf. 30:26). The Chronicler's statement may be one of kind more than totality, since he is probably referring to the centralized celebration of the Passover linked to the Jerusalem temple. Chronicles inserts "the days of the prophet Samuel" (35:18) for "the days of the judges" in 2 Kings 23:22, presumably because Samuel is the prototypical "priest-seer" for postexilic Judaism.

In keeping with his thematic emphasis on "all Israel," the Chronicler uses the name "Israel" to refer to the divided kingdoms of Israel and Judah as recorded in 2 Kings 23:22. For him, the Passover is a unifying festival in the life of Israel since it brings the king, the priests, the Levites, and all the people together in fellowship over a ritual meal (2 Chron. 35:18). The repetition of the date formula ("the eighteenth year of Josiah's reign," 35:19) is part of an inclusio or envelope construction linking the events of the religious reforms associated with finding the law scroll and the Passover celebration (see comments on 34:8).

Battle report of Josiah's death (35:20–25). The expression "after all this" (35:20) cues the reader that some time has elapsed since Josiah's celebration of the Passover. Specifically, the narrative leaps chronologically from the Passover festival in Jerusalem in 622 B.C. to Josiah's death in battle at Megiddo in 609 B.C. The Chronicler expands the report of Josiah's death found in 2 Kings 23:29–30 in order to offer a theological commentary on the tragic event. Given the dominant theme of the retribution principle in Chronicles, Josiah's death poses a narrative problem for the writer, namely, how to explain the untimely end of a righteous king.

According to Begg, the battle report of Josiah's death broadly fits the pattern of previous death reports for other kings such as Asa and Jehoshaphat.[31] The Chronicler uses a four-part structure in order to censure Josiah and to demonstrate that the untimely death of a righteous king is not incongruous with the retribution principle. (1) Josiah's death is construed as an example of *immediate* judgment for sin (35:22). (2) Josiah is portrayed after the manner of earlier kings who started well but later stumbled into sin (e.g., Joash and Uzziah). (3) As with predecessors like Rehoboam (11:1–4) and Ahab (18:16–22), Josiah hears a "warning speech" through a spokesman for God prior to his fatal military misstep. (4) Finally, as with Asa, Jehoshaphat, and Hezekiah, the Chronicler contrasts successful religious reform with an impending external military threat forcing the king into a life-and-death decision.

---

31. C. Begg, "The Death of Josiah in Chronicles: Another View," *VT* 37 (1987): 1–8.

By way of historical background, we must remember that the military might of the ancient superpower of Assyria is now on the wane, while the greatness of the Babylonian Empire is swiftly and brutally on the rise.[32] Only a year prior to Josiah's ill-advised campaign against Pharaoh Neco (610 B.C.), the Babylonians forced the last Assyrian king, Ashur-uballit, to flee the capital city of Haran and set up a provisional government in Carchemish. Pharaoh Neco apparently seeks passage through Palestine to bring his large army to reinforce the beleaguered Assyrian army for a final stand against the Babylonians at Carchemish (35:20).

Pharaoh Neco indicates he has no quarrel with Josiah or Judah; he simply wants a right of way through Judah so he can show loyalty to his Assyrian ally (35:21). The Megiddo pass lies on the international coastal highway, an ancient trade route connecting Egypt with Syria, northern Mesopotamia, and Anatolia. The site of Megiddo guards this bottleneck on the route through the Mount Carmel foothills. To meet up with the Assyrians at Carchemish, Neco must move his army through the Megiddo pass. It is at this strategic location that Josiah (foolishly) chooses to intercept Pharaoh Neco and the Egyptian army.

The key statement in the Chronicler's rendition of Josiah's death is the clause "he would not listen to what Neco had said" (35:22). Previously, Josiah was commended by Huldah the prophetess for his responsiveness to God (34:27). Now he actually stands in opposition to God's word spoken through Pharaoh Neco—to his own destruction (35:21b). But how is King Josiah to discern that the Egyptian king is delivering a message from God? The text provides no answer, but we must assume that somehow through the ministry of God's Spirit, Josiah could recognize the divine origin of the truth and the authority of Neco's speech.

Ironically, Josiah goes into battle disguised much like the ploy of King Ahab of Israel (35:22a; cf. 18:28–34). Like Ahab, Josiah is pierced by an arrow and severely injured during the heat of the battle (35:23). According to 2 Kings 23:29, he dies in battle at Megiddo. The expanded report in Chronicles has Josiah dying in Jerusalem (2 Chron. 35:24b). The logical harmonization of the two reports suggests that Josiah is mortally wounded in battle at Megiddo and probably dies in transit to Jerusalem from loss of blood, so that he is declared "dead on arrival" in his capital city.

The Chronicler is careful to note that Josiah receives a proper burial in the "tombs of his fathers" (i.e., the equivalent of a "state funeral," 35:24). In this regard, the words of Huldah's prophecy over Josiah are fulfilled: He is

32. See further Saggs, *The Greatness That Was Babylon;* idem, *The Might That Was Assyria* (London: Sidgwick & Jackson, 1984).

buried in the tombs of his fathers in peace (i.e., Judah's unilateral engagement of the Egyptians in battle ends when Josiah dies; cf. 34:28).

Josiah has been a popular king, for "all Judah and Jerusalem" mourn his death (35:24). In fact, the prophet Jeremiah (a contemporary of Josiah) composes laments for the slain king that continue to memorialize his legacy to the time of the Chronicler. We should not confuse these laments with the book of Lamentations, also written by Jeremiah, according to Jewish tradition, during or after the destruction of Jerusalem. The shock wave of Josiah's death sends tremors through Judah from which the nation never recovers. Not only do his religious reforms die with him in battle, but also the kingdom of Judah itself will soon "die" in the Babylonian onslaught.

Concluding regnal résumé (35:26–36:1). This concluding résumé contains two formulas: the historical source citation formula (35:26–27) and the succession formula (36:1). The Chronicler repeats 2 Kings 23:28, 30b, with two exceptions. (1) He expands the clause "all he did" into "acts of devotion, according to what is written in the Law of the LORD" (2 Chron. 35:26; cf. 34:2). The expression "acts of devotion" is better rendered "covenant loyalty" (ḥesed), commemorating the covenant-renewal ceremony convened by Josiah and ratified by all Judah (34:29–31). (2) The Chronicler also adds the phrase "in Jerusalem" to the succession formula (36:1), presumably to remind his audience that God made good on his promise to restore his people and his name in that city. On the phrase "the people of the land," see comments on 33:25.

THE PREACHING OF THE CHRONICLER. We have already noted that the peculiar literary genius of the Chronicler lies in his ability to retell Israelite history as a sermon. According to Rex Mason, the essential features of the sermon include an appeal to some recognized source of authority, a proclamation of some theological teaching about the person and works of God, an appeal for some kind of response on the part of the audience, and the use of rhetorical devices designed to arouse the interest of the audience and engage them in the message topic.[33]

(1) The Chronicler cites two authoritative historical sources in his review of the reigns of the Kings Manasseh, Amon, and Josiah. The "annals of the kings of Israel" (33:18) and the "book of the kings of Israel and Judah" (35:27) are documents belonging to the royal archives and portions of which are now a part of the Old Testament books of 1 and 2 Kings. A third resource,

---

33. Rex Mason, "Some Echoes of the Preaching in the Second Temple? Tradition Elements in Zechariah 1–8," ZAW 96 (1984): 223–25.

the "records of the seers" (33:19) proves more difficult to identify. Clearly it is widely recognized as a reliable historical document compiled by the school of the prophets.

(2) This section of Chronicles highlights certain character traits of God, especially his compassion and mercy in responding to those who humble themselves and offer prayer seeking God's forgiveness (i.e., Manasseh, 33:12–19; Josiah, 34:27). God is portrayed as one who listens and is moved to benevolent action on behalf of the penitent (33:13). Conversely, God's righteousness in not acquitting the guilty is demonstrated in his response to Amon, who "increased his guilt" before God by refusing to humble himself (33:23).

(3) The repeated theme of this literary unit is repentance, or more specifically, "humbling oneself" before God (33:12, 19, 23; 34:27). The biblical term used (*kn*^{c}) denotes a change of heart and attitude from a posture of defiance to submission toward God and principles of righteousness. The idea of repentance in the Old Testament, then, is basically that of turning around or returning to a point of departure. The "turn" of repentance and conversion consists of turning *from* something and turning *toward* something.[34] Theologically, repentance is turning away from self and sin to God in utter humility and dependence.

Of special interest to the Chronicler are the immediate moral consequences of human behavior. Manasseh's sin leads to his exile and imprisonment in Assyria (33:10–11). Later, Manasseh's repentance leads to his restoration as king of Judah (33:12–13). Seemingly, all this would have been a great encouragement to the Chronicler's audience. Yet, curiously, Chronicles is a sermon without an application since the books contain no direct reference to the writer's own time period. The writer preaches from the examples of repentance in the lives of the Judahite kings of Manasseh, Amon, and Josiah but makes no direct appeal to the citizens of postexilic Jerusalem to respond in like manner.

(4) Finally, the Chronicler employs the literary or rhetorical approach of "storytelling" as the means of capturing and maintaining audience interest in his message. By storytelling we mean the use of the genre of biblical narrative as the primary vehicle for preaching the sermon. Biblical narrative may be separated (somewhat artificially) into two categories: heroic narrative and epic narrative.[35] Chronicles is primarily epic narrative in that it is national rather than familial or tribal history, tends to emphasize cause-and-effect sequences more than plot development, contains commentary offered by

34. William Barclay, *Turning to God: A Study of Conversion in the Book of Acts and Today* (repr. of 1964 Epworth ed.; Grand Rapids: Baker, 1972), 26–30.

35. Ryken, *How to Read the Bible as Literature*, 75–81.

the narrator, and often notes how God acts through human agents (e.g., prophet, king).[36]

Biblical narrative "presents a theology—that is, a proclamation about God—told by means of narrative."[37] For Mathews, this means that "historical narrative is narrative theology" because the biblical writers assume the role of God's prophet and present a theological interpretation of Hebrew history.[38] The audience's intuited understanding of the Chronicler's application is a key ingredient in the art of preaching through the medium of biblical narrative. Narrative theology is a subtle but most powerful literary technique for penetrating the heart and mind of the hearer (or reader) with the truth claims of the preacher's message.

Two characteristics of biblical narrative are especially important to the subliminal approach in evoking the desired response from the writer's audience. (1) The first is related to the idea of plot development, a central feature of storytelling. The plot of a story is a coherent sequence of related events moving toward closure. The essence of a story plot is conflict moving toward resolution.[39] By his careful selection, arrangement, and reshaping of the narrative events associated with Manasseh, Amon, and Josiah, the Chronicler encourages his audience to consider the history of Judah during this time as a type of theological commentary on the divine response to human repentance. For the Chronicler, the resolution of the conflict (i.e., the seeming failure of the divine promise concerning the Davidic covenant after the return from exile) is found in the continuity of repentance and blessing as exhibited in the lives of certain kings of Judah.

(2) The second characteristic is linked to the role of the Chronicler as "narrator" (whether overt or covert) of the events in his retelling of Israel's history. Typically, the narrator speaks in the third-person in biblical narrative, leaving personal judgment and moral commentary to the subtle influences of literary structure and the dialogue of the main characters. According to Bar Efrat, the narrator tends to "hint at things—in delicate and indirect ways—rather than stating them explicitly. The method of the biblical narrator requires a constant mental effort on the part of the reader, involving careful thought and attention to every detail of the narrator."[40]

---

36. Eugene H. Merrill, "History," in *Cracking Old Testament Codes*, ed. D. Brent Sandy and Ronald L. Giese (Nashville: Broadman & Holman, 1995), 91.

37. Kenneth A. Mathews, "Preaching Historical Narratives," in *Reclaiming the Prophetic Mantle*, ed. George L. Klein (Nashville: Broadman, 1992), 25.

38. Ibid., 27.

39. Ryken, *How to Read the Bible as Literature*, 40.

40. Shimon Bar-Efrat, *Narrative Art in the Bible* (Bible and Literature Series 17; Sheffield: Sheffield Academic Press, 1989), 45.

The same holds true for the Chronicler's readers (or hearers). As narrator, the Chronicler persuades the audience to understand the history of Israel from his theological viewpoint, a viewpoint (sometimes) different from those of the participants in the story. Point of view is crucial for the interpretation of the narrative because it is the ideological and theological lens through which the audience comprehends the events of the plot of the story. By recounting the stories of repentance and subsequent divine blessing associated with Kings Manasseh and Josiah, as well as the divine judgment resulting from Amon's failure to heed the word of God and repent, the Chronicler delicately and indirectly persuades his audience that humbling themselves before God in repentance would be in their best interests too!

PREACHING REPENTANCE. According to John Stott, the preacher is called to both comfort and disturb people.[41] Admittedly, the latter task is an unpopular one. Nevertheless, it is necessary at times for the servant of God to confront his audience. The tradition of the prophet as "conscience" for God's people has its roots in the ministry of the Old Testament prophets, who were called both to "uproot and tear down" and to "build and to plant" (Jer. 1:10).

The preacher both comforts and disturbs the audience through the act of preaching, the proclamation of the Word of God. The messenger must deliver the message of the One who sends the servant—not an invented message (cf. Amos 3:8; 2 Peter 1:21). For Stott, contemporary preaching builds bridges between two worlds: the Word or Holy Scripture and the world of everyday life.[42] The preacher "earths" the Word in the world by communicating God's truth with relevance and pertinence to our ever-changing society.

The "preaching" of Chronicles informs contemporary preaching at two levels. (1) In terms of content, the disturbing message of preaching is the call to repentance. (2) In terms of style, the narrative approach permits the preacher to locate the disturbing message in a larger story that also includes the message of comfort.

We have defined repentance as an "about face," a turning away from sin, self, and death to righteousness, God, and life (Jer. 31:18–20; Luke 3:8–14). The effects of the Fall are still manifest in the world, as the both the psalmist and the apostle Paul observe that "all have turned aside ... there is no one

---

41. John R. W. Stott, *Between Two Worlds: The Art of Preaching in the Twentieth Century* (Grand Rapids: Eerdmans, 1982), 305.

42. Ibid., 138–44.

who does good" (Ps. 14:3; Rom. 3:12). One need only pick up a daily newspaper or turn on a local television news broadcast to verify the biblical assessment of the human condition. The real question, then, is not one of why anyone should repent of sin and turn to God. Rather, the crucial questions are twofold: Who can truly forgive sin and restore human dignity and purpose? When is it too late to repent and turn to God?

There is a sense in which the story of Manasseh's repentance foreshadows that of the believing thief in the Gospel (33:12−13; cf. Luke 23:40−43). Both stories answer the crucial questions by illustrating the point that the God of the Bible can truly forgive sin and that his door of salvation and restoration is always open. The old and new covenants alike portray God as one who is gracious, merciful, compassionate, and slow to anger—not desiring that anyone should perish but that all should repent and live (Ezek. 18:32; cf. Ex. 34:6−7; John 3:16; 2 Peter 3:9). The lyrics of an old nineteenth-century Christian hymn capture the truth of this biblical teaching: "There is a wideness in God's mercy like the wideness of the sea; there's a kindness in His justice which is more than liberty."

Scott has aptly reminded us that the preacher's call to repentance, in any age, must be both personal and corporate. That is, corporate or community repentance "for social sin and the defects of accepted morality" goes hand in hand with personal repentance for sin and rebellion against God and his holy law.[43] Beyond this, the call to repentance is necessarily coupled with the summons to believe and live in God's way—the way that leads to life and "fruitful" living (cf. Matt. 7:13−20). The enduring reality that encourages the prophets in their ministry and saves them from despair as heralds of God's "disturbing" word—the idea of humanity's capacity for repentance—should sustain today's preacher in like manner.[44]

Barclay furthers the discussion by developing the idea that today's preacher should also be sustained by what he calls "the great challenge and privilege of the Christian."[45] That great challenge and privilege are partnering with God in the ministry of the conversion of individuals to Christianity, and this partnership is necessary because the primary means of conversion in the early church was the preaching of the gospel.

Repentance does not necessarily suspend the consequences of personal or corporate sin. The kingdom of Judah was destroyed and the Hebrews were exiled in Babylonia despite Josiah's national revival (36:15−19). As Heschel has warned, God's forgiveness must not be mistaken for indulgence or

---

43. Scott, *The Relevance of the Prophets*, 218.
44. Heschel, *The Prophets*, 1:185.
45. Barclay, *Turning to God*, 31.

complacency.[46] Nor are we to be seduced by the preaching of "cheap grace" decried by Bonhoeffer.[47] Lest we tame God and fashion him after our own image, it is important to remember he is loving and faithful, but he is also terrible and dangerous. We would do well to recall Lucy's conversation with Mr. and Mrs. Beaver about the great lion Aslan of Narnia fame:

> "Then he isn't safe?" said Lucy.
> "Safe?" said Mrs. Beaver. "Who said anything about safe? Course he isn't safe. But he's good. He's the King."[48]

Indeed, the God of the Bible is holy and just; but he is also "gracious and compassionate, slow to anger and rich in love. The LORD is good to all; he has compassion on all he has made" (Ps. 145:8–9). The glorious message of the Bible, unique among all the holy books of the world's religions, is that God's anger, though provoked by human sin, may be revoked by human repentance. Happily, assuredly God returns to those who return to him (Zech. 1:3; Mal. 3:7).

The Chronicler also provides instruction on preaching style. A. W. Tozer wrote about those who preach the "old cross" and those who preach the "new cross."[49] The old cross is the symbol of death, representing the abrupt and violent end of a human being. It "slays the sinner" and makes no compromise, modifies nothing, and spares nothing. It strikes the "victim" cruel and hard—and completely. The new cross does not slay the sinner but attempts to redirect him or her into a cleaner and happier way of living. It saves one's self-respect and offers the individual a new and improved "old life."

The message of the Christian church today must be the "old cross" of Tozer. Indeed, "the message of the cross is foolishness to those who are perishing, but to us who are being saved it is the power of God" (1 Cor. 1:18). Again, Paul says that those in Christ have died to sin because we have been buried with him through baptism in his death (Rom. 6:1–4). True repentance slays the sinner and creates a new person in Jesus Christ (2 Cor. 5:17).

Much like the Old Testament prophets, the preacher today is called to "slay the sinner" with the words of God's righteous judgment (e.g., Hos. 6:5). There is still a place for the fiery and confrontational ministry of a John the Baptist-like evangelist. A dark world will always need the uncompromising witness to the "true light" (John 1:7–9). Yet contemporary North American society has experienced a shift in communication paradigms. The multiple forms of

---

46. Heschel, *The Prophets*, 2:65.
47. Dietrich Bonhoeffer, *The Cost of Discipleship* (New York: Macmillan, 1963), 45.
48. C. S. Lewis, *The Lion, the Witch, and the Wardrobe* (New York: Macmillan, 1950), 75–76.
49. Warren W. Wiersbe, ed., *The Best of A. W. Tozer* (Grand Rapids: Baker, 1978), 175–76.

electronic media utilized to both entertain and inform our technological society have profoundly influenced the "language" of communication. For example, today's audio-visual communication especially appeals to the hearts and feelings of the audience. This contrasts starkly with the notational form of communication that appeals chiefly to the intellect and reason.[50]

The emergence of what is now called "symbolic language" is directly related to this cultural shift in communication paradigms. According to Babin, symbolic language is a language of stories, images, suggestions, and inferences.[51] This is also the language of biblical narrative, a language that hints at things "in delicate and indirect ways."[52] The Chronicler reminds us that at times the preacher can "slay the sinner" indirectly with stories and personal examples of repentance couched in biblical narrative. There is an important place for the use of symbolic language in the church today as people reconnect with the idea of story and imagination as a result of the electronic media.

Naturally, the indirect communication of story and image is never a substitute for the direct communication of the prophetic call to repentance. Rather, it is complementary. This is why indirect communication is usually interpreted for the audience (e.g., Jesus' interpretation of the parable of the sower; cf. Matt. 13:18). The Chronicler's audience knows the history of Israel from the Kings' parallels and the books of the major and minor prophets. His indirect call to repentance through the story of Hebrew history is contextualized for his audience by the shared national experience culminating in the Babylonian exile and the restoration of Judah. Like the parables of Jesus, however, the indirect communication of story as found in biblical narrative has much to commend it for the ministry of Christ's gospel in our postmodern society. The indirect communication of the Bible was often prompted by historical or theological crises. The shift in the historical paradigm from the modern world to a postmodern world seems such a historical crisis, with considerable "theological fallout" for the Christian church.

(1) It places the onus on the audience (whether reader or hearer) to enter the story and search for personal meaning and application. Thus, indirect communication becomes both clue and snare because it simultaneously informs and conceals. For those with "ears to hear," indirect communication of biblical narrative incites curiosity and excites the imagination. It becomes an invitation to the "seeker" to enter the mystery of the kingdom of God (cf. Col. 1:26−27).

---

50. See Pierre Babin, *The New Era in Religious Communication* (Minneapolis: Fortress, 1991), 31.
51. Ibid., 149.
52. Bar-Efrat, *Narrative Art in the Bible*, 45.

(2) Indirect communication dulls the ears and pronounces judgment on the "outsider," those who have willfully chosen not to "see" and "hear" God's truth (cf. Ezek. 24:3—14). In quoting Isaiah the prophet, Jesus indicated that some have already "closed their eyes" and "hardly hear with their ears" and thus have hearts that have become "calloused" (Matt. 13:15; cf. Isa. 6:9—10). The implicit answer to the question posed to Jesus by his disciples as to why he spoke in parables is really that of winnowing the faithful from the unfaithful by means of indirect communication (Matt. 13:10—13). This is no doubt a hard teaching, but it serves to further our understanding of the gospel of Jesus Christ as a "stumbling block" and a "rock" that makes people fall (1 Cor. 1:23; 1 Peter 2:8).

(3) This approach gives a preeminent place to the work of the Holy Spirit in drawing people into a conversation with God. One aspect of the genius of indirect communication is its ability to break down "defense mechanisms" in the audience as the reader or hearer gets caught up in the story. This means the "punch line" often has far greater impact for the "insider" or the person of faith than truth expressed by more direct means of communication.

Perhaps the best example of this is Nathan's explanation to King David of the parable about a poor man who had but one ewe lamb (2 Sam. 12:1—6). What else could David say but "I have sinned against the LORD" (2 Sam. 12:13)? What else could have prompted David to write about the experience of his own repentance with such depth of feeling and force of spiritual conviction as in Psalm 51? In a way, the Chronicler anticipates the later ministry of Jesus, who "did not say anything to them without using a parable" (Mark 4:34).

2 Chronicles 36:2–21

JEHOAHAZ WAS TWENTY-THREE years old when he became
king, and he reigned in Jerusalem three months. ³The king
of Egypt dethroned him in Jerusalem and imposed on
Judah a levy of a hundred talents of silver and a talent of gold.
⁴The king of Egypt made Eliakim, a brother of Jehoahaz, king
over Judah and Jerusalem and changed Eliakim's name to
Jehoiakim. But Neco took Eliakim's brother Jehoahaz and carried him off to Egypt.

⁵Jehoiakim was twenty-five years old when he became king,
and he reigned in Jerusalem eleven years. He did evil in the
eyes of the LORD his God. ⁶Nebuchadnezzar king of Babylon
attacked him and bound him with bronze shackles to take him
to Babylon. ⁷Nebuchadnezzar also took to Babylon articles
from the temple of the LORD and put them in his temple there.

⁸The other events of Jehoiakim's reign, the detestable
things he did and all that was found against him, are written in
the book of the kings of Israel and Judah. And Jehoiachin his
son succeeded him as king.

⁹Jehoiachin was eighteen years old when he became king,
and he reigned in Jerusalem three months and ten days.
He did evil in the eyes of the LORD. ¹⁰In the spring, King
Nebuchadnezzar sent for him and brought him to Babylon,
together with articles of value from the temple of the LORD,
and he made Jehoiachin's uncle, Zedekiah, king over Judah
and Jerusalem.

¹¹Zedekiah was twenty-one years old when he became
king, and he reigned in Jerusalem eleven years. ¹²He did evil
in the eyes of the LORD his God and did not humble himself
before Jeremiah the prophet, who spoke the word of the
LORD. ¹³He also rebelled against King Nebuchadnezzar, who
had made him take an oath in God's name. He became stiff-
necked and hardened his heart and would not turn to the
LORD, the God of Israel. ¹⁴Furthermore, all the leaders of the
priests and the people became more and more unfaithful, following all the detestable practices of the nations and defiling
the temple of the LORD, which he had consecrated in
Jerusalem.

¹⁵The LORD, the God of their fathers, sent word to them through his messengers again and again, because he had pity on his people and on his dwelling place. ¹⁶But they mocked God's messengers, despised his words and scoffed at his prophets until the wrath of the LORD was aroused against his people and there was no remedy. ¹⁷He brought up against them the king of the Babylonians, who killed their young men with the sword in the sanctuary, and spared neither young man nor young woman, old man or aged. God handed all of them over to Nebuchadnezzar. ¹⁸He carried to Babylon all the articles from the temple of God, both large and small, and the treasures of the LORD's temple and the treasures of the king and his officials. ¹⁹They set fire to God's temple and broke down the wall of Jerusalem; they burned all the palaces and destroyed everything of value there.

²⁰He carried into exile to Babylon the remnant, who escaped from the sword, and they became servants to him and his sons until the kingdom of Persia came to power. ²¹The land enjoyed its sabbath rests; all the time of its desolation it rested, until the seventy years were completed in fulfillment of the word of the LORD spoken by Jeremiah.

Original Meaning

THE BABYLONIANS SACKED the city of Nineveh in 612 B.C. and then deposed the remnants of the Assyrian political establishment from Haran in 610 B.C. Thus Assyria's reign of terror in the ancient Near East came to an end. This colossal event, one the prophet Jonah longed to see and the prophet Nahum eventually witnessed, did not really bring peace to the peoples of Syria and Palestine. The resulting vacuum of political power in the Levant was quickly filled, as Pharaoh Neco II of Egypt marched to Carchemish on the Euphrates River. He intended to join with the Assyrian ruler Asshur-uballit in a last-ditch attempt to repulse the Babylonians and help restore Assyrian control in the western sector of the disintegrating empire. King Josiah's ill-fated attempt to intercept Neco at Megiddo only delayed the defeat the Egyptians experienced at Carchemish.

Although the Egypto-Assyrian alliance failed to save the Assyrian Empire, Neco's campaign did result in Egyptian control of Syria-Palestine. It is unclear whether King Josiah was obligated to oppose Pharaoh Neco II as a vassal of Babylonia or if he acted independently. In either case, his death meant the end of political autonomy for Judah. His successor, Jehoahaz, was dethroned by Neco and deported to Egypt. Neco placed Eliakim (or Jehoiakim), the brother of Jehoahaz, on the throne, and Judah became a vassal state to the pharaoh. Judah remained under Egyptian control until 605 B.C.

The Last Four Kings of Judah

Jehoahaz, son of Josiah	three months, 609 B.C.	exiled to Egypt
Jehoiakim, son of Josiah	609–598 B.C.	deported to Babylonia briefly/ died in office (or assassinated?)
Jehoiachin son of Jehoiakim	three months, 597 B.C.	exiled to Babylonia
Zedekiah, uncle of Jehoiachin	597–587 B.C.	exiled to Babylonia

The Babylonian armies of Nabopolassar and his son Nebuchadnezzar met Pharaoh Neco at Carchemish in 605 B.C. and routed the Egyptians. A short time later they dealt the Egyptians a second and more costly defeat near Hamath. The death of Nabopolassar and the accession of Nebuchadnezzar as king of Babylonia in 604 B.C. mark the emergence of a new superpower in ancient Mesopotamia. Given this new threat from the east, King Jehoiakim shifted his allegiance to Nebuchadnezzar, and Judah became a vassal of Babylonia in 603 B.C. (cf. 2 Kings 24:1).

King Nebuchadnezzar and Pharaoh Neco battled again in 601 B.C. The resulting stalemate between Babylonia and Egypt afforded Jehoiakim the opportunity to throw off the yoke of vassalage and rebel against Nebuchadnezzar. The Babylonian king was occupied with rebellion elsewhere in his kingdom and was unable to retaliate against Judah until December 598 B.C., the very month King Jehoiakim died.[1] Jehoiachin succeeded his father as king of Judah but surrendered to Nebuchadnezzar after a three-month siege (2 Kings 24:10–11; 2 Chron. 36:9). Jehoiachin was deported to Babylonia along with the queen mother, other high-ranking officials, and numerous craftsmen and artisans (2 Kings 24:12–17). Jehoiachin's uncle, Mattaniah (also called Zedekiah) was installed as a puppet king in his stead by the Babylonians.

Zedekiah was a weak king, unable to control the resurgent nationalism in Judah and apparently easily manipulated by the nobles and advisers around

---

1. John Bright (*A History of Israel*, 4th ed. [Louisville: Westminster John Knox, 2000], 327) is among those who suggest King Jehoiakim was assassinated amid hopes of gaining milder treatment from the Babylonians.

him. After a series of political missteps, Zedekiah finally rebelled against the king of Babylon in 589 B.C. The Babylonian response was swift and thorough. King Nebuchadnezzar lay siege to Jerusalem early in 588 B.C. The end came in July of 587 B.C., with the carnage so appalling and the devastation so sweeping that survivors could only sit aghast in silence as they mourned "the Daughter of Zion" (see the book of Lamentations).

This concluding section of the Chronicler's narrative poses only minor interpretive problems. The only textual problem of note is the reference to the age of Jehoiachin when he becomes king (36:9). The majority of Hebrew manuscripts reads "eight," but the NIV agrees with most commentators in correcting the scribal error by inserting the number "eighteen" cited in the ancient versions (cf. 2 Kings 24:8, which reads "eighteen").

The identification of Zedekiah as Jehoiachin's "uncle" is probably a case where the Hebrew word "brother" should be understood in the broader sense of "relative" (2 Chron. 36:10; cf. 2 Kings 24:17; this means the genealogy of Josiah in 1 Chron. 3:15—16 mentions two different Zedekiahs). There is no need to suspect the accuracy of the Chronicler's report of Jehoiakim's being bound in bronze shackles and taken to Babylon, despite the fact 2 Kings 24:1 does not mention the event. Perhaps Jehoiakim is required to go to Babylon to participate in Nebuchadnezzar's victory parade as a conquered and vassal king (after the example of Manasseh during the reign of Esarhaddon of Assyria, 2 Chron. 33:11).[2]

The four brief accounts of the reigns of Jehoahaz (36:2—4), Jehoiakim (36:5—8), Jehoiachin (36:9—10), and Zedekiah (36:11—14) summarize the deadly game of "musical thrones" that sees the end of the kingdom of Judah. These four reports, totaling fourteen verses, are much less detailed than the parallel narrative in 2 Kings 23:31—24:20. A fifth report, the "obituary" of Judah, is an abbreviated account of the fall of Jerusalem to the Babylonians (2 Chron. 36:15—21; cf. 2 Kings 25:1—21; Jer. 52:4—27).

No doubt the compiler assumes his audience has knowledge of the earlier record, but this does not fully explain his haste to tell the story of Zedekiah and the destruction of Jerusalem by the Babylonians. The Chronicler's reduction in reporting the material from 2 Kings indicates some special purpose in retelling Judah's history. According to Selman, the reigns of the last four kings of Judah, compressed into a single presentation, underscore "the increasingly unstoppable threat of exile."[3] On a more positive note, it is also possible that the Chronicler's brevity in treating the end of kingship in Judah is intended

2. See Donald J. Wiseman, *Notes on Some Problems in the Book of Daniel* (London: Tyndale, 1965), 18.

3. Selman, *1 Chronicles*, 36.

to highlight the exemplary reign of Josiah, "thus leaving a fresher memory in the reader's mind of the possibility of faithfulness and blessing."[4]

This final section of the Chronicler's history is driven by both a documentary impulse (i.e., telling *what* happened) and the literary impulse (i.e., telling *how* it happened).[5] The references to Jeremiah the prophet (36:12, 21) may indicate the Chronicler's dependence on the book of Jeremiah as a source for this portion of his history. In any event, the repetition of the twin themes of the exile of the last Judahite kings and the repeated plundering of the Lord's temple explains *what* happens to the kingdom of Judah (36:4, 6–7, 10, 18, 20). The descriptions of King Zedekiah (who does not humble himself and will not turn to the Lord, 36:12–13; cf. 7:14) and the priests and all the people (who are unfaithful, 36:14; cf. 30:8) illustrate *how* all this happens to Judah.

Curiously, the Chronicler fails to report the death formulas for the last kings of Judah as recorded in the Kings account (e.g., "and there he [Jehoahaz] died," 2 Kings 23:34; and "Jehoiakim rested with his fathers," 24:6; etc.). Kingship just fades into oblivion, as if the Chronicler seeks to represent the stories of the four kings as simply "different manifestations of the same phenomenon."[6] In so doing, the Chronicler offers his audience hope because he leaves open the possibility for the restoration of Israelite kingship as predicted by Jeremiah (Jer. 33:15–16) and Ezekiel (Ezek. 34:23).

Three important themes or emphases emerge from the Chronicler's report concerning the last kings of Judah, the fall of Jerusalem, and the Babylonian exile. (1) According to Selman, the brevity of the narrative describing the reigns of the last kings of Judah indicates a special purpose in the Chronicles, namely, "the increasingly unstoppable threat of the exile."[7] The Chronicler's acknowledgment of the inevitability of the Exile is important for two reasons. (a) It affirms the character of God as a God of justice (cf. Jer. 30:11; Nah. 1:3). (b) It prevents "spiritual paralysis" in the restoration community by defusing the "what if" questions that later generations might raise when looking back at the Exile and its aftermath.

The Exile is also a comprehensive punishment of Judah's sins, in that there is "no remedy" for God's wrath (36:16), and the "remnant" who escape the sword suffer exile (36:20).[8] It is possible that the Chronicler has in mind

---

4. McConville, *I and II Chronicles*, 266.
5. Ryken, *How to Read the Bible As Literature*, 33.
6. Selman, *2 Chronicles*, 545.
7. Selman, *1 Chronicles*, 36.
8. The word "remedy" in 36:16 is derived from the same root as the word translated "heal" in 7:14 (*rp'*). Context suggests God has voided the promise to "heal" the land, making petition for God's intervention futile.

Malachi's understanding of divine judgment as a raging fire that both destroys the wicked and purifies the righteous (Mal. 3:1–4).

(2) The historian of 2 Kings identified Manasseh as the culprit responsible for the Babylonian exile (2 Kings 24:3–4). The Chronicler, however, extends blame to the entire nation, not to any one individual. King Zedekiah, the priests, and the people are all unfaithful to God and equally accountable for the fall of Judah (2 Chron. 36:14).[9] The corporate interpretation of the Exile is a key component in the "all Israel" theology of the Chronicler. The culpability for the Exile belong to all Israelites, especially those generations from Kings Manasseh to Zedekiah.

Likewise, all Israelites are heirs of God's promises for the restoration of Israel announced by the prophets. The Chronicler knows that his generation will be successful in obeying the word of the Lord only by recognizing their vicarious relationship to the tragic events of the past and the anticipated blessings of the future (cf. Rom. 8:17, "we share in his sufferings . . . that we may also share in his glory"). The general categories of sins attributed to the people ("detestable practices" and "defiling the temple," 2 Chron. 36:14) serve as warnings to the Chronicler's contemporaries. God's people are always at risk of those things that are "idolatrous" (i.e., any substitute for God; cf. Jer. 7:9–11) and those things that are "irreverent" (i.e., any denial of God's holiness; cf. Jer. 32:34).

(3) The Chronicler implicitly addresses the retribution principle conditioning the Mosaic covenant by noting the cause-and-effect relationship between Judah's desecration of the temple (36:14) and the despoiling of the temple by the Babylonians (36:18). The response of divine blessing for obedience to the stipulations of God's covenant and the response of divine judgment for violation of the same frame Israel's relationship to Yahweh (Lev. 26; Deut. 28; cf. Paul's teaching on "sowing and reaping" in Gal. 6:7–8). The references to God's messengers and prophets further underscore the emphasis on the retribution principle in the Chronicler's assessment of the fall of Jerusalem.

The blessings and curses theology of the Mosaic covenant is foundational to prophetic ministry because it is on this basis that these divine messengers forecast either blessing or judgment for God's people (e.g., Isa. 1:10–20; Jer. 9:13–16). The series of participles describing the people's response to the message brought by God's servants ("mocking . . . despising . . . scoffing," 2 Chron. 36:16 NRSV) suggests this is habitual behavior, making the

---

9. Selman, 2 Chronicles, 549, who contends that Israel's "unfaithfulness" (Heb. ma'al, i.e., failure to give God his due and usurping it for oneself) is the chief cause of the Babylonian exile.

rejection of the prophetic voice a theme in Kings and Chronicles (2 Kings 17:12–14; 24:2; 2 Chron. 24:19).

The Chronicler hurries past the last four kings of Judah to report the fall of Jerusalem for good reason (36:15–21). His audience knows all too well the tragic story of the sack of the city of David and the pillaging and destruction of Solomon's temple. They do not need a reminder of the fall of Jerusalem as much as a statement of justification for the Exile. The Chronicler needs to guard against wrong thinking and bad theology, lest God be blamed for Judah's calamity.

Essentially, the Chronicler offers his generation a twofold rationale for Judah's expulsion from the land of the promise. (1) Both king and people have rejected God's word spoken by his prophetic messengers (36:16). (2) The people of Judah have failed to keep the covenant stipulation of giving the land "its sabbath rest" (36:21; cf. Lev. 25:1–7). Here again the compiler assumes his audience has a working knowledge of the Torah and the Prophets in the intertwining of the covenant curse (Lev. 26:34) and the word of Jeremiah (Jer. 29:10).

More important theologically, the Chronicler understands the Exile as God's work. The Lord himself brought the Babylonians against Judah and handed his people over to Nebuchadnezzar in fulfillment of the words of Jeremiah the prophet (36:17, 21; cf. Jer. 25:8–11; 29:10). It is of vital importance that the Chronicler affirm God's faithfulness to his Word. The restoration period of Israelite history witnesses a shift away from divine revelation by means of prophetic utterance to priestly instruction based on previous revelation from God now inscripturated (e.g., Ezra's exposition of the Torah, Neh. 8:1–3). The postexilic generation needs assurance that God keeps his Word, whether it be a word of blessing or judgment (Ps. 33:4–5).

THE RETRIBUTION PRINCIPLE. This passage, perhaps more than any other in the books of Chronicles, illustrates the inherent instructional value of Old Testament history clearly recognized by Paul (Rom. 15:4; 1 Cor. 10:11). The topic of the Exile provides an entree for visiting any number of theological issues, given the magnitude and complexity of that catastrophic event in Hebrew history. Our study of this section of Chronicles will address a single subject, that aspect of divine judgment known as the retribution principle.

The biblical principle of retribution assumes predictable patterns of divine response to human behavior. In general, conformity to God's expectations brings reward while disobedience to his commands results in punishment.

God's blessing or judgment of Israel is conditioned by her "faith quotient," demonstrated by obedience to covenant legislation. These blessings for obedience and curses for disobedience were outlined for Israel as part of the covenant-renewal ceremony for that first post-Exodus generation of Hebrews (cf. Deut. 28). God's response to corporate Israel and the nations generally was framed by the retribution principle. The poetry and wisdom literature of the Old Testament indicate this is also God's primary method for dealing with individuals (e.g., Job 4:8–9; Prov. 11:5). In the New Testament, Paul summarizes the retribution principle with the popular proverb: "A man reaps what he sows" (Gal. 6:7).

But this is not the whole story. The divine judgment (or blessing) of Israel and the nations was clumsy in the sense that Israel's covenant relationship with Yahweh resulted in a shared or corporate identity for the Hebrew people.[10] As a covenant community, the "one" and the "many" in ancient Israel were inseparably related, as is illustrated in the story of Achan (Josh. 7). Sometimes this "shared identity" spanned generations, eventually engendering a certain fatalism among the Hebrews (e.g., Ex. 20:5–6; cf. Ezek. 18:1–2).

The New Testament extends the concept of shared identity to the church as a covenant community (cf. 1 Cor. 5). Ultimately, the application of the retribution principle in any specific historical context meant the righteous within the larger community were likely to share the same fate as the wicked in terms of divine judgment. Conversely, the wicked within the community may have shared the prosperity of the larger community in terms of divine blessing granted to the righteous. In either case, one might impugn God's justice.

At times the Hebrews complained that the retribution principle was inoperative and that divine justice had been suspended (e.g., Hab. 1:2–4). On other occasions the faithful contended that the principle had been inverted— that is, the arrogant were blessed and the righteous were cursed (e.g., Mal. 3:14–15). These examples from the Old Testament prophets introduce a theological concept known as "theodicy," a term applied to the efforts to justify the ways of God to humanity, especially in relationship to the problem of evil. Questions associated with theodicy, especially the reasons for the suffering of the righteous, are central to the story of Job. Theodicy is also an important theme in the laments of the Psalms, as the Hebrew poets pondered the prosperity of the wicked (e.g., Ps. 73:3).

The problems raised by theodicy are not peculiar to the writings of the Hebrews in the ancient world. The literature of the Egyptians and the

---

10. See Robinson, *Corporate Personality in Ancient Israel.*

Mesopotamians includes similar "Job" stories, reflections on the problem of evil and the experience of human suffering.[11] The Old Testament actually advances numerous theodicies or explanations to justify God's dealings with humanity, as summarized below:

1. Retributive—just punishment for sin (Gen. 3:16–19; 6:5–7; Deut. 30:15–19; cf. Gal. 6:7)
2. Disciplinary—corrective affliction (Deut. 8:3; Prov. 3:11–12)
3. Probationary—God's testing of the heart (Deut. 8:2–3; Job 1:6–12; 2:10)
4. Temporary or apparent—in comparison with the good (or bad) fortune of others (Ps. 73; Jer. 12:1; Mal. 3:15)
5. Inevitable—a result of the Fall (Job 5:6–7; Ps. 14:1–4)
6. Necessarily mysterious—God's character and plan are inscrutable (Job 11:7; 42:3; Eccl. 3:11)
7. Haphazard and morally meaningless—time and chance happen to all (Job 21:23, 25–26; Eccl. 9:11–12)
8. Vicarious—one may suffer for another or for the many (Deut. 4:21; Ps. 106:23; Isa. 53:3, 9, 12).[12]

At best these responses are only a partial resolution to a vexing theological puzzle. This is true because the ways of God remain mysterious and the mind of God is ever inscrutable (cf. Job 9:10; Isa. 55:8–9). The Scriptures do offer some consolation, however, in our endeavor to explain the ways of God in his creation. According to the psalmist, one important key to understanding theodicy is worship, especially prayer (Ps. 73:17). The Chronicler must have understood all this, since he brings perspective to God's dealings with ancient Israel by framing his review of Hebrew kingship with an emphasis on prayer and temple worship.

THEODICY. Reflective writings on the topic of theodicy are not limited to the Hebrew Bible or the ancient world. The topic remains central to religious and philosophical discussions grappling with the meaning of human existence. Theodicy, especially the retribution principle, raises theological questions about the existence of God and his

---

11. See V. H. Matthews and D. C. Benjamin, *Old Testament Parallels: Laws and Stories from the Ancient Near East*, 2d ed. (New York: Paulist, 1997), 203–28.

12. Adapted from R. B. Y. Scott, *The Way of Wisdom* (New York: Macmillan, 1971), 144–47.

justice, his goodness, and his omnipotence. Human suffering and the reality of death cut across the barriers of time, culture, and religious tradition. One relatively recent example is the popular book by Rabbi Harold S. Kushner, *When Bad Things Happen to Good People*.[13]

Rabbi Kushner's personal odyssey into the "unfair distribution of suffering in the world" was prompted by a pediatrician's diagnosis of his three-year-old son Aaron. Aaron was stricken with progeria, a condition known as "rapid aging." An inexplicable and tragic illness, Kushner recalls learning from the doctor's report that, "Aaron would never grow much beyond three feet in height, would have no hair on his head or body, would look like a little old man while he was still a child, and would die in his early teens."[14]

The senselessness of his child's malady drove Kushner to wonder about the justice of God and to question his fairness. Contemplation on his child's misfortune caused Kushner to challenge his understanding of God as an all-wise and all-powerful parent figure, who rewarded good people and punished bad people. Specifically, Kushner tells us he doubted the equity of the retribution principle because "tragedies like this were supposed to happen to selfish, dishonest people,"[15] not to rabbis following God's ways and doing God's work. Finally, the rabbi reasoned that even if he deserved punishment for some secret sin, why should God make his innocent child suffer in his stead?

Rabbi Kushner is to be commended for his honesty and his courage in addressing human pain and suffering, life and death—grappling "hand to hand" with theodicy out of his personal experience. Surely we as Christians could profit from this proactive Jewish approach to the "wrongs" of life that echoes the lament of the psalmist and the complaint of the prophet. Sadly, his humanistic conclusions are weak and misguided, informed more by popular psychology than by rigorous theology. Not only do they misrepresent God (the God of the Hebrew Bible), but also in the end they offer little hope to those struggling with the vicissitudes of this life. Essentially Rabbi Kushner concludes:

- God is a God of goodness and justice.
- God is not a God of power and might; there is a chaotic randomness in the universe that lies outside of God's control.
- People turn to God for encouragement and comfort, not to be judged or forgiven, not to be rewarded or punished.

---

13. Harold S. Kushner, *When Bad Things Happen to Good People* (New York: Schocken, 1981).

14. Ibid., 2.

15. Ibid., 3.

- Human beings are free moral agents fully responsible for their actions; God will not intervene to interrupt, overturn, or take away human freedom.
- The goal of religion is to remove the guilt of sin and failure and to help people feel good about themselves.
- The wrongs of life are the result of Fate, not God.
- Without the response of human love, God only exists as creator—not as God.
- Human beings respond to God in love not because he is perfect but because he is the author of beauty and the source of strength, hope, and courage.
- The purpose of religion is to help human beings forgive and love God when they discover he is not perfect.

The Chronicler, however, knows no such religion and no such God. One need only examine the petitions and doxologies in Chronicles to recognize that the Israelites of the Old Testament world prayed to a God uniquely different from the one to whom Rabbi Kushner prays. The prayers of David (1 Chron. 29:10–19) and Solomon (2 Chron. 6:14–42) reveal a God who:

- is the everlasting God
- is ruler of all the earth
- possesses all strength and power
- tests the hearts of his people to encourage integrity and loyalty
- hears and responds to the prayers of his people
- judges the guilty and establishes the innocent
- controls the elements of nature and circumstances of life
- upholds the cause of the righteous
- turns to those who turn to him and forgives their sin

This does not mean that the disturbing questions raised by a thoughtful discussion of theodicy simply evaporate once we recite a catechism of divine attributes. The Chronicler knows as much when he quotes David: "I am the one who has sinned. . . . What have they done? . . . Let your hand fall upon me and my family, but do not let this plague remain on your people" (1 Chron. 21:17). But it does mean that we as human beings may not devalue God because we cannot understand or completely explain the conundrum of why "bad things" sometimes happen to "good people." As Job learned, the creature does not inherently possess (nor earn by righteous behavior) any "credential" entitling one to evaluate the Creator on his application of justice in a fallen world (Job 40:8; 41:11; cf. Isa. 55:8–9).

The Chronicler affirms the theological paradox taught throughout the literature of the Old Testament: Yes, God is Almighty, infinitely powerful

(1 Chron. 16:25–26; cf. Ps. 89:8–18); and yes, God is Father, eternally good (1 Chron. 16:34; cf. Ps. 100:5; Isa. 9:6). So what does all this mean for the problem of evil, for theodicy? As Jehoshaphat came to learn, there are times when we can only acknowledge God as Judge and admit our own inability and powerlessness, ultimately trusting in the God of justice (cf. 2 Chron. 20:12).

Thankfully, the Christian has an advantage over the Old Testament faithful in the discussion of theodicy because we have "the rest of the story." The record of the new-covenant fulfillment of the old-covenant promise offers at least a partial solution to the problems raised by theodicy in the form of biblical theology, especially in the area of Christology. For example, Job longed for an advocate from heaven who might vindicate him in his suffering (Job 16:19). The disciples of Jesus affirmed the realization of Job's hope when they testified that they believe that Jesus came from God (John 16:30).

Interestingly, however, this Advocate from heaven does not decree the end of human suffering. Rather, he bluntly informs his followers that "in this world you will have trouble. But take heart! I have overcome the world" (John 16:33). This means the righteous should not necessarily expect to escape the problem of evil in this fallen world. Instead, they are assured God will uphold them in their suffering by the help of his Holy Spirit (1 Cor. 10:13; Rom. 8:9–11). Only a sovereign God of infinite power and eternal goodness is able to use human sufferings to cultivate godly virtues in the righteous that lead to the crown of life (Rom. 5:3–4; James 1:12).

Beyond this, the New Testament frames the discussion of human pain and suffering in the context of worship, broadly speaking. The prophet Isaiah recognized that God created human beings for the praise of his glory (Isa. 43:7). The apostle Paul provides insight on what it means for human beings to glorify God when he writes: "My grace is sufficient for you, for my power is made perfect in weakness" (2 Cor. 12:9). For this reason Paul rejoiced in his sufferings (deserved or undeserved) because it was then that the power of Christ was manifest in his life as a testimony to the power of God in the world (2 Cor. 12:10). Another illustration is God's choosing the weak, foolish, and lowly things of this world to confound the proud and induce faith in the humble (1 Cor. 1:27–29).

It is also important to remember that in addition to the response of biblical theology, Christian theologians and apologists have probed the questions raised by theodicy for centuries. One treatise especially helpful is *The Problem of Pain* by C. S. Lewis.[16] Lewis offers at least partial answers to the intellectual problem raised by human suffering in an essay that addresses:

---

16. C. S. Lewis, *The Problem of Pain* (orig. 1962; New York: Touchstone, 1996); for a more "existential" treatment (i.e., anecdotal or experiential approach), see P. Yancey, *Where Is God When It Hurts?* (Grand Rapids: Zondervan, 1977); Paul Brand and Philip Yancey, *Pain: The Gift Nobody Wants* (Grand Rapids: Zondervan, 1993).

- the interplay of human free will with what he terms the relatively independent and "inexorable Nature" created by God, so that Lewis concludes: "To exclude the possibility of suffering which the order of nature and the existence of free wills involve … you find that you have excluded life itself"[17]
- the idea of divine goodness contrasted with human goodness, recognizing that the human notion of "kindness" is not coterminous with the biblical revelation of divine "love" and that love may cause pain because its object may need alteration to become fully lovable
- the reality of "original sin," the abuse of free will that ruined humanity inherently, so that one can only speak of "good" people in the most relative of terms, given the present reality of a "corrupted" humanity, and that God's goodness must sometimes be remedial and corrective
- the fact that divine "testing" through pain does engender faith and induce obedience in rebellious human beings, demonstrating "that the old Christian doctrine of being made 'perfect through suffering' is not incredible"[18]
- the admission that there is a paradox about "tribulation" in Christianity that ultimately finds its resolution in the Incarnation—that marvelous mystery of God becoming a human being, living among his own creatures, and suffering for them vicariously so that all sin, suffering, and pain might be abolished and God's goodness might once again have full reign in his creation

Finally, according to Lewis, the Christian doctrine of suffering best explains the almost "schizoprehenic" nature of humanity that worships the material world and yet craves a better world. He concludes:

> The settled happiness and security which we all desire, God withholds from us by the very nature of the world: but joy, pleasure, and merriment He has scattered broadcast…. Our Father refreshes us on the journey with some pleasant inns, but will not encourage us to mistake them for home.[19]

---

17. Lewis, *The Problem of Pain*, 31.
18. Ibid., 94.
19. Ibid., 103.

2 Chronicles 36:22–23

I N THE FIRST year of Cyrus king of Persia, in order to fulfill
the word of the LORD spoken by Jeremiah, the LORD
moved the heart of Cyrus king of Persia to make a proclamation throughout his realm and to put it in writing:

²³"This is what Cyrus king of Persia says:

"'The LORD, the God of heaven, has given me all the
kingdoms of the earth and he has appointed me to build
a temple for him at Jerusalem in Judah. Anyone of his
people among you—may the LORD his God be with
him, and let him go up.'"

THE CLOSING PASSAGE of Chronicles is an excerpt
from the decree of Cyrus recorded in Ezra 1:1–
3 (cf. 6:3–5).[1] By way of genre analysis, the unit
is generally considered a report (i.e., a self-con-
tained prose narrative about a single event or situation in the past).[2] Scholars stand divided on the question as to whether the concluding paragraph of
the book is an appendix (i.e., a later expansion of the Chronicler's work) or
an epilogue (i.e., a formal finale original to the Chronicler).[3] It is clear that
the quotation of Cyrus's decree functions as a coda, offering a hopeful summary statement to the Chronicler's history and directing the audience (or
reader) to the continuation of the story of the repatriation of Jerusalem found
in the books of Ezra-Nehemiah. It seems only logical to regard the epilogue
as the work of the Chronicler since he retells the history of Israel as a theology of hope for his postexilic audience.

The Chronicler deliberately breaks off the text of the decree and concludes abruptly with the clause "and let him go up" (36:23; cf. Ezra 1:3).[4] This
repetition of the Cyrus decree in Chronicles serves to splice together two

---

1. For an alternative paragraph structure marking the beginning of the epilogue with
36:21, see Selman, *2 Chronicles*, 550.

2. See the glossary in De Vries, *1 and 2 Chronicles*, 434.

3. For an example of the former see Williamson, *1 and 2 Chronicles*, 419; for the latter see
Selman, *2 Chronicles*, 551.

4. T. C. Eskenazi ("The Chronicler and the Composition of 1 Esdras," 48 *CBQ* [1986]:
39–61) cites this feature as evidence that Chronicles and 1 Esdras have a common author;
cf. Allen, *1, 2 Chronicles*, 443.

documents originally separate (Chronicles and Ezra-Nehemiah). This permits the later reader to make the transition historically to the accounts of the aftermath of Cyrus's edict, namely, the eventual rebuilding of God's temple in Jerusalem (cf. Ezra 3:7–13; 6:14–15).

According to Selman, this dangling quotation is designed to emphasize the reader's (or audience's) response to the book—namely, "to exercise faith in God's promises."[5] While this may be the case implicitly, it seems that the wordplay on the last word of the quotation (and the book, 36:23) calls attention to the activity of worship. The verb "go up" (*ʿalah*) is also the primary root for the "burnt offering" (*ʿolah*), one of the animal sacrifices required by the law for atoning for sin (cf. Lev. 1:3–17). Thus, the Chronicler's closing paragraph becomes a directive to his own audience to "go up" to the temple now built, "offer up" appropriate worship to God, and in this way rebuild Judah and Jerusalem spiritually. Israel's hope for the future lies both in an unswerving faith to the promises of God and in the proper worship of God.

The epilogue includes a date formula, "the first year of Cyrus king of Persia" (36:22; the year is 538 B.C.). The famous clay barrel or inscribed cylinder of Cyrus records his conquest of Babylon without a battle and his overturning of the foreign policy of previous regimes.[6] The ancient superpowers of Assyria and Babylonia practiced a policy of deporting select elements of conquered populations to Mesopotamia. Local deities were absorbed into the Mesopotamian pantheon, and the religious custom of the empire was imposed on the subjugated nation or people group (cf. 2 Kings 16:10–14). Persian policy implemented by Cyrus permitted displaced people groups to repatriate their homelands if they so desired. In addition, he sought to placate the gods of these people groups by encouraging the traditional worship of local deities.

Although the Hebrews are not specifically mentioned in the text of the Cyrus Cylinder, the decree includes those Israelites previously exiled by the Assyrians and Babylonians. The document cited by the Chronicler is most likely a formal extension of the original decree for this specific people group. Such authorization from the central government would have been necessary before the governor of the province in question for relocation approved resettlement.[7] The Chronicler calls attention to widespread publication of this

---

5. Selman, 2 *Chronicles*, 551.

6. For an English translation of the Cyrus cylinder, see Matthews and Benjamin, *Old Testament Parallels*, 193–95.

7. This fact is attested by the copies of letters sent to the Persian king by various lower-tier administrators from the satrap that included the province of Judah (e.g., Ezra 4:7–22; 5:6–17); cf. Jon L. Berquist, *Judaism in Persia's Shadow* (Minneapolis: Fortress, 1995), esp. 60–61, 132–35.

decree to emphasize the fact that this is not an isolated event in the transition from Babylonian to Persian control of Mesopotamia and Syria-Palestine.
The emphasis on the writing or documentation of the proclamation signifies
that the edict is vested with the full weight of Persian statecraft.

According to Ezra 1, King Cyrus restores numerous articles taken by the
Babylonians as booty from the temple of Yahweh to the first band of returnees
under the leadership of Sheshbazzar. This is yet another way in which God
"moves the heart of Cyrus" for the benefit of his chosen people (2 Chron.
36:22). No doubt the threefold repetition of "Cyrus king of Persia" is intended
to call to mind Isaiah's word about Cyrus as God's "shepherd" for Israel (Isa.
44:28). Well in advance of the fact, God through the prophet Isaiah named
Cyrus as the subduer of nations and deliverer of the exiles from the land of
Judah (Isa. 45:1–4, 13).

This echo of the oracles of Isaiah is yet another reminder from the Chronicler that God's word is sure. Even more, the restoration community in
Jerusalem can be assured of God's ongoing sovereignty over the nations. By
the time of the Chronicler, King Cyrus is long dead and little more than a
fading memory as a symbol of Persia's past greatness. Yet the temple is now
rebuilt in Jerusalem and God's people are once again settled in their land.[8]
Although still under Persian control, postexilic Judah has the guarantee of
God's word for complete restoration and the historical evidence that Israel's
God controls the destinies of the nations.

Jeremiah is a prominent figure in the last chapter of Chronicles. Three
times he is identified as the prophet who spoke the word of the Lord
(36:12, 21, 22). In two of these instances, emphasis is placed on the divine
fulfillment of Jeremiah's prophetic word (36:21, 22). Jeremiah was a prophet
to the Judean monarchy from 627 B.C. until sometime after 586 B.C. The
Chronicler credits him for the prominent role he played in the reforms of
King Josiah after the discovery of the Book of the Law in 622 B.C. (cf.
2 Chron. 34:14–33). He is also an eyewitness to the destruction of
Jerusalem by the Babylonians and the likely composer of the book of
Lamentations.

More important, Jeremiah announces the new covenant promised by
God for the restoration of Israel after the judgment of the Babylonian exile
(cf. Jer. 31:31–34). In view of this, the Chronicler's accent on this prophet
becomes a stroke of genius as the conclusion to his theology of hope for
postexilic Judah. His litany of the divine fulfillment of the word of Jeremiah
concerning judgment, exile, and restoration to the land serves as a subtle

---

8. Dillard, 2 *Chronicles*, 302, has noted a certain irony in the fact that the building of both
the first and second temples were subsidized by funds from Gentile nations.

reminder that God will indeed work to fulfill the rest of Jeremiah's oracles—
especially that word of the new covenant!

The excerpt from Cyrus's edict calling for the rebuilding of Yahweh's
temple in Jerusalem is probably a veiled reference to the fulfillment of Isaiah's prediction that Cyrus will be God's agent for restoring Jerusalem after
the Exile (Isa. 44:28). Cyrus the Great was king of Persia from 539–530 B.C.
The unexpected phrase "king of Persia" is used of Cyrus three times in the
epilogue. Rather than assume the interpolation of a later editor or narrator,
it seems more likely the expression is original to the Chronicler as an intra-
textual echo to the visions of Daniel. There "kings of Persia" are mentioned
within Daniel's scheme of four world empires that must appear on the stage
of history before God establishes his kingdom (Dan. 8:20; 11:2; cf. 2:39). The
emphasis on Cyrus as the "king of Persia" reminds the postexilic community
that the second of those four Mediterranean basin superpowers is already on
the scene and that God's irrepressible plan for the nations continues to move
forward.

The title "God of heaven" is a postexilic epithet for the God of Israel.[9]
There is some question as to what Cyrus means by it—whether a reference
to one of the several great gods who brought him to power or a statement
of Yahweh's uniqueness among the deities of the ancient world.[10] Based on
the Chronicler's affirmation of the inability of the highest heavens to contain God, it seems likely he expects his audience to understand the latter
(cf. 2:6; 6:18).

This suggestion is confirmed in the use of the standard messenger formula
("this is what [Cyrus king of Persia] says") typically found as an introduction
to prophetic speech in the Old Testament (cf. Isa. 44:6, 24; 45:1). In one
sense, not only is King Cyrus Yahweh's "shepherd," but he is also Yahweh's
"prophet" in his proclamation permitting the restoration of Jerusalem and
the rebuilding of the temple. The aftermath of Cyrus's decree—the waves of
Jews emigrating from Mesopotamia to Palestine as a type of second exodus
and the rebuilding of the Jerusalem temple—is recorded in the books of
Ezra-Nehemiah.

---

9. The title "God of heaven" is used in official documents and in the Jews' dealings with
Gentiles (see Joseph Blenkinsopp, *Ezra-Nehemiah* [OTL; Philadelphia: Westminster, 1988],
75; cf. Ezra 5:12; 7:12, 21, 23; Jonah 1:9; the phrase also occurs frequently in the Ele-
phantine papyri).

10. Cf. F. Charles Fensham, *Ezra and Nehemiah* (NICOT; Grand Rapids: Eerdmans, 1982),
43–44.

Bridging Contexts

THE KINGDOM AND THE WORD OF GOD. The Hebrew worldview as portrayed in the Old Testament tends to reduce human experience and the issues of life to polar opposites such as good or evil (Amos 5:14), life or death (Deut. 30:15), justice or oppression (Isa. 1:17), wisdom or folly (Eccl. 2:13), and so on. The Chronicler's epilogue offers another such antithesis in the juxtaposition of the phrases "the God of heaven" and "all the kingdoms of the earth" embedded in the speech of Cyrus (2 Chron. 36:23). These categories establish contrasts between the divine and human realms, between one Realm and many realms.

Charles Colson has updated the Chronicler's discussion in his contemporary analysis of kingdoms in conflict, the kingdom of God and the kingdoms of this world.[11] He aptly reminds us that as human beings we are irresistibly "religious" and "political" and that any mediation of the conflict between the rival kingdoms must seriously consider both "the nature of [hu]man[ity] and the nature of God and His rule over the world."[12] According to Colson, the Bible is the primary source for information about who we are as human beings and who God is as our Creator and Redeemer.

The Chronicler also understands that rival kingdoms are in competition for the loyalty of men and women, vying for control of the human heart and intellect. He also recognizes that the only effective means for mediating the polarity of the divine and human realms is the Word of God. This is evidenced, in part, by the repetition of the so-called "prophetic word formula," emphasizing "the word of the LORD spoken by Jeremiah" (2 Chron. 36:21, 22).

In fact, variations of this prophetic word formula occur more than a dozen times in the Chronicles (1 Chron. 10:13; 17:3; 22:8; etc.). This has prompted Allen to comment that the epilogue attests the Chronicler's "tremendous regard for the Word of God," affirming Isaiah's declaration that the "word of our God stands forever" (Isa. 40:8).[13] This premium on the surety of God's Word is a foundational principle in the Chronicler's theology of hope for the restoration community. What better way to validate those promises for the restoration of Israel and a new covenant relationship with Yahweh spoken prior to the Exile by that same prophet Jeremiah (cf. Jer. 31:31–34)?

But what if there is no "word of the LORD spoken" by some divinely appointed prophetic figure? By the time of the Chronicler the prophetic voice has been silent in the Jewish community. No messenger from God is

11. Charles Colson, *Kingdoms in Conflict* (Grand Rapids: Zondervan, 1987).
12. Ibid., 49.
13. Allen, *1, 2 Chronicles*, 443.

prefacing oracles with the prophetic word formula. How are the faithful in restoration Judah to mediate the conflict between the two realms, the kingdom of God and the kingdoms of this world? Perhaps Rabbi Heschel is correct in his observation that "no word is God's final word" (i.e., "the word of God never comes to an end").[14] I suspect the Chronicler might agree with Rabbi Heschel on at least two accounts.

(1) The Chronicler's message is largely "borrowed" from the written works of earlier prophets and kings who spoke "the word of the LORD." The Chronicler truly believes that the word of the Lord stands forever (Isa. 40:8) because he assumes the words of God once spoken and preserved command equal authority when "preached" to a later generation of God's people (see further the Chronicles as "sermon" in the introduction).

(2) The Chronicler recognizes God's Word is not the exclusive domain of the Hebrew prophets, kings, or sages. Interestingly, he utilizes a variation of the prophetic word formula to introduce the decree of Cyrus in his epilogue ("This is what Cyrus king of Persia says," 36:23). The Chronicler knows that in his sovereignty God has innumerable "mouthpieces" at his disposal, including rulers of kingdoms like Cyrus the Great. This leads Wilcock to conclude that "to know the Chronicler's God is to know the God of all history."[15] The Chronicler wants to make certain his audience knows this truth as well. The Jewish community needs to be reminded that the God of all history is still appointing rulers to do his bidding in fulfilling his promises for the complete restoration of his people, even as he spoke through King Cyrus of Persia to rebuild the Jerusalem temple.

DIVINE PRESENCE. The crisis in practical theology experienced by the Chronicler, given the disparity between the rule of "the God of heaven" and the rule of "the kingdoms of the earth," remains an unresolved issue for the faithful of God today. The nations still conspire against the Lord (Ps. 2:1–2), and stories of wars and rumors of wars around our globe are still front-page news (Matt. 24:6).

On the one hand, the Bible declares with certainty that God is the sovereign Lord of the nations (cf. Ps. 22:28; 30:10; Isa. 40:15, 17). Yet on the other hand, the "Assyrias, Babylonias" and "Persias" of contemporary history still rage against God and persecute the church of Jesus Christ. This side of the second advent of our Lord, the Chronicler's solution for reconciling the

14. Heschel, *The Prophets*, 1:194.
15. Wilcock, *The Message of Chronicles*, 288.

biblical doctrine of God's sovereignty with the political reality of the nations roaring like the waves of the sea as they churn up the mud and mire of wickedness and rebellion against God is still worthy of careful consideration (cf. Isa. 17:12–13; 57:20–21).

(1) The Chronicler affirms God's presence among his people (36:23). God is with those who trust his Word and pledge loyalty and obedience to him, those whose hearts are "fully committed to him" (16:9). In fact, Allen suggests that the Chronicler's rephrasing of Ezra 1:3 is intentional, designed expressly to emphasize the "enabling presence" of God.[16]

This truth of the divine presence in the midst of the faithful is the great hope of the postexilic restoration community, namely, the Lord's returning and dwelling among his people again (Hag. 2:4–5, 7; Zech. 1:16–17). All this is in fulfillment of the promise of Ezekiel's temple vision, renaming the city of Jerusalem "the LORD is there" (Ezek. 48:35). The idea of God's presence is perhaps the great theme of the Bible, beginning with the intimate fellowship with God experienced by that first human pair (cf. Gen. 3:8–9) and ending with paradise regained when God himself will live with his people (Rev. 21:3). More than this, we experience what the Chronicler could only anticipate through the word of the prophets as Immanuel has indeed come (John 1:14; cf. Isa. 7:14) and the deposit of the Holy Spirit has been given as the pledge that God will once again have an "address" among his people (Eph. 1:13–14).

(2) The epilogue of Chronicles concludes with the clause "and let him go up" (36:23). The quotation of King Cyrus's proclamation is broken off in mid-sentence. Again, Allen conjectures that this is the Chronicler's way to say "the end" or "but that's another story."[17] This may well be the case. What better way for the Chronicler to conclude his sermons and prepare his audience for "the rest of the story" found in the books of Ezra and Nehemiah?

(3) But there is something even more significant in the incomplete citation of Ezra 1:3 in the Chronicler's epilogue. The expression "let him go up" is both an invitation and a directive to participate in temple worship. The psalmist uses the verb "go up" (ʿlh) to depict ascending the Temple Mount and worshiping in God's holy place (Ps. 24:3; 122:4). Like the psalmist, the Chronicler recognizes that the formal worship of Yahweh is the integrating component of life lived in a fallen world. It is only as the psalmist (here Asaph) experiences God in temple worship that he can gain perspective on

16. Allen, *1, 2 Chronicles*, 443–44 (lit., "the Lord his God is with him"). Unfortunately, the NIV's "may his God be with him" obscures this fact in its attempt to harmonize 2 Chron. 36:23 with Ezra 1:3.
17. Ibid., 443.

the seeming incongruities between the experiences of the wicked and the righteous (cf. 73:13–17).

There is a sense in which the Chronicler's epilogue brings closure to the discussion of theodicy in the previous section that recounts the exile of Judah (36:2–21). It is almost as if he has sensed his audience cannot let go of the memory of that tragic event or the corporate blame they harbor toward God for allowing it to happen.

Just prior to the Babylonian exile the prophet Habakkuk called the people of Judah to a similar experience. Given the impending invasion of King Nebuchadnezzar and his marauding hordes, Habbakuk encouraged the people to gain perspective on God's plan for Israel and the nations by acknowledging his presence in his holy temple and revering him in silence (Hab. 2:20). Only as the finite contemplates the Infinite One, only as the creature ponders the Creator, only as the filthy consider the Holy One, can the temporal take on meaning in the light of the eternal. The Chronicler's call for postexilic Judah to "go up" to the temple and worship makes the apostle Peter's words all the more penetrating when he says:

> But you are a chosen people, a royal priesthood, a holy nation, a people belonging to God, that you may declare the praises of him who called you out of darkness into his wonderful light. (1 Peter 2:9)

Appendixes

Appendix A: Maps of Old Testament Israel

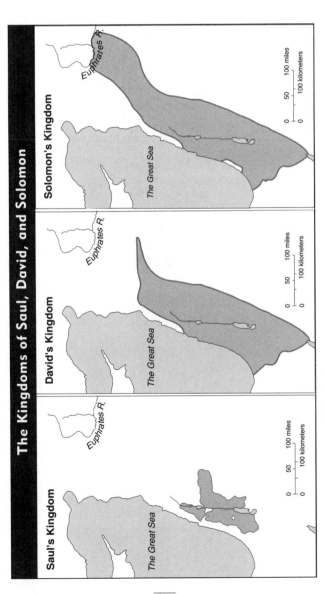

From Hill and Walton, *A Survey of the Old Testament*, page 221.

Divided Monarchy

From Hill and Walton, *A Survey of the Old Testament*, page 237.

Postexilic Judah

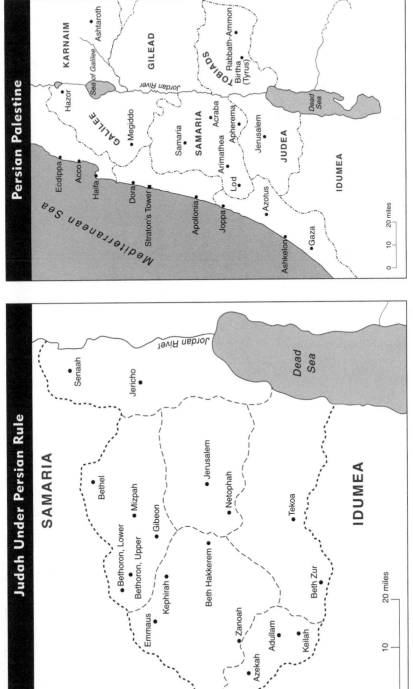

Persian Palestine

Judah Under Persian Rule

From Edwin Yamauchi, "Ezra-Nehemiah," *The Expositor's Bible Commentary* (Grand Rapids: Zondervan), 4:597.

Appendix B: The Hebrew Religious Calendar

Equivalents of the Julian Calendar

Julian Calendar	*Babylonian-Jewish Calendar*
Mar/Apr	Nisan; preexilic Hebrew name ʾAbib (Ex. 12:2)
Apr/May	Iyyar, preexilic Hebrew name Ziw (1 Kings 6:1)
May/June	Sivan
June/July	Tammuz
July/Aug	Ab
Aug/Sept	Elul
Sept/Oct	Tishri; preexilic Hebrew name ʾEtanim (1 Kings 8:2)
Oct/Nov	Marhesvan; preexilic Hebrew name Bul (1 Kings 6:38)
Nov/Dec	Kislev
Dec/Jan	Tebeth
Jan/Feb	Shebat
Feb/Mar	Adar

Jewish Religious Calendar: Festivals

Month	*Date*	*Festival*
Nisan	1	New Moon (Num. 10:10)
	10	Selection of Passover lamb (Ex. 12:3)
	14	Passover lamb killed (Ex. 12:6); Passover begins (Num. 28:16)
	15	First day of Unleavened Bread (Num. 28:17)
	16	Firstfruits (Lev. 23:10)
	21	End of Passover and Unleavened Bread (Lev. 23:6)
Iyyar	1	New Moon (Num. 1:18)
Sivan	1	New Moon (Num. 1:18)
	6	Pentecost (50 days after Firstfruits); Feast of Weeks (Lev. 23:15–21)
Tammuz	1	New Moon (Num. 1:18)
Ab	1	New Moon (Num. 1:18)
	9	Day of mourning for destruction of temple
Elul	1	New Moon (Num. 1:18)
Tishri	1	New Moon, New Year, Feast of Trumpets (Lev. 23:24; Num. 29:1–2)

	10	Day of Atonement (Lev. 23:26–32; the fast in Acts 27:9)
	15–21	Feast of Tabernacles (Lev. 23:33–43)
Marhesvan	1	New Moon (Num. 1:18)
Kislev	1	New Moon (Num. 1:18)
	25	Feast of Dedication of the temple (1 Macc. 4:52ff.), Hanukkah, or Feast of Lights, an 8-day festival (John 10:22)
Tebeth	1	New Moon (Num. 1:18)
Shebat	1	New Moon (Num. 1:18)
Adar	1	New Moon (Num. 1:18)
	14–15	Feast of Purim (Est. 9:21)

Jewish years are counted according to the World Era, beginning with the creation of humanity (estimated to be the year 3761 B.C.). Thus Israel once again became a nation, an autonomous political state, after World War II in the year 5709 (or A.D. 1948). Rather than counting time from the birth of Christ, Jewish convention indicates the years before Christ as B.C.E. (Before the Common Era) and the years following Christ's birth as C.E. (The Common Era). On ancient calendars, see Jack Finegan, *Handbook of Biblical Chronology*, rev. ed. (Peabody, Mass.: Hendrickson, 1998). For an in-depth discussion of the development of the events comprising the Hebrew religious calendar, see Abraham P. Block, *The Biblical and Historical Background of the Jewish Holy Days* (New York: Ktav, 1978); and Peter S. Knobel, ed., *Gates of the Seasons: A Guide to the Jewish Year* (New York: Central Conference of American Rabbis, 1983).

Appendix C: Comparative Chronology of Hebrew Kingship

The United Monarchy

The Dynasty of Saul
  Saul (?–1011 B.C.)
  Ish-Bosheth (1011–1009 B.C.)
The Dynasty of David
  David (1011–971 B.C.)
  Solomon (971–931 B.C.)

The Divided Monarchy

The Kings of Israel (Northern Kingdom)

King	Hayes and Hooker	Thiele	Bright	Cogan and Tadmor
Jeroboam	927–906	931–910	922–901	928–907
Nadab	905–904	910–909	901–900	907–906
Baasha	903–882 (880)	909–886	900–877	906–883
Elah	881–880	886–885	877–876	883–882
Zimri	7 days	885	876	882
Omri	879–869	885–874	876–869	882–871
Ahab	868–854	874–853	869–850	873–852
Ahaziah	853–852	853–852	850–849	852–851
Jehoram (Joram)	851–840	852–841	849–843/2	851–842
Jehu	839–822	841–814	843/2–815	842–814
Jehoahaz	821–805	814–798	815–802	817–800
Jehoash (Joash)	804–789	798–782	802–786	800–784
Jeroboam II	788–748	793–753	786–746	789–748
Zechariah	6 months	753–752	746–745	748–747
Shallum	1 month	752	745	747
Menahem	746–737	752–742	745–737	747–737
Pekahiah	736–735	742–740	737–736	737–735
Pekah	734–731	752–732	736–732	735–732
Hoshea	730–722	732–722	732–724	732–724

The Kings of Judah (Southern Kingdom)

King	Hayes and Hooker	Thiele	Bright	Cogan and Tadmor
Rehoboam	926–910	931–913	922–915	928–911
Abijah	909–907	913–911	915–913	911–908
Asa	906–878 (866)	911–870	913–873	908–867
Jehoshaphat	877–853	872–848	873–849	870–846
Jehoram	852–841	853–841	849–843	851–843
Ahaziah	840	841	843/842	843–842
Athaliah	839–833	841–835	842–837	842–836
Joash (Jehoash)	832–803 (793)	835–796	837–800	836–798
Amaziah	802–786 (774)	796–767	800–783	798–769
Azariah (Uzziah)	785–760 (734)	792–740	783–742	785–733
Jotham	759–744	750–732	750–735	758–743
Ahaz	743–728	735–716	735–715	743–727
Hezekiah	727–699	716–687	715–687/6	727–698
Manasseh	698–644	697–643	687/6–642	698–642
Amon	643–642	643–641	642–640	641–640
Josiah	641–610	641–609	640–609	639–609
Jehoahaz	3 months	609	609	609
Jehoiakim	608–598	609–598	609–598	608–598
Jehoiachin	3 months	598–597	598/7	597
Zedekiah	596–586	597–586	597–587	596–586

Chronologies for the Hebrew monarchies will vary between one and ten years, depending on the source consulted. The sources cited here are J. H. Hayes and P. K. Hooker, *A New Chronology for the Kings of Israel and Judah* (Atlanta: John Knox, 1988); E. R. Thiele, *The Mysterious Numbers of the Hebrew Kings*, rev. ed. (Grand Rapids: Zondervan, 1983); J. Bright, *A History of Israel*, 4th ed. (Louisville: Westminster John Knox, 2000); M. Cogan and H. Tadmore, *Second Kings* (AB 11; Garden City, N.Y.: Doubleday, 1988). The dates for the kings of the divided monarchies of Israel and Judah in this commentary are based on the work of E. R. Thiele (with minor variations).

Appendix D: Sacrifice in the Old Testament

The Sacrificial System

Name	Portion Burnt	Other Portions	Animals	Occasion or Reason	Reference
Burnt offering	All	None	Male without blemish; animal according to wealth	Propitiation for general sin; demonstrating dedication	Lev. 1
Meal offering or tribute offering	Token portion	Eaten by priest	Unleavened cakes grains, must be salted	General thankfulness for first fruits	Lev. 2
Peace offering a. Thank offering b. Vow offering c. Freewill offering	Fat portions	Shared in fellowship meal by priest and offerer	Male or female without blemish according to wealth; freewill, slight blemish allowed	Fellowship a. For an unexpected blessing b. For deliverance when a vow was made on that condition c. For general thankfulness	Lev. 3 Lev. 22:18–30
Sin offering	Fat portions	Eaten by priest	Priest or congregation: bull; king: he-goat; individual: she-goat	Applies basically to situation in which purification is needed	Lev. 4
Guilt offering	Fat portions	Eaten by priest	Ram without blemish	Applies to situation in which there has been desecration or de-sacrilization of something holy or there has been objective guilt	Lev. 5:1–6:7

From John H. Walton, *Chronological Charts of the Old Testament*, rev. ed. (Grand Rapids: Zondervan, 1994), 21 (used by permission).

Occasions for Sacrifice

Animals to be offered	Bullocks	Rams	Lambs	Goats
Occasions for Offerings				
Daily (morning & evening)			2	
Additional offerings on the Sabbath			2	
New Moons	2	1	7	1
Annual Festivals				
Unleavened Bread (daily offering)	2	1	7	1
Total for 7 days	14	7	49	7
Weeks (Firstfruits)	2	1	7	1
1st day of 7th month	1	1	7	1
Day of Atonement	1	1	7	1
Tabernacles: Day 1	13	2	14	1
Day 2	12	2	14	1
Day 3	11	2	14	1
Day 4	10	2	14	1
Day 5	9	2	14	1
Day 6	8	2	14	1
Day 7	7	2	14	1
Day 8	1	1	7	1
Total for 8 days	71	15	105	8

Number of animals to be offered at the public sacrifices, daily, weekly, and at festivals.

The two lambs on the Sabbath are additional to the usual daily two.

The total for seven days refers to the seven days of the Festival of Unleavened Bread (i.e., 2 bullocks per day for 7 days = 14).

Similarly, the total for eight days refers to the eight days of the Feast of Tabernacles (*i.e.,* 1 goat per day for 8 days = 8 goats).

Chart of the occasions laid down for public sacrifice and offerings (Num. 28–29). Taken from *New Bible Dictionary,* 3d ed., ed. I. Howard Marshall, A. R. Millard, J. I. Packer, and D. J. Wiseman; copyright © 1996, Universities and Colleges Christian Fellowship, Leicester, England. Used by permission of InterVarsity Press, P.O. Box 1400, Downers Grove, IL, 60515. www.ivpress.com.

Appendix E : Index of Synoptic Parallels in Chronicles and Samuel-Kings

David

	1 Chronicles	*2 Samuel*
Saul's death	10:1–14	[*1 Sam.*] 31:1–13
David hears of Saul's death		1:1–16
David's lament for Saul and Jonathan		1:17–27
David anointed king over Judah		2:1–7
War between the houses of David and Saul		2:8–3:1
David's sons born at Hebron	[3:1–4a]¹	3:2–5
Abner sides with David		3:6–21
Joab murders Abner		3:22–39
Ish–Bosheth murdered		4:1–12
David becomes king over Israel	11:1–3	5:1–5
David conquers Jerusalem	11:4–9	5:6–10
David's mighty men	11:10–47	[23:8–39]
Warriors join David at Ziklag	12:1–23	
Others join David at Hebron	12:24–41	
Bringing back the ark	13:1–14	[6:1–11]
Hiram helps David	14:1–2	5:11–12
David's children born at Jerusalem	14:3–7	5:13–16
David defeats the Philistines	14:8–17	5:17–25
David brings the ark to Jerusalem	15:1–16:6	6:1–19a
David's psalm of thanksgiving	16:7–36	
Levites appointed for the ark	16:37–43	6:19b–23
God's covenant with David	17:1–15	7:1–17
David's prayer	17:16–27	7:18–29
David's military victories	18:1–13	8:1–14
David's officials	18:14–17	8:15–18
Defeat of Ammonites and Arameans	19:1–19	10:1–19
Siege of Rabbah	20:1a	11:1
David and Bathsheba		11:2–27
Nathan rebukes David		12:1–25
David captures Rabbah	20:1b–3	12:26–31
Amnon and Tamar		13:1–22

1. Texts out of chronological sequence are [bracketed].

(cont.)	*1 Chronicles*	*2 Samuel*
Absalom's revenge and flight		13:23–29
Absalom returns to Jerusalem		14:1–33
Absalom's conspiracy		15:1–16:14
Advice of Hushai and Ahithophel		16:15–17:23
David at Mahanaim	[2:17]	17:24–29
Absalom's death		18:1–19:8a
David returns to Jerusalem		19:8b–44
Sheba rebels against David		20:1–22
David's officials	[18:15–17]	20:23–26
Gibeonites avenged		21:1–14
Wars against the Philistines	20:4–8	21:15–22
David's song of praise		22:1–51
Last words of David		23:1–7
David's mighty men	[11:10–47]	23:8–39
Warriors join David at Ziklag	[12:1–23]	
Others join David at Hebron	[12:24–41]	
David numbers the fighting men	21:1–27	24:1–25
Temple site chosen	21:28–22:1	
David's preparations for the temple	22:2–23:1	
Divisions of the Levites	23:2–32	
Divisions of the priests	24:1–31	
Divisions of the singers	25:1–31	
Divisions of the gatekeepers	26:1–19	
Treasurers and other officials	26:20–32	
Army divisions	27:1–34	
David's plans for the temple	28:1–29:9	
David's prayer	29:10–19	

		1 Kings
Abishag brought to David		1:1–4
Adonijah assumes the throne		1:5–27
David names Solomon king	29:20–22	1:28–53
David's charge to Solomon		2:1–9
Death of David	29:26–30	2:10–12

Solomon

	2 Chronicles	*1 Kings*
Solomon's throne established		2:13–46
Solomon asks for wisdom	1:1–13	3:1–15
Solomon's wise ruling		3:16–28

Divided Monarchy

	2 *Chronicles*	1 *Kings*
(cont.)		
Yahweh appears to Elijah		19:9b–18
Call of Elisha		19:19–21
Ben–Hadad attacks Samaria		20:1–12
Ahab defeats Ben–Hadad		20:13–34
A prophet condemns Ahab		20:35–43
Naboth's vineyard		21:1–29
Jehoshaphat king of Judah	17:1–19	
Micaiah prophesies against Ahab	18:1–34	22:1–40
Jehu rebukes Jehoshaphat	19:1–3	
Jehoshaphat appoints Judges	19:4–11	
Jehoshaphat defeats Moab and Ammon	20:1–30	
End of Jehoshaphat's reign	20:31–21:3	22:41–50
Ahaziah king of Israel		22:51–53

	2 *Chronicles*	2 *Kings*
Yahweh's judgment on Ahaziah		1:1–18
Elijah taken up to heaven		2:1–12a
Elisha succeeds Elijah		2:12b–25
Moab revolts		3:1–27
Elisha and the widow's oil		4:1–7
Elisha and the Shunammite woman		4:8–37
Elisha's miracles for the prohets		4:38–44
Namaan healed of leprosy		5:1–27
Axhead made to float		6:1–7
Elisha traps blind Arameans		6:8–23
Famine in besieged Samaria		6:24–7:2
The siege lifted		7:3–20
Shunammite woman's land restored		8:1–6
Hazael murders Ben–Hadad		8:7–15
Jehoram king of Judah	21:4–20	8:16–24
Ahaziah king of Judah	22:1–6	8:25–29
Jehu anointed king of Israel		9:1–13
Jehu kills Jehoram		9:14–26
Jehu kills Ahaziah	22:7–9	9:27–29
Death of Jezebel		9:30–37
Ahab's family killed		10:1–17
Ministers of Baal killed		10:18–36
Athaliah and Joash	22:10–23:21	11:1–20
Joash repairs the temple	24:1–16	12:1–16
Wickedness of Joash	24:17–27	12:17–21

Scripture Index

Subject Index

Author Index

Praise for the NIV Application Commentary Series

"This series promises to become an indispensable tool for every pastor and teacher who seeks to make the Bible's timeless message speak to this generation."
—Billy Graham

"It is encouraging to find a commentary that is not only biblically trustworthy but also contemporary in its application. **The NIV Application Commentary** series will prove to be a helpful tool in the pastor's sermon preparation. I use it and recommend it."
—Charles F. Stanley, Pastor, First Baptist Church of Atlanta

"**The NIV Application Commentary** is an outstanding resource for pastors and anyone else who is serious about developing 'doers of the Word.'"
—Rick Warren, Pastor, Saddleback Valley Community Church, Author, *The Purpose-Driven Church*

"**The NIV Application Commentary** series shares the same goal that has been the passion of my own ministry—communicating God's Word to a contemporary audience so that they feel the full impact of its message."
—Bill Hybels, Willow Creek Community Church

"**The NIV Application Commentary** series helps pastors and other Bible teachers with one of the most neglected elements in good preaching—accurate, useful application. Most commentaries tell you a few things that are helpful and much that you do not need to know. By dealing with the original meaning and contemporary significance of each passage, **The NIV Application Commentary** series promises to be helpful all the way around."
—Dr. James Montgomery Boice, Tenth Presbyterian Church

"If you want to avoid hanging applicational elephants from interpretive threads, then **The NIV Application Commentary** is for you! This series excels at both original meaning and contemporary signficance. I support it 100 percent."
—Howard G. Hendricks, Dallas Theological Seminary

"**The NIV Application Commentary** series doesn't fool around: It gets right down to business, bringing this ancient and powerful Word of God into the present so that it can be heard and delivered with all the freshness of a new day, with all the immediacy of a friend's embrace."
—Eugene H. Peterson, Regent College

"This series dares to go where few scholars have gone before—into the real world of biblical application faced by pastors and teachers every day. This is everything a good commentary series should be."
—Leith Anderson, Pastor, Wooddale Church

"This is THE pulpit commentary for the 21st century."
—George K. Brushaber, President, Bethel College & Seminary

"Here, at last, is a commentary that makes the proper circuit from the biblical world to main street. **The NIV Application Commentary** is a magnificent gift to the church."
—R. Kent Hughes, Pastor, College Church, Wheaton, IL

Look for the NIV Application Commentary *at your local Christian bookstore*

GRAND RAPIDS, MICHIGAN 49530 USA
WWW.ZONDERVAN.COM

"Academically well informed ... this series helps the contemporary reader hear God's Word and consider its implications; scholarship in the service of the Church."
—Arthur Rowe, Spurgeon's College

"The NIV Application Commentary series promises to be of very great service to all who preach and teach the Word of God."
—J. I. Packer, Regent College

"The NIV Application Commentary series will be a great help for readers who want to understand what the Bible means, how it applies, and what they should do in response."
—Stuart Briscoe, Pastor, Elmbrook Church

"The NIV Application Commentary meets the urgent need for an exhaustive and authoritative commentary based on the New International Version. This series will soon be found in libraries and studies throughout the evangelical community."
—Dr. James Kennedy, Ph.D., Senior Minister,
Coral Ridge Presbyterian Church

"... for readers who want a reliable synthesis with a strong emphasis on application.... [Provides a] freshness that can benefit students, teachers, and (especially) church leaders ... makes good devotional reading, precisely because it emphasizes the contemporary application.... This approach refreshes and challenges the reader, and would make helpful material for sermon-preparation or Bible study.... At a time when many pastors are deeply in need of inspiration and encouragement, these volumes ... would be a good investment for congregations, even if it means adding a line to the annual budget."
—Christianity Today

"This commentary needs to be given full marks for what it is attempting to do. This is to provide a commentary for the English reader that takes exegesis seriously and still has space left for considerations of what the text is saying in today's world.... One will understand everything that one reads. May its tribe increase!"
—Journal of the Evangelical Theological Society

"... a useful, nontechnical commentary.... In the application section are illustrations, which, to pastors seeking a fresh approach, are worth the price of the book.... Other useful features include same-page footnotes; Greek words transliterated in the text of the commentary; and an attractive, user-friendly layout. Pastors and Bible teachers who want to emphasize contemporary application will find this commentary a useful tool."
—Bookstore Journal

"... one of the most helpful commentary sets from recent years."
—Alabama Southern Baptist Convention

"Some commentaries build walls that isolate you back in the ancient world. The NIV Application Commentary builds bridges that make the Bible come alive with meaning for contemporary life—and the series does so concisely, clearly and accurately. No wasted words or academic detours—just solid help and practical truth!"
—Warren Wiersbe

Look for the NIV Application Commentary at your local Christian bookstore

ZONDERVAN™
GRAND RAPIDS, MICHIGAN 49530 USA
WWW.ZONDERVAN.COM

Bring ancient truth to modern life with the
NIV Application Commentary series

Covering both the Old and New Testaments, the **NIV Application Commentary** series is a staple reference for pastors seeking to bring the Bible's timeless message into a modern context. It explains not only what the Bible means but also how that meaning impacts the lives of believers today.

Genesis
John H. Walton
ISBN: 0-310-20617-0

Psalms Volume 1
Gerald H. Wilson
ISBN: 0-310-20635-9

Exodus
Peter Enns
ISBN: 0-310-20607-3

Ecclesiastes, Song of Songs
Iain Provan
ISBN: 0-310-21372-X

Judges, Ruth
K. Lawson Younger
ISBN: 0-310-20636-7

Jeremiah, Lamentations
J. Andrew Dearman
ISBN: 0-310-20616-2

1 & 2 Samuel
Bill T. Arnold
ISBN: 0-310-21086-0

Ezekiel
Iain M. Duguid
ISBN: 0-310-20147-X

1 & 2 Chronicles
Andrew E. Hill
ISBN: 0-310-20610-3

Daniel
Tremper Longman III
ISBN: 0-310-20608-1

Esther
Karen H. Jobes
ISBN: 0-310-20672-3

Hosea, Amos, Micah
Dr. Gary V. Smith
ISBN: 0-310-20614-6

Available at your local Christian bookstore

ZONDERVAN™

GRAND RAPIDS, MICHIGAN 49530 USA

WWW.ZONDERVAN.COM

Bring ancient truth to modern life with the
NIV Application Commentary series

Covering both the Old and New Testaments, the **NIV Application Commentary** series is a staple reference for pastors seeking to bring the Bible's timeless message into a modern context. It explains not only what the Bible means but also how that meaning impacts the lives of believers today.

Mark
David E. Garland
ISBN: 0-310-49350-1

Galatians
Scot McKnight
ISBN: 0-310-48470-7

Hebrews
George H. Guthrie
ISBN: 0-310-49390-0

Luke
Darrell L. Bock
ISBN: 0-310-49330-7

Ephesians
Klyne Snodgrass
ISBN: 0-310-49340-4

James
David P. Nystrom
ISBN: 0-310-49360-9

John
Gary M. Burge
ISBN: 0-310-49750-7

Philippians
Frank Thielman
ISBN: 0-310-49300-5

1 Peter
Scot McKnight
ISBN: 0-310-49290-4

Acts
Ajith Fernando
ISBN: 0-310-49410-9

Colossians, Philemon
David E. Garland
ISBN: 0-310-48480-4

2 Peter, Jude
Douglas J. Moo
ISBN: 0-310-20104-7

Romans
Douglas J. Moo
ISBN: 0-310-49400-1

1&2 Thessalonians
Michael W. Holmes
ISBN: 0-310-49380-3

Letters of John
Gary M. Burge
ISBN: 0-310-48620-3

1 Corinthians
Craig L. Blomberg
ISBN: 0-310-48490-1

1&2 Timothy, Titus
Walter L. Liefeld
ISBN: 0-310-50110-5

Revelation
Craig S. Keener
ISBN: 0-310-23192-2

2 Corinthians
Scott J. Hafemann
ISBN: 0-310-49420-6

Available at your local Christian bookstore

GRAND RAPIDS, MICHIGAN 49530 USA
WWW.ZONDERVAN.COM

We want to hear from you. Please send your comments about this book to us in care of zreview@zondervan.com. Thank you.

GRAND RAPIDS, MICHIGAN 49530 USA

WWW.ZONDERVAN.COM